Walter Jost is associate professor of English at the University of Virginia. *Michael J. Hyde* is University Professor of Communication Ethics at Wake Forest University.

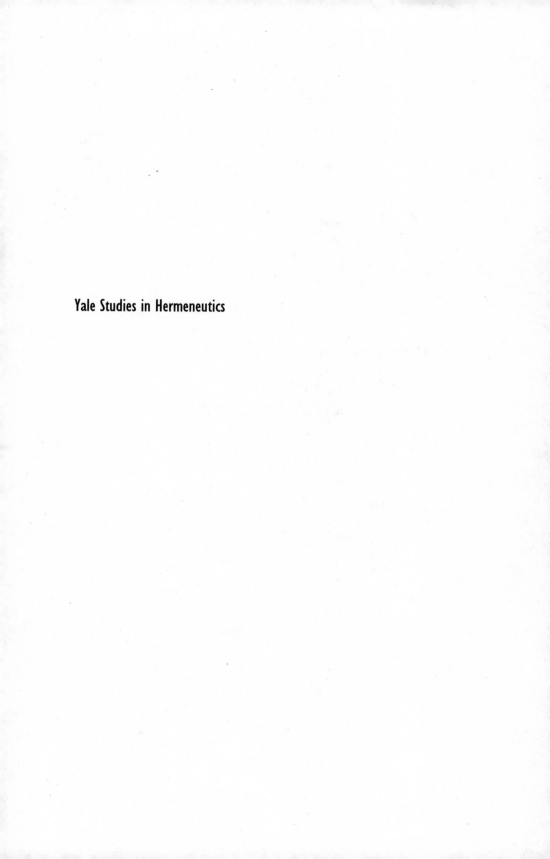

Yale Studies in Hermeneutics

Yale Studies in Hermeneutics

Joel Weinsheimer, Editor

Rhetoric and Hermeneutics in Our Time: A Reader

Edited by Walter Jost and Michael J. Hyde

1997

Yale University Press

New Haven and London

Printed in the United States of America.

Library of Congress Cataloging-in-Publication Data

Rhetoric and hermeneutics in our time :
    a reader / edited Walter Jost and
    Michael J. Hyde.
        p.   cm.—(Yale University studies in
            hermeneutics)
    Includes bibliographical references and
        index.
    ISBN 0–300–06836–0 (cl : alk. paper)
    1. Hermeneutics—History—20th
century.   2. Rhetoric—Philosophy—
History—20th century.   I. Jost, Walter.
II. Hyde, Michael J.   III. Series.
    BD241.R457   1997
    121'.686—dc21   96–45205
                    CIP

A catalogue record for this book is available from the British Library.

The paper in this book meets the guidelines for permanence and durability of the Committee on Production Guidelines for Book Longevity of the Council on Library Resources.

10 9 8 7 6 5 4 3 2 1

For our parents: Wally and Jeanne Jost and Claire Hyde

A word has meaning against the context of a sentence. A sentence has meaning against the context of a language. A language has meaning against the context of a form of life. A form of life has meaning against the context of a world. A world has meaning against the context of a word.
—Stanley Cavell, *The Senses of Walden*

Contents

Prologue

At mid-century E. R. Curtius, adverting to the study of rhetoric in his magisterial *European Literature and the Latin Middle Ages,* boldly pronounced not only that "as an independent subject, it has long since vanished from the curriculum" but that "in our culture, rhetoric has no place."[1] Only a few years later, related sentiments were expressed by the Oxford scholar C. S. Lewis. Lewis was, among other things, a Renaissance specialist for whom the modern ignorance of rhetoric as a subject of study presented the single greatest obstacle to our properly approaching the literature of the distant past.[2] For Lewis, as for Curtius, the ancient system of rhetorical *topoi,* speech genres, levels and types of style, and so on had long ago "penetrated all literary genres," becoming the "common denominator" (*ELLM* 70) of European literature, even its very foundation (despised by many as a "cellar"; *ELLM* 79), whose classical and medieval sources needed to be understood for an appreciation of the Western literary legacy. Certainly neither Curtius nor Lewis was seeking to reintroduce rhetoric as an independent university pursuit, although both possessed the literary historian's knowledge of the once-pervasive influence of rhetoric across the liberal arts curriculum. Nevertheless, while the ancient coin of rhetoric may always have been valued by a knowledgeable few, rhetoric itself was considered by most to have gone out of circulation long before, to have become effaced, ineffective, above all anachronistic—which is to say backward, out of its proper time.

Half a century after Curtius's assessment, the fortunes of rhetoric have so been reversed that another Renaissance scholar, Richard Lanham, has observed that "during the last twenty years, rhetoric has moved from the periphery to the center of our intellectual focus."[3] Arm in arm with what we have come to know as the art of interpretation—or hermeneutics—rhetoric enables a new understanding of understanding as well as new modes of comprehension and exchange between familiar and distant texts, across intellectual boundaries, and into foreign literatures, new curricula, and changing canons. The title of this book, accordingly, can be understood as virtually tautological, for ours is a time in which rhetoric and hermeneutics have achieved a parallel influence and momentum (if not always willing acceptance) across the academic horizon. Indeed, in light of the massive social, cultural, intellectual, and economic conflicts defining both the modern and postmodern age, it can no longer occasion much surprise that these two disciplines should have inspired and continue to inspire such widespread and diverse response. After all, both rhetoric and hermeneutics thrive, each in its own way, on the conflicts of interpretations and opinions that now enliven every field of endeavor in or out of academe. They thrive as well on a practical "being-in-the-world" (as Heidegger calls it) that for some is skeptical and resistant and for others receptive—filled with anxiety, to be sure, but filled also with, in Richard Bernstein's words, "a perennial impulse of wonder."[4] Our aim in this volume is to show the novice and expert alike what some versions of contemporary rhetoric and hermeneutics look like and to propose how the two can be thought of together, for each not only presupposes but extends and corrects the other.

In spite of the flourishing of sophisticated debates in monographs and journals over the definition and scope of each of these terms, no one until now has initiated a dialogue between thinkers interested in both rhetoric and hermeneutics. Such a dialogue seeks to clarify the points of contact and separation of the two and their common principles, problems, and aims, as well as their different means and strategies. Hermeneutics has become in our time variously a philosophical, literary, and critical problematic. It is at once a problem of method, broadly conceived (hermeneutic phenomenology, reader-response criticism), of philosophic claims to truth (the interpretive nature of human being), and of the skeptical resistance to both method and truth (the epistemological instability of being, language, self, and so on, or the exposure of the threat of systematic, ideological distortion in our communication).[5] Hermeneutics did not always command such scope; it evolved (in a nonteleological way, as Jean Grondin has noted)[6] from a chiefly exegetical concern with the Bible, a concern that first extended to all texts, then to all problems of understanding in the so-called human sciences, and finally to the philosophic concern with understanding and interpretation as such. These methodological and philosophical views were developed over the nineteenth and twentieth centuries chiefly by German thinkers—Friedrich Schleiermacher, Wilhelm Dilthey, Friedrich Nietzsche, Martin Heidegger, Hans-Georg Gadamer—partly in response to the philosophical totalizations of Immanuel Kant, G. W. F. Hegel and Edmund Husserl. Having appropriated parts of this tradition and corrected some of its errors, contemporary hermeneutics provides revolutionary directions for study not only in philosophy but across the disciplines, and, in our view, it promises further insights and possibilities, particularly as it is drawn into closer discussion with rhetoric.

As for rhetoric, it was, again, Curtius who noted (with scholarly understatement) that "Germans appear to have an innate distrust of it" (*ELLM* 62)—a remark that perfectly captures Kant's and Hegel's dismissive comments about rhetorical topics and tropes but that is misleading when it comes to Gadamer's later recognition of the vast common ground between our two subjects: "I would like to see more recognition of the fact that this is the realm hermeneutics shares with rhetoric: the realm of arguments that are convincing (which is not the same as logically compelling). It is the realm of practice and humanity in general."[7] Gadamer's allusion here to the realm of practice and humanity in general suggests the genuinely daunting scope of rhetoric and hermeneutics. It is a realm, however, whose range is entirely consistent with Roman and Renaissance conceptions of rhetoric and increasingly so with philosophical, literary, and critical conceptions of hermeneutics, reminding us that neither rhetoric nor hermeneutics can ever be a strictly proprietary project. Rather, each is intrinsically a transdisciplinary effort whose most creative work may lie not behind us but in the present and future, especially as rhetoric and hermeneutics come to be better understood as mutually constitutive enterprises.

Most readers interested in a book like this will affirm the centrality of rhetoric and hermeneutics to human *praxis*. But they will also admit the difficulties involved in identifying just what these contested concepts mean. As editors, we have tried to avoid both a dogmatic imposition of definitions on the one hand and a laxity of conception on the other. We do not suppose that our readers are experts in either field, nor that they (any more than our contributors!) can or should be expected to agree about how best to define *rhetoric* or *hermeneutics*. In fact, in these two disciplines conceived in their fuller forms, such attempts at essentialist definitions have already been ruled out by the disciplines themselves. Our practice has rather been to use both terms as rhetorical topics of invention—that is, as indeterminate concepts whose intellectual histories and uses can be employed to suggest new lines of inquiry. This openness avoids philosophically unwarranted ontologizing or reifying of the terms' meanings as well as a flat-footed collapsing of either term into the other.

Indeed, even those theologians (e.g., Schleiermacher, Bultmann), philosophers and critical thinkers (e.g., Heidegger, Gadamer, Ricoeur, Habermas, Lacan, Foucault), and more "literary" thinkers and critics (Kierkegaard, Nietzsche, Burke, Derrida, de Man) who explicitly use or invoke the two disciplines and their histories cannot offer ready answers about what the disciplines entail and how they might be thought of together. In Kierkegaard, for example, all rhetoric or public speaking, "all persuasiveness, all bargaining, all direct attention by means of one's own person,"[8] is consistently consigned to the junk heap of public opinion and manipulation—in other words, convicted of the age-old charge of pandering to the masses. And yet throughout Kierkegaard's work, one finds elaborate and thoughtful theory and practice of indirect communication and truth as subjectivity. In word and deed if not in name, then, Kierkegaard throws rhetorical persuasion and hermeneutic interpretation into passionate embrace. Historically, this and similar disorienting maneuvers make for a complex, even fragmented narrative for our two disciplines, a complexity far beyond any neat summary to which our essays could (or perhaps should) aspire. Nevertheless, as a way of moving closer here to defining topically (or pragmatically) the two concepts, we offer a further line of thinking that illustrates how the relations between rhetoric and hermeneutics have been obscured. Because the title of this book directs attention to the importance of time (and timing) in rhetoric and hermeneutics, let us turn briefly to Heidegger's account of time as a way of indicating the unforeseen advantages that might be gained by thinking about rhetoric and hermeneutics together.

In *The Genesis of Heidegger's Being and Time,* Theodore Kisiel recounts Heidegger's gradual breakthrough, over approximately twelve years, to a new conception of time. This new account not only organizes but grounds Heidegger's entire transcendental analysis of *Dasein;*[9] Kisiel, retrieving Heidegger's 1922–23 terminology, designates it "the kairology of Being."[10]

As students of philosophical hermeneutics are aware, Heidegger's profound innovation challenges the adequacy of our everyday notion of time as *chronos,* the strict succession of punctual "nows" that fade as if eternally into the past and the future. In stark contrast, Heidegger reveals temporality as the very structure of human being or, more accurately, of the ontological structure of human being as "care" (*Sorge*)—that which enables us to respond to (or rather toward) our own possibilities. The *toward* in this formulation signals the ontological priority of the future against any mythic punctilious present in Heidegger's account of temporality; it is futural "possibility" that constitutes our "anticipation" and that activates our ongoing "retrieval"—or, as Gadamer and Ricoeur put it, our "appropriation"—of the past. In this way, our present is always already (primordially) endowed with both the past and the future in the project of our possibilities. Thus Kisiel: "A new and different sense of time concentrated on the moment which is at once my unique lifetime. How? By 'at once' (equiprimordially) forerunning the possibility of my death and repeating the possibility of my birth (heredity, inheritance, heritage)."[11] Time or "temporality" as *kairos,* therefore, which Heidegger derives chiefly from the early Christian concern with the "fullness of time"—the Second Coming as an existential rather than neutral or objectively given moment—is configured not as a horizontal forced march but as a self-appropriating circle of understanding and care.

Now, the point here is that what remains lurking in Kisiel's account of Heidegger's kairology of Being is the fact that *kairos,* as students of rhetoric are aware, is a vintage rhetorical concept deriving from pre-Socratic drama, philosophy, and oratory, particularly that of Pythagoras, Empedocles, and (implicitly) Gorgias. In Greek drama and literature *kairos* embraced various meanings: brevity, proportion or moderation (as in Hesiod's "Observe good measure, and proportion [*kairos*] is the best of all things"), what is suited to the moment, the expedient, effective, correct, or appropriate.[12] In later rhetorical theory *kairos* was elaborated as the "appropriate" (*to prepon*), "decorum" (e.g. in Cicero), and Renaissance-humanist *sprezzaturra,* all three of which involve the orator's practical ability to adapt to circumstances and audiences without relying on theoretical rules.[13] Originally, however, *kairos* referred to the principle and power (*dunamis*) by which the opportune moment calls forth an intuitive, appropriate response from the rhetor (instead of the rhetor initiating an action after conscious assessment of the situation). It is a power of invention or discovery (*heuresis*) irreducible to calculation and logic that ends the stasis of contending *logoi* at the critical moment in which decision and action are demanded. As such *kairos* remains beyond the control of the rhetor, coming rather as a gift or even magic (*goetia*). In short, the emphasis falls on *kairos* as receptivity; in later theory it falls on *to prepon* and decorum as artful activity.

To be sure, Kisiel shows that Heidegger himself is not unaware of the link between rhetoric and *kairos,* at least as this link appears in Aristotle's *Rhetoric.* Given his task of tracking Heidegger, however, who seems never to have mentioned (for example) Pythagoras or Gorgias in his courses or in his writings in the twenties, it is understandable that Kisiel would not speculate on possible connections to these thinkers. Still, the fact remains that potentially interesting but unseen affiliations hold between the pre-Socratics and Heidegger, especially regarding Heidegger's own considerable emphasis on "listening to" and hearing the call of conscience (in *Being and Time*) and the call of Being and of language (in his later writings). This would seem to resemble Gorgias's stress on rhetorical invention as a power that one receives, chiefly by listening and hearing rather than by speaking.[14] More important, on such an angle of approach we conceivably gain a perspective by which to measure how selectively (and perhaps unwittingly) Heidegger has drawn from the rhetorical tradition of *kairos* to inform his own philosophical hermeneutics. Whether the objection voiced by many to the later Heidegger is correct—that a kind of quietist passivity threatens to preclude practical thought and action—nevertheless, an active passivity is quite familiar to the early, and foreign to the later, *kairotic* tradition of rhetoric. This passivity diminished as *kairos* developed in Aristotle and Cicero, who emphasized enthymematic probabilities, civic responsibilities, the rhetor as agent, topics as agency, and invention as a human initiative. Thus Kisiel (selectively) notes: "Almost perversely, Heidegger's interest in rhetoric gravitates toward [hearing], in which speaking has its end. For speaking finds its completion in the communication, in being received or accepted by the auditor who undergoes or 'suffers' the speech. A seemingly marginal topic, the 'suffering' and resulting 'passion' (Gr. *pathos*) of the listener, is made central."[15] In fact, this gravitation to hearing retrieves Gorgias's invaluable contribution to the history and theory of rhetoric and hermeneutics, although at the same time it risks losing the active involvement of speaker in the rhetorical situation.

Dimly and from afar, then, rhetorical reverberations of the hermeneutic of time as *kairos* suggest what otherwise specialist attention to hermeneutics alone, or to rhetoric alone, conceals: namely, that our very being-in-the-world is inseparably hermeneutical and rhetorical in complex ways and that a multifaceted speaking as well as listening constitutes our situation. Our own time is an epoch of corporate capitalism and technologism, of vulgarization and breakdown. But it is also a time of deep reflection on linguistic interpretation: on persuasion, "conversion" across paradigms or worldviews, propaganda, and more invidious forms of deception and power, as well as on forms of the electronic word and the new multimedia. It is, accordingly, a time in which we need both to listen to and to discuss what Gadamer calls the "deep inner convergence" between rhetoric and hermeneutics.[16] David Tracy makes this same point in his chapter in this volume: "It now seems clear that hermeneutical thinkers must both acknowledge and engage rhetorical theories and vice versa."[17] What in turn seems called for (appropriate to) such a time, therefore, what has seemed fitting to the editors and authors involved in this book, is the need to open up new *topoi* for debate and discussion, new connections and extensions that have not yet been brought fully to light. For Aristotle, dialectic was "critical" (*Metaph.* 1004b 17–27), while its "counterpart," rhetoric, was exploratory and "inventional" in its use of topics to investigate and determine a given matter. To many of the contributors to this volume, the task at hand now includes identifying hermeneutics (in its modern forms) as a further counterpart to rhetoric and rhetoric to hermeneutics and seeing both as features or dimensions of all thought and language, not only as the special methods or abilities of political *praxis*. In this way this book is meant to encourage the general drift of thinking about the relations of rhetoric and hermeneutics, and particularly to provide some of the signposts by which those identified with one discipline can make their way to and within its counterpart.

In other ways as well the book is intended to remind us that rhetoric and hermeneutics are themselves supremely *kairotic,* that is, temporal, situated, and motivated enterprises. In this regard our appropriation of each discipline by means of the chapters in this book is itself limited and motivated in two obvious ways. First, we sought scholars working in several different disciplines, and we are confident that we have located those whose chapters represent some of the most interesting and provocative work being done today. Second, our editorial effort is itself temporal because historical, a product of our own "effective historical consciousness" (Gadamer) behind or in addition to our authors' own divergent heritages. In our introduction, and in our selection of the chapters that follow, we have been guided by an implicit faith in or acknowledgment of a middle way between the so-called metaphysics of presence and the *mise-en-abîme* that is asserted by some to be its only alternative and by a rhetorical concern with conscience and possibility as found, for example, in Heidegger and Levinas as the place of places. Within the limits of our choices and commitments, we believe that these chapters, both in how our authors interpret and argue and in what they discuss, profitably reflect on, even as they reflect, contemporary preoccupations.

Of course, we recognize that the reassuring phrase "our time" threatens to become a self-deceiving shibboleth, for it is in fact a deeply problematic expression. What value is the appeal to "our," some will ask, if it does not directly, aggressively, even single-mindedly feature the oppressed and marginalized, the non-Western, the colonized, women, children—in a word, the Other? We are aware that what the term *our* in the title designates is potentially paradoxical. What "we" seem to share in this time, what is common to us, is our sense of fracture and incommensurability, precisely a lack of common places and possibly a diminishing common interest in discovering them. In addressing this plight as an opportunity for action, however, our authors do bridge some of our shared gaps and *aporias* without trying to minimize or deny them. In this way they seek to reconstitute themselves, and their readers, without recourse to fix-it-all theories or damn-it-all skepticisms.

In fact, this metaphor of bridging is employed by Gadamer and others to define hermeneutics: "Hermeneutics may be defined as the attempt to overcome [the] distance in areas where empathy [is] hard and agreement not easily reached. There is always a gap that must be bridged."[18] Less figuratively, we propose to follow Gerald Bruns's exemplary practice of calling hermeneutics "a family of questions about what happens in the understanding of anything, not just of texts but of how things are."[19] Such a move allows for both a familiar typology of hermeneutics—as "method, philosophy, and critique"—as well as for the scope of its historical manifestations (classical, Enlightenment, romantic, modern, postmodern).[20] As philosophy, hermeneutics interprets not only human being but being in all its manifestations as interpretive understanding (uncovering "as-structures," i.e., seeing something-as-something, "seeing-as"); hermeneutics discusses what it is to reveal *die Sache selbst* beyond the reach, as Richard Bernstein has put it, of both an impossible objectivism and a vicious relativism (although no one has shown exactly how this is accomplished). As method, hermeneutics codifies the more or less indeterminate rules and procedures of the interpretation of texts and text analogues, transferring Gadamer's insights into the work of art to the understanding of history and all texts. And as social critique, hermeneutics offers a means of challenging the manifest content of all messages; hermeneutics claims to be able to police its own claims to truth, maximizing the possibilities for freedom from distortion (although the issues involved, for example, in the Gadamer-Habermas debate have hardly been resolved).

Following Bruns, we can also think of rhetoric as comprising a family of questions about what is involved in influencing oneself and others regarding (the interpretation of) any indeterminate matter.[21] Precisely because rhetoric operates within the realm of the indeterminate, it is characterized by a fundamental instability, the "play" within its scope of possibilities for meaning and action that Richard Lanham rather awkwardly calls a "bi-stable oscillation."[22] In other words, the rhetorician ranges between the poles of conflicting possibilities for argument and appeal and aims at what Robert Frost calls "a momentary [which is to say timely, *kairotic*] stay against confusion." In rhetoric this play repeats itself in all of rhetoric's features. The rhetorical topic, for example, is equivocal, or two-termed, or contradicted by another topic, and it is always itself a standing indeterminacy. The rhetorical trope upsets the literal proposition, decenters conceptual argument, and calls into question empirical fact and rational first principle. Argument occurs on either side of a question, stabilizing a position, but only for a moment, until it starts up all over again. From style to substance and back to style, from word to world, theory to practice, *sic et non,* a continuum of possibilities blurring into and constituting each other—word unto world without end.

Unfortunately, even in our hyper-rhetorical times, many promoters of rhetoric and hermeneutics would transform this play among situated (*weltliche*) possibilities, this movement between movement and stasis, into either a "free play" of (non)positions said to be merely arbitrary and fictional or into a totalitarian politics of power whose options are reduced to coercion and will. In our view this alternative is false and barren, although certainly both whim and power are part of, and limits to, rhetoric. Instead, what is characteristic about the rhetorician is her ability deliberately to choose an *appropriate* stance, achieved in part, without doubt, by listening to the situation—now given more to open-endedness and indeterminacy, now to closure and decision, *as the particular case requires.* Too often this situated competence is enslaved to uniquely nonrhetorical interests, fascinations, fashions, and agendas. Our own stay against this confusion acknowledges the deeper rhetorical truths of deconstruction while joining with Cornel West in his assessment of our contemporary situation: "In this world-weary period of pervasive cynicisms, nihilisms, terrorisms, and possible extermination, there is a longing for norms and values that can make a difference, a yearning for principled resistance and struggle that can change our desperate plight."[23]

Above all, both rhetoric and hermeneutics occupy the realm of the nonexpert and nontheoretical, as Victoria Kahn explains in Chapter 7. This is the field of everyday action and thought, the contested premises of our shifting home. Expert theory of any kind isolates aspects of this field for special treatment, building its structures of observations, ideas, rules, and laws, but always at the risk of leaving behind those myriad indeterminate parts that combine to make up the whole man or woman, the whole action or event or situation or story or life, however much we argue about its character and shape and significance, and however much such wholes are riddled with gaps, *aporias,* and absences. Rhetoric, like hermeneutics, returns us to this contested and finite whole of everyday existence, in comparison with which all theory, though far-reaching and powerful in its appropriate uses, is existentially thin and feeble.

In our time hopeful signs are emerging. Gradually we are recognizing that rhetoric and hermeneutics offer the means for a renovated liberal education—a distinctly rhetorical *paideia* (in Lanham's phrase) whose value inheres not in theory, nor in a fixed canon, nor in excessive worry over lack of consensus on what is taught, nor even, as Mark Turner urges, in the common cognitive structures of our pervasive metaphorizing.[24] Rather, rhetorical education inheres in how we understand and interpret the indeterminate wholes of our practical lives, those concrete indeterminacies whose interpretations are aided by theory only when that theory cleaves to the matrix of shared, if contested, everyday beliefs, values, experiences, emotions, events, metaphors, images, and narratives with which rhetoric and hermeneutics are uniquely concerned. We need to concentrate on what we are conflicted about and how we become conflicted about such things. In our view this orientation to "how" is cultivated chiefly by rhetorical and hermeneutic training in interpretation and persuasion; it is stabilized (for the moment) in our varied understandings of our own and others' dynamic traditions. In our time, accordingly, rhetoric and hermeneutics should be understood to range from specific arts whose handbooks articulate rules and strategies of invention, address, and application to the broadest possible conceptions of rhetoricality (in Bender and Wellbery's phrase) and rhetoricity (in Charles Altieri's) as dimensions of human existence.[25] Like Lanham and others in our time, we believe—pace Curtius and Lewis—that rhetoric and hermeneutics can reclaim not only their former exalted place in a liberal-arts curriculum but also the nonfoundational grounds of the curriculum itself, of the whole curriculum as a shifting panorama of everyday, indeterminate wholes requiring our interpretations and identifications. Indeed, we believe that only rhetoric and hermeneutics, properly redefined, can show how the principled subject-matter disciplines presuppose the nonexpert realm of *praxis* and practical reasoning and how they must, in the beginning and in the end, be responsible to them. This is the overall orientation of the chapters that follow.

The introduction is broadly designed to locate the major themes explored more deeply in the subsequent chapters. Roughly parallel with the division of the introduction, the book is divided into four sections. This scheme provides sites for rhetoric and hermeneutics to interact with and influence each other. Part I locates different versions of or approaches to the rhetorical and hermeneutic situation and the competences required by them. Part II suggests ways to think about those competences as matters for both invention and application, including ways to think about these terms as mutually implicative. Part II naturally leads to Part III in the way that topics naturally lead to arguments and their premises and further suggests that arguments and narratives (like topics and tropes) presuppose one another in various ways. On the surface Part IV correlates less closely with the fourth section of our introduction. But at a deeper level each investigates where the "possibility of morality" resides.

Particularly in our own time, rhetoric and hermeneutics have been concerned with the importance of conversation in our everyday lives, a truth that was brought home to us again and again in the course of this work through talks with Joel Weinsheimer. From the beginning Joel offered encouragement, support, and practical wisdom, which we are pleased to acknowledge here. We also thank John Campbell of the University of Washington, Richard Harvey Brown of the University of Maryland, Ed Block, Jr., of Marquette University, and Wendy Olmsted of the University of Chicago for their thoughtful readings of the introduction. Finally, we express our gratitude to our manuscript editor, Susan Laity, for her unfailing good sense in matters of style and *dispositio*.

No less essential to rhetoric and hermeneutics are the disposition of charity and the attitude of play. Our families provided both, encouraging us to do this work but requesting us on occasion to stop—for which gifts, among many others, we thank them.

NOTES

1 E. R. Curtius, *European Literature and the Latin Middle Ages* (Princeton: Princeton University Press, 1953; rpt. 1990), 62. Hereafter cited in the text as *ELLM*.

2 C. S. Lewis, *English Literature in the Sixteenth Century* (Oxford: Oxford University Press, 1954), 61.

3 Richard Lanham, *The Electronic Word: Democracy, Technology and the Arts* (Chicago: University of Chicago Press, 1993), 71.

4 Richard Bernstein, *The New Constellation: The Ethical-Political Horizons of Modernity/Postmodernity* (Cambridge: MIT Press, 1991), 28.

5 There are numerous, widely available anthologies and other collections in hermeneutics across the disciplines; most contain useful bibliographies. For helpful overviews of the historical and intellectual ranges of hermeneutics, see Gerald L. Bruns, *Hermeneutics Ancient and Modern* (New Haven: Yale University Press, 1992), Jean Grondin, *Introduction to Philosophical Hermeneutics* (New Haven: Yale University Press, 1994), 170–228. For some specifically literary uses, see William V. Spanos, ed., *Martin Heidegger and the Question of Literature: Toward a Postmodern Literary Hermeneutic* (Bloomington: Indiana University Press, 1976).

6 Grondin, *Introduction to Philosophical Hermeneutics*, 3.

7 Hans-Georg Gadamer, *Wahrheit und Methode* (Tübingen: J. C. B. Mohr, 1960); *Truth and Method*, 2d rev. ed., trans. Joel Weinsheimer and Donald G. Marshall (New York: Continuum, 1993), 568. For a helpful bibliography of rhetorical scholarship, see Winifred Brynat Horner, ed., *The Present State of Scholarship in Historical and Contemporary Rhetoric*, rev. ed. (Columbia: University of Missouri Press, 1990).

8 Søren Kierkegaard, *Concluding Unscientific Postscript*, trans. David F. Swenson and Walter Lowrie (Princeton: Princeton University Press, 1941), 221.

9 *Dasein* is a term of art that does exact, useful work for Heidegger, but which we can render here as "human being."

10 Theodore Kisiel, *The Genesis of Heidegger's* Being and Time (Berkeley: University of California Press, 1993), 421.

11 Ibid., 438.

12 See William H. Race, "The Word [*Kairos*] in Greek Drama," in *Transactions of the American Philological Association,* ed. Douglas E. Gerber, vol. 3 (Chico, Calif.: Scholars Press, 1981), 197–213. Other helpful works include Mario Untersteiner, *The Sophists,* trans. Kathleen Freeman (Oxford: Basil Blackwell, 1954); G. B. Kerferd, *The Sophistic Movement* (Cambridge: Cambridge University Press, 1981); Jacqueline De Romilly, *Magic and Rhetoric in Ancient Greece* (Cambridge: Harvard University Press, 1975), and *The Great Sophists in Periclean Athens,* trans. Janet Lloyd (Oxford: Clarendon Press, 1992); Edward Schiappa, *Protagoras and Logos: A Study in Greek Philosophy and Rhetoric* (Columbia: University of South Carolina Press, 1991), esp. 73–74; Dale L. Sullivan, "Kairos and the Rhetoric of Belief," *Quarterly Journal of Speech* 78 (1992), 317–32; and Eric E. White, *Kaironomia: On the Will-to-Invent* (Ithaca: Cornell University Press, 1987). Given its provenance in rhetoric, it is significant that *kairos* does not appear in F. E. Peters's historical lexicon, *Greek Philosophical Terms* (New York: New York University Press, 1967), for the constellation of values it elevates—time, contingency, invention, adaptation to audience and occasion, persuasion—are just the values philosophers from Plato to Hegel have resisted.

13 On *sprezzaturra* see Victoria Kahn, "Humanism and the Resistance to Theory," Chapter 7, this volume. See also Lanham, *Electronic Word,* 148. For a different approach to the term, see Frank Kermode, *The Sense of an Ending: Studies in the Theory of Fiction* (New York: Oxford University Press, 1967), 46–50.

14 This line of thought is pursued in interesting ways by Stanley Cavell in *The Senses of Walden* (Chicago: University of Chicago Press, 1982, expanded edition), 88: "*Walden,* in its emphasis upon listening and answering, outlines an epistemology of conscience."

15 Kisiel, *Genesis,* 296–97.

16 Hans-Georg Gadamer, "The Hermeneutics of Suspicion," in *Hermeneutics: Questions and Prospects,* ed. Gary Shapiro and Alan Sica (Amherst: University of Massachusetts Press, 1984), 55.

17 David Tracy, "Charity, Obscurity, Clarity: Augustine's Search for Rhetoric and Hermeneutics," Chapter 12, this volume.

18 Gadamer, "Hermeneutics of Suspicion," 57. Heidegger glosses *hermeneuein* as "the exposition which brings tidings because it can listen to a message": Martin Heidegger, "Dialogue with a Japanese," in Heidegger, *On the Way to Language,* trans. Peter D. Hertz (New York: Harper and Row, 1971), 29.

19 Gerald L. Bruns, "On the Tragedy of Hermeneutical Experience," Chapter 3, this volume.

20 See Josef Bleicher, *Contemporary Hermeneutics: Hermeneutics as Method, Philosophy, and Critique* (London: Routledge, 1980).

21 In *Aristotle's* Rhetoric: *A Theory of Civic Discourse* (New York: Oxford University Press, 1991), 7, George Kennedy has something like this in mind when he writes: "Rhetoric, in the most general sense, is the energy inherent in emotion and thought, transmitted through a system of signs, including language, to others to influence their decisions or action."

22 Lanham, *Electronic Word*, 82.

23 Cornel West, *The American Evasion of Philosophy: A Genealogy of Pragmatism* (Madison: University of Wisconsin Press, 1989), 4. Cf. Henry Staten, *Wittgenstein and Derrida* (Lincoln: University of Nebraska Press, 1984), 126–27: "If there is any skepticism in Derrida, it is a moral not an epistemological skepticism—not a doubt about the possibility of morality but about an idealized picture of sincerity that takes insufficient account of the windings and twistings of fear and desire, weakness and lust, sadism and masochism and the will to power, in the mind of the most sincere man." For compatible accounts, see Richard Bernstein, *The New Constellation;* Christopher Norris, *Derrida* (Cambridge: Harvard University Press, 1987); and Drucilla Cornell, *The Philosophy of the Limit* (New York: Routledge, Chapman, and Hall, 1992).

24 Lanham, *Electronic Word,* esp. chaps. 4 and 7; Mark Turner, *Reading Minds: The Study of English in the Age of Cognitive Science* (Princeton: Princeton University Press, 1991). For related accounts see Walter Jost, *Rhetorical Thought in John Henry Newman* (Columbia: University of South Carolina Press, 1989), esp. chap. 6: "'A Comprehensive View': The Role of Rhetoric in Liberal Education"; and David Bromwich, *Politics By Other Means: Higher Education and Group Thinking* (New Haven: Yale University Press, 1992), esp. chap. 4.

25 John Bender and David E. Wellbery, eds., *The Ends of Rhetoric: History, Theory, Practice* (Stanford: Stanford University Press, 1990); Charles Altieri, "Rhetorics, Rhetoricity, and the Sonnet as Performance," *Tennessee Studies in Literature* 25 (1980): 1–23. See also Hans-Georg Gadamer, "Rhetoric and Hermeneutics," Chapter 1, this volume.

Introduction

Rhetoric and Hermeneutics:
Places Along the Way

Walter Jost and Michael J. Hyde

Our purpose in this introduction is twofold. On the one hand we propose several ways in which rhetoric and hermeneutics might support each other—that is, contribute to thinking about the philosophic character as well as the practical strategies involved in both interpretation and persuasion. On the other hand we seek to set forth general lines of inquiry and argument that are explored in the chapters that follow and that we hope will stimulate readers of this book to further questions and inquiries of their own.

As our means of structuring both our chapter and the book as a whole, we explore four sites or places (*topoi*) at which rhetoric and hermeneutics intersect: first, the situated competences of the two; second, the fundamental and correlative capacities of invention and application; third, the mutual implication of arguments (topics) and metaphor and narrative (tropes); and fourth, the call of conscience understood as the *topos* of *topoi,* the place of places that opens up the human world "as" a world of values, commitments, ideals, agendas, interests, and needs and that, in so doing, summons us to ourselves and to others. More specifically, we focus in the first and last sections on Heidegger and Levinas, respectively, and in the second section on Gadamer and Vico, as central figures responsible for opening up many of the issues currently at stake. The third section includes in its discussion such thinkers as Ludwig Wittgenstein and Stanley Cavell, who have been unfortunately neglected by those interested in rhetoric and hermeneutics. The introduction culminates in a speculative meditation on the concept of conscience as a *topical* "first principle" for both disciplines. With this concept, in other words, we are suggesting neither a self-evident truth nor some determinate (e.g., religious) content, nor even a "universal topic" of the type sought by Vico, but rather what might be called a "temporal topic" of the sort investigated by Kenneth Burke or Mikhail Bakhtin. Although we do not explicitly refer to conscience in the first three sections, the concept underwrites our entire effort, for we argue that conscience is the sine qua non underwriting all rhetorical and hermeneutical thought and activity.

RHETORIC AND HERMENEUTICS: SITUATED COMPETENCES

Because of the contingency of human existence, we inhabit a world where the practice of rhetoric is genuinely necessary. The point has been made by many theorists, among them Hans Blumenberg: "Lacking definitive evidence and being compelled to act are the prerequisites of the rhetorical situation."[1] Indeed we are rhetorical beings, creatures who are capable of dealing symbolically with particular matters that we recognize as pressing and that require careful deliberation and judgment, but whose meaning and significance are presently ambiguous, uncertain, and contestable. The history of rhetoric defines a tradition made up of a vast array of observations describing the ways symbolic action has taken form in such situations. This tradition is also marked by an equally vast array of theoretical prescriptions based on these observations that promote rhetoric to the status of an art and that offer direction for cultivating the ability to engage this contingency—what we might call our rhetorical competence. One of the earliest accounts of the importance of such competence for establishing and maintaining our social well-being is offered by Isocrates: "Because there has been implanted in us the power to persuade each other and to make clear to each other what we desire, not only have we escaped the life of wild beasts, but we have come together and founded cities and made laws and invented arts; and, generally speaking, there is no institution devised by man which the power of speech has not helped us to establish. For this it is which has laid down laws concerning things just and unjust, and things honorable and base; and if it were not for these ordinances we should not be able to live with one another."[2] As exemplified here, associating rhetorical competence with the creation and preservation of a community's moral ecology is a commonplace of the rhetorical tradition, one that works as a major source of legitimation for teachers of rhetoric. When "the power to persuade" becomes the all-too-easy target it is made out to be in, for example, Plato's *Gorgias* and *Sophist* and later in Descartes, Locke, Kant, and Hegel, this competence is dissociated from its declared connection with the morality of a community or culture (and more broadly with the human orientation to ideals as guides for behavior).

The rhetorical tradition has had much to say about rhetorical competence in the narrower sense: the civic-minded power to persuade. Conceptualized in terms of the canons of the art of rhetoric, for example, rhetorical competence has been specified as a proficiency in handling the five stages of composing and presenting a speech: *inventio* (invention), *dispositio* (arrangement), *elocutio* (expression), *memoria* (memory), and *pronuntiatio* or *actio* (delivery), as well as an ability to handle the formal divisions of the speech: *exordium* (introduction), *narratio* (narration), *partitio* (division), *confirmatio* (proof), *refutatio* (refutation), and *conclusio* (conclusion). Most important, these canons and divisions serve to organize arguments from the substantive facts and issues of the case, the emotions of the audience, and the character of the speaker.[3]

Knowing how to put these things to use when confronting the contingent demands of a situation may facilitate a person's attempts to be persuasive (what one critic has called the "external" goals of the practice), but for the ancients, rhetorical competence could also function as an integrative social influence between the self and others (the "internal," ethical-political goal of the practice).[4] Beginning with the Sophists, training in rhetorical competence has had as one of its internal goals increasing people's chances of getting an equal hearing for their ideas such that they and their contributions might be recognized and respected as important to the sociopolitical workings of a community.[5] Moreover, as Aristotle would have us understand in expanding on this point, the service provided to the community by its members' rhetorical competence extends beyond mere persuasion to include the development of judgment (*krisis*) and practical wisdom (*phronesis*). Rhetorical competence lends itself to collaborative deliberation and reflective inquiry (including the self-deliberations of individual members). In the rhetorical situation an audience is not set at a distance. Rather, it is acknowledged, engaged, and called into the space of practical concerns. By facilitating civic engagement, rhetorical competence helps sustain and enrich the knowledge of any public, and thus a community's own competence. Through the deliberative rationality of rhetorical practices, a community can recognize itself and judge whether to admit the epistemological and moral claims of those who are attempting to influence it.[6]

Hence, in its very functioning, rhetorical competence gives expression to the communal character of the self's existence and in so doing allows all concerned to "know together" (Gr. *sun-eidesis;* Lat. *con-scientia*). For us as for the Greeks, maintaining the health of our communal existence requires nothing less.

There is another art, however, in addition to rhetoric, that asks us to attend to the nature and importance of rhetorical competence (again narrowly defined). It is the art of understanding, or hermeneutics, an art that, as the philologist and founder of modern hermeneutic theory Friedrich Schleiermacher points out, "at once depends upon and presupposes composition," whether spoken or written.[7] Here Schleiermacher associates the composition of a text with the art of presentation (rhetoric), an art that enables the author to explicate his subject matter so that it may be understood by others. Hence, Schleiermacher maintains that "hermeneutics and rhetoric are intimately related in that every act of understanding is the reverse side of an act of speaking [or writing], and one must grasp the thinking that underlies a given statement."[8]

The hermeneutical task being emphasized here defines a fundamental goal of Schleiermacher's theory of interpretive understanding. In order to gain the fullest access to the intended meaning in a given text, the reader must attempt to reconstruct and reexperience the distinctive mental processes that were at work in its composition. Schleiermacher points to the author's particular style as a major source of evidence for comprehending these processes. He writes: "Thoughts and language are intertwined, and an author's distinctive way of treating the subject is manifested by his organization of his material and by his use of language."[9] An appreciation of the rhetorical competence that informs the text is therefore needed by the interpreter.

It seems fair to say, then, that the hermeneut is herself something of a rhetorical critic. With Schleiermacher, however, one must be careful in advancing this ambiguous claim. For the Greeks, as for many contemporary theorists, rhetorical criticism is naturally an effort in rhetorical competence broadly understood: the critic is deeply involved in the process of crafting a composition that is intended to be persuasive but which is *also* devoted to cultivating judgment and practical wisdom in others.[10] In contrast, Schleiermacher maintains that hermeneutics is basically a philosophical endeavor; it "deals only with the art of understanding, not with the [interpreter's] presentation of what has been understood."[11] Yet, as Kurt Mueller-Vollmer notes, this position is not without its problems: "Schleiermacher viewed hermeneutics as the 'art of understanding' where 'understanding' is elevated to the art of a scholarly discipline. . . . However, it seems doubtful whether hermeneutics, by excluding from its agenda the element of presentation, can still fulfill the task which Schleiermacher envisions. For the art of the philologist consists largely in generally accepted procedures, assumptions, verbal strategies, an institutionalized body of knowledge and the tacit agreement on standards for hermeneutic competence. The presentation of one's understanding is an integral part of the art in question."[12]

In fact, then, hermeneutics and rhetoric are more intimately related than Schleiermacher believed, for what he failed to realize was that the art of understanding, dedicated as it is to advancing the hermeneutic competence of those interested in being part of its scholarly enterprise, must itself employ the practice of rhetoric to disclose clearly and to justify any truth claim regarding the authorial intentions of a given text. "Convincing and persuading," writes Gadamer, "are obviously as much the aim and measure of understanding and interpretation as they are the aim and measure of the art of oration and persuasion."[13] In its relation with the art of understanding, rhetorical competence must be acknowledged as something more than an object of study, something more than a passageway of stylistic signposts directing the reader back to the subjective confines of an author's thought. Of course rhetorical competence can include a concern with the author's subjective thought; but Schleiermacher's exclusive focus on this goes against the grain of the deeper (less subjectivistic) rhetorical intentionality that we now recognize is at work in the text. As Calvin Schrag reminds us: "The distinctive stamp of rhetorical intentionality is that it reaches out toward, aims at, is directed to the other as hearer, reader, and audience. This intentionality illustrates not the theoretical reflection of cognitive detachment but rather the practical engagement of concrete involvement."[14] The rhetorical competence that informs a text leads hermeneutics in the direction it must go to reach out and engage others so that its declared understanding of a particular subject matter can be shared, agreed with, or disputed. This is how hermeneutics achieves practical significance: by returning, with the help of rhetoric, from the workings of the mind to the everyday world of situated, practical concerns.

One might describe this returning as a homecoming for hermeneutics, since the everyday world that it now inhabits, as Heidegger has shown, is the place where the art of understanding is first practiced.[15] Before it is converted into the abstract and formal rules, logics, and laws of theoretical knowledge, with its penchant for "knowing-that," human understanding assumes the more primordial and performance-based form of a person's "knowing-how" to deal with the immediacy of his or her everyday, goal-directed activities. As creatures of know-how, that is, with the tacit and unreflective ability to cope successfully with our problems, we embody and exhibit a hermeneutic competence for coming to see and involve ourselves with the world. This competence or interpretive outlook is one of "circumspection," concern with the world in such a way that it becomes and remains useful for our purposes. Here things first manifest themselves *as* "equipment." With the writing of this introduction in mind, for example, we approach our computers not as objects present to our eyes but as instruments and materials of work ready to our hands. As they come into the "circumspective interpretation" of our know-how, we appreciate the computers *as* tools that, when handled well, facilitate a specific task.

Heidegger terms this the "existential-*hermeneutical* 'as'" of primordial understanding (know-how): it is the original, albeit unthematized and nonverbalized, articulation (*Rede*) of our everyday, situated comportment with environed things (*BT* 200–201ff.). We live lives that necessitate the hermeneutical competence of such comportment in order to be skilled at living, to do what is appropriate to perform a job well. Hermeneutical competence is productive of and maintained by the practical wisdom (*phronesis*) that is based in a given culture's "hermeneutical situation" (its world of perspectival understanding) and that forms the habit of right insight into human action.[16] The relation between rhetoric and hermeneutics is rooted in this existential situation of circumspective concern. Rhetoric, too, is a type of know-how, a complex competence that gives expression, among other things, to our ability to be persuasive, to make known the useful and the inexpedient, the fitting and the improper, the just and the unjust, thereby enabling us to engage others in collaborative deliberation about contestable matters. In this way the know-how of rhetorical competence not only draws from a culture's historically based hermeneutical situation, it also contributes to the advancement of this intersubjective domain of understanding. In Heidegger's terms, the know-how of rhetorical competence must therefore be appreciated as having much to do with "the everydayness of Being with one another," with our "publicness." Heidegger credits Aristotle's *Rhetoric* with providing "the first systematic hermeneutic" of this communal character of existence. Moreover, like Aristotle, Heidegger would have us understand how our everyday way of being with others defines a realm of emotional orientations and attachments (i.e., moods) that are constantly "attuning" us to situations we are a part of and that are forever unfolding before our eyes. Hence, in offering a gloss of the *Rhetoric*, Heidegger writes: "Publicness . . . not only has in general its own way of having a mood, but needs moods and 'makes' them for itself. It is into such a mood and out of such a mood that the orator speaks. He must understand the possibilities of moods in order to rouse them and guide them aright [i.e., in a right or just manner]" (*BT* 178).[17]

Philosophy has long been critical of rhetoric because of its association with emotion. The criticism typically has a Platonic ring to it: by catering to an audience's emotions, rhetoric inhibits people from developing intelligence based on a rational knowledge (*episteme*) of reality; it thereby encourages the masses to become "the greatest of all sophists."[18] From the standpoint of hermeneutic ontology, however, this view of the matter is far too negative and simplistic. For, as Heidegger makes clear in his analysis of mood, the fundamental workings of human emotion have an important role to play in the constitution of experience. That is, emotions provide the perspectives for seeing the world "as" interesting, as something that matters and that warrants interpretation. By virtue of this function, we are able to comport with things and with others. Human emotion must therefore be seen as something that informs and gives focus to the "circumspective interpretation" of the primordial understanding of know-how. Or as Heidegger puts it: "Understanding always has its mood" (*BT* 182).

As a type of know-how, rhetoric is perforce associated with the hermeneutical workings of emotion. If rhetoric is to perform its most worthy function of trying to move people toward situated goods, it must cast a concerned eye on how its public is circumspectively and thus emotionally involved with the immediate situation. This is how the orator maximizes the chance that those comprising his or her audience will take an interest in what is being said, so that they too may have a say in determining whether their extant ways of seeing, interpreting, and being involved with things and with others might be changed for the better. Without the formation of such a common interest, collaborative deliberation is all but impossible.

Heidegger is correct: the orator (by which we mean more generally any rhetorically competent individual in any practical setting) must understand the possibility of moods in order to rouse them and guide them in a right or just manner. Such rhetorical competence operates in the immediacy of the present, in the lived space of the here and now, in the existential and practically oriented world of know-how. Rhetoric offers an interpretive understanding of this world; it articulates and thus makes explicit something about how people are faring in their everyday relationships with things and others and how they might think and act in order to understand better and perhaps improve a particular situation. The interpretive understanding that belongs to rhetorical discourse thereby shows itself as a "derivative mode" of the primordial, hermeneutical "as" of circumspective interpretation. Heidegger discusses this derivative mode of interpretive understanding in terms of how it operates as an "assertion," as "apophantic" discourse (*apophansis:* to make manifest) that *points out* something by *predicating* it in a definite way, such that what is being talked about can be *communicated* and shared with others (*BT* 196–99).

Now, rhetorical discourse certainly makes use of assertions. All the more do the discourses of logic and science. There is, however, an important difference between the apophantic mode of operation of these latter and related discourses and that of rhetorical discourse.[19] Heidegger directs us toward an understanding of this difference with his analysis of how the assertions of logic and science bring about a "levelling of the primordial 'as' of circumspective interpretation" (BT 198–201). One sees this phenomenon unfolding, for example, when physicians, trained to abide by and express the scientifically oriented "voice of medicine," engage in the practice of "properly" writing up a patient's medical case history.

Medical case histories are rooted in the "illness stories" of patients. Such stories, according to Eric Cassell, "are different from other stories because they almost always have at least *two* characters to whom things happen. They always have at least a *person* and that person's *body*."[20] Of these two characters, it is the body, the rhetorical-hermeneutic place (*topos*) where disease dwells, that must assume priority as a matter of interest to the physician. Directed by this priority, the physician can now begin constructing a story that will—or at least should, so far as his peers are concerned—cut like a scalpel through the personhood of the patient, thereby leaving intact only those portions of the patient's history that can be used to make a good case about some disease, in some body, in some bed. Medical case histories mark out an effort in dissection directed toward offering a depersonalized perception and account of the patient. They are prized for their self-effacing objectivity and efficiency, both of which are registered via the antiseptic language of "disease theory" and what it has to say about such things as angina pectoris, rheumatic mitral valvular disease, and oat cell carcinoma of the lung. Medical case histories employ a language that tells a body story, not a person story. From the standpoint of medical science, these two stories are not meant to go together. They employ different language games, their respective characters are incommensurate. Indeed, the idiosyncratic subjectivity of the "person" gets in the way of the scientific objectivity of the "body." When this occurs, the medical matter may become too time-consuming, too existential, too uncertain and opinionated. The Hippocratic *Law* tells us: "There are in fact two things, science and opinion; the former begets knowledge, the latter ignorance."[21] Medical case histories offer stories that are Law-abiding.

Those of us who have benefited from a physician's ability to tell such a story can testify to its importance. When complaints surface, however, they often bear on the fact that, during an encounter with the medical profession, the patient was treated by physicians whose scientific conditioning and outlook blinded them to the difference between physiology and life. What tends to be forgotten when such blindness occurs is that patients are people and should be treated as people. A diseased body is also a *lived* body that brings to the medical encounter a host of personal concerns, involvements, and values (a world of know-how) that the patient may wish to have taken into account in the design of a treatment. Patients have the right to do this; they have the right to affirm who they are while in the presence of Medicine. As suggested above, it is this large dimension of the patient's humanity that is left out of the picture of a body story. Here, then, is an instance of the leveling of the primordial "as" of circumspective interpretation. The assertions of a body story point out and predicate their object in a restrictive way. Their apophantic mode of operation, as Heidegger would say, "no longer reaches out into a totality of involvements" (*BT* 200), into the patient's, or person's, hermeneutically informed world of know-how.

One may, of course, speak of the rhetoric of body stories. Determining *how* a text means is a genuine rhetorical concern. But in this case, what is actually being referred to is a mode of discourse that has been dislodged from that world in which rhetoric's genuine calling originates. Rhetoric makes its living first and foremost *in* the world of know-how. It discovers the materials that are needed for its work from how people are involved with the everyday concerns and contingencies of life. Here the available means of persuasion are found, and people await the acknowledgment of their particular interests by those who engage them in collaborative deliberation about contestable matters. The effectiveness of rhetoric is dependent on its staying in touch with this emotionally attuned realm of *praxis*, of the person. For only then can it attend to, with the hope of clarifying and improving, its audience's active relationships with things and with others. Rhetoric's apophantic mode of operation is directed by this hope; its assertions must tell of the world of know-how. Hence, in its most elucidating and epiphanic moments, it is not uncommon for the assertions of rhetoric to assume a poetic nature. Heidegger tells us that "poetry, creative literature, is nothing but the elementary emergence into words, the becoming uncovered, of existence as being in the world [of know-how]. For the others who before it were blind, the world first becomes visible by what is thus spoken."[22] In Heidegger's sense a poetic interpretation can serve rhetoric well. When used in an appropriate, fitting, and engaging—that is, rhetorically competent—manner, a display of poetic or hermeneutic competence may help us improve the ways others are presently seeing, interpreting, and involving themselves with the situational matters at hand. In short, as a type of know-how or hermeneutical competence, the practice of rhetorical competence must cultivate in others the practical wisdom that is advanced and sustained by such competences and that no community can afford to be without. The social, political, and moral welfare of our everyday Being-with-others, of our publicness, is a major concern of rhetoric.

There are, of course, less noble ways of thinking about rhetoric. In his description of how publicness defines a world of common sense and common *praxis,* for instance, Heidegger tends to emphasize its "mass"-like (Plato), "crowd"-like (Kierkegaard), and "herd"-like (Nietzsche) propensity to bring about a mindless conformity in its adherents. That rhetoric can and does play a role in sustaining our publicness is undeniable. With Heidegger, then, it can be said that those who theorize and practice the orator's art are involving themselves with a *techne* whose way of being admits more than a modicum of inauthenticity (*uneigentlichkeit*).[23] A similar assessment of rhetoric is announced by Gadamer when he speaks of the art as "that which is other than the factical matter of our propositions," as "that which possesses the purely operational and ritual function of exchange through speaking, whether in oral or written form," and thus as a "pseudotext" that "is devoid of meaning."[24] Rhetoric, to be sure, is capable of existing in such a fallen state, and the teachings of philosophical hermeneutics can be employed to remind and warn us of this fact. But these teachings also enable us to develop an appreciation of how rhetoric admits a competence for addressing others such that, when the situation calls for it, they can be roused and guided "in a right or just manner."

RHETORICAL INVENTION AND HERMENEUTIC APPLICATION

In this section our immediate task is to shed some light on how—that is, with what specific intellectual, emotional, and imaginative means—people become active in rhetorical and hermeneutic situations, what it means for them to become competent as strategic readers and speakers. What specifically gives their activity intellectual, as well as moral, discipline and resolve in the face of indeterminacy? The question is at once methodological and existential, concerned with intellectual skill and competence (or tact) motivated and informed by ready moral commitment and conscience—what one literary thinker has aptly described as "competence, supported by an instinct."[25] Accounts of rhetoric and hermeneutics in our own time offer various approaches to this problem, but one locus classicus, Gadamer's *Truth and Method,*[26] reflects on, and embodies, both rhetoric and hermeneutics in ways that critics have not explicitly thematized, and that will allow us to suggest how figures like Vico and Burke, along with Gadamer, help us to think out new connections.[27]

It is significant that Gadamer begins *Truth and Method* by appropriating central concepts of the humanist tradition (*Bildung, sensus communis,* judgment, taste), for these have been rhetorical preoccupations from the Sophists on. And it is significant that Gadamer turns to Vico at the beginning of his book, and again in the afterword, and that he focuses on Vico's major treatise on rhetoric and rhetorical education, *De nostri temporis studiorum ratione* (On the study methods of our time, 1709).[28] For Gadamer, Vico "makes a good starting point" (*TM* 19) in considering the problematic of hermeneutics by suggesting how the defense of rhetoric against "critical" (Cartesian, deductive) philosophy might be extended to the understanding and defense of hermeneutics against latter-day versions of rationalist philosophy. Rhetoric aims at "the grasp and moral control of the concrete situation" (*TM* 21), not at abstract, universal knowledge ("science" and its attendant expertise), just as hermeneutics does: "Practical knowledge . . . . is directed towards the concrete situation. Thus it must grasp the 'circumstances' in their infinite variety. This is what Vico expressly emphasizes about it" (*TM* 21). Students of rhetoric will recognize in those circumstances what ancient rhetoricians called the *peristaseis* or *circumstantia* of a case—the occasion, audience beliefs and values, the unique array of facts—toward which orators directed all their efforts. We might generalize and say that such rhetorical doctrines have always already operationalized many of the contemporary hermeneutic (philosophic) reflections on *praxis*, while the latter deepen and extend traditional rhetorical theory in ways not yet appreciated. Either way, the question is not "What is abstractly true or right?" but "What is true or right or good in this unique case?" Even this formulation suggests a division in kind between the two questions, as if the general question were about (philosophic, nonrhetorical) truth, and the specific question about passing probabilities (mere rhetoric). Against this division Cicero in *De oratore* has both Crassus and Antonius bridge the split by requiring the general as well as the particular to become the subject matter of oratory, insofar as the orator prevents philosophic abstraction from severing its ties to practical and public concerns, "the manners, minds, and lives of mankind." The holistic ground of the ethical-political is accessible to all, what Vico called *sensus communis*: "the real power of eloquence is such, that it embraces the origin, the influence, the changes of all things in the world, all virtues, duties, and all nature, so far as it affects the manners, minds, and lives of mankind."[29]

Gadamer's position is similarly unified, for, like Cicero's and Vico's, it stabilizes the general in the particular, in the circumstances of one's own situation, time and place: Theory-with-a-capital-T is returned to diverse historical practices, and hermeneutic philosophy does its best work by helping other fields keep themselves tethered to specific common enterprises and the contest of beliefs and values comprising them. In fact, there is an important parallel that

goes undiscussed both in *Truth and Method* and among students of hermeneutics generally. This is the parallel between what Vico identifies as the fundamental activity of rhetoric, namely *inventio,* seeing the available means of
persuasion (*Methods* 14); and what Gadamer calls "the fundamental problem
of hermeneutics," namely *applicatio,* the always provisional fulfillment of distanciated meaning in the interpretive act (*TM* 307ff.). The sort of parallel we
are suggesting is hinted at in Bacon's *Advancement of Learning* (1605), where
Bacon defines rhetorical invention in a way that Vico approved, as "remembrance . . . *with an application*"—and which, in the spirit of Vico, we can philosophically deepen and bring full circle by defining hermeneutic application as
"remembrance—*with an invention.*"[30] Such a move is also implicitly sanctioned by Gadamer in his afterword to *Truth and Method:* "I would like to see
more recognition of the fact that this is the realm hermeneutics shares along
with rhetoric: the realm of arguments that are convincing (which is not the
same as logically compelling). It is the realm of practice and humanity in general. . . . The arts of rhetoric and argumentation (and their silent analogue,
thoughtful deliberation with oneself) are at home here. If rhetoric appeals to
the feelings, as has long been clear, that in no way means it falls outside the
realm of the reasonable. Vico rightly assigns it a special value: *copia,* the abundance of viewpoints" (*TM* 568).[31]

In other words *copia,* "the abundance of viewpoints" constituting the material of *sensus communis* and the source of rhetorical invention, was, in the classical rhetorical tradition that Vico appropriated, the source of the *ars topica,*
the art of topics (in our own time we might call topics the art and ability of Heidegger's "hermeneutic-as" or Wittgenstein's "seeing-as").[32] Allowing for a distinction between tacit and unthematized "first-stage" topics and consciously
organized and deployed "second-stage topics,"[33] we can say that conscious
rhetorical invention is remembrance by means of (second-order or reflective)
topics and the application of their content to a new case or text. Hermeneutic
application, accordingly, is the remembrance of cases or texts with a topical invention. What then, more specifically, are topics, and what might such a parallel suggest for both rhetoric and philosophical and literary hermeneutics?

In the rhetorical tradition topics has always named a more or less tacit,
more or less articulatable ability to negotiate social and cultural "identifications" (to use Kenneth Burke's term) or *sensus communis* (to use Vico's). Topics are the places—issues, values, commitments, beliefs, likelihoods—that we
hold in common with others, that we dwell in and argue over, and that we use
reflectively to find the issues and premises of a specific case. The source of
their power resides in the fact that they are Janus-faced. Horizontally or temporally they retrieve or recall the past and yet are *applied* toward an indetermi-

nate present and future (thus topics *as such* cannot be accused of political conservatism, although Aristotle may have held as much).[34] Vertically or intellec-
tually they are terms, propositions, figures, fables, cases of some generality
(their verbal form is secondary, for it varies with the kind of indeterminacy in
which they are involved)[35] that are accessible to all of those engaged in specific
concrete cases and particulars; in this way they escape the charge of social elit-
ism or academic preciosity. The philosopher Bernard Lonergan is a neglected
thinker who, without himself mentioning the rhetorical tradition, appreciates
how topics draw from, and then work on, *sensus communis*: "Common sense,
unlike the sciences, is a specialization in the particular and concrete. It is common without being general, for it consists in a set of insights that remain incomplete, until there is added at least one further insight into the situation at
hand; and, once that situation has passed, the added insight is no longer relevant, so that common sense at once reverts to its normal state of incompleteness."[36] Hence topics are insights that are *kept incomplete* and whose very deficiency *enables* inquirers to deploy their understanding within a new
situation. This situation is one they do not yet fully understand and need to explore to persuade others, and themselves, of what they jointly will find and
make persuasive within that space.

Implied in such an account is a further tension. Rhetoricians often speak of
second-stage topics as an art (*techne*) or systematic technique, whose form is
the compilable list of general headings and propositions all-too-familiar in the
history of rhetoric, and whose downward tendency is toward memorization
and mechanical use. On the other hand, first-stage topics can be the focus of a
cultivated faculty (*dunamis*) or sense or skill or function, whose upward drift is
a self-levitation into romantic genius and mystery but whose proper, nonrule-
governed exercise is, as we have said, practical competence and more or less
tacit conscientiousness and know-how (instinct).[37] The tension between these
two aspects can be heard in Vico: "Those who [instinctively] know all the *loci*
[*topoi*], i.e., the lines of argument to be used, are able (by an operation not unlike reading the printed characters on a page) to grasp extemporaneously the
elements of persuasion inherent in any case or question" (*Methods* 15). To
grasp extemporaneously is to have achieved, through diligence and education
(*Bildung*), an essentially uncodifiable ability of discernment, of taste, of decorum. To *teach* this ability, however, as Vico and others also wished to do, one
must refer students to second-stage lists, examples, and exercises to learn by
creative imitation. This tension should be instructive, but it periodically collapses into a dichotomy favoring one side or the other.

As list and teachable technique, for example, second-stage topics provide a
repertoire of responses to practical *aporias,* a relatively stable inventory of

contradictory historical or social thought and behavior to which the thoughtful inquirer turns for *re*-sources—sources that can be used again and again on opposite sides of a question as new problems occur. Aristotle's *Rhetoric* I, 3–15, and II, 1–25—in other words, no less than two-thirds of the book—is just such a general inventory, one that Aristotle recognizes can be added to or subtracted from as the scene of its employment changes. More specific inventories or catalogues in principle would include all "how-to" manuals: *The Federalist Papers,* or Benjamin Cardozo's *Nature of the Judicial Process,* or Kierkegaard's *Concluding Unscientific Postscript,* or any number of such texts normally unrecognized as "rhetorics," that is, as collections of topical resources for situated practical thought.

When topics (as list or repertoire) get too uniformly or finely determined in their meanings, however, they cease to function as rhetorical places and become something else, namely mere facts, or principles of a determinate inquiry, or ideology. Pursued productively, these generate or otherwise become a part of abstract knowledge or science and its expertise, produced from selected stable and recurrent aspects of some greater indeterminate whole and pursued *apart* from that whole and its competing interpretations. (In truth, all theory must be taken to some extent topically in order to be of practical use.) Performed ineptly or sophistically, however, the application of theory to practice begets a Raskolnikov, whose claim to bring a "new word" is no longer a topical invention but rather a brute coercion that crushes all inquiry and situated competence under the hatchet blows of the isolated individual will.[38] Here, authentic ideals of conscience are no longer responsible to shared, if contested, places. Instead, they are perverted into simple success or failure in the assertion of one's own or another's power. Less extreme versions of the will-to-power and the politics of topical rhetoric similarly refer invention to personal preference and already defined interests. In contrast, genuine topics help us discover what we say we *ought* to be interested in, what our "ownmost" situation *is not yet understood to be* (and never totally understood to be), by virtue of our refusal to permit them to freeze into *either* determinate principles or unprincipled determinisms. We do this by staying open to analogical extrapolations of what is already known or done or believed. In this regard the art of topics must resist attempts to freeze it into determinate lists, rules, "knowledge," and stay open, by way of application, to novel ideas, images, and narratives.[39]

First-stage topics, as a natural competence and cultivated ability to discern the new by means of (or in) the old, is an ability ultimately beyond all codifiable arts of rhetoric. As such, first-stage topics tend to lose coherence and identity and to shade off into the particularities of a "well-stocked mind," a "liberal education," claims to omnicompetence, and (historically) a creativity aligned with romantic expressivism and, at the other end of the line, a hermetic free play of language. Pursuing topics intelligently, we can get, for example, Heidegger's later meditations on the way poetry *opens up* a region (*Gegend*) or place (*Ort*) hitherto unsuspected in daily thought and speech: topics understood now at the level of world disclosure.[40]

By contrast, Ivan Karamazov's Grand Inquisitor pursues topics in a way that decisively forecloses intelligence. For the Grand Inquisitor, inquisitiveness is not rhetorical inquiry into the indeterminate nature of God or man but rather dogmatic imposition, not by anti-rhetorical coercion but by hyper-rhetorical (sophistical) seduction, aiming to relieve the "audience" of mankind of its burden of thought and freedom—which is to say, its genuinely open-ended situation in the world. On Ivan's account the natural human desire to respond inventively to the call of conscience is not reduced to the success or failure to master others but imperceptibly removed from the public sphere and hidden behind a cloud of "miracle, mystery, and authority."[41] Less extreme versions of this approach convert topics into the negotiable agreements of interpreting communities deciding—as if it were a matter for decision—in what conscience will be said to consist. By contrast, an authentic topics acknowledges the already inhabited spaces of our own enduring acknowledgments (our forms of life) while insisting on our continued testing of these according to the call of a shareable conscience informed—and corrected—by the full panoply of established thought and value in the world, which is to say, *across* forms of life. In this respect topics is an inexhaustible power to examine continuously "all" of the relevant means of persuasion. Thus Vico states that "the most eulogizing epithet that can be given to a speech is that it is 'comprehensive': praise is due to a speaker who has left nothing untouched, and has omitted nothing from the argument, nothing which may be missed by his listeners" (*Methods* 15).

Now, in hermeneutic *applicatio*, Gadamerian "prejudices," selected and organized within what Heidegger calls "forestructures of understanding" (*BT* 191), effectively function as first-order inventional *topoi* of our understanding and interpretation of ourselves and the world. When it comes to reading distanciated texts, as Gadamer explicitly recognizes, "the grasping of the meaning of the text takes on something of the character of an independent productive act, one that resembles more the art of the orator than the process of mere listening."[42] Philosophic treatises that account for these structures can thus profitably be taken up within the history of rhetoric as well as hermeneutics, while their actual *uses* by these philosophers are also rhetorical inventions themselves, within and upon the *sensus communis* of those involved.[43] For

Gadamer, as for Vico and Cicero, the paradigm for application and invention alike is law. The problem to be solved is the relation subsisting between an established but distant rule or text and a novel and urgent case. The question becomes this: If we cannot be said to "apply" what we do not *in some sense* already have, and yet if new prejudices and a new situation preclude mechanical replication of the old rule in our possession, how then is application undertaken? *In what sense* do we "have" our traditions and texts? And why should their employment be called inventive?[44]

It may seem an impoverished answer to recall that the possession of a topical ability resists theoretical formulation, that this ability of invention/application consists of *incomplete* insights that only find completion in the judgment of those involved in concrete situations—in other words, that we are, in Blumenberg's phrase, "beings of deficiency" whose impoverishment, however, *is* our *virtu*.[45] For this is as close as we come to formulating what will never fully formulate. The hermeneutic reader employs her topical prejudices to explore, say, a distanced text, *in that way disclosing new topics* (and sometimes "old" topics in new ways) in texts that often seem placeless, strange, or eccentric (*a-topon*) to the reader.[46] To borrow Bakhtin's term, the "exotopic" text is not strictly or *wholly* "elsewhere" but rather enters our horizon and offers further, unforeseen topics that cut across the bias or horizon of the inquiring reader.[47] In this way retrieval of the old is equally an unfolding of the new, for although one has in one sense "had" both the text and the topics used in approaching it, the two together disclose new applications, new places, for inquiry and action.[48] A statute, for example, unfolds over time by prompting hitherto unthought trajectories of extrapolation, often analogical, while a poem can assume new effects by pointing out new implications of standing words, thoughts, and actions.

In this regard the single, historical common term that brings invention and application together is the "appropriate." In Greek rhetoric the rhetor aims at finding *to prepon,* what is right and fitting for the situation, which in Cicero and Quintilian becomes "decorum," the master principle of rhetoric analogous to ethical *prudentia* or *phronesis*—that right judgment in practical cases that Gadamer celebrates in Aristotle, Vico, and the humanist tradition and that has often been referred to as "tact."[49] In hermeneutics, similarly, the appropriate becomes "Appropriation": in Heidegger, *Ereignis* is the "event of Appropriation" that comes as a gift to the alert listener, the gift of what is *atopon;* in Gadamer, it is the fusion of horizons that are never, as Bruns notes, "unified or identical or subsumed into a higher or wider perspective";[50] and in Ricoeur, appropriation is a "making-our-own" (*Aneignung*) of what we only imperfectly had before and what incorporates a dialectic between reader and text resistant to ideological domination by the subject *over* the text. Ricoeur writes: "Far from saying that a subject, who already masters his own being-in-the-world, projects the *a priori* of his own understanding [*topoi,* prejudices] and interpolates this *a priori* in the text, the revelation of new modes of being—or, if you prefer Wittgenstein to Heidegger, new "forms of life"—gives the subject new capacities [new *topoi*] for knowing himself."[51]

In this way hermeneutic application, like rhetorical topics, uses an established *sensus communis* to work toward a new but nonunitary (nontotalized) *sensus communis*—to find commonly acceptable ways to tolerate and inquire within plural senses and plural communities. The virtue of bringing rhetoric to bear on this issue, as Charles Altieri points out in his chapter in this volume, resides in the way that rhetorical doctrine keeps us tied to inexpert matters and values common in principle to all, to debate and contest over our places, and, as Wendy Olmsted notes in her chapter in this volume, to inferences and arguments, e.g., in analogical extensions of a form of life. Rhetoric brings us back to a language of agents and agencies in which questions about who we are become repeatedly reworked in the places where we work. Topics provide an orientation and an ability to handle both settled social identifications and possible novel perspectives and values and in that way resist self-complacency with meaning and history outside of the reach of power and ethics-politics.

The virtue of bringing hermeneutics to bear on rhetoric, conversely, resides, as Palmer, Schrag, and Bruns variously recognize in their respective chapters in this volume, in the way that hermeneutics opens new *topoi* of reading and reception. *Topoi* such as "appropriation/application," for example, transform the problematic of ancient *inventio,* or of eighteenth-century "criticism" (another term of the humanist tradition) by suggesting historicized extensions of rhetorical practice. That is, where rhetoric can threaten to dissolve its different kinds of "stay against confusion" in sheer "momentariness," versions of Heidegger's "moment of Appropriation" place rhetorical action within historical time and its abiding (if contested) calls of conscience. The question then becomes: How do we discriminate among those calls, and which do we respond to?

RHETORICAL ARGUMENT AND HERMENEUTIC DISCLOSURE

We have said that, when we think of topics solely in their received classical sense as second-order topical catalogues or systems of invention, we are likely to reach a false estimate of their character and worth. The reason is that the notion of "system" is often taken to privilege concepts, beliefs, propositions, rules, and logical arguments by which a rhetor actively intervenes in a rhetorical and hermeneutic situation.[52] Regarding decisions to be made, moreover, such systems aim at consensus through judgment, while, regarding the act of reading or interpretation, they tend to presuppose stable narrators and to frame readers as more or less subservient to traditions and texts, as well as to supposedly stable semantic meanings or authorial intentions.[53] The opposite tack is to take topics as a generalized ability or dimension of creative strategizing always already in play in thought or language beyond authorial control (i.e., eclipsing the author altogether). On that approach any independent identity or integrity for the concept tends to be denied. In "The Rhetoric of Temporality," for example, Paul de Man perceives an antinomy in romantic rhetoric between a purportedly stable symbol and a pervasive and unstable allegory aligned with other figures and ultimately with irony. In his view all of us are constrained to opt for the latter, explicitly subordinating systematic and traditional *topoi* to the service of those disorienting and disruptive figures and tropes.[54] "Rhetorical intervention" gives way not to rhetorical-hermeneutic "disclosure," the evocation of the contested hermeneutic "as-structures" of our existence and world, but to deconstructive "deferral," the endless questioning of any authoritative grounds for meaning. Against what is arguably most important in the rhetorical tradition, de Man threatens to reduce "rhetoric" to an unstable figurality in which topics and proofs ("ideas") are subordinated to and finally subsumed by unauthorized and unstable tropes ("images"),[55] while the hermeneutics of reading is similarly reduced to the grammatical iterability of signifiers (*différance*).

Like Heidegger, Gadamer, and Ricoeur, Kenneth Burke travels a parallel but fundamentally different route from de Man. Burke too explores the interplay between "idea" and "image," but in a way that he finds consistent with the pragmatic bent of classical rhetoric rather than with the transcendental turn of romantic expressivism. Burke writes: "In keeping with the genius of Hazlitt's expression, 'ideas of the imagination,' we began thinking that there should be a term for ideas and images both. 'Titles' (or 'epithets') seemed to meet the requirement. For the rhetorician uses 'titles' (either imaginal or ideological) to identify a person or a cause with whatever kinds of things will, in his judgment, call forth the desired response. He will select such titles in accordance with the bias of his intention and the opinions of his audience. But what are such titles (or 'entitlings' or 'identifications') but another term for the Aristotelian 'topics,' which shift so easily and imperceptibly between ideas and images that you wonder how the two realms could ever come to be at odds?"[56]

On this view topics are not only memory places whose images enable systematic storing of information, as de Man suggests; nor are they exclusively generators of commonsense opinions (*doxa*) and probable arguments (*en-*

doxa).[57] Rather, they are what Michael Leff has called "mobile strategies that promote the substance of inquiry."[58] They are inventional re-sources for persuasion or identification that generate or open onto a *range* of materials: from concepts and arguments at one end, whose purpose is to support claims persuasively and whose excellence is *prudentia* or *phronesis;* to images, tropes, and figures at the other end, whose purpose is to "disclose," "evoke" or "show forth" (*epi-deixis*) the topical first principles of all thought and action rather than to argue, and whose excellence is not rational *phronesis* ("insight," right judgment) but an unrationalizable *kairos* (timeliness, appropriateness) attuned to the situation that one encounters.[59] For de Man, again, this range of idea and image is an opposition that quickly collapses into the hegemony of untrustworthy figures (as symbol collapses into irony, as ontological grammar gives way to strategic rhetoric), destabilizing any claims to authoritative persuasiveness or proof.[60] But for Burke and others the range of rhetorical materials generated by *topoi* remains a continuum—a holding-in-tension—of the sort caught by another American *grammaticus-rhetoricus,* Stanley Cavell: "My interest, it could be said, lies in finding out what my beliefs mean, and learning the particular ground they occupy. This is not the same as providing evidence for them. One could say it is a matter of making them evident."[61] The continuum, in short, is equally a rhetorical and hermeneutic one, between topics commonly received as places for arguments ("providing evidence"), and tropes and other techniques used as means of disclosure, the display of "worldly" phenomena in Heidegger's sense ("making them evident"). This conception of things extends far beyond the deictic self-display of language.

It is not possible to demonstrate here Burke's insight that classical rhetoricians recognized and used a similar continuum of rhetorical materials. *Dispositio* and *narratio,* for example, were for the ancients not merely artificial embellishments, much less (merely or exclusively) unstable pitfalls for authors and audiences, but rather substantive resources in league if not always on a level with arguments for making one's case.[62] Regarding that genre of rhetoric most steeped in these techniques of showing (of *narratio*)—namely epideictic rhetoric—Quintilian has said: "Indeed I am not sure that this is not the most important department of rhetoric in actual practice" (*Institutio* 2.1.10). The question we are after now is how to rethink rhetorical topics and tropes in light of contemporary hermeneutic reflection on the disclosure that occurs in understanding and interpretation. To bring out what is at stake, we wish to shift the discussion from the more familiar level of textual interpretation to a more foundational level of understanding our "world" as the understanding of practical "forms of life."

In Cavell's distinction, it may be noticed, the author hints that giving evidence (via arguments) and making evident (via images, tropes, examples, fables, analogies, snippets of conversation, hypotheticals, and much else besides)[63] operate together on two different levels. The first is the more common level of our "beliefs" and their uses in typical problem cases or texts interpreted within stable forms of life and their language games (following Cicero, Vico, and Gadamer we can think of a law case as the paradigm). The second is the deeper level of the "grounds" or basis of these beliefs that locate a form of life in the first place.[64] What we wish to sketch out here, if only programmatically, is that on this more "foundational level," tropes and other nonlogical strategies initially evoke or show forth the world in ways inseparable from, but not reducible to, logical arguments and proofs. Like de Man, in other words, Cavell and Burke recognize that world (whether immanent or transcendent) can no longer be thought of as a self-presence made manifest in, for example, the symbol. But for these latter thinkers, as for Heidegger, world does not wash away in endless figurality. As David Tracy has put this last point: "A rhetoric of the tropes cannot simply replace persuasive argument [topics]."[65]

Perhaps plate tectonics offer an apt metaphor for the condition we are in: continents shift, yet we do not tumble into the ocean for all that. On the contrary, what stability we enjoy is owing to our grounds being free enough to adjust in response to ongoing change (though not, of course, without considerable psychic disturbance). In our own dynamic times it may appear retrograde to reintroduce a term like "world" or a phrase like "grounds of our beliefs." But Wittgenstein provides us with an exemplary practice of such retrieval and application when he speaks in this way: "Something must be taught us as a foundation."[66] Like Cavell, Wittgenstein is proposing no facile foundationalism when he speaks of foundations: "The difficulty is to realize the groundlessness of our believing" (*OC* 166); or again: "At the foundation of well-founded belief lies belief that is not well-founded" (*OC* 253). How do we square these seemingly contrary statements in a way that illuminates both rhetoric (i.e., inventional topics and the arguments and tropes they generate) and hermeneutics (the retrieval, application, and appropriation of "atopic" and "exotopic" texts and traditions)?

One of Wittgenstein's responses to our question is this: "Knowledge is in the end based on acknowledgement" (*OC* 378). The rhetorical-hermeneutic version of this is to say (1) that the paradigm of deliberative rhetoric is from the beginning based on an *epideictic* rhetoric of tropes, examples, and narratives, just as (2) explicit hermeneutic interpretation is always already grounded in the concernful understanding of one's horizonal articulations (*Rede*)—that is, in how the world appears always already structured or "jointed."[67] Of course here the question becomes: What does Wittgenstein mean by "acknowledgement," what sorts of things are "acknowledged" rather than "known," and how do they come to be so? Throughout *On Certainty* we encounter examples like this: "Why do I not satisfy myself that I have two feet when I get up? There is no why. I simply don't. This is how I act" (*OC* 148). In *The Claim of Reason* Stanley Cavell extends considerable effort to show that we do not know that other human beings are in fact human in the way, for example, that we know that this narrow yellow object on the desk is a pencil.[68] In neither Cavell nor Wittgenstein, however, is this an attempt to circumvent or waylay investigation of fundamental beliefs and practices. Rather, it is the reverse: their works constitute a rhetorical-hermeneutic *showing-forth*, a disclosing by means of invention *and* application of arguments *and* examples/tropes, a disclosing not only of the beliefs we hold but of the practices we engage in (or that engage us) in the world in which we live. Cavell and Wittgenstein both offer, in short, a "confession" or testimonial of how the world appears to them (qua member of a culture or form of life) and by extension to us: "All the philosopher, this kind of philosopher, can do is to express, as fully as he can, his world, and attract our undivided attention to our own."[69] For, when the authors say we do not know that we have two feet or that another person is a human being, their aim is to point out that our relations to these matters are more stable than the terms *knowledge* and *argument* allow.

Such an *epideixis*-as-confession, we have indicated, does not preclude giving reasons why the terms *know* and *knowledge* do not apply. In *On Certainty* Wittgenstein gives two such reasons. First, there are no argumentative premises we could cite that are better established than the claim being made about feet or people and that would make the claims a product of *argument*. Second, any attempt to doubt the claim presupposes experience with doubting and claiming, that is, presupposes involvement in a language game and a form of life as *already given,* thereby contradicting itself. Such argumentation and example giving are hardly apodictic proofs; they are also not (nor were they meant to be) epistemological defeats of skepticism. Rather, they are modes of a hermeneutic-rhetorical disclosure that brings grammar (rules, structures, conditions of meaning) and rhetoric (contingency, response) together. Such appeals do not so much lead to rhetorical conclusions as constitute rhetorical *topoi* and tropes—shared, agreed-upon places and anecdotes and examples and stories within which reasoning and arguing, claiming and concluding take place and within which "doubting" and "knowing" are first defined, but which are not themselves susceptible to any final argumentative justification, the attempt at which would clearly lead to an infinite regress. They are neither rational nor irrational but that which locates both; doubt about them presupposes them. They are agreements "in judgments" (*OC* 140)[70] and in practice ("forms of life"; *PI* 241), what Cavell calls agreements in our "attunements" (*CR* 32 passim).

If what rhetoricians call the rhetoric of "good reasons" ultimately fails at these deeper levels, fails because what will count as good and what will count as reasons are the very issues at stake, then the by-now familiar questions return: What do we say to someone who believes in slavery, or denies basic freedoms to women or children or homosexuals or other races? How does a religious believer speak to an unbeliever and vice versa? Wittgenstein places such questions in an explicitly rhetorical setting: "Where two principles really do meet which cannot be reconciled with one another, then each man declares the other a fool and a heretic. . . . I would 'combat' the other man,—but wouldn't I give him reasons? Certainly, but how far do they go? At the end of reasons comes *persuasion*"(*OC* 611, 612). Or again: "I can imagine a man who had grown up in quite special circumstances and been taught that the earth came into being 50 years ago, and therefore believed this. We might instruct him: the earth has long . . . etc.—We should be trying to give him our picture of the world. This would happen through a kind of *persuasion*" (*OC* 262). What kind of persuasion does Wittgenstein mean? For *persuasion* here cannot be construed as the antithesis to criteria, rules, arguments, knowledge, insofar as we have indicated that actual employment of grammatical criteria, arguments, and so on themselves always involve rhetorical occasions and appropriateness of response among practical speakers: contingent rhetorical occasions are the fuller settings within which philosophic criteria are derived and from which they can never be free (except in Theory).

Although Wittgenstein does not extrapolate on this point, a provocative but unfortunately neglected essay by the philosopher Raphael Demos entitled "On Persuasion" (1932) anticipates many of the later claims forwarded by philosophers as diverse as Thomas Kuhn, Richard Rorty, Richard Bernstein, and Charles Taylor.[71] Against sheerly relativistic ("ethnocentric") notions that theory "creates" its facts *simpliciter,* and thus circularly confirms itself in a prison house not of language but of cultural practices, Demos argues both that divergent theories or worldviews may equally explain the "facts" and that "to explain facts is not enough; a theory must be true" (OP 226). Again, such truth is not an easy matter of superior arguments, since the very ideas of argument and reason are contested. For Demos, as for Wittgenstein, the superiority of one theory or worldview over another resides rather in the "cumulative force of minute considerations" (OP 228); ultimately "it is a conflict between patterns. Persuasion is not a mechanical process, but a living growth in which elements are gradually assimilated, and ultimately modify those very tissues which assimilate them" (OP 228).[72]

What is persuasion, such that arguments and reason giving require tropes, examples, stories, and style to ground our beliefs and practices? For Demos persuasion is a matter of our "realizing" the pattern of accumulated particulars—coming to an experience of this pattern beyond merely intellectual understanding— and this realization is achieved by "evocation":

> Often the reason why so much discussion among individuals is futile is that what one person realizes vividly, the other does not. Evocation is the process by which vividness is conveyed; it is the presentation of a viewpoint in such a manner that it becomes real for the public. It is said that argument is the way by which an individual experience is made common property; in fact, an argument has much less persuasive force than the vivid evocation of an experience. The enumeration of all the relevant points in favor of a theory and against its opposite can never be completed; far more effective is it to state a viewpoint in all its concreteness and in all its significant implications, and then stop; the arguments become relevant only after this stage has been completed (OP 229).73

There are two points here: first, that one realizes something vividly, and second that *what* one realizes is a "pattern" or "whole" within which everything else makes sense, what Wittgenstein called "systems" or the "inherited background" (*OC* 94) of our practice and knowledge: "We do not learn the practice of making empirical judgments by learning rules: we are taught *judgments* and their connexion with other judgments. A *totality* of judgments is made plausible to us" (*OC* 140); "When we first begin to *believe* anything, what we believe is not a single proposition, it is a whole system of propositions. (Light dawns gradually over the whole.)" (*OC* 141); "It is not single axioms that strike me as obvious, it is a system in which consequences and premises give one another *mutual* support" (*OC* 142). Charles Taylor terms such patterns our moral "frameworks," whose supports are our "hypergoods," that is, those "strong evaluations" or intuitions of goods that we believe deserve admiration and adherence beyond our own desires and wishes—in short, that belong to human beings *as* humans.74 For Taylor as for the others we have treated, adherence to these frameworks is a matter of practical reason, and also consists in the vivid realization of some whole, but with this addition: that there be an "epistemic gain" in converting from A to B. As with Cavell, this transition (or persuasion) for Taylor is grounded in (inter)personal confession and story: "Practical reasoning . . . is a reasoning in transitions. It aims to establish, not that some position is correct absolutely, but rather that some position is superior to some other": "This form of argument has its source in biographical narrative. We are convinced that a certain view is superior because we have *lived a transition* which we understand as error-reducing and hence as epistemic gain. I see that I was confused about the relation of resentment and love, or I see that there is a depth to love that I was insensitive to before. But this doesn't mean that we don't and can't argue. Our conviction that we have grown morally can be challenged by another. It may, after all, be illusion. And then we argue; and arguing here is contesting between interpretations of what I have been living."[75]

After Heidegger and Wittgenstein and Cavell, after Saussure and Derrida and de Man, such deictic (disclosive) rhetoric can never again be understood as the unmediated presencing of self or world: in different ways all of these thinkers have established the differential "as"-structures of our *praxis* and perception and the historical multiplicity and contest concerning which of those structures will count (however momentarily) as "true." Topics or tropes may function as places or evocations but not as irrefutable arguments or transparent symbols of a transcendent order. To allow this, however, is not to stop investing in our arguments, nor (*per impossible*) to attempt to do without them altogether. Rather we look to bring our talk back "home" (to use the postromantic language of Wittgenstein and Cavell) to the realm where our arguments (including nonfictional examples and fables) actually cause the work of the world to be undertaken (and challenged) in the first place. We return to practices and their recalcitrant conditions of action and reaction, as John Dewey long ago advised. Thus we can agree with Richard Bernstein that Derrida, for example, "is always encouraging us to question the status of what we take to be our center, our native home, our *arche*"; but we also must not forget, as many are inclined to do, Bernstein's further notice: "In one of his most beautiful and loving essays, his homage to Levinas (from whom he appropriates so much), Derrida writes of—this time playing off Heidegger against Levinas—the respect for the other *as what it is:* other. Without this *acknowledgement, which is not a knowledge,* or let us say without this 'letting be' of an existent (Other) as something existing outside me in the essence of what is (first in its alterity), no ethics would be possible."[76] In the following section we seek to further Derrida's playing off of Heidegger against Levinas, keeping both in the region (place) of the rhetorical notion of home, that is, as the ongoing search for a community's nonfoundational practices.

THE CALL OF CONSCIENCE

We spoke of such a homecoming earlier when we noted how the rhetorical competence that informs a text directs the "art of understanding" back to its existential and hermeneutical origins, to the everyday world of situated concerns and practices. Here rhetoric discovers the materials (topics) that are needed for its timely and appropriate application of know-how. Here evocative displays of our comportmental relationships with things and with others are set forth, and persuasive arguments aimed at collaborative deliberation and practical wisdom are invented. In discussing these related activities of rhetorical competence with the help of hermeneutical theory, our aim has been to indicate in a small way how the enterprises of rhetoric and hermeneutics can be thought of together for the illumination of both. With this goal in mind, we now wish to consider one final matter that, although it has implicitly supported our entire discussion, has yet to be specifically detailed as a common point of reference for these enterprises. That matter is conscience.[77]

It may fairly be said that rhetoric's lifelong troubles, its ongoing critique by philosophy, begin with a certain interpretation of the call of conscience advanced by Socrates.[78] The "prophetic voice" of this call commanded his "service to God" (23b), which he took to mean that his life's calling must be that of "leading the philosophical life" (28e), of "elucidating the truth" for others (29d), and encouraging them "not to think more of practical advantages than of . . . [their] mental and moral well-being" (36c). "I am," said Socrates to those who accused him of corrupting the minds of the youth, ". . . a gift from God" (31a). He could not say this if he did not believe it to be true, for "the voice," his daemon, always spoke up and prevented him from committing any wrongdoing (40a–b). When the call came, lying was out of the question, as was any involvement in the politics of public life, "corrupted" as they were by the teachings of those who were eloquent but unwise, who were skilled in the oratorical practice of making "the weaker argument defeat the stronger" by employing "flowery language . . . decked out with fine words and phrases" (17b–18b), but who apparently felt no shame as they engaged themselves in such a crowd-pleasing and unconscionable rhetorical exercise, and who, as evidenced by Socrates' trial, could pose a serious threat to his life. Unfortunately, Socrates did not escape this threat. During his defense, accordingly, he had little trouble admitting to his fellow citizens that "no man on earth who conscientiously opposes either you or any other organized democracy, and flatly prevents a great many wrongs and illegalities from taking place in the state to which he belongs, can possibly escape with his life. The true champion of justice, if he intends to survive even for a short time, must necessarily confine himself to private life and leave politics alone" (31e–32a).

When Socrates drank his dram of hemlock and Plato assumed his mentor's "calling," the destiny of the rhetorical tradition was more or less set. From that time forward, those who wished to speak more favorably of the orator's art would have to answer to charges of sophistry brought by these two Greeks, by clarifying how rhetoric will not serve only as a vehicle (and a whipping boy) for

the more or less rhetorical arguments of philosophers. Rhetoric has a necessary and legitimate role to play, not only in creating, sustaining, and correcting
the (im)moral ecology of the body politic, but also in illuminating our contested (topical) nature as human beings.

With what it has to tell us about the call of conscience, philosophical hermeneutics provides a way for rhetoric to affirm and develop this point. As students of his works are well aware, Heidegger makes much of the matter in
Being and Time. Here one learns that the call (*Ruf*) of conscience is itself made
possible by what Heidegger describes as the essential meaning of human
being (*Dasein*): "temporality." As selves who are always in the process of becoming that which we are, time is of the essence. For Heidegger, the call of
conscience arises from the temporality of our existence and summons us to become authentically concerned with this essential nature of our being, to assume the personal and ethical responsibility of affirming our freedom through
resolute choice. *Being and Time* is devoted in great part to describing how this
is so. The description, to say the least, is quite involved. Given the space limitations of this introduction, accordingly, we shall discuss only a few of Heidegger's observations, which help establish how the call of conscience, hermeneutics, and rhetoric are related.

Conscience calls: we begin here. With Heidegger's ontological assessment
of the matter, however, it becomes clear that the call of conscience is something other than what the discourses of religion and morality would have us
believe. Indeed, according to Heidegger, conscience calls, but the sound of
its voice is silence—the silence of our ongoing "projective" involvement with
the temporal process of becoming and understanding what we are: our possibilities. "The discourse of the conscience never comes to utterance," writes
Heidegger; "Only in keeping silent does the conscience call" (*BT* 342–43).
This call, then, is not to be confused with some existent institutionalized discourse that speaks to us of the good and the bad. Rather, the call of conscience is always already at work before any practical prescriptions and in-
junctions are announced, for the call discloses itself first and foremost as "the
giving to understand" of human being's temporality, of its existence, of its
openness to Being. The call of conscience is *this* disclosure; it thereby exhibits that formal structure of discourse (*Rede*) whose function is to point out,
uncover, and make manifest something about the world.[79] The call of conscience is a primordial saying (*logos*) that originates in the temporal openness
of that being (*Dasein*) whose concern for its Being enables it to perceive and
care enough about what it is hearing. Maintaining a rhetorical outlook on this
matter, it can also be said that the call of conscience operates topically: what
it discloses, evokes, shows forth with its "saying" is the human being's funda-

mental *placement* in the world, the way it is always "on the way" (*unterwegs*) toward understanding what can or will be in its life but is "not yet." The call of conscience constitutes a commonplace presupposed by all others; its saying opens us to the openness of our existence, the source of our inventional resources.

We are attuned to this saying most dramatically in moments of anxiety—when, for example, our daily progress in the everyday world of circumspective concern and know-how is impeded, if not stopped altogether by occurrences (e.g., a serious illness) that disrupt our accustomed routines and relationships with things and with others. Then, if only for an anxious moment, we must confront the authenticity of our potentiality-for-Being, for then we are called upon to anticipate our possibilities, to assume the responsibility of affirming our freedom through resolute choice, and thus to become personally (i.e., authentically) involved in the re-creation of a meaningful existence in order to restructure our lives. To engage in this life-giving activity is, for Heidegger, to have heard and responded to the call of conscience—a call that makes its presence known with "the momentum of a push" and that thereby arouses *Dasein* to become concerned with the truth of its temporal existence and with the decisive challenge of living this truth in some meaningful way.[80] The call of conscience, in other words, calls on our ability to discover those inventional resources (topics) whose material can sustain for the time being a responsible form of life.

Heidegger describes *Dasein*'s ability to hear and respond to the call of conscience in a responsible manner as a "wanting to have a conscience." In wanting to have a conscience, however, we perforce must come to terms with our guilt. According to Heidegger, "The call of conscience has the character of an *appeal* to *Dasein* by calling it to its ownmost potentiality-for-Being-its-Self; and this is done by way of *summoning* it to its ownmost Being-guilty" (*BT* 314). As beings who are always caught up in the temporal and topical process of making choices about the future, we can never escape the guilt that we are. For in choosing and actualizing certain existential possibilities, we are necessarily sacrificing others. And because, as selves, we are our possibilities, the sacrifice makes us forever guilty of acts of omission. Conscience calls us to this ontological situation of "Being-guilty," for "to hear the call authentically, signifies bringing oneself into a factical taking-action," whereby choices *must* be made (*BT* 341). Hence, Heidegger points out that our "essential Being-guilty is, equiprimordially, the existential condition for the possibility of the 'morally' good and for that of the 'morally' evil—that is, for morality in general and for the possible forms that this may take factically. The primordial 'Being-guilty' cannot be defined by morality, since morality already presupposes it for itself."

Like the call of conscience that summons us to it, "*Being*-guilty is more primordial than *any knowledge* about it" (*BT* 332).

Conscience calls us to assume the responsibility of affirming our freedom through resolute choice; it thereby summons us to deal with our guilt. Heidegger emphasizes that this constitutes a "personal" undertaking on the part of a human being; but he also admits that it has much to do with *others*. Responding to the call is not an act that detaches a human being "from its world" and isolates it "so that it becomes a free-floating 'I.'" On the contrary, the resoluteness that shows itself with one's response "is always the resoluteness of some factical *Dasein* at a particular time." Wanting to have a conscience is a situated occurrence that "brings the Self right into its current concernful Being-alongside what is ready-to-hand, and pushes it into solicitous Being with Others" (*BT* 344)—in other words, that makes a human being a *human* being, one who engages responsibly in the things and affairs of his or her world. But now the self is in the position of taking on the additional responsibility of becoming a voice of conscience for those who are willing to hear, as it makes use of the inventional resources (tropes, stories, arguments) that have been deemed appropriate for evoking a worldview and making a case. Abiding by what Heidegger notes about "the [authentic] solicitude which leaps forth and liberates," such a voice must maintain what it considers its own correct point of view, while at the same time encouraging, by way of "considerateness" (*Rücksicht*) and "forbearance" (*Nachsicht*), an authentic response from the Other. In Heidegger's terms, the goal here is to have all concerned "devote themselves to the same affair in common," "become authentically bound together," and in that way enable each other to disclose the situation at hand (*BT* 159).

In Heidegger's analysis of the call of conscience, we learn how the resolute self is responsible for bringing about an authentic community by calling upon others to assume the responsibility of affirming *their* freedom through resolute choice. In doing this, the resolute self not only displays a willingness to test before others the integrity of its affirmed authenticity—a test that Heidegger maintains must be taken time and again—but also engages others in the related tasks of trying to cultivate all that is good in their heritage, such that they too might have a say in the establishing of their collective destiny. Summarizing this entire process, Heidegger notes: "Only in communicating and in struggling [with others] does the power of destiny become free" (*BT* 436).

We submit that such an interpersonal engagement directed toward the cultivation of community is something that calls for what we have been describing in this chapter as the practice of rhetorical competence—a practice that, as Heidegger once put it, has a role to play in the ethical task of guiding us "in a right or just manner." Rhetoric offers itself as a response to the contingent demands of a situation; it functions with an eye and ear attuned to the needs of others; in the midst of disputational contexts it provides an opportunity for collaborative choice; its ultimate aim is not merely manipulation and persuasion but the enactment of deliberation and judgment and the cultivation of practical wisdom and *kairotic* appropriateness. Rhetoric, in other words, helps promote civic engagement and civic virtue; it thus lends itself to the task of enriching the moral character of a people's communal existence. Or to put all this somewhat differently: in the hands of one who has heard the call of conscience and who is now willing to test the integrity of his chosen point of view by "communicating" and "struggling" with others, rhetoric can sound a call that acknowledges our comportmental relationship with things and with others and that summons us to choose, to act, and perhaps to change our lives for the better. Upon hearing this call we may, of course, find its voice to be "guilty" of maintaining a wrong point of view. Yet, to the extent that this voice displays "considerateness" and "forbearance" toward us, it nevertheless provides time and space for an authentic response such that a codisclosing of the situation becomes possible.

Conscience calls a person to choose, to make a decision about some matter of interest. Rhetoric helps to ensure that the integrity and "truthfulness" of this decision are brought before the Other to be shared, tested, agreed with, or disputed. Heidegger would have us remember that human existence is marked with an indelible communal character: "The world of *Dasein* is a *with-world* [*Mitwelt*]. Being-in[-the-world] is *Being-with* Others" (*BT* 155). Rhetoric pays homage to this essential feature of the Self's existence, of its way of "dwelling" here on earth. As beings who are capable of hearing and responding to the call of conscience, we also have an obligation to dwell rhetorically. Our Being-with Others demands as much.

Heidegger has little to say about the ways and means of this obligation. In developing his philosophy he is more concerned with discovering how the self can enter into a genuine "conversation" with Being than he is with detailing how the self can display a competence for initiating and sustaining such a conversation with others.[81] As a practice that by its very nature is *other-oriented,* rhetoric is inclined to be on the lookout for philosophies that speak highly of the importance of acknowledging and caring for the other. Within the tradition of philosophical hermeneutics, we know of no one more devoted to this task than Emmanuel Levinas. For here is a philosopher who would have us understand that the call of conscience originates not in "the temporality of Being" but rather in "the temporality of the interhuman," in the "face-to-face" encounter between the self and the other. This encounter, according to Levinas, defines the primordial domain of ethics—a domain where the self, exist-

ing as it does in constant "proximity" to the other, is always in the situation of
trying to come to terms with the otherness or alterity of the other, with what
the self can never totally be in mind and body, with a fundamental *difference*
embedded in life that forms the existential basis of all forms of social critique
because its mere presence "calls into question" the self's egoist tendencies and
know-it-all attitudes. Levinas equates this never-ending event of questioning
with the call of conscience—a call whose voice signifies "the revelation of a resistance to my powers" and to "my glorious spontaneity as a living being."[82]
The distinctiveness of the other, the sheerness of its "face," raises the issue of
accountability: Am I being just with my freedom to do and say what I will?
Otherness calls upon the self to attest to the particular subjectivity that it is.
Levinas puts it this way:

> I am defined as a subjectivity, as a singular person, as an "I," precisely because I am
> exposed to the other. It is my inescapable and incontrovertible answerability to the
> other that makes me an individual "I." So that I become a responsible or ethical "I"
> to the extent that I agree to depose or dethrone myself—to abdicate my position of
> centrality—in favor of the vulnerable other. . . . The ethical "I" is subjectivity pre-
> cisely in so far as it kneels before the other, sacrificing its own liberty to the more
> primordial call of the other. . . . I can never escape the fact that the other has de-
> manded a response from me before I affirm my freedom not to respond to his de-
> mand.[83]

With the call of the other, of conscience, the self is obliged to respond in the
manner of Adam, Abraham, and Moses: "Here I am," for your sake. With the
call, the self's situation becomes "religious."[84] The other warrants considerateness and forbearance (Heidegger), to be sure; but it also deserves sympathy for the plight of its body, for its pain and suffering. The experience of "the
flesh" is nowhere developed in Heidegger's hermeneutic reading of the call.
Levinas, on the other hand, cannot say enough about it. Steeped in the Hebraic tradition of biblical exegesis, he interprets the face of the other as calling
for unconditional devotion to its oftentimes desperate needs. "Morality,"
writes Levinas, "comes to birth not in equality, but in the fact that infinite exigencies, that of serving the poor, the stranger, the widow, and the orphan, con-
verge at one point of the universe."[85] This point is the other, who faces the self
and issues a call.

Heidegger is attuned to a call that makes its way through "one's own" (the
self's) existence. Levinas hears it differently: the call of conscience comes
from the other. Like Derrida and Ricoeur, we think it worth considering
whether these two perceptions are as at odds as Levinas seems to suggest.[86]
Still, what Levinas has to say about the face-to-face encounter offers a signifi-

cant extension of Heidegger's all-too-brief treatment of how the call of conscience is related to the indelible communal character of human existence. It is tempting to see this extension as providing further support for the importance of recognizing the worth of our rhetorical competence—a competence that aids the self in its attempts to acknowledge others and engage them in collaborative deliberation. But Levinas refuses to grant such support. For he equates rhetoric with "ruse, emprise, and exploitation," and accuses its "enthusiasm" for "eloquence" as being a much too common occurrence that inhibits our ability to hear the one true "discourse" that never goes away: the primordial call of the other, the saying (*logos*) of the face, the call of conscience.[87] If there is any way to salvage a positive assessment of rhetoric in Levinas's thought, it comes from one of his many essays ("Everyday Language and Rhetoric Without Eloquence") devoted to elucidating the importance of the saying of the face. Levinas's phrase "rhetoric without eloquence" seems to suggest that the former of these two can exist without the latter. Clearly, not all rhetoric is eloquent in the obvious senses of the word. In the context of Levinas's essay, however, we might conceive of such a noneloquent rhetoric in an untraditional way. Might it be the case that the saying of the face—that which calls into question the self's freedom and beckons it toward the other—is itself a rhetoric without eloquence, the most primordial rhetoric of all? Levinas does not say.

Hermeneutics, rhetoric, and conscience. Heidegger helps us understand how these things go together, but he could have said more. Levinas helps to remedy this deficiency, but not without ridiculing rhetoric. Heidegger stops short in commending this art. Levinas goes too far in condemning it. In this introduction we have tried to overcome both these tendencies and establish a middle ground between them. The chapters that follow may be read as providing additional directives for advancing this project.

NOTES

1 Hans Blumenberg, "An Anthropological Approach to the Contemporary Significance of Rhetoric," trans. Robert M. Wallace, in *After Philosophy: End or Transformation?* ed. Kenneth Baynes, James Bohman, and Thomas McCarthy (Cambridge: MIT Press, 1987), 441.

2 Isocrates, *Antidosis,* trans. G. Norlin (Cambridge: Harvard University Press, 1982), 253–56.

3 For a historical treatment of these matters, see Brian Vickers, *In Defence of Rhetoric* (New York: Oxford University Press, 1989).

4 See Eugene Garver, *Aristotle's Rhetoric: An Art of Character* (Chicago: University of Chicago Press, 1994).

5 John Poulakos, "The Possibility of Rhetoric's Early Beginnings," the Van Zelst Lecture in Communication, Northwestern University, School of Speech, May 14, 1991.

6 See *Aristotle's Rhetoric: A Theory of Civic Discourse,* trans. George A. Kennedy (New York: Oxford University Press, 1991), bk. I, 1354a, 1355a–b; bk. II, 1381a. Also see Aristotle, *The Politics of Aristotle,* trans. Ernest Barker (New York: Oxford University Press, 1979), 1252b30, 1253a13–15, 1253a29–30, 1281b1–6. For comprehensive treatments of Aristotle's theory of rhetoric, see, for example, W. M. A. Grimaldi, *Studies in the Philosophy of Aristotle's Rhetoric* (Columbia: University of Missouri Press, 1983); Thomas B. Farrell, *Norms of Rhetorical Culture* (New Haven: Yale University Press, 1994), and Garver, *Aristotle's Rhetoric.*

7 Friedrich Schleiermacher, *Hermeneutics: The Handwritten Manuscripts,* ed. Heinz Kimmerle, trans. James Duke and Jack Forstman (Missoula, Mont.: Scholars Press, 1977), 97.

8 Ibid., 97.

9 Ibid., 148–49.

10 See Michael J. Hyde and Craig R. Smith, "Hermeneutics and Rhetoric: A Seen but Unobserved Relationship," *Quarterly Journal of Speech* 65 (1979): 347–63.

11 Schleiermacher, *Hermeneutics,* 96.

12 Kurt Mueller-Vollmer, "Introduction" ("Language, Mind, and Artifact: An Outline of Hermeneutic Theory since the Enlightenment"), in Mueller-Vollmer, ed., *The Hermeneutics Reader: Texts of the German Tradition from the Enlightenment to the Present* (New York: Continuum, 1990), 12.

13 Hans-Georg Gadamer, "On the Scope and Function of Hermeneutical Reflection," trans. G. B. Hess and R. E. Palmer, in Gadamer, *Philosophical Hermeneutics,* ed. David E. Linge (Berkeley: University of California Press, 1976), 24. See Chapter 15 (retitled) in this volume.

14 Calvin O. Schrag, *Communicative Praxis and the Space of Subjectivity* (Bloomington: Indiana University Press, 1986), 198–99.

15 See, for example, Heidegger, *Being and Time,* trans. John Macquarrie and Edward Robinson (New York: Harper and Row, 1962), 95–122. Hereafter cited in the text as *BT.* For lucid analyses of Heidegger's thinking on this point, see W. B. Macomber, *The Anatomy of Disillusion: Martin Heidegger's Notion of Truth* (Evanston, Ill.: Northwestern University Press, 1967), esp. 34–44; and Hubert L. Dreyfus, *Being-in-the-World: A Commentary on Heidegger's* Being and Time, *Division I* (Cambridge: MIT Press, 1991), esp. 184–214.

16 Heidegger describes the ontological structure of a culture's hermeneutical situation as consisting of a "fore-having," a "fore-sight," and a "fore-conception." The fore-having is the realm of possibilities that a culture makes available to its members in advance of any particular act of interpretation that may be performed by a member of the culture. This intersubjective realm of understanding constitutes the parameters of being wherein the members of the culture learn to think and behave in ways that other members can sensibly comprehend. The fore-sight is an abstraction of the fore-having; it originates when members of a culture appropriate the cul-

ture's fore-having and, in so doing, formulate specific "points of view" that guide the interpretation of a certain object. Consequently, these points of view are also in advance of any particular act of interpretation; they are the orientations we bring to the scenes of interpretation that allow us to make sense of what we see. A "prejudice," for example, is an ontic representation of what is here being designated ontologically as a point of view (the fore-sight of understanding). The fore-conception is how we structure the linguistic possibilities of our fore-sight in advance of an act of interpretation. A categorical system that, for example, is used in conducting a scientific experiment or a rhetorical analysis is an example of fore-conception. (See *BT*, 188–95.) All interpretation operates within the "forestructure" (fore-having, fore-sight, fore-conception) of understanding. As interpretation develops understanding, understanding shows itself in both a synchronic and diachronic form. Understanding is synchronic in that any particular act of interpretive understanding is a structuring of language at a specific moment in time; it becomes situation bound. Understanding is diachronic because, once it is situated by interpretation, it goes beyond the particular interpretation and contributes to the historical tradition that moves language through time. (See Paul Ricoeur, *The Conflict of Interpretations: Essays in Hermeneutics,* ed. Don Ihde [Evanston, Ill.: Northwestern University Press, 1974], esp. 27–96; and Paul Ricoeur, *Interpretation Theory: Discourse and the Surplus of Meaning* [Fort Worth: Texas Christian University Press, 1976].) Taken together, the synchronic and diachronic dimensions of understanding (with their corresponding forestructure) constitute the hermeneutical situation of any given culture and of human existence in general. The meaning of human existence, as it develops in and through interpretive understanding, always occurs within the hermeneutical situation. The same can be said about a person's hermeneutical competence.

17 The bracketed phrase here corresponds to the original German: "in der rechten Weise." See Martin Heidegger, *Sein und Zeit* (Tübingen: Max Niemeyer, 1979), 138–39. While Macquarrie and Robinson translate the phrase as "aright," we suggest that a less condensed translation is more appropriate. The German *recht* can refer to the moral sense being emphasized in our reading (as when, for example, one says "es ist nicht recht von dir," "it's wrong or unfair of you"). Moreover, if one is to credit Heidegger's gloss of the *Rhetoric* as being right, just, and fair, then our suggested translation is appropriate because, for Aristotle, rhetoric has a moral role to play in the workings of the polis.

18 Plato, *The Republic of Plato,* trans. Francis M. Cornford (New York: Oxford University Press, 1979), XXI, vi, 487b–497a.

19 For a discussion, see Walter Jost, "Philosophic Rhetoric: Newman and Heidegger," in Gerard Magill, ed., *Discourse and Context: An Interdisciplinary Study of John Henry Newman* (Carbondale: Southern Illinois University Press, 1993), 54–80.

20 Eric J. Cassell, *Talking with Patients,* volume 2: *Clinical Technique* (Cambridge: MIT Press, 1985), 15. What is being noted about medical case histories in this and the following paragraph is based on an analysis in Michael J. Hyde, "Medicine,

Rhetoric, and the Euthanasia Debate: A Case Study in the Workings of a Postmodern Discourse," *Quarterly Journal of Speech* 79 (1993): 201–24.

21 W. H. S. Jones, *Hippocrates (Law),* Vol. 2 (London: William Heinemann, 1923), sec. 4.

22 Martin Heidegger, *The Basic Problems of Phenomenology,* trans. Albert Hofstadter (Bloomington: Indiana University Press, 1982), 171–72.

23 See, for example, Michael J. Hyde and Craig R. Smith, "Aristotle and Heidegger on Emotion and Rhetoric: Questions of Time and Space," in *The Critical Turn: Rhetoric and Philosophy in Postmodern Discourse,* ed. Ian Angus and Lenore Langsdorf (Carbondale: Southern Illinois University Press, 1993), 68–99. These authors, like many others, fail to consider how Heidegger's ontological assessment of the "the call of conscience" works to question this common interpretation. For an essay that develops this point, see Michael J. Hyde, "The Call of Conscience: Heidegger and the Question of Rhetoric," *Philosophy and Rhetoric* 27 (1994): 374–96. We discuss the call of conscience later in this introduction.

24 Hans-Georg Gadamer, "Text and Interpretation," trans. Dennis J. Schmidt and Richard Palmer, in *Dialogue and Deconstruction: The Gadamer-Derrida Encounter,* ed. Diane P. Michelfelder and Richard E. Palmer (Albany: State University of New York Press, 1989), 106. Perhaps this unflattering conception of the orator's art has something to do with Gadamer's "encounter" with Derrida, that postmodern rhetorician who, as evidenced in his contributions to the encounter, is unreceptive to Gadamer's hermeneutical way of getting at the "truth" of a text's subject matter.

25 David Bromwich, *A Choice of Inheritance: Self and Community from Edmund Burke to Robert Frost* (Cambridge: Harvard University Press, 1989), 265.

26 Hans-Georg Gadamer, *Wahrheit und Methode* (Tübingen: J. C. B. Mohr, 1960); *Truth and Method,* 2d rev. ed., trans. Joel Weinsheimer and Donald G. Marshall (New York: Continuum, 1993), 568. Further references in the text will be to this edition, cited parenthetically as *TM.*

27 In a review of *Truth and Method* (abridged as "Hans-Georg Gadamer's Truth and Method," trans. and ed. Marvin Brown, *Philosophy and Rhetoric,* 13 [Summer 1980]: 160–80; the original review first appeared in *Göttingische Gelehrte Anziegen,* 218, nos. 3–4, [1966]), Klaus Dockhorn makes a similar point (161). But Dockhorn's emphasis throughout (and Gadamer's emphasis in his approving reference to Dockhorn's review in Chapter 15, this volume) falls on emotion (*pathos*). As we explain below, this potentially reinforces the tired misconception that rhetoric's task in life is chiefly to manipulate feelings for personal gain. Our emphasis here falls on *logos*—or more accurately, on the competence or know-how involved in locating and exploring topics to find the substance (*logos*), as well as the *ethos* and *pathos*, of a specific case. This is what Ernesto Grassi (after Vico and Heidegger) calls "topical philosophy," and what Kenneth Burke makes central both to his grammar and rhetoric of motives.

28 Giambattista Vico, *On the Study Methods of Our Time,* trans. Elio Gianturco

(Ithaca: Cornell University Press, 1990). Further references in the text will be to this edition, cited parenthetically as *Methods*. For an excellent account of Vico's thought, which has influenced our project here, see Donald Philip Verene, *Vico's Science of Imagination* (Ithaca: Cornell University Press, 1981), esp. chap. 6, "Rhetoric."

29 Cicero, *On Oratory and Orators,* trans. and ed. J. S. Watson (Carbondale: Southern Illinois University Press, 1970), 213.

30 Francis Bacon, *The Advancement of Learning,* ed. G. W. Kitchin (London: J. M. Dent and Sons, 1973), 127, emphasis added. See also Victoria Kahn, "Humanism and the Resistance to Theory," Chapter 7, this volume.

31 See also Hans-Georg Gadamer, "Rhetoric and Hermeneutics," Chapter 1, this volume: "Admittedly, what Vico was argumentatively defending is the educative function of rhetoric, always living—though less in the actual practice of eloquence and the expertise that values it than in redirecting the rhetorical tradition to reading classical texts." As hinted earlier, this account of rhetoric cuts against Heidegger's interest in the *pathe* in Aristotle's *Rhetoric,* inasmuch as ontic feelings (and ontological moods) in Heidegger tend to become dissociated from the practical *activity* required of the speaker to discover what is relevant and persuasive in some contingent case (or text)—in a word, from rhetorical *inventio*. For a concrete illustration of what we are suggesting here and what Gadamer is talking about, see David Tracy, "Charity, Obscurity, Clarity: Augustine's Search for Rhetoric and Hermeneutics," Chapter 12, this volume: "Thus the paradox: a proper hermeneutics is simultaneously a new rhetoric of discovery or invention."

32 See *Methods,* 15: "Criticism is the art of true speech; 'ars topica,' of eloquence [*copia,* copiousness]." Cf. Cicero, *Topica,* 386–87. Also Ernesto Grassi, "Critical Philosophy or Topical Philosophy? Meditations on the *De nostri temporis studiorum ratione,*" in *Giambattista Vico: An International Symposium,* ed. Giorgio Tagliacozzo and Hayden V. White (Baltimore: Johns Hopkins University Press, 1969); Victoria Kahn's chapter, this volume; and Calvin Schrag's chapter, this volume: "Not only is there the otherness of the interlocutor/addressee/reader, there is also the otherness of the *topoi,* the topics, which have to do with the plethora of beliefs, practices, and institutions that congeal into a variety of forms of life."

33 See Theodor Viehweg, *Topics and Law,* trans. W. Cole Durham, Jr. (Frankfurt am Main: Peter Lang, 1993), 22–23:

"When one stumbles upon a problem somewhere, one can of course simply proceed in the manner that arbitrarily selects views [*topoi*] at will more or less in a trial and error fashion. . . . Observation teaches us that in everyday life we nearly always proceed in this way. Also, in such cases more precise investigation would show that certain leading views guide the particular orientation at the time in question. But these are not made explicit. For purposes of overview we will call this procedure *first stage Topics.*

"The uncertainty of this approach is readily apparent, and makes it understandable that one seeks a resource which in its simplest form would always be available as a repertoire of views. Thus arise *topoi*-catalogs. We will refer to a procedure that uses this type of catalog as *second stage Topics*."

34 See Garver, *Aristotle's Rhetoric*, 81.

35 Ibid., 82: "The diversity of answers given by commentators to the question, 'What is a topic in Aristotle's *Rhetoric?*,' suggests not confusion but the possibility that what topics are and how they function vary with the purpose for which they are employed and the manifold on which they are used." For additional light on topics, see Richard McKeon, "Creativity and the Commonplace," *Philosophy and Rhetoric* 6 (1973): 199–210; Nancy Struever, "Topics in History," *History and Theory* 19 (1980): 66–79; Walter Jost, "Teaching the Topics: Character, Rhetoric, and Liberal Education," *Rhetoric Society Quarterly* 21 (Winter 1991): 1–16; and Michael C. Leff, "Recherches américaines sur les lieux," in *Lieux Communs, topoi, stéréotypes, clichés,* ed. Christian Plantin (Paris: Editions Kime, 1993), 506–17.

36 Bernard Lonergan, *Insight: A Study of Human Understanding,* 3d ed. (New York: Philosophical Library, 1970), 175.

37 See Quintilian, *Institutio Oratoria,* trans. H. E. Butler, 4 vols. (Cambridge: Harvard University Press, 1985), vol 2: 5.10.100: "But as it is not in itself sufficient to know that all proofs are drawn from either persons or things, . . . so he who has learned that arguments must be drawn from antecedent, contemporary or subsequent facts will not be sufficiently instructed in the knowledge of the method of handling arguments to understand what arguments are to be drawn from the circumstances of each particular case; especially as the majority of proofs are to be found in the special circumstances of individual cases and have no connexion with any other dispute, and therefore while they are the strongest, are also the least obvious, since, whereas we derive what is common to all cases from general rules, we have to discover for ourselves whatever is peculiar to the case which we have in hand" (257–59). The nuanced sensibility required by topics is echoed again and again in unforeseen places: what the French call *le bon sens,* Pascal's *esprit de finesse,* Newman's "illative sense," Polanyi's "tacit knowledge," and the hermeneutic tradition's *subtilitas applicandi.*

38 Fyodor Dostoevsky, *Crime and Punishment,* ed. George Gibian (New York: Norton, 1989), 222, 224.

39 For good examples of this, see Albert R. Jonsen and Stephen Toulmin, *The Abuse of Casuistry: A History of Moral Reasoning* (Berkeley: University of California Press, 1988).

40 In "The Topology of Being," in Otto Pöggeler, *Martin Heidegger's Path of Thinking,* trans. Daniel Magurshak and Sigmund Barber (Atlantic Highlands, N.J.: Humanities Press, 1987), 227–42, Pöggeler refers to poetry and thinking (in Heidegger's senses of these terms) as an "emplacing" (topologizing): "Emplacement means to interrogate what has been thought regarding the unthought in it, to allow the unthought to be expressed in word" (238). For a similar discussion that explicitly adverts to the rhetorical tradition, see Otto Pöggeler, "Metaphysics and the Topology

of Being in Heidegger," in *Heidegger: The Man and the Thinker*, ed. Thomas Shee-
han (Chicago: Precedent, 1981), 173–85; also William L. Nothstine, "'Topics' as
Ontological Metaphor in Contemporary Rhetorical Theory and Criticism," *Quarterly Journal of Speech* 74 (1988): 151–63; Michael R. Heim, "Topics, Topicality and
the New *Topos*," *Philosophy Today* (Summer 1981): 131–38; and idem, "Philosophy as Ultimate Rhetoric," *Southern Journal of Philosophy* 19 (Summer 1981): 188:
"The common cultural context, prior to argumentative or judgmental assertion, is
explored as the site where meaning appears. . . . This is the *topos* of existential
rhetoric, the indexical *Da* of *Dasein*."

41 Fyodor Dostoevsky, *The Brothers Karamazov*, trans. Richard Pevear and Larissa
Volokhonsky (New York: Knopf, 1992), 255.

42 "Rhetoric, Hermeneutics, and Ideology-Critique," Chapter 15, this volume.

43 See Viehweg, *Topics and Law*, 30: "Interpretation is a part of Topics"; also Walter
Jost, "Philosophic Rhetoric: Newman and Heidegger," in *Discourse and Context*,
54–80.

44 Cf. Hans-Georg Gadamer, *Truth and Method*, 324–30, 518ff.; and idem, "Rhetoric
and Hermeneutics," Chapter 1, this volume.

45 Hans Blumenberg, "An Anthropological Approach to the Contemporary
Significance of Rhetoric," *After Philosophy*, 428–58. It is this selfsame incompleteness that Richard Lanham keeps in the forefront of his own rhetorical consciousness when, discussing the rhetorical problem of how we know when to stop amplify-
ing some subject matter, he writes: "When we come to the crucial question of when
enough is enough, of when *brevitas* should supervene, the rhetorical [as theoreti-
cal-technical] wisdom is bankrupt. . . . You decide [rather] by that broad range of intuition which the rhetorical paideia trained you for but never could specify" (*The
Electronic Word: Democracy, Technology and the Arts* [Chicago: University of
Chicago Press, 1993], 75). See also Drucilla Cornell, *The Philosophy of the Limit*
(New York: Routledge, Chapman and Hall, 1992), 111: "Without a simple origin the
very process of discovery of legal principles from within the *nomos* will . . . involve
invention."

46 See Gadamer's essay, "Rhetoric, Hermeneutics, and Ideology-Critique," Chapter
15, this volume.

47 See Tzvetan Todorov, *Mikhail Bakhtin: The Dialogical Principle*, trans. Wlad
Godzich (Minneapolis: University of Minnesota Press, 1984), 99.

48 This reading counters that of John D. Schaeffer, *Sensus Communis: Vico, Rhetoric,
and the Limits of Relativism* (Durham, N.C.: Duke University Press, 1990), who
reads Gadamer as a latter-day Enlightenment *philosoph* resistant to contingent
rhetorical commonplaces and provisional truths.

49 For an excellent account see Michael Leff, "Decorum and Rhetorical Interpretation: The Latin Humanistic Tradition and Contemporary Critical Theory," *Vichi-
ana* 3 (1990): 107–26.

50 Gerald L. Bruns, *Hermeneutics Ancient and Modern* (New Haven: Yale University
Press, 1992), 237.

51 Paul Ricoeur, "Appropriation," in Ricoeur, *Hermeneutics and the Human Sciences*, ed. and trans. John B. Thompson (Cambridge: Cambridge University Press, 1981), 192.

52 Cf. Roland Barthes, "The Old Rhetoric: An Aide-Mémoire," in *The Semiotic Challenge*, trans. Richard Howard (New York: Hill and Wang, 1988), 22: "Aristotle's rhetoric is above all a rhetoric of proof, of reasoning, of the approximative syllogism (enthymeme); it is a deliberately diminished logic, one adapted to the level of the 'public,' i.e., of common sense, of ordinary opinion." Also Burke, "The Rhetorical Situation," 268: "I never cease to marvel at the systematic treatment of 'persuasion' in the *Rhetoric* of Aristotle. I have in mind his way of listing the 'places' (topics, *topoi*) which a speaker can utilize in the attempt to persuade or dissuade, to praise or blame, to build up a character or to smear him, and the like. But the whole process was so deliberate it didn't seem to cover kinds of situations which were not characterized by the clear, formal purposiveness that classical books on rhetoric were primarily concerned with."

53 Cf. Wayne Booth, *The Rhetoric of Fiction* (Chicago: University of Chicago Press, 1960; rev. 1990), and Booth, *A Rhetoric of Irony* (Chicago: University of Chicago Press, 1974). For a critique of such a rhetoric of reading, see Paul Ricoeur, *Time and Narrative*, 3 vols. (Chicago: University of Chicago Press, 1990), 3, 164 and passim.

54 Paul de Man, "The Rhetoric of Temporality," in *Blindness and Insight* (Minneapolis: University of Minnesota Press, 1983), 187–91. See also "The Rhetoric of Tropes (Nietzsche)" and "The Rhetoric of Persuasion (Nietzsche)" in de Man, *Allegories of Reading: Figural Language in Rousseau, Nietzsche, Rilke, and Proust* (New Haven: Yale University Press, 1979), 103–18; 119–31.

55 De Man, "Rhetoric of Temporality," 189, 191.

56 Kenneth Burke, *A Rhetoric of Motives* (Berkeley: University of California Press, 1969), 86.

57 For an example of speaking of topics this way, see Harold Bloom, *The Western Canon: The Books and School of the Ages* (New York: Harcourt, Brace, 1994), 39: "The greatest authors take over the role of 'places' in the Canon's theater of memory, and their masterworks occupy the position filled by 'images' in the art of memory."

58 Michael Leff, "Recherches américaines sur les lieux" (author's original).

59 For Vico's similar views, see Donald Phillip Verene, *Vico's Science of Imagination*, 159ff., 172, passim; also Ernesto Grassi, "Rhetoric and Philosophy," *Philosophy and Rhetoric* 9 (1976): 200–216.

60 For what we take to be de Man's inadequate gloss on Burke's project, see "Semiology and Rhetoric," in *Allegories of Reading*, 8. See also Paul de Man, "The Resistance to Theory" in de Man, *The Resistance to Theory* (Minneapolis: University of Minnesota Press, 1986), esp. 14–21.

61 Stanley Cavell, "Knowing and Acknowledging," in *Must We Mean What We Say?* (Cambridge: Cambridge University Press, 1976), 241. For Cavell's challenge to de Man's disjunction of grammar and rhetoric (or, said otherwise, de Man's collapse of

grammatical conditions for meaning into rhetorical instability *simpliciter*), see "The Politics of Interpretation (Politics as Opposed to What?)," in *Themes Out of School: Effects and Causes* (Chicago: University of Chicago Press, 1980), 27–59. For a similar attempt to unite topics and tropes, see Michel Meyer, *Rhetoric, Language, and Reason* (University Park: Pennsylvania State University Press, 1994), esp. 155–56.

62 For one such account, see John D. O'Banion, *Reorienting Rhetoric: The Dialectic of List and Story* (University Park: Pennsylvania State University Press, 1992).

63 See Stanley Cavell, "The Style of the *Investigations*," subsection of "The Availability of Wittgenstein's Later Philosophy," in *Must We Mean What We Say?* 71: "There are questions, jokes, parables, and propositions so striking (the way lines are in poetry) that they stun mere belief."

64 A similar tack is pursued by Charles Altieri, *Canons and Consequences: Reflections on the Ethical Force of Imaginative Ideals* (Evanston, Ill.: Northwestern University Press, 1990), 87 passim, who recognizes different levels of embedding to our social purposes and practices.

65 David Tracy, *Plurality and Ambiguity: Hermeneutics, Religion, Hope* (Cambridge: Harper and Row, 1987), 62.

66 Ludwig Wittgenstein, *On Certainty,* ed. G. E. M. Anscombe and G. H. von Wright, trans. Denis Paul and G. E. M. Anscombe (New York: Harper and Row, 1969), sec. 449. Hereafter cited as *OC*.

67 For support, see Richard Shusterman, "Beneath Interpretation," in *Pragmatist Aesthetics: Living Beauty, Rethinking Art* (Oxford: Basil Blackwell, 1992), 114–35; and Lawrence W. Rosenfield, "The Practical Celebration of Epideictic," in *Rhetoric in Transition: Studies in the Nature and Uses of Rhetoric,* ed. Eugene E. White (University Park: Pennsylvania State University Press, 1980), 140.

68 Stanley Cavell, *The Claim of Reason: Wittgenstein, Skepticism, Morality and Tragedy* (Oxford: Oxford University Press, 1979). Hereafter cited as *CR*.

69 Stanley Cavell, "Aesthetic Problems of Modern Philosophy," in *Must We Mean What We Say?* 96; also see idem, "The Availability of Wittgenstein's Later Philosophy," 71: "Wittgenstein chose confession. . . . It contains what serious confession must: the full acknowledgement of temptation . . . and a willingness to correct them and give them up." Cf. Charles Altieri, "Rhetorics, Rhetoricity and the Sonnett as Performance," *Tennessee Studies in Literature* 25 (1980): 3: "Both Wittgenstein and Derrida make powerful cases that it is rhetoric rather than logic that becomes the central focus of philosophical inquiry once the contradictions appear inescapable in an empiricist ontology based on logical simples"; and Richard Shusterman, "Wittgenstein and Critical Reasoning," *Philosophy and Phenomenological Research* 47 (September 1986): 102: "Wittgenstein confessed that much of his own philosophical argumentation is just persuading his audience or readers to see a particular phenomenon in a particular way, much as the critic tries to persuade his readers to see a work of art in a particular way. 'What I'm doing is *also* persuasion. If someone says, "There is no difference," and I say "There is a difference," I am persuading; I am saying I don't want you to look at it like that.'" See also Ludwig

Wittgenstein, *Lectures and Conversations on Aesthetics, Psychology and Religious Belief,* ed. Cyril Barrett (Berkeley: University of California Press, n.d.), 27. Such argumentation is not paradigmatically deliberative in nature but epiphanic or epideictic in an extended sense—a showing forth. On the epiphanic in modern art and literature, see Charles Taylor, *Sources of the Self: The Making of the Modern Identity* (Cambridge: Harvard University Press, 1989), 418–93.

70 See also Ludwig Wittgenstein, *Philosophical Investigations,* 3d edition, trans. G. E. M. Anscombe (New York: Macmillan, 1968), sec. 242. Hereafter cited as *PI.*

71 Raphael Demos, "On Persuasion," *The Journal of Philosophy* 29 (April 1932): 225–32. Cited in the text as OP.

72 For a similar holistic account of truth, see John Henry Newman, *An Essay in Aid of a Grammar of Assent,* ed. I. T. Ker (Oxford: Clarendon Press, 1976).

73 Cf. *PI* 122: "A main source of our failure to understand is that we do not command a clear view of the use of our words.—Our grammar is lacking in this sort of perspicuity. A perspicuous representation produces just that understanding which consists in 'seeing connexions.' Hence the importance of finding and inventing intermediate cases." See also Altieri, *Canons and Consequences,* 97–98. On the relation of "vividness" to "vivacity" in George Campbell and David Hume, and to *enargeia* in Aristotle, see Walter Jost, "On Concealment and Deception in Rhetoric: Newman and Kierkegaard," *Rhetoric Society Quarterly* (Winter–Spring 1995): 51–74.

74 In *The Claim of Reason,* 111, Cavell develops his own version of this line of thought: "But now we are thinking of convention not as the arrangements a particular culture has found convenient, in terms of its history and geography, for effecting the necessities of human existence, but as those forms of life which are normal to any group of creatures we call human, any group about which we will say, for example, that they *have* a past to which they respond. . . . Here the array of 'conventions' are not patterns of life which differentiate human beings from one another, but those exigencies of conduct and feeling which all humans share. Wittgenstein's discovery, or rediscovery, is of the depth of convention in human life; a discovery which insists not only on the conventionality of human society but, we could say, on the conventionality of human nature itself, on what Pascal meant when he said 'Custom is our nature' (*Pensées,* #89)."

75 Taylor, *Sources of the Self,* 72, emphasis added. This would seem to be Demos's position; it is similar to Ronald Dworkin's view that Judge Hercules will seek the most comprehensive legal theory available, one that both makes sense of the facts and that "goes on" with the overall project of law consistent with the best political view of justice. Although Wittgenstein's position need not, at all points, entail the idea that there is one "best account" of myriad "forms of life" (one might have, for example, motivations other than "epistemic gain" for wanting to persuade someone to one's own worldview), much of what Wittgenstein says allows for Taylor's line of argument, without which, as Richard Harvey Brown has argued, one forfeits all hope of exposing any forms of consciousness as false: "Such a forfeiture is displayed in Peter Winch's essay, 'Understanding a Primitive Society' (1970), in which Winch

virtually precluded the possibility of cross-cultural anthropological comparison" (*Social Science as Civic Discourse: Essays on the Invention, Legitimation, and Uses of Social Theory* [Chicago: University of Chicago Press, 1989], 41). For more on this issue, see Steven Mailloux's chapter in this volume.

76 Richard Bernstein, *The New Constellation: The Ethical-Political Horizons of Modernity/Postmodernity* (Cambridge: MIT Press, 1992), 183, 184–85, emphasis added. See also Jacques Derrida, "Afterword" to *Limited Inc* (Evanston, Ill.: Northwestern University Press, 1988).

77 Much of what follows here is based on Michael J. Hyde, "The Call of Conscience: Heidegger and the Question of Rhetoric," *Philosophy and Rhetoric*, 27 (1994): 374–396, and on idem, *The Call of Conscience: Philosophy, Rhetoric, and the Euthanasia Debate* (Columbia: University of South Carolina Press, forthcoming), which includes a revised version of that essay. On conscience understood as a rhetorical *topos*, see Walter Jost, *Rhetorical Thought in John Henry Newman* (Columbia: University of South Carolina Press, 1989), esp. chaps. 2 and 7. For the authors, "conscience" works somewhat as *caritas* does for Augustine; see David Tracy, "Charity, Obscurity, Clarity: Augustine's Search for Rhetoric and Hermeneutics," Chapter 13, this volume: "*Caritas*, then, as both *ethos* and *logos*, will also prove to be the central new rhetorical principle of discovery (*inventio*) for both the signs of *eros* in the search for true wisdom in the classics of the pagans and the signs of *agape* in the new classics, the Scriptures."

78 Our discussion of this interpretation is based on Plato's *Apology*, trans. Hugh Tredennick, in Plato, *The Collected Dialogues of Plato*, ed. Edith Hamilton and Huntington Cairns (Princeton: Princeton University Press, 1961).

79 See Heidegger, *Being and Time*, 196, where he discusses the "pointing out" character of discourse. For a comparison of Heidegger and Wittgenstein on these and related matters, see Stephen Mulhall, *On Being in the World: Wittgenstein and Heidegger on Seeing Aspects* (London: Routledge, 1993).

80 Cf. Michael Zimmerman, *Eclipse of the Self: The Development of Heidegger's Concept of Authenticity* (Athens: Ohio University Press, 1981), 75: "The phenomenon of conscience testifies that human existence has the power of self-correction. In Aristotelian terms, human beings have their own *telos* and move towards its full manifestation. Our *telos* is to become open to our possibilities: existence yearns to be truthful. . . . Conscience is the sign that our temporal openness is dissatisfied with functioning deficiently."

81 Critiques of Heidegger typically make much of this point; see, for example, Paul Ricoeur, *Oneself as Another*, trans. Kathleen Blamey (Chicago: University of Chicago Press, 1992), 349: "By stressing the ontology of guilt (of being-in-debt), Heidegger dissociates himself from what common sense most readily attaches to the idea of debt, namely that it is owed to someone else—that one is responsible as a debtor—finally, that being with one another is public." Richard Bernstein maintains that there is a "danger" with Heidegger because his project virtually "closes off the space for attending to the type of thinking and acting that can foster human solidarity and

community." Hence Bernstein would have us remember what he feels that the later Heidegger forgets: "Our dialogue, and communicative transactions, are not only with Being itself, but with other human beings." "Heidegger on Humanism," in Richard Bernstein, *Philosophical Profiles: Essays in a Pragmatic Mode* (Philadelphia: University of Pennsylvania Press, 1986), 208, 219. For a response to this kind of objection, see Fred Dallmayr, *Language and Politics* (Notre Dame, Ind.: University of Notre Dame Press, 1984), 191.

82 Emmanuel Levinas, *Totality and Infinity: An Essay on Exteriority*, trans. Alphonso Lingis (Pittsburgh: Duquesne University Press, 1969), 84.

83 Emmanuel Levinas, "Ethics of the Infinite," trans. Richard Kearney, in *Dialogues with Contemporary Continental Thinkers: The Phenomenological Heritage*, ed. Richard Kearney (Manchester: Manchester University Press, 1984), 62–63.

84 Levinas develops this point throughout his philosophy; see, for example, his *Ethics and Infinity: Conversations with Philippe Nemo*, trans. Richard A. Cohen (Pittsburgh: Duquesne University Press, 1985), 85–122; and his *Otherwise than Being, or Beyond Essence*, trans. Alphonso Lingis (Boston: Kluwer, 1991), 144–65.

85 Levinas, *Totality and Infinity*, 245.

86 See Jacques Derrida, "Violence and Metaphysics: An Essay on the Thought of Emmanuel Levinas," in his *Writing and Difference*, trans. Alan Bass (Chicago: University of Chicago Press, 1978), 79–153; and Paul Ricoeur, *Oneself as Another*, esp. 297–356.

87 See Emmanuel Levinas, *Totality and Infinity*, 70–72, and "Everyday Language and Rhetoric Without Eloquence," in his *Outside the Subject*, trans. Michael B. Smith (Stanford: Stanford University Press, 1994), 135–43.

Part I
Locating the Disciplines

I

Rhetoric and Hermeneutics

Hans-Georg Gadamer

Translated by Joel Weinsheimer

In the context of lectures to the Jungius Society, one could scarcely pick a theme that sounds more inapposite than that of rhetoric and hermeneutics. For what distinguishes Jungius—and not just in the eyes of Leibniz, who entered into genuine partnership with this great pathbreaker of seventeenth-century science—is a decisive departure from dialectical and hermeneutic modes of proceeding and a turn toward empiricism and demonstrative logic (albeit purged of slavish devotion to Aristotle). Jungius was not simply raised in the culture of humanistic pedagogy grounded on dialectic and rhetoric; later he still ascribed it propaedeutic value and viewed the strengthening of "the dialectical and hermeneutic capacity" as important, especially to polemical theology (cf. his 1638 correspondence with Jac Lagus). Admittedly, this statement appears in a letter and is meant more in a teacherly and diplomatic way than as a real appraisal, for Jungius was actually trying to win over his former student to the methodology and logic of science. But even so, his flexibility indicates that, for a man of science of that time, rhetorical education remained a matter of course. It is only against this background that we can begin to appreciate the special achievement of men like Jungius, this pioneer of a new scientific attitude.

"Rhetoric" has a thematic interest of its own, however, not just as background to anyone who wants to understand the epistemological and scientific fate of the *humaniora* before they were constituted in the form of the romantic *Geisteswissenschaften*. In this connection, the role of hermeneutic theory, more or less secondary, is far less consequential than that of the ancient, medieval, and humanistic tradition of rhetoric. As part of the trivium, rhetoric led a life that went virtually unnoticed because it was so obvious. This means, however, that inconspicuous changes in the old were gradually paving the way for the new historical sciences. As developed by Luther, Melanchthon, and Flacius in the course of their defense against the tridentine Counter-Reformation attack on Lutheranism, through the initial stages of rationalism and the Pietism opposing it, up to the rise of the historical worldview in the age of romanticism, the history of hermeneutic theory unfolded not as a species of epistemology and theory of science but under the pressure of the theological controversies ignited by the Reformation. It was indeed the primary issue of the modern historical human sciences, seen from the viewpoint from which this history was written by Wilhelm Dilthey and Joachim Wach.

Now, a hermeneutic truth allied to the concept of fore-understanding comes into play here. Even research into the history of hermeneutics is governed by the universal hermeneutic law of fore-understanding. By way of introduction, we can see its impact in three examples.

The first is precisely what underlies Dilthey's "Studien zur Geschichte der Hermeneutik," the prize essay selected by the Berlin Academy of Sciences that Dilthey wrote as a young scholar. Only a few parts of this essay, along with the abridged version of 1900, were known before it finally saw print in 1966, thanks to Martin Redeker's edition of the incomplete second volume of Dilthey's *Life of Schleiermacher*.[1] There Dilthey offers a masterly presentation of Flacius, furnished with copious documentation. He examines Flacius's hermeneutic theory and evaluates it by applying the standard of his increasingly self-conscious historical sense and the scientific methods of critical historiography. Measured against this standard, Flacius displays brilliant premonitions of the truth mixed with inexplicable slips back into narrow dogmatism and vacuous formalism. This would be the last word on the subject if in fact interpreting Holy Scripture presented no other problem than that recognized by historical theology of the liberal period to which Dilthey belonged. In being applied to the New Testament, the praiseworthy intention of understanding every text from its context and of resisting dogmatic pressure ultimately leads to the dissolution of the canon, if, like Schleiermacher, one foregrounds "psychological" interpretation. For then every New Testament author is viewed from the hermeneutic standpoint of the context, thus undermining the principle of *sola scriptura* that undergirds Protestant dogma. Dilthey implicitly approved of this inference. It underlies his critique of Flacius, in that he views the latter's exegetical deficiencies as owing to an unhistorical and abstract logical conception of the whole of Scripture or the canon. Similarly, the tension between dogmatics and exegesis reveals itself in other parts of Dilthey's exposition, especially in his critique of Franz and in his insistence that the context of Scripture as a whole takes priority over that of individual texts. Since Dilthey, criticism of historical theology during the past half century, climaxing in the concept of the kerygma, has made us more receptive to the legitimacy of the canon and therefore, too, of Flacius' dogmatic interests.

The effect of fore-understanding on research in hermeneutic history is further exemplified in the distinction introduced by L. Geldsetzer between dogmatic and zetetic hermeneutics.[2] By distinguishing interpretation bound by dogma and fixed by institutions and their authority from undogmatic, open, inquiring interpretation of texts that, under certain conditions—including the task of interpretation—leads to a verdict of *non liquet* [neither guilty nor innocent], the history of hermeneutics takes on a form that betrays a fore-understanding shaped by modern theory of science. Inasmuch as it underwrites theology's dogmatic interests, the new hermeneutics comes into considerable proximity to a juristic hermeneutics that conceives of itself dogmatically—as carrying out policies that have been fixed in laws. Yet it remains a question whether juristic hermeneutics misunderstands its own nature when, in the effort to discover the law, it ignores the zetetic element in legal interpretation and views legal hermeneutics as essentially subsuming a case under a general law that is already given as such. Here recent insight, decisively assisted by Hegel, into the dialectical relation of law and case may have altered our fore-understanding of legal hermeneutics. The role of adjudication has always limited the provenance of the subsumption model. Adjudication actually serves the end of rightly interpreting the law (and not merely rightly applying it). The same is all the more true for interpretations of the Bible—and, mutatis mutandis, the classics—which have been relieved of all practical purposes. As the "analogy of faith" is not dogmatically fixed or pregiven for biblical interpretation, so too the language that conveys a classic text to a given reader is not appropriately conceived by modeling one's thought on the epistemological concept of objectivity and considering the text's exemplariness to be merely a figment of narrow dogmatism. The distinction between dogmatic and zetetic hermeneutics strikes me as itself dogmatic, and it ought to fall prey to hermeneutic dissolution.

A third interesting kind of fore-understanding that causes the history of hermeneutics to appear in a particular light is briefly developed by Hasso Jaeger in an erudite contribution to the history of early hermeneutics.[3] Jaeger places Dannhauer at the point where the word *hermeneutics* first occurs, along with the idea of broadening Aristotelian logic with the logic of interpretation. He views Dannhauer as the final spokesman for the humanistic *res publica literaria* before rationalism rigidified it, and irrationalism and modern subjectivism spread their noxious blooms from Schleiermacher through Dilthey to Husserl and Heidegger (or worse). Amazingly, the author mentions neither the connection between the humanistic movement and the Reformation's principle of *sola scriptura* nor the definitive role that rhetoric plays in the whole problematic of interpretation.

Now, there can be no doubt, as Dilthey was well aware, that this Reformation principle itself, no less than its theoretical defense, corresponds to a broad humanistic practice that departs from scholastic pedagogy with its appeal to ecclesiastical authority and instead demands reading the original text itself. Moreover, this principle belongs to the greater humanist context, the rediscovery of the classics, which, of course, especially meant the classical Latin of Cicero. This was not merely a theoretical discovery, however; it was just as much a function of *imitatio,* the renovation of classical oratory and stylistics. Thus rhetoric is omnipresent.

Yet there was something strange about the rebirth of declamation. How could there be a renaissance of classical oratory without its classical space— the *polis* or *res publica?* After the end of the Roman republic, rhetoric lost its political centrality, and during the Middle Ages it formed part of the academic culture overseen by the church. It could not experience a renewal of the kind for which humanism strived without undergoing a much more drastic alteration of function, for the rediscovery of classical antiquity was connected with two things, both pregnant with consequences: the invention of printing and, following the Reformation, the explosion of reading and writing connected to the doctrine of universal priesthood. Thus began a process that finally, over the course of centuries, not only eliminated illiteracy but at the same time led to a culture of silent reading that demoted the spoken word and even words read aloud to the second rank. This was an immense event of introversion of which we have only recently become truly aware, now that the mass media have opened the way for a new orality.

Thus the humanistic revitalization of rhetoric, appealing more to Cicero and Quintillian than to Aristotle, soon left its origins behind and entered into new fields of influence that altered its shape and effect. Its overall theoretical form could be conceptualized as a logic of probability, and it was locked in indivisible unity with dialectic. As such it was freed from the school of logical formalism and from theological dogma based on authorities. The logic of probability, however, gauged itself so much by the criterion of logic that in the long run it could not threaten the precedence of the logic of necessity exemplified by Aristotle's *Analytics*.

Thus a dispute like that between rhetoric and philosophy in classical antiquity came to be repeated once again in the Renaissance. It was less philosophy, however, than modern science and the logic of judgment, conclusion, and proof corresponding to it that contested the validity and applicability of rhetoric and that were victorious in the long run.

A poignant witness to the pressure of the new science is the defense of the necessity of rhetoric that Giambattista Vico felt compelled to make even in Naples, so proud of its traditions.[4] Admittedly, what Vico was argumentatively defending is the educative function of rhetoric, always living—though less in the actual practice of eloquence and the expertise that values it than in redirecting the rhetorical tradition to reading classical texts.

Something new ultimately occurs here, however, even if only in the study of ancient oratory: namely, the new hermeneutics that offers an account of textual interpretation. Now, in one respect rhetoric and hermeneutics are intimately related: being able to speak, like being able to understand, is a natural human capacity that develops to the full without the conscious application of rules, although natural talents, along with their proper cultivation and practice, come into play.

So it really amounts to a fundamental narrowing of the matter when classical rhetoric refers only to the conscious practice that occurs in *writing* speeches, and thus divides oratory into the legal, political, and epideictic genres. In this connection, it is highly characteristic that the *praeceptor germaniae*, Melanchthon, added a new genus, the *didaskalikon* or educational lecture.[5] Even more characteristic, however, is that Melanchthon considered the proper use of rhetoric, the classical *ars bene dicendi,* to consist precisely in the fact that young people could not get along without the *ars bene legendi*—i.e., the ability to compose and evaluate speeches, longer disputations, and above all books and texts.[6] At first this sounds like a merely ancillary reason for learning and cultivating readiness of speech. But in the course of Melanchthon's presentation, reading as such—as well as the transmission and appropriation of the religious truths found in religious texts—gradually comes to take precedence over the humanistic ideal of imitation. Thus Melanchthon's lectures on rhetoric decisively affect the new Protestant educational system.

So the task of rhetoric had shifted toward hermeneutics, even though no full awareness of the change had occurred, and the word *hermeneutics* had not

yet come into use. The great heritage of rhetoric had an effect on the new business of textual interpretation in several decisive respects. Just as for Plato's students true rhetoric could not be divorced from a true knowledge of things
(*rerum cognitio*) without falling into absolute nothingness,[7] so also the patent
presupposition operative in interpreting texts is that the text being interpreted
contains the truth about things. During the early revival of rhetoric in the age
of humanism, guided entirely by the ideal of imitation, this may have seemed
obvious. Certainly it was so for the kind of hermeneutics we are considering,
for to Melanchthon as well as to the first founder of Protestant hermeneutics,
Flacius Illyricus, the theological controversy over the understanding of Holy
Scripture was the fundamental motive. For that reason, the question could not
arise of whether the art of understanding is called upon to disclose the true
meaning of a false sentence, for example. This situation changes in the seventeenth century with the rise of methodological consciousness—on which Zab-
arella exercised great influence—and correlatively, dependence on hermeneutics in scientific theory alters as well. We can observe this in Johann
Dannhauer, who censures rhetoric in the appendix and tries to ground the
new rhetoric by drawing on Aristotelian logic. Of course, this does not mean
that the content of what he says was completely independent of the rhetorical
tradition, for the latter in fact provided the model for textual interpretation.

If we consider Melanchthon next, we find that the Lutheran principle of
sola scriptura is a self-evident presupposition of his course on rhetoric and
plays a role in its content, though it does not govern the flow of argument,
which is conducted completely in the manner of the peripatetic school. Melanchthon attempts to justify the meaning and value of rhetoric entirely in its
new application to reading, as we have described. "For no one can mentally
comprehend longer expositions and complicated disputations who is not supported by a kind of art that informs him about how the parts are ordered and
articulated, as well as about the intentions of the speaker and a method of explicating and clarifying obscure matters."[8] Here Melanchthon is also certainly
thinking about theological controversy, but he is wholly following the Aristotle
of the medieval and humanistic tradition when he relates rhetoric very closely
to dialectic; and that means assigning it no special sphere but rather underscoring its general applicability and utility.

"The first and most important thing is the main intent and central viewpoint or, as it is called, the *scopus* of the discourse."[9] Thus Melanchthon introduces what became a dominant concept in the later hermeneutics of Flacius, a
concept he derives from the methodical introduction to Aristotle's *Ethics*.
Clearly Melanchthon is no longer thinking of speaking in the narrower sense,
when he talks about the Greeks' attempt to raise questions at the beginning of

all their books (sic!). Knowing the basic intent of a text is essential to an adequate understanding of it. This point, moreover, is fundamental to the most important doctrine that Melanchthon establishes, which is undoubtedly his doctrine of the *loci communes*. He introduces it as part of *inventio* and thereby follows the ancient tradition of *topic*, although he is quite aware of the hermeneutical issues it implies. He emphasizes that this most important chapter, "which contains the beginning and end of the whole art,"[9a] does not simply contain a fund of insights, of which the orator or teacher should acquire as many as possible; such *loci*, properly assembled, constitute the whole of knowledge. This amounts to an implicit hermeneutic critique of the superficiality of a rhetorical *topic*.[10] On the other hand, it serves the end of justifying his own procedure, for Melanchthon grounded early Protestant dogma on a sensible selection and collection of Holy Scripture's touchstone passages: the *loci praecipui* that first appeared in 1519. Later Catholic criticism of the Protestant principle of *sola scriptura* is not entirely justified in charging that the reformers' principle is illogical because it sets up these dogmatic *sententiae*. It is true that choice always implies interpretation and thus has implications for dogma, but the hermeneutic distinction of early Protestant theology consists in its claim that its abstract dogmas are legitimated from Scripture itself and its intent. Another question, of course, is to what extent Reformation theologians followed their basic principle.

The point of *sola scriptura* was to repress allegorical interpretation (although it remained somewhat unavoidable with respect to the Old Testament, just as it is still recognizable today in the form of so-called typological interpretation). An explicit reference to Luther's exegetical practice in interpreting Deuteronomy and the prophets will serve to illustrate the continuing validity of his principle. Melanchthon states: "This does not communicate mere allegories, but first of all history itself is related to the *loci communes* of faith and works, and only then do allegories result from these *loci*. But no one can follow this procedure who is not unusually learned."[11] Even this compromise confirms our interpretation that the principle of *sola scriptura* maintains its fundamental position.

We could go further in identifying elements of rhetoric within the principles of later hermeneutics, but perhaps a general consideration suffices at this point. It concerns the new task of reading. In contrast to spoken discourse, the written or reproduced text is deprived of all the kinds of interpretive assistance that a speaker takes care to offer. These can all be grouped under the concept of proper emphasis. The totality of understanding is encapsulated in the ideal case—never completely realized—of perfect emphasis, and everyone knows how hard it is to utter a sentence with really appropriate intonation. At one point Dannhauer rightly remarks, written "literature is made intelligible in virtually no other way than by a living teacher. Who can actually read the old manuscripts of the monks without such help? The punctuation can be understood only on the basis of orators' prescriptions concerning periods, commas, and colons." This passage confirms that the new help in reading provided by punctuation depends on the old art of articulation governed by rhetoric.

The full breadth of this problem, though, is not genuinely understood until the advent of Pietist hermeneutics as it develops from August Hermann Franke through J. Rambach and his followers. For it is here that the old chapter in classical rhetoric, the awakening of affects, is first recognized as a hermeneutic principle. Rooted in the inmost moods of the mind, affect is intrinsic to all discourse; we are familiar with this experience: "Spoken with different affects and gestures, the same words widen their range, sometimes developing completely different senses." In thus taking cognizance of the affective modulation of all discourse (and especially preaching) lies the root of the "psychological" interpretation founded by Schleiermacher and ultimately of all theories of empathy. As Rambach puts it, for example: "The interpreter needs to take on the spirit of the author to such an extent that he slowly becomes like his second I."

Here, however, we are getting ahead of ourselves. The first hermeneutic self-awareness is already brought to fruition by Flacius in the Reformation. He too was first of all a philologist and humanist who had been won over to Luther and the Reformation. It was his indisputable achievement to have brought hermeneutics to the defense of the Lutheran principle of *sola scriptura* against the Tridentine theologians' attacks. His defense of the primacy of Scripture had to wage battle, as it were, on two fronts: on the one hand, against humanism's ideal of Ciceronian style, which did not fit the Bible; on the other, against the Counter-Reformation charge that the Holy Scripture is generally unintelligible unless it is unlocked with the help of the church's traditional teachings. To open the Scriptures without the later keys of dogma is the basic intention of the key composed by Flacius, his so-called *Clavis scripturae sacrae*. Here he treats the sources of difficulty in Scripture thoroughly and receives ironic praise from his Catholic critic Richard Simon for his effort—as well as for being so well read in the Church fathers. Now, for Flacius the most important difficulty in Scripture, underlying the whole principle of *sola scriptura,* does not lie in the general difficulties posed by any text written in a foreign language. This side of the matter Flacius explicates fully, since he was a leading Hebrew and Greek scholar who therefore felt he had special competence in the area; fundamentally more important is a religious reason for difficulty. "According to holy doctrine, all men are naturally not only slow and dull;

they are, in addition, strongly inclined to the opposite of what it says; we are not only incapable of loving, honoring and understanding it; we consider it silly and impious, and shrink far away from it."

Here a central motif of all hermeneutics, namely, the task of overcoming and assimilating the strange, receives a special, indeed unique formulation, one to which all other kinds of textual strangeness—whether of language, historical outlook, or form of expression—are subordinate. For here what is at issue is the ur-motif of Protestantism: the opposition of law to the promise of grace. We make it too easy for ourselves when we call the hermeneutics grounded thereon dogmatic because of this dogmatic interest. Certainly it is intended to assist Christian faith and acceptance of the gospel, but it nevertheless remains a purely hermeneutic effort. It consists in perfecting and justifying the Protestant principle of *sola scriptura,* the application of which confirms the religious supposition of justification by faith alone.

We would be taking an artificially narrow perspective if we viewed the task of interpreting texts through the prejudices of modern scientific theory and the criterion of scientificity. The interpreter's task *in concreto* is never merely a logical-technical transmission of the sense of some discourse, where the question of the truth of what it says is completely disregarded. Any attempt to understand the sense of a text means taking up the challenge that it presents. Its truth claim is therefore the presupposition of the whole enterprise, even when better understanding results in a critique of the sentence and shows it to be false. We can also observe this in the way Flacius designs his hermeneutics. He knows how much of a challenge the gospel presents. It is neither superfluous nor dogmatically narrow for him to enumerate all the conditions necessary to rightly understand Holy Scripture. At issue, to cite one example, is not just the pious expectation that we will listen to God's Word, as Flacius demands, but rather the condition that our soul will be free of all cares, which is expressly necessary in all difficult cases. Or along with the advice to memorize things that are not completely understood, "in the hope that God will make them clear to us one day," he suggests another piece of advice that is true generally and valid for every reader: keep in mind, first of all, the *scopus,* purpose, and intention of the whole text.

Such general recommendations do not reduce the uniqueness of Holy Scripture's claim; rather, the claim is properly foregrounded by applying them. "We must keep in mind that this book contains not only the kind of doctrine books usually contain, but also these two: the law and the gospel. The nature of each is opposed to the other, to be sure, yet they are consonant in that while the law exposes our sinfulness, it indirectly encourages us to accept forgiveness (from the savior)." Even this is a hermeneutic matter. It signifies that the Bible demands a special kind of assimilation, namely the believer's acceptance of the glad tidings. That is the *scopus* according to which Holy Scripture has to be read, even when someone approaches it simply as a historian, or an atheist considers it false—on Marxist grounds, for example. This kind of text, like every other, must be understood according to its intention.

In every case—though especially in preaching, which so revitalizes the Scripture that its tidings are renewed—reading and interpreting Scripture come under the kerygmatic claim of the gospel. A hermeneutic consciousness needs to be aware of this fact, and it does not justify calling Flacius's hermeneutic theory dogmatic. It offers nothing less than an adequate theoretical grounding for the principle of *sola scriptura* that Luther established. Flacius's hermeneutic theory does not offend against humanist and philological principles of correct interpretation when it understands a religious text as religious tidings. It requires no dogmatic suppositions about content that cannot be derived from the text of the New Testament but instead possess authority superior to it. The whole of his hermeneutics follows from this one principle. Only the context can really determine the sense of individual words, passages, etc.: "Ut sensus locorum tum ex scopo scripti aut textus, cum ex toto contextu petatur." Here the front-line position in the polemic against all doctrinal tradition that is not text-based is completely clear. It is a corollary of the fact that Flacius, like Melanchthon, follows Luther in warning against the perils of allegory. The doctrine of the *scopus totius scripti* is intended to guard against succumbing to precisely this temptation.

If we look more closely into the matter, the classical conceptual metaphors of rhetoric are here being summoned to prevent Scripture from being dogmatically subordinated to the doctrinal authority of the church. The *scopus*, designated as the head or visage [*Gesicht*] of the text, is often clear just from the title, but it emerges primarily from the basic lines followed by the course of thought. This suggestion takes up and extends the old rhetorical viewpoint of *dispositio*. One needs to pay special attention, so to speak, to where the head, breast, hands, and feet are, and how the individual members and parts cooperate in the whole. In this connection Flacius speaks of the "anatomy" of the text. This is pure Plato. Instead of mere sequences of words and sentences, every discourse must be organized like a living being with its own body, so that it lacks neither head nor foot; rather, the inside and outside exist harmoniously and contribute to the whole. This is what the *Phaedrus* says (264c). Even Aristotle is following this rhetorical construct when he describes the structure of a tragedy: *hosper zoon hen holon*.[12] Our German expression "das hat Hand und Fuss" comes from the same tradition.

It is also pure Plato to say (and Aristotle has offered explanation and grounding for the fact) that the essence of rhetoric is not exhausted in formulatable rules of art or technique. The teachers of rhetoric whom Plato is criticizing in the *Phaedrus* occupy themselves with something prior to rhetoric proper. For the real art of rhetoric can neither be prescinded from knowledge of the true nor from knowledge of the "soul." By this he means the spiritual situation of the listener, whose affects and passions the discourse awakens to the ends of persuasion. This is what the *Phaedrus* teaches, and so the whole of rhetoric up to the present day follows from the principle of the *argumentum ad hominem* in everyday colloquial use.

Now, it is true, however, that in the age of rationalism and the new science that unfolded in the seventeenth and eighteenth centuries, the tie between rhetoric and hermeneutics was loosened. Most recently, Hasso Jaeger has in notable fashion called attention to the role played by Dannhauer's *Idea boni interpretis*.[13] Dannhauer appears to have been the first to use the word *hermeneutics* terminologically, clearly relying on the eponymous text of Aristotle's organon. This shows that Dannhauer is claiming to have furthered and fulfilled what Aristotle had begun in his *Peri hermeneias*. As he says himself, he aims "to extend the province of the Aristotelian organon by adding a new city." His orientation, then, is toward logic, which—as a further part, a broader philosophical science—is meant to displace interpretation, and that in so general a way that it will take precedence to theological, like legal, hermeneutics, just as logic and grammar are prior to all special application. Thus Dannhauer leaves out everything that he calls oratorical interpretation, namely, the application and utility that one strives for with a text and that is generally called *accomodatio textus,* and he tries through hermeneutics to bring about in understanding generally a human and logical infallibility equal to that of logic. This inclination toward a new kind of logic is what leads him to parallel hermeneutics with analytical logic and expressly foreground the latter. Both parts of logic, the analytical and hermeneutical, have to do with truth, and both teach how to avoid falsehood. But they are distinguished by the fact that hermeneutics teaches how to discover the true meaning of a false sentence, while analysis can derive a true conclusion only from true premises. The former, then, has to do only with the "meaning" of sentences and not with the correctness of what they say.

Dannhauer is perfectly aware of the difficulty here: the sense intended by the author need not be clear and univocal. This, precisely, is human weakness: that a single speech can have many meanings. But he claims that with sufficient effort such polysemy can be dissolved. We can see how rationalistic his thinking is in this matter when he proposes that the ideal of hermeneutics is to change and, as it were, metamorphose illogical discourse into logical. The point, he suggests, is to situate that kind of discourse—for example, the poetical—in its proper light, so that it can deceive no one. Its true place, however, is within logical discourse, pure statement, categorical judgment, the proper way of speaking.

Extolling such a logical orientation as the true realization of the idea of hermeneutics, as Jaeger does, strikes me as mistaken. Dannhauer, a Strassburg theologian of the early seventeenth century, thinks of himself as a student of Aristotle's organon, which has freed him from the confusions of contemporary dialectic. Yet if we look beyond Dannhauer's affiliation with theory of science and examine what he says, we can see that he shares almost everything with Protestant hermeneutics; and if he ignores its connection with rhetoric, he does so in reliance on Flacius, who, he thinks, had devoted sufficient attention to this side of the matter. As a Protestant theologian, he in fact explicitly shares an appreciation of the significance of rhetoric. In his *Hermeneutica sacrae scripturae* he cites whole pages of Augustine in order to show that Holy Scripture can hardly be described as merely artless (as would appear from the viewpoint of the Ciceronian rhetorical ideal); rather, it possesses a special kind of eloquence appropriate to men of the highest authority, men almost divine. We can see that the humanistic canons of rhetorical style still retain their validity here, because the Christian theologian opposes them—like Augustine—only by defending the Bible's high rhetorical standards. What the rationalist reorientation of hermeneutics' methodological self-understanding brings about in terms of new content, then, does not affect the substance of the hermeneutic undertaking at all, as based on the principle of *sola scriptura*. Dannhauer continually refers to the contested theological questions and insists, just like other Lutherans, on the fact that the capacity for hermeneutics, and thus the possibility of understanding Holy Scripture, is common to all humankind. For him too, the cultivation of hermeneutics serves to defend against the papists.[14]

However, regardless of whether one models one's methodological self-consciousness on the pattern of logic or of rhetoric and dialectic, in either case the *Kunst* [art] of hermeneutics has a universality that transcends all particular forms of application—to the Bible, to the classics, or to legal texts. This is implied in both orientations and is grounded in the special problematic implied in the concept of a *Kunstlehre* [rules of art] and the development of that concept, first introduced by Aristotle. Compared to "pure" instances of *techne* or *Kunstlehre*, rhetoric as well as hermeneutics seem to be special cases. Both are concerned with the whole verbal universe, not with determinate and limited fields of production. Correlatively, they progress more or less continuously from the natural, general human capacity for speech and understanding to conscious use of the rules for speaking and understanding. But this has another important aspect that can be seen neither from the viewpoint of modern science nor that of the concept of *techne:* to divide the "pure art" from the natural and social conditions of everyday practice is possible only to a limited extent. In the case of rhetoric this means that, divorced from the natural situation and natural practice, merely learning and knowing the rules does not help anyone achieve real eloquence; and it means, conversely, that a discourse that just follows the rules, without having any appropriate content, remains empty sophistry.

Transposing this to hermeneutics, we find that the art of good interpretation is concerned with a special intermediate category, namely, discourse fixed in writing or print. On the one hand, this means that understanding is made more difficult, even when the verbal and grammatical preconditions are met completely. The dead word must still be reawakened in living speech. On the other hand, this fixity means that things are made easier insofar as what is fixed presents itself unchanged to repeated attempts to understand it. What is at stake here, however, is not merely adding up the advantages and disadvantages of fixity. To the extent that hermeneutics concerns itself with interpreting texts, and texts are designed for reading aloud or silently, it remains the case that in every instance the task of interpreting and understanding cooperates with the art of writing. So in the early period of oral culture a special art of writing was instituted to provide a textual basis for appropriate oral delivery. This is an important stylistic device, one that played a decisive role in the classical period of the Greeks and Romans both. Special helps to reading, punctuation, and articulation became possible and necessary with the general increase in silent reading and especially with the emergence of print. Clearly, what was expected of the art of writing also changed. Paralleling the explanation of the decline of eloquence that Tacitus offers in the *Dialogues* is the theory that the art of printing explains the decline of epic literature and the alteration in the art of writing that corresponds to the alteration in the art of reading. We can see how far both rhetoric and hermeneutics are distinguished from the knowledge conceived on the hand-based model of manufacture, to which the concept of a *Kunstlehre (techne)* is connected.

The problematic involved in the concept of a *Kunstlehre* is still discernible in Schleiermacher, even when it is applied to rhetoric and hermeneutics. The interface between understanding and interpretation is exactly like that between speaking and giving speeches. In both cases the part played by conscious application of rules is so subordinate that in rhetoric and hermeneutics, as in logic, it seems better to speak of achieving a theoretical consciousness—

that is, giving a "philosophical" account—that is more or less unconnected to any functional application.

Here it is necessary to recall the special place in the mind occupied by practical philosophy, according to Aristotle. It is called *philosophia,* and that word always designates a kind of "theoretical" rather than practical interest. Nevertheless, as Aristotle emphasizes in the *Ethics,* it is not an effort undertaken for the purpose of mere knowledge, but instead an *arete*—that is, something acquired for the purpose of practical being and doing. Now, it strikes me as quite noteworthy that the same thing might be said of what Aristotle calls *poeitike philosophia* in the sixth book of the *Metaphysics* and that clearly comprehends poetics as well as rhetoric. Neither is it a simple kind of *techne* in the sense of technical knowledge. Both indeed depend on a universal human capability. Their special position vis à vis the *technai* is admittedly not so clearly indicated as is the idea of practical philosophy, which is characterized by being polemically contrasted to the Platonic idea of the good. Yet I think it might be maintained as consistent with Aristotle's thought that the special position of poetic philosophy can be defined by analogy to practical philosophy. In any case, history has borne out this relation; for the trivium, which is divided into grammar, dialectic, and rhetoric and includes poetics under the rubric of rhetoric, possesses a similar universality, by contrast to more specialized ways of making and producing things, as these are related to *praxis* generally and the kind of rationality that governs it. Far removed from the claim to be sciences, these components of the trivium are nevertheless "free" arts—that is, they belong among human *Dasein*'s basic forms of behavior. They are not something that people do or learn so that they become people who have learned it. This capacity for *Bildung* belongs to the possibilities of humanity as such, to what everyone is or can be.

It is this, ultimately, that marks the significance of the relation between rhetoric and hermeneutics that we are considering. Neither the art of interpreting nor that of understanding is a specific skill one can acquire in order to become one of those who have learned it, like a kind of professional interpreter; rather they belong to human being as such. To that extent, the so-called *Geisteswissenschaften* appropriately bear and carry the name of *humaniora* or humanities. This may have been obscured by the monopoly of method and science typical of modernity. In truth, however, a culture that has assigned a leading place to science and therefore to the technology based on it can never entirely explode the larger framework—the social *Mitwelt*—in which human beings are constituted. In this larger framework, rhetoric and hermeneutics have an unassailable and all-encompassing place.

NOTES

Bracketed information and notes that carry the letter *a* have been supplied by the translator.

1 Wilhelm Dilthey, *Leben Schleiermachers*, 2:595.

2 See Geldsetzer's extremely informative introductions to his reprints of Thibaut, xxx–xliii, and Flacius.

3 [Hasso Jaeger, "Studien zur Frühgeschichte der Hermeneutik,"] *Archiv für Begriffsgeschichte* 18 (1974): 35–84.

4 G. Vico, *De ratione studiorum* [*On the Study Methods of Our Time*, trans. Elio Gianturco (Ithaca: Cornell University Press, 1990)].

5 [Philipp] Melanchthon, [*Opera quae supersunt omnia*, ed. C. G. Bretschneider (Halle: Schwetschke and Sons), 1846; rpt. New York: Johnson Reprint, 1963)], vol. 13, [*Ad historiam profanam et philosophiam spectantia*, part 4: *Elementorum rhetorices*], pp. 423ff.

6 Ibid., p. 417.

7 Ibid.: *rerum cognition ad docendum necessaria:* Plato, *Phaedrus*, 262c.

8 Melanchthon, vol. 13, pp. 417ff.

9 Ibid., pp. 442f.

9a Ibid., p. 470.

10 Apparently the students of Melanchthon were less fully aware of this issue. This is what I conclude from Johannes Sturm, *Linguae latinae resolvendae ratio* (1581): "Neo tempore valde occupati fuimus adolescentes in instituendis locis communibus. Corrogavimus quaedam ex eo libro Erasmi, quem edidit de ratione discendei. Phillipus honorificae memoriae etiam tradidit quosdam locos communes et alii alios locos communes omnium rerum. . . . Vobis hi loci instar memoriae seu recordationes." Melanchthon's students, then, were not clear on the hermeneutic dimension involved in collecting *loci*.

11 Melanchthon, vol. 13, p. 452.

12 Aristotle, *Poetics*, 23.1.1459a20.

13 H. Jaeger, "Studien zur Frühgeschichte der Hermeneutik," *Archiv für Begriffsgeschichte* 18 (1974): 35–84, esp. pp. 41ff. [Note added by author in 2d ed.]

14 For the above mentioned Sturm there is no question of depending on Aristotle. Sturm actually warns against Jesuits "ut magis sint Aristotelici quam theologi."

2

Rhetoric—Poetics—Hermeneutics

Paul Ricoeur

Translated by Robert Harvey

The difficulty in the theme submitted here for investigation results from the tendency of the three disciplines of the title to overlap with one another to the point that they let themselves be led on by their totalizing aims at covering the entire terrain. What terrain? That of discourse, articulated in configurations with more extended meaning than the sentence. By this restrictive clause, I wish to situate these three disciplines at a higher level than that of the theory of discourse considered within the limits of the sentence. At this level of simplicity, the definition of discourse is not the object of my investigation, even though it constitutes its presupposition. I ask that the reader grant (in accordance with Emile Benveniste and Roman Jakobson, J. L. Austin and John Searle) that the first unit of meaning in discourse is not the sign under the lexical form of the word, but rather the sentence, i.e., a complex unit which coordinates a predicate on a logical subject (or, using P. F. Strawson's categories, which unites an act of characterization by a predicate and an act of identification by positing a subject). Thus taken into employ in its basic units, language may be defined by the phrase "someone says something about something to someone." Someone says: a speaker makes something happen, that is, an utterance, a speech-act whose illocutionary force adheres to precise constitutive rules which alternately make of it a statement, an order, a promise. Something about something: this relationship defines the statement as such, by uniting a meaning to a reference. To someone: the word addressed by the speaker to the interlocutor turns the statement into a communicated message. It falls to a philosophy of language to distinguish within these coordinated functions the three major mediations which make it so that language is not unto itself its own end: the mediation between man and world, the mediation between man and another man, the mediation between man and himself.

It is upon this common background of discourse, understood as a unit whose meaning is found on the level of the sentence, that the three disciplines whose rival and complementary aims we shall now compare stand out. Through them, discourse takes on its properly discursive meaning, that is, an articulation by means of units of meaning which are more vast than the sentence. The typology we shall try to institute is irreducible to that proposed by Austin and Searle: indeed, a typology of speech-acts in terms of the illocutionary force of utterances becomes established at the sentence level of discourse. Thus a new type of typology superimposes itself upon those of speech-acts, a typology of properly discursive, that is, hyperphrastic, usage of discourse.

RHETORIC

Rhetoric is the oldest discipline of the discursive usage of language. It was born in Sicily in the sixth century before our era.[a]

A few major features characterize rhetoric. The first of these defines the center from which the aforementioned realm unfolds. When it comes time to assess the ambition of rhetoric to cover the entire field of the discursive use of language, this first feature should not be lost sight of. What defines rhetoric first are certain typical situations of discourse. Aristotle defines three which regulate the three genres of the deliberative, the judicial, and the epideictic. Three locations are thus designated: the assembly, the tribunal, and commemorative gatherings. Specific audiences thus constitute the privileged *addressees* of the art of rhetoric. They have in common the rivalry of opposite discourses between which it is important to choose. In every case, the idea is to get one judgment to prevail over another. In each of these situations, a controversy calls forth the cutting edge of decision. One can speak in a broad sense of litigation or of a trial even in the epideictic genre.

The second criterion of the art of rhetoric consists in the role played by argumentation, i.e., a mode of demonstration situated halfway between the constraint of the necessary and the arbitrariness of contingency. Between the proof and the sophism there reigns the probable argument whose theory Aristotle inscribed in dialectic, thus making of rhetoric the "antistrophe," that is, the rejoinder of dialectic. It is precisely in the three aforementioned typical situations that it behooves us to isolate a reasonable discourse, halfway between the demonstrative discourse and the violence hidden in the purely seductive discourse. We can already see how argumentation may conquer, step by step, the entire field of practical reason (where the preferable calls for deliberation, whether it is a matter of ethics, law, or politics) and—we shall see this later, when rhetoric is carried to its limits—the entire field of philosophy as well.

However, a third feature tempers the ambition to prematurely amplify the field of rhetoric: the orientation toward the listener is not at all abandoned by the argumentative regimen of discourse; the aim of argumentation remains persuasion. In this sense, rhetoric can be defined as a technique of persuasive discourse. The art of rhetoric is an art of operative [*agissant*] discourse. The speaker aspires to conquer the assent of his audience and, if the situation is appropriate, to incite that audience to act in the desired manner. In this sense, rhetoric is illocutionary and perlocutionary at the same time.

But how does one persuade? A last feature helps us to state precisely the contours of the art of rhetoric surprised at the "seat" from which it radiates. The speaker's orientation toward the audience implies that he begins with conventional ideas that he shares with it. In this, argumentation has little creative function: it transfers the agreement granted to premises onto conclusions. All the intermediary techniques (which, moreover, can be very complex and refined) remain a function of the real or presumed agreement of the audience.

Finally, we must say a word about elocution and style, to which the moderns have had far too great a tendency to reduce rhetoric. We cannot disregard them, however, precisely because of the orientation toward the listener. The figures of style—turns of phrase and tropes—extend the art of persuasion into an art of pleasing even when they are in the service of argumentation and do not sink into simple ornamentation.

This description of the seat of rhetoric readily reveals its ambiguity. Rhetoric has never ceased to oscillate between a threat of a fall from grace and the totalizing claim in pursuance of which it aspires to equal philosophy.

Let us begin with the threat of the fall from grace: all the features we have just described indicate that in discourse there is a certain vulnerability and a propensity toward pathology. The shift from dialectic to sophistry delineates, in Plato's eyes, the most important tendency of rhetoric. From the art of persuasion one moves without transition to the art of deceit. The preliminary agreement upon acknowledged ideas shifts to the triviality of prejudice; from the art of pleasing one moves to that of seducing, which is none other than the violence of discourse.

Political discourse is assuredly the most inclined to these perversions. What is called ideology is a form of rhetoric. But it must be said of ideology what is said of rhetoric: it is the best and the worst. The best: the whole set of symbols, beliefs, and representations which, by way of acknowledged ideas, ensures the identity of a group (nation, people, party, etc.). In this sense, ideology is the discourse itself of the imaginary constitution of society. But this is the same discourse that takes a turn toward perversion as soon as it loses contact with the first account concerning founding events and becomes a discourse justifying the established order. We are not far from the function of dissimulation and illusion that Marx denounced. It is thus that ideological discourse illustrates the decadent path of the art of rhetoric: from the repetition of the first foundation to justifying rationalizations, then to mendacious falsification.

However, rhetoric has two tendencies: one of perversion and one of sublimation. It is upon the latter that the totalizing claim of rhetoric asserts itself. Rhetoric stakes its all on the art of argumentation, along the lines of the probable, unrestricted by the social constraints heretofore described.

The supersession of what we have named the typical situations (with their specific audiences) occurs in two stages. In the first stage, the whole human order can be annexed by the rhetorical field in that what is considered ordinary language is nothing but the functioning of natural languages in ordinary situations of conversation; now, conversation puts particular interests into play— particular interests really being those passions to which Aristotle devoted book 2 of his *Rhetoric*. Thus, rhetoric becomes the art of "human, all too human" discourse. But this is not all: rhetoric may claim the whole of philosophy for its magistery. We need only consider the status of first propositions in all philosophies: being hypothetically undemonstrable, they can proceed only from a weighing up of the opinions of the most competent, thus aligning themselves under the banner of the probable and of argumentation. This is what Chaim Perelman maintained throughout his work. For him, the three fields of rhetoric, argumentation, and first philosophy intersect.

I cannot say that this pretension to all-inclusiveness is illegitimate, and even less can I say that it is refutable. I simply wish to stress two points first: that it seems to me that rhetoric can free itself entirely neither from typical situations which isolate its generative seat nor from the intention which defines its finality. Concerning the initial situation, it must not be forgotten that rhetoric has claimed the right to command the public use of the word in the typical situations described by the political, legal, and the festive assemblies. In relation to these audiences, that of the philosopher, by Perelman's own admission, can only be a universal audience, i.e., virtually all of humanity, or, at the least, its competent and reasonable representatives. It is to be feared that this extrapolation beyond typical situations corresponds to a radical change in the discursive realm. As for the finality of persuasion, it cannot be sublimated to the point of fusion with the disinterest of authentic philosophical discussion either. Indeed, I am not naive enough to believe that philosophers free themselves not only from the constraints but also from the pathology which infect our debates. What remains is that the aim of philosophical discussion, in its most honest forms which prevail in the typical situations described above (if it is equal to what we have called the universal audience), transcends the art of persuasion and of pleasing.

This is why it is necessary to consider other constitutional seats of discourse, other arts of composition and other aims of discursive language.[1]

POETICS

If we do not confine ourselves to opposing rhetoric and poetics (in the sense of writing with rhythm and versification), it may appear difficult to distinguish between the two disciplines. If we return once again to Aristotle, *poiesis* means production or manufacturing of discourse. Now, is not rhetoric also an art of composing discourse, thus a *poiesis?* Furthermore, when Aristotle considers the coherence which renders the plot of the tragic, comic, or epic poem intelligible, is he not saying that the assembly or juxtaposition (*sustasis*) of actions must satisfy verisimilitude and necessity (*Poetics* 1154a.33–36)? Even more surprising, does he not say that in pursuance of the meaning of the probable and the necessary, poetry teaches universals and thus proves to be more philosophical and of a more elevated character than history (1451b.5)? There can be no doubt then that poetics and rhetoric intersect in the region of what is probable.

But if they thus intersect, it is because they come from different origins and make their way toward different goals.

The initial place from which poetry radiates is, according to Aristotle, the fable or the plot the poet invents when he borrows the material for his episodes from traditional narratives. The poet is an artisan not only of words and sentences but of plots which are fables or fables which are plots. The localization of this nucleus—which I call the initial site of diffusion or of extrapolation of the poetic mode—is of the utmost importance for the confrontation that follows. At first glance, this site is restricted, since it covers only the epic, the tragedy, and the comedy. But it is precisely this initial reference which allows the opposition between the poetic act and the rhetorical act. The poetic act is the invention of a fable plot; the rhetorical act, an elaboration of arguments. Indeed, there is poetry in rhetoric to the extent that "finding" an argument (*euresis* in book 1 of *The Rhetoric*) is the same as a true invention. And there is rhetoric in poetry to the extent that, for every plot, one can find a corresponding theme or thought (*dianoia* is Aristotle's expression). But the accent does not fall in the same place: the poet does not argue, *stricto sensu,* even if his characters argue; argument serves only to reveal the character insofar as he contributes to the progress of the plot. And the rhetorician does not create any plot or fable, even if a narrative element is incorporated into the presentation of the case. Argumentation remains fundamentally dependent upon the logic of the probable, i.e., of the dialectic in the Aristotelian (and not in the Platonic or Hegelian) sense, and of the topic, i.e., of the theory of *loci* or *topoi,* which are schemes of conventional ideas appropriated to typical situations. On the other hand, the invention of the fable plot remains fundamentally an imaginative reconstruction of the field of human action—an imagination or reconstruction to which Aristotle applies the term *mimesis,* i.e., creative imitation. Unfortunately, a long, hostile tradition has led us to think of imitation as a copy or a replica of the identical. And thus we understand nothing in the crucial declaration of Aristotle's *Poetics* according to which the epic, the tragedy, and the comedy are imitations of human action. However, precisely because *mimesis* is not a copy but rather a reconstruction through creative imagination, Aristotle does not contradict himself. He explains himself perfectly when he defines *mimesis* by emplotment, and the plot itself as "the arrangement (*sustasis*) of incidents" (*Poetics,* chapter 6).

What then is the initial nucleus of poetics? It is the relation between *poiesis, muthos,* and *mimesis:* in other words, it is the relation "production/fable/plot/creative imitation." As creative act, poetry imitates to the exact degree that it engenders a *muthos,* or fable plot. It is this invention of a *muthos* which must be opposed to argumentation, insofar as it is the generating nucleus of rhetoric. Whereas the ambitions of rhetoric find their limit in its attention to the listener and its respect for conventional ideas, poetics points to the breach of newness that the creative imagination opens in this field.

The other differences between the two disciplines issue from the last one. I have characterized rhetoric not only by its method (argumentation) but also by its relation to typical situations and by its persuasive aim. On these two points, poetics differs. The epic or tragic poem's audience is brought together by the recitation or by the theatrical representation. The audience is a people not in the role of arbiters of rival discourses but as offered to the cathartic process exercised by the poem. *Catharsis* must be understood as an equivalent of medical purging and religious purification: a clarification carried out by intelligent participation in the *muthos* of the poem. Catharsis must, finally, be opposed to persuasion. Contrary to all seduction or flattery, it consists in the imaginative reconstruction of the two basic emotions by which we participate in any great deed: fear and pity. Fear and pity are in turn metaphorized, in a way, by this imaginative reconstruction in which, thanks to *muthos,* the creative imitation of human action consists.

Thus understood, poetics too has its seat of diffusion: the *poiesis/muthos/mimesis* nucleus. From this center, it can radiate and cover the same field as rhetoric. In the political domain, while ideology bears the stamp of rhetoric, utopia bears that of poetics, to the extent that utopia is nothing other than the invention of a social fable capable, it is believed, of changing life. And philosophy? Is it not also born under the sun of poetics? Does not Hegel himself say that philosophical and religious discourses have the same content and differ only as the concept differs from representation (*Vorstellung*)—a prisoner, as it is, of narration and symbolism? Does not Perelman vindicate me just a little bit in the "Analogy and Metaphor" chapter of *The Realm of Rhetoric?* Speaking of the creative aspect connected to analogy, the model, and the metaphor, he concludes in these terms: "Philosophical thought, incapable of empirical verification, develops by an argumentation that aims to have certain analogies and metaphors accepted as central elements in a world view" (125).

Conversion of the *imaginary* is the central aim of poetics. With it, poetics stirs up the sedimented universe of conventional ideas which are the premises of rhetorical argumentation. At the same time, this same breakthrough of the imaginary shakes up the order of persuasion, from the moment it becomes less a matter of settling a controversy than of generating a new conviction. Henceforth, the limit of poetics is, as Hegel knew, the powerlessness of representation to equal the concept.

HERMENEUTICS

What is the initial seat of foundation and dispersion of our third discipline? I shall start with the definition of hermeneutics as an art of interpreting texts. Indeed, a special art is required as soon as the geographical, historical, and cultural distance which separates the text from the reader gives rise to a situation of misunderstanding which can only be overcome in a plural reading, that is, a multivocal interpretation. Under this fundamental condition, interpretation—the central theme of hermeneutics—is seen to be a theory of multiple meaning.

I shall take up a few points concerning this initial insertion. First, why the insistence on the notion of text or of the written work? Is there not a comprehension problem in conversation, in the oral exchange of the word? Is there not misunderstanding and incomprehension in what claims to be dialogue? Most certainly. But the face-to-face presence of interlocutors allows the play of question and answer to gradually rectify mutual understanding. With regard to this play of question and answer, a case can be made for a hermeneutics of conversation. But that would only be a pre-hermeneutics in that the oral exchange of the word does not reveal a difficulty that only writing gives rise to—that is, severed from its speaker, the meaning of discourse no longer coincides with the latter's intention. Henceforth, what the author wanted to say and what the text signifies undergo separate destinies. The text, which according to Plato's *Phaedrus* is a sort of orphan, has lost its defender, which was its father, to confront alone the adventure of reception and reading. With regard to this situation, Wilhelm Dilthey, one of hermeneutics' theoreticians, wisely proposed reserving the term of interpretation for the comprehension of works whose discourse is fixed by writing or deposited in monuments of culture which lend to meaning the support of a sort of inscription.

And now, what text? It is here that, if it must be distinguished from that of rhetoric or poetics, the originary place [*lieu originaire*] of the work of interpretation must be recognized. Three places have successively stood out. First, in our Judeo-Christian culture, there was the canon of the biblical text. This origin [*lieu*] is so decisive that many readers are tempted to identify hermeneutics with biblical exegesis. This identification is not quite true, even in this limited framework [i.e., the Bible], because exegesis consists in the interpretation of a well-defined text, whereas hermeneutics is that of a secondary discourse concerning the rules of interpretation. Nevertheless, this first identification of the originary place of hermeneutics is not without reason or effects. Our concept of "figure," as Erich Auerbach analyzed it in his famous article "Figura," remains largely tributary of the first Christian hermeneutics, applied to the reinterpretation of the events, characters, and institutions of the Hebraic Bible in the terms of the proclamation of the New Alliance. Then, the complicated edifice of the four meanings of the Scripture was developed with the Greek Fathers and the entirety of medieval hermeneutics. Four meanings which are four levels of reading: literal or historical, tropological or ethical, allegorical or symbolic, anagogic or mystical. Finally, for the moderns, a new biblical hermeneutics issued from the incorporation of classical philological sciences and ancient exegesis. It is at this stage that exegesis rose to its authentic hermeneutical level, that is, to the task of transferring the core of meaning that the texts took on with respect to a cultural situation—which has ceased to be ours—into a modern cultural situation.

Here, we are beginning to see the outlines of a problematic not specific to biblical or even, generally, religious texts: the struggle, as I described earlier, against misunderstanding born of cultural distance. Henceforth, to interpret is to translate a signification from one cultural context to another according to a putative rule of equivalence of meaning. It is at this point that biblical hermeneutics merges with the two other modalities of hermeneutics. Indeed, already in the Renaissance, and especially from the seventeenth century onward, philology of classical texts constituted a second field of interpretation autonomous from the former one. Here, as in the former, the restitution of meaning revealed itself to be a promotion of meaning, a transfer or, as I have just said, a translation in spite of, or even in favor of, the temporal or cultural distance. The problematic common to exegesis and philology proceeds from this special relationship between text and context in which the text can reputedly decontextualize itself, that is, free itself from its initial context in order to recontextualize itself in a new cultural situation while preserving a presumed semantic identity. The hermeneutic task consists, then, in approaching this presumed semantic identity equipped solely with the resources of decontextualization and recontextualization of meaning. Translation, in the broad sense of the term, serves as model for this precarious operation. Recognition of the third seat of hermeneutics is an opportunity to better understand what this operation consists of. We now are dealing with legal hermeneutics. A legal text is never without a process of interpretation—jurisprudence—which innovates within the lacunae of written law and especially in new situations not anticipated by the legislator. Jurisprudence thus provides the model of an innovation which is at the same time a tradition. It happens that Perelman is one of the most remarkable theoreticians of the relationship between law and jurisprudence. Now, the recognition of this third hermeneutical seat is the opportunity also for an enrichment of the concept of interpretation such as it has been instituted in the two previous seats. Jurisprudence shows that cultural and temporal distance is not only an abyss to be bridged, but a *medium* to pass through. All interpretation is a reinterpretation constituting a living tradition. No transference, no translation without a tradition—that is, a community of interpretation.

Such being the threefold origin of the hermeneutical discipline, what relationship does it have with the two other disciplines? Once again, the phenomena ranging from encroachment and overlapping to a claim of all-inclusiveness come up for examination. Compared to rhetoric, hermeneutics also possesses argumentative phases, in that it must always explain more for the purpose of understanding better and also in that it behooves it to settle rival interpretations, and even rival traditions. But its argumentative phases remain a subset of a more vast project, which is certainly not that of re-creating a situation of univocity by thus settling in favor of a privileged interpretation. The example of the four meanings of the Scripture is, in this respect, very instructive; and, before the latter, the wise decision of the early Christian church to allow the four Gospels, whose differences in intention and organization are obvious, to subsist side by side. Faced with this hermeneutical freedom, one could say that the task of an art of interpretation, compared to one of argumentation, is less to win acceptance for one opinion over another than to allow a text to signify as much as it *can:* not to signify one thing rather than another but to "signify more," and thus to make us "think more" according to Kant's expression in the *Critique of Judgment (mehr zu denken)*. In this respect, hermeneutics (whose project, I have said, is less to persuade than to open the imagination) seems to me closer to poetics than to rhetoric. It too calls upon the productive imagination in its demand for a surplus of *meaning*. Moreover, this demand is inseparable from the work of translation, of transfer, which is linked to the recontextualization of a meaning transmitted from one cultural space to another. But then why not say that hermeneutics and poetics are interchangeable?

This too may be said, inasmuch as the problem of semantic innovation, as I liked to say in *The Rule of Metaphor,* is at the core of both. The initial difference must, however, be stressed between the applications of this semantic innovation in hermeneutics and its applications in poetry. I shall reveal this difference in the very heart of poetry.

Aristotle's insistence on identifying *poiesis* with the assembly or juxtaposition of the fable plot should be recalled. The work of innovation thus resides inside the unity of discourse which makes up the plot. Moreover, even though *poiesis* was defined as *mimesis* of action, Aristotle will no longer make any use of the notion of *mimesis,* as if it were enough to disconnect the imaginary space of the fable from the real space of human action. It is not a real action that you see there, the philosopher suggests, but only a simulacrum of action. This disjunctive, rather than referential, use of mimesis is so characteristic of poetics that it is this sense which has prevailed in contemporary poetics, where the structural aspect of *muthos* has been retained while the referential aspect of fiction has been abandoned. Against structural poetics, it is this challenge that hermeneutics takes up. I would like to state that the function of interpretation is not only to have a text signify something else or even signify everything it can and signify always something more (to take up the expressions already used), but its function is to unfold what I now call the world of the text.

I readily admit that this task is not the one which romantic hermeneutics, from Schleiermacher to Dilthey, liked to emphasize. For them, it was a matter of reactualizing inspired subjectivity hidden behind the text in order to make themselves contemporary with that subjectivity and to equal it. That path is today closed. And it became so precisely by the consideration of the text as an autonomous space of meaning and by the application of structural analysis in this purely textual sense. But the alternative does not lie with a psychologizing hermeneutics or with a structural or structuralist poetics. If the back door of the text is closed, that is, the side of its author's biography, the front door, if I may say so (i.e., the side of the world it discloses), is open.

I am well aware of the difficulties in this argument, which I defended in *The Rule of Metaphor*. Nevertheless, I maintain that the power of reference is not an exclusive feature of descriptive discourse. Poetic works point to a world as well. If this argument appears difficult to defend, it is because the referential function of the poetic work is more complex than that of *descriptive* discourse and even, in a sense, paradoxical. Indeed, the poetic work unfolds a world only under the condition that the reference of descriptive discourse be deferred. The poetic work's power of reference then appears as a secondary reference by means of the deferral of the primary reference of discourse. The poetic reference may thus be characterized, as Jakobson has said, as an *undoubled* [*dédoublée*] reference. There is some truth in the widely accepted thesis in literary criticism that in poetry, language has a relationship only to itself. By deepening the abyss that separates signs from things, poetic language celebrates itself. It is for this reason that poetry is commonly held to be a discourse without reference. The thesis that I am maintaining here does not negate the preceding one but rather is based upon it. It posits that the deferral of the reference (as defined by the norms of descriptive discourse) is the negative condition for a more fundamental mode of reference to be brought out.

It will still be objected that the world of the text is yet a function of the text, its signified, or, in Benveniste's words, its *intenté*. However, the hermeneutic moment is the work of thought by which the world of the text faces what we conventionally call reality in order to redescribe it. This confrontation may range from denial or even destruction (which is still a relation to the world) to the metamorphosis and the transfiguration of the real. It is here as it is with models in science whose ultimate function is to redescribe the initial *explanandum*. This poetic equivalent of redescription is the positive *mimesis* lacking in a purely structural theory of poetic discourse. The impact between the world of the text and, simply, the world, within the space of reading, is the ultimate stake of the productive imagination. It engenders what I would dare to call the productive reference proper to fiction.

It is with this task in mind that hermeneutics can, in turn, erect a totalizing, or even totalitarian, claim. Wherever meaning constitutes itself within a tradition and demands a translation, interpretation is at work. Wherever interpretation is at work, a semantic innovation is at stake. And wherever we begin to "think more," a new world is both discovered and invented. But this totalizing claim must, in its turn, be subjected to the trial of criticism. Hermeneutics has to be brought back to the center from which its claim arose, that is, the foundation-bearing [*fondateurs*] texts of a living tradition. Now, the relation between a culture and its textual origins falls under another sort of criticism: the criticism of ideologies, illustrated by the Frankfurt School and its successors, Karl-Otto Apel and Jürgen Habermas. What hermeneutics tends to be unaware of is the more fundamental relationship between language, work, and power. For hermeneutics, it is as if language were an origin without origin.

This criticism of hermeneutics at its very source becomes, at the same time, the condition by which the rights of the two other disciplines are recognized. We have seen that these disciplines radiate from different seats.

In conclusion, it seems to me that one must leave each of these three disciplines undisturbed in their three respective birthplaces, which are irreducible one to another. And there is no superdiscipline which would totalize the whole field covered by rhetoric, poetics, and hermeneutics. Lacking this impossible totalization, one can only locate the noticeable points of intersection between the three disciplines. But each discipline speaks for itself. Rhetoric remains the art of arguing with a view to persuading an audience that one opinion is preferable to its rival. Poetics remains the art of constructing plots with a view to broadening the individual and collective imaginary. Hermeneutics remains the art of interpreting texts within a context distinct from that of the author and from that of the texts' original audience with a view to discovering new dimensions to reality. Arguing, fashioning [*configurer*], redescribing: such are the three major operations whose respective totalizing aims are mutually exclusive, but the finiteness of whose original sites condemns them to complementarity.

NOTES

Editor's note: the opening paragraph, as follows, has been deleted: "The following study arises from a lecture given in 1970 at the Institut des Hautes Etudes in Belgium in the presence and under the presidency of Professor [Chaim] Perelman. This lecture having never been published, it is an honor to be invited by [Perelman's] friends and disciples to join in the homage to the man who for several decades was the master philosopher of Brussels."

a. Editor's note: the following sentence has been deleted: "Furthermore, throughout his work and right up to its most compact expression under the title *The Realm of*

Rhetoric, Professor Perelman took rhetoric for his guide in the exploration of philosophical discourse itself."

1 In *The Realm of Rhetoric* (Notre Dame: University of Notre Dame Press, 1982) Perelman affords a place to modalities of argumentation that are confined to what I shall later call poetics: the analogy, the model, and the metaphor. He also affords a place to interpretative procedures that pertain to what will later be held to be an illustration of the discipline of hermeneutics.

3

On the Tragedy of
Hermeneutical Experience

Gerald L. Bruns

Breakdown and failure reveal the true nature of things.
—Karl Jaspers, *Tragedy Is Not Enough*

Hermeneutics is made up of a family of questions about what happens in the understanding of anything, not just of texts but of how things are. This is different from the usual question about how to make understanding happen, how to *produce* it the way you produce a meaning or a statement where one is missing. For hermeneutics, understanding is not (or not just) of meanings; rather, meaning is, metaphorically, the light that a text sheds on the subject (*Sache*) that we seek to understand. Think of *Sache* not as an object of thought or as the product or goal of conceptual determination but as a question that comes up or confronts you—a question not of your own devising and perhaps one you don't know how to put into words, like the questions of horror and death that hover and loom from life's onset. No one thinks up questions like these; rather they encroach and bear down, and we just find ourselves exposed to them. Frequently the *Sache* of thinking makes itself felt as just this sort of question without words; it is that which resists conceptual framing and leaves one dumbstruck with its evasions. Hermeneutics has to do with these evasions. However, it is not a method of preventing or outwitting them. It is not always the case that what happens in understanding is that one understands something in the sense of grasping or solving it. What happens, what happens also or instead, is that one *always* confronts the limits—in Gadamer's language, the finitude or historicality, the situatedness—of understanding itself.

In the essay "Text and Interpretation," which was part of his so-called encounter with Derrida, Gadamer characterized these limits in terms of the "impenetrability of the otherness of the other."[1] For Schleiermacher the task of hermeneutics had been to (explain how to) understand the other, as if from inside the other's own subjective condition. After Gadamer, however, we would say that in understanding, we encounter the other in its otherness, not as an object in a different time and place but as that which resists the grasp of my knowledge or which requires me to loosen my hold or open my fist. It is what will not be objectified before me. Whether I take the other ethically as a person (Levinas) or thoughtfully, thinkingly, as a subject matter, like the question of language (Heidegger), what happens in understanding is that I always experience the refusal of the other to be contained in the conceptual apparatus that I have prepared for it or that my own time and place have prepared for it; and of course this alters my own relation to this framework, not to say my own self-relation or my own standing. So one could say that what happens in understanding is not so much the familiarization of the other as self-estrangement. But perhaps it is enough to say that in this event one is left unguarded or exposed to the other as well as to oneself and the world, which is now implicated in the strangeness of the other.

It is not easy to say what sort of experience this is, however, partly because of the limitations of the concept of experience. When Gadamer's *Truth and Method* was first published (1960), the notion of experience, among other cherished ideas, had already begun to disappear from our conceptual horizon. Reasons for this include the development of structuralism, which redesigned Kant's theory of the transcendental subject as a concept of a total system immanent in its results. Henceforward experience would only be a metaphor of surface structure. Moreover, structuralism provided the language for powerful new interpretations of Marx, Nietzsche, and Freud, which Paul Ricoeur summarized with the phrase "hermeneutics of suspicion." Crucially, critiques of ideology, deconstruction, and psychoanalysis make complete sense only when defined critically against various German philosophies of the spirit, where the concept of experience is a fundamental category. In the German idealist tradition, experience is the domain of the creative subject. It is where we form the world and ourselves in it. For example, in 1957 Robert Langbaum argued that modern literature is a "poetry of experience," that is, a poetry of worldmaking and the formation of new values to replace an obsolete cultural inheritance.[2] The romantic motto is: there is nothing outside of experience. But now we say that everything is outside of it; it is an empty concept, a category of false consciousness. History, for example, never occurs at the level of experience.

The foremost philosopher of experience was Wilhelm Dilthey, for whom *Erlebnis*, usually translated as "lived experience," is the basic unit of time, history, and human culture. Experience here is not of phenomena or of objects like desks and chairs; it is the existence of human subjects within a temporal order that cannot itself be objectified the way empirical data can, because one can never stand outside of temporality and observe it as it goes by (like Willard Quine's "passing show"). Rather, one can enter into it only in reflection, and what one encounters then is not experience itself but only the mediating constructions produced by experiencing subjects.

For experience in the romantic sense is essentially expressive. It produces works or narratives of itself that make possible the reexperiencing of all that happens. This reexperiencing—Dilthey's *Nacherleben*—is the task of hermeneutics or, more broadly, of the hermeneutical disciplines that Dilthey called the *Geisteswissenschaften*. In Dilthey's theory what distinguishes hermeneutical understanding from scientific explanation is that understanding can never occur at an analytical distance; it always means living through what is understood. Its goal is the intelligibility of what cannot be conceptualized or reduced, namely, human life in all its singularity. The point is that in the romantic view what calls for understanding is never just a text but another subject. The text is always understood as a mediation between subjects of historical experience. The thought that one can never work through these mediations to relive the experience that produced them, the idea that one mediation simply opens onto another, is what separates us from Dilthey.

Now in *Truth and Method,* in the context of Heidegger's historicizing of the romantic subject, Gadamer has harsh words for Dilthey, whom he sees as clinging to a Cartesian theory that conceives the subject as disengaged from history and sustaining itself entirely from within. This criticism is not entirely just, but it is true that *Nacherleben* implies something like an out-of-body hermeneutics, through which the interpreter is able to escape his or her historicality and enter into the subjectivity of another. "By transposing his own being experimentally, as it were, into a historical setting," Dilthey says, "the interpreter can momentarily . . . reproduce an alien life in himself [*Nachbildung fremden Lebens in sich herbeizuführen*]."[3] This reproduction of the other in oneself is what Gadamer wants to reexamine in the light of Heidegger's historicism. We can never extricate ourselves from our own historical situation. We always read the other from within our own time and place. But what happens in this reading? Gadamer's idea is that we always encounter the resistance of the other to the way we make sense of things and that this encounter has important critical consequences. We cannot reproduce an alien life in ourselves without risk to our self-identity.

Indeed, Gadamer's critique of Dilthey does not do away with experience but simply brings it down to earth. Gadamer works along the lines of Heidegger's readings of Hegel, perhaps not so much the early lectures on Hegel's *Phenomenology of the Spirit* (first delivered in 1930–31) as on "Hegel's Concept of Experience" (1942–43), first published in *Holzwege* (1950). The second text is a close reading of the ten pages or so that make up Hegel's introduction to *Phenomenology*, in which experience is characterized as a reversal of consciousness (*Umkehrung des Bewusstseins*).⁴ Experience here is *Erfahrung* rather than *Erlebnis,* but it also means living through an event as against merely responding to it as a spectator. Hegel stresses that his idea "does not seem to agree with what is ordinarily meant by experience" (p. 79/p. 55), and Heidegger emphasizes that this is because experience has nothing to do with empirical knowledge, nor is it anything like Husserl's phenomenological experience, where experience is still reducible to the self-evidence of objects.⁵ For in Hegel's idea nothing is acquired, nothing is grasped or objectified in its essence; instead, *everything is taken away.*

Hegel thinks of *Erfahrung* as a reversal of consciousness that elevates it to a higher ground called philosophy or science. The model of this reversal has to be something like the Copernican Revolution, but as Heidegger reads him, Hegel is interested mainly in the truth that consciousness discovers about itself in this event. Experience as *Umkehrung* is, to be sure, a movement of enlightenment for Hegel, who calls it "a way of the Soul which journeys through . . . its own configurations as though they were stations appointed for it by its own nature, so that it may purify itself for the life of the Spirit, and achieve, finally, through a completed experience of itself, the awareness of what it really is as such" (p. 72/p. 49). But the way of purification is (as always) through suffering and destitution. What consciousness discovers about itself is that its knowledge of the world, and so of itself, is not "real knowledge." As Hegel says, the journey that consciousness undergoes, its experience of itself, "has a negative significance for it." "The road can . . . be regarded as the pathway of *doubt,* or more precisely as the way of despair" (p. 72/p. 49). Experience does not simply lead to hesitation and uncertainty; it is a "thoroughgoing skepticism" (p. 72/p. 50), a self-alienation in which "consciousness suffers violence at its own hands" (pp. 74–75/p. 51). Not to put too fine a point on it, experience is essentially satirical, a self-unmasking, as if reason could only discover the truth of things, and so of itself, when it sees that it is a fool.

For Gadamer the understanding of a text always has the structure of a reversal. At the most elementary level there is "the experience of being brought up short by the text" that is essential to philology or to any effort to determine what a text is saying.[6] Just when we think we have the meaning of a text pinned down, it confronts us with something that puts our understanding in question. At a higher level, the classical text, as Gadamer says, "is something that resists historical criticism" (p. 287), that is, it refuses to be contained in the contexts that our research arranges for it; it is always breaking free of our constructions and intervening in our own situation. Indeed, a recurrent theme of the history of interpretation is that the understanding of a text always requires, in some sense, a conversion to the text's way of thinking, and what this means is that we always end up having to reinterpret ourselves, and even change ourselves, in the light of the text. To understand a text is not only to grasp its meaning; it is to understand the claim that it has on us. Most often this claim is critical in the strong sense, as when a text exposes us to our prejudices, by which Gadamer means not only our private, subjective dispositions but, more important, the conceptual frameworks we inhabit and to which we appeal when we try to make sense of things. More is at stake in interpretation than interpretation. What would it be for a text to explode the conceptual world of the one who seeks to interpret it?

This is really what is at issue in *Truth and Method* in the chapter called "The Concept of Experience and the Essence of Hermeneutical Experience," a chapter that more than thirty years later remains pretty much unread. Here Gadamer emphasizes the negativity of experience. Paraphrasing Hegel, Gadamer calls *Erfahrung* "skepticism in action" (p. 353) because it throws what one knows, or rather what one is, into question, that is, into that open place of exposure where everything is otherwise than usual. In experience one does not acquire anything, unless it is experience itself, where being experienced is not the same as being in possession of something objective and determinate; rather, experience is always of limits and refusal. This is why it is so hard to communicate experience, as from parents to children. Experience in this sense can only be put into stories; it cannot be contained within propositions or underwritten by the law of contradiction. It has the universality of proverbs rather than of principles. It is never rule-governed. Experience is inevitably painful, because it entails the defeat of will or desire, the breakdown of design or expectation, of power or projection, but this breakdown is also an opening, even a sort of emancipation or releasement. Gadamer thinks of it in terms of insight, where insight means less a metaphysical grasp of something, however, and less an illumination of transcendence than an "escape from something that had deceived us and held us captive [*ein Zurückkommen von etwas, worin man verblendeterweise befangen war*]" (p. 338/p. 356), a release, say, from some prior certainty or ground, some vocabulary or framework or settled self-understanding; or say that the hermeneutical experience always entails an "epistemological crisis" that calls for the reinterpretation of our situation, or ourselves—a critical dismantling of what had been decided.[7] Thus the negativity of hermeneutical experience is not merely nugatory and ironic or logically absurd; it is a negativity that places us in the open, in the region of the question. Were we to ask what a hermeneutical experience is like, Gadamer would certainly point us to Plato's dialogues, where Socrates is seen reducing the cultural experts of Athens to bewilderment or *aporia*. We call *aporia* "undecidability," but it is what Gadamer means by openness. Openness is not the open-mindedness of the liberal enlightenment, which is mostly a condition of disengagement that comes from having reflected ourselves out of the world. For Gadamer openness is a condition of exposure in which one's conceptual resources have been blown away by what one has encountered. In this event one finds oneself radically situated with no place to hide. Now insight and recognition become, as Gadamer likes to say, inescapable.

Hence the relevance of tragedy, as Gadamer himself suggests when he refers to the motto of Aeschylus, *pathei mathos,* learning through suffering (p. 356). Learning what, however? The traditional thought is that tragedy is always about self-knowledge, as when Oedipus learns the terrible truth about himself. But of course, to speak strictly, there never was a time when Oedipus did not know the truth about himself. Self-knowledge was never something that Oedipus lacked. His problem is that self-knowledge was never enough. More accurately, his relation to himself is neither a relation of knowing nor a relation to a self. What Oedipus knows is his name, that is, the name he has made for himself: Oedipus, "wise above all other men to read / Life's riddles and the ways of Heaven" (ll. 33–34). (Remember, he is famous for having solved the riddle of the Sphinx.) There is nothing false about this name, as the action of the play confirms, but the paradox is that the action confirms the identity of Oedipus by estranging him from it. This self-estrangement begins when Oedipus is asked to live up to his name, be the same man still, emancipate Thebes (again) from its curse, which he does of course; but this time *he* is the curse as, in fact, he knows well enough, though he doesn't see it yet, for he has heard more than once, and from no less than the oracle at Delphi, what his fate was to be, that he was to murder his father and marry his mother, else why did he flee from Corinth?

Oedipus never misunderstands himself—he will always be the man who solved the riddle of the Sphinx—but this self-understanding cannot contain the other that his fate inscribes. The story of Oedipus is about the implacable reality of this otherness, its inescapability as Fate. Fate is not just the inevitability of events; it is the otherness of identity, or reality, that which we seek to avoid but meet willy-nilly at the crossroads. It is this other that Oedipus must finally acknowledge; this is the meaning of the recognition scene. Exactly what this means, what it comes to, is that the self of Oedipus must now abide with this other, who becomes his sole society and the region of his exile. As if the point about Oedipus were that he is no longer the same as us, being no longer the same as himself. Sameness is just what he is exiled from; he can never be the same again, although nothing about him has changed (except his self-interpretation). Recall that the hermeneutical genius of Oedipus was that he was able to solve the riddle of the Sphinx by seeing himself in it, recognizing himself as human (the secret of the riddle); but the action of the play takes us to the limits of this self-recognition. Now Oedipus is required to acknowledge what lies on the other side, beyond self-recognition, of which he now deprives himself, because by blinding himself he can no longer see himself in the eyes of his children, where recognition means kinship. One could say that Oedipus encounters the limits of self-understanding, or that his self-understanding encounters the limits of the human or the same, which is to say, the limits of the speakable. The double meaning of his blindness is that what he can no longer see is himself as one of us. He understands himself as belonging elsewhere, beyond the reach of language. "Drive me at once beyond your bounds, where I / Shall be alone, and no one speak to me" (ll. 1375–76). But Oedipus was always already beyond this threshold. That is the meaning of Fate, which inscribes not our identity (in the sense of kinship) but our difference (in the sense of the mark that singles us out, separates us, like the difference the name "Oedipus" inscribes: "lame-footed," the sign that links him to his fate). Miasma or pollution is the social form of this difference that Thebes cannot abide. Oedipus is uncontainable. In his otherness, he is reality. It is this, if anything, that he understands.

One can clarify some of this by appealing to Stanley Cavell's writings on tragedy, most notably "The Avoidance of Love: An Essay on *King Lear*." Cavell's idea is that in tragedy we discover the moral or truth of skepticism, which is that "the human creature's basis in the world as a whole, its relation to the world as such, is not that of knowing, anyway not what we think of as knowing."[8] Each of Shakespeare's great plays starts out with a will-to-certainty—a will to be absolutely certain of the world, to have it absolutely present to one's mind and senses, to make it subject to one's knowing, hence to bring it or keep it under control. The lesson of tragic action is the refusal of the world to be subjected in this way. This refusal is summarized by Cordelia's answer to Lear ("Nothing, my Lord" [1.1.89]), but one could just as well refer to Desdemona's inaccessibility to the demands that Othello's doubt places upon her, her ines-capable otherness that Othello would either know or destroy. Like the skeptic, Cavell says, the tragic hero finds that the world "vanishes exactly with the ef-fort to *make* it present" (*Disowning Knowledge,* p. 94). What he learns, or needs to learn, is to forgo the knowing that presentness calls for. But how "do we learn that what we need is not more knowledge but the willingness to forgo knowing? For it sounds to us as though we are being asked to abandon reason for irrationality . . . or to trade knowledge for superstition. . . . This is why we think skepticism must mean that we cannot know the world exists, and hence that perhaps there isn't one (a conclusion some profess to admire and others to fear). Whereas what skepticism suggests is that since we cannot know the world exists, its presentness to us cannot be a function of knowing. The world is to be *accepted;* as the presentness of other minds is not to be known, but ac-knowledged" (p. 95).

Acknowledgment is how we connect up with reality as historicality or limit. It is what happens in hermeneutical experience, where understanding is an achievement not of objective consciousness but of openness and answerabil-ity, where openness means exposure. "Experience," Gadamer says, "teaches us to acknowledge the real." What is recognized is reality as other, not as the same: reality as that which is more Fate than Fact. "The genuine result of expe-rience," Gadamer says, "is to know what is. But 'what is,' here, is not this or that thing, but 'what cannot be done away with [*was nicht mehr umzustossen ist*]' (Ranke)" (*Truth and Method,* pp. 339–40/p. 357). Tragedy is what does away with everything except "what is." This is, so to speak, the key to its philosophi-cal, or at all events critical, nature as a hermeneutics of the inescapable. If we think of Shakespeare's great plays, we see that tragic learning (*pathei mathos*) is always a radical divestiture in which nothing is left to the tragic figure, every-thing is taken away, leaving the person radically exposed to reality, as if the whole category or project of presentness were reversed. What is it to be pre-sent to reality? It takes a Macbeth or Lear to know. The whole movement of *King Lear* is to expose Lear to his own otherness. His daughters are the first to do this, but from the start he encounters his other in the unmaskings of his Fool:

Lear: Doth any here know me? This is not Lear:
Doth Lear walk thus? speak thus? Where are his eyes?
Either his notion weakens, his discernings
Are lethargied—Ha! waking? 'tis not so.
Who is it that can tell me who I am? (1.4.246–50)

(To which Lear's Fool darkly replies: "Lear's shadow.") But above all there is the unforgettable image of Lear naked before the storm:

Lear: Why, thou wert better in thy grave than to answer with thy uncovered body this extremity of the skies. Is man no more than this? Consider him well. Thou owest the worm no silk, the beast no hide, the sheep no wool, the cat no perfume. Ha! here's three on's are sophisticated! Thou art the thing itself: unaccommodated man is no more but such a poor, bare, forked animal as thou art. Off, off, you lendings! come, unbutton here. [*Tearing off his clothes.*] (3.4.105–13)

One wants to say that hermeneutical experience always entails the event of exposure that belongs to tragedy. Cavell even suggests that exposure is exactly what happens to us in reading the text of a tragic drama. "I have more than once suggested," Cavell says, "that in failing to see what the true position of a character is, in a given moment, we are exactly put in his condition, and thereby implicated in the tragedy." But how? "What is the medium of this drama, how does it do its work upon us?" One could, Cavell says, describe it this way: "The medium is one which keeps all significance continuously before the senses, so that when it comes over us that we have missed it, this discovery will reveal our ignorance to have been willful, complicitous, a refusal to see" (*Disowning Knowledge,* p. 85), that is, a failure not of exegesis but of acknowledgment. Understanding a tragic action, Cavell says, is "different from the experience of comprehending meanings in a complex poem or the experience of finding the sense of a lyric. These are associated with a thrill of recognition, an access of intimacy, not with a particular sense of exposure. The progress from ignorance to exposure, I mean the treatment of an ignorance which is not to be cured by information (because it is not caused by a lack of information), outlines one motive to philosophy; this is a reason for calling Shakespeare's theater one of philosophical drama" (p. 85).

This seems close to what Gadamer said in *Truth and Method* about the tragic effect, that is, about the way tragedy (on Aristotle's analysis) appropriates its audience and exposes it to the tragic experience. I mean the idea that the tragic audience is not kept at a distance by tragic representation but is, on the contrary, overwhelmed and transformed by it. Thus Aristotle speaks of the pity and fear (*eleos* and *phobos*) that tragedy induces in the audience. Gadamer takes these in the sense of misery and apprehension, the anguish and cold horror that come over us when we see someone rushing to his destruction. "Misery and apprehension [*Jammer und Bangigkeit*]," Gadamer says, "are modes of ekstasis, being outside oneself, which testify to the power of what is being played out before us" (p 124/pp. 130–31). Yet what can it mean to say that tragedy is *kathartic,* that it "purifies" us of these disturbances? Gadamer says:

It seems clear to me that Aristotle is thinking of the tragic pensiveness that comes over the spectator in tragedy. But pensiveness is a kind of relief and resolution, in which pain and pleasure are peculiarly mixed. How can Aristotle call this condition a purification? What is the impure element in feeling, and how is this removed in the tragic emotion? It seems to me that the answer is as follows: being overcome by misery and horror involves a painful division [*Entzweiung*]. There is a disjunction [*Uneinigkeit*] with what is happening, a refusal to accept [*Nichtwahrhabenwollen*] that rebels against the agonizing events. But the effect of the tragic catastrophe is precisely to dissolve this disjunction with what is [*diese Entzweiung mit dem, was ist*]. It effects the total liberation of the constrained heart. We are freed not only from the spell in which the misery and horror of the tragic fate had bound us, but at the same time we are free from everything that divides us from what is. (pp. 124–25/p. 131)

In Cavell's language, we may imagine that the tragic audience is distributed along a moral plane between "acknowledgment and avoidance" (*Claim of Reason*, p. 329) and that the resolution of the tragic action means not just the working out of catastrophe but the overcoming of that "refusal to accept" that Gadamer identifies as our characteristic response to the unfolding of what happens (call it our characteristic response to reality as Other or as Fate: we are always fleeing Corinth). Again the idea is that tragic knowledge is closer to what Cavell calls acknowledgment and what Gadamer calls hermeneutical experience than it is to what we normally think of as knowledge, namely, knowledge as conceptual representation. "Tragic pensiveness," says Gadamer, "does not affirm the tragic course of events as such, or the justice of the fate that overtakes the hero but rather a metaphysical order of being that is true for all. To see that 'this is how it is' is a kind of self-knowledge for the spectator, who emerges with new insight from the illusions in which he, like everyone else, lives. The tragic affirmation is an insight that the spectator has by virtue of the continuity of meaning in which he places himself" (*Truth and Method*, pp. 125–26/p. 132). The point to understand is that tragic affirmation is not pretty; it means acknowledgment not just of the difficulty but of the horror of life. Tragic knowledge thus entails what elsewhere is called the "critique of the subject." It is emancipation from false consciousness achieved not by methodological application or analysis but by hermeneutical experience, that is, by the encounter with the otherness of reality, or with that which refuses to be contained within—kept at bay by—our conceptual operations and results. The difference between hermeneutical experience and logical forms of critique, however, is just the difference between tragedy and comedy, between the cold shock of recognition and the joyful exuberance of liberation from the constraints of historicality. In hermeneutical experience there is little comfort, unless it is simply that now we know how awful things can get. Tragic serenity consists of being beyond surprise.

In antiquity it was philosophy's claim that it alone would safeguard us against tragedy. The counterclaim is that tragedy cures us of philosophy. This comes out in Martha Nussbaum's *Fragility of Goodness*, which tries to situate Aristotle's account of tragedy within the framework of Plato's attempt in his middle dialogues to imagine a life secured against disaster (beyond herme- neutical experience).[9] For Plato the goal of the good life is to become ration- ally self-sufficient, impervious to events or circumstances, essentially sealed off from adversity (which is to say, from other people). It is not that terrible things cannot happen to the good or just man; it is that these terrible things cannot deprive him of his self-possession, his sense of being at home with him- self; catastrophe cannot deprive him of his well-being and self-sameness. So Socrates is not just not a tragic figure; he is, as Nietzsche figured him, anti- tragic. I mean that Plato seems to have set out to create a character to whom tragedy could never happen. The Socratic good life is free from pity and fear. Socrates would have never fled from Corinth. He would never have met him- self at the crossroads. Otherness never accrues to Socrates. (Recall the un- Lear-like image from the *Symposium:* Socrates standing motionless for hours in the snow, impervious to the cold.) His ignorance is never fatal and neither, one is tempted to say, is his death. Whereas for Aristotle (on Nussbaum's read- ing) the good life is exactly what risks tragedy by not sealing itself off; on the contrary, risk is essential to the good life precisely because what the good life requires is openness and responsiveness to what cannot be controlled, namely the world of action, events, and other people. As Nussbaum says, for Aristotle there are "central human values"—friendship, for example, and justice—that "cannot be found in a life without shortage, risk, need, and limitation. Their nature *and* their goodness are constituted by the fragile nature of human life" (p. 341). Whether Aristotle would go so far as the chorus in *Antigone*—"Noth- ing very great comes into the life of mortals without disaster"—is arguable, be- cause his view of life (like Nussbaum's) is comic rather than tragic, but his con- ception of the good life as exposed to the world rather than sealed off in philosophical asceticism led him to seek in tragic drama the experience of what it is to be fully human, as if this were of greater philosophical importance than the experience of unqualified *eudaimonia.*

Of course Nietzsche thought that on this precise point Aristotle had con- founded everything, missing not only the musical foundations of tragedy but the purpose, which is to induce in us an experience of transcendental joy:

Let the reader invoke, truly and purely, the effects upon him of genuine musical tragedy by harkening back to his own experience. . . . He will remember how, watching the myth unfold before him, he felt himself raised to a kind of omniscience, as though his visual power were no longer limited to surfaces but capable of penetrating beyond them; as though he were able to perceive with utter visual clarity the motions of the will, the struggle of motives, the mounting current of passions, all with the aid of music. Yet, though he was conscious of a tremendous intensification of his visual and imaginative instincts, he will nevertheless feel that this long series of Apollonian effects did not result in the blissful dwelling in will-less contemplation which the sculptor and epic poet—those truly Apollonian artists—induce in him by their productions. He will not have felt that justification of the individuated world which is the essence of Apollonian art. He will have beheld the transfigured world of the stage and yet denied it, seen before him the tragic hero in epic clarity and beauty and yet rejoiced in his destruction. He will have responded profoundly to the events presented on the stage and yet fled willingly into that which passes understanding. He will have considered the actions of the hero and yet divined in them a higher, overmastering joy.[10]

Hence W. B. Yeats's notion of tragic gaiety—"Hector is dead and there's a light in Troy; / We that look on but laugh in tragic joy."—which subsumes even the tragic heroes themselves:

All perform their tragic play.
There struts Hamlet, there is Lear,
That's Ophelia, that Cordelia;
Yet they, should the last scene be there,
The great stage curtain about to drop,
If worthy their prominent part in the play,
Do not break up their lines to weep,
They know that Hamlet and Lear are gay;
Gaiety transfiguring all that dread.[11]

Nietzsche says: "In thus retracing the experience of the truly responsive listener we gain an understanding of the tragic artist, of how, like a prodigal deity of individuation, he creates his characters—a far cry from mere imitation of nature—and how his mighty Dionysiac desire then engulfs this entire world of phenomena, in order to reveal behind it a sublime esthetic joy in the heart of original Oneness" (p. 133). The "spirit of the sublime," Nietzsche says, "subjugates terror by means of art" (p. 52).

Yet what is missing from hermeneutical experience, what this experience fatally lacks, is precisely the sort of distancing factor that informs the Nietzschean-Yeatsian theory of tragedy. Here again Cavell is helpful. In "The

Avoidance of Love" he says that our experience of *King Lear* is different from
our experience of Racine's *Phèdre* or Ibsen's *Hedda Gabler:*

> In *Phèdre* we are placed unprotected under heaven, examined by an unblinking
> light. In *Hedda Gabler,* we watch and wait, unable to avert our eyes, as if from an ac-
> cident or an argument rising at the next table in a restaurant, or a figure standing on
> the ledge of a skyscraper. In *King Lear* we are differently implicated, placed into a
> world not obviously unlike ours (as Racine's is, whose terrain we could not occupy),
> nor obviously like ours (as Ibsen's is, in whose rooms and rhythms we are, or re-
> cently were, at home), and somehow participating in the proceedings—not listen-
> ing, not watching, not overhearing, almost as if dreaming it, with words and gestures
> carrying significance of that power and privacy and obscurity; and yet participating,
> as at a funeral or a marriage or inauguration, confirming something; it could not
> happen without us. It is not a dispute or a story, but history happening, and we are
> living through it; later we may discover what it means when we discover what a life
> means. (*Disowning Knowledge,* p. 97)

Participating, not watching, not listening, not overhearing—or reading. Cavell
says that my relationship to the characters on the tragic stage is not (or not just)
literary or aesthetic, much less cognitive. That is, they are not just present to
me in the usual theatrical or imaginative or projective fashion; rather, I belong
to their present, am present to *them,* meaning that they have a claim on me,
not just on my attention but on *me.* What sort of claim is this? And how am I to
respond? I am, to be sure, in a theater, in the dark, present at what transpires;
but part of the tragic *ekstasis* is that the dark no longer conceals me: I am outside the distance between the stage and my self-possession, facing the characters not so much as if they were real but as if my separateness from them no
longer derives from their ontological peculiarity as aesthetic objects or fictional representations. It is now a human separateness, something different
from aesthetic distance or the cognition of a disengaged, punctual ego; it is
something intimate and harrowing, like a cold sweat. (Cavell writes: "Calling
the existence of Lear and others 'fictional' is incoherent [if understandable]
when used as an explanation of their existence, or as a denial of their existence.
It is, rather, the name of a problem: *What* is the existence of a character on the
stage, what kind of [grammatical] entity is this?" [p. 103].)

Cavell wants to say that tragedy, or at all events this tragedy, exposes me to
this fact of (my) human separateness; that is, *King Lear* does not simply show
or disclose or teach or illustrate this separateness, it is *die Sache Selbst,* the
tragic *ekstasis.*

> Catharsis, if that is the question, is a matter of purging attachment from everything
> but the present, from pity for the past and terror of the future. My immobility, my

transfixing, rightly attained, is expressed by that sense of awe, always recognized as the response to tragedy. In another word, what is revealed is my separateness from what is happening to them; that I am I, and here. It is only in his perception of them as separate from me that I make them present. That I make them *other*, face them.

And the point of my presence at these events is to join in confirming this separateness. Confirming it as neither a blessing nor a curse but a fact, the fact of having one life—not one rather than two, but this one rather than any other. I cannot confirm it alone. Rather, it is the nature of this tragedy that its actors have to confirm their separateness alone, through isolation, the denial of others. What is purged is my difference from others, in everything but separateness. (*Disowning Knowledge,* p. 109)

I am external to the world, and (radically) to others—not, however, as a transcendental spectator ("We that look on but laugh in tragic joy")—but rather as confined in myself and in my horror as events unfold, belonging to a time in which I do not intervene, which knows nothing of me: "Their fate, up there, out there, is that they must act, they are in the arena in which action is ineluctable. My freedom is that I am not now in the arena. Everything which can be done is being done. The present in which action alone is possible is fully occupied. It is not that my space is different from theirs but that I have no space within which I can move. It is not that my time is different from theirs but that I have no present apart from theirs. The time in which that hint is laid, in which that knowledge is fixed, in which those fingers grip the throat, is all the time I have. There is no time in which to stop it" (pp. 110–11). And then it is too late, in a twinkling it is over, vanished, leaving me divested of the world, staring blankly at the darkness that has me all to itself. Cleansed I certainly am, as of everything but the extremity of my being human. "Because the actors have stopped," Cavell says, "we are freed to act again; but also compelled to. Our hiddenness, our silence, and our placement are now our choices" (pp. 114–15).

In an essay entitled "Politics as Opposed to What?" Cavell speaks of the scene of interpretation as a drama of "reading and being read."[12] His example is from psychoanalysis, where "the situation of reading has typically been turned around, that it is not first of all the text that is subject to interpretation but we in the gaze or hearing of the text" (p. 200). An analogous case would be the reading of a Platonic dialogue, in which our understanding of the text is of the way the text appropriates us, makes us answerable to its interrogations; and for Gadamer this is the model of all eminent texts and of tradition as well (*Truth and Method,* pp. 362–79). Cavell understands this hermeneutical situation as being redemptive or therapeutic, rather (for him) like the reading of Wittgenstein's *Philosophical Investigations,* which like tragedy cures us of philosophy, or (for Wittgenstein) like the reading of the *Tractatus Logico-Philosophicus,* which cures us of itself.[13] One moral at least is that our relation to tragic drama is not one of reading, although of course it is not one of *not* reading; rather, we are taken by the text out of our usual position with respect to it, so that, among other things, as an expression of our understanding it would no longer be enough to give a reading of it, checking ourselves against the text, as if that were simply to go on as before (as if we hadn't read it correctly). We could put this another way by saying that our understanding of tragedy can be satisfied not by our reading of it but only by our actions in the world. If we go on as before, we are, Cavell would say, evading the text. In this respect tragedy resembles the law and the Scriptures, which we understand only insofar as we understand where they have taken us, and where we go from here. Understanding a text means being resituated not only in relation to the text but with respect to the present and future.

The concept of hermeneutical experience thus sheds some useful light on the idea that we understand differently if we understand at all. This does not mean that we periodically assign new meanings to a text or that the text, as someone might put it, is susceptible to indefinitely many interpretative readings (all at once?). *King Lear* has never meant anything except what it says, except when revised so that Cordelia might be allowed to live. But now it seems far from clear that our understanding of this or any text can be adequately characterized as a grasp of meanings. The concept of meaning has always seemed overpriced for the return we get on it. So much, indeed, seems to have been conceded over the centuries by grammarians, logicians, and various sorts of philosophers of language who, against the principle of Ockham's Razor, find themselves having to multiply categories of meaning—literal versus figurative, meaning versus significance, deep versus surface structure—just to keep pace with the sorts of things hermeneutical experience exacts from us. Perhaps this only means that, as with everything else, the extension of the concept of meaning cannot be closed by a frontier. If we understand differently when we understand at all, it is because of the way a text like *King Lear* resituates us in the world—exposes us to it despite our best conceptual defenses, for example the idea that poetry makes nothing happen, or maybe deprives us of these defenses, which we sometimes mistake for meanings.

NOTES

1 Hans-Georg Gadamer, "Text and Interpretation," in *Hermeneutics and Modern Philosophy,* ed. Brice Wachterhauser, trans. Dennis J. Schmidt (Albany: State University of New York Press, 1986), 385.

2 Robert Langbaum, *The Poetry of Experience: The Dramatic Monologue in Modern Literary Tradition* (New York: Norton, 1963).

3 Wilhelm Dilthey, "The Development of Hermeneutics" (1900), in *Gesammelte Schriften*, vol. 5, 330; Dilthey, *Selected Writings*, ed. H. P. Rickman (Cambridge: Cambridge University Press, 1976), 258.

4 G. W. F. Hegel, *Werke in zwanzig Bänden* (Frankfurt: Suhrkamp, 1970), vol. 3, 79; Hegel, *Hegel's Phenomenology of the Spirit*, trans. A. V. Miller (Oxford: Oxford University Press, 1977), 55. Parenthetical references in text will be to these editions.

5 G. W. F. Hegel, *Hegel's Concept of Experience*, trans. Kenley Royce Dove (New York: Harper and Row, 1970), 124–29. See Husserl, *Experience and Judgment: Investigations in a Genealogy of Logic*, trans. James S. Churchill and Karl Ameriks (Evanston, Ill.: Northwestern University Press, 1973), 27–63.

6 Hans-Georg Gadamer, *Wahrheit und Methode*, 2d ed. (Tübingen: Mohr, 1965); *Truth and Method*, 2d ed., trans. Joel Weinsheimer and Donald G. Marshall (New York: Continuum, 1989), 268. Parenthetical references in text will be to these editions.

7 See Alasdair MacIntyre, "Epistemological Crises, Dramatic Narrative, and the Philosophy of Science," *Monist* 60, no. 4 (October 1977): 453–72. For a more linear, less apocalyptic view of experience, see Günther Buck, *Lernen und Erfahrung* (Stuttgart, 1969), which follows Husserl's conception of "perceptual experience," where the negativity of experience simply produces an alteration or expansion of horizons without any critical transformation. See also Buck, "The Structure of Hermeneutic Experience and the Problem of Tradition," trans. Peter Heath, *New Literary History* 10, no. 2 (Autumn 1978): 31–47. Horizonal change, Buck says, "presents itself . . . as a movement from narrower and more specific to wider and more general horizons. A nullified anticipation, in being discredited, frees our view for a more embracing anticipation that arises, as it were, behind it. This process seems repeatable at will. We can think of no final horizon that experience could ever go beyond. The unsteadiness induced by negative experience is always contained within the higher-order steadiness of wider horizons" (p. 38). But the idea of an "epistemological crisis" means that the way we inhabit these horizons undergoes a break and calls for a reinterpretation of ourselves and our history.

8 Stanley Cavell, *The Claim of Reason: Wittgenstein, Skepticism, Morality, Tragedy* (New York: Oxford University Press, 1971), 324. Cavell's essays on Shakespeare have been gathered together in *Disowning Knowledge in Six Plays of Shakespeare* (Cambridge: Cambridge University Press, 1987). Further references to these books are cited parenthetically in the text. See Gerald L. Bruns, "Stanley Cavell's Shakespeare," *Critical Inquiry* 16, no. 1 (Spring 1990): 612–32.

9 Martha Nussbaum, *The Fragility of Goodness: Luck and Ethics in Greek Tragedy and Philosophy* (Cambridge: Cambridge University Press, 1986), esp. the superb reading of *Antigone*, 51–82. See p. 70 on the chorus in *Antigone*: "For these people experience the complexities of tragedy while and by being a certain sort of community, not by having each soul go off in isolation from its fellows; by attending to what

is common or shared and forming themselves into a common responding group, not by reaching for a lonely height of contemplation from which it is a wrenching descent to return to political life." Further references are cited parenthetically in the text. See my discussion of Nussbaum's book, "Tragic Thoughts at the End of Philosophy, *Soundings* 72, no. 4 (Winter 1989): 694–724.

10 Friedrich Nietzsche, *The Birth of Tragedy and the Genealogy of Morals,* trans. Francis Golffing (Garden City, N.Y.: Doubleday Anchor, 1956), 131–34. Further references are cited parenthetically in the text.

11 W. B. Yeats, "The Gyres" and "Lapus Lazuli," in *The Collected Poems of W. B. Yeats* (New York: Macmillan, 1983), 293, 295.

12 Stanley Cavell, "Politics as Opposed to What?" in *The Politics of Interpretation,* ed. W. T. J. Mitchell (Chicago: University of Chicago Press, 1983), 199. Further references are cited parenthetically in the text.

13 Cavell appropriately cites here Stanley Fish's "Aesthetic of the Good Physician," in *Self-Consuming Artifacts: The Experience of Seventeenth-Century Literature* (Berkeley: University of California Press, 1972), esp. 13: "To read the *Phaedrus,* then, is to use it up; for the value of any point in it is that it gets *you* (not any sustained argument), to the next point, which is not so much a point (in logical-demonstrative terms) as a level of insight. It is thus a *self-consuming artifact,* a mimetic enactment in the reader's experience of the Platonic ladder in which each rung, as it is negotiated, is kicked away. The final rung, the level of insight that stands (or, more properly, on which the reader stands) because it is the last, is, of course, the rejection of written artifacts, a rejection that, far from contradicting what has preceded, corresponds exactly to what the reader, in his repeated abandoning of successive states in the argument, has been doing." Reading carries us to the limits of reading, as philosophy to the limits of philosophy.

4

Toward a Hermeneutics Responsive
to Rhetorical Theory

Charles Altieri

I would like to begin by quoting Hans-Georg Gadamer and Friedrich Schleiermacher on the connection of rhetoric and hermeneutics. First Gadamer:

> Thus the rhetorical and hermeneutical aspects of human linguisticality interpenetrate each other at every point. There would be no speaker and no such thing as rhetoric if understanding were not the lifeblood of human relationships. There would be no hermeneutical task if there were no loss of agreement between the parties of a "conversation" and no need to seek understanding. The connection between hermeneutics and rhetoric ought to serve, then, to dispel the notion that hermeneutics is somehow restricted to the aesthetic-humanistic tradition alone and that hermeneutical philosophy has to do with a "life of the mind" which is somehow opposed to the world of "real" life and propagates itself only in and through the "cultural tradition."[1]

Now Schleiermacher:

> Hermeneutics and rhetoric are intimately related in that every act of understanding is the reverse side of an act of speaking, and one must grasp the thinking that underlies a given statement.

Dialectics relies on hermeneutics and rhetoric because the development of all knowledge depends on both speaking and understanding.[2]

Both make the important move of using rhetoric to bind hermeneutics to the model of spoken conversation rather than to the writerly domain of textuality. But Gadamer is far more "rhetorical" in making his point, largely because he is under severe pressure from Jürgen Habermas to show that hermeneutics is not an abstract exercise in ontology, with little relevance to social praxis. And, ironically, it is that effort at eloquence that betrays how limited his grasp of rhetoric is.[3] Rhetorical theory teaches us that not all speech can be confined to the structure of conversation, since as much is hidden as is exposed; so we must learn to beware of the seductive effect of our own loquaciousness. If we contrast Gadamer's statement, for example, to the simplicity of Schleiermacher's, we find its conversational aspect severely overdetermined by competitive anxiety and compensatory self-projection. Scratch the conversational model and find lurking interest and fear in intricate conjunctions.

Therefore I wish to use the limitations of Gadamer's position, as well as of the more radical versions of his "ontological" stance that replace speech models with ideals of textuality, in order to restore the force, if not the specific doctrines, of traditional philological and romantic hermeneutics, whose insistence on psychology and efforts at provisional identifications seem to me fundamental to grasping the rhetorical dimension of human expressions and to projecting the ethical and social implications of our hermeneutical reflections. This rhetorical dimension includes, but cannot be reduced to, the need for a suspicious attitude. Tempting as Gadamer's pieties make the occasion, I doubt we need another Paul de Man, or even another John Caputo, although their critical attitudes will help sustain my own insistence on the dangers of idealizing dialogue as a model for political values. We must build into hermeneutics an awareness of how slippery its dialogical ideals are, since, once we leave the sphere of intimate relations, communication is rarely an end in itself but rather is enmeshed in the pursuit of personal interests and the seduction of both ourselves and other people. If we can make theory responsive to the ways that understanding adapts to these complex webs of interests and fears, we will also be able to develop a much richer, more contoured ethical language than Gadamer's, without yielding the social field to Habermasian formalism.[4] For if we know what to suspect we also know what we have to handle to reach agreement or even to be responsive to differences among cultural groups. So we should have a much clearer sense of the tasks performed by what we might call the other, constitutive half of rhetoric, that which is devoted to finding ways of creating community and exploring our powers to bring the symbolic into accord with actual desires, needs, and interests. Ultimately, our coming to appreciate this dimension of rhetoric will serve as a social aesthetic that can enable us to recognize the intricate bonds that social life fosters.

To accomplish these ends we must challenge the tendency of the now-dominant ontological hermeneutics codified by Gadamer to characterize dialogue simply in terms of how we adapt to an irreducible abstract otherness that we must learn to honor both for its own singularity and for how it teaches us to recognize the contingency of our own stances. Rhetorical theory leads otherwise: rather than idealizing the other for its mysterious independence, it invites us to make provisional speculations on the other as active agent, about whom we must make practical hypotheses because the hermeneutic event involves intricate paths of cooperation and conflict.[5] Even when we grant the importance of recognizing contingency, we cannot stop there but must understand both the fears and the ways of addressing those fears that grasping the full dynamics of rhetorical actions affords us. And that means that we also cannot be content with Habermas's efforts to subsume rhetoric under philosophy by treating communicative competence as establishing rational political ideals. Unless we beg the question by assuming the equality we intend to prove, it is by no means clear that Nietzsche's views are any less well grounded idealizations of rhetorical possibilities. So I will have to be content to demonstrate how attention to rhetoric can influence our views of agency and sociality, without using rhetoric to ground any set of normative claims.

To make my case I will begin by contrasting two versions of ethos—that promulgated by ontological hermeneutics and that which we can project from the idealized rhetorical theory I have been invoking. I conceive this enterprise as staging a test for determining whether we can use those rhetorical concerns about agency to foster a version of philological and romantic hermeneutics better suited than the ontological stance to the fostering of a rich and supple model of human agency, of expressive force, and of the bonds extending from intersubjective to more general social structures. Then I will shift to the agonistic mode by setting the concerns of a hermeneutics oriented toward the rhetorical directly against the model of ontological hermeneutics projected in Gerald Bruns's learned and powerfully argued *Hermeneutics Ancient and Modern*.[6] His is the strongest case I know for the values that can be elaborated by insisting on what we might call a hermeneutical poetics of culture rather than a rhetoric, so it makes a good basis for developing an alternative view of the impact rhetoric can have on our theorizing.

Bruns proves helpful in establishing the basic distinctions we need in order to pursue the relevant comparisons. He accepts the now-standard distinction between "transcendental" romantic hermeneutics and the "ontological" position emerging from Heidegger's work, but he also sharpens our awareness of the philosophical implications involved in that distinction. All hermeneutics, Bruns argues, is devoted to clarifying the concept of *Verstehen,* or understanding (p. 1). Consequently, hermeneutic theory is always in some tension with rationalist and empiricist versions of philosophy because for them efforts at understanding are shadowy preludes to the real work of description and argument that secures knowledge. Hermeneutics must show why understanding is a distinct realm, with its own specific criteria for descriptions and with its own access to process and to values that are lost or suppressed when we focus on the kinds of third-person criteria that secure knowledge claims. Hermeneutics, in other words, is doomed to occupying the fuzzy but crucial margin where hypotheses about psychology are called upon to clarify the processes that go into producing and attending to (or adjusting to) meanings.

Given the vagueness and importance of these issues, it is not surprising that hermeneutics after Luther has developed two competing sets of what Bruns calls "regulating questions" (p. 4). The transcendental tradition, epitomized in Schleiermacher's and Wilhelm Dilthey's very different models, concentrates on how we develop knowledge claims about the interior life of those whose situations, cultural frameworks, and lifeworlds differ radically from those shaping the inquirer's prejudices or cultural grammars. The ontological tradition, on the other hand, shifts from ideals of knowledge to a problematics of intimacy based on how the audience comes to apply what it can perceive as dynamic features that emerge as it works with a given body of materials. This second approach "does not stop with the determination of meanings but is an ongoing critical reflection in which we see ourselves and what matters to us in the light of the text, even as we see the text in the light of ourselves and of our interests" (p. 11). So meaning "is, metaphorically, the light that a text sheds on a subject (*Sache*) that we seek to understand" (p. 179). Then we can distinguish mundane and sublime versions of engaging this light—the former in Gadamer's concerns for effective history and the negotiation of our prejudices; the latter in Heidegger's focus on "'undergoing an experience with language'"—so that we are taken "out of the propositional attitude in which we assert our mastery over words and things" and resituated "in an attitude of listening" that leaves us "open and vulnerable" to the possibilities of belonging "in the grasp of what is said" (pp. 155–57).

With the options cast this way it is hard not to prefer the second approach, since it promises a more complex relational sense of what provokes and rewards efforts at understanding. Yet that very temptation makes me cautious. This is why I wish to specify the ethos sustained by and sustaining Bruns's stance—in part because we can then elaborate what claims need to be defended and compared to alternatives and in part because we can then help resist the tendency in all claims about "relational" processes to grow vague in defining just what we can determine about the specific properties being related.

Ontological hermeneutics, both mundane and sublime, are most striking in the ethical possibilities they afford for the modes of agency they describe. Minimally, they avoid every form of subjectivism—whether the subjectivism be attributed to the inferiority of the author or to the demands of the interpreter. One might even say that the author and interpreter become effective collaborators in addressing a problem or situation, since all the emphasis is on who one becomes when exposed to the activity that the text can perform in one's world. Consequently, one is constantly aware of the various contingencies at play in the interaction: the very process of application offers the potential for the mutual recognition of both how each pole is singular and how each singularity nonetheless impinges on other lives. Responsibility, then, is also no longer an abstract fidelity to rules or to the practices that provide criteria for knowledge. If the locus of meaning is the force by which applications of texts take hold in the world, then responsibility is measured by the intensity of a responsiveness aware both of its dependency on what enables its thinking and of its own distance from that other. Responsibility becomes inseparable from acknowledging the singularity and hence the freedom of the other (pp. 260–65).

Obviously, this ethos brings with it substantial social values. We have already seen how the application of texts encourages the recognition of the limitations of one's own position while granting the other its irreducible difference and singularity—without this, the application would only repeat the agent's own basic values. We can also see how authority and power need no longer reside in some abstract set of rules or demands. Authority is continually asserted, and continually tested, by the Levinasian notion of the claim that the other has on me by virtue of how I learn to feel myself dependent on its call (p. 211). Bruns can then use all these values to place the entire Heideggerian project within two general social frameworks. At one pole he shows how hermeneutics had to change in order to handle what Nietzsche had wrought of his Lutheran and romantic heritage. Claims to "know" another's meaning became inseparable from the assertion of a will to power working within the will to truth. But Heidegger shifted "the question of understanding from the theoretical plane of seeing from a perspective to the practical plane of involvement and participation in ongoing action" (p. 9). At the other pole, it becomes clear that the best way to appreciate the sociality basic to our efforts at understanding is to examine moments of crisis rather than those of achieving agreement (p. 3). For then we cannot take social bonds for granted, nor can we rely on conventional agreement: instead, as Stanley Cavell argues, we must attend to how in the search for applicable criteria we discover, and learn to value, what is involved in being active members of working social units (p. 117).

What difference does it make to bring rhetoric into the picture? To answer that, we must first put pressure on the ease with which Gadamer tries to link the domains of rhetoric and hermeneutics, admitting as different only the demand for immediate effects basic to the rhetor's actions. In fact, other significant differences emerge, even if we collapse different traditions within rhetorical theory and concentrate only on the broad outlines they share. 1) Where most hermeneutic theories emphasize how the responder can fully interpret a text or utterance, most rhetorical theory, Ciceronian and Sophistic alike, concentrates on what the composing agent can do in order to produce certain effects on the audience. 2) Correspondingly, where hermeneutic theory dwells on how we can hear what the other is saying—whether that involves specifying how we grasp the speaker's meaning and apply a text or appreciating what is involved in undergoing an experience with language—most rhetorical theory occupies itself with how an author can move or position those auditors so that they will be disposed to perform certain actions. For rhetorical theory, meaning is not a central concern: what matters is how the control over meaning can be deployed, at times by wielding ambiguity rather than engaging it and at times by manipulating the other rather than being content with communication. And that is why Habermas is wrong to claim that rhetoric can be confined within the model of conversation. It is perhaps better to ally rhetoric with social interactions as analyzed by Erving Goffman, since in Goffman, communication is not an end in itself but an instrument allowing agents to carry out certain projects. And where conversational ideals stress intimate relations, usually among equals, rhetorical perspectives are more amenable to a range of differences in status or knowledge between speaker and auditor. These differences range from the fear and suspicion de Man celebrates in Rousseau's "Second Discourse" to the notions of awe and exemplarity invoked by Longinus. 3) To appreciate the status of the message in the two disciplines we might look at how figures of speech are characteristically treated. In hermeneutics, figures are means of sharpening disclosures that emerge in the process of understanding, so that, as Bruns brilliantly develops it, allegory becomes for author and interpreter a vehicle for exploring the possibility of making connections between different cultural domains (pp. 85–87). Rhetorical theory shares this concern with figures as means of generating force, but it redefines force so as to keep it under the author's control. For this theory, simply achieving understanding or facilitating applications is not enough; instead the emphasis lies at one pole on powers of persuasion and seduction, at the other on the capacity figures have to construct frames of mind crucial to the fostering of social harmony. 4) If rhetorical theory treats communication as primarily instrumental rather than as an end in itself, then we cannot be content with developing practical attitudes from idealized communication situations. We also have to understand how society can function by our learning to share structures of suspicion (or emulation); thus, one form of honoring the otherness of the other consists in maintaining a respectful wariness of the kind that shapes interactions in, for example, Restoration theater. 5) One practical consequence of these differences is the challenge rhetorical theory posits for hermeneutic uses of the concept of tradition. Hermeneutics tries to place rhetoric within tradition, so how rhetoric functions simultaneously unfolds aspects of a culture and invites inquiry into how we might come to agree, since we share the language in which the dispute arises. But even Ciceronian rhetoricians must begin with a recognition that claims about tradition are aspects of the *topoi* they manipulate in order to develop the kinds of consensus that serve their interests or projects. The more general the argument about tradition, the more likely it is to be in the service of some particular program. It is prudent, therefore, to distrust all general claims about tradition as a precondition for negotiating concrete claims to continuity.[7]

Perhaps the strongest way to establish the stakes involved in these differences is to notice the contrasting modes of discourse toward which the two orientations gravitate. Hermeneutics seems always linked to theology, whether the frame be interpreting sacred texts or, as in Bruns's account of Heidegger, the importance of negative theology as a model for transgressing toward the unnameable (p. 223). But rhetoric cannot sponsor or even ally with theology unless, as with Augustine, it is subsumed under an allegorical hermeneutics. Because rhetoric has to face the fact that the author is interested and partial (even if seeking consensus), understanding particular speech acts cannot be a matter simply of responding to a full *Logos*. Rather, understanding involves how we stage utterances within a theater composed of human wills vacillating between cooperation and conflict. Consequently, as Burke reminds us, the rhetorician must treat even theological claims as elements within this human drama, suspecting that theology produces its absolute object because of the unreasonably ideal and abstract demands it makes on our concepts of understanding.

If these differences over theology themselves prove too abstract, we can see essentially the same structure of differences emerging in more subtle terms if we compare how hermeneutics and rhetoric interact with poetics. Even romantic hermeneutics privileges a poetics of empathy. But ontological hermeneutics is more radical. For the Heideggerian line, poetics is the paradigmatic field for hermeneutics because poetry demands that we experience the full power and otherness of language while insisting also on the intimate engagement with the field of thinking afforded by that otherness. Even more important, poetics becomes fundamental to ethics because it exemplifies a sharp distinction between idle talk and authentic voice exposed to what can be disclosed about being as it follows the paths language opens for it.

But that distinction also severely limits the ethical claims of ontological hermeneutics because it cannot let ethical values be tainted by the conventionality and collective structures of concern embodied in that idle talk. Consequently, this hermeneutic tradition cannot quite capture the complex interrelation between individuation and conventionality that is basic to any ethical framework compatible with the ways that our speech acts manipulate public grammars. Authenticity requires singularity. To secure a singularity not consumed by convention one must turn to something like Cavell's demand for constant efforts at self-ownership, which then become difficult to place back within public space (except by vague claims about responsiveness). For rhetoric, on the other hand, poetics matters primarily as a technical domain deepening the rhetor's knowledge of what can move audiences. The major affinity between rhetoric and poetics consists in a shared interest in how figures of speech work. But that interest can open into ethical considerations that hermeneutics has yet to address. Following Longinus, rhetorical theory can examine how individuals win respect or secure personal identities by virtue of how their speaking engages public expectations for their actions. Here responsibility takes the form of the power to elicit response rather than the power to respond. And that emphasis on eliciting response, I have argued in *Subjective Agency*, provides the model of agency necessary for a full expressivist morality emphasizing the values involved in how we carry into practice the verbal characterizations of ourselves that we offer to different audiences.[8] Both an ethics of care and an ethics of principle can be grounded in terms of specific commitments that require certain actions if we are to maintain the identities we consider central.

I cannot claim that philological and romantic hermeneutics provide an adequate picture of how these rhetorical concerns might be recovered within our accounts of understanding. But I can say that this tradition in hermeneutics lays the foundations for such work, requiring only that we modify the psychology we employ for describing both authors and audiences and that we be more ambitious in linking self-projection to moral responsibility. The following passage from Schleiermacher should help us appreciate what those foundations offer: "In order to complete the grammatical side of interpretation it would be

necessary to have a complete knowledge of the language. In order to complete
the psychological side it would be necessary to have a complete knowledge of
the person. Since in both cases such complete knowledge is impossible, it is
necessary to move back and forth between the grammatical and psychological
sides, and no rules can stipulate how to do this."[9]

Now we must expand both the grammatical and psychological dimensions
of understanding, building on a grasp of what cannot be accomplished within
ontological hermeneutics. To engage the grammatical we cannot simply distinguish authentic from idle speech or convention from compelling otherness.
We must attempt to find public contexts to share, so that the grammar manifests itself as the glue of social life. In doing so, we can replace romanticizing
the other with specifying how distinctions emerge between what we can determine and what seems irreducibly and perhaps fascinatingly unrecoverable
in our encounters with other persons. And this, in turn, enables us to give determinate content to the ways hermeneutics also clarifies our own limits, since
we can specify different levels of comprehension and different degrees of confidence in our understanding. Similarly, rhetoric insists on treating texts as acts
and hence as inviting something more than reflections on how they might become vehicles for the audience's ontological explorations. And to attend to the
range of these actions, as well as to the investments embodied in them, we
need to develop intricate and flexible psychological predicates while constantly testing for what these predicates cannot handle. Hermeneutics responsive to rhetoric is also hermeneutics forced to build its sense of sociality
around a complex weaving of mutual understanding and mutual fear, with the
fear a fundamental factor in the accords we manage to develop.

This psychological orientation requires that hermeneutics concerned with
rhetorical matters occupy an intricate boundary where the otherness of the
other elicits two distinct dramas. At one pole the other appears as an interlocutor before whom responsibility becomes something more determinate and
more public than simple responsiveness. Dialogue with others becomes a vehicle by which the agents create a context for specifying what their moral values are and for working out expectations that bind them to specific principles,
as well as to more vague and general modes of caring. Historical knowledge of
Longinus makes it possible both to clarify our own relation to his principles
and to share with others an idealized projection of a possible judge whose values carry over into principles that the actor is willing to be measured by. And
concrete understandings with our own actual associates allow practical versions of the same dynamic.

At the other pole, hermeneutics helps clarify where personal ethics must
end and where the more complex blend of principle and prudence that char-

acterizes political life must begin. For just about any psychology we bring to bear that attends to rhetoricity will focus attention not only on what the other seeks as communication but also on what the other intends to achieve by way of that communication. Therefore gestures toward openness must be correlated with the means of protecting ourselves. And that need itself can become something we share, so that there emerges within politics its own prudential principles that do the work of ethics, even though a powerful sense of shared values is rarely available. When that sense is not available, we can locate mutual understanding in terms of what we know we cannot know yet can specify as *différends* or at least as areas of contention. However, for such understandings to be effective we must neither romanticize our capacity to empathize nor demonize the otherness of the other as some condition entirely separate or alienated from what we bring to the situation.

I am embarrassed to be assuming a position that claims wisdom on such large and important matters. So I feel that I should conclude by justifying these gestures, if only on the grounds that there are substantial stakes in keeping alive alternatives to Heideggerian and Derridean versions of hermeneutics. As tests for my claims, then, I would like to take up specific arguments in Bruns's book, since I consider it a powerful and humane rendering of what that position can make available. If I am right, a hermeneutics attentive to rhetorical agency ought to be able to mark the limitations of the ontological tradition and offer competing claims that are at least as plausible and more valuable for certain purposes. Specifically, I will isolate three themes in Bruns's book: his shaping of a binary opposition between philosophy and radical interpretation, the resulting tendency to base his ethical ideals on possibilities of granting and coming to terms with the singularity of the other, and his projection of an idealized notion of tragic affirmation as his basic overall reflective attitude for coming to terms with all that this sense of otherness entails. These three themes provide so tight a mutually reinforcing structure that they all become problematic if the grounding binary opposition proves inadequate.

Bruns is careful to note that his is a radical position. He grants that there are other roles for hermeneutics to play, especially in showing, as Paul Ricoeur does, how texts "expose our actual world to alternative possibilities" and hence also serve the critical task of showing that the limits of our world "are historical and contingent" (p. 140). But, he continues, "One will always fall short of the dark reality of hermeneutics if one simply stops where Ricoeur and others seem to stop," without asking how this way of thinking reduces the work of textuality to "the bare narrative function of projecting a possible world onto the space of interpretation." The full power of hermeneutics requires a coming to terms with its own primal scene—its genesis in "the moment when philosophy confronts poetry or whatever is not itself—whatever is resistant to itself: that which refuses to be philosophized" (p. 221). And that resistance is most pronounced in the power of textuality to exceed those frames of intentionality and visions of self-identity that traditional philological and romantic hermeneutics impose upon it. Heidegger, followed by Jacques Derrida, celebrates the force by which the work of art "remains within the world as a breach, a rupture, a shaking that allows nothing to settle into place" and hence sets off by contrast the "task philosophy sets for itself": "to interrupt this event, to close the breach, to preserve the identity and self-sameness of the world, that is, to set logical limits to the Open." Bruns then concludes: "If the work of the work of art is to set up a world, the task of philosophy is to stabilize this event, perhaps to cut it off as if to prevent the endless dissemination of worlds" (pp. 234–35).

How dark is this darkness? How compelling is the dichotomy Bruns establishes between what he calls Ricoeur's "hermeneutics of appropriation" and this resistance to all appropriation in the name of unsettlement? And, finally, how can rhetorical theory help us show how important and varied the task of settlement is? One might begin empirically by pointing to Nelson Goodman's *Ways of Worldmaking* as a powerful example of why philosophy cannot be contained within Bruns's picture—not because philosophy does not seek limits and definitions but because the limits can play roles that go far beyond simply containing the disruptive force of the poetic and the textual. Both Goodman and Wittgenstein, as well as Spinoza and even Kant and Hegel, share with Derrida a fascination for the ways that limits can also be passages, containment also the generation of new event-fields. So we have to challenge the binary oppositions on which Bruns's entire value scheme is based.

To do that we must first specify the abstract logic for his case. As Wittgenstein put it, interpretation occurs when we have lost our way and must make hypotheses about how to proceed in a particular case. Therefore interpretation begins where philosophical categories wobble or simply fail to connect directly to concrete situations. But the difference need not involve radical opposition: we need not speak of what "refuses to be philosophized" in order to indicate that some aspects of the world are not amenable to our work with concepts (recall Wittgenstein on knowing the aroma of coffee or learning to ride a bicycle). Indeed, the one thing philosophy seems to have learned from its history of failures is to be circumspect in creating polarities: making worlds is also a matter of balancing parts of worlds. In this particular case we have to realize that understanding is a much broader topic than interpretation, for much of our understanding takes place without the self-reflexive thematizing interpretation calls for. And, as Wittgenstein, Polanyi, and others have shown, the basic principles involved in such understanding can be taken up by philosophy, even though philosophy is generically blocked from specifying how judgment works in particular cases. Therefore even when we insist on what makes interpretation different from such understandings, there is no need for sharp boundaries. Although our appreciation of the singular must always be won against the tendency to impose categorical understanding, there is no reason philosophy cannot honor that struggle or even help us appreciate what is at stake in recognizing that singularity. Philosophical reflection simply offers a different, more generalizing orientation that nonetheless can complement, or even sponsor, hermeneutic concerns for concrete specificity. Think of the way that Spinoza's purely abstract mind returns in Gilles Deleuze's critique of categorical thinking; or recall how rich Kant is on the productive energies that allow significant individuation—in practical actions and in the ways genius works to produce those features of art works that become central to Heidegger's aesthetics.

These aspects of my critique do not depend on rhetorical theory. However, if we turn to that theory we find an entirely different angle on what is problematic in Bruns's binary between radical hermeneutics and philosophical thinking. His resistance to concepts is so thorough that in the end he can value only event-qualities or forces that are manifest as resistance. Because all general claims about the needs, powers, and possible ends that agents pursue smack to him of philosophy, and because he refuses to grant the importance of a rhetorical theater for specifying and negotiating these issues, he cannot propose any general language to help clarify why or how this active resistance takes place; he cannot clarify specific stakes involved in judging such resistance or in warranting various degrees of acquiescing to or acknowledging the existing conceptual orders; and, most important, he cannot give strong, socially workable models of how the recognition of such resistance might foster a more socially practicable set of values and identifications.

All my complaints take sharper focus if we examine his treatment of the "other," the one character who still seems capable of being heroized in a wide range of contemporary theoretical discourses. Bruns's heroizing takes its departure from Levinas's treatment of the other as the one "'who can sovereignly say no to me,'" setting in opposition not simply a force of direct resistance but "the very *unforseeableness* of his reaction" (p. 210): "What comes down to us from the past says no to us, is not obsolete but refractory and resistant, excessive with respect to interpretation, satirical with respect to our allegories, and so it will not serve as foundation and testimony, background or thesis; indeed it will not serve at all except to draw us out of ourselves, leaving us, Oedipus-like, exposed and possibly horrified at our own image" (p. 211). From this account Bruns draws three basic values: that we can learn from such others how relativism is insufficient because the other has the power to compel self-criticism (p. 7), that this notion of otherness provides a useful model for imagining how to imagine the singularity fundamental to freedom (pp. 260–65), and that this satiric relation of other to self comprises the dark repressed side of the apparent generosity by which hermeneutics tries to generate empathy for such others.

It is worth mentioning that Bruns's own superb readings of the past do little to make good on any of these principles. He is far too busy doing a traditional job of showing how thoroughly we can in the present come to recognize and value the intricate intelligence and complex sensibilities that cultural traditions preserve, for it is only by the depth and lucidity of such sympathy that we can appreciate the past sufficiently to let what emerges as different play against what emerges as parallel needs and quests. So from this perspective the other is far more accessible than Bruns grants—largely because the very category of "other" exhibits Bruns's antiphilosophy doing exactly what philosophy does at its worst. By asking the term to do so much work, Bruns ends up totalizing what in fact is a complex set of strands that cannot be lumped under any single category defining identity or difference—as is evident in his striking account of what remains Other in Socrates' "terrible reserve" and "self-possession" (p 45).[10]

Here the ontological tradition in hermeneutics most clearly comes into conflict with rhetorical theory. Where ontology is trapped in terms like *same, relative,* or *other,* rhetorical analysis concentrates on how actions play among those various conditions. And rather than posit static poles, its concern is always with flexibility and malleability: claims to identity can be manipulated for the interests of difference, and fears about irreducible differences can be negotiated in ways that establish provisional shared concerns. That provisionality, I hasten to add, cannot be criticized in terms of some more abstract claim about identity, or nonidentity, because rhetorical theory calls our attention to states where those attributions do not have any stable referents. Instead, the relevant speech acts implicate aspects of cultural grammars that are continually being worked into new combinations.

I am even more interested in the ways rhetorical thinking helps us flesh out what is dark about hermeneutics. For by focusing on wills and orientations toward actions, rhetoric reminds us that the limitations in our understanding extend far beyond our inability to penetrate or contain what is excessive and singular. From a rhetorical perspective, the other's capacity to say "no" is not its most threatening feature. When we fear a "no" we try to keep our distance, and we can hope to work out rapprochements honoring those necessary distances. But suppose the other wants a "yes" from me, despite my incomplete knowledge of who he or she is or of what I am being asked to enter. Cavell would say that this is the moment when I must face the possibility of skepticism and try to work toward some kind of atonement. This, however, presupposes that there is a corresponding "yes" latent in the other's "no." In contrast, rhetorical theory is more likely to speak of adjustment than atonement, largely because it is less concerned with the singularity basic to the ontology of freedom than it is with the desires for power basic to the agent's biological and social urges to extend its field of interests.

For rhetoric the problem is not quite the otherness of the other but the ways in which one cannot quite distinguish between the otherness of the other and an all-too-frightening likeness in its will to power or willingness to deceive (by playing at likeness or at otherness). Given that view we need to cultivate social attitudes that are not only aware of their own limitations but capable of a wariness that never collapses into cynicism and of an openness that can celebrate minor reciprocities and hope perpetually for more.

When Bruns turns to this question of overall attitude he shifts between an idealization of the mode of consciousness that tragedy cultivates and an interest in the forms of freedom made possible by treating otherness as a satire of our own prejudices. Here I will take his sense of the tragic attitude as the more comprehensive stance, since it provides a way of accommodating to the satiric. Moreover, his arguments about tragic affirmation seem necessary to address two crucial problems in his thinking—the level of generality his theorizing occupies (which takes the place of a hermeneutics attentive to continual adjustments in degrees of understanding) and the fact that his rigid understanding of otherness leaves little room for the chance-sensitive sociality characteristic of comedy.

Bruns is very good on tragedy. Combining Gadamer and Cavell, he roots tragedy in the irreducible otherness "which resists the grasp of my knowledge or which requires me to loosen my hold or open my fist" (p. 180). For one is then "left unguarded" and exposed to a world now "implicated in the otherness of the other." No fantasy of control or self-sufficiency can suffice. Tragedy matters, then, because it is the genre where such fantasies break down. Gadamer insists that tragic catharsis is not a matter of maintaining distance but of giving way to the pity and fear that arise as we see someone rushing toward destruction. Catharsis does purify, but only by resisting the temptation to deny what the agonizing events make visible. Full tragic catharsis "'dissolves the disfunction with what is,'" and hence frees us from both the specific illusions driving the tragic fate and, more generally, "'everything that divides us from what is'" (p. 188). Cavell then fleshes out the psychology by which we can engage the pure present tense of the tragic dilemma so fully that we can also face the limits of our own separateness. When we return to the world, we do so entirely exposed to it, despite our best conceptual defenses; therefore, we are required to take complete responsibility for our relation to it (pp. 193–94). Only then are we capable of a "tragic serenity" that "consists of being beyond surprise" (p. 189): "What is it to live through not just the *ébranlement* of one's concepts but the complete destruction of one's world? Tragic drama is the concrete working out of this question. In so doing, it acknowledges the horror of life, is responsive and open to it, does not refuse to mourn. What philosophy (including philosophy of religion)—what Caputo—objects to is tragedy's refusal to propose solutions to the problem of this horror. But one could just as well take it that tragedy is making a claim against philosophy: namely that living through the destruction of the world discloses . . . what cannot be done away with by means of philosophy, much less philosophy of religion" (p. 227).

In my view there are two serious problems here. The first is as daunting as it is obvious: suppose that sometimes what is disclosed requires our having to close our fist rather than open it?[11] Bruns cannot address this possibility because his view of tragedy remains that of the spectator interested in some general reflective attitude rather than that of the agent who must make particular decisions to act in certain ways. All Bruns's talk of contingency and exposure, all his proclamations about literally becoming King Lear remain generalized versions of contingency, or even of Lear, who is far more concerned with his daughters and his own shame than he is with understanding fatality.

The second problem follows from this. I think Bruns mistakes the force of Caputo's (and Habermas's) objections. The issue is not whether tragedy can resist philosophy, at least insofar as it engages a certain confidence in philosophy that can also be resisted from within philosophy—think of Willard Quine and Nelson Goodman as cures for overconfidence. Rather, Caputo is asking whether even resisting philosophy on this level of abstraction affects how we move from facing the problem of horror in general to grappling with particular horrors. Bruns would probably respond that we are unlikely to face the full terror of particular horrors until we learn to work through our defenses against being exposed to the various dark truths about our condition. But how many times do we need to learn this lesson, at least in the generalized way that Bruns characterizes it? Ultimately, the issue is not one of knowledge but of disposing our wills. So long as we represent these horrors in a language of exposure and otherness, we have recourse only to such abstract philosophical and antiphilosophical formulations. But if we attach wills, purposes, and combative strategies to such horrors, and if we recognize them as embodiments of various aspects of specific conflicts, then we can build on the honesty that tragedy cultivates.

The true alternative to the kind of confident generalizing philosophy that Bruns condemns is not some equally abstract antiphilosophy but an insistence that philosophy engage other discourses in offering perspicuous representations that indicate how it might help clarify issues or characterize the needs and demands that bring agents to their stands on such issues. For the rhetorician, the understanding of tragedy must give way to a tragic understanding of the limits of understanding, for understanding is simultaneously not effective enough to bridge our differences and so effective that it overcomplicates what might be resolved more simply, were we to negotiate without worrying about what we think we know. Rhetoric offers a practical alternative to tragedy's imperial abstractness, as long as we can use our practical wariness as a means of fully honoring those social bonds we manage to establish.

NOTES

1 Hans-Georg Gadamer, "Rhetoric, Hermeneutics, and the Critique of Ideology: Metacritical Comments on *Truth and Method*," in Kurt Mueller-Vollmer, ed., *The Hermeneutics Reader: Texts of the German Tradition from the Enlightenment to the Present* (New York: Continuum, 1985), 280. Jürgen Habermas's critique of Gadamer, "On Hermeneutics' Claim to Universality," is also included in this anthology.

2 Friedrich Schleiermacher, *Hermeneutics: The Handwritten Manuscripts,* ed., Heinz Kimmerle, trans. James Duke and Jack Forstman (Missoula, Mont.: Scholars Press, 1977), "Introduction," 96.

3 Gadamer has a difficult task. For while Habermas is concerned directly with the "connection between language and practice" (*Hermeneutics Reader,* 297), Gadamer concentrates on the possibility of establishing a *phronesis* that integrates individual understanding with individual judgment. Gadamer therefore can be only indirectly social, so long as he refuses to grant the need for specific methods by which to secure the social negotiations of one's understandings. For Gadamer the relevant issue is not the principle of communicative competence but the capacity of individuals to grasp communicative possibilities. So his version of rhetoric is confined to talk about creativity. He cannot even acknowledge Habermas's concern for rhetoric as the art of creating consensus because he has no vehicle for understanding the social status of one's own understandings. But this also means that he can be far more complex than Habermas about how specific aspects of understanding affect concrete social bonds.

Gadamer's *Truth and Method* (2d rev. ed., trans. Joel Weinsheimer and Donald Marshall [New York: Crossroad, 1989]) does not strengthen his case on rhetoric.

There, when he speaks about rhetoric he unfailingly links it with the ideals of humanism, so that rhetoric becomes the complement of hermeneutics. What rhetors compose in the quest of understanding, hermeneuts dispose by revealing to us the terms and conditions by which we come to appropriate our own humanity.

4 Let me be clear that rhetorical theory will not resolve problems that arise in debates about whether we can or should construe authorial intentions or about how intention is positioned within tradition. Instead, the rhetorician clarifies what is possible and what is at stake if we are to employ *topoi* pertinent to establishing intentions. But by doing that the rhetorician makes it difficult to be satisfied with conversational models of meaning, even when we are dealing with actual conversations, since she also brings to bear methods for attending to figures that play a central role in how the arts and legal practices establish meanings.

5 I shall be quite loose in calling upon rhetorical theory because I am not interested here in determining which theories are best. Instead, I take the entire domain of theories as having degrees of pertinence for various aspects of understanding understanding—Quintillian on figures, Gorgias and his modern heirs on suspiciousness, Enlightenment figures like Diderot and Lord Chesterfield on the need for combining wariness with limited openness, and Kenneth Burke on the flexible range of possible scenarios and plays on identity and difference that comprise the human barnyard.

6 Gerald Bruns, *Hermeneutics Ancient and Modern* (New Haven: Yale University Press, 1992). Future references will be cited parenthetically in the text.

7 Bruns handles the vagueness of Gadamer on "tradition" by making the term a locus for reflexive inquiry rather than a specific, arguable thesis. For an impressive attempt to make Gadamer's idea of tradition do practical work in legal studies see Francis J. Mootz III, "Rethinking the Rule of Law: A Demonstration That the Obvious Is Plausible," *Tennessee Law Review* 61 (1993): 69–195.

8 Charles Altieri, *Subjective Agency: A Theory of First-Person Expressivity and Its Social Implications* (Oxford: Blackwell, 1994). In this book I also offer extensive critical commentary to support the claim I make above about Cavell, as well as to clarify the claims about ethics and the relation between responsibility and responsiveness that I develop below.

9 Schleiermacher, "Introduction," 100.

10 It is instructive to compare Bruns's Levinasian other to Jean-François Lyotard's *différend*. Treating otherness in terms of *différends* is much more compatible with rhetorical theory because there is less totalizing of what we encounter, more capacity to locate the otherness in specific traditions or practices, and a specific rationale for action because the *différend* is primarily a measure of what cannot be understood as a grievance. Therefore we can at least hope to eliminate some *différends* by learning to hear the other. There are no necessary ontological boundaries, only circumstances, possible goodwill, and luck. Yet, like Bruns, Lyotard vacillates between taking the *différend* as primarily something to be overcome, and hence a problem to be handled by enlightened sociality, and taking it as primarily something to be cele-

brated because of its resistance to dominant categories. Because I believe that there is no theoretical way to adjudicate such options, I propose the rhetorician's casuistry as the best possible reflective stance.

11 Ezra Pound claims that the modern world has developed shame about violence and hence cannot produce individuals who are sure of their own identities. Without quite endorsing that, or without quite saying that the individuality is worth the violence, I would like to connect Bruns here to Wordsworth's *Borderers,* since the play cannot let itself follow out its own tragic logic by having the protagonist kill his oppressive father. Pound might have called this the demise of classical drama.

5

What Hermeneutics
Can Offer Rhetoric

Richard E. Palmer

Rhetoric and hermeneutics today have achieved, as our editors point out in the Prologue, an impressive prominence across disciplines; indeed, they parallel each other in more than influence and multidisciplinary significance. They are parallel generically, they are interwoven historically, and they have experienced a remarkable expansion in theory and self-understanding in the last half of the twentieth century.[1] In each case, however, that expansion has been achieved, for the most part, in isolation from the other. Now it is time to renew old ties and explore what each can offer the other. My aim here is to affirm the desirability of a dialogue between rhetoric and hermeneutics, to reemphasize the long and interwoven history of rhetoric and hermeneutics, showing their essential interconnectedness, and to ask more specifically what hermeneutics can offer the already promising *rhetorica rediviva* of today. To carry out this last aim, I shall offer twenty *topoi* that spell out my vision of a rhetoric informed by hermeneutics.

THE INTERCONNECTIONS OF RHETORIC AND HERMENEUTICS

The Need and Desirability of a Dialogue

There can be little doubt that a continuation of the dialogue between rhetoric and hermeneutics could be fruitful today and is still needed in spite of what has already been accomplished. Admittedly, rhetorical theory in the United States has already displayed an openness to European thought. For instance, Chaim Perelman and L. Olbrechts-Tyteca's *New Rhetoric* (on "argumentation") and James Murphy's *Rhetoric in the Middle Ages* have broadened the horizons of contemporary rhetorical thinking by renewing our familiarity with ancient and medieval European rhetoric. Thomas M. Conley's *Rhetoric in the European Tradition* is another evidence of openness to European thought, and the collection *The Rhetorical Tradition: Readings from Classical Times to the Present,* by Patricia Bizzell and Bruce Herzberg, has further expanded the "rhetorical tradition" by offering a representation of ancient, medieval, and modern texts. Also, four of the theorists discussed in *Contemporary Perspectives on Rhetoric,* by Sonja K. Foss, Karen A. Foss, and Robert Trapp, are Europeans.[2] Finally, we should credit two journals, *Philosophy and Rhetoric* and the *Quarterly Journal of Speech,* that have, over the past quarter of a century, offered many articles that bring the treasures of Continental thinking to our shores.

Yet despite this exciting turn toward Europe in American rhetorical theory, and the reaching out to philosophy, linguistics, and social science, it appears to me that the promise of a new relation to hermeneutics, and particularly to Gadamerian hermeneutics, has not been fully realized. For instance, four of the five most recent figures in Bizzell's and Herzberg's *Rhetorical Tradition* (1990) are French: Michel Foucault, Jacques Derrida, Hélène Cixous, and Julia Kristeva. No German theorists associated with hermeneutics are shown there to be fertilizing the tradition of twentieth-century rhetoric. Neither Jürgen Habermas nor Hans-Georg Gadamer appear. I am far from wishing to exclude the French contributors from the hermeneutic tradition, but where are Gadamer and Habermas?[3] A glance at two collections of essays in rhetorical theory also reveals only a little dialogue with German hermeneutics. Foss, Foss, and Trapp's *Contemporary Perspectives on Rhetoric* crosses the Rhine to include Habermas but not Gadamer, and it devotes only a page to hermeneutics—as an influence, along with positivism, on Habermas. To me, this hardly suggests a consciousness of what Gadamer's philosophical hermeneutics could offer to contemporary rhetorical theory. Conley's *Rhetoric in the European Tradition* gives only limited attention to Perelman and Habermas, with a nod to Ernesto Grassi. Herbert Simons's *The Rhetorical Turn: Invention and Persuasion in the Conduct of Inquiry* indirectly recognizes the influence of European hermeneutics when it turns at the outset to Richard Rorty, who clearly puts hermeneutical thinking in the same camp with rhetoric. And although the four selections devoted to philosophy that conclude *The Rhetorical Turn* do mention Gadamer and Habermas, the dominant philosophical influence in the volume seems to be pragmatism—especially that of Joseph Margolis—not Gadamerian or Habermasian hermeneutics. This suggests that even where an effort was made to consider European philosophers and theorists, the reception of German hermeneutics into American rhetorical theory remains incomplete. There have been other important efforts to bring in a consideration of Gadamerian hermeneutics. Yet in spite of what Michael Hyde, Walter Jost, Larry Grossberg, Stanley Deetz, Richard Lanigan, and others have already presented in public lectures and written in *Philosophy and Rhetoric, Rhetoric Society Quarterly,* the *Quarterly Journal of Speech, Man and World,* and elsewhere, it seems to me that a clear articulation of what hermeneutics could offer the reborn rhetoric of today is still needed. A brief consideration of a suggestive reference to "three turns" by Richard Rorty will further illustrate this point.

Richard Rorty was perhaps the first major American philosopher to appreciate the philosophical import of German hermeneutics. In chapter 7 of his *Philosophy and the Mirror of Nature,* significantly titled "From Epistemology to Hermeneutics," Rorty distinguishes two basic styles of philosophy, the foundationalist and the nonfoundationalist, or hermeneutical. He defines hermeneutics "not as a discipline, nor a method of achieving the sort of results epistemology failed to achieve, nor a program of research" but rather as a "style of thought" found in a number of major modern thinkers.[4] Hermeneutics entails a recognition of incommensurability, an understanding that the contributions to discourse may not be neatly subsumable under clear categories. He identifies this approach with "the holistic, antifoundationalist, pragmatist treatments of knowledge and meaning which we find in Dewey, Wittgenstein, Quine, Sellars, and Davidson" (p. 317). With sweeping strokes he describes a style of thinking and a set of assumptions that are radically at variance with the modern Cartesian-Newtonian paradigm of conclusions whose certainty is based on clear demonstrations, and at the same time he shows a clear and essential link between German hermeneutical thinking and American pragmatism. Although he does not refer to it, Rorty's dichotomy between the two basic styles of thinking parallels that in *The New Rhetoric* between a logic of demonstration and what Perelman and Olbrechts-Tyteca call "argumentation," a way of reasoning based on persuasiveness. In any case, the kinship of the "new rhetoric" with the philosophical assumptions and style that Rorty describes as the hermeneutical is clear. Yet the implications of German hermeneutics, perhaps precisely because of Rorty's close linking of hermeneutics with American pragmatism, were not realized even in the philosophically oriented chapters in that volume.

At the beginning of the Iowa Symposium on the Rhetoric of the Human Sciences (1984), Rorty, whose paper later appeared in *The Rhetoric of the Human Sciences*,[5] observed that efforts to reconceive inquiry in the human sciences seem to have been marked by three turns. First, there was the linguistic turn, followed by the interpretive turn, and finally the rhetorical turn.[6] Rorty himself had been associated with the first two turns by virtue of *Philosophy and the Mirror of Nature* and an earlier volume, *The Linguistic Turn*.[7] In Iowa he opened a seminal symposium on the rhetorical turn and its meaning for inquiry in the human sciences. His formulation of three turns is pregnant with meaning, but we need to avoid what might be called the assumption of succession: it is not the case that the linguistic turn was eclipsed by the interpretive and then the rhetorical turn. Rather, all three turns are still having their effect. As Thomas Kuhn's *Structure of Scientific Revolutions* shows, the implications of any new paradigm are only gradually understood and absorbed. The three turns are not yet fully grasped—are still being "received," as we say in hermeneutics in reference to "reception-history." In terms of helping to overcome the illusions of scientific objectivity, these were important turns: the linguistic turn took away the transparency of language and, by focusing on it, revealed language as a conditioning matrix for all thought. Language is a game with rules, a game of doing/saying and listening/understanding, a game involving "performative" utterances. The belief in objectivity suffered a further blow with the interpretive turn, when it was discovered that our interpretations were themselves interpretations of interpretations all the way down. Nietzsche had already pointed out that there is no escape from interpretation and Heidegger observed in *Being and Time* that everything we understand is always already interpreted, so understanding cannot escape the "hermeneutical circle."[8] The rhetorical turn, then, does not simply follow after or replace the other two; it builds on them. But the understanding and reception of both the linguistic turn and the interpretive turn are still incomplete; their implications and ramifications are still sinking in. Thus, as the rhetorical turn makes us aware of the pragmatic and interest-laden dimensions of speaking in inquiry, rhetorical theory must continue to resist the objectivizing models and scientific assumptions about language and interpretation. This does not mean that objectivity is useless and that recent empirical studies must be rejected; rather, objectivity is radically incomplete, and this fact needs to be continually remembered. The three turns have been incomplete turns, whose implications are still unfolding and need to be spelled out.

Of course, a turn need not be 90 or 180 degrees; it may only register a slight shift in direction (*Wendung*). But when Heidegger used the metaphor of a turn (*Kehre*) after *Being and Time* (1927) and *Kant and the Problem of Metaphysics* (1929), the term pointed to a profound philosophical change. Heidegger was referring to his desertion of transcendental philosophy, of the metaphysical terminology and metaphors of Kant, Fichte, Hegel, and even Husserl and transcendental phenomenology—of the whole "language of metaphysics" since Plato. Heidegger did not shrink from the radical, apocalyptic conclusion that he stood at the end of philosophy itself and of the doing of philosophy, if philosophy entailed a continuation of the old metaphysics.[9] Instead, he reconceived "thinking" so radically that it no longer referred to previous philosophy or to "calculative thinking" but rather became a kind of meditative receptivity to "what offers itself" to thought. As he put it provocatively in the first lecture of *What Is Called Thinking?* "Science does not think [*Die Wissenschaft denkt nicht*]."[10]

Significantly, Gadamer did not follow Heidegger on his path away from philosophy into poetry (especially into Hölderlin's vision of his era, which Heidegger took up) and away from the "language of metaphysics."[11] Rather, in his lectures during the 1950s preparatory to *Truth and Method* (1960), Gadamer chose to make hermeneutics his focal point and a "new hermeneutics" the goal of his inquiry.[12] Hermeneutics was a term Heidegger used as early as 1919 and again in *Being and Time* in reference to his own project. Gadamer had been Heidegger's assistant in Marburg from 1923 to 1928, when Heidegger returned to Freiburg, and he was familiar with the term. Almost in tandem, Gadamer in *Truth and Method* offered a new hermeneutic about the time Perelman and Olbrechts-Tyteca offered their volume, *The New Rhetoric* (1958). These two works are parallel in many ways. They both challenge the hegemony of scientific objectivity and offer a new basis and conception of argument. In Perelman and Olbrechts-Tyteca the basis was probability and persuasiveness; in Gadamer the appeal was to "what we have all experienced" rather than to a foundational axiom. Both works appealed not to the rules and assumptions of the "new science" in the tradition of Descartes but to the conditions of speaking to an audience and also to Aristotle's practical philosophy, which prescribed different rationalities for different subject matters. But the historical accident of simultaneity meant that Perelman and Olbrechts-Tyteca did not and could not call on Gadamer's hermeneutics for support of their vision of a new rhetoric.

Interwoven Histories and Generic Overlaps

Rhetoric and hermeneutics are generally thought to be both conceptually and historically separate. Conceptually, they appear distinct: rhetoric has to do with speaking well and hermeneutics with understanding and interpreting a text. Historically, rhetoric seems to have the priority, since it can be traced back to ancient Greek rhetoric. But if one does not insist on the exact term, hermeneutics stretches back to antiquity also—if one includes ancient Hebrew treatises on how to interpret the Torah, ancient treatises on dream interpretation like Artemidorus's *Oneiretikon,* the writings of the Stoic allegorizers who instructed listeners to Homer on how to interpret the gods, or the ancient writings on the interpretation of legal documents. True, these works did not have the umbrella term *hermeneutics* to unite them, but they constitute a body of ancient texts that must be included in any history of hermeneutics as methods for interpreting texts. Conceptually, there is also some overlap. The Greek verb *hermeneuein* seems to refer to oral interpretation, i.e., rhetoric. Indeed, *hermeneuein* contains three distinct meanings of interpretation in Greek antiquity: to say (as in oral interpretation), to translate (as in translating a language), and to explain (to make a thing clear). Ion, the proud young interpreter of Homer who was interviewed by Socrates in the *Ion,* was a *hermeneut,* an oral interpreter. To interpret orally is to understand and say. Yet Socrates in that dialogue succeeded to his own satisfaction in showing Ion that he did not truly "understand" what he was doing, thus did not truly have the only knowledge that counted as knowledge (*episteme*) for Socrates, theoretical knowledge.

This raises the issue of the tension between rhetoric and philosophy in Plato. Ion was able to move his audience not by his knowledge but by the power of his words, which were "understood" in one sense by him, according to Socrates, only through the inspiration of the muse and without passing through a theoretical comprehension. In a parallel way Socrates in the *Gorgias* disputed Gorgias's claim to teach virtue through oratory on the grounds that the orator sought more to please and persuade his hearers than to bring them to a painful truth. Orators, according to Socrates, were more like pastry cooks than doctors, but a true statesman should advocate what is best rather than what is pleasant. The Sophists' training in oratory, in Socrates' view, did not prepare their followers for choosing the best. Thus, according to Socrates in *The Republic,* the training for rule should be that given the seeker of truth, the "lover of wisdom"—the philosopher. This well-known Platonic distinction seems to set up an irreconcilable generic difference between rhetoric and philosophy. And between hermeneutics and philosophy also, insofar as hermeneutics is a method or an art (a *techne*). Rhetoric, for Plato, lacks philosophical depth and philosophy lacks rhetorical power and splendor. Socrates began his defense at his trial, according to the *Apology,* by disclaiming any skill in oratory—but not in dialectic. Hence, both rhetoric and a certain kind of hermeneutics suffer at the hands of Socrates and his quest for knowledge.

The modern-era specialization of rhetoric into the art of speaking (and writing) seems to further separate it from modern philosophy, with its quest for the a priori, the deepest, truest first principles. And again the same may also be said to a lesser degree of modern hermeneutics because its modern specialization into rules and methods for the explication of texts, beginning with the Protestant hermeneutical manuals, also seems to separate it from the quest for philosophical reflection on understanding. Only in the eighteenth and nineteenth centuries, as hermeneutics focused not on the types of texts and the types of problems in interpreting them but on the general preconditions for understanding well, did hermeneutics move toward a philosophy of understanding. And in the latter part of the twentieth century, as rhetoric focused not only on the devices and techniques of effective speaking but also on the preconditioning elements in speaking—on what speaking does and can do—it moved toward what one could call a philosophy of speaking. Such a philosophy inquires into the types and conditions of persuasion and proof; it distinguishes, with Perelman and Olbrechts-Tyteca, proof under the aegis of demonstration from persuasiveness under the aegis of persuasive argumentation. As the new rhetoric reflects on its task, it encounters the question of how people come to know things and how it can best cause another person to know these things or become persuaded of these things in order to reach agreement in understanding (also an important phrase in hermeneutics). So the new rhetoric does not shy away from epistemology. Speaking is not specialized and separated from understanding but must be taken along with the process of understanding for an adequate philosophical reflection on speaking as such and on what it does and is able to do.

The significance of this move to include epistemology (and, elsewhere, dialectic) in rhetorical theory should not be missed. For in the period from ancient times to the Renaissance, rhetoric included the art of thinking (dialectic) and of how to read texts (now specialized into hermeneutics). But the modern era brought with it a specializing of rhetoric that focused on the art of speaking well and that of writing well as an extension of this. Rhetoric was no longer seen as involving the hermeneutical task of rightly interpreting texts. Yet in the late twentieth century, when a phenomenology and an ontology of speaking have become of interest to both rhetoric and hermeneutics—and also to philosophy—the disciplinary barriers make less sense. At the same time, the recovery of a more encompassing view of rhetoric—one more like that found in antiquity, in the Middle Ages, and in the Renaissance—has become a focus of rhetorical interest. This interest in historical recovery represents the reclaiming of a long neglected view of rhetoric. Because of this, the teaching and transmitting of the "rhetorical tradition" becomes not just a loyal repetition but an effort at recovery, an active engagement with the tradition, a kind of deconstruction, in order to recover dimensions of rhetoric that have been lost, to discover what has been "covered over" by a specialized view of rhetoric that uncritically adopts conventional ways of viewing language and communication. In this endeavor, philosophy today becomes not the antagonist of rhetoric but its friend, its therapist, its means of breaking the spell of a modern tradition of overspecialization. The idea of a journal of *Philosophy and Rhetoric* begins to make sense. Because philosophy also has a great deal to learn from rhetoric, there is the opportunity for a mutually beneficial conversation, even cross-fertilization. An important part of twentieth-century philosophy that can prove useful to rhetoric is philosophical hermeneutics, for it reflects on a process that was disregarded in the modern era but had previously been an integral part of rhetoric.

The story of modern-era hermeneutics (since the Reformation) parallels that of rhetoric. With the Reformation a set of directions for interpreting Scripture without reference to the canonical fathers was required; rule manuals were published, and in the period preceding the romantic era, biblical hermeneutics was closely tied, in terms of its methods of exegesis, with classical philology. In the early nineteenth century, the height of German idealism and romanticism, Friedrich Schleiermacher made a major conceptual move away from the specialization of hermeneutics into techniques of interpretation and toward a more general reflection on understanding. He complained that the hermeneutics of his day (including classical philology) was an unsystematic amalgam of conflicting rules for dealing with different kinds of problems in different kinds of texts. He proposed stepping back from the specific problems and looking at the general conditions for understanding in ordinary conversation. In an early fragment from 1805 he notes: "The way in which a child construes the meaning of a new word"—from the grammar, the speech situation, the purpose of the utterance—"that is *Hermeneutik*."[13] In a critical dialogue with the Enlightenment-oriented classical philology of his day Schleiermacher developed and presented in his lectures of 1819 and 1829 what he called a general hermeneutics (*allgemeine Hermeneutik*). In a deeper sense, he argued, the very *style* of the utterance conveys the "soul" of the other person, the "dark thou," in all its individuality. But in order to sense the individual stylistic deviations from the norm, the mark of individuality, one had to know the norms of language (the words, the grammar), the genre, and even the situation of the utterance. Here, Schleiermacher is speaking not of specific problems or types of texts but of the universal conditions for understanding utterances, spoken or written—the conditions for a conversation. Hermeneutics thus moves away from rules and methods and toward a philosophy of language as it happens in living conversation between two souls, two individualities.

A half-century later, a biographer of Schleiermacher's named Wilhelm Dilthey renewed Schleiermacher's project of a general hermeneutics, first by writing a prize essay reviewing the development of hermeneutics from the Reformation to Schleiermacher and later by proposing hermeneutics as a methodological foundation for the human sciences. But Dilthey inserted hermeneutics into the context of his own life philosophy (*Lebensphilosophie*). Hermeneutics, according to his 1900 essay, "The Rise of Hermeneutics," involved the right construing of "expressions of lived experience fixed in writing [*schriftlich fixierte Erlebnisäusserungen*]."[14] Following Hegel, Dilthey viewed writing as the external expression of the human intellect and spirit: an externalization in a law, a work of literature, or a religious text. To interpret any one of these involved delving into its connection with *life* (the *Lebenszusammenhang*), i.e., the "context of" or "connection to" life. What was needed at that time, Dilthey argued, was a "critique of historical reason" that offered an epistemological and methodological foundation for the human and social sciences equivalent to the one argued in Kant's *Critique of Pure Reason*, which had given the natural sciences a philosophical foundation and warrant. It was Dilthey's hope that methods would arise out of this foundational hermeneutics that would enable interpretations of objects, texts, or actions in the social sciences, fine arts, and humanities to be as objectively "valid" as determinations were in the natural sciences.

But, as Gadamer points out in detail in *Truth and Method,* setting this goal of an objective validity equivalent to that of the natural sciences made scientific objectivity a model for understanding in the *Geisteswissenschaften* (human sciences, including the social sciences), in spite of Dilthey's own insights into the contextuality of understanding in history and life. It remained for Heidegger and Gadamer to free hermeneutics from the methodological mission of providing correct interpretations of texts and to place the "event" of understanding in its full intentional, existential, phenomenological, historical, ontological, and linguistic context. This meant redefining, even reconceiving, being, time, human being and doing, language, thinking, poetry, truth, and many other concepts that modern scientific reason had bent to its measure and purposes. The thinking through of these reconceptions is the unfulfilled agenda that hermeneutic philosophy can offer rhetoric today. *Truth and Method* puts forward its interpretation of the consequences of these reconceptions and thus remains an indispensable document for rhetorical theorists. For it offers its own unfolding of the complex process of understanding: as embedded in traditional ways of seeing and understanding, in words and grammar that bear the stamp of those previous ways of seeing and being in the world, and in expectations and preconceptions that one brings to specific tasks of understanding. The German term for this prior set of understandings is *Vorverständnis,* preunderstanding, a preliminary sense that is the basis for understanding anything at all. Gadamerian hermeneutics makes a claim to universality, claiming to focus on the way understanding happens always and everywhere, high and low, complex and simple, in oral conversation or in relation to a written text. Understanding is dialogical, according to Gadamer. Even the understanding of an artwork is a dialogue, a language game embedded in traditional expectations, and thus a process in which one can be surprised, contradicted, overwhelmed. A description in universal terms of the understanding-situation, the understanding-process, the understanding-*event* is what hermeneutics offers rhetoric. The specialization of hermeneutics into discrete disciplinary methods is transcended but not replaced through a universal, philosophical hermeneutics.

Gadamer's "Rhetoric and Hermeneutics"

No stronger testimony to the generic connectedness and historical interwovenness of rhetoric and hermeneutics can be found than Gadamer's remarkable essay "Rhetorik und Hermeneutik" (1976), translated into English for the first time in this volume. The source of the generic connectedness lies in two basic capacities of human beings. Gadamer observes that "in one respect rhetoric and hermeneutics are intimately related: being able to speak, like being able to understand, is a natural human capacity that develops to the full without the conscious application of rules, although natural talents, along with their proper cultivation and practice, come into play."[15] To speak well *presupposes* the capacity to understand and articulate that understanding. To understand, for Gadamer, entails not only grasping the inflections that accompany spoken utterance but also supplying those inflections as one reads a written utterance (*TM* 378ff.). This means that even silent reading is in principle an "oral interpretation." To read a Dostoevsky novel like *The Brothers Karamazov,* for instance, with its tense dialogues, is to bring its words back to living speech. This is the hermeneutic process. Yet without this process there could be no rhetoric because without an understanding of the matter at hand, there could be no assembling of the best arguments. We are dealing with two closely related, interdependent capacities.

But Gadamer's essay goes further to speak about the historical interwovenness of Reformation hermeneutics and Renaissance rhetoric. The hermeneutical treatises of Flacius and Melanchthon simply borrow from the rhetorical tradition transmitted from antiquity through the Middle Ages and presupposed in their education. The methods of understanding texts are those already present in their education in rhetoric. Gadamer asserts: "'Rhetoric' has a thematic interest of its own, however, not just as background, to help us understand the epistemological and scientific fate of the *humaniora* before they were constituted in the form of the romantic *Geisteswissenschaften*. In this connection, the role of hermeneutic theory, more or less secondary, is far less consequential than that of the ancient, medieval, and humanistic tradition of rhetoric. As part of the trivium, rhetoric led a life that went virtually unnoticed because it was so obvious." Gadamer here uses the word *fate* advisedly, for the story of rhetoric during this period shows it becoming increasingly specialized in the art of speaking well while losing its larger pedagogical role in the humanistic education in the classics. But during the Renaissance, hermeneutics as the art of reading the classics correctly was included in rhetoric. Only under the pressure of the Reformation did hermeneutics take on a separate life of its own. As Gadamer shows in the case of Flacius and Melanchthon, the principles they applied to achieve an autonomous discipline of text interpretation were those of the humanistic revival of rhetoric in which they had been educated.

As the influence of the "new science" was increasingly felt, Gadamer notes, the "educative function [*Bildungsfunktion*] of rhetoric" was defended by Giambattista Vico. This view of rhetoric remains relevant today, Gadamer argues, not so much in terms of the art of speaking as in the turning of the rhetorical tradition to *the reading of classical texts*, which brings us back to the hermeneutical teachings in the tradition of humanistic rhetoric. Gadamer explicitly laments the narrowing of rhetoric to an art either of reading written speeches aloud or to an art of political public speaking. While Melanchthon added to rhetoric the teaching lecture (*genos didaskalikon*), he emphasized that in rhetoric the classical *ars bene dicendi* (art of speaking well) could never renounce the *ars bene legendi* (art of reading well), which comprises, says Gadamer, "the ability to compose and evaluate speeches, longer disputations, and above all books and texts"; Gadamer here cites Melanchthon's *Elementorum Rhetorices* (Elements of rhetoric). Gadamer notes that *bene legendi* is not just a supplementary matter for Melanchthon but rather that "in the course of Melanchthon's presentation, reading as such—as well as the transmission and appropriation of the religious truths found in religious texts—gradually comes to take precedence over the humanistic ideal of imitation." Indeed, he quotes Melanchthon as putting the matter even more strongly: "'For no one can mentally comprehend longer expositions and complicated disputations who is not supported by a kind of art that informs him about how the parts are ordered and articulated, as well as about the intentions of the speaker and a method of explicating and clarifying obscure matters.'" Gadamer adds that Melanchthon is completely consistent with the medieval and Renaissance humanistic tradition when he chooses not to confine rhetoric in a narrow, special area but puts rhetoric and dialectic together and emphasizes their general applicability and usefulness.

Gadamer goes on to discuss another principle of rhetoric as understood by Renaissance humanists and found in Melanchthon—"the main intent and central viewpoint or, as it is called, the *scopus* of the speech"—which in modified form becomes a major doctrine of Melanchthonian hermeneutics. Gadamer points out how significantly Melanchthon's rhetoric is involved with right *reading*. He notes that "In contrast to spoken discourse, the written or reproduced text is deprived of all the kinds of interpretive assistance that a speaker takes care to offer. These can all be grouped under the concept of proper emphasis. The totality of understanding is encapsulated in the ideal case—never completely realized—of perfect emphasis." And to have the right emphasis one needs to understand the *scopus,* eventually the *scopus totius scripti:* the purpose and intention of the whole text.

This leads Gadamer to note the centrality of the task of reading for Protestant hermeneutics. Indeed, the Scripture's clarity, emphasized by Luther, depends on right reading. And Flacius' important *Clavis scripturae sacrae* (1545), the first major work of Protestant hermeneutical reflection, supported in a detailed and concrete presentation the principles of Protestant exegesis of the Scriptures. Where did he suddenly come up with the principles for the *Clavis?* From the rhetoric taught him by the humanists! As Gadamer remarks, Flacius "was first of all a philologist and humanist who had been won over to Luther and the Reformation." The intention of the *Clavis* was to show that the Scripture was understandable as a text without the help of the canonical tradition of the Roman Church. As Gadamer later puts it, "If we look more closely into the matter, the classical conceptual metaphors of rhetoric are here being summoned to prevent Scripture from being dogmatically subordinated to the doctrinal authority of the church." Even as hermeneutics focuses on the task of reading, apparently separating itself from rhetoric, it makes use of the "the conceptual metaphors of classical rhetoric." Such is the interwovenness of rhetoric and early modern hermeneutics, that even in the separation of hermeneutics there was extensive borrowing from classical rhetoric.

In conclusion, the historical interwovenness of rhetoric and hermeneutics in the Renaissance and Reformation is due to the wholesale adoption of the principles of textual interpretation already present in the rhetoric taught by Renaissance humanists that were taken over into the hermeneutical treatises of the Reformation and post-Reformation Protestantism. The direction of influence in this case was clearly from rhetoric to hermeneutics. Their essential interrelatedness is between understanding and speaking, two capacities that depend on and require each other. The separation and specialization of these capacities that developed from the seventeenth through the mid-twentieth centuries came about in part through the force of the paradigms of modern scientific thinking that encouraged specialization and the breaking down of problems into separate parts, following Descartes's recommendation in his *Discourse on Method*. In the twentieth century, a change in the reigning scientific paradigm, beginning with relativity and uncertainty theory in quantum physics, signaled the beginning of another paradigm shift, toward a more holistic paradigm for thinking. One aspect of this complex historical shift was the move toward a more holistic view of rhetoric as found in the "new rhetoric" and an interest in pragmatism, sociology of knowledge, and other extra-rhetorical studies. Along with this came renewed interest in the ancient, medieval, and Renaissance rhetorical tradition and therewith a broader conception of rhetoric. This has laid the foundation for a dialogue with a hermeneutics that has moved beyond three centuries of mere rules and methods of text interpretation. It is my argument that there are resources in hermeneutics, broadly conceived, that could be helpful to the new rhetoric. I shall present this argument as a set of twenty *topoi*.

VISION OF A RHETORIC INFORMED BY HERMENEUTICS

What would a rhetoric informed by or inclusive of hermeneutics—aware of a tradition of hermeneutics stretching back to antiquity and especially aware of nineteenth- and twentieth-century philosophical hermeneutical reflection—look like? Here is a vision of such a rhetoric formulated as twenty *topoi*. It should be emphasized that this proposal as a whole is not meant to exclude other fruitful influences on contemporary rhetoric that are presently at work. Many of my *topoi* are suggestive rather than essential to the overall vision of a rhetoric informed by hermeneutics, and several represent position-taking with regard to various topics. But they spell out in more detail how various dimensions, problems, and debates of hermeneutics with its critics might bear on a new alliance with rhetoric or might foster a rhetoric informed by hermeneutics. All answer in various ways the question "What would such a rhetoric look like"?

1. A rhetoric informed by hermeneutics would be aware of the buried history of hermeneutics within rhetoric in ancient, medieval, and Renaissance humanist education. But it would also be aware that the scope of hermeneutics is such that it includes writings on the interpretation of religious, literary, and legal texts in both Hebrew and Greek antiquity, and perhaps those in other ancient cultures.

2. A rhetoric informed by hermeneutics would recognize the generic interrelatedness of understanding and speaking and thus of the art of reading and the art of speaking, as we have seen in Gadamer's discussion of Melanchthon and Flacius.

3. Such a rhetoric would see how the capacity to formulate utterances in language is linked to the capacity to understand utterances in language, such that the one is inconceivable without the other. The art of speaking requires the art of understanding to penetrate the matter to be spoken, and the art of understanding requires the art of speaking to articulate what has been understood. Without speaking understanding is mute; without understanding speaking is empty.

4. Such a rhetoric would challenge the interpretive presuppositions of a science-driven, demonstration-oriented modern era. In it, Perelman and Olbrechts-Tyteca's *New Rhetoric*—and rhetoric as an epistemic project—would receive further support from Heidegger, Gadamer, Ricoeur, and other hermeneutical theorists. It is notable that Gadamer in his essay "Rhetoric, Hermeneutics, and the Critique of Ideology" also grasps the importance of rhetoric for contemporary hermeneutical reflection when he asks: "Where, indeed, but to rhetoric should the theoretical examination of interpretation turn? Rhetoric from oldest tradition has been the only advocate of a claim to truth that defends the probable, the *eikos* (versimile), and that which is convincing to the ordinary reason, against the claim of science to accept as true only what can be demonstrated and tested!"[16] Gadamer explores the rich resources of Aristotle's practical philosophy for hermeneutics not only in *Truth and Method* but in a number of later writings, such as the essays collected in his *Reason in the Age of Science*.[17] In his return to Aristotle's practical philosophy, he supplies further philosophical support (beyond that found in American pragmatist philosophers) for the parallel move in the new rhetoric.

5. Such a rhetoric would react sharply against the narrowing of its scope in the modern era, just as philosophical hermeneutics has reacted against the narrowing of its scope in the nineteenth and twentieth centuries. This histori-

cal parallel offers more than a common ground today; it also calls for a more inclusive vision in both rhetoric and hermeneutics. It even suggests a possible closer academic alliance, such as a department of rhetoric and hermeneutics, or a department of rhetoric and interpretation theory.

6. Such a rhetoric would find religious hermeneutics from the Reformation to the present to be of interest, especially the assumption that (a) the text contains a truth that challenges and enriches the self-understanding of the reader and is even capable of transforming the reader's self-consciousness and perception of the world. The implications of this are most obvious in relation to works of literature, especially the classics, and in the fine arts. And the assumption that (b) the principles of ancient rabbinic hermeneutics, such as the Seven Rules of Hillel, the Thirteen Rules of Ishmael, and Baraita of the Thirty-Two Rules, have a more general application in terms of rhetorical argumentation.[18]

7. Such a rhetoric would not disdain juridical hermeneutics both as it has been formulated in antiquity and as it has developed in modern times under other rubrics. For instance, there is the basic hermeneutical problem of bridging the gap between a text with legal force and an individual case that may be subsumed under a certain principle. The problematic character of subsumption itself in legal demonstration and proof would be a theme of such a new rhetoric. Gadamer's philosophical hermeneutics makes the moment of *applicatio,* so indispensable to juridical hermeneutics, central to adequate understanding in general. This, too, has implications for rhetoric, as the editors have shown in the Introduction to this book.

8. A rhetoric informed by hermeneutics would find inspiration in Schleiermacher's vision of the communicative situation. Schleiermacher turned to the conditions for conversation to see how understanding and misunderstanding take place. He was interested in understanding as an ongoing process interrupted by misunderstandings. The goal of hermeneutics, for Schleiermacher, was to avoid misunderstanding. Schleiermacher's hermeneutics also involved, beyond all rules, an element of "divination" or "guessing," of finding in the style of an utterance clues to the individuality of the utterer. The work of Manfred Frank is important in this regard.[19] For Schleiermacher and for hermeneutics in general, the hermeneutical problem is one of overcoming alienation and strangeness. The alienation to be confronted may be produced by the distance in historical time between the interpreter and the text; it may arise because of an alterity of language or cultural assumptions; ultimately, for Schleiermacher, it arises from the otherness of the other, the "dark thou."

9. A hermeneutically informed rhetoric would find inspiration in Dilthey's sense of the historical embeddedness and contextuality of every text, law, re-

ligious belief, or work of art. I would want to explore the special dynamics of encountering that historicality and contextuality within one's own historical consciousness and moment in history. For rhetoric this means that the matrix of a historically situated understanding becomes central to one's thinking, speaking, and selection of arguments about an issue.

10. A hermeneutically informed rhetoric would find inspiration in Nietzsche, who, like Dilthey, denied that there was any metaphysical world behind our present phenomenal world. Nietzsche asserted the endlessness of interpretation and its interest-guided character. Habermas early in his career grasped the hermeneutical significance of Nietzsche and collected his epistemological writings in one volume.[20] Nietzsche's views on interpretation fascinated Heidegger in the thirties and later fascinated Derrida and, indeed, a whole generation of French writers in the 1960s and 1970s.[21] Their implications move in the direction of a postmodern hermeneutics, as Alan Schrift has shown.[22] The writings of Nietzsche could also enable the rhetorical theorist to leap radically beyond the parameters of most twentieth-century views of language and interpretation, just as they inspired French visions of a new philosophical perspective.

11. A rhetoric informed by hermeneutics would be continually aware of the difference between meditative and calculative thinking. It would know what Heidegger meant by his provocative sentence in the first lecture of *What Is Called Thinking?* "Science itself does not think and cannot think" (p. 8). From Heidegger hermeneutics and a hermeneutically informed rhetoric learns that creative thinking requires a special talent for listening and hearing, and these require a special openness, an openness difficult to achieve in the metaphors and framework of modern calculative consciousness.

12. Such a rhetoric would learn from Heidegger's "Letter on Humanism" that "we have not begun to ponder carefully enough the essence of action [*das Wesen des Handelns*]."[23] To do so, one cannot accept Jean-Paul Sartre's "Existentialism is a Humanism" with its philosophy that "you are what you do." In his "Letter on Humanism" Heidegger was replying to Sartre's famous essay and to a letter from Jean Beaufret asking how to work for a rebirth of humanism. For Heidegger, neither humanism nor any other ism, including existentialism, was the answer. Rather, the task was rethinking the prevailing conceptions of human being-in-the-world, action, being, history, and speaking. This does not mean the interpreter cannot also gain a great deal from pragmatist philosophical thinking about action or about performative utterance from J. L. Austin or about meaningful action as text from Paul Ricoeur. But all these leave out "the turn" toward new concepts of human being-in-the-world, history, and poetic speaking in the later Heidegger.

13. A rhetoric that is fully informed by Heideggerian hermeneutics must go back to his explorations of understanding and language in *Being and Time*. It would be aware of what Heidegger accomplished for hermeneutics in that work beyond merely seeking the meaning of Being, and it would know why that accomplishment was important. It would know what it means for rhetoric to live and understand everything, including one's own being, in a prediscursive totality of relations.

14. A rhetoric informed by hermeneutics would explore the later Heidegger's understanding of language, art, and truth as disclosive. It would grasp the implications of Heidegger's famous proposition, "Language speaks [*Die Sprache spricht*]," as well as his luminous assertion, "Language is the house of Being" ("Letter on Humanism," p. 217). It would ponder his interpretation of Stefan George's line, "Where the word breaks down no thing may be [*Kein ding sei wo das wort zerbricht*]" and explore what it means for rhetoric that an artwork "sets up a world" and a viewer or hearer steps into its space.[24] Such a rhetoric would explore critically the implications of Heidegger's ascribing agency to language itself. Although such assertions do not constitute a view of language that should be accepted uncritically, they do bring into view new aspects of the being and doing of language and of art.

15. A rhetoric informed by hermeneutics would draw on Ricoeur's rich contributions to hermeneutics. A few of these would be: (a) his distinction between a "hermeneutics of the sacred," which takes the text as an access to a higher truth, and a "hermeneutics of suspicion," which, with Marx, Freud, and Nietzsche, goes behind the text to the interests guiding its formation; (b) his essay on meaningful action as text, which would include a gesture, a ceremony, or a work of art from today, yesterday, or antiquity, from our culture or another, as well as the whole movement from text to action; (c) his discussion of the difference between understanding and explaining; (d) his incisive and extensive explorations of metaphor; and (e) the idea from *Time and Narrative* that there are kinds of truth that cannot be reduced to a principle, axiom, or thesis; rather, they can only be conveyed by means of a story, a narrative.[25]

16. A hermeneutically informed rhetoric would have to go into both sides of the Gadamer-Habermas debate—and learn from both. It would consider (a) the significance of Gadamer's claims regarding the universality of hermeneutics; (b) Habermas's criticism that Gadamer falls into an "idealism of language" and Gadamer's reply; (c) Habermas's ideal model of a compulsion-free, undistorted communication in an ideal "communicative situation" and what this brings to light; (d) why Gadamer takes issue with this strategy as counterfactual and no longer dealing with "living language"; and (e) Gadamer's charge that Habermas cherishes the prejudices of Enlightenment thinking, including

the assumption that prevailing views are dogmatic and must be overcome by reason.

17. A rhetoric informed by hermeneutics would have room for Michel Foucault's critique of power and knowledge in, say, *Power/Knowledge,* building as it does on Nietzsche but using in an archaeology of knowledge an especially developed form of structuralist analysis. Such a rhetoric would look at the systems of representation and the historical account of other systems of exchange found in *The Order of Things* because speaking itself is a form of representation.[26] In *The Birth of the Clinic,* Foucault criticizes notions of discourse centered around the "scientifically structured discourse about an individual" in twentieth-century clinical practice: "The mindless phenomenologies of understanding mingle the sand of their conceptual desert with this half-baked notion" and dissolve into "the feebly eroticized vocabulary of 'encounter' and the 'doctor-patient relationship.'"[27] Elsewhere, he offers an attack on the "constraining role" of "the multiplicity of commentaries" he finds in the psychiatric and penal system.[28] He develops his arguments ever more fully in subsequent writings, such as *Power/Knowledge.* The question of the author is another issue Foucault develops by the virtual elimination of him or her. And his illuminating analyses of systems of representation, of discipline and punishment, of systematic suppression of social deviation, and of the treatment of women, the sick, and social outcasts are important to understanding the hidden constraints and exercises of power in a range of interpretive situations from medicine to criminal justice. These are of direct relevance to interpreting texts. Foucault's exposure of the hidden constraints in discourse facilitates the understanding of the interpretation of texts, persons, and discourse. It should be emphasized that Nietzsche's and Foucault's multiple contributions to our understanding of the interpretive context of modern thought are not threats to hermeneutics but additions to hermeneutic sophistication. They should not be taken as invalidating or rendering irrelevant other contributions to hermeneutical reflection in this century; rather, they supplement, extend, and enrich our knowledge of the interpretive matrix in which understanding and speaking take place. They "transform the hermeneutic context," as the title of a collection of French writings has put it.[29]

18. A hermeneutically informed rhetoric would interpret deconstruction as a special form of hermeneutics. Deconstruction is not an alternative to hermeneutics but a special form of it—a way of dealing with texts, a way of regarding language—with its own insights into the nature of language. Deconstruction argues that the nature of language is covered over when one takes "oral presence" as one's guide to the nature of language rather than writing and its structure of reference to what is absent. One thereby introduces a "metaphysics of

presence" into one's view of language. *Différance* is basically a nonmetaphysical, pseudotranscendental structure within language itself. Several English-speaking interpreters of Derrida—Rodolphe Gasché, Irene Harvey, Christopher Norris, Alan Schrift, and John D. Caputo—have made Derrida more available to English-speaking readers in his philosophical dimensions, but there has been a tendency by some literary critics to adopt the strategy of deconstruction without its philosophical underpinnings and by others to attack Derrida as undermining traditional humanistic assumptions.[30] Both alternative responses bypass the hermeneutical significance of deconstruction. A hermeneutically informed rhetoric will inquire into the deconstructionist project from a philosophical point of view, going back to Heidegger's project of *Destruktion* and to Derrida's early critique in *Speech and Phenomena* of Edmund Husserl's view of language. It is vital not to fall into facile antagonism to deconstruction but rather to understand what is at issue in the deconstructionist view of language, logocentrism, speaking, and oral presence. Superficially, these would make deconstruction an enemy of rhetoric as the art of the spoken word. Yet the point of deconstruction is more subtle than this and has to do with a structural difference hidden in the referentiality of language. This difference is found in both spoken and written language, but because this is so, the analysis of writtenness is able to dispel certain metaphysical presuppositions about language as "presence." Philosophically, Derrida's thought itself calls into question, as had Heidegger's thought before him, certain axioms of the ontological tradition since Plato. Such a rhetoric as I have in mind would not lose what deconstruction has to offer by rejecting Derrida out of hand.

19. A rhetoric informed by hermeneutics would study the dynamics of the encounter between Gadamer and Derrida at the Sorbonne in April 1981.[31] Gadamer was eager to enter into dialogue with Derrida, but Derrida was clearly reluctant and unprepared to enter into dialogue with Gadamer. Gadamer ended up bitterly disappointed, and both acknowledged afterward that nothing much happened. Studying what did and did not take place reveals what prerequisites are necessary for a dialogue to "take place" at all. Such issues as goodwill, common ground, respect for the other, conflicting interests, and the unwanted implication of compromise or willingness for a rapprochement arose. The reflections on Derrida's project in several of Gadamer's subsequent essays are also of interest.[32] Essentially, Gadamer reproaches Derrida for taking his lead from Husserl's view of language and from semantic theory. This leads to a semiotic view of language that neglects those dimensions that emerge when one reflects on living language.

20. Finally, such a hermeneutically informed rhetoric would welcome the pragmatist contributions of William James, Charles S. Peirce, John Dewey,

J. L. Austin, John Searle, and Ludwig Wittgenstein to the understanding of language use. It would acknowledge that the tradition of American pragmatism from Peirce to Richard Rorty and Joseph Margolis is tremendously important for rhetorical theory without allowing pragmatism to disqualify the hermeneutical insights of Schleiermacher, Nietzsche, Dilthey, Heidegger, Gadamer, Habermas, and Derrida. Indeed, the kinship between American pragmatism and German hermeneutics needs to be emphasized. Both build their reflection on an empirical reference back to concrete experience and doing. Both recognize that meaning resides in the situation and in the goals of persons in a situation, not outside and beyond them in a metaphysical realm. Both appeal to the Aristotelian practical philosophy as a forerunner of their thought. Both see the communicative experience in terms of a language game. But Heidegger and Gadamer see language as more than an exchange of signs and as more than a tool for doing things performatively with language. These two thinkers start with understanding rather than with speaking, and each discusses the ontology of understanding and of language in terms of a speaking that one hears rather than a doing that one does, and of speaking in its highest forms as a medium of new disclosure, of enabling one to see things in a new way, of setting up a world.

A rhetoric instructed by hermeneutics, then, recognizes that listening and understanding go with, indeed should precede, every act of speaking well. If speaking is usually a response to something, there is no escape from the task of understanding. A rhetoric informed by hermeneutics would not view understanding as something transparent and unproblematical to be hurried over or taken for granted in the preparation for speaking; rather, understanding would be seen as a basic component of our being-in-the-world and the matrix of our speaking. For hermeneutics, a certain agency resides in the language itself. As Heidegger puts it, "Language speaks." Understanding this speaking has its own difficulties and requirements and deserves the attention of the rhetorical theorist. A hermeneutically informed theorist would realize that our view of understanding also involves our presuppositions with regard to agency, language, history, and ultimately, human being-in-the-world. The "communicative situation" has gotten more complex—richer and deeper.

A renewal of the partnership between rhetoric and hermeneutics offers still other advantages for rhetoric. The historical focus in hermeneutics on the interpretation of texts reinforces the linking of rhetoric with its earlier tradition, which included moral education, philology, and the task of interpreting the classics. Thus it reemphasizes the *humanistic* history of rhetoric. This proposed renewal of the once-broad scope of rhetoric represents a deepening of rhetoric, both historically, philosophically, and humanistically. Historically it recalls long-forgotten dimensions to rhetoric. Philosophically it makes available philosophical hermeneutics, a major current in twentieth-century philosophy. Humanistically, it reestablishes contact with works of literature, law, theology, and Greek philosophy.

This is not the hour to dump the classics of the Western rhetorical, literary, and philosophical tradition overboard. The classics remain classic, and we need to respect and explain the fact that for generations Homer, Dante, and Shakespeare have continued to speak—and will continue to do so if they are not drowned out in a brave new world of television violence and ignorance of the past. The fact that respect for the great works of the past seems to have fallen off in the culture of our day should give us pause to reexamine our present perspective, even in academic disciplines. We need to be sensitive to the elements in our present culture and in our philosophical attitude that devalue the past. In hermeneutics, the present is not the definitive and final standpoint for evaluating the past. For hermeneutics, oriented as its reflection is to texts from the past, history is not a detritus stretching into the distance behind us but continuously alive and operative in our understanding. Reading today seems to be in decline. Earlier in our educational tradition, we sought meaning not just in conversation with friends, nor from the mass media, but in conversation with the classics. Hermeneutics reminds rhetoric why that conversation may still be valuable.

It has something to do with truth and the love of truth. I do not have in mind the embalming preservation of "timeless truths" alluded to by Caputo in ridicule of philosophical hermeneutics but a respectful dialogue with the texts that puts us in contact with the wisdom in our tradition.[33] When our understanding in reading a text rings true, it is not because we have reclaimed a timeless truth straight from the heaven of metaphysics but because the experience preserved in the words of an utterance reverberates with our own experience and becomes persuasive, compelling. A rhetoric informed by hermeneutics would be a rhetoric for which the texts of our tradition still contain something worth understanding and experiencing.

NOTES

In its original form, this chapter was a paper presented to the Central Illinois Philosophers Group in Springfield, Ill., on March 29, 1995. I am indebted to the following members of the group for helpful suggestions and corrections: George Agich, Robert Becker, Harry Berman, Meredith Cargill, Royce Jones, Marcia Salner, Larry Shiner, Eric Springsted, and Peter Wenz. I also wish to thank my student assistant, John C. Werry, for secretarial help.

1 Although the theory develops apace in both disciplines, I am told that many of the theorists and practitioners themselves feel a certain placelessness or marginalization, even denigration, in relation to the traditional disciplinary categories in higher education.

2 See Chaim Perelman and L. Olbrechts-Tyteca, *The New Rhetoric: A Treatise on Argumentation,* trans. John Wilkinson and Purcell Weaver (Notre Dame: University of Notre Dame Press, 1969); James J. Murphy, *Rhetoric in the Middle Ages: A History of Rhetorical Theory from St. Augustine to the Renaissance* (Berkeley: University of California Press, 1974); Thomas M. Conley, *Rhetoric in the European Tradition* (New York: Longman, 1990); Patricia Bizzell and Bruce Herzberg, eds., *The Rhetorical Tradition: Readings from Classical Times to the Present* (Boston: St. Martin's, 1990); Sonja Foss, Karen A. Foss, and Robert Trapp, *Contemporary Perspectives on Rhetoric,* 2d ed. (Prospect Heights, Ill.: Waveland Press, 1991).

3 Also, where are selections from the area of speech communication in the twentieth century—selections by such authors as Lloyd F. Bitzer, Charles Willard, Walter Fisher, Ernest Bormann, Kathleen Hall Jamieson, and Herbert A. Wichelns? Do they belong to the rhetorical tradition of the twentieth century? They do if we consult Edward P. J. Corbett, James L. Golden, and Goodwin F. Berquist, eds., *Essays on the Rhetoric of the Western World* (Dubuque, Iowa: Kendall/Hunt, 1990), which contains chapters by these authors. I am grateful to my colleague in speech communication at MacMurray College, Meredith Cargill, for references in the area of speech communication and extensive editorial suggestions on this chapter.

4 Richard Rorty, *Philosophy and the Mirror of Nature* (Princeton: Princeton University Press, 1979), 315. Further page references will be cited parenthetically in the text.

5 Richard Rorty, "Science as Solidarity," in John S. Nelson, Allan Megill, and Donald M. McCloskey, eds., *The Rhetoric of the Human Sciences: Language and Argument in Scholarship and Public Affairs* (Madison: University of Wisconsin Press, 1987), 38–52.

6 Herbert W. Simons, *The Rhetorical Turn: Invention and Persuasion in the Conduct of Inquiry* (Chicago: University of Chicago Press, 1990), vii.

7 Richard Rorty, ed., *The Linguistic Turn: Recent Essays in Philosophical Method* (Chicago: University of Chicago Press, 1967).

8 Martin Heidegger, *Being and Time,* trans. John Macquarrie and Edward Robinson (New York: Harper and Row, 1962), §32.

9 See his *The End of Philosophy,* trans. Joan Stambaugh (New York: Harper and Row, 1973).

10 Martin Heidegger, *What Is Called Thinking?* trans. Fred D. Wieck and J. Glenn Gray (New York: Harper and Row, 1968), 8; German text, *Was heisst Denken?* (Tübingen: Max Niemeyer, 1954), 4. Further references will be cited parenthetically in the text. See also his "The Origin of the Work of Art," in *Basic Writings,* ed. David Farrell Krell, rev. and expanded ed. (San Francisco: HarperCollins, 1993): "Science is not an original happening of truth, but always the cultivation of a domain of truth already opened" (187).

11 See Gadamer's "*Destruktion* and Deconstruction," in Diane P. Michelfelder and Richard E. Palmer, eds., *Dialogue and Deconstruction: The Gadamer-Derrida Encounter* (Albany: State University of New York Press, 1989), esp. 106ff. This is one of three essays by Gadamer in that volume discussing his and Derrida's relationship to Heidegger: cf., "Letter to Dallmayr" (93–101), "*Destruktion* and Deconstruction" (102–13), and "Hermeneutics and Logocentrism" (114–25).

12 See Gadamer, *Truth and Method*, 2d ed., rev. trans. Joel Weinsheimer and Donald G. Marshall (New York: Crossroad, 1989). Cited hereafter in the text as *TM*.

13 Friedrich Schleiermacher, "Aphorism on Hermeneutics from 1805 and 1809/10," and "*The Hermeneutics:* Outline of the 1819 Lectures," trans. Roland Haas and Jan Wojcik, in *The Hermeneutic Tradition: From Ast to Ricoeur*, ed. Gayle L. Ormiston and Alan B. Schrift (Albany: State University of New York Press, 1990), 68 and 52.

14 Wilhelm Dilthey, "The Rise of Hermeneutics," trans. Fredric Jameson, in *The Hermeneutic Tradition*, ed. Ormiston and Schrift, 101–14.

15 Hans-Georg Gadamer, "Rhetorik und Hermeneutik," *Gesammelte Werke*, vol. 2 (Tübingen: J. C. B. Mohr, 1986), 280; Eng. trans. Joel Weinsheimer, "Rhetoric and Hermeneutics," Chapter 1, this volume. Further references will be to this translation.

16 Hans-Georg Gadamer, "On the Scope and Function of Hermeneutical Reflection," in Gadamer, *Philosophical Hermeneutics*, ed. and trans. David E. Linge (Berkeley: University of California Press, 1976), 24. See also Chapter 15, this volume.

17 Hans-Georg Gadamer, *Reason in the Age of Science*, trans. Frederick G. Lawrence (Cambridge: MIT Press, 1981), esp. "Hermeneutics as a Theoretical and Practical Task," 113–38.

18 A valuable text in this regard is Louis Jacobs, *Jewish Biblical Exegesis* (New York: Behrman House, 1973). Also see Gerald L. Bruns, *Hermeneutics Ancient and Modern* (New Haven: Yale University Press, 1992). A basic reference is Hermann L. Strack, *Introduction to the Talmud and Midrash* (New York: Athenaeum, 1931).

19 See Manfred Frank's work on Schleiermacher's hermeneutics, *Das individuelle Allgemeine: Textstrukturierung und Interpretation nach Schleiermacher* (Frankfurt: Suhrkamp, 1977), which needs to be translated, as well as his *Die Unhintergehbarkeit von Individualität* (Frankfurt: Suhrkamp, 1986).

20 Friedrich Nietzsche, *Erkenntnistheoretische Schriften*, ed. Jürgen Habermas (Frankfurt: Suhrkamp, 1968). See also Habermas's *Knowledge and Human Interests*, trans. Jeremy J. Shapiro (Boston: Beacon, 1971), esp. the appendix.

21 See Martin Heidegger, *Nietzsche*, 4 vols., trans. David F. Krell (New York: Harper and Row, 1979–1987).

22 Alan Schrift, *Nietzsche and the Question of Interpretation: Between Hermeneutics and Deconstruction* (New York: Routledge, 1990).

23 "Letter on Humanism," in Heidegger, *Basic Writings*, 217. Hereafter cited parenthetically in the text.

24 See Heidegger's "The Nature of Language," in *On the Way to Language*, trans. Peter D. Hertz (New York: Harper and Row, 1971), 60ff.

25 See Paul Ricoeur: (a) *Freud and Philosophy: An Essay on Interpretation* (New Haven: Yale University Press, 1970); (b) "The Model of the Text: Meaningful Action Considered as a Text," *Social Research* 38 (1971): 529–62; and *Du text à l'action: Essais d'herméneutique* (Paris: Editions du Seuil, 1986); (c) "What Is a Text? Explanation and Understanding," in Ricoeur, *Hermeneutics and the Human Sciences*, ed. and trans. John B. Thompson (Cambridge: Cambridge University Press, 1981); (d) *The Rule of Metaphor*, trans. Robert Czerny (Buffalo: University of Toronto Press, 1977); and (e) *Time and Narrative*, vols. 1–2, trans. Kathleen McLaughlin and David Pellauer, and vol. 3, trans. Kathleen Blamey and David Pellauer (Chicago: University of Chicago Press, 1984–1988).

26 See Michel Foucault, *Power/Knowledge: Selected Interviews and Other Writings, 1972–1977*, ed. Colin Gordon (New York: Pantheon, 1980); Foucault, *The Archaeology of Knowledge*, trans. A. M. Sheridan Smith (New York: Random House, 1972); Foucault, *The Order of Things: An Archaeology of the Human Sciences* (New York: Vintage, 1975).

27 Michel Foucault, *Birth of the Clinic: An Archaeology of Medical Perception*, trans. A. M. Sheridan Smith (New York: Vintage, 1975), xiv.

28 See Foucault, *Madness and Civilization: A History of Insanity in the Age of Reason*, trans. Richard Howard (New York: Tavistock, 1967).

29 Gayle L. Ormiston and Alan D. Schrift, eds., *Transforming the Hermeneutic Context: From Nietzsche to Nancy* (Albany: State University of New York Press, 1990).

30 See Rudolphe Gasché, *The Tain of the Mirror: Derrida and the Philosophy of Reflection* (Cambridge: Harvard University Press, 1986); Irene E. Harvey, *Derrida and the Economy of Différance* (Bloomington: Indiana University Press, 1986); Christopher Norris, *Derrida* (Cambridge: Harvard University Press, 1987); Alan D. Schrift, *Nietzsche and the Question of Interpretation: Between Hermeneutics and Deconstruction* (New York: Routledge, 1990); John D. Caputo, *Radical Hermeneutics: Repetition, Deconstruction, and the Hermeneutic Project* (Bloomington: Indiana University Press, 1987).

31 See Diane P. Michelfelder and Richard E. Palmer, *Dialogue and Deconstruction: The Gadamer-Derrida Encounter* (Albany: State University of New York Press, 1989). I have elsewhere discussed the contrasts between Gadamer and Derrida. See, for example, Richard E. Palmer, "Improbable Encounter: Gadamer and Derrida," *Art Papers* 10 (Jan.–Feb. 1986): 36–39; Palmer, "Gadamer and Derrida as Interpreters of Heidegger: On Four Texts of Gadamer and Four Texts of Derrida," in *The Question of Hermeneutics*, ed. Timothy J. Stapleton (The Hague: Kluwer, 1994), 255–305.

32 These are included in Michelfelder and Palmer, *Dialogue and Deconstruction*.

33 See Caputo, *Radical Hermeneutics*, 111. Caputo states his purpose in this lively volume, which is quite relevant to the project of a rhetoric informed by hermeneutics, as follows: "I want to defend an ethics which arises from cold hermeneutics, hermeneutics without comfort, which issues from the salutary interplay of Heidegger and Derrida" (239).

6

Hermeneutical Circles, Rhetorical Triangles, and Transversal Diagonals

Calvin O. Schrag

The aim of this essay is to provide a thought experiment on how to maneuver an alliance of hermeneutics with rhetoric. I argue that hermeneutics is delimited by the practice of rhetoric, and in turn both hermeneutics and rhetoric need to be refigured within the space of transversal communication.

HERMENEUTICS AND THE SEARCH FOR MEANING

Hermeneutics as theory and practice of interpretation stimulates an economy of meanings, latent as well as manifest, that is at play in texts and actions, in text analogues and action analogues, while it addresses both actual and potential misunderstandings. Hermeneutics constitutes its operating matrix as a part-whole relationship and finds its root metaphor in the circle. The aim of hermeneutical understanding is to comprehend the part through the whole and the whole through the part. Whether dealing with a text complex or a configuration of action, the hermeneut attends to the parts of the text and particular acts in relation to other parts and other acts, all of which have meaning only recursively as they are placed back into the context of a configurative whole. Meaning is garnered to the degree that an intercalation of part and whole is achieved, evincing the circularity of movement from part to whole and whole to part. Charles Taylor articulates this point with some felicity when, addressing the matter of the circularity of text interpretation, he states the case as follows: "The circle can also be put in terms of part-whole relations: we are trying to establish a reading for the whole text, and for this we appeal to readings of its partial expressions; and yet because we are dealing with meaning, with making sense, where expressions only make sense or not in relation to others, the readings of partial expressions depend on those of others, and ultimately of the whole."[1]

There is, however, another display of circularity in the hermeneutical undertaking. Not only is there a circular to and fro between part and whole, there is also a circularity of interpretive understanding in the variation and expansion of perspectives on the part-whole configuration itself. Within this circularity of perspectives there is only a movement between and among perspectives; there is no movement beyond perspectivity to a vantage point outside the circle of understanding. To be sure, advances and refinements in the quest for meaning are possible through a revision of perspectives that results from an encounter with other perspectives, but there appears to be no exit from the circularity of perspectivity as such. This marks another dimension of the circularity of hermeneutical thought and discourse.

It is of vital importance, however, that we not mistake the circularity of hermeneutical thought and discourse for the obtrusive *circulus vitiosus* that invalidates linear and quantitative calculating and reckoning. The hermeneutical circle is not a "vicious circle," an aberration of proper entailment that would be avoidable by carefully attending to the rules of inference. Hermeneutics is not governed by the rules of linear/representational thinking. True, such rules may have utility in an analytical explanation of the constitutive parts of a portion of text or a pattern of action and in this manner contribute to the understanding of a part-whole complex. Such would be the case, for example, in attending to the rules of grammar in analyzing an obscure and problematic sentence structure within a wider portion of text. The comprehension of a perspective on a part-whole intercalation, however, proceeds not from rules of method somehow determined in advance but rather from a *taking as* posture. Hence, the propriety of the vocabulary of the "hermeneutical as." A text under consideration is *taken as* a certain genre of discourse—for example, a scientific document, a political satire, a homily, a historical account, a piece of fiction, a treatise on morality. A display of behavior is *taken as* an expression of meaningful action—a friendly gesture, a physical threat, an obscene sign, a cry for help.

Whether interpreting a text or an action, there is always a foregrounding of both the texture and range of meanings that come to bear. The task of hermeneutics is to sort out, consolidate, describe, and redescribe these meanings by attending to the partial expressions as they relate to other partial expressions in pursuit of an understanding and articulation of the whole. Indeed, different perspectives on the integration of part and whole may arise, requiring a "correction" of any particular perspective through a contrastive comparison with another actual or possible perspective. This strategy of correction is not a matter of landing on the correct perspective and finally getting it right but rather a dynamics of opening up new possibilities through which delivered perspectives might be enriched. But there is no escape from the circling from part to whole nor from the circularity of revisable perspectives. Given this state of affairs, Heidegger's advice may be peculiarly judicious: "What is decisive is not to get out of the circle but to come into it in the right way."[2]

The consequences of the hermeneutical requirement to come into the circle in the right way, one soon finds out, are both broad and deep. The scope of hermeneutics does appear to enjoy a kind of ubiquity, prompting some hermeneuts to speak of a "universal hermeneutics."[3] One can readily observe that hermeneutics has spread its mantle over a variety of discourses and disciplines. In the pantheon of Hermes one finds hermeneutics of the social sciences and hermeneutics of the natural sciences; hermeneutics of texts and hermeneutics of action; hermeneutics of jurisprudence and hermeneutics of medical practices; hermeneutics of culture forms and hermeneutics of *Existenz*. The range of hermeneutics is broad. It is also deep. In each of the discourses and disciplines that exhibit its traces it goes all the way down. There is no terminus ad quem in the hermeneutical project, no end point, no coming to rest in a brute, isolated, hard-knob, indubitable *fact*. Indeed, there are no facts without interpretation. Facts become facts only when they are *taken as* such within a constituted disciplinary matrix. The interior dynamics of hermeneutics is that of a progression from one interpretation-fact complex to another. This is the sense in which interpretation goes all the way down. Clearly, it does not go all the way down in the sense of reaching a stable foundation of incorrigible facts and unimpeachable assertoric claims. In this respect, hermeneutics is antifoundationalist both in attitude and strategy. The break with epistemological foundationalism is decisive.[4]

The entwinement of fact and interpretation and the ensuing rupture with epistemological foundationalism have certain consequences for the classical problem of meaning and reference as defined in the annals of modernity. Hermeneutics remains a quest for meaning, but the understanding and use of *meaning* is significantly refigured. Meaning is no longer understood simply as a concept or a set of concepts issuing from an insular and sovereign cogito seeking commerce with an epistemic "object" (physical body, sense datum, intuited essence, proposition, etc.). Hermeneutics effects a *Verstellung*, a dissimulation, of both the knowing subject and the object as known. The subject-object dichotomy as enframed by modern epistemology is dismantled from both sides, as it were. The abstract Cartesian thinking subject is refashioned into an embodied, self-interpreting, discursive, and agentive subject; the object of reference is reinscribed as a figure-against-a-background. In the move from objectifying ostensive reference to hermeneutical reference, the referent is no longer determined as an isolatable and self-identical datum but is refigured as that which shows itself against the contours of an intentionality-laden background. Discourse remains discourse about something, but the "aboutness" in question does not turn on the isolation of discrete properties and relations. The aboutness, the terminus of reference, if you will, is more global, having to do with the *world-as-experienced* in perception, discourse, and action.

Let us suppose that a portion of discourse turns on the life and times of former president John F. Kennedy. John F. Kennedy as the proper referent at issue in the discussion has its aboutness, its power of indication, fulfilled only through the insinuation of a background of political institutions and social practices that situate Kennedy as "the former president of the United States." One could say, in the vocabulary of phenomenology, that what is referred to is John F. Kennedy's "being-in-the-world." Meanings put into play by self-interpreting speakers and actors find their fulfillment in a reference to a *lifeworld*. Such is the route of hermeneutical reference, which, as I have argued elsewhere, is complemented by a hermeneutical self-implicature, through which the subject, deconstructed as an epistemological sovereign ego-cogito, is reclaimed as an implicate in the life of discourse and action.[5]

Although the response of hermeneutics to the classical problem of meaning and reference, by way of a refiguration of the problem itself, comprises a notable advance, there are certain emergent issues in this response that require further critical attention. To be sure, within a hermeneutical posture there is a move beyond epistemological protocols of verification and truth conditions legislated in advance of inquiry; however, there remains a gesture in the direction of coherence as a quasitheory of truth, given the strong commitment to holism. In its antifoundationalist stance, hermeneutics severs relations with the classical representational theory of knowledge and the correspondence theory of truth. However, it continues to make purchases on the coherence theory of truth in defining the project of interpretive understanding as one of integrating part with whole and whole with part.

This appetition for a holism, in both practical and theoretical understanding, confers a certain privilege upon unity and totality. The dynamics of hermeneutical understanding is that of a shuttling to and from parts and wholes, oriented toward an agreement on the meaning of a particular part-whole configuration. But this accentuation of a quest for unity and solidarity of agreement among the community of interpreters invites a troublesome *aporia* in the face of insurmountable conflicts of interpretation. It is precisely at this juncture, where the orientation toward common understanding and shared perspectives encounters a conflict of interpretation—or, indeed, as in some cases, a radical dissensus—that delimitation of the hermeneutical project is required. We need to effect a shift of inquiry standpoint, involving a suspension of the heavy demands for unity, coherence, and consensus in our sundry projects of understanding and explanation. The hermeneutical circle lacks the requisite resources for productively addressing conflicts of interpretation. Its presuppositions do not allow a move to the outside of the circle, to a supplementary standpoint from which resolutions to conflict situations and ruptures of consensus would be productively addressed. Might such a delimitation of and supplement to the hermeneutical circle be found in the rhetorical triangle?

THE CONSEQUENCES OF RHETORIC

Although the hermeneutical demand is both broad and deep in its orientation toward a solidarity of consensus against the backcloth of a valorization of unity and totality, it encounters difficulties in dealing with the intrusion of difference in situations of conflicts of interpretation. Let us now explore possible resources in rhetoric for addressing the difficulties occasioned by the event of difference within the hermeneutical economy.

It is important to keep in mind that hermeneutics and rhetoric have traveled together over a considerable length of time. Heidegger has called our attention to Aristotle's *Rhetoric* as comprising "the first systematic hermeneutics of the everydayness of Being with one another."[6] Gadamer, and on this point quite in accord with Heidegger, concludes that "the rhetorical and hermeneutical aspects of human linguisticality completely interpenetrate each other."[7] If such is indeed the case, then it would clearly follow that Gadamer's call for a "universal hermeneutics" needs to be supplemented with a call for a "universal rhetoric." Rhetoric, like hermeneutics, goes all the way down and all the way back. They enjoy a co-primordial ubiquity.

Surely there is a close connection between hermeneutics and rhetoric. Yet the one cannot be simply analyzed into the other. They overlap, they interconnect, they supplement each other; but one cannot be reduced to the other. As

Paul Ricoeur has well stated, rhetoric and hermeneutics each speaks for itself. "Rhetoric remains the art of arguing with a view to persuading an audience that one opinion is preferable to its rival. . . . Hermeneutics remains the art of interpreting texts within a context which is distinct from that of the author and from that of the texts' original audience with a view to discovering new dimensions of reality."[8] Closely related yet distinct, the required task thus becomes the articulation of the lines of force and vectors of interplay that stimulate the amalgamated hermeneutical-rhetorical economy.

The thesis I wish to propose concerning the hermeneutic-rhetoric connection is that rhetoric at once delimits and enriches hermeneutical understanding in accentuating the role of the other and the play of difference. In performing this service rhetoric reins in the hermeneut's strong proclivities to unity, solidarity, and consensus. The recognition of alterity and difference, in turn, has certain consequences for addressing the *aporia* of the conflict of interpretations, which hermeneutics by itself is unable to resolve.

The role of the other and the play of alterity in the rhetorical situation come to prominence through the triangulation of rhetor and interlocutor intersecting the *topoi* that occasion the discourse. Whereas the root metaphor of hermeneutics is the circle, the root metaphor of rhetoric is the triangle.[9] Rhetoric, properly understood as collaborative discourse and action designed for the purpose of persuasion, is a project of communication to, for, and with *the other*. The aim of rhetoric is communication. The modes of this communication vary from confronting the face of the other in a dialogic transaction, to addressing a wider audience on issues of public concern, to the uses of texts and the technology of telecommunication, to forms of personal behavior and institutional action. In attending to the modes of persuasive communication in the rhetorical situation it is important to recognize the integrity of a rhetoric of action that is not simply reducible to a rhetoric of the spoken or the written word. One persuades by actions as well as by words. Kenneth Burke's notion of "administrative rhetoric" is particularly illustrative of this point.[10]

The alterity at issue in the dynamics of persuasive communication is inscribed on two nodal points in the triangulation of the rhetorical economy. Not only is there the otherness of the interlocutor/addressee/reader, there is also the otherness of the *topoi*, the topics, which have to do with the plethora of beliefs, practices, and institutions that congeal into a variety of forms of life. Language is already on the scene and social practices and institutions are already in play when a rhetor engages an interlocutor. Various meanings and lifestyles are already extant, insinuated within the delivered discourses and practices. When a rhetor seeks to persuade an interlocutor to vote for a particular candidate for a state or national office, the meanings of democracy and representational government are already inscribed in a lifeworld that antedates their conversations. When an adherent to a religion of the East engages an adherent to a religion of the West in dialogue, the background of religious thought and practices that divide East and West impinge, sometimes obtrusively, upon the participants in the dialogue. It is thus that the rhetorical situation exhibits an alterity that antedates the otherness in the rhetor-interlocutor dyad, an alterity of lifeworld horizons to which each in different ways responds.

The lifeworld, with its multiple patterns of meaning, is indeed the proper referent in the rhetorical situation, enabling one to speak of a dynamics of "rhetorical reference" that at once delimits, supplements, and enriches the dynamics of the circularity of "hermeneutical reference." Rhetorical reference is centrifugal rather than centripetal, adventitious, coming from the outside as it were, impinging upon rhetor and interlocutor alike, effecting an incursive disclosure, setting the requirement for each speaker to respond to the discourses and actions of a lifeworld that is not of his or her doing. Rhetoric thus finds its occasion not in a condemnation to subjective freedom (à la Jean-Paul Sartre) nor even in a condemnation to meaning (à la Maurice Merleau-Ponty) but more specifically in a condemnation to responsibility (à la Emmanuel Levinas) in which mortals—indeed, by virtue of their mortality—are called upon to respond to discourses and actions that are always already extant.

The requirement to respond to an incursive alterity of multiple and often heterogenous beliefs and practices confers upon rhetoric its peculiar dynamics of communication—a communication that remains an existential struggle because of the diversity of perspectives that define our sociohistorical inherence. Given the multiplicity and heterogeneity of voices that invade the rhetorical situation, our projected goals of solidarity and consensus will need to be somewhat attenuated. It may be that the principle of unity that informs the ontology of the part-whole framework of hermeneutical inquiry will require modifications, as will the hermeneutical definition of understanding as a quest bent upon the attainment of solid agreement. The realities of the rhetorical situation appear to be such that any privileging of unity and totality and any prescription of a consensual solidarity will inevitably lead to a profound metaphysical disappointment.

The topography of rhetoric is more amenable than that of hermeneutics to the settlements of otherness on its terrain, and it is thus more ready to accept diversity and difference. In its dealings with diversity and difference, rhetoric is required to experiment with new strategies of argumentation and persuasion, probing possibilities for new forms of behavior and social organization. It is thus that rhetoric is able to place a premium on novelty, invention, and creativity. It supplements the weight placed on tradition in hermeneutical understanding by experimenting with the new and the untried. It conserves the past without succumbing to conservativism. It speaks from the past as it heeds the call of the future. In this manner rhetoric is forced to reckon with time, effecting a preserving function in its liaison with the discursive and institutional practices of the tradition as it engenders a creating function in its projection of new forms of discourse and action.[11]

In its distanciation from the discursive and institutional sediments within the tradition, intervening while it invents, rhetoric is able to supply a needed critical function, a standpoint for critique of tradition, convention, and ideology. The rationality of rhetoric finds a decisive expression in this critical function. One of the principal tasks of rhetoric is to bring traditional beliefs and practices to the bar of critical discernment and evaluation. We are thus able to find in this posture of critique what Hans Blumenberg seeks when he sets out to find in rhetoric "a form of rationality itself—a rational way of coming to terms with the provisionality of reason."[12] Inventing the new does not necessitate a toppling of the old, but it does call for a critical assessment and a mustering of arguments for an acceptance of some practices and cultural forms and a jettisoning of others. The rhetorician J. Robert Cox sees the critical principle of rhetoric emerging from a "dialectic of repetition and disavowal," which provides a space for a *critical* appropriation of traditional forms of life. Thanks to the dynamics of disavowal, the contents of a tradition are always placed under scrutiny, questioned, reevaluated, refigured, or indeed overturned.[13]

Cognizant of the incursion of alterity and the need for a critical assessment of the delivered contents of the tradition, rhetoric effects a delimitation of hermeneutics without simply jettisoning it. Rhetoric is more like a supplement to and complement of hermeneutics than a displacement of it, addressing the *aporia* of the conflict of interpretations bequeathed by hermeneutics in such a manner as to problematize the ideals of solidarity and consensus in recognition of the need to live with multiplicity and difference. Yet there is a troublesome tendency that travels with this delimitation of the quest for common understanding and solidifying agreement while accentuating the multiple, the different, and the other. The tendency is to valorize and celebrate difference over sameness to the point that the hermeneutic problematic of the conflict of interpretations is stood on its head. The consequences of such an embrace of difference is that conflict, the disruption of consensus, no longer poses a problem; the problem is placing a value on agreement and collaborative activity in the first place. Indeed, the proper disposition of discourse is then seen as being dissensus rather than consensus, disagreement rather than agreement.

This tendency has found its most illustrious avatar in the "rhetorical agonistics" proposed by the arch postmodernist Jean-François Lyotard. Rhetorical agonistics portrays rhetoric as a veritable agon, a war of minds and wills bent toward conflict rather than dialogue. Lyotard separates the "partisans of agonistics" from the "partisans of dialogue," extolling the economy of difference over the economy of sameness.[14] What underwrites the economy of rhetorical agonistics, if indeed one can speak of underwriting on such matters as these, is what Lyotard has named the *différend,* which as distinct from a litigation is an irremediable conflict between two parties that resists resolution for want of a common rule of judgment.[15]

It should be noted that a consequence of some effect ensues from Lyotard's rhetorical agonistics, namely, that the proper end of discourse is dissensus rather than consensus, paralogy rather than commensurability. "As I have shown in the analysis of the pragmatics of science, consensus is only a particular state of discussion, not its end. Its end, on the contrary, is paralogy."[16] This rhetorical turn to an economy of agonistics, privileging dissensus over consensus, issues a bankruptcy notice to any hermeneutic of meaning oriented toward mutual understanding and solidarity in thought and discourse. The apparently ineradicable multiplicity and heterogeneity of beliefs and practices, courting at every juncture an irremediable conflict of interpretations and institutional programs, forestalls anything that would approximate a consensus or a meeting of minds. The hermeneutical circle is ruptured by a dissolution of its economy of coherence and unity—its appetition for part-whole totalization; it is replaced by a triangulation of rhetor, interlocutor, and heterogeneous practices, producing a situation in which the rhetor remains at war with the interlocutor in the face of insurmountable *différends.* The partisans of agonistics thus provide a somewhat curious resolution to the hermeneutical *aporia* of conflicting interpretations. Conflict, which for the hermeneut, as a partisan of dialogue, is a negativity to be avoided, becomes for the partisan of agonistics a state of affairs to be cultivated.

TRANSVERSAL COMMUNICATION

In this section I propose to delimit and resituate the hermeneutical and rhetorical tasks discussed in the previous sections in an effort to think beyond the resultant *aporias* in each. This will involve a reconsideration of the aims of discourse and the dynamics of communication by way of experimentation with a new grammar and a new root metaphor. The grammar is that of transversality, and the root metaphor is the diagonal instead of the circle or the triangle. Admittedly, the concept of transversality is not of recent invention. For some time it has been an underlaborer in the disciplines of mathematics, physics, physiology, anatomy, psychology, and philosophy. One of the more prominent philosophical uses of transversality occurs in Sartre's existentialist description of consciousness as a "play of transversal intentionalities."[17] Sartre's project is to displace a self-identical consciousness, grounded in a transcendental ego, with a consciousness that overruns any stable presence of consciousness by way of concrete transversal intentionalities that bind it to past consciousness through a recursive functioning.

The sense of transversality as it plays in the multiple disciplines is diagonal transgression, lying across, extending over surfaces and lines, longitudinal mass, bands of fibers, vertebrae, or moments of consciousness. In their lying across and extending over, transversal vectors and lines of force exhibit a convergence without coincidence, a conjuncture without identity. The root metaphor of the diagonal is thus peculiarly apt, conveying the sense of cutting across and intersecting without coming to rest at any particular point, surface, or moment.

Although Sartre's appropriation of the figure of transversality in his description of the dynamics of consciousness is insightful and has its own rewards, the figure has a wider applicability in the arenas of discourse and action that mark out our variegated communicative engagements. Transversality as a feature of our social practices of discourse, action, and institutional involvements defines the dynamics of moving across multiple contexts and forms of human association, oriented toward an understanding of these multiple contexts without violating their otherness. Transversal thought and communication recognizes the integrity of the beliefs and practices of the other and critically engages the other so as to enhance an understanding of that which is one's own. It enriches both self-understanding and the understanding of the other. The principle task is not to change the beliefs and practices of the other (although this may result from an ongoing communication) but rather to understand the other. In its orientation toward an enriched understanding of self and other, transversal communication continues the hermeneutical project of seeking the better understanding (*Besserverstehen*) that was proposed by Wilhelm Dilthey. However, it does so without the heavy ontological investments in a unity-based holism that defined the classical hermeneutical program.

The dynamics of transversality is such that due regard is given to the particularity and historical specificity of social practices and culture forms. It proceeds in recognition of the contextuality and conditionality of the multiple knowledge claims and valuations that define our historical situatedness. Claims for contextless and unconditioned sources of universal truths are rendered problematic. Thought is informed by the *trans*-versal rather than the universal. However, the recognition of the contextuality and historical specificity of our beliefs and practices need not catapult us into a historical relativism that views all thought and action as simply determined by the particular-ities of our personal and social existence. Such would be the case only if we failed to distinguish the *context conditioned* from the *context determined*. To say that the amalgam of our thought, discourse, and action is context condi-tioned is to recognize that a variety of cultural and historical influences inform what is believed, asserted, and practiced. But this surely is not to say that the totality of human thought and action is determined by particular contexts, which themselves would house, in a mysterious fashion, causal or quasi-causal forces that produce thought in the way electricity produces light. The trans-versal feature of thought and action enables a movement both *within* and *across* traditional beliefs and practices. Thought and action remain contextu-alized, but they are not determined by the particularities of any specific con-text within any specific tradition. It is thus that transversal lines of force are able to create a passage between the Scylla of a vacuous universalism and the Charybdis of an anarchic historicism. Transversal thought is *trans*-historical, neither ahistorical nor historicist, neither suspended above the historical nor suffocated within it.

Against the backdrop of the space and dynamics of transversality, effecting convergences without coincidence, situated betwixt and between the claims for universality and identity on the one hand and the valorization of particular-ity and difference on the other, I intend to address the resultant *aporias* in the hermeneutical and rhetorical endeavors. Because of its ontological commit-ments to unity and totality, marginalizing heterogeneity and alterity, herme-neutical understanding overdetermines the requirement for agreement and solidarity, thus lacking the resources to deal with conflicts of interpretation. Rhetoric, cognizant of the irruption of otherness and the play of multiplicity, supplements interpretation with argumentation and defines the field of our communicative practices as a battlefield, an agon of disputation, in which the most forceful argument has the best chance to persuade, if only for the mo-ment.

To put the matter simply, we need to find a way of maneuvering between the imperatives of consensus and the celebration of dissensus, between solid agreement and intractable discord, between the commensurable and the in-commensurable. Transversal communication is peculiarly fitted for the task, splitting the difference, as it were, between the partisans of dialogue and the partisans of agonistics, moderating the hermeneutical appetitions for unity and common understanding while mitigating the combative posture of rhetoric.

There are a number of points that require special emphasis in this particu-lar task, which is one of splitting the difference between consensus and dissensus. A point to be underscored is the need for a refiguration of the phenomenon of intersubjectivity, accenting the "inter" rather than the "subjective" side of the phenomenon. Intersubjectivity must no longer be understood as the end result of a phenomenological constitution on the part of a monadic, constituting subject, whereby the other is called to presence via the projection of an alter ego and an accompanying analogical transfer of sense. Rhetoric has done well to recognize the exteriority of the other, encountered in advance of constitution, and announced by way of an intrusion of social practices and cultural forms of life that are alien to the projects of subjectivity. Yet the differences that are inscribed through the incursion of alterity need not congeal into the impermeability of a Lyotardian *différend*. Indeed a *différend* in the guise of an *absolute* exteriority, impermeable and nonrelational, remains at most a limit to thought and to the experience of a lifeworld. The array of differences encountered in the lifeworld—the other self, the other text, the other set of mores, the other institution, the other culture—turn on a *topos*, a topography, a space of engagement, a being-with-that-which-is-other, that binds, however loosely, rhetor and interlocutor, citizen and alien, friend and foe.

It is thus that Lyotard's sharp demarcation of "partisans of dialogue" from "partisans of agonistics," against the backdrop of an intractable *différend,* appears to be somewhat overdrawn. Apparently the partisans of agonistics wage war not only on the partisans of dialogue but also on each other. But then in what sense do they continue to function as partisans? Whence issues the collaborative zeal to march shoulder to shoulder as party affiliates? If the agon is so firmly entrenched in the economy of discourse, how is it that one partisan of agonistics is able to communicate with another? Have we not learned from Plato that there needs to be honor even among thieves? Might it not be that one can learn from Lyotard (in a somewhat serendipitous manner to be sure) that even a rhetorical agonistics requires a measure of collaboration and solidarity among its partisans?

The point to be underscored at this juncture is that a new sketch of the terrain of intersubjectivity is needed to account for being with others in the midst of conflict and strife. As antagonist I wage a war with a protagonist, registering total disagreement, to the point of rupturing the dialogue and eventually removing myself from the conversation. But what I cannot do is remove him or her from the intersubjective space we share. The facticity of the situation is such that "the other," whether protagonist or antagonist, remains inscribed as "the one with whom one differs." Even in the throes of disagreement, partisans of dialogue and partisans of agonistics continue to face each other as they announce to the world, "*We* cannot agree!"

It is on this new topography of intersubjectivity as a we-experience amid occurrent differences that something like an ethic of transversal communication is able to take root—an ethic that is able to tolerate differences in its response to the diversity of beliefs and practices. The dynamics of such an ethic resides in the cognition of the alterity of the other as an *acknowledgement* of the other as other. The grammar of acknowledgement is already a mixed grammar, both descriptive and normative. Acknowledging the other is at once a demonstration, by discourse or action, word or deed, that one has *knowledge of* and *respect for* the rights, claims, and authority issuing from the other; *regard* for incurred debts, promises, and duties; and an *avowal* of the integrity of the other as other. All these senses, in mixing the descriptive and the prescriptive, travel with the event of acknowledgment. Acknowledging the other as other is a mode of being-with-others, an event of intersubjectivity within a concrete lifeworld, that is already infused with moral predicates. Contextualized within an ethos that defines the character of rhetor and interlocutor alike, acknowledgment conveys respect for the integrity of the other, soliciting the ethical as the requirement for a fitting response to the discourses and the actions of the other that are always already in force.

The economy of transversal communication, stimulated by the ethic of the fitting response, refigures both the hermeneutic orientation toward understanding and the rhetorical stance on alterity, effecting a passage between the unacceptable alternatives of pure consensus and unqualified dissensus as the proper ends of discourse. The search for understanding, the appetition for agreement and shared meaning, the drive toward solidarity—these all remain. However, the hermeneutical project is recast in such a manner as to become a struggle with irremovable risks, given the play of difference in the diverse agenda of beliefs and social practices. This recasting enables an acceptance of the conflict of interpretations and the clash of convictions as indigenous features of existence in a cosmopolitan lifeworld.

These conflicts of interpretations and clashes of convictions in public life arise from intricate interlacings of political, economic, moral, and religious perspectives. Such is the case in the longstanding divergent points of view separating the British Crown and the Irish Republican Army, the Palestinian Arab and the Zionist Jew, the Eastern Orthodox Serb and the Catholic Croat, the Eastern mystic and the Western rationalist. To demand consensus amid such profound differences is to court resignation and cynicism. Each perspective is shaped within a hermeneutical circle of agreed-upon beliefs and practices, and each perspective is bounded by another hermeneutical circle exterior to it. There are no trade routes from the circulating beliefs and practices in the one economy to another. Any opening of routes from one circle to another will require a diagonal extending across the multiple circles of interpretation, a transversal communicative performance that seeks an understanding of that which is other without aspiring to a coincidence of perspectives. The other understood transversely is the other understood *in spite of* differing commitments and points of view. Transversal communication is bent neither toward a solid agreement with the other nor toward a displacement of the other.

The rhetoric of transversal communication labors within the space between the rhetor and the interlocutor, but it does not seek to fill this space by establishing a point of identity through conversion or coercion, nor does it strive to annihilate the space of the other. The proper end of the rhetoric of transversal communication is convergence without coincidence, conjuncture without identity; it exhibits a self-understanding that works with an understanding of the other, geared to possible agenda for collaboration in spite of difference. Amid the heterogeneity of discursive and institutional practices, it acknowledges the other as a coinhabitant of a common earth. It is thus that transversal communication can split the difference between consensus and dissensus. The diagonal of transversality ruptures the closure of the hermeneutical circle as it keeps the triangulation of rhetoric from subjugation to an absolute exteriority.

NOTES

1 Charles Taylor, *Philosophy and the Human Sciences: Philosophical Papers* (Cambridge: Cambridge University Press, 1985), 18.

2 Martin Heidegger, *Being and Time,* trans. John Macquarrie and Edward Robinson (New York: Harper and Row, 1962), 195.

3 See particularly Hans-Georg Gadamer, "The Universality of the Hermeneutical Problem," in Gadamer, *Philosophical Hermeneutics,* trans. David E. Linge (Berkeley: University of California Press, 1976), 3–17.

4 For an extensive critical discussion of the *aporias* of epistemological foundationalism, see Richard Rorty, *Philosophy and the Mirror of Nature* (Princeton: Princeton University Press, 1979), esp. chap. 7, "From Epistemology to Hermeneutics," 315–56.

5 See Calvin O. Schrag, *Communicative Praxis and the Space of Subjectivity* (Bloomington: Indiana University Press, 1986), esp. parts I and II.

6 Heidegger, *Being and Time,* 178.

7 Gadamer, "Rhetoric, Hermeneutics, and Ideology-Critique," in *Philosophical Hermeneutics,* 25. See Chapter 15, this volume.

8 Paul Ricoeur, "Rhetoric—Poetics—Hermeneutics," in *From Metaphysics to Rhetoric,* ed. Michel Meyer (Dordrecht: Kluwer, 1989), 149. See Chapter 2, this volume.

9 For an extended discussion of the figuration of the triangle in rhetoric and communication, see James L. Kinneavy, *A Theory of Discourse* (New York: Norton, 1971).

10 Burke uses the designator *administrative rhetoric* to describe a rhetoric that illustrates a dynamics of persuasion not confined to discursive forms. His example is
Theodore Roosevelt sending the United States fleet to Germany on a "goodwill mission"—ostensibly a friendly visit but more specifically an unequivocal message
warning the German emperor of Roosevelt's military buildup. See Kenneth Burke,
Language as Symbolic Action (Berkeley: University of California Press, 1968), 301.

11 For a discussion of the role of invention in rhetoric, see Michael J. Hyde and Craig
R. Smith, "Aristotle and Heidegger on Emotion and Rhetoric: Questions of Time
and Space," in *The Critical Turn: Rhetoric and Philosophy in Postmodern Discourse,* ed. Ian Angus and Lenore Langsdorf (Carbondale: Southern Illinois University Press, 1993), 68–99.

12 Hans Blumenberg, "An Anthropological Approach to the Contemporary Significance of Rhetoric," trans. Robert M. Wallace, in *After Philosophy: End or Transformation?* ed. Kenneth Baynes, James Bohman, and Thomas McCarthy (Cambridge: MIT Press, 1987), 452.

13 J. Robert Cox, "Cultural Memory and the Public Moral Argument," The Van Zelst
Lecture in Communication (Evanston, Ill.: Northwestern University School of
Speech, 1987), 10. Cox's vocabulary of "dialectic of repetition and disavowal" is informed by Heidegger's use of *Wiederholung* and *Widerruf* in working out the dynamics of historical understanding. Cox has shown that these two moments are operative in the dynamics of the rhetorical art.

14 Jean-François Lyotard, *The Differend: Phrases in Dispute,* trans. George Van Den
Abbeele (Minneapolis: University of Minnesota Press, 1988), 26.

15 "As distinguished from a litigation, a differend [*différend*] would be a case of conflict
between (at least) two parties, that cannot be equitably resolved for lack of a rule of
judgment applicable to both arguments" (Lyotard, *Differend,* xi).

16 Jean-François Lyotard, *The Postmodern Condition: A Report on Knowledge,* trans.
Geoff Bennington and Brian Massumi (Minneapolis: University of Minnesota
Press, 1984), 66.

17 Jean-Paul Sartre, *The Transcendence of the Ego: An Existentialist Theory of Consciousness,* trans. Forrest Williams and Robert Kirkpatrick (New York: Noonday
Press, 1957), 39. The grammar of transversality has also received intermittent usage
in the French scene of postmodern thought, in particular, by Gilles Deleuze and
Félix Guattari. For a sustained discussion of the uses of transversality in postmodern philosophy as well as of the applicability of the concept for understanding the
dynamics of reason in communicative praxis as an interplay of discourse and action,
see Calvin O. Schrag, *The Resources of Rationality: A Response to the Postmodern
Challenge* (Bloomington: Indiana University Press, 1992), esp. chap. 6, "Transversal Rationality," 148–79.

Part II

Inventions and Applications

7

Humanism and the
Resistance to Theory

Victoria Kahn

I am not bound, said the Count, to teach you how to acquire grace or anything else, but
only to show you what a perfect courtier ought to be.
—Castiglione, *Il Cortegiano*

In a seminal 1982 article Paul de Man claimed that the resistance to theory on
the part of conservative literary historians and critics is simply the "displaced
symptom" of a resistance to theory at the heart of theory itself.[1] Theory in this
second sense is defined as metalanguage that takes as its object the rhetorical
or tropological dimension of language which inevitably interferes with the
cognitive or semantic functions of grammar and logic. Whereas we ordinarily
identify theory with a comprehensive system of axioms and principles of deductive reasoning or with a Kantian epistemological critique of the conditions
of the possibility of knowledge, theory in de Man's sense must be equated with
a certain conception of rhetoric in which the privileged trope is irony, defined
as the indeterminacy or the undecidability of meaning. When we recall with
de Man that the humanities have traditionally been defined in terms of the
trivium of grammar, rhetoric, and logic (dialectic), the conservative resistance

to theory can be seen as a resistance to the way rhetoric puts in question the epistemological stability of language and, with language, the trivium itself.

De Man's definition of theory is by his own admission a historical one (post-1960). But it is also critical of traditional literary history insofar as the latter takes for granted the possibility of understanding, which the conflict between the rhetorical and grammatical/logical modes of language undermines. Thus, the problem of theory and its resistance is not fixed to any one historical period, according to de Man, but is relevant to all periods—that is to say, to the problem of periodization itself.

Interestingly, this double meditation on history is reflected in the history of de Man's article itself, which, de Man tells us, grew out of a request from the Modern Language Association for an overview of contemporary trends in literary criticism. The commissioned article was never published. "The Resistance to Theory" thus refers both to the MLA's resistance to de Man's article and to the original article, which, in arguing against the *intelligibility* of theory, proved to be singularly incompatible with the pedagogical aims of the MLA. This publishing nonevent points to contemporary debates about the relation of theory to pedagogy: debates about the desirability, even the possibility, of "doing theory" and of teaching theory in the graduate curriculum. But in problematizing the notion of literary history by reference to the trivium, and specifically to rhetoric, de Man's article also allows us to see its relevance for the study of the literature of earlier periods—in particular, the pedagogical imperative of Renaissance humanism. Whether or not we finally accept the deconstructive notion of theory that de Man presents, the tension he identifies at the heart of theory can serve as a useful topic of invention with respect to the humanist conventions of reading and interpretation. For, as we shall see, humanism can be defined in the first instance as a rhetorical practice that resists theory conceived of as an epistemological project; but this first resistance is part of a more complicated, pedagogically motivated resistance to theory conceived of as undecidability. Finally, a survey of some of the humanist texts that exemplify these resistances can help us in turn to see the relevance of sixteenth-century debates on method to the current critical scene.

THEORY AND PRACTICE

To those familiar with the work of Bernard Weinberg and Baxter Hathaway, the identification of Renaissance humanism with a resistance to theory must at first glance seem dubious.[2] For if this identification is correct, what are we to make of the many sixteenth-century "trattati di poetica e retorica," the treatises on imitation and commentaries on Aristotle's *Poetics,* the proposed reform of dialectic in the work of Valla and Agricola, the codification of rhetorical and logical forms of argument in English handbooks? In all these works there is a discourse of a certain generality that we associate with theory.

On the other hand, Paul Oskar Kristeller, one of the most eminent scholars of the Renaissance, has insisted that while the humanists shared a general interest in moral philosophy, humanism is not properly thought of as a philosophical or theoretical movement. Humanist works, he observes, "often seem to lack not only originality, but also coherence, method, and substance, and if we try to sum up these arguments and conclusions, leaving aside citations, examples, and commonplaces, literary ornaments and digressions, we are frequently left with nearly empty hands. Thus I have not been convinced by the attempts to interpret these humanistic treatises as contributions to speculative thought."[3] Are these two perspectives opposed? Or is there something about Weinberg's and Hathaway's Age of Criticism that is resistant to theory in Kristeller's sense?

In attempting to answer this question, a first step might be to historicize our original notion of theory as speculative thought and to ask whether the humanists intended to make a contribution to this realm of inquiry. To the extent that theory is identified with scholasticism, the answer must be no. For again and again, the humanists attack the scholastics for trying to formulate necessary and universal propositions about God's existence and the structure of his creation. Such speculation, according to the humanists, is both illegitimate and useless: illegitimate because human reason cannot know the divine, and useless because even if we were to have contemplative knowledge, such abstractions would not help us direct our earthly civic affairs.[4]

This double complaint is reflected in the humanist critique of scholastic discourse, both for its pretensions to reflect adequately the structure of the cosmos[5] and for its neglect of the rhetorical, that is, affective and communicative dimension of language, which is essential to human society and civic life.[6] These complaints, in other words, are directed not simply against the ignorance of the norms and elegantiae of classical Latin but against the important human consequences of such ignorance. The reified ontological vocabulary of scholasticism cannot, by definition, allow for a flexible and pragmatic response to the demands of human society. Yet as Valla argues forcefully in his *Dialecticae disputationes*, a logic or dialectic that is to be useful must be referred to the social, linguistic criterion of usage, or *consuetudo*.[7] Furthermore, to the extent that logic is referred to usage, it becomes identical with those forms of argument that derive from or aim at producing consensus: rhetorical syllogisms, commonplaces, arguments from probability or opinion. Logic, in short, becomes topical and takes as its aim persuasion or conviction rather than apodictic certainty. The humanist resistance to theory is thus in the first instance a resistance to scholastic logic.

But if as a result of the humanist reform of dialectic, rhetoric takes the place of logic as the most important member of the trivium, this does not mean that the humanists would share de Man's conclusion that the trivium has now become epistemologically unstable. For if theory is identified with the epistemological unreliability or undecidability of rhetorical language, then the humanists wish both to acknowledge this potential instability and to resist it. This second resistance takes the form of the claim that if theoretical cognition is unfounded and useless, another kind of knowledge is both possible and desirable: the practical knowledge of human affairs, of social and linguistic praxis. The humanists call this kind of knowledge *phronesis,* or prudence, thereby identifying it with the Aristotelian faculty of practical reason or judgment in matters that require deliberation and choice.[8]

Aristotle opposes prudence on the one hand to *theoria,* or speculation, and on the other to *techne,* or productive knowledge. Like *theoria,* prudence is an intellectual virtue, but whereas theory includes the intelligence of first causes and the necessary and universal knowledge of their consequences (*NE,* 1139a 25; 1139b 15; *Posterior Analytics,* 1.71b 9–72b 4), prudence is concerned with action within the realm of contingent human affairs. These affairs can never be the object of scientific certainty, only of practical deliberation. In this, prudence draws near to *techne.* But while the aim of technical knowledge is to produce an artifact, prudence has no other aim than itself: "In matters of action, the principles or initiating motives are the ends at which our actions are aimed" (*NE,* 1140b 15). Thus, Aristotle concludes, prudence "is not a pure science because matters of action admit of being other than they are, and it is not an applied science or art, because action and production are generically different" (*NE,* 1140b). To secure its own realm of action, then, prudence must resist being assimilated to the claims of *theoria* on the one side and those of *techne* on the other.

Although the humanists adopted the Aristotelian definition of prudence, they also followed Cicero in arguing that the prudent man is one who knows how to use the rhetorical skills of persuasion to achieve his practical ends. Yet although the orator or prudent man must be able to argue on both sides of a question, he will in any particular case choose one side or the other. The further assumption, however, is that by the exchange of opinions—by argument *in utramque partem* between individuals—we can arrive at a socially useful, pragmatic truth. Thus, although Cicero recognized that argument *in utramque partem* could take the form of irony if both sides or points of view were maintained at the same time, for the early humanists the potential undecidability of irony was held in check by social constraints. Giovanni Pontano, for example, sees Socrates' ironic indirection not as an instance of the rhetoric that puts in question the possibility of meaning and action but rather as a rhetorical invitation to his audience to assume an attitude of ethical moderation. But even more significant, he turns irony into the chief social grace or decorum by identifying it with *urbanitas*.[9] In a move that is characteristic of the humanists as a whole, the epistemological threat of skepticism is contained by the practice of social consensus.

THEORY AND EXAMPLES

Because the realm of practice and choice is also for Cicero and the humanists the realm of rhetoric, the faculty of prudence finds its rhetorical equivalent in the rule of decorum.[10] This rule does not function as a philosophical axiom or as the major premise of a syllogism; it does not subsume particulars or logically entail a necessary and universal conclusion. The rule of decorum cannot be theorized because it is always already the application of the rule. Thus George Puttenham writes in the *Arte of Poesie:* "This decencie is therfore the line and levell for al good makers to do their busines by. But herein resteth the difficultie, to know what this good grace is, and wherein it consisteth. . . . The case then standing that discretion must chiefly guide all those businesse, since there be sundry sortes of discretion all unlike, even as there be men of action or art, I see no way so fit to enable a man truly to estimate of [decencie] as example."[11]

Puttenham's recourse to examples in his discussion of decorum is instructive. Just as prudence or decorum cannot be defined once and for all in the form of "scholastical precepts" (271) but must instead be *instanced* in particular examples, so the author who wishes to educate the reader's judgment so as to make that judgment more prudent or decorous must also make use of examples. Puttenham's reflection on the resistance of decorum to theorizing, and the consequent necessity of examples, thus leads us to the center of the humanist pedagogical program: the humanist resistance to scholastic theory (which is at the same time a resistance to the epistemological threat irony may pose to ethics) takes the form of a practice of examples or of an exemplary practice, on the assumption that such examples will involve the reader in a practice of interpretation that is essential for the active life.

The authorial recourse to examples presupposes a faculty of imitation (whether of nature or of prior texts). As Roger Ascham writes in *The Scholemaster,* "Imitation is a faculty to express lively and perfectly that example which ye go about to follow."[12] But such exemplary texts also require an imitative response on the part of the reader. Accordingly, Ascham imagines a "very profitable book" on imitation, "containing a certain few fit precepts unto the which should be gathered and applied plenty of examples out of the choiceth authors of both the tongues. This work would stand rather in good diligence for gathering and right judgement for the applying of those examples than any great learning or utterance at all" (127). Contrary to the commonplace books, which are assembled by "common porters, carriers, and bringers of matter and stuff together" (128), and which "do not teach you *how it is done*" (129; my italics),[13] Ascham's examples would illustrate an activity of judgment by the fact of their having been selected and presented in a certain order (130). Yet as an example of such exemplary practice he refers the reader to Erasmus's *Chiliades, Apothegmata,* and *Similiae,* texts that impress us less by their order than by their disorderliness. What, then, is the force of these examples?

That contemporary readers were struck and disturbed by the disorder of Erasmus's works is apparent in sixteenth-century editions of these texts. Conrad Lycosthenes, for example, in his 1557 edition of the *Parabolae sive similiae* classifies Erasmus's similitudes according to theme in order to make the book easier to use. Erasmus himself, however, was careful to insist on the quite different principle of selection that had gone into this work—the "colligendi explicandique laborem" that distinguished his text from ordinary commonplace books.[14] His aim was not to present all the similitudes he could gather in a logical or thematic order but to give the reader a taste (*gustus*) of these and thus inspire him to seek them in further reading.[15]

Erasmus's *De copia* also deliberately refuses the systematic order Lycosthenes and his readers demanded. But again, this refusal cannot be explained by authorial laziness or carelessness. Rather, it is inseparable from Erasmus's sense that, as Terence Cave has argued, *copia* is less a repertoire of technical rules for amplification than a generative principle or *practice*. Not surprisingly, then, Erasmus introduces a distinction within the notion of *copia* (*copia* of words versus copia of things) only to deprive it of any *theoretical* significance: "Although these [*copia* of words and *copia* of things] can be observed anywhere, so closely combined that you cannot tell them apart at all easily, so much does one serve the other, so that they might seem to be distinct only in theory [*praeceptis*], rather than in fact and in use [*re atque usu*], nevertheless, for the purpose of teaching, we shall make the distinction in such a way that we cannot deservedly be condemned for hair splitting in distinguishing, nor, on the other hand, for negligence."[16] The rest of the work bears out these remarks, for book 2, on the *copia rerum,* concerns examples of linguistic rather than non- or prelinguistic amplification. Furthermore, there is no evident order to Erasmus's examples. Finally, Erasmus's aim, as in the *Parabolae,* is not for the reader to memorize his examples but for him to understand the principle, or *ratio,* informing them. This is particularly obvious in Erasmus's discussion of the *ratio colligendi exempla.* Taking the example of Socrates' death and drawing a variety of morals from it, Erasmus shows us how this and all other examples can be used *in utramque partem (LB* l. 102 AC). Erasmus's work, then, deliberately eschews logic not to appear more perfectly aesthetic but to act more effectively upon the reader, to be more conducive to practice. To read these texts, as Ascham argues, is to *use* them (131). Only through use do they give rise to "right and deep judgement in all kinds of learning" (128).[17]

If Erasmus's pedagogical works are eclectic or chaotic in appearance, other exemplary Renaissance texts seem self-contradictory as well. And this is true not only of an obvious paradoxical encomium like Erasmus's *Encomium Moriae.* As many critics have remarked, the examples ostensibly adduced to illustrate general theoretical claims in, for example, Sidney's *Apology,* Machiavelli's *Il Principe,* or Montaigne's *Essais,* do not simply "fail" to illustrate general precepts but, in failing, succeed in questioning their subordinate status as mere illustrations of theory.[18] Examples in humanist and humanist-influenced texts are resistant to theory because they call for judgment and use rather than naive or slavish imitation. As Karlheinz Stierle has argued, they are problematizing rather than illustrative or problem solving.[19] Like the pragmatic order of Erasmus's texts, they invite us not to imitate or avoid single examples of virtue or vice but to imitate the example of the author's discretion as embodied in the rhetorical practice of the text as a whole. But as the case of Lycosthenes suggests, these self-contradictory texts also pose special problems for their readers. The example of Castiglione's *Il Cortegiano* can serve to illustrate my point.

If the humanists' pragmatic and problematizing examples are responsible for the self-contradictory appearance of many Renaissance texts, they also give rise to the temptation to theorize this (in)coherence. As an editor faced with a compendium of exempla, Lycosthenes could choose to reorganize his text thematically. The problem is somewhat different for the interpreter of an exemplary narrative. Here at least two options are open: one can either reduce the examples to mere ornament and thus ignore them or attempt to bring some kind of order to the examples by privileging one sort over another. An instance of the former is Kristeller's remark cited at the beginning of this chapter. To read *Il Cortegiano* from Kristeller's perspective would be to "leave aside" the text in its entirety. An instance of the latter is Eduardo Saccone's interpretation of *Il Cortegiano;* because Saccone actually reads Castiglione's examples, it will be instructive to look more closely at his argument.[20] As we shall see, Saccone's reading is important both because he points to a significant problem of interpretation in Castiglione's work—the incompatibility of the examples of the courtier's graceful behavior, or *sprezzatura*—and because his own interpretation exemplifies a resistance to that incoherence, a resistance, as de Man's article suggests, that a certain conception of theory shares with the pedagogical imperative. (I shall return to the problematic pedagogy of these incompatible examples at the end of this chapter.)

As Saccone and others have argued, *sprezzatura* is not a quality but an ability; it cannot be simply defined, it must be enacted. Thus Canossa's reply to Gonzaga's request for a definition: "I am not bound to teach you how to acquire grace or anything else, but only to show you what a perfect courtier ought to be," is itself an example of the *sprezzatura* for which there can be no pedagogical precept or abstract rule. It is appropriate, then, that readers of *Il Cortegiano* should focus on the examples of *sprezzatura* in their attempt to understand this paradoxical disdainful grace, this art that conceals art.

As dissimulation or artfulness, *sprezzatura,* like irony, is inherently ambiguous and equivocal. This ambiguity necessarily introduces the question of the audience, for to be successful the courtier must conceal his artfulness, but for it to be appreciated as *sprezzatura,* his concealment must be perceived. *Sprezzatura,* then, seems to presuppose, Saccone argues, a double audience. Yet when we turn to the examples of this ability, we see that they are not easily reconcilable.

In one case we are presented with an orator who conceals his art lest the people should "fear that they could be duped by it" (43–44). In another case, we are shown a courtier who disguises himself as a person of low birth at a country festival, thereby showing "a certain *sprezzatura* in what does not matter: all of which adds much charm . . . because the bystanders immediately take in what meets the eye at first glance; whereupon, realizing that here there is much more than was promised by the costume, they are delighted and amused" (103). The example of the orator presupposes a double audience: the naive auditors who perceive only the artlessness of the orator's performance and those in the know, who admire the artfulness (483). But in the second example, according to Saccone, there is only a single audience, and the ambiguity of a single performance is resolved temporally in the gradual realization that the lowly individual is really a courtier. This second example is allegorical, not ironic, and thus not a true illustration of *sprezzatura*. And yet in his own reading of the example of the orator Saccone has already reduced irony to univocality, for the division of the audience actually means that neither experiences *sprezzatura* as irony: rather, one auditor perceives it as art and the other as nature. In short, having articulated the principle of the resistance to theory par excellence—that is, the principle of irony (whether humanist or de Manian), Saccone cannot resist the temptation to theorize that resistance. At the same time, however, he allows us to see that the irreconcilability of Castiglione's examples may itself be the best example of the irony of *sprezzatura,* the best example of a practice of decorum for which there can be no theoretical rule.

THEORY AND METHOD

Castiglione's *Il Cortegiano* and Erasmus's pedagogical works were received in England as the arts or handbooks that the latter, at least, were intended to be. But the precise nature of this reception also points to a shift within the humanist pedagogical tradition: specifically, to the efflorescence around the mid-sixteenth century of debates concerning the status of method in humanist discourse. These debates signal one of the ways the resistance to the humanist resistance to theory begins to make itself felt.[21]

The humanists' interest in pedagogy, in ever-more efficient ways or methods of conveying knowledge to their students, led to an examination of a number of classical texts on method (e.g., Socrates' remarks in the *Phaedrus,* Aristotle's *Posterior Analytics,* and Galen's *Ars parva*), which the humanists then interpreted in terms of their own rhetorical preoccupation with invention or the finding of arguments.[22] In the beginning of the sixteenth century, then, while the Greek term *methodus* had no precise philosophical meaning, the humanists tended to identify it with the general pursuit and teaching of knowledge, that is, with the pragmatic arts of communication as both the means and ends of instruction. Method was technical only in the general sense that it involved the knowledge of the appropriate means to achieve a particular end. Furthermore, contrary to the classical notion of *techne,* humanist method gradually came to suggest orderliness, speed, and efficiency.[23] Thus Erasmus writes a *Ratio seu methodus compendio ad veram theologiam perveniendi* (1520), which provides the reader with the essential tenets of his Christian humanism but which could hardly be said to have as its aim the reduction of religion to an art in the classical sense.[24]

Also in the sixteenth century, and partly in opposition to the humanist conception of method, another, more scientific conception of method grew up.[25] This notion was modeled on Aristotle's demonstrative or apodictic logic rather than on rhetoric, and it was concerned with, in Hobbes's words, "the knowledge of [logical] consequences."[26]

In one sense, this scientific conception of method departs even more than the humanist conception from the Aristotelian notion of *techne.* But as a logic that permits of, but is not identical with, technical application, it also points up the structural homology between the classical notions of *techne* and theory: the fact that in both cases abstract principles take (epistemological) precedence over practice or the application of such principles.[27] Such a conception of method finds its apotheosis in Descartes, who opposes the apodictic certainty guaranteed by "la vraie méthode" to persuasion "par l'exemple et par la coustume"[28] and who argues that the true model of philosophical method is mathematical reasoning.

This conflict between two notions of method is instructive with regard to the humanist pedagogical program. Clearly, some degree of method appealed to the humanists' desire for educational reform, but the precise nature and aims of that reform necessitated an ambivalence about method as well. For when method is equated with logic or with *techne*, practical deliberation is perforce excluded. The attempt to formalize or systematize the judgment of decorum is thus bound to fail, since it will by definition usurp the function of decorous or prudential judgment. That the humanists were aware of this danger is apparent in Ascham's remarks in *The Scholemaster*:

> Indeed, books of commonplaces be very necessary to induce a man into an orderly general knowledge, how to refer orderly all that he readeth *ad certa rerum capita* and not wander in study. And to that end did Petrus Lombardus the Master of Sentences and Philip Melanchthon in our days write two notable books of commonplaces.
>
> But to dwell in *epitomes* and books of *commonplaces,* and not to bind himself daily by orderly study to read with all diligence principally the best doctors, and so to learn to make true differences betwixt the authority of the one and the counsel of the other, maketh so many seeming and sunburnt ministers as we have.[29]

Yet when we turn to the English logic and rhetoric handbooks of Ascham's day, many of them seem concerned precisely with conflating authority and counsel: with providing the student who does not "read" in Ascham's sense with a practical manual of style and argument.

As we see when we compare Puttenham's *Arte of English Poesie* with Leonard Cox's *Rhetoric,* or Petrus Ramus's and Abraham Fraunce's logics, one reason for the great number of such handbooks is the growth of the middle class and the consequent demand for the democratization of learning in the form of easily accessible techniques. In addressing courtiers, then, Puttenham's *Arte* only *seems* to be atypical of the late sixteenth-century handbooks, and his own remarks suggest why. The true courtier, he writes, does not need precepts because he is already in the know; that's how he knows he's a courtier (282, 295). Precisely this paradox points up the ambivalent function of the courtesy books. On the one hand, Puttenham's humanistic refusal of theory could be interpreted as an aristocratic gesture, a gesture that, by denying the effort we associate with the *acquisition* of skills, also refuses to make learning accessible to the "common people."[30]

Thus Frank Whigham has argued that "the first employment of courtesy literature was the repression of . . . [social] mobility" (18). On the other hand, as Whigham goes on to point out, in codifying and thus making available the rules and signs of courtesy, such literature also "aroused" and, I would add, educated the "ambition" (20) of the nonaristocratic. In the end, Puttenham's aim may not have been so far from that of Roland MacIlmaine, the English translator of Ramus's *Logike,* who complains of "the envious, that thinkethe it not decent to wryte any liberall arte in the vulgar tongue" (8)[31] and who argues that the "ready and easy way" of Ramus's single method will make logical skill available to all. In a similar vein, Fraunce inquires in the preface to *The Lawiers Logike* (1588), "Coblers bee men, why therefore not Logicians? and Carters have reason, why therefore not Logike? *Bonum, quò communius, co melius.*"[32] Given the widespread popular interest in method and precepts, it is not surprising that Ramus's reform of logic and rhetoric found a receptive audience in England.

Ramus's concern with method is in one sense the culmination of humanist pedagogy, for, as Walter Ong has shown, theory in Ramus's system is identified with the pedagogical content or usefulness of theory. Pedagogy, in other words, is not simply the means of instruction: it is the subject matter as well.[33] But Ramism also marks the death of humanism, for although the Ramist reform of the arts curriculum seems to derive in part from the humanist interest in method, it actually results in the subordination of invention and disposition to logic, as well as the reduction of rhetoric to elocution, now conceived of, in the best of all possible worlds, as inessential.

Thomas Sloan has suggested that Ramus's insistence on logic as the only legitimate form of address betrays an anxiety about the power of rhetoric to appeal to the passions. But the elimination of *logos* and *pathos* from rhetoric was not the only consequence of Ramus's reform. For the "one and only method" also does away with judgment, that is, with *reading* in Ascham's sense of the word. If there is only one method, there can be no choice, no practical deliberation. If all realms of inquiry are to be methodized, then it is no longer prudence but *techne* that is the standard and measure of all things. Finally, as Ong has argued, in such a world there can be no dialogue or debate, no sense of decorum as the infinity of possible methods.[34]

Not surprisingly, with this technical model of judgment comes a reevaluation of the status of the example. Illustrative examples are now, as they later were for Kant, superfluous; the use of examples as a form of logical argument is allowed, in which case they no longer, as far as Ramus is concerned, have the status of illustrations. Accordingly, Ramus's textbook on geometry provides the student with theorems but no examples; and Ramus's *Logike* reduces examples (including those from poetry) to instances or forms of logic.[35]

When we return to the English rhetorical handbooks, we can see that, like Ramus's *Logike,* these treatises also betray an anxiety about the use of figurative language—a use that requires practical judgment or discretion and that may involve an appeal to the passions. Peacham's *Garden of Eloquence,* for example, associates the control of the potential waywardness of figurative language with the maintenance of the social hierarchy. The fanatical—from our point of view—codification of tropes and figures in this work includes in every discussion of a particular figure a "caution" against the abuse of that figure. It is instructive to compare Castiglione's ironic treatment of *sprezzatura* or Pontano's remarks on *urbanitas* with Henry Peacham's sober advice concerning irony: "It ought to be forescene, that this figure is not to be used without some urgent cause, or to iest without some fit occasion, nor often used, lest he that useth it be either taken for a common mocker, or else for such a one, as men can not tell how to understand him, or when to beleeve him. Neither is it a meete forme of speech for every sort of people to use, especially of the inferior toward the supperior, to whom by some reason he oweth dutie, for it is against the rule of modestie and good manners, either to deride his better, or to iest with him in this forme and maner."[36]

Even Puttenham, whose *Arte of English Poesie* places rhetorical figures within the larger context of a general theory of poetry, shares Peacham's nervousness about the social and political consequences of rhetoric. Though he does not provide us with a caution against the misuse of every figure, he does define figurative language in general as an abuse or trespass of literal language. For this reason, he goes on to tell us, "the grave judges *Areopagites* . . . [forbade] all manner of figurative speaches to be used before them in their consistorie of Justice, as meere illusions to the minde, and wresters of upright judgement [of the judge]" (166). Furthermore, he remarks that linguistic ambiguity has been known to lead to rebellion, a complaint that will later be taken up by Jonson and Hobbes.[37] But because poets are pleaders rather than judges, their abuses do not deceive; instead they "dispose the hearers to mirth and solace" (167).[38] And yet, even Puttenham feels obliged to give some warning against the vices of speech (256–67), "because we seem to promise an art [in writing this treatise] . . . and to th' end [that] we may not be carped at by these methodicall men" (257). It is significant, in this light, that although Puttenham approves of artifice throughout his work (see 150), in the end he distinguishes between "method" as that which aids nature, and "imitation" as an artifice that is contrary to nature.[39] Although he does not develop this notion of method, his brief discussion suggests affinities with Ramus's method as the systematization of *natural* reason.

In terms of the preceding argument for the humanist resistance to theory, then, these English handbooks of rhetoric and logic represent a kind of midway point between the early humanists' emphasis on practice—specifically on a variety of rhetorical practices that from a logical point of view seem inconsistent or contradictory—and a subsequent disenchantment with humanism, a dissatisfaction that takes the form in the seventeenth century of a return to logic divorced from rhetoric and, more important, to a conception of theory as scientific demonstration based on the model of mathematical reasoning. To the extent that these handbooks aim to present the reader with a technique, they point to an ambivalence at the center of the humanist pedagogical project, an ambivalence caused by the resistance of prudence or practical reason to the classical notions of *theoria* and *techne*. Such handbooks both answer to and undermine the early humanists' concern with method.

THE RESISTANCE TO HUMANISM'S RESISTANCE TO THEORY

It is one of the ironies of the reception of the humanist resistance to theory that this resistance was itself perceived as too theoretical. Machiavelli's remarks in chapter 15 of *Il Principe* are probably the most famous example of this complaint: "Since I intend to write something useful to an understanding reader, it seemed better to go after the real truth [*verità effettuale*] of the matter than to repeat what people have imagined. A great many men have imagined states and princedoms such as nobody ever saw or knew in the real world, for there's such a difference between the way we really live and the way we ought to live that the man who neglects the real to study the ideal will learn how to accomplish his ruin, not his salvation."[40] But if Machiavelli perceives his humanist predecessors as too idealistic and prescriptive, other critics of humanism objected that humanism was not theoretical, by which they meant logical, enough. Such a view finds its first powerful exponent in Bacon, by whom even method—whether rhetorically or Ramistically conceived—is found wanting.

Bacon's critical revision of the humanists' rhetorical conception of method is apparent in his use of humanist terminology against itself. He divides his program for the advancement of learning according to the traditional rhetorical categories, but in doing so, he extends the meanings of these terms far beyond the realm of rhetoric: "The *Arts intellectual* are four in number; divided according to the ends whereunto they are referred: for man's labour is to *in-*

vent that which is sought or propounded; or to *judge* that which is invented; or to *retain* that which is judged; or to *deliver over* that which is retained. So as the art must be Four: *Art of Inquiry* or *Invention: Art of Examination* or *Judgment: Art of Custody* or *Memory:* and *Art of Elocution* or *Tradition*."[41] Thus, for example, invention retains its rhetorical definition as the finding of arguments, but it acquires the new and more important meaning of the finding of arts (127): "Neither is the method or the nature of the traditional material only to the *use* of knowledge, but likewise to the progression of knowledge" (140; cited in Howell, 370). Elocution, on the other hand, is no longer identified with figurative language but rather with method as the communication of one's knowledge.

Yet while Bacon retains the Ramist emphasis on logic as the "sole custodian of method in communication" (Howell, 374), he objects to the *premature* methodizing of Ramus's single way (32). In addition to a magisterial method of communication that hands down the conclusions of one's research, it is necessary to devise a "probative" method (140), that is, one that conveys knowledge in the order in which things were discovered and thereby incites to further learning.

Bacon's attempt to formulate a method that is more pedagogically effective than that of Ramus depends on the reintroduction of the division between knowledge and pedagogy that Ramus had done much to close. Similarly, Bacon's refusal of the traditional sixteenth-century distinction between theoretical and practical knowledge appears at first glance to be part of the humanist insistence on the unity of the active and contemplative lives (35).[42] But whereas prudence or praxis is the model of cognition for early humanists, Bacon subordinates action to theoretical speculation and thus reduces practical reason to technology, that is, to the productive knowledge of *techne*. As Bacon writes in the *Novum Organum* (Aphorisms, 3): "Human knowledge and human power meet in one; for where the cause is not known the effect cannot be produced. Nature to be commanded must be obeyed; and that which in contemplation is as the cause is in operation as the rule."[43] That later readers perceived Bacon's return to theory—his resistance to practice in the humanist sense—is apparent in Kant's acknowledgment of Bacon and his followers in the epigraph and the second preface to the *Critique of Pure Reason:* "They learned that reason has insight only into that which it produces after a plan of its own, and that it must not allow itself to be kept, as it were, in nature's leading strings, but must itself strew the way with principles of judgement based upon fixed laws, constraining nature to give answer to questions of reason's own determining" (B xiii). Clearly, this monological constraint of nature is incompatible with the early humanists' resistance to theory, their insistence on intersubjective dialogue or rhetoric *in utramque partem* as the model of human cognition and action.

THEORY AND PEDAGOGY

With the late twentieth-century revival of interest in rhetoric, the questions of method and of the relation of theory to practice—specifically the practice of interpretation—are once again at the center of literary studies. If we now return to *Il Cortegiano*, we can see how the interpretive problem posed by *sprezzatura* provides us with an allegory of contemporary critical debate. Take *sprezzatura* as a figure for the resistance to theory in de Man's double sense. On the one hand, Gonzaga's refusal to give precepts represents the conservative and aristocratic disdain for theory: the refusal, say, of the academic establishment to examine its own critical presuppositions. (*Sprezzatura*, as Castiglione tells us, is never disinterested.) On the other hand, *sprezzatura* can be a figure for the irony of a de Man, who refuses the pedagogical imperative because of its incompatibility with the resistance or irony at the heart of theory itself. The first position might be described as a theory that hides a theory (the orator's New Criticism); the second as a theory that undoes theory (the disguised courtier's deconstruction). Although the representatives of these two positions seem to be opposed, their shared identity as courtiers points to a fundamental similarity: a concern with a formalist analysis that obscures or refuses to name its political and ideological interests. Finally, in both cases, though for different reasons, literature is "untainted by history."[44]

But there are other positions in the court of criticism as well. While de Man equates one kind of theory with method, Jonathan Culler opposes the two, claiming that theory offers a general account of literature ("its forms, its components, their relations"), whereas method aims to resolve local problems of interpretation.[45] This distinction derives from Culler's desire to shift the focus of literary studies from specific acts of interpretation to the study of the rules and conventions governing all interpretation. Not surprisingly, such a view of theory, unlike de Man's, is presented as compatible with the pedagogical imperative and thus, apparently, with method in the humanist sense. Culler, then, is like Ottaviano, who, in book 4 of *Il Cortegiano*, provides *sprezzatura* with a humanistic defense against the charges of self-interested deceit on the one hand, and mere aesthetic formalism on the other, by casting the prince as a governor and the courtier as a pedagogue. As Cesare Gonzaga complains, "Truly, signor Ottaviano, one cannot say that your precepts are not good and useful; nevertheless, I should think that if you were to fashion your prince accordingly, you would rather deserve the name of a good schoolmaster than of a good Courtier" (319). Teaching theory on the graduate level, Culler argues, will allow the student to engage in interdisciplinary studies and thus provide a practical defense of the continuing relevance of the trivium within the university curriculum as a whole.

Culler's portrayal of the role of theory in responding to the economic pressures of the job market, and to the declining status of the humanities, reflects both our humanist desire to make the liberal arts useful and relevant and our post-humanist ambivalence about practice, our turn toward a technical conception of pedagogy. Departments of literature no longer train their students in philology because there is no demand for such learning. Universal education has led to a catholic, generalizing approach to the liberal arts, one that in turn gives rise to the demand for easily accessible techniques of reading and interpretation. One form this Ramist technology of the liberal arts may take is the "ready and easy way" (or version) of theory, even of a theory of undecidability or indeterminacy. In an article on the history of practical criticism, Geoffrey Hartman offers the humanist response to the scientific or technological model of literary theory: "To methodize indeterminacy would be to forget the reason for the concept."[46] The problem, for both Hartman and Culler—and it is the humanist dilemma—is how theory can resist its assimilation to method and still be useful or practical.

Finally, there is a more moderate position to be taken with regard to the separation between theory and practice implied by some of Culler's pronouncements. A number of respondents to a 1982 article against theory remind us that if theory and method are different, theory and practice can and should be articulated dialectically.[47] Theory has for too long been associated with (even as it reacts against) the Kantian search for the epistemological grounds of interpretation—with the subordination of practice to a speculative model of the truth.[48] This Kantianism finds its courtier representative in the figure of the neoplatonist Bembo, for whom "knowledge must always precede desire" (336), and whose goal is "contemplation of the universal intellect" (354). The aim of the dialectical critic, however, is to formulate theory as a "metapractice," or "practice about practice," one that is necessarily bound up with desires, interests, intentions to persuade.[49]

This dialectical articulation of theory and practice should be distinguished from de Man's conception of the irreducible moment of practice at the center of theory, or the interference of the rhetorical and cognitive dimensions of the text. For although many "dialectical" critics would applaud de Man's equation of rhetoric with the impossibility of reading a text in terms of phenomenological categories (cognition as vision), they would not identify this impossibility with the undecidability of meaning. In fact, one could argue that such an identification is the consequence of a frustrated desire for contemplation of the "universal intellect." Terry Eagleton suggests as much when he writes: "Meaning may well be ultimately undecidable if we view language contemplatively, as a chain of signifiers on a page; it becomes 'decidable' . . . when we think of language as something that we do, as indissociably interwoven with our practical forms of life."[50]

Accordingly, the dialectical articulation draws near to the humanist pragmatic resistance to theory and thus to the humanist conception of the pedagogical imperative. At the same time it points up the tie between this imperative and the (re)turn to literary history on the part of many literary theorists. If the goal of humanist pedagogy is to educate the judgment, the faculty of decorum, it necessarily involves the determination of what is appropriate at a given moment and in a given historical context. Accordingly, Federico Gonzaga advises the courtier to "consider well what he does or says, the place where he does it, in whose presence, its timeliness" (98), and earlier, Ludovico remarks on the sense of historical difference that will inform every correct imitation of antiquity: "Cicero in many places reprehends many of his predecessors, and in censuring Sergius Galba declares that his orations have an antique cast to them; . . . so that, if we attempt to imitate the ancients servilely, we shall not be imitating them. And Virgil, who (as you say) imitated Homer, did not imitate him in language" (53–54).[51]

If we now return to de Man's remarks about literary history, cited at the beginning of this essay, we may be able to see the humanists' rhetorical sense of history and their dialogical or dialectical sense of the relation of theory to practice as a via media between the reified periodization of conservative literary historians, on the one hand, and de Man's skepticism on the other. Like Emilia's gentle reminder to Bembo in *Il Cortegiano*, "Take care, messer Bembo, that with these thoughts your soul, too, does not forget your body" (357), the revival of interest in humanist rhetorical theory, and in the humanists' rhetorical conception of history, can serve to remind us that *theoria* is not our only "theoretical" option. Roland Barthes was writing as a Renaissance humanist and a contemporary theorist of literature when he claimed that "the theory of the text can coincide only with a practice of writing."[52]

NOTES

Epigraph: Baldassare Castiglione, *The Book of the Courtier* (Il Cortegiano), trans. Charles Singleton (New York, 1959), 41. Count Ludovico Canossa is speaking to Federico Gonzaga. Further references are to this edition and will be cited parenthetically in the text.

1 De Man's article, "The Resistance to Theory," was published in *The Pedagogical Imperative*, ed. Barbara Johnson, *Yale French Studies* 63 (1982): 3–20. I owe the germ of this chapter to a conversation with Debra Fried of Cornell University. Thanks are due as well to the Society for the Humanities at Cornell, under whose auspices this chapter was written.

2 See Bernard Weinberg, ed., *A History of Literary Criticism in the Italian Renaissance*, 2 vols. (New York, 1961); idem., ed., *Trattati di poeticae e retorica del Cinquecento*, 4 vols. (Bari, 1974); Baxter Hathaway, *The Age of Criticism* (Ithaca, 1962).

3 Paul Oskar Kristeller, "The Humanist Movement," in *Renaissance Thought: The Classic, Scholastic and Humanistic Strains* (New York, 1961), 17–18.

4 On the first point, see the *Epistolario di Coluccio Salutati*, ed. Francesco Novati, *Fonti per la storia d'Italia*, 4 vols. (Rome, 1891–1911), 3:447; 4:176. On the second, see Salutati, *De Nobilitate legum et medecine*, ed. Eugenio Garin (Florence, 1947), 32, 136, and passim. See also the general preface to Valla's *Dialecticae disputationes* for his criticism of Aristotle for not engaging in civic affairs (in *Opera omnia*, ed. Eugenio Garin, 2 vols. [Basel, 1540; Turin, 1962], 1:644).

5 I am thinking here of the medieval scholastic definition of truth as "adequatio intellectus et rei."

6 See Salutati, *Epistolario*, 1:179–80; 3:606–10; 4:142; and Leonardo Bruni, *Ad Petrum Paulum Histrum Dialogus*, in *Prosatori latini del Quattrocento*, ed. Eugenio Garin (Milan, 1952), 60.

7 See Valla, *Dialecticae disputationes*, Preface 3, *Opera omnia* 1:731. See also Valla's *In eundem Pogium libellus secundus*, *Opera omnia*, 1:385. On this appeal to *consuetudo*, see Salvatore I. Camporeale, *Lorenzo Valla: Umanesimo e teologia* (Florence, 1972), esp. 149–71; and Nancy Struever, "Lorenza Valla: Humanist Rhetoric and the Critique of the Classical Languages of Morality," and Charles Trinkaus, "The Question of Truth in Renaissance Rhetoric and Anthropology," both in *Renaissance Eloquence*, ed. James J. Murphy (Berkeley, 1983), 191–206, 207–20.

8 The following quotations from the *Nicomachean Ethics* (hereafter abbreviated *NE*) are taken from the translation by Martin Ostwald (New York, 1962).

9 See Cicero, *De oratore*, 2.47.269ff.; and Giovanni Pontano, *De sermone*, ed. S. Lupi and Risicato (Ligano, 1954) book 2, chap. 7.65: "Those who use irony moderately, in those things which are public and manifest to all [i.e., without the intention to deceive], are seen to be urbane [*urbanos*] and to win a certain favor or esteem [*gratiam*] among their fellow citizens." See also book 6, p. 197, on Socrates.

10 See Cicero, *De officiis*, 1.43.153, and *Orator*, 21.71–72.

11 George Puttenham, *The Arte of English Poesie* (Kent, Ohio, 1970), 268, 270. U's and v's have been regularized. All further quotations will be from this edition and pagination will be indicated in the text. For similar reflections on the difficulty of providing a rule of imitation, see the passages cited by Thomas M. Greene in his chapter "Sixteenth-Century Quarrels: Classicism and the Scandal of History," in *The Light in Troy: Imitation and Discovery in Renaissance Poetry* (New Haven, 1983), esp. 171.

12 Roger Ascham, *The Scholemaster* (1570), ed. Lawrence V. Ryan (Ithaca, 1967), 114. Further references will be given in the text.

13 See Philip Sidney's remarks in *An Apology for Poetry,* ed. Geoffrey Shepherd (Manchester, Eng., 1973), 101: The poet "so far substantially . . . worketh, not only to make a Cyrus which had been a particular excellency as Nature might have done, but to bestow a Cyrus upon the world to make many Cyruses if they will learn aright, why, and how that maker made him."

14 See Erasmus, *Parabolae sive similiae,* in *Opera omnia,* ordo 1, tome 5, ed. Jean-Claude Margolin (Amsterdam, 1975), p. 94, l. 65; cf. p. 92, ll. 44–51. On Lycosthenes, see Margolin's introduction, 34–75; on the difference between the *Parabolae* and ordinary commonplace books, see 8.

15 See *Parabolae,* p. 94, ll. 66–70. See also Erasmus's remarks on the purpose of his *Adagia,* in *Opera omnia,* ed. J. Leclerc (Leiden, 1703–6; rpt. Hildesheim, 1962), vol. 2, 711 CD; 712E–713D. Henceforth this edition will be referred to as *LB*.

16 Erasmus, *On Copia of Words and Ideas,* trans. Donald B. King and H. David Rix (Milwaukee, Wis., 1963), chap. 7, p. 16; *LB,* vol. 1, 6 AB. On the *De copia,* see Terence Cave, *The Cornucopian Text: Problems of Writing in the French Renaissance* (Oxford, 1979), 3–34. On the example of Socrates' death, referred to below, see Marion Trousdale, "A Possible Renaissance View of Form," *ELH* 40 (1973): 179–204.

17 See Ben Jonson, *Timber or Discoveries,* in Ben Jonson, *Works,* ed. C. H. Herford, Percy Simpson, and Evelyn Simpson, 11 vols. (Oxford, 1925–52), 8:628: "Now, that I have informed you in the knowing these things [respecting reading]; let mee leade you by the hand a little farther, in the direction of the use; and make you an able Writer by practice."

18 See Margaret Ferguson's chapter on Sidney in her *Trials of Desire: Renaissance Defenses of Poetry* (New Haven, 1982); Eugene Garver, "Machiavelli's *The Prince:* A Neglected Rhetorical Classic," *Philosophy and Rhetoric* 13 (1980): 99–120. I am grateful to Nancy Struever for sharing with me her unpublished "Machiavelli and the Critique of the Available Languages of Morality in the Sixteenth Century," now published in revised form in her *Theory as Practice: Ethical Inquiry in the Renaissance* (Chicago, 1992), 147–81. On Montaigne, see Karlheinz Stierle, "L'Histoire comme exemple, l'exemple comme histoire," *Poétique* 10 (1972): 176–98.

19 Stierle, "L'Histoire," esp. 186–87, 193.

20 Eduardo Saccone, "*Grazia, Sprezzatura* and *Affettazione* in Castiglione's *Book of the Courtier,*" *Glyph* 5 (1979): 34–54.

21 In *Light in Troy,* Thomas Greene charts an analogous development in sixteenth-century debates about imitation, specifically the imitation of Cicero. Greene shows how in a number of treatises in the second half of the century, the flexible standard of the judgment required for successful imitation gives way to a concern with method and inflexible rules. See esp. 176ff.

22 This paragraph relies on the discussions of method by Walter Ong, *Ramus, Method, and the Decay of Dialogue* (Cambridge, Mass., 1958); and Neal W. Gilbert, *Renais-*

sance Concepts of Method (New York, 1960). See also Cesare Vasoli, *La Dialettica e la retorica dell'Umanesimo: 'Invenzione' e 'Metodo' nella cultura del XV e XVI secolo* (Milan, 1968); as well as his "La Retorica e la dialettica umanistiche e le origini delle concezione moderne del 'metodo,'" *Il Verri* ser. 4, vol. 35 (1970): 250–306. Ong writes that Hermogenes is one source of the humanists' rhetorical conception of method (231). He cautions us about the fluidity of such terms as *methodus, ars,* and *doctrina* in the sixteenth century (156ff.); see also Gilbert (60).

23 Gilbert, *Concepts of Method,* 66.

24 The *Ratio* was originally published in 1519; the term *methodus* was added to the title in 1520.

25 Gilbert, *Concepts of Method,* xxiv, 13, and passim.

26 Thomas Hobbes, *Leviathan,* ed. C. B. Macpherson (Harmondsworth, Eng., 1975), pt. 1, chap. 5, p. 115.

27 See *Nicomachean Ethics,* 1141a 10ff., where Aristotle discusses the use of the term *sophia* to describe the technical knowledge involved in art or craftsmanship, as well as the knowledge of theoretical wisdom (which includes the intelligence of first principles and the scientific knowledge of *theoria*). See also Ostwald's note 24 in the same text. On this similarity between *theoria* and *techne,* see Hannah Arendt, *The Human Condition* (Chicago, 1958), 301–4, esp. 301–2: "The decisive point of similarity, at least in Greek philosophy, was that contemplation [*theoria*], the beholding of something, was considered to be an inherent element in fabrication [*techne*] as well, inasmuch as the work of the craftsman was guided by the 'idea.'"

28 René Descartes, *Discours de la méthode,* ed. Etienne Gilson (Paris, 1930), 19.

29 Ascham, *Scholemaster,* 107. See Francis Bacon, *The Advancement of Learning,* ed. G. W. Kitchen (London, 1973), 135, for a similar warning against the dangers of commonplace books; as well as Erasmus's *De copia,* book 1, chap. 9, on the necessity of forming a storehouse of *copia* through the reading of primary texts.

30 The phrase is taken from the prefatory letter *to The Logike of The Moste Excellent Philosopher P. Ramus Martyr,* trans. Roland MacIlmaine (1574), ed. Catherine M. Dunn (Northridge, Calif., 1969), 9. Further references will be given in the text. There has been much discussion of the audience of Puttenham's work, in particular of how his discussion of rhetorical figures codifies modes of social interaction in the Elizabethan period. See Daniel Javitch, *Poetry and Courtliness in Renaissance England* (Princeton, 1978); Louis Adrian Montrose, "Of Gentlemen and Shepherds: The Politics of Elizabethan Pastoral Form," *ELH* 50 (1983): 415–59; and Frank Whigham, *Ambition and Privilege: The Social Tropes of Elizabethan Courtesy Theory* (Berkeley, 1984).

31 MacIlmaine continues: "Thou seest (good Reader) what a grounde they have to defend their opinion, and howe they labour only to roote out all good knowledge & vertue, and plante mere ignorance amongest the common people" (9). See also Leonard Cox, *The Arte or Crafte of Rhetoryke* (ca. 1530), ed. Frederic Ives Carpenter (Chicago, 1899), who writes that his work will be useful for students, lawyers, ambassadors, and preachers (41).

32 Abraham Fraunce, *The Lawyer's Logic,* ed. R. C. Alston (Menston, Eng., 1969), preface.

33 See Ong, *Ramus,* 156–67, esp. 161, on Ramus's identification of *methodus* and *theoria.* See also Lisa Jardine, *Francis Bacon and the Art of Discovery* (Cambridge, 1974), 29, for a similar remark about Agricola. See also the definition of dialectic at the beginning of Ramus's *Logike:* "Dialecticke otherwise called Logicke, is an arte which teachethe to dispute well"; and Melanchthon (quoted in Ong, 159): "Dialectic is the art or way of teaching correctly, in order, and lucidly" (*Erotema dialectices,* book 1).

34 Thomas O. Sloan, "The Crossing of Rhetoric and Poetry in the Renaissance," in *The Rhetoric of Renaissance Poetry from Wyatt to Milton,* ed. Thomas Sloan and Raymond B. Waddington (Berkeley, 1974), 212–42. Paradoxically, although Ramus ideally excludes prudential judgment from his single method, he recognizes the need for a kind of prudence in addressing a recalcitrant audience, one for whom the light of reason has been obscured. The "prudential method" thus allows for all those rhetorical devices of indirection, whether in figurative language, invention, or disposition, that are antithetical to logic strictly conceived. The significant difference between the Ramist and humanist conceptions of prudence is that what was for the humanists a necessity—the practical faculty of deliberation and choice in contingent affairs—has with Ramus become an object of contingency and choice. Prudence is no longer essential but is, like figurative language, ornamental.

35 See Kant's remarks on the superfluousness of examples in the first preface to the *Critique of Pure Reason,* trans. Norman Kemp Smith (London, 1950), A viii–ix. On Ramus's geometry textbook, see Gilbert, *Concepts of Method,* 85. On the example as a form of logical argument see Ramus's *Logike,* book 2, chap. 16, pp. 56–58.

36 Henry Peacham, *The Garden of Eloquence (1593), A Facsimile Reproduction* (Gainesville, Fla., 1954), 36.

37 Puttenham, *English Poesie,* 267. See also Jonson, *Timber or Discoveries,* 593, and Hobbes, *De cive,* in *English Works,* ed. Sir Thomas Molesworth, 2 vols. (London, 1839–45), 2:xiii; as well as *Leviathan,* chap. 17, p. 226.

38 This defensive move is analogous to the one Sidney makes in his *Apology* (123–24), when he claims at one moment that poetry is mere play. See Margaret Ferguson's discussion of this strategic move in *Trials of Desire,* esp. 151.

39 This is not to say that Puttenham always uses the term *imitation* in a pejorative sense; see, for example, *English Poesie,* 20.

40 Niccolò Machiavelli, *The Prince,* trans Robert M. Adams (New York, 1977), 44.

41 Bacon, *Advancement of Learning,* 122. On Bacon's use of rhetorical terminology, see Jardine, *Francis Bacon,* and Wilbur Samuel Howell, *Logic and Rhetoric in England, 1500–1700* (New York, 1969), 364–76.

42 See Jardine, *Francis Bacon,* 97–98.

43 Francis Bacon, *Works,* ed. J. Spedding, R. L. Ellis, and D. D. Heath, 15 vols. (Cambridge, Mass., 1857–61), 8:67–68.

44 Terry Eagleton, *Literary Theory: An Introduction* (Minneapolis, 1983). See also 146 on the similarities between New Criticism and deconstruction.

45 Jonathan Culler, "Literary Theory in the Graduate Program," in his *The Pursuit of Signs: Semiotics, Literature, Deconstruction* (Ithaca, 1981), 210–26, esp. 218.

46 Geoffrey H. Hartman, "A Short History of Practical Criticism," in his *Criticism in the Wilderness: The Study of Literature Today* (New Haven, 1980), 269. The whole essay is relevant to the dilemma of the humanities discussed by Culler.

47 Steven Knapp and Walter Michaels's "Against Theory" appeared in *Critical Inquiry* 9 (1982): 723–42. The responses to it appeared in *Critical Inquiry* 9 (1983): 727–800.

48 See in particular the articles by Jonathan Crewe, "Toward Uncritical Practice," 748–59, esp. 750, on the necessity of a dialectical conception of the relation of theory to practice; and Adena Rosmarin, "On the Theory of 'Against Theory,'" 775–83, esp. 776ff., on the Kantian epistemological conception of theory, both in *Critical Inquiry* 9 (1983).

49 Steven Mailloux, "Truth or Consequences: On Being Against Theory," *Critical Inquiry* 9 (1983), 766. The notion of dialectic here and in the following paragraph is not Hegelian, but dialogical, mutually determining. I am not claiming that all the respondents to Knapp and Michaels agree, but rather that some of the respondents point to a nonexclusive, nonhierarchical conception of the relation of theory to practice.

50 Eagleton, *Literary Theory*, 146–47.

51 Erasmus's remarks in the *Ciceronianus* on the correct imitation of Cicero are representative of this dialectical or dialogical conception of history: "What effrontery would he have then who required us always to speak in a Ciceronian style? Let him first restore to us the Rome which existed at that time; let him restore the senate and the senate house, the conscript fathers, the knights, the people in tribes and centuries. . . . Since then the entire arena of human affairs has been altered, who today call speak well unless he greatly diverges from Cicero? . . . Wherever I turn, I see everything changed" (cited by Greene, *Light in Troy*, 182).

52 Roland Barthes, "From Work to Text," in his *Image, Music, Text*, trans. Stephen Heath (New York, 1977), 164.

8

Rhetoric, Hermeneutics, and Prudence in the Interpretation of the Constitution

Eugene Garver

Recently I have been listening to the Minnesota legislature debate whether to extend protection against discrimination to homosexuals. Much of the public debate turns on whether homosexuality is a matter of choice or destiny. Politicians, it appears, think that law is subordinate to metaphysics. Former Justice Blackmun was criticized for maintaining that the Supreme Court need not decide the metaphysical question of when human life begins. Had he tried, wouldn't his arguments have sounded as ridiculous as those of the Minnesota politicians? Should questions of law and justice depend on metaphysics?

As a practical argument becomes more philosophical, technical, or precise, it becomes worse. Aristotle advises the rhetorician: "Do not seek enthymemes about everything; otherwise you do what some of the philosophers do whose syllogisms draw better known and more plausible conclusions than their premises."[1] Should we lower our expectations? ("Let's be realistic and admit that the law is nothing but power and irrational desire. We have to protect our way of life against foreign invaders.") Or should we rather assume that the cure for bad philosophy is better philosophy and more exact scientific determination of the beginning and end of life, or the genetic basis for homosexuality?

The dispute over how to respond to the fact that the more philosophical or scientific a practical argument gets, the worse it becomes, is a reenactment of the ancient battle between philosophy and rhetoric over which one is allowed to claim practical wisdom. There are times when philosophy and science seem unnecessary because rhetoric in its most minimal, least reflective sense—argument on both sides of a question—produces satisfactory results. There are times when such rhetorical practice is challenged and therefore seems to require a theory to back it up. Philosophy supplants rhetoric and gives practical argument a sure foundation. Dissatisfaction with rhetoric moves people to philosophy, and disappointment at what they find there moves them back to rhetoric. Slogans like "Justice: political, not metaphysical," the priority of democracy to philosophy, antifoundationalism, and "The end of philosophy" are rediscoveries of the revenge rhetoric periodically takes on philosophy.[2] Legal "realism" reenacts sophistical rhetoric's suspicion of ideas and claims that there is nothing beyond argument or beyond winning an argument. The philosophic "realism" of natural law continues the philosophical project of judging reasoning in terms of how well it represents a truth that is independent of that reasoning.

Rhetoric's victories over philosophy are often as short-lived as those of philosophy over rhetoric, which is why the struggle seems interminable. My antiphilosophical parable about homosexual rights shows that the raising of the stakes in practical debate from political accommodation to metaphysical determination often looks irreversible. There is a common and powerful fear that once we give up sure methods and indisputable principles, we are reduced to caprice, a belief that Richard Bernstein has named the Cartesian Anxiety.[3] People want their opinions to have the strongest possible backing, and they won't be talked out of such a desire. Once they have tasted the waters of philosophy, no matter how diluted or recycled, innocence is hard to regain. If I wish to discriminate against homosexuals, and I know that my feelings of revulsion cannot be shown in public, I have to find reasons, such as the distinction between nature and choice, to support my desires. Whether Kant was right in arguing that theoretical reason contains a drive for system that makes reason's reach exceed its grasp, *practical* reason seems inevitably to get ahead of itself and to claim accomplishments beyond its capacities.

In spite of the pervasiveness of such philosophical ambitions and rhetorical responses, prudence need not be a prize over which philosophy and rhetoric contend. It evades that fight and becomes its own master when the internal values of the practice of argument and the forms of practical argument themselves are the best way of embodying our ethical aspirations.[4] Rhetoric argues both sides of a question. Nature and choice can each be a reason both for and against extending protection against discrimination to homosexuals. As Michael McConnell says, "It used to be thought that sexuality was entitled to constitutional protection because each person should be free to choose the objects of his or her affection. Now it is more often argued that sexuality is entitled to constitutional protection because it is not a choice, but something inherent in the person's nature, which cannot be changed."[5]

Rhetoric by itself is consequently incomplete, but it does not have to be replaced by philosophy. Rhetoric can evolve into civility instead. The recognition that there are alternative reasonable solutions, conclusions, and judgments is an advance over thinking that anyone who disagrees with you or reaches a different conclusion from you must be dishonest or stupid. This civilizing side of rhetoric means it need not be either antiphilosophically sophistic or foundationally philosophical. Rhetoric can become a form of prudence.

The emergence of prudence from this ethical alternative to both philosophy and rhetoric gives slogans like "Justice: political, not metaphysical" an ethical, rather than simply an antiphilosophical, meaning. Aristotle invents *ethos* as the thing that completes *logos* and *pathos,* the more obvious items of the trio, and so circumvents those sterile polemics between Plato and the Sophists. The discovery of the ethical is Aristotle's contribution to the history of rhetoric and the history of prudence. Rather than present Aristotle's discovery of the ethical, I wish here to show how the ethical reemerges as an alternative to reason and passion in late twentieth-century discussions of constitutional hermeneutics when the interpretation of the Constitution becomes a principal home for prudent thought and action.

Because political questions become subjects for litigation in the United States, these perennial questions about prudence, philosophy, and rhetoric have become questions about legal and hermeneutic argument. Popular polemics about constitutional interpretation replicate old struggles between rhetoric and philosophy over where to locate *phronesis*. These reenactments quickly become rituals, however, which is why the polemics between people like Stanley Fish or Robert Bork and their opponents often appear to be sleepwalking through arguments we have all heard before. But alongside these rituals are discussions of constitutional hermeneutics that rediscover some of the ethical dimensions of rhetoric and prudence and that discover new insights into prudence in contemporary circumstances.

Hermeneutics is the attitude we adopt toward texts when we put two distinct demands on them. We wish our interpretations to be faithful to the text, and we want the result of the interpretation to be true, as well as to achieve further goals, such as justice. Hermeneutics is an attitude toward a text that we hope will be not only binding but *rationally* binding on us.[6] The idea of rational fidelity has, under different guises, been developed as a central problem for constitutional hermeneutics by several thinkers. Sanford Levinson calls the object of his inquiry "constitutional faith." Joseph Vining proposes to distinguish the authoritative from the authoritarian. Paul Kahn asks whether reason and will, or reason and history, can coexist in constitutional interpretation.[7] Rational faith, obedience and loyalty, constitutional faith, and the authoritative are different ways of framing the problem of constitutional hermeneutics and hence of constitutional prudence today. They are variations on the theme of the hermeneutic circle. The problem of the hermeneutics of rational fidelity can also be seen as a nuanced development of Aristotle's distinction between constitution and contract, the political parallel to his ethical distinction between true friendship and a friendship of utility.

Determining the meaning of a contract is easier than exploring the hermeneutics of the Constitution, because we have lower expectations for contracts. A contract may be minimally rational, but a constitution is supposed to embody ideals as well as desires. A contract satisfies the wishes of its parties, but a constitution is binding on people other than the ratifying parties, and so obligation and fidelity must come from reason. "Any state that is properly so called . . . must pay attention to virtue; for otherwise the community becomes merely an alliance, . . . a guarantee of men's just claims on one another, not designed to make the citizens virtuous and just."[8] Loyalty to the constitution consists in rational fidelity, allegiance both to the purposes of the constitution and, I shall show, to the argumentative methods for accomplishing those purposes. In constitutional hermeneutics, we seek rational allegiance to an old document that governs us as citizens.

Rational fidelity requires a strong conception of community and the Constitution. A robust sense of hermeneutics as reading a constitution rather than a contract develops alongside a conception of rhetoric as a practice, not just a technique for getting what you want. The point of a contract is to have limited purposes that therefore leave the parties unchanged; constitutions embody concern for the parties' moral education and virtue: "In contracts for the exchange of commodities and military alliances . . . [the parties] associate on the same footing when they came together as they did when they were apart. . . . Political fellowship exists for the sake of noble actions, not merely for living in common" (*Politics*, III.5.1280b25–1281a4). If citizenship could be reduced to a contract, then prudence would be replaced by purely instrumental rhetoric. When society is reduced to a contract, prudence is replaced by purely instrumental rhetoric.[9]

Let me illustrate the idea of rational fidelity with a second parable. In 1994

I published an article on Aristotle's analysis of natural slavery.[10] I proposed, as a hermeneutical thought-experiment, to treat his justification of slavery in the same way one would consider his arguments against the possibility of a void, that is, as an attempt to lay a conceptual foundation for a conclusion that we—contemporary readers of Aristotle—know in advance to be false. We read parts of Aristotle's *Physics* with the same suspension of interest in truth that we might read about Azande magic. I wondered whether we could read his analysis of slavery that way too, or whether my readers and I might be threatened by the possibility that if his arguments were strong enough, we might become committed to a possible truth that would be unwelcome. There is the uncomfortable possibility that we might live in the same moral community as Aristotle, even if not in the same scientific community; to have as a fellow citizen someone who intelligently assaults some of our deepest values is a possibility we would rather not face.

In contemporary constitutional hermeneutics, we seek rational allegiance to an old document that governs us as citizens. We have decided in advance that the document governs us—while for Aristotle's *Politics* there is only a remote possibility, and for his *Physics* none at all—and search for rational allegiance. The hermeneutical idea of rational fidelity is intelligible, I shall show, only with a sense a prudence and rhetoric where the ethical exists alongside the emotional and the rational.[11]

In what follows, I wish to show how three aspects of prudence emerge from the rhetoric and hermeneutics of contemporary jurisprudence. I shall ignore those easy polemics about theories of interpretation proposed by Bork and Fish and take a more Aristotelian approach by looking instead at what I take to be the best in contemporary discussions of constitutional hermeneutics and prudence. The three features of contemporary prudence are: (1) pluralism, (2) the distinction between legitimacy and justice, and (3) the rediscovery of the ethical. All have roots in classical rhetoric. The best contemporary jurisprudential theory and practice articulate them in characteristically modern ways, so I shall try to illustrate both the continuities between past and present and the peculiar demands that prudence faces today.

PLURALISM

Pluralism has been the great twentieth-century American development in prudence. Pluralism, at least initially, pushes prudence toward rhetoric and away from philosophy. Rhetoric as a faculty of proving both sides of a question is at home with interest-group pluralism. But when rhetoric and interpretation become subject to reflection, pluralism can be converted from contract to constitution, and rhetoric from antiphilosophy to ethical and prudent philosophy.[12]

Pluralism has been present in American politics from the beginning. The *Federalist Papers* argued against the received idea that homogeneity is necessary for successful democracy and freedom, claiming instead that heterogeneity is the guardian of freedom. The battle between Federalist and anti-Federalist over heterogeneity and homogeneity translates the ancient battle between rhetorical-sophistical powers and philosophic wisdom into an American form, where it continues today in fights between liberal advocates of a neutral state that accommodates differences and conservative proponents of homogeneity either of the nation or of local communities that practice racial, religious, or sexual discrimination. The American Founders took the pluralism of interests and factions out of the realm of contract by developing the institutional pluralism of separation of powers and a federal system.

That same battle between rhetoric and philosophy, between Federalist and anti-Federalist, is played out again in disputes about whether there must be a single method for interpreting the Constitution or whether pluralism has a place there too. The pluralism of modes of argument is an even more thoroughgoing remedy to the pluralism of interests, as rhetoric develops from an instrument of power to be used for purposes prior to rhetoric into a rhetorical culture of argument, and the plural community evolves from the adoption of a peace treaty to the adoption of a constitution.[13] That constitutional interpretation employs a variety of kinds of argument is as undeniable as that pluralism of interests and beliefs characterized the United States from the beginning. At issue is whether this variety should be replaced by a single correct method, or whether the variety itself is essential to rational fidelity and modern prudence.

Philip Bobbitt's *Constitutional Interpretation* (1991) and his earlier *Constitutional Fate* (1982) are perfect places to look at the relations between philosophy and rhetoric as they encounter the twentieth-century fact of pluralism and the specifically American phenomenon of political questions becoming legal questions and legal questions ultimately turning on hermeneutics.[14] Rather than survey the entire field of constitutional hermeneutics, I would like to concentrate on Bobbitt's articulation, for the three features of contemporary prudence—pluralism, the distinction between legitimacy and justice, and the rediscovery of the ethical—are all prominent in his account. When Levinson speaks about constitutional faith, Vining distinguishes the authoritative from the authoritarian, and Kahn wonders about the synthesis of reason and will, it is not immediately obvious that prudence and constitutional hermeneutics require plural modes of interpretation and argument. Bobbitt's formulation is thus more suited to my purpose of showing what prudence and prudent rhetoric can be today.

My parables of Minnesota politicians on homosexuality and Aristotle on slavery both come into play in considering Bobbitt's "grammar" of "six different modes of Constitutional argument," a system that specified six forms of constitutional argument that permitted one to map any constitutional proposition onto a field of legitimacy" (*CI,* x). Like rhetoric and unlike logic, this grammatical analysis distinguishes legitimacy from justice: an interpretation can be well-formed and grammatically correct, yet not produce justice. Bobbitt's grammar, like Kenneth Burke's *Grammar of Motives,* qualifies as a rhetoric, for it not only shows how to distinguish well-formed from deficient statements, but it ties those modes of argument to purposes for which they are appropriate. By showing how each mode is purposive, he shows how arguments are legitimating, and not merely rule-following, as a narrower form of grammar might be.

Let me run through Bobbitt's six modes. In *Constitutional Interpretation,* they generate six distinct arguments concerning the constitutionality of using private money to fund such secret policies as aid to the Nicaraguan Contras. One can, first, argue *historically* that Article 1 of the Constitution "provides the link between government operations and the democratic mandate by requiring that all funding take place by statute, that is, by the actions of persons who can be turned out by the voters every biennium. . . . To circumvent Article I by relying on non-appropriated funds . . . is to strike at the heart of this idea" (72). *Structural* argument begins from the fact that "the people and not the state are sovereign" (73). Secret policies make it impossible for the people to be sovereign. Moreover, the constitutional separation of powers requires cooperation rather than unilateral action, and "that cooperation makes the difference between power and law" (75).

A *textual* argument can be made for "quasi-private entities to conduct paramilitary operations" because Congress can grant letters of marque and reprisal. But the text is "equally clear" on forbidding "off-budget funding" (75). There are *prudential* arguments, perhaps easier for nonlawyers to generate, as to why "the Enterprise" was an irresponsible idea. It just doesn't look good when it's exposed. *Doctrinal* argument invites us to look for relevant precedents and analogies. Is the government's using private funding for the Contras analogous to a city's taking private donations instead of taxes to run an art museum, or is it similar to a city's allowing a privately funded and operated police force to aid in the public purpose of reducing crime?[15]

Finally, there are *ethical* arguments against such a policy. The "patriotic and highly intelligent men and women [who carried out Reagan's policies] replaced their country's vision of itself, as expressed in law, with their own vision for it. . . . The Enterprise did not reflect a commitment to serve the nation's policies whatever they might be" (81).

There are two ways of understanding the methods of constitutional interpretation. The first claims that any legitimate method of interpretation must be justified by a theory of politics, of interpretation, of history, or of democratic values.[16] That line of argument makes metaphysics prior to rhetoric and prudence, subordinating hermeneutics to epistemology. The other way makes these modes of argument themselves ultimate, needing no such foundation. They are not ultimate premises but ultimate modes of reasoning. This is the priority of politics to epistemology, of rhetoric to philosophy. If we take that line, the question we shall have to face is whether sophistic rhetoric or ethical rhetoric constitutes constitutional interpretation.

The pluralism of modes of argument shifts the center of attention and the locus of valuation from substantive principles to argument as an activity, as well as to forms of argument. The prudent and rhetorical concentration on forms of argument, instead of on substantive principles or ideologies, allows fidelity to the Constitution rather than subordination of the Constitution to a theory or favored object of belief. Rational fidelity demands allegiance to the written Constitution, but the identity, meaning, rationality, and justice of "the Constitution" are located by these modes of argument, rather than by the methods we use to denote an extra-argumentative object. Since the forms of argument are not premises, as in philosophical antirhetoric, they are not themselves the objects of argument and dispute but instead are powers for generating such objects. The methods can be fundamental to a rhetorical culture of argument and justice that needs no further backing.[17] This is, of course, the hermeneutic circle, but with a prudential and practical turn.

The six modes of interpretation Bobbitt offers do not follow from a theory of justice or hermeneutics but emerge from the developing practice of constitutional argument and interpretation. They are not, then, antiphilosophical rhetorical tools of power but elaborations of a rhetoric of prudence. Any sort of fidelity to a text requires historical and textual interpretation; limited government inevitably demands some sort of structural interpretation; two hundred years of interpretation generate doctrinal modes of reasoning as decisions accumulate and organize themselves, and the demands for *rational* fidelity ensure the legitimacy of prudential and ethical arguments.

Constitutional argument has to be grounded in the plural modes rather than in a derivation from principles superior to the Constitution itself. None of these six hermeneutic modes can account for its own operation. None is self-justifying, any more than the Constitution is self-interpreting. There is no textual argument for textualism, no ethical argument for ethical argument.[18] To argue otherwise is to make a theory or set of principles superior to the Constitution itself. A theory of contracts that would justify an ideology of original intent, for example, would then become authoritative over the Constitution. Instead, from the constitutional idea of justice under law follows, first, the focus on modes of argument and, second, a system of multiple modes of argument. Given plurality, we have three possibilities. We abandon ourselves to relativism as the triumph of rhetoric over philosophy, we turn to philosophy and against argument to console ourselves against the Cartesian anxiety, or we focus on the modes and practices of argument as themselves the locus of value and the source of legitimacy. It is this third, ethical alternative that allows prudence to overcome the opposition of philosophy and rhetoric.

Plural modes of judicial argument, therefore, are a constitutional requirement. This argument follows the opposite direction from what we might expect. After all, the constitutional rule of law historically emerged as a remedy to the civil war created by the lethal competition among sects of Christianity. Historically, plurality might lead to the rule of law, limited government, and a written constitution, but my argument suggests the opposite: a conception of justice that ties it to these legal institutions makes pluralism inevitable. Given the facts of plural interests and competing sects, limited government and a written constitution are good ideas, but limited government and a written constitution require this more robust, intellectual form of pluralism. The intellectual pluralism of rhetorical, argumentative pluralism prevents interest-group pluralism from being reduced to instrumental reason that satisfies preferences, which would be the victory of rhetoric over philosophy.[19] Justice through law and rational fidelity require argumentative pluralism. The development of plural modes of argument from the heterogeneity of interests rationalizes and civilizes those interests. Pluralism moves from being a fact of life we must grudgingly accept to an opportunity for the development of new facets of prudence.

JUSTICE AND LEGITIMACY

Bobbitt's pluralistic scheme shows what prudence must look like in the face of contemporary rhetorical and hermeneutic problems. It is, first, a purposive pluralism of modes of argument that requires, second, the distinction between legitimacy and justice and issues, finally, in the double senses of the ethical—a narrow conception, where the ethical is a mode of argument in its own right, and a wide one, which characterizes the whole field of constitutional interpretation. I would like now to turn from pluralism to the distinction between legitimacy and justice.

This distinction is a fundamental contribution rhetoric and hermeneutics make to practical reason. Bobbitt, like many others, introduces the distinction by comparing it to grammar: sentences can be grammatically correct without being true, but it is through being grammatically correct that they become candidates for truth. Only with such a distinction is rational fidelity possible. Limited government's distinction between sovereign and state, and hence legitimacy and justice, is a rediscovery and adaptation to contemporary circumstances of Aristotle's distinctions between instrumental reason and constitutive reason, and between internal and external ends. These distinctions need to be made more explicit today than they were for Aristotle, and doing so is an advance that modern ethics and politics makes over Aristotle's version, just as modern constitutional democracy is an advance over the polis.

The separation of legitimacy from justice directs attention to judicial argument, the locus of legitimacy, and away from the motives and results of arguments, which might be the loci of justice. Turning attention to legitimacy has great advantages. It grants legitimacy to those who lose arguments and allows them to see themselves and be seen by others as part of a community. This makes pluralism appealing even to those whose inclinations are more sophistical or philosophical. As Bobbitt puts it: "The multiplicity of incommensurate modalities . . . allows different groups in America to claim the Constitution as their own in the face of reasoned but adverse interpretations" (*CI*, 158). Or as Aristotle puts it: "People become hostile to an individual human being who opposes their impulses even if he is correct in opposing them; whereas a law's prescription of what is decent is not burdensome."[20]

But equally, the separation of legitimacy from justice should be troublesome because the judicial autonomy that results from focus on argument insulates judicial arguments and decisions from motives and results, and protects the people who interpret the Constitution from criticism. Perhaps this is what legitimate argument and rational fidelity to the Constitution mean—but where is justice? By directing attention to the plural modes, aren't we directing attention *away from justice* and creating a separation between the lawful (or legitimate) and the just?

When Aristotle defines rhetoric as the art of finding in each case the available means of persuasion, he distinguishes such activity from another kind of success, that of actually persuading a particular audience, and so distinguishes the internal ends of a practice from the external ends that motivated it. He draws an analogy to medicine: a doctor can do everything medically possible to heal a patient, and yet the patient can die. The operation would be deemed a success according to its own internal standards of art, thus putting the doctor beyond censure. But that is hardly consolation to the patient or his family. Do we wish to follow Aristotle in constructing a rationale for protecting a profession from external, lay criticism? An advocate or a judge who demonstrates the legitimacy of an argument or a decision by claiming that it relied on a structural argument is not only evading the question of justice but denying our right to raise such a question. Hermeneutics is protected by a hermeneutic circle. Outsiders have no place to criticize judicial argument and decision.

The accusations that the legitimacy/justice distinction protects constitutional interpretation from criticism in the name of justice resemble charges that we are putting our faith in process values or craft values.[21] But the idea of craft values that are distinct from the purposes they serve makes sense only under an instrumental conception of argument. *Both* sophistical rhetoric and foundational philosophy embody such instrumental conceptions: sophistical rhetoric because rhetoric uses argument to achieve purposes given prior to argument, and philosophy because the test of a good argument is whether it reaches a good end. The prudent relation between activity and its purposes is not the instrumental relation of means to end.

In antiphilosophic rhetoric, there can be only external relations between constitutional argument and justice. Even when constitutional arguments are assumed in the long run to result in justice (because of the invisible hand of the adversary system), there is no intrinsic connection between clever argument and just result. In sophistic rhetoric, we try anything, because winning is the only thing. These are modes of argument suitable for a state of nature and a world of contracts. Successful judicial argument determines the lawful. If you want justice, you must look elsewhere. The legal realists offer this vision of legal argument. Lawyers are not accountable for their clients' purposes and are therefore free to make tactical choices against the wishes of their clients. In constitutional interpretation, similarly, what is just and what will win the argument are independent.

In philosophy, the relation between argument and justice is, by contrast, so tight that the results of argument are beyond criticism. I began by saying that in matters of *praxis,* the more philosophical, technical, or precise the argument becomes, the worse it becomes, and we can see this thesis proven here. The philosopher claims that with the right method and the right principles, justice follows necessarily. If I correctly follow the rules of deductive argument, I have constructed a valid argument. Following legitimate procedures authorizes their conclusions and so places them beyond criticism. This is philosophy ministering to Cartesian anxiety and disarming rhetoric. Someone who admits that an argument is valid and yet criticizes it because she does not like the result misunderstands the nature of such an argument. It would be like someone following and accepting a proof in Euclid and then checking whether two triangles really were equal. Under this conception of judicial argument, successful arguments issue in justice because that is what justice is—the conclusion of a successful judicial argument.

In prudence, as opposed to sophistical rhetoric and foundational philosophy, constitutional interpretation and arguments have the autonomous value of legitimacy, but this autonomy will not mean a protection from criticism or a substitution of craft values for substantive ones. The relation between legitimacy and justice is the practical relation between an internal and a given end developed by Aristotle. This relation is not only found in his definition of rhetoric, with its analogy to medicine, but it is also at work in the virtues. Courage could be defined as saving one's city, but one can be courageous in defeat. This contradictory definition is impossible in the other two conceptions of the relation between practice and result. Praise accrues to the courageous man not for winning the battle but for mastering his fear and fighting, that is, for achieving his internal end. There are even times when the given end, justice or saving the city, might best be reached by someone other than the courageous man or the constitutional hermeneut. "It is quite possible for brave people not to be the best soldiers. Perhaps the best will be those who are less brave, but possess no other good, for they are ready to face dangers, and they sell their lives for small gains" (*Nicomachean Ethics,* III.9.1117b17–20).

The intrinsic, practical relation between argument and justice *is* the Constitution. The Constitution is a practice, a form of *praxis*.[22] To argue with rational fidelity to the Constitution is to act justly. In continuing to seek justice through constitutional hermeneutical argument, we are reenacting the ratification of the Constitution. We have rational fidelity to the document by becoming parties to it, something that is clearly impossible for contracts. That is how prudent argument operates in the hermeneutic circle. Instead of the image of the doctor avoiding litigation because the patient died, we have the jurisprudential practice of referring to *dissents* as authorities. If constitutional hermeneutic arguments were good only when successful—that is, if we collapsed the distinction between justice and legitimacy—then referring to dissents as authorities would be incoherent. A dissent can be more authoritative than a majority opinion because we value the argument, not simply the result. I can have rational fidelity toward Chief Justice Holmes's dissent in *Abrams v. United States,* but I might view the majority opinion in *Korematsu v. United States* as at most a binding precedent, requiring fidelity but not worth my rational faith.[23]

When legitimacy and justice are related poetically and externally the way a craft is related to its products, then hermeneutics creates an analogous distinction between meaning and application or appropriation. Under that conception, meaning is to legitimacy as appropriation or use is to justice. The judgment of legitimacy, like the determination of meaning, should, in such an understanding, be neutral with respect to justice. A single meaning can have different applications in different circumstances, just as a single statement can sometimes be a threat, sometimes a warning, sometimes an argument, and sometimes a bribe, without changing meaning. A neutral method and a neutral expert could determine legitimacy along with meaning. Legitimacy, like meaning, would not change with time, as justice would. If *Dred Scott* once was legitimate, it still is.[24] Legitimacy is a field for experts, while the determination of justice is a question left for citizens.

Prudential argument and hermeneutics have to reject the separation of meaning and application in favor of the distinction between legitimacy and justice. I take this as a contribution that Aristotle's *Rhetoric* and Bobbitt's consideration of the plural modes of constitutional argument can make to hermeneutic theory. A legitimate argument is an argument that aims at justice, and judgments about its legitimacy have to take into account this purposive nature. Legitimacy is not a craft value, judged by experts and protected from judgments by outsiders. It is said that forgeries that fool contemporaries are transparent failures to later generations. If the distinction between a legitimate and an illegitimate argument is the ethical distinction of whether the argument aims directly at an external end, then it can be apparent to us (as it may not have been to his contemporaries) that Justice Taney's argument in *Dred Scott* was illegitimate. It violated the constitutional ethos by using argument as an instrument to purposes outside itself. Similarly, a legitimate argument against *Brown v. Board of Education* could have been made in 1954 but the "same" argument would be illegitimate today.[25]

Prudence offers a different understanding of the relation between legitimacy and justice than either sophistical rhetoric or foundational philosophy. If I claim that my preferred method always results in justice—from a philosophical point of view—this would be proof that my method is the right one. But if I look at the matter prudently, I recognize that the coincidence between my conception of justice and the results of my argument are grounds for accusing me of special pleading and rationalizing. This is what it means for philosophic argument to be too strong for *praxis*. On the other hand, if my preferred method consistently generates manifestly unjust results, then it is no defense to say that those results are legitimate and that I have therefore done my job. I could no longer have rational faith in the Constitution. I would be living under a regime in which hermeneutics and prudence would be impossible.

Rhetoric and philosophy both posit ahistorical relations between justice and legitimacy. Prudence historicizes that relation. For the first sixty years of the Constitution, slavery was a peripheral issue, and its presence in the Constitution was seen as a political compromise that did not make the Constitution itself less fundamentally just. Slavery was an accidental, not an essential, feature of the Constitution, one to which we were bound as we are to the terms of a contract, not a constitution. When slavery and its expansion become such a central issue that its presence in the Constitution was more than an embarrassment, it created a rational crisis of faith. People had to choose between loyalty to the Constitution and adherence to ideals of justice, a choice that could be considered a pretty good definition of civil war, in which legitimacy and justice are at odds. Rational fidelity to the national government and its Constitution become impossible.[26] Frederick Douglass's attitude to the Constitution was the same as the attitude I hold toward Aristotle's defense of slavery—Douglass offered obedience without there being a rational claim on him; my interpretation of Aristotle yields understanding without allegiance.

Similarly, *Brown v. Board of Education* quickly became a touchstone for all subsequent theories of judicial hermeneutics. Because it is seen as just, any theory of constitutional interpretation must also view it as legitimate by showing how it follows from that theory. *Brown* stands as an embarrassment for single-minded advocates of original intent, who need a considerable apparatus of epicycles to save their hypothesis. Successful constitutional argument forces us to modify our ideas of justice. A constitutional argument that leaves our ideas of justice untouched is not a prudent argument but a sophistical one. Plural modes of argument "allow changes to come without requiring that the Constitution be repudiated, when a precedent has been rightly decided within a particular mode, but has come to mean something unacceptable in the world within which it must operate" (*CI*, 158).

Prudential methods lie between inadequate rhetorical and philosophical methods. The aims of prudential methods are partly—but only partly—defined by their methods, just as the successful use of the methods is partly—but only partly—defined by success at reaching the external end. To interpret a text, one must try to understand it, but one should not have a determinate sense of its meaning in advance.[27] The prudent relation between internal and external ends, between finding the available means of persuasion and persuading, between acting generously and actually benefiting someone, is more complicated than rhetoric or philosophy would have it.[28] To prudence, the existence of choice and responsibility is a sign of a correct account of *praxis,* while to antirhetorical philosophy and antiphilosophical rhetoric, choice is a sign of incompleteness and failure. History and choice are part of a prudent understanding of constitutional hermeneutics, but they are not part of its alternatives. The battle between rhetoric and philosophy comes from and flourishes in the absence of the ethical. Both philosophy and rhetoric engender desires for an absence of the ethical: the hope that rhetorical power by itself is enough, and the hope that philosophical wisdom will substitute for prudence. Both seek to eliminate judgment, philosophy by algorithmic methods, and rhetorical *techne* by substituting craft values of ingenuity and virtuosity for virtue.

The separation of legitimacy from justice locates constitutional argument and interpretation between rhetoric and philosophy, in the practical and the ethical. I want to *do* justice, and I want it to be *justice* that I do. Aristotle says that people care about and love things because they are theirs and because the things are in fact lovable (*Politics*, II.1.1262b22–23), but we do not wish those to be two separate sources of value. We want the things that we decide are just actually to be just, not merely to be things that we prefer and can impose on others. We want to achieve justice in a way that bears an intrinsic relation to those just accomplishments. We want our community to be just but just through our own efforts.

With the distinction between legitimacy and justice in hand, let me return briefly to the arguments about whether to extend the constitutional protection against discrimination to homosexuals. There are no legitimate constitutional arguments about "nature" or "choice" because those are not terms of prudence. "The decision has a legal grammar, a grammar surprisingly like that of 'reasonable care,' 'malice aforethought,' 'notice,' 'unconscionability,' and not at all like that of 'pro-choice' or 'right-to-life'" (*CI*, 178). Although saying this seems to be a way of protecting professional expertise against concerned citizens, we can now see it as a way of changing our understanding of justice from something that exists prior to argument, and indeed to the Constitution, to justice as an activity constituted in part by the activity of constitutional hermeneutics. Forcing ourselves to abandon the language of nature and choice and adopt the language of due process and equal protection forces us into an argumentative community. This is moral progress.

THE DISCOVERY OF THE ETHICAL

I said at the beginning of this chapter that Aristotle's great achievement in the *Rhetoric* is to place the ethical alongside the logical and the pathetic. He identifies the artful in rhetoric with the argumentative, and he then defines the ethical in terms of the argumentative. Neither of these moves is obvious. We need to use both—the identification of the legitimate with the six modes of constitutional argument and the further identification of the legitimate with the ethical—to understand what prudence, rhetoric, and constitutional hermeneutics can mean today.

For Aristotle, the ethical is one of the three sources of proof (along with the rational and the emotional); at the same time, all persuasion that falls within the art of rhetoric is ethical. Similarly, Bobbitt identifies legitimacy with argument, but it takes ethical criteria to demarcate the legitimate. He introduces the ethical by contrasting the hermeneutics of the "businessman, who is anxious to get from point 'a' to point 'b,' and who has a very clear idea of where 'b' is located, [for whom] the law is simply a set of rules that imposes certain costs on doing business," with the public official for whom "law is a map, a set of directions in a contentious democracy where there are many different views of where 'b' lies, or even what it is" (*CI*, 80). The businessman has to obey the laws; the public official has to execute them faithfully. It is only when argument is ethical that the rhetoric available to serve any master is replaced by prudent argument that is its own master, as constitution replaces contract. Any mode of argument can be used the way the businessman uses law or the way the public official, with something that could accurately be called *civic virtue,* interprets it. The difference is ethical.

I would like to explore four parallels between *ethos* as a mode of proof in Aristotle's *Rhetoric* and Bobbitt's presentation of the ethical as one of his six modes of constitutional argument. First, Aristotle stresses that the *ethos* that is the most persuasive kind of proof is internal to the speech itself, not to the reputation of the speaker. Bobbitt similarly restricts the ethical to constitutional ethos. Second, in both cases, the ethical emerges as only one source of proof or mode of argument. Third—in a way that follows from the second—ethical argument as a distinct mode of argument is relatively rare, and dangerous. Usually argument becomes ethical by virtue of being argumentative and aiming at its internal end. Finally, the person who argues ethically is trying to achieve the internal end of argument, to make a legitimate case, while the one who argues unethically aims directly at the external end of winning the case.

To take the first parallel, Aristotle distinguishes between *ethos* produced by the argument and *ethos* as a preexistent property that hearers impute to speakers. Even though such imputation may well be far more persuasive, it is not part of the art of rhetoric (*Rhetoric*, I.2.1356a5–13). This might seem to be fastidiousness on Aristotle's part, but when applied to constitutional interpretation, the distinction between internal, argumentative—constitutional—and external *ethos* becomes a substantive and important distinction. Bobbitt distinguishes between constitutional *ethos* and other ethical values that judges might hold. "The principal error one can make regarding ethical argument is

to assume that any statute or executive act is unconstitutional if it causes effects that are incompatible with the American cultural ethos. This equates
ethical argument, a constitutional form, with moral argument generally. . . .
The 'morality' of the American constitutional system is, broadly speaking, that
of the values of limited government, forbearance and pluralism" (*CI*, 20–21).
There is all the difference in the world between arguing about discrimination
against homosexuals in terms of a private preference for privacy and arguing
about it in terms of a constitutional disagreement about the limits of government. There can be legitimate ethical arguments on both sides of the latter
question. An ethical argument that the Constitution is concerned with state
action and so cannot interfere with private preferences has to be met by an
ethical argument that political privileges and immunities cannot be denied by
a majority to a minority.

Second, in both the *Rhetoric* and contemporary constitutional hermeneutics, the ethical emerges only as one source of proof or mode of argument
among others. At the beginning of the *Rhetoric,* Aristotle says that his predecessors concentrated on emotional appeals and so ignored arguments *and* denied the existence of ethical appeals. Similarly, the ethos internal to the practices of constitutional argument is a spirit committed to reading the
Constitution as a constitution, not as a contract. Internal ethos is by that fact
committed to the other forms of argument as well. To argue ethically is necessarily to be a pluralist with regard to argument. The constitutional hermeneut
who argues historically, textually, or prudentially *may* be a pluralist, but the
ethical reasoner *must* be.[29] Aristotle's *phronimos* did not have to be a pluralist,
but the prudent constitutional reasoner today must be.

To erect ethical argument as a distinct mode of argument or source of proof
makes explicit what is already present in plural legitimate argument, in an art
of rhetoric with its own internal ends or the constitutional hermeneutics of rational fidelity. The ethical, both in Aristotle's *Rhetoric* and in contemporary
constitutional hermeneutics, is difficult to isolate as a distinct mode of proof
because its operation is so often tacit, negative, and regulative.[30] The textual-
ist, for example, denies that a right to privacy can be found in the Constitution,
which contains no words about privacy. The argument from ethos claims that
the right to privacy can be found in the constitutional ethos of limited government itself. No one would suggest that the government could order women to
have more children or that some people, chosen by lot, must spend their lives
in military service. Ethical arguments reject such possibilities before they are
even raised, which is why it is usually tacit, negative, and regulative.

In the third parallel, we can offer an even stronger conclusion. The
Rhetoric shows how direct ethical arguments are prone to backfire. "Trust me;

I'm not a crook" is rarely successful; argument is for the most part ethical by being argumentative, that is, by aiming at its internal end. In *Constitutional Fate*, Bobbitt offers two examples of ethical argument from concurring opinions in a single case, and they show that ethical argument generally becomes less legitimate when made explicit and self-conscious. "The *Griswold* case gave us two opinions [that] employed ethical argument, one quite studiedly and quite unfortunately and the other successfully and unobtrusively" (*CF*, 172).[31] Bobbitt regards these juxtapositions of adjectives as accidental, that is, that good ethical arguments can be made self-consciously and explicitly as well as unobtrusively. He believes that the studied nature of Justice Goldberg's concurring opinion did not *cause* its weakness and that the unobtrusiveness of Justice Harlan's was not of the essence. But the parallel to the *Rhetoric* suggests that it is a peculiarity of ethical argument that it works best when modifying, restraining, and regulating the other modes.

To argue legitimately is to accomplish the internal end of constitutional interpretation, but that internal end is in part a means to, and in part constitutive of, the given end of justice. We argue prudently in order to do justice. The activity of constitutional fidelity constitutes, as all practices do, a community and culture, in this case a community and culture of argument. Unlike philosophy and rhetoric when they define themselves as polemical opposites, prudential argument requires moral as well as intellectual virtues. (This is why philosophers and rhetoricians are put to death: their activities are seen as incompatible with citizenship, while *phronimoi* are accused only of being conservative.) The internal values of legitimate argument bar totalitarian ambitions and legislate civility. They make possible a community of disagreement; thus, argumentative pluralism makes possible communities of plural interests and aspiration, instead of communities where those interests are simply united by a contract or a peace treaty. This is what Aristotle meant when he said that citizens are concerned about one another's virtue, while members of commercial contracts or defensive alliances are not. To argue prudently is to be by the nature of the activity part of a community.

I can now make my fourth and final point. The ethical does double duty: it is one mode of argument among others, and yet at the same time all legitimate argument is ethical. For Aristotle, whether an appeal is part of the art of rhetoric is ultimately an ethical question. Argument functioning as instrumental reason in aid of an external end is not ethical. Applied to contemporary constitutional hermeneutics, this is quite a powerful conclusion. The difference between a legitimate textual, historical argument and an illegitimate one is ultimately an ethical difference between argument as constitutive and argument as a means. A person whose methods of argument always lead to conclusions that coincide with a political platform is arguing as unethically as one who is indifferent to whether the results of argument are just.

I have tried to give a new and more historically sensitive sense to the distinctions between letter and spirit and between contract and constitution. The hermeneutic task is to find a meaning for the Constitution to which one can give rational fidelity. Rhetoric is a neutral power equally available in the service of any purpose external to itself—that is the sense of the rhetorical from which we began and against which philosophy is in perennial revolt. Prudent rhetoric is not that same rhetoric oriented to good ends but a rhetoric that locates its value and its allegiance to the forms of argument themselves, while always mindful that the forms are purposive forms, aiming at a justice they do not define.

Aristotle's *phronesis* is illuminated when we see how it reappears and how it is transformed in a different context. This contemporary Aristotelian vision of constitutional hermeneutics, rhetoric, and *phronesis,* in which pluralism, the internal ends of argument, and the ethical dimensions of argument develop together, is an advance over the more popular sophistical and philosophical constructions of constitutional interpretation. The latter pretend that the superiority of their position is metaphysical, not ethical. Each therefore tries to establish its own position by refuting the other. The ethical enters their accounts only as warnings concerning external ends: strict constructionists are racists and their opponents wish to impose antireligious equality on us. My arguments in favor of *phronesis* have been ethical arguments. Ethically, it is possible to combine the desire for stability that motivates philosophy's quest for certainty with the desire for autonomy that motivates rhetoric's desire for self-assertion. On my account, constitutional hermeneutics, rhetoric, and *phronesis* develop the intellectual and emotional abilities most likely to advance justice.

NOTES

Earlier drafts of this chapter benefited from readings by Philip Bobbitt and James B. White.

1 Aristotle, *On Rhetoric: A Theory of Civic Discourse,* trans. George A. Kennedy (New York: Oxford University Press, 1991), III.17.1418a10.
2 John Rawls, "Justice as Fairness: Political Not Metaphysical," *Philosophy and Public Affairs* 14 (1985): 223–51. The replacement of philosophy by more modest and political principles has been a major theme in the work of Richard Rorty. See, e.g., "The Priority of Democracy to Philosophy," in Merrill Peterson and Robert Vaughn, eds., *The Virginia Statute of Religious Freedom* (Cambridge: Cambridge

University Press, 1988), and reprinted in Alan R. Malachowski, *Reading Rorty* (Oxford: Blackwell, 1989).

3 Richard Bernstein, *Beyond Objectivism and Relativism* (Philadelphia: University of Pennsylvania Press), 1983.

4 Recall Alasdair MacIntyre's definition of a practice: "A coherent and complex form of socially established cooperative human activity through which goods internal to that form of activity are realized in the course of trying to achieve those standards of excellence which are appropriate to, and partially definitive of, that form of activity, with the result that human powers to achieve excellence, and human conceptions of the ends and goods involved, are systematically extended" (*After Virtue*, 2d ed. [Notre Dame: Notre Dame University Press, 1984], 187). In *Aristotle's Rhetoric: An Art of Character* (Chicago: University of Chicago Press, 1994), I show in detail what it means to regard rhetoric as a practice in this sense. My other claims about the *Rhetoric* in this chapter are developed and defended in that book.

5 Michael W. McConnell, "Religious Freedom at the Crossroads," in Geoffrey R. Stone, Richard A. Epstein, and Cass. R. Sunstein, eds., *The Bill of Rights in the Modern State* (Chicago: University of Chicago Press, 1992), 173, n. 250.

6 Gerald Bruns, *Hermeneutics Ancient and Modern* (New Haven: Yale University Press, 1992), 11: "What is understood in a text is never reducible . . . to another's meaning, rather what one understands, in the light of another's meaning, is a subject matter. . . . Because of who we are and how we are situated the text has a claim on us, and part of what we understand is the substance and force of this claim, and also how we are going to respond to it." See also 65–66: "A text, after all, is canonical not in virtue of being final and correct and part of an official library but because it becomes *binding* on a group of people. The whole point of canonization is to underwrite the authority of a text, not merely with respect to its origin as against competitors in the field—this, technically, would simply be a question of authenticity—but with respect to the present and future in which it will reign or govern as a binding text."

7 Sanford Levinson, *Constitutional Faith* (Princeton: Princeton University Press, 1988). Prior to Levinson is Hugo Black's *A Constitutional Faith* (New York: Alfred Knopf, 1968). Joseph Vining's distinction in *The Authoritative and the Authoritarian* (Chicago: University of Chicago Press, 1986) is posed initially as a distinction between two kinds of texts: some of the texts that organize and control our lives "offer access to a mind," "evidence of the workings of a mind" (i.e., those that are "authoritative;" 12), while others ("authoritarian") do not." Vining eventually makes the difference one of community. The idea of rational fidelity is also parallel to the synthesis of reason and will that Paul Kahn traces in *Legitimacy and History: Self-Government in American Constitutional Theory* (New Haven: Yale University Press, 1992). As Kahn points out, to the extent that reason is sufficient to determine justice, a written constitution becomes unnecessary. The Founders described their act of constitution-making as one of deliberation and choice based on reason, but those who come after them seem forced to choose between obeying either the rea-

son or the will of the Founders. While our projects have many affinities, Kahn would find my exposition of rational fidelity overly optimistic.

8 Aristotle, *Politics*, trans. Carnes Lord (Chicago: University of Chicago Press, 1984), III.5.1280a5–12.

9 The distinction between contract and constitution, and so between the kinds of interpretation appropriate to each, has been present since the beginnings of judicial review, in *Marbury v. Madison*, where Chief Justice Marshall claims that the Constitution is the vehicle through which the people "establish, for their future government, such principles as, in their opinion, shall most conduct to their own happiness. . . . [It] is the basis on which the whole American fabric has been erected."

10 Eugene Garver, "Aristotle's Natural Slaves: Incomplete *Praxeis* and Incomplete Human Beings," *Journal of the History of Philosophy* 32 (1994): 1–22.

11 Similarly, in his exposition of Ronald Dworkin's theory of constitutional hermeneutics, whose function is to understand the law as being the best it can be, Cass Sunstein notes that "the evaluative dimension comes in trying to make the law *the best* it can be. The descriptive part comes in trying to make the law the best it can be. . . . A statement about what 'the law is,' therefore, cannot be rigidly separated from a statement about what 'the law should be.' 'What the law is' turns out to be a part, in part, of what people think it should be'" (Cass R. Sunstein, *The Partial Constitution* [Cambridge: Harvard University Press, 1993], 112). See also David Hume: "Whatever speculative errors may be found in the polite writings of any age or country. . . . There needs but a certain turn of thought or imagination to make us enter into all the opinions which then prevailed, and relish the sentiments or conclusions derived from them. . . . [But the] case is not the same with moral principles as with speculative opinions. . . . I cannot, nor is it proper I should, enter into such sentiments . . . and where a man is confident of the rectitude of that moral standard by which he judges, he is justly jealous of it, and will not pervert the sentiments of his heart for a moment, in complaisance to any writer whatsoever" (*Essays: Moral, Political, and Literary*, ed. Eugene F. Miller [Indianapolis: Liberty Classics, 1987], 252–53).

12 As is now explicit in his *Political Liberalism*, the project of Rawls's work has been precisely to convert pluralism from a modus vivendi to a form of justice. As will become clear, I seek to effect that same conversion for constitutional hermeneutics and rhetoric.

13 Sunstein, *Partial Constitution*, 23–24: "The framers' belief in deliberative democracy drew from traditional republican thought, and . . . departed from the tradition in the insistence that a large republic would be better than a smaller one. It departed even more dramatically in its striking and novel rejection of the traditional republican idea that heterogeneity and difference were destructive to the deliberative process. For the Framers, heterogeneity was beneficial, indeed indispensable; discussion must take place among people who were different. It was on this score that the Framers responded to the antifederalist insistence that homogeneity was necessary to a republic." The debate between Jürgen Habermas and Hans-Georg Gadamer, as reported by Richard Bernstein, reenacts this dispute over whether

phronesis requires a background of agreement in order to function. See Richard Bernstein, *Philosophical Profiles* (Philadelphia: University of Pennsylvania Press, 1986), 71–72: "Habermas can be used to highlight some of the difficulties in the very appeal to *phronesis*. For Gadamer himself has stressed that *phronesis* involves a mediation and codetermination of the universal and the particular. In the context of ethical and political action, by the 'universal' Gadamer means those principles, norms, and laws that are founded in the life of the community and orient our particular decisions and actions. Gadamer stresses how all such principles and laws require judgment and *phronesis* for their concrete application. This makes good sense when there are shared *nomoi* that inform the life of a community. But what happens when there is a breakdown of such principles, when they no longer seem to have any normative power, when there are deep and apparently irreconcilable conflicts about such principles, or when questions are raised about the very norms and principles that ought to guide our *praxis?* What type of discourse is appropriate when we question the 'universal' element—the *nomoi*—that is essential for the practice of *phronesis?*"

14 Philip Bobbitt, *Constitutional Interpretation* (Oxford: Blackwell, 1991), and *Constitutional Fate: Theory of the Constitution* (New York: Oxford University Press, 1982). References to these books appear within the text as *CI* and *CF,* respectively.

15 It is worth noting that structural and doctrinal arguments are those most absent from the sorts of hermeneutics influenced by Gadamer, who downplays the institutional context of interpretation.

16 For the grounding of interpretation in a theory of interpretation, see E. D. Hirsch, *The Aims of Interpretation* (Chicago: University of Chicago Press, 1976). For the grounding of interpretation in a theory of politics, see Ronald Dworkin, *Taking Rights Seriously* (Cambridge: Harvard University Press, 1977).

17 Robert Post, "Theories of Constitutional Interpretation," *Representations* 30 (1990): 24. "What is authoritative is neither more nor less than our common commitment to the flourishing of the mutual enterprise of nationhood. . . . The radical and paradoxical implication of this perspective is that the Constitution explicitly loses its character as a specific document or a discrete text. It becomes instead, as Karl Llewellyn bluntly put it, a 'going Constitution,' a 'working Constitution' which has a content that 'is in good part utterly extra-Documentary,' and which represents the *'fundamental* framework' of the 'governmental machine.' In this way the Constitution is transformed into what Kant might call the 'regulative' idea of the enterprise of constitutional adjudication, the 'imaginary focus from which the concepts' of that enterprise 'seem to proceed, even though there is nothing knowable at that focus.'

"The Constitution as a regulative idea defines the *telos* and shape of constitutional interpretation; it demands a continual effort to articulate the authority of our 'fundamental nature as a people' and hence concomitantly to summon 'us to our powers as co-founders as to our responsibilities' in the full knowledge that 'how we are able to constitute ourselves is profoundly tied to how we are already constituted by our own distinctive history.'" Post's quotations are from (1) Karl Llewellyn, "The Constitution as an Institution," *Columbia Law Review* 34 (1934): 14–15, 26; (2) Immanuel Kant, in J. N. Findlay, *Kant and the Transcendental Object: A Hermeneutic Study* (Oxford: Oxford University Press, 1981), 241; and (3) Hanna Pitkin, "The Idea of a Constitution," *Journal of Legal Education* 37 (1987): 167–69. See also the epigraph to Post's article by Claude Lefort: "Modern democracy invites us to replace the notion of a regime founded upon laws, of a legitimate power, by a notion of a regime founded upon the *legitimacy of a debate as to what is legitimate and what is illegitimate*—a debate which is necessarily without any guarantor and without any end" (*Democracy and Political Theory,* trans. David Macey [Minneapolis: University of Minnesota Press, 1988], 39).

18 *CF,* 228: "The more carefully we examine the actual uses of the Constitution in constitutional decision, the sharper becomes the conflict between those uses and our requirement that they follow inexorably from a constitutional command." See also Vining, *The Authoritative and the Authoritarian,* 156. For an opposed point of view, compare Robert Bork, *The Tempting of America,* 176.

19 This reversal is a modern working out of the problem about justice posed in Plato's *Republic,* book 2. Justice may come into existence because of the need for cooperation in the division of work, but true justice makes such divisions among natures possible.

20 Aristotle, *Nicomachean Ethics,* trans. Terence C. Irwin (Indianapolis: Bobbs-Merrill, 1985), I.9.1180a23–24.

21 Vining, *The Authoritative and the Authoritarian,* 224: "Lawyers, being so aware of processes, are prone to making the mistake of thinking that since outcomes are contingent there is only process left to hold onto, and that commitment to law is commitment to process, or, as it is called in law, procedure. Law *is* procedure, it is sometimes said. But since there can be no real commitment to process—when one embraces one's child, husband, wife, or lover, one does not fold one's arms around a process—the result is that there is no real commitment to law. Lawyer's mistake in thinking contributes greatly to the relativism and emptiness they so often espouse and suffer so needlessly. Process is not all that is left when particular outcomes are seen to be contingent." See also Jerold S. Auerbach, "What Has Teaching of Law to Do with Justice?" *NYU Law Review* 53 (1978): 457–74.

22 John Dewey, *Essays in Experimental Logic* (Chicago: University of Chicago Press, 1918), 311: "Society not only continues to exist *by* transmission, *by* communication, but it may fairly be said to exist *in* transmission, *in* communication. There is more than a verbal tie between the words, common, community, and communication. Men live in a community in virtue of the things which they have in common; and communication is the way in which they come to possess things in common. . . . A democracy is more than a form of government; it is primarily a mode of associated living, of conjoint communicated experience."

23 *Abrams v. United States,* 250 U.S. 616 (1919); *Korematsu v. United States,* 323 U.S. 214 (1944).

24 David Hoy, "Hermeneutical Critique of the Originalism/Nonoriginalism Distinction," *Northern Kentucky Law Review* 15 (1988): 494–95: "Application as the necessary inherence of a text in some context, is not a second, subjective moment in coming to understand the text. There may be a further operation where the interpreter has the option of making the text explicitly relevant. If we call this appropriation rather than application, we can, then, see that there may be times when interpreters may have to try to avoid making the text seem relevant, perhaps because they want to let less well understood features of the text become more problematic for us than they have been. Thus, on Gadamer's theory, application is not an option and is not subjective. But appropriation (e.g., making the text seem more rather than less relevant) is an optional strategy, such that it can be used or avoided." See also Michael J. Perry, "Why Constitutional Theory Matters to Constitutional Practice (and Vice Versa)," in Gregory Leyh, ed., *Legal Hermeneutics: History, Theory, and Practice* (Berkeley: University of California Press, 1992), 241–68.

25 *Dred Scott v. Sandford*, 60 U.S. 393 (1856); *Brown v. Board of Education*, 347 U.S. 483 (1954).

26 Kahn, *Legitimacy and History*, 36: "When the issue of slavery became critical to the life of the nation, this idea of exceptionality [of slavery in the Constitution] was threatened. As the nation confronted constitutionally legitimated inequality, the scientific foundation of the whole constitutional edifice came under tremendous stress."

27 *CI*, 166: "Our values do not necessarily precede our choices; rather, making decisions actualizes and in some cases even precipitates our values. Before all choices, there are no values, only vague attractions, repulsions, attitudes.... It is not that values are a precondition for making choices, but rather the other way around."

28 Technically, for Aristotle the relation between legitimacy and justice is the relation between potency and act, as is his relation between virtue and happiness. Legitimate arguments are those that, when successful, establish justice. This does not mean that legitimate arguments are necessarily just, any more than it means that the virtuous man is automatically happy. It does mean, first, that it is only through virtue that one achieves happiness and, second, that our best way of understanding happiness is through understanding virtue. The relation between legitimacy and justice is weaker, however, for we believe that we have alternate ways of both knowing what justice is and, occasionally, securing it. That difference comes from the fact that we have many legitimate ways of arriving at justice.

29 Post's "responsive" mode of interpretation has many similarities to Bobbitt's "ethical." Although he does not use my language, he does assert something similar: that this mode is necessarily self-conscious and pluralistic; it necessarily distinguishes legitimacy from justification. "Responsive interpretation is unique, for it alone explicitly thematizes this relational nature of constitutional authority. Both historical and doctrinal interpretation purport to submit to a Constitution whose authority is independent and fixed, either in the preexisting consent of the ratifiers or in the preexisting rules of controlling precedents. Although this submission is illusory, it is an

illusion capable of disarming dissent. Responsive interpretation, however, disavows this illusion, and frankly locates constitutional authority in the relationship between the Constitution and its interpreters. As a consequence responsive interpretation generates an intense and singular kind of political dynamics" ("Theories of Constitutional Interpretation," 29–30).

30 *CF,* 95: "There is an almost utter absence of the discussion of ethical arguments *as arguments* in the teaching of constitutional law. Either they are instead regarded as disreputable reflections of the moral and political positions of the judge who lacks sufficient willpower to keep them properly cabined or they are indulged by both the cynical and the sentimental for being what 'real' judging is all about, having little to do with the competition of arguments *per se.*"

31 *Griswold v. Connecticut,* 381 U.S. 479 (1965); in this case the Court held that privacy rights invalidated state laws prohibiting the sale of birth-control devices.

9

Hermeneutical Rhetoric

Michael Leff

"Hermeneutical rhetoric" is the counterpart of Steven Mailloux's "rhetorical hermeneutics." In an article bearing that title and more extensively in his book *Rhetorical Power,* Mailloux offers an "anti-theory theory" of interpretation that situates literary hermeneutics within the context of rhetorical exchange.[1] Traditional literary theory, Mailloux argues, relies upon a general conception of interpretation as the basis for justifying particular interpretative acts. Such "theory" takes two forms—"textual realism," where meaning is found in the text, and "readerly idealism," where meaning is made through intersubjective agreements among a community of interpreters. As theories, these positions are diametrically opposed, but, Mailloux maintains, both are theoretical precisely because they share the assumption that standards of interpretation must refer to a general ground that exists outside the context of a particular interpretative act; in one case, the text itself acts as a constraint on meaning, and in the other case, shared conventions constrain and shape meanings—but both alike seek to justify interpretations through something extrinsic to the specific context in which the interpretative work occurs. And, Mailloux contends, both fail to meet their own standards; they suffer "radical embarrassments" because they cannot offer theoretically coherent accounts of how interpretation works in practice.[2]

Moreover, Mailloux denies that the problems of idealism and realism can be solved either by combining the two or by displacing both in favor of some other theory. The problem is theory itself and the answer is to stop doing it. In its place, Mailloux advocates a form of "interpretative neo-pragmatism" that views interpretation as a grounded rhetorical process:

> Such a hermeneutics views shared interpretative strategies not as the creative origin of texts but rather as historical sets of topics, arguments, tropes, ideologies, and so forth which determine how texts are established as meaningful through rhetorical exchange. Such communities are actually synonymous with the conditions in which acts of persuasion about texts take place. Concepts such as "interpretative strategies" and "argumentative fields" are, we might say, simply descriptive tools for referring to the unformalizable context of interpretative work, work that always involves rhetorical action, attempts to convince others of the truth of explications and explanations.[3]

In other words, contexts always enter into interpretation, and because contexts are theoretically indeterminate, they cannot be formalized and subjected to standards extrinsic to the ground of a particular rhetorical exchange. Interpretative theory is only a species of rhetorical politics, and rather than attempting to resolve interpretative controversies by rising above them, hermeneutics ought to ground itself within rhetorical histories; it ought to provide thick descriptions of interpretative practices that are mindful of the shifting political positions of those who engage in them.[4]

As this brief summary indicates, Mailloux's rhetorical hermeneutics not only alters conventional notions about the theory-practice relation, but it also blurs distinctions between the political and the literary. Nevertheless, his position clearly and self-consciously emerges from within a specific disciplinary context. His argument begins with debates about theory and meaning in literary studies, and, although he extends his interests into the domain of politics, his focal point remains the problem of interpretation per se and his dominant referent is literary texts. The adjective-noun relation in rhetorical hermeneutics indicates this emphasis. Mailloux, that is, works through rhetoric to generate a more sophisticated conception of the hermeneutic enterprise.

Because of my own disciplinary interests, I would like to reverse this orientation so that the stress falls on rhetoric. Hence, I wish to reverse the position of the adjective and the noun and propose a hermeneutical rhetoric. The focal interest here centers on rhetorical practice as manifested in texts that directly and overtly engage political circumstances. And this change in focal object also suggests a different motive—a shift from how rhetoric constrains under-standing of texts to how interpretative processes become inventional re-sources in texts that purport to address extraverbal reality. To put the point simply: where Mailloux asks how rhetorical strategies enter into hermeneutic activity, I ask how hermeneutical strategies enter into the production of politi-cal rhetoric.

This antithesis is too simple and tidy to serve as anything other than a provi-sional distinction between disciplinary perspectives. In critical practice, the two orientations are not easily separated, and whoever begins with one almost inevitably becomes entangled with the other. Mailloux's book illustrates this fluidity as it moves from a consideration of theoretical texts to literary texts to texts generated in Senate hearings, and at every phase of this movement, sim-ple distinctions between production and interpretation give way to an analysis that reveals how the two processes blend in the communicative context. Like-wise, my interest in the production of political discourse must necessarily pro-ceed through an interpretative process grounded within a disciplinary com-munity. The hermeneutic strategies of the rhetor are not just there to be plucked out of a text; to locate and assess them, I must engage in interpretative work and offer explanations and arguments rhetorically appropriate to the community of rhetorical critics. Thus, a complex interaction between herme-neutic inquiry and rhetorical exchange operates in both disciplinary contexts, whatever the differences between the two in their initial orientations. Or, from a broader perspective, we might say that all interpretative work involves participation in a rhetorical exchange, and every rhetorical exchange involves some interpretative work.

These considerations might tempt us to close the circle at either point in-differently and to regard rhetorical hermeneutics and hermeneutical rhetoric as two ways of saying the same thing. But I believe that this would be a serious mistake, for it would disregard one of Mailloux's fundamental premises. Hold-ing that practice has priority over theory—indeed that theory is a form of prac-tice—Mailloux's argument proceeds through "rhetorical histories," and it is anchored in the disciplinary history of literary studies. Rhetorical criticism (in speech communication) and literary hermeneutics (in literary disciplines) have had significantly different histories, and scholars in the two domains typ-ically engage in significantly different practices. Even if these distinctions are arbitrary and counterproductive (although I don't think they always are), they remain a practical fact that cannot be ignored. Consequently, we would distort Mailloux's project if we simply transposed its results into rhetorical criticism. Instead, we need to develop a hermeneutic (in Hans-Georg Gadamer's sense of the term) that recognizes the "otherness" of disciplinary interests while it

opens space for fusing these differences into new perspectives. This effort requires recognition of points of resistance as well as affinity; it is for this reason
that I propose to make hermeneutical rhetoric a counterpart rather than a species or a genus of rhetorical hermeneutics.

INVENTION, INTERPRETATION, AND IMITATION
IN THE RHETORICAL TRADITION

Hermeneutical rhetoric entails a realignment of the relation between interpretation and production in the rhetorical tradition, as that relation is now
generally conceived. At present, the dominant view is that classical rhetoric
must be sharply distinguished from contemporary criticism because of the
productive/performative emphasis of the one, and the hermeneutic/interpre-
tative emphasis of the other. The earliest version of this distinction, so far as I
know, appeared fifteen years ago in Jane Tompkins's influential essay "The
Reader in History: The Changing Shape of Literary Response."[5] Tompkins
notes a number of similarities between classical literary criticism formed on
the rhetorical model and contemporary reader-response theory. But she also
identifies a crucial difference: contemporary critics, she observes, take "meaning to be the object of critical investigation," whereas classical critics are concerned with language as power and not as signification. Hence, their purpose
in studying texts is not to understand the texts' meaning but to identify techniques useful for future rhetorical production. In the classical approach, the
goal of criticism is to enhance the reader's inventional skills as writer or
speaker rather than to treat the text as a privileged locus of meaning.[6]

More recently, Dilip Gaonkar has adopted a similar perspective as the basis
for constructing a disciplinary history of rhetorical criticism. For Gaonkar,
classical rhetoric deals with production and looks forward to the making of a
text. By contrast, contemporary rhetoric, as it has followed in the wake of the
"interpretative turn," has adopted a hermeneutic goal and seeks to interpret
texts that have already been made. The two orientations, he argues, are distinct, and the productionist vocabulary of classical rhetoric therefore offers a
thin and inherently flawed basis for contemporary rhetorical criticism. Yet
after conducting a detailed reading of the literature, Gaonkar concludes that
practicing critics still rely heavily, though often unconsciously, on the assumptions and techniques embedded in the classical model of production. The use
of this model, he notes with regret, has persisted despite the overt renunciation of neo-Aristotelianism; the resulting tension between unrecognized presuppositions and professed interpretative objectives has had a debilitating effect on the critical work in the discipline.[7]

The distinctions drawn by Tompkins and Gaonkar have the merit of clarity, and up to a point they are plausible and useful. Classical rhetoric and the criticism associated with it surely place emphasis on reading as a resource for future production rather than as an exercise in assigning meaning. Moreover, the technical apparatus of classical rhetoric is intended mainly as a guide to rhetorical performance and production, and its application to critical interpretation does raise problems that often have been neglected. And Gaonkar rightly emphasizes the persistence and magnitude of these problems in the disciplinary history of modern rhetorical criticism.

Nevertheless, if these paired distinctions between periods and focal interests indicate plausible differences of tendency, they are misleading when considered as global and essential oppositions. Production and interpretation, as we have learned from Mailloux, cannot be isolated from each other, and just as contemporary interpretative theories emerge through rhetorical production, so also the productive emphasis in classical rhetoric has its hermeneutic moments. Unfortunately, modern rhetorical critics, who have concentrated almost exclusively on the technical lore of classical rhetoric, have failed to appreciate the way interpretation and production interact in the full program of traditional rhetorical education. And Gaonkar, because he begins with a strong and unqualified binary opposition between production and interpretation, assumes that the problems in applying classical rhetoric to interpretative work stem from the productive essence of that rhetoric. He does not consider that these difficulties might result from the way modern scholars interpret the tradition, and thus he falls victim to the disease of conceptual rigidity he intends to cure.

The appropriation of classical rhetoric by modern critics was not the result of unmediated contact with the essence of the tradition. It occurred within an academic milieu that favored—almost demanded—foundationalist conceptions of theory and method.[8] Modern critics left the impress of their prejudices and needs on the tradition, selecting and interpreting its elements to conform with their interest in abstract theory and objective methodology. Not surprisingly, then, they isolated the preceptive lore as almost the sole focus of attention and treated the precepts as theoretical principles capable of objective, somewhat mechanical application to texts. Other aspects of classical rhetorical education—its extensive program of reading, for example, or its compositional exercises and its rather antitheoretical stress on pragmatic judgment—were largely ignored. The result was a critical program that had little interpretative energy. The fault here, however, was less a consequence of the original model than of the way the model had been reconstructed. Moreover, the efforts to reform rhetorical criticism have typically proceeded through efforts to displace rather than reinterpret the older tradition.

Yet, Gaonkar's binary analysis notwithstanding, the contemporary hermeneutic turn invites such reinterpretation. By denying that texts have fixed, objective meanings, the new hermeneutics opens space for the concepts of probability, social exchange, and situated interests to become matters of serious concern. And, as we have noted in Mailloux's work, these concepts undermine the assumption that interpretation and production are distinct activities. Underscoring these points of affinity between rhetoric and hermeneutics, Gadamer argues that "the grasping of the meaning of the text takes on something of the character of an independent productive act, one that resembles more the art of the orator than the process of listening. Thus it is easy to understand why the theoretical tools of the art of interpretation (hermeneutics) have been to a large extent borrowed from rhetoric."[9] Gadamer, however, has never elaborated this relation between traditional rhetoric and hermeneutics, and I suspect that the reason is indicated in this passage. He emphasizes the productive (rhetorical) aspect of interpreting a written text, but because he seems to regard rhetoric as an oral art (defined by the speaker-hearer relationship), the idea of a hermeneutic component in rhetoric may be foreign to him. If, however, we take a broader view and consider how a program of reading and criticism entered into rhetorical education, we might perceive how hermeneutic processes of understanding through application can enter into the primarily productive economy of the rhetorical system.

In classical rhetoric, the doctrine of *imitatio* provided the most obvious intersection between the reading of texts and the production of persuasive arguments. Although this doctrine held a prominent place in traditional rhetoric, modern scholars have only begun to give it serious attention, and it is sometimes badly misunderstood because of the aversion to "imitation" that we have inherited from romantic thought. *Imitatio* is not the mere repetition or mechanistic reproduction of something found in an existing text. It is a complex process that allows historical texts to serve as equipment for future rhetorical production. Classical literary criticism, drawn into the orbit of rhetorical functionalism, largely served as a vehicle for developing productive skills through *imitatio,* and Tompkins notes that this orientation militated against reading literary texts as free-standing units, but she underestimates the role that interpretation played within this rhetorical approach to literature.

The function of rhetorical education, at least in its more liberal versions, was to impart the practical judgment and linguistic resources needed to adapt to changing circumstances. Eloquence demanded the capacity to make the appropriate response to concrete situations, and hence propriety (*prepon* or *decorum*) in rhetoric, like prudence in ethics, could not be reduced to theoretical rules. Rules were general, but rhetorical cases were particular and could not be resolved simply by theoretical knowledge. Consequently, the preceptive lore of rhetoric did not constitute a theory or method in the modern sense of these terms. Instead, the body of precepts served as an armamentarium of possible strategies, whose potential could be realized only as they were used in actual rhetorical production. Thus, a knowledge of rhetoric limited to abstract principles would yield what Quintilian called a "dumb science."[10] The goal of the system was not to generate theory but to assist in developing a faculty for judging when to use a strategy and how to embody it appropriately in a particular case.

Given the limitations of theoretical instruction, *imitatio* played a vital role in rhetorical education, for it could show what the rules could not tell. In the first phase of this process, the reader would learn to identify strategies and forms as actually embodied in a historical text and to judge their significance relative to the construction of the text as a whole and its situated rhetorical purposes. In the second phase, such strategies and forms would be reembodied in a new composition addressed to a different situation. Throughout both phases, invention and interpretation interact with each other. Significant features of the historical text must not only be recognized but be applied to an understanding of how they function in the rhetorical metabolism of that text—something that implies an inventive act on the part of the reader—and then, as reader becomes writer, interpretative judgment must be used to determine whether, when, and how these strategies can be appropriated for new uses. And within this practice, the interplay between understanding and production creates an organic connection between the historical text and the new composition; the old text leaves its impression on the rhetor's product, but the rhetor's productive act has left its interpretative impression on the original. In her astute analysis of classical *imitatio*, Rita Copeland summarizes this complex development when she observes that "the relationship between model and copy, like that of lineage, is predicated on the act of invention; the model, or ancestor, discovers and posits the ground for future invention. Such an evolutionary pattern is enabled or sustained by the very interpretative community which it creates. Hence, to justify the imitative enterprise, the copy produces, not conspicuous likeness of the original, but rather what is understood and revalued in the original."[11]

As Copeland's remarks suggest, *imitatio* can become something much more than a technical classroom exercise. In practice, of course, it is sometimes used for limited and technical stylistic purposes, but it can also function as an important resource for developing extended arguments. Or again, through a process similar to Kenneth Burke's "casuistic stretching," imitation of the structure and language of an old text may help introduce radically new ideas. Even more broadly, historical texts may serve as political and moral as well as artistic paradigms—paradigms that embed themselves deeply into the rhetorical performance and help constitute the persona of the rhetor.

At all these levels, but especially in cases that involve a strong political and ethical tendency, *imitatio* functions as a hermeneutical rhetoric that circulates influence between past and present. As the embodied utterances of the past are interpreted for current application, their ideas and modes of articulation are reembodied, and old voices are recovered for use in new circumstances. Hermeneutic rhetoric, then, is at once a mechanism for technical production and a vehicle for achieving what J. Robert Cox calls the invention of usable traditions.[12]

This capacity for stable innovation—for building community through tradition without becoming mired in a staid traditionalism—marks the most significant feature of hermeneutic rhetoric as constructive counterpart to rhetorical hermeneutics. In formulating a rhetorical hermeneutics, Mailloux strips hermeneutics of a foundational basis by situating it in rhetorical practice. This conception leaves him open to the charge of pernicious relativism, and Mailloux attempts to blunt this charge by arguing that acknowledgment of the contingency of rhetorical politics "is not to avoid taking a position. Taking a position, making an interpretation, cannot be avoided. Moreover, such historical contingency does not disable interpretative argument, because it is the only ground it can have. We are always arguing at particular moments in specific places, to certain audiences. Our beliefs and commitments are no less real because they are historical, and the same holds for our interpretations."[13]

This endorsement of positioned argument in place of argument fixed against a standard outside historical circumstance fits comfortably within the rhetorical tradition. Yet when focused upon interpretation, this position has greater power for diagnostic and descriptive purposes than for invention. Rhetorical hermeneutics can provide thick descriptions of how interpretative practices change at different times and in different rhetorical communities, but it offers no account of how members of a community can invent new interpretative strategies while remaining within that community. In other words, Mailloux teaches us how we enter into rhetorical situations, but his program does not consider how we can alter them. Taking a stand within a contingent situation seems to reflect either the existing communal structures of argument and belief or an idiosyncratic, wholly subjective reaction against those standards. Hermeneutical rhetoric, however, focuses upon interpretation as a source of invention and suggests how traditions can be altered without destroying their identity. It offers a view of community as a locus of deliberating subjects who change themselves and one another by renewing and revaluing moments in their history.

This sketch of hermeneutical rhetoric has proceeded along abstract, theoretical lines, but I have argued that the concept cuts across the bias of theory and practice and manifests itself through concrete application. Consequently, it is best explained by reference to particulars; in the remainder of this chapter, I would like to illustrate the concept through a case study—specifically, Abraham Lincoln's use of the Declaration of Independence as a ground and vehicle for dealing with issues of his own time. I have selected this case because I believe it offers a clear instance of hermeneutical rhetoric and because the texts in question have already received detailed and expert study from many interpreters.[14] I have little new to say about Lincoln's use of the Declaration, but I hope to indicate how some of the existing interpretations can be synthesized and supplemented through the concept of hermeneutical rhetoric.

A CASE STUDY IN HERMENEUTICAL RHETORIC

Lincoln's most famous reference to the Declaration appears in the opening sentence of the Gettysburg Address: "Four score and seven years ago our fathers brought forth on this continent, a new nation, conceived in Liberty, and dedicated to the proposition that all men are created equal."[15] These words are so familiar, so comfortably imprinted in memory, that we normally do not pause to consider how Lincoln, without naming the Declaration, positions himself in relation to it. A moment's reflection, however, reveals that the relation is both complex and controversial. When Lincoln says that the nation was brought forth "four score and seven years ago," he confidently asserts something that is not a simple historical fact. It is equally possible to date the origin of the nation at other times and in respect to other documents, such as the Articles of Confederation or the Constitution. Thus, Lincoln selects a particular text to represent the origins of the American people, to locate their most fundamental principles, and to frame his own rhetorical effort.

Lincoln's sentence also recalls the language of the Declaration's second paragraph, which begins: "We hold these truths to be self-evident: That all men are created equal; that they are endowed by their Creator with certain unalienable rights; that among these are life, liberty, and the pursuit of happiness." Again Lincoln is selective, using some of the key terms from the original while omitting others. More important, he not only places the phrase "all men are created equal" in an emphatic position, he alters its epistemological status. While Jefferson holds the principle to be a self-evident truth, Lincoln regards it as a proposition to which the nation is dedicated. As several commentators have explained, this difference is significant, and I shall return to it later. For my present purposes, however, it is enough to note that the Gettysburg Address does not open with an elegantly neutral reference to the Declaration but with a carefully selected and nuanced view of how the document should be understood.

Once we recognize these rhetorical complications, it should come as no surprise that interpreters of the Gettysburg Address have reached very different conclusions about how Lincoln stands in relation to the Founding Fathers. Edwin Black, for example, holds that the speech expresses "a profound conservatism. The first sentence having announced the historical founding of a destiny, the speech serves the perpetuation of that original purpose." It is concerned with "the conservation of a political idea and with the republic that instantiates it."[16] Other readers, including a number of conservatives, reach the opposite conclusion. For them, the traditional language and the appeal to traditional authority disguise a radical purpose—"a startling new interpretation of that principle of the founders which declared that 'all men are created equal.'"[17] Distorting the teachings of the fathers for his own immediate political purposes, Lincoln, according to M. E. Bradford, constructs an "imaginary history" and then uses it as an instrument to transform the Union into a "unitary structure."[18] Still other readers find in the speech a complex blend of traditional and innovative elements. Thus, for Garry Wills, the Gettysburg Address is a revolutionary text, forever altering the self-perception of Americans as a people. But Wills argues that Lincoln effects this revolution through a rhetoric of correction rather than radical subversion. By reinterpreting the Declaration, Lincoln discovers a way to "correct the Constitution itself without overthrowing it."[19] For Glen Thorow, the Address sustains a complex, lively interaction between past principles and current interests, and "in apparently repeating the principles of the Declaration of Independence, Lincoln subtly changes their meaning."[20] Lincoln, Thorow maintains, does not simply invoke the authority of the Fathers; he interprets "their advice in light of their deeds for the present time."[21]

This third position, especially as Thorow articulates it, represents Lincoln as engaging in something very similar to the kind of hermeneutical rhetoric I have described earlier. From this perspective, past and present—interpretation of an old text and rhetorical invention for current purposes—work together simultaneously. Having established the Declaration as a point of reference (in fact, as the originary point of reference for the nation), Lincoln is constrained by that document, but he can also open space to reinterpret it and redefine the nation. Thus, the rhetorical power of the Gettysburg Address, in some large measure, results from the circulation of influence between Lincoln's words and the words of the original he both copies and reinvents. Thorow and Wills both offer useful readings of the speech in terms of this interaction. Thorow is precise and comprehensive in noting how Lincoln's text follows and departs from the Declaration, but he does not connect the text with its antecedents in Lincoln's antislavery rhetoric of the 1850s—a matter of real importance in understanding the "new birth of freedom" Lincoln announces at Gettysburg. Wills offers a detailed account of this connection, but his reading of the Address is less sensitive to its internal structure and to the hermeneutic energy it develops. In what follows, I hope to combine the virtues of both approaches and offer a more fully realized description of the intersection between rhetoric and hermeneutics in Lincoln's discourse. For this purpose, I need to begin with Lincoln's use of the Declaration in the period preceding his election to the presidency.

On August 17, 1858, shortly before his first debate with Stephen Douglas, Lincoln delivered a campaign speech in Lewistown, Illinois. Included in it was one of his most impassioned appeals to the Declaration of Independence. In that document, Lincoln said, the "Fathers of the Republic" revealed nothing less than

> their majestic interpretation of the economy of the Universe. This was their lofty, wise, and noble understanding of the justice of the Creator to His creatures.
>
> Yes, gentlemen, to all His creatures, to the whole great family of man . . . they erected a beacon to guide their children and their children's children, and the countless myriads who should inhabit the earth in other ages. . . . While pretending no indifference to earthly honors, I do claim to be actuated in this contest by something higher than an anxiety for office. I charge you to drop every paltry and insignificant thought for any man's success. It is nothing; I am nothing; Judge Douglas is nothing. But do not destroy that immortal emblem of Humanity—the Declaration of American Independence.[22]

This passage comes from a campaign speech, and its language is inflated, the sentiments hyperbolic. Nevertheless, it is difficult to deny their sincerity, for Lincoln repeats them so often and, in his more reflective moments, grounds them in an economical and precise logic. Three years before his senatorial campaign, in a letter to his friend Joshua Speed, Lincoln had written: "Our progress in degeneracy appears to me to be pretty rapid. As a nation, we began by declaring that 'all men are created equal.' We now practically read it 'all men are created equal, except negroes.' When the Know-Nothings get control, it will read 'all men are created equal, except negroes, and foreigners, and catholics.' When it comes to this I should prefer emigrating to some country—to Russia, for instance, where despotism can be taken pure, and without the base alloy of hypocracy."23

For Lincoln, then, the Declaration was not just a historical document, but "a living creed."24 Its principle of equality, as he understood it, was the universal, eternal, and essential bedrock of American democracy, or of any other self-governing polity. Any exception to or limitation on this principle subverted liberty, because it sanctioned the exercise of tyrannical control by one individual or group over another. The proposition that "all men are created equal," therefore, constituted the basis for political morality, and unless the public accepted and acted in accordance with this proposition, free government would inevitably erode and degenerate into tyranny.

This conception of the Declaration and the centrality of equal political rights did not emerge through philosophical contemplation. It was generated in and through the political controversies of the 1850s, when slavery emerged as the dominant issue nationally, and in the state of Illinois, where opinion was sharply divided. If, as Richard Hofstadter has said, the Declaration "was the primary article of Lincoln's creed,"25 that creed was itself developed within the crucible of political debate. Thus, Lincoln's immediate political purposes shaped his views of the Declaration and offered "political ammunition" for him as a controversialist.26 Merging interpretation and invention, Lincoln used the Declaration as a rhetorical instrument to build a political constituency for himself and to discredit his opponents, the most notable of whom was Douglas.

In countering Douglas's program of popular sovereignty, which attempted to drain the moral charge from the slavery issue, Lincoln repeatedly cited the plain language of the Declaration; slavery was not consistent with the moral truth that all men are created equal, and those who believed in the Declaration could not assume an ethically neutral position concerning slavery. Thus, Douglas's misguided effort to diffuse this issue did not offer a middle course. Instead, Lincoln argued, it was a radical deviation from the wisdom of the founders and a threat to the most fundamental principle of a free government; Douglas was attempting to "blow out the moral lights around us."

The plain language of the Declaration, however, was open to more than one interpretation, and Douglas responded with a vigorous counterattack based upon well-known historical evidence. When the Declaration was enacted, slavery was legal in all thirteen colonies, and many of the signers of the Declaration, including Jefferson himself, owned slaves. Consequently, unless the founders were the worst sort of hypocrites (and thus not worthy of credence), they could not have meant to include blacks in the phrase "all men are created equal." In the debate at Galesburg, Douglas charged that Lincoln's "Chicago doctrine"—his claim that the "negro and the white are made equal by the Declaration of Independence and by Divine Providence—is a monstrous heresy. The signers of the Declaration of Independence never dreamed of the negro when they were writing that document. They referred to white men, to men of European birth and European descent, when they declared the equality of all men." For Douglas, "this government was made by our fathers on the white basis. It was made by white men for the benefit of white men forever, and was intended to be administered by white men for all time to come." Thus, it was Lincoln who had distorted the sentiments of the founders and who, by assuming that he was "a wiser man than those who framed the government," threatened to subvert the edifice they had constructed.[27]

Douglas's argument rests upon assumptions that are unacceptable to a twentieth-century reader, but at the time and in the context of its utterance the argument carried substantial weight. Lincoln could not credibly claim the authority of the founders and of the Declaration without fashioning an effective reply. Moreover, the strictly historical parts of Douglas's argument were undeniable—the Declaration was written and promulgated by men who lived in a society that sanctioned slavery, and many of them were slave owners. Consequently, Lincoln needed to discover an interpretative perspective that deemphasized inferences based on the literal historical record and that stressed ethical principles relevant to the issues of his own day. His answer to this problem was a hermeneutic tour-de-force that first appeared in a speech he delivered in June 1857 and that he repeated verbatim in the final debate at Alton. After accusing Douglas of "doing violence to the plain unmistakable language of the Declaration," Lincoln commented:

> I think the authors of that notable instrument intended to include all men, but they did not intend to declare all men equal in all respects. They did not mean to say that all were equal in color, size, intellect, moral developments, or social capacity. They defined with tolerable distinctness in what respects they did consider all men created equal—equal in "certain inalienable rights, among which are life, liberty, and the pursuit of happiness." This they said, and this they meant. They did not mean to assert the obvious untruth that all were then actually enjoying equality, nor yet, that they were about to confer it immediately upon them. In fact, they had no power to confer such a boon. They meant simply to declare the right, so that the enforcement of it might follow as fast as circumstances should permit. They meant to set up a standard maxim for free society, which should be familiar to all, and revered by all; constantly looked to, constantly labored for, even though never perfectly attained,

constantly approximated, and thereby constantly spreading and deepening its influence, and augmenting the happiness and value of life to all people of all colors everywhere.[28]

In this remarkable passage, we witness hermeneutical rhetoric at work, as Lincoln constructs a vehicle for connecting the past utterance with its present application so that meaning and use interact. The principle of equality is not a statement of fact, but a maxim—a truth that we ought to use in measuring and directing our actions. This truth is eternal and universal, but we may never realize it, and we can never understand it except as it applies to circumstances that no one, not even the wise men who formulated the principle, could foresee. It is an ideal that we must constantly pursue although we cannot know where it will lead us. We do not grasp this truth in detached isolation, but we enact it through our political and ethical judgments, deepening and spreading its meaning, altering its precise content, through time and circumstance. The principle that all men are created equal is a legacy from our fathers but not a legacy that comes in the form of a fixed and finite property that can be measured, catalogued, and stored. Rather, we have been bequeathed a principle we can understand only through use. The founders, then, have left us a maxim that establishes a universal standard for a free society—a minimal principle of human respect and dignity—but it is a maxim that we renew and revalue in our constant effort to sustain the legacy of a free society under the pressure of constantly changing circumstances. The meaning of the maxim is not fixed at the moment of its utterance but develops in and through the nation's history.

Lincoln's argument was not an abstract exercise in hermeneutics per se. It was a positioned response framed within a heated political controversy and designed to do partisan work. Nevertheless, his partisan position reflected and embraced a general conception of history and the proper interpretation of historical texts. As David Zarefsky argues, Lincoln regarded history not as a documentary record but as a dynamic force "projected forward into the future from motives uncovered through a reflective reading of the past."[29] This perspective allowed Lincoln to effect a dissociation between "empirical description and ideal principle, between the Declaration as fact and as norm."[30] And when he argued that the phrase "all men are created equal" was a moral norm, he suggested that its verification must "come over time in the life of the country."[31] In the Gettysburg Address, the principle specifically assumes this meaning as the moral norm becomes a proposition.

As I noted earlier, the opening sentence of the Gettysburg Address both echoes and alters the language of the Declaration. In the Declaration, the principle that "all men are created equal" is held as a self-evident truth. In Lincoln's version, it is a proposition to which the nation is dedicated. A self-evident truth requires no proof; it is verified as it is uttered. A proposition, however, "may be true or false and must be proven one or the other."[32] But there is a paradox here, for Lincoln had frequently and emphatically maintained that equality in political rights was the most fundamental principle of the nation. How, then, could it be proven true? What proof could be adduced to verify the most basic and essential premise of a system?

The second sentence of the Address answers this problem by framing the issue in national history: "Now we are engaged in a great civil war, testing whether that nation, or any other nation so conceived and so dedicated, can long endure." What is to be proved, then, is not the truth of the proposition per se—the question is not Are all men created equal? Rather, the question is whether the proposition can be verified in human history—Can a nation dedicated to it endure?

In raising this question, Lincoln implicitly calls attention to the historical distance between the Founding Fathers and his own generation. They founded the nation on the basis of a self-evident truth, but as the terrible fact of the Civil War demonstrates, repeated assertion of that truth is not enough to bind and sustain the nation through time. The principle that "all men are created equal" remains essential to the identity of the American people—it is the genetic link connecting later generations to the Fathers. But if later generations are to act on this principle appropriately, they must reinterpret it and make it relevant to their own circumstances. The progeny, then, stand in a complex, equivocal relationship to the Fathers. They are both identified with and other than the Fathers. Speaking eighty-seven years after the birth of the nation, Lincoln acknowledges his patrimony, but he cannot simply restate the principles of the founders. If he is to preserve these principles, he must change them—or, more precisely, he must change the way the public mind conceives and applies them. What was fitting and proper for one time and purpose must change to meet the demands of other times and purposes.

The structure of the Gettysburg Address, I believe, explicates and enacts this complex, equivocal relationship between generations by creative equivocation of the verb *dedicate*. That verb appears six times in this short speech and, as Edwin Black has shown, its meaning shifts significantly at different points in the text. The most dramatic shift—and the one Black stresses—occurs between the second paragraph and the third, "where the dedication of the cemetery is transformed into the dedication of the audience."[33] In the second paragraph, Lincoln speaks of the literal purpose of the occasion, which is to "dedicate" (to hallow or consecrate) a final resting place for the dead. In the third, however, he speaks to a larger and more appropriate purpose, which is for the living to rededicate themselves (commit or devote themselves) to the unfinished work the dead have "so nobly advanced." But there is yet another sense of this term that appears in the text. In the opening sentence, Lincoln says that the founders dedicated the nation to the proposition of political equality. In this sense, *dedicate* means to set apart or designate something for a special purpose. The Fathers, that is, dedicated the nation by setting it apart and giving it a special mission through recognition of the principle of equality. Their progeny, on the other hand, must rededicate the nation by committing themselves to that principle and applying it to the work ahead—the work of proving the moral truth of that principle through their actions.

In the unfolding rhetorical economy of the speech, the shifting senses of *dedicate* establish a complex relationship between the living and the dead that applies not only to the audience and the fallen soldiers but also to the audience and the founders of their nation. At its point of origin, the nation was set apart and given a special mission by the founders, and this mission was to prove the proposition that "all men are created equal." The nation is now engaged in a civil war testing whether a nation set apart in this way can endure; more immediately, those who "have come together" at Gettysburg are engaged in consecrating a cemetery for the men who gave their lives for that nation, and it is "altogether fitting and proper" that they do so.

To this point, Lincoln's text proceeds in a straightforward direction, progressively moving from past to present, progressively narrowing the focus to the immediate occasion, and finally affirming the propriety of its conventional purpose. But then comes a peripety. "But in a larger sense, we cannot consecrate—we cannot hallow—this ground." The occasion demands something more than a memorialization of the dead. It requires that the living commit themselves to the purpose to which the dead were devoted. Thus, the living most appropriately honor the dead not by consecrating their graves but by projecting their spirit into the future and dedicating themselves to the still unfinished work. Thus, at the present moment and in the present occasion, Lincoln defines and then redefines the purpose of both his speech and his audience, turning from a piety that sets the dead apart in consecrated ground to one that reaffirms their example through action. It is in just this sense that Lincoln calls for the nation to rededicate itself to the principles of the Fathers. Rather than hallowing or consecrating these principles, the nation must dedicate itself to them. Rather than repeating and conserving the words of the Fathers, the living must imitate them, giving them new meaning in the effort to prove the proposition that sets the nation apart and gives it an identity and mission. It is for the living to realize a "new birth of freedom" and to ensure that "government of the people, by the people, for the people shall not perish from the earth."

In sum, the Gettysburg Address follows and extends the rhetorical trajectory of Lincoln's earlier antislavery speeches. In the debates of the 1850s, Lincoln had sought to justify a specific and controversial attitude toward slavery through his interpretation of the Declaration of Independence. The same strategy appears in the Gettysburg Address, but it is directed toward a more general end. The focus shifts from justification of an attitude about a specific issue to justification of a perspective about how attitudes ought to evolve in a free society. The conception of history implicit in the earlier discourses manifests itself explicitly in the structure of the Gettysburg Address, and it is coupled with metaphors that disclose a conception of the nation as a living organism. Structurally and metaphorically, the Address establishes a generational relationship between Lincoln and the Founding Fathers in which the Fathers offer models for rhetorical and political imitation. That is, the Fathers provide the genetic basis for national identity, but their words cannot simply be copied nor their actions repeated; their legacy can be preserved only through renewal and revaluation as historical circumstances demand. In all of Lincoln's discourse, the Declaration stands as the model of models, representing the moment of national origin and the source of the nation's most fundamental principle. The course of history and the tendency of present events are charted against the standard established in the Declaration. That standard, however, is not fixed in time or conceptual space. It is a maxim or proposition that guides and tests conduct without controlling it, and thus the authority of the Declaration merges with contemporary sensibilities, while, at the same time, these sensibilities enter into the understanding of the authority of the Declaration. This circulation of influence between past and present allows Lincoln to change tradition without destroying it, and it illustrates what I have called a hermeneutical rhetoric.

NOTES

1 Steven Mailloux, "Rhetorical Hermeneutics," in *Interpreting Law and Literature: A Hermeneutic Reader*, ed. Sanford Levinson and Steven Mailloux (Evanston, Ill.: Northwestern University Press, 1988), 345–62, and Mailloux, *Rhetorical Power* (Ithaca: Cornell University Press, 1989).

2 Mailloux, *Rhetorical Power*, 4–14.

3 Ibid., 15.

4 Ibid., 16–18.

5 Jane Tompkins, "The Reader in History: The Changing Shape of Literary Re-

sponse," in *Reader Response Criticism: From Formalism to Post-Structuralism,* ed. Jane P. Tompkins (Baltimore: Johns Hopkins University Press, 1980), 201–32.

6 Ibid., 202–6.

7 Dilip Gaonkar, "The Idea of Rhetoric in the Rhetoric of Science," *Southern Communication Journal* 58 (1993): 258–95.

8 For a detailed account of how these forces influenced critical theory, see William L. Nothstine, Carole Blair, and Gary A. Copeland, "Professionalization and the Eclipse of Critical Invention," in *Critical Questions: Inventions, Creativity, and the Criticism of Discourse and the Media,* ed. William L. Nothstine et al. (New York: St. Martin's Press, 1994), 15–70.

9 Hans-Georg Gadamer, "On the Scope and Function of Hermeneutical Reflection," trans. G. B. Hess and R. E. Palmer, in *Philosophical Hermeneutics,* ed. David E. Linge (Berkeley: University of California Press, 1976), 24. See also Chapter 15 in this volume.

10 Quintilian, *Institutio Oratoria,* trans. H. E. Butler (Cambridge: Harvard University Press, 1931), V.10.119.

11 Rita Copeland, *Rhetoric, Hermeneutics, and Translation in the Middle Ages: Academic Traditions and Vernacular Texts* (Cambridge: Cambridge University Press, 1991), 27.

12 J. Robert Cox, "Cultural Memory and Public Moral Argument," The Van Zalst Lecture in Communication (Evanston, Ill.: School of Speech, Northwestern University, 1987).

13 Mailloux, *Rhetorical Power,* 180–81.

14 Among the works dealing with this topic, I have been most influenced by Glen E. Thorow, *Abraham Lincoln and American Political Religion* (Albany: State University of New York Press, 1976), David Zarefsky, *Lincoln, Douglas, and Slavery in the Crucible of Debate* (Chicago: University of Chicago Press, 1990), and Garry Wills, *Lincoln at Gettysburg: The Words that Remade America* (New York: Simon and Schuster, 1992). In writing about Lincoln's discourse of the late 1850s, I rely heavily on Zarefsky. My reading of the Gettysbury Address is greatly indebted to Thorow, and my thought about the connection between the earlier speeches and the Gettysburg Address depends in great part upon Wills.

15 I quote from the text in Abraham Lincoln, *Speeches and Writings,* ed. Don Fehrenbacher, 2 vols. (New York: Library of America, 1989), 2:536. All subsequent references to the Gettysburg Address are to this edition.

16 Edwin Black, "Gettysburg and Silence," in *Readings in Rhetorical Criticism,* ed. Carl R. Burgchardt (State College, Pa.: Strata, 1995), 557–58; reprinted from the *Quarterly Journal of Speech,* 80 (1994): 21–36.

17 *Willmoore Kendall Contra Mundum,* ed. Nellie D. Kendall (Arlington, Tex.: Arlington House, 1971), 69; quoted in Wills, *Lincoln at Gettysburg,* 39.

18 M. E. Bradford, "Against Lincoln: An Address at Gettysburg. Commentary on 'Lincoln and the Economics of the American Dream,'" in *The Historian's Lincoln: Pseudohistory, Psychohistory, and History,* ed. Gabor S. Boritt (Urbana: University

of Illinois Press, 1988), 111. Also see Bradford, "The Gnosticism of Lincoln's Political Rhetoric," *Modern Age* 23 (1979): 10–24.

19 Wills, *Lincoln at Gettysburg*, 147.

20 Thorow, *Lincoln and American Political Religion*, 65.

21 Thorow, "Abraham Lincoln and American Political Religion," in *The Historian's Lincoln*, 142.

22 Abraham Lincoln, "Speech at Lewistown, Illinois," August 17, 1858, in *The Collected Works of Abraham Lincoln*, ed. Roy P. Basler, 8 vols. (New Brunswick, N.J.: Rutgers University Press, 1953), 2:546.

23 Abraham Lincoln, letter to Joshua F. Speed, August 24, 1855, in *Speeches and Writings*, 1:363.

24 Zarefsky, *Lincoln, Douglas, and Slavery*, 149.

25 Richard Hofstadter, "Abraham Lincoln and the Self-Made Myth," in Hofstadter, *The American Political Tradition and the Men Who Made It* (New York: Vintage, 1973), 130.

26 Ibid., 130.

27 Stephen Douglas, "Opening Speech in the Galesburg Debate," October 7, 1858, in *Created Equal? The Complete Lincoln-Douglas Debates of 1858*, ed. Paul M. Angle (Chicago: University of Chicago Press, 1958), 294. Douglas had made similar remarks in the Jonesboro Debate; see Angle, 201.

28 Abraham Lincoln, "Speech on the Dred Scott Decision," Springfield, Illinois, June 27, 1857, in *Speeches and Writings*, 1:398.

29 Zarefsky, *Lincoln, Douglas, and Slavery*, 164.

30 Ibid., 152.

31 Ibid., 153.

32 Thorow, *Abraham Lincoln and American Political Religion*, 72. This paragraph and the next follow Thorow, 72–78.

33 Black, "Gettysburg and Silence," 555.

10

Subtilitas Applicandi in
Rhetorical Hermeneutics:
Peirce's Gloss and Kelly's Example

Nancy S. Struever

Hans-Georg Gadamer begins the chapter in *Truth and Method* entitled "The Rediscovery of the Hermeneutical Problematic" with a significant tactic: he cites the eighteenth-century Pietist J. J. Rambach's definition of hermeneutics as tripartite, as a *subtilitas intelligendi, explicandi, applicandi,* or subtlety in knowing, interpreting, and applying. What is essential in this stipulation of application as faculty are the recognition of the interpreter as agent and the focus on the activity of inquiry: not only does the sense of the object text find its full and concrete form only in interpretation but the interpreter of the text is part of the meaning he apprehends; his situation, his present experience, is vital, incorporated, and combined with the tradition he studies in the text he produces.[1] Although it would seem obvious that subtlety of application is necessarily a sophisticated rhetorical capacity, Klaus Dockhorn, in his review of the first edition of *Truth and Method,* chose to insist on this necessity. Dockhorn's review notes the citation and the emphasis on agency and argues for the central role of rhetoric in hermeneutics. In making his case for the essentially rhetorical nature of good hermeneutical inquiry, Dockhorn invokes the ancient quarrel of rhetoric and philosophy; rhetoric is the second classical *Bildungs-*

weg, the "other" formation that has an ontic theory of affect as its center because it has communication—application—as its goal. From the rhetorical
telos of persuasion, the commitment to labor in the domain of fixation of belief, follows the characteristic investments of rhetoric: the engagement with
affect, with all psychological sources of motive; the affirmation of decorum—
the strict attention to the appropriate—because beliefs are formed, held, and
dissolved only as specific and time bound; and the constraint of the creation of
"social and affective" knowledge by means of dialogic interaction.[2] If Gadamer can be said to insist on an exclusive hermeneutic focus on the relation to
the past as the only source of edification, Dockhorn gives an account of the
process of edification.

To be sure, later on Gadamer criticizes Wilhelm Dilthey's definition of
rhetoric as an auxiliary discipline, merely supportive of the hermeneutical task
of analysis.[3] Dilthey, in his more compressed account, assumes that rhetoric is,
as art, parallel to hermeneutics as art; interpretation is the *kunstmassige Verstehen von schriftlich-fixierte Lebensausserungen,* and hermeneutics is the
Kunstlehre for this understanding of textually fixed life expressions; hermeneutics and criticism, aesthetics and rhetoric, ethics and politics are all essential to an essentially historical understanding.[4] But Dilthey also emphasizes
subtlety: the historical example of hermeneutical skill is the "personal and genial virtuosity" of the philologue; the prime modern exemplar is Friedrich
Schleiermacher, who combines philological virtuosity with strong philosophical capacity and who engaged in the epistemological definition of *Verstehen,* in
turn the fundamental proceeding for all further operations in the *Geisteswissenschaften.*[5]

Thus Dilthey, Gadamer, and Dockhorn raise two connected issues: What is
the place of rhetoric in hermeneutics? and What is the status of rhetorical hermeneutics in inquiry in general? To confront these issues, I shall subtend a
nineteenth-century philosophical gloss and a twentieth-century historio-
graphical example, arguing that C. S. Peirce's account of the logic of inquiry in
general situates and justifies rhetorical hermeneutics as well-motivated inquiry and that the political-historical investigations of George Armstrong
Kelly illustrates the Peircian gloss: Kelly's work is rhetorical hermeneutics in
its most useful, and subtle, sense.

Dilthey's contribution was the linkage of philosophical seriousness and
hermeneutic perspicacity. But Peirce also combines philology and philosophy; he demonstrates a genial philological virtuosity in his brilliant critique of
contemporary (German!) philology, "The Logic of Drawing Testimony from
Ancient Documents."[6] As a pragmatist philosopher, he is, of course, interested in application, in practical values, but his philosophical elucidation is of

the impurity, the difficulty of inquiry in general.[7] I shall argue that this elucidation of difficulty describes subtlety as value and thus strengthens
Gadamer's definition. By considering the issues of topic, method, and application in first Peirce and then Kelly, I hope to demonstrate the usefulness of
their "impure" hermeneutics.

A PEIRCIAN GLOSS: "THERE IS NO DISTINCTION OF MEANING SO FINE AS TO CONSIST IN ANYTHING BUT A POSSIBLE DIFFERENCE OF PRACTICE"

The great series of articles that appeared in the *Monist* (1891–93) that includes "The Architecture of Theories," "The Doctrine of Necessity Examined," "The Law of Mind," "Man's Glassy Essence," and "Evolutionary Love,"
are brief, programmatic essays engaged in the most far-reaching cosmological
revisionism; in the appended "Reply to the Necessitarians," Peirce offers an
autobiographical fragment: "I was brought up in an atmosphere of scientific
inquiry, and have all my life chiefly lived among scientific men. For the last
thirty years, the study which has constantly been before my mind has been
upon the nature, strength, and history of methods of scientific thought." I
would emphasize his focus on the *history* of scientific thought. By "science" he
means, of course, thought that carries the community of inquirers forward in
its problem-solving efforts, efforts that include those of philosophers.[8]

Peirce's interest in the history of philosophy was in no way divorced from his
daily work for many years in largely computational efforts in the physical sciences. The *Monist* articles attempt an architectonic summary and fold in the
extraordinary historical implications of Darwinian evolutionary theory, abandoning a "mechanical" philosophy for a philosophy of life and thus of growth:
"The only possible way of accounting for the laws of nature and for uniformity
in general is to suppose them results of evolution. This supposes them not to be
absolute, not to be obeyed precisely."[9] The articles shift interest to a mathematical logic that deals in probability, as well as to the spontaneity, variety, and
indeterminacy in nature. A powerful theory of continuity dominates his account of both nature studied and mind studying—a mind defined as a continuum of feelings, of affections of ideas—and the habitual actions of those general ideas.[10] Peirce's insistence on continuity of matter and mind, that is
resonant of the classical connection of body and soul, glosses Dockhorn's insistence on the centrality of affect in all discursive practices. Dockhorn's use of
Heidegger's comment that the theory of affect has scarcely improved since
Aristotle reveals, I believe, Dockhorn's assumption that an Aristotelian psychology, as found in the *De anima*, which posits the unity of body and soul and

the continuity of the soul's faculties (sensitive, imaginative, memorative, fantastic, rational), justifies the classical rhetorical program of elaboration and mastery of needful affective strategies. Peirce does not retain the Aristotelian hierarchical ordering of faculties, but he does maintain that the Cartesian dualism of body and mind subverts all useful inquiry models; the Peircian revival of continuity, with its claim that "matter is but effete mind," justifies, among other things, a rhetorical revival.[11]

At the same time, Peirce's historical commitment is surely pertinent to a rhetorical-hermeneutical program. Although his "Logic of Drawing Testimony" is his most explicit account of historical methodology, and thus of the hermeneutical task, his appropriation of evolutionary theory (where "the idea of growth is primordial," along with its corollary, science as movement, as evolving thought patterns within a community of inquirers) makes his project completely historical. "Community" and "temporicity" are the two defining constraints of inquiry.[12]

Peircian notions of rhetoric, however, are also central to his project. While late twentieth-century interest in Peirce can be read as primarily a series of appropriations, or misappropriations, of his semiotics of icon, index, and symbol, a manuscript that was not published in his lifetime, "Ideas, Stray or Stolen, about Scientific Writing, No. 1," suggests the importance of rhetoric as one of the trivial arts, as "methodeutic." He defines rhetoric as "the science of the essential conditions under which a sign may determine an interpretant sign of itself and of whatever it signifies, or may, as a sign, bring about physical results."[13] But this places rhetoric in the center of his pragmatist project; Peircian inquiry is practical activity considered only under the rubric of action: inquiry, in short, that requires *subtilitas applicandi*. Further, rhetorical pertinence is threefold: rhetoric structures application; rhetoric proffers the analytic method that Gadamer and Dilthey stress; and, most important, rhetoric, as the method that deals with beliefs, focuses the inquirer on generative knowledge—belief—rather than on the dead certainties that represent only the residue of defunct inquiry. Topic, method, application are rhetorically reinforced.

Topic   Peirce's primary devotion is to inquiry itself: when he claims that "the sole motive, idea and function" of thought is to produce beliefs and that "the soul and meaning of thought . . . can never be made to direct itself toward anything but the production of belief," he immediately engages rhetorical interests. If the purpose of thought is to produce belief, "the essence of belief is the establishment of a habit, and different beliefs are distinguished by the different modes of action to which they give rise. . . . The whole function of thought is to produce habits of action." But this in turn engages hermeneutical interests: "Thus we come down to what is tangible and practical, as the root of every real distinction of thought, no matter how subtle it may be; there is no distinction of meaning so fine as to consist in anything but a possible difference of practice."[14]

Method   But this, of course, has direct effect on his notion of method; his reply to his necessitarian critics claims that the formal certainty of the a priori strategy they espouse is only "imaginary"; formal analysis produces formal, that is, mental, "brain-spinning" results.[15] Further, Peirce's insistence on the irregularity, the diversity, uncertainty, and specificity of the world, is an insistence on a flexible—indeed, decorous—method. But the emphasis on variety as task is rhetorical, and his methodological response is rhetorical as well. "Reply" contains a strong assertion of the rhetorical canon of decorum: "My method of attacking all problems has ever been to begin with an historical and rational inquiry into the special method adapted to the special problem." The insistence on appropriateness is the essence of his architectonic proceeding: specificity guarantees system; his tychism assumes that chance "makes room for a principle of generalization, or tendency to form habits."[16]

Application   In Peircian inquiry, it is not simply the case that subtlety, tact, or decorum is a desirable capacity of the inquirer; rather, the whole life of inquiry is a life of application. In the *Monist* articles, evolutionary theory assumes growth as pervasive, and "the perfect illustration of growth is the development of a philosophical idea by being put into practice."[17] Peirce's "social theory of reality" claims that "the real is the idea in which the community eventually settles down"; the inquirer is engaged, bound to, a group practice. But the community of inquiry is time bound in a stringent way; open-endedness is stipulated: "We cannot be quite sure the community ever will settle down to an unalterable conclusion on any question; . . . nor can we presume any overwhelming *consensus* of opinion will be resolved on every question."[18] Growth stipulates that the practitioner either thwarts or strengthens communal effort, that the inquirer is committed in and to a history of investigative habits of action. Yet, although the evolutionary model dominates, Peirce disowns the *progressive* metaphor of a Cartesian cast, the figure of the gradual, proper replacement of belief by certain knowledge, as false psychologistically.[19] Belief is indispensable as it energizes and motivates the actions of inquiry. Most important, belief transpires in a supraindividualist practice, "independent of the vagaries of me and you."[20] There is a peculiar reversal of emphasis here: it is not so much that he derives "community" from an epistemological construct; rather, he insists on the dependence of epistemology on community, on the biological constructs of life, of generation and growth, and of affective, interactive growth. There is but one law of mind: "Ideas tend to spread continuously, and to affect certain others which stand to them in a peculiar relation of affectability."[21]

KELLY'S EXAMPLE: THE CORRELATION OF RELIGION AND POLITICS

Dockhorn's notion of rhetorical hermeneutics is far from the simplistic uses of rhetorical analysis in contemporary historical theory and practice. George Armstrong Kelly's last three books, *Politics and Religious Consciousness in America* (1984), *Mortal Politics in Eighteenth-Century France* (1986), and *The Humane Comedy* (posthumous; 1992) are far from this fashionable rhetorical formalism, but close to the thick program Dockhorn enunciates.[22] All three treat, in a magisterial manner, the unfashionable thesis of the importance of the intrication of religion and politics in modernity. *The Humane Comedy* and *Mortal Politics* present an intriguing symmetry: in *The Humane Comedy*, Kelly's motivating postulate is that "religion is a major and much-neglected path towards understanding French liberalism and its discriminations" (*PRC* 35). In *Mortal Politics*, Kelly uses politics as a focus on religion: as a regular legal sponsor of death in war or criminal justice, the state has a great impact on the primary religious concern of consoling humanity in the face of mortality (*PRC* 11ff.). In *Politics and Religious Consciousness*, however, Kelly had already defined his program, which requires nothing less than the recovery of an investigative role from the past. There he announced that his models were first Charles-Louis Montesquieu, then Alexis de Tocqueville. Montesquieu claimed to write about religion not as a theologian but as a political writer, an *écrivain politique;* both he and Tocqueville write about religion from the perspective of politics (*PRC* 15; *HC* 36). Tocqueville is not simply model but hero; Kelly admires his combination of an elegant skepticism and a rooted conviction of the centrality of belief in political problematic. Tocqueville's genius is to focus on the interaction of freedom and control and the interdependence of religion and politics as control systems.

Topic   I argue that Kelly's Tocquevillian approach is a double engagement, with belief as both subject and object. First, belief is *topic;* Kelly's program is the correlation of religion and politics, and the danger of concentrating on an uncorrelated politics is the neglect of the entire domain of belief, which Hannah Arendt has defined as the operative domain of politics, rather than simply the eschewal of its subset, religious faith.[23] The correlated domain is, in fact, Dockhorn's domain of "social and affective knowledge," which is essential to the political writer. Second, belief is *investigative constraint:* it is for the political writer a web of practical obligation that modifies investigative process. Thus, Kelly's double approach to belief is Peircian: when Peirce asserts that the purpose of thought is to establish belief and that the function of belief is to give rise to habits of action, he does not discriminate between actions of inquiry and actions *tout court;* although his purpose is to describe inquiry, the fixation of belief, the development of habits, are omnipresent human—indeed, biological—interests.

Just so, in the *Humane Comedy* Kelly's liberal protagonists are deeply concerned with describing the range of beliefs but deeply concerned as well in their own engagements in a domain of beliefs, with personal sincerity, social "confidence" in communication. Because Kelly assumes that the transactions of politics and the transactions of inquiry occur within a web of beliefs and habits of action, his account is not overly preoccupied with the gains in factual certainty or the slippages into factual error of his liberal theorists; neither does it project a simplistic opposition of "rationality" and "error" in maps of political choice. Rather, the *Humane Comedy* delivers a rhetorically discriminating account of the tangle of religious and political beliefs, the argumentation charged with the definitions of faith and superstition, dogma, manners, and morality that define French liberal thought.

Note the organization of the *Humane Comedy:* the first two chapters contrast the liberal initiatives of Benjamin Constant and Tocqueville as liberal confrontations of religion with "the health and strength of a free society at stake" (*HC* 84). Chapter 3 is the most complex and the most rewarding. It argues, counterintuitively, that the nineteenth century, like the seventeenth century, was a "religious century," a time of rebuilding (*réveil*), although within the limits of the essential privacy of the new, postrevolutionary and post-Enlightenment identity (85; cf. *MP* 290–91), a privacy that compels political theoretical disarray. Every attempt of the liberal Catholic or Protestant at useful diagnostic correlation falls into the error of partisanship. Kelly marks the fatal ambiguities of liberal Catholicism: although political liberty is the source of its regeneration, the movement remains committed to the supremacy of Christian belief as goal (*HC* 125, 127). In a Quixotic response, the Protestant Guizot assigns the minoritarian (3 percent) Protestants the task of liberalizing Catholicism (109). As Kelly sums up, "the perplexities of floating a common faith and morale, a legitimizing agency for the liberal state, on the deceptive buoyancy of traditional religion," generates "technical difficulties, ideological rancors, logical puzzles" (142, 154). Chapters 4 and 5 report bizarre manifestations of liberalism's "resources of spirituality" (93). "Philosophy as Civil Religion" describes an attempt at a double alliance of philosophy and religion and philosophy and politics, which is primarily a daft effort to domesticate dogmas as theories (154); this is exemplified in the "eclecticism" of Victor Cousin, something very like an American "great books" fancy stretched into a cult, constituting itself within the academic framework overhauled by the revolution and empire. It is a "lay religion," a "halfway-dogma" (167), administered by an educational bureaucracy: in sum, academic politics as a surrogate for thought. Chapter 5 is a brilliant analysis of the powerful rhetoric of Alphonse de Lamartine's poetry as one of the vehicles for the "dementia" of liberalism (181); his poetry is a war, "liberalism waged against liberals": poetry as surrogate for analysis (219).[24] The sixth and last chapter describes what is, by now, the familiar liberal retreat from "political competition to spheres of culture and criticism" (222), a retreat to Parnassus, executed with consummate skill by the elderly Tocqueville, Ernest Renan, and Gustave Flaubert.

I would emphasize the continuity of *The Humane Comedy* with Kelly's earlier texts. In *Mortal Politics,* Kelly grapples with the nature of secular belief; the French Revolution, among other things, raised the stakes of "the risk of death as a commemorative or punitive symbol ratifying society's moral judgements in a period of high crisis" (235). And, indeed, Kelly appropriates Tocqueville's thesis of continuity in French politics; the burden of the latter's argument is that secularization, the joint product of the Enlightenment and the revolution, only replaced one kind of myth with another (xxi), one extravagance of assertion with another.[25] But this critique, too, is Peircian: for Peirce, fixation of belief, energized knowledge, is the end of inquiry; what is to be avoided is not belief, which is ineluctable, but an "extravagant absoluteness of assertion," which belongs to an infant stage of intellectual development and which Peirce sees in the Necessitarian opponents to his philosophy.[26] And this extravagance Kelly detects not only in the French Revolution, not only in the French liberals, but, in his earlier work on America, in the American contemporary "secularist" investigations of their own religion and politics.

Method   Kelly's two statements in the *Politics and Religious Consciousness,* that he is engaged simply in "a theoretical investigation" (*PRC* 201) and that he is dedicated to "a recovery of a balanced orientation" to religion and politics, a "task of reconstruction" (5), are not contradictory. And when he claims that recent sociology has produced a "secular body of theory that, in the waning of theology, has endowed religion with new credentials and new weapons" (16), he is making note of studies that exacerbate contest, rather than nourish balance. To a certain extent, the "new weapons" are the unwitting product of secularist ideologies. Yet Kelly is not in the armaments industry; his purpose in his focus on religion and politics as sacred and profane "control systems" is to restore religion and politics in a correlation; it is a hermeneutic project of explicating contestatory as well as reinforcing practices (177), a precise account of powerfully interactive matrices.[27]

Correlation requires an inclusive method, an enriched program, with the range of topics that Gadamer insists is essential to hermeneutical investigation: from communication strategies to institutional manipulations, from personal interventions to the weight of religious and political traditions and the intrusion of revolutionary moments. "Enriched" and responsive: a series of flexible *topoi,* repetitively invoked, direct the readings of texts and the argumentative line: odd *topoi*—combinatory, localist, action oriented, formation sensitive. Kelly's description of French localism, for example, conveys a localism of irritating detail, of a parochial smugness that the French elites seem unable to evade; he notes how their intellectual elites, as opposed to the German, are "casually recruited" (*HC* 145) and thus debilitatingly parochial and inbred. His topical flexibility responds to a Peircian texture. When Peirce insists that the immense majority of the relations the scientist confronts are fortuitous and irregular, he supports the value of a rhetorical perspective; when he assumes "an element of indeterminacy, spontaneity, or absolute chance in nature," he also describes the texture of probabilism, spontaneity, and variety that the rhetorician self-consciously addresses.[28] In the same way, Kelly attunes his account to the instances of particularist response to the bizarre, labile situations of French politics from 1820 to 1860.

I am arguing that Peirce's gloss and Kelly's example promote a strong, as opposed to merely formalist, rhetorical/hermeneutic project: only the most idiosyncratic, most peculiarly "rhetorical" tactics are useful. To be sure, a great deal of the *Mortal Politics* is simply straightforward rhetorical analysis of a variety of genres: funeral sermons, secular eulogies, the "dialogues of the dead," revolutionary music and speeches.[29] Yet Gadamer's emphasis was on *subtlety* of knowing, interpreting, applying, recalling: Kelly's subtlety stems from a tact that replaces a pious valuation of tidiness or cleanliness. Subtlety, indeed, accompanies a Tocquevillian taste for the intractable and difficult (*HC* 82–84). Kelly's subtlety counters the clean rationalism of secularist Anglophone political history. There the judgmental opposition of belief and knowledge tends to reduce and even erase problems before they can be described adequately or actively entered. This tidiness creates a "loss of problems"; we can contrast Kelly's sense of the complex intrication of elements that the tidy secularist attempts to keep in clear antagonism. In a sense, the secularist's beliefs are more intrusive in his account because they force moralistic judgments of "bad" beliefs and allow secularized beliefs to proceed undiscounted and unchecked. They are "formalist" in the Peircian sense of "imaginary," "mental" all the way down; progress becomes the replacement of the confusion of belief with reason by means of the gainful employment of rational institutions and formal theories.

Finally, recall Peirce's methodological dictum: all distinctions in meaning become distinctions in practice. Rhetoric should save the inquirer from the futility of a career that consists simply in playing with meanings. Here Kelly illumines what a rhetorical hermeneutics is *not:* it is not a merely negative hermeneutic, a rhetorical unmasking of technique, a demystification, a deconstruction. Kelly is not exemplary of the current practice, with its perverse acceptance of a reductionist definition of rhetoric; his rhetoric is not, in short, a postmodern formalism with its excessive preoccupation with matters of style, with narrative form and metaphor. For this predicates a thin layer, a skin of formal operations that either betrays a deeper layer of artifice motives or represents the elements of verbal play, that constitutes in its entirety the message of the text. The negative hermeneutic authenticates the career of the accomplished wordplayer, obsessed with reflexivity and defined by terminal self-concern.[30] Thus the rhetorical work of Culture Criticism is predominantly shop talk; it is an exchange of internal memos on the discipline problems of the guild, quarrels that are singularly uninteresting to nonmembers. Yet the Cultural Critics' Parnassian retreat from political persuasion is simply a retreat to another kind of persuasion. But where Gadamer at one point seems to limit the role of rhetoric to demystification, Kelly seems to regard demystification as an occupational disease; the elite that he calls "the knowledge estate" purveys and lives within a new language "which is the unhappy consciousness itself" (*PRC* 251).[31] Kelly warns of the difficulty of climbing back up from demystification critique to correlative reconstruction.

Application   I have noted Gadamer's insistence that legal and theological hermeneutics furnish the model for hermeneutics in general; I am arguing that Kelly's political writing *is* legal and theological hermeneutics. Fundamental in Gadamer's account is the recognition of application as an integral element of all understanding; in legal and theological work "there is the essential tension between the text set down . . . and the sense arrived at *by* its application in the particular moment of interpretation, either judgement or preaching. . . . A law is not there to be understood historically, but to be made concretely valid through being interpreted" (*in seiner Rechtsgeltung durch sie Auslegung konkretisieren*).[32]

We must combine, then, Gadamer's insistence on the inquirer's status as agent, and Peirce's notion of a community of inquirers; Kelly's account of the political writer is an account of an agent working within a community. The idea is that good legal, theological, or political hermeneutics require a specific sense of one's audience as "appliers," as persons engaged in practice; the legal scholar directs her discourse to other scholars but finally to judges, lawyers, administrators of law. The theological scholar directs her discourse to other scholars but necessarily to those engaged in the "delivery" of faith. This hermeneutics has a double temporal subtlety: to work in the domain of belief requires a devotion to the temporal dimension of political activity that the ahistorical domain of accumulated, residual certain knowledge, "dead certainties," lacks; to "apply" restores temporal subtlety to the community of inquiry's self-definitions; truth as Peircian supraindividual truth requires time.

The central chapter of *Politics and Religious Consciousness* is "Disenchantment," which summarizes the modern disintegrative and powerful forces: secularization, privatization, differentiation, bureaucratization, and, oddly, nostalgia. Disenchantment, Kelly argues, troubles politics as well as religion in America, a thesis whose correctness strikes us more readily in 1996 than in 1984. But what is of particular interest is his use of the theorists of force: the linear succession of his choices creates a community practice. His use of the works of Harvey Cox, Gabriel Vahanian, David Bellah, Talcott Parsons, Peter Berger, Thomas Luckmann, and Judith Shklar attempts to shift accepted conventions of how theory can be applied; indeed, in this case, Kelly also pinpoints the nonapplicability of impoverished scholarly strategies. Kelly addresses these theorists *as if* their works responded to a community at large; he employs their ideas *as if* they will correct, or be corrected by, ephemeral discourse. Still, Kelly finds much of their work "inapplicable"; Bellah's Civil Religion is in fact a fiction, the imaginary product of an unimaginative academic discourse. Kelly is not accusing the theorists of lack of desire to impinge; rather, he is accusing them of irresponsibility. "Because politics . . . is a universal field of everyone's transactions, the responsibility of translation from theory to practice is very great" (192). Scholars' accounts of American religious practices and malpractices should not be complicitous or antagonistic paraphrase but intrusive reconstructions, forcing debate.

The difficulty is that political "science" as investigative community is cathected to a non-Peircian natural science, a science that is invested with "translation" difficulties. Kelly observes that these are not the difficulties of subversion, the Kuhnian "historicization of scientific truth," "for these recondite interpretations do not reach the ordinary man" but are those of the "conceptual exoticism" of normal science. "Is it easier to believe in four hundred elementary particles (many of them merely theorized) than in the Holy Trinity?" For most people, he claims, science is seen as a threatening as well as an ameliorating force. They hold a "dualistic faith" (*PRC* 180). Thus Kelly's political writing is to political science as rhetoric is to philosophy; like Dockhorn's classical rhetoricians and philosophers, Kelly and the scientists share seriousness of intent, but they disagree on the issue of purity, or at least on the value of purity achieved by detachment from the community at large—a detachment that sets a task of demarcating an investigative community by means of recondite, thus exclusionary, fictions.

AN AMERICAN PROGRAM?

In Kelly's work, I have argued, the theoretical possibilities of hermeneutics become practical initiatives but without recourse to, indeed, perhaps antagonistic to, German theoretical justifications. The juxtaposition of Peirce's gloss and Kelly's example may suggest an American modification.

If we return to Dockhorn, we find the argument that rhetorical interests dominate, justify, hermeneutics; rhetorically sophisticated work is hermeneutically perspicacious; a sound hermeneutical project has implicit in it the rhetorical formation. Not logical but rhetorical formation is useful; rhetoric confronts variety instead of reducing it; it engages specificity with decorous response, instead of stigmatizing decorum as relativist; and it singles out belief as of essential interest in the understanding of action.

If we return to Peirce, we again find rhetorical canons and values as generating well-motivatedness in inquiry, for Peirce recognizes that not only is all observation theory laden but all investigation is application laden as well. "Practical" in his pragmatism is not a thin, prudential notion, but a thick investigational commitment. Pragmatism is an American philosophical school, and the claim that good hermeneutics is essentially practical is, I would argue, specifically American as well. If we consider the work of another American, a contemporary of Kelly's, Michael Walzer, we find that the dominating concern of each of their political investigations is the correlation of religion and politics, which entails the stipulation of the centrality of the problematic of belief; and we find as well a double amplification of *subtilitas applicandi*.[33]

For Kelly, the political writer in the Tocquevillian mode writes "politically," persuasively; he succeeds or fails not as rhetorically confrontational but as confronting rhetorically, engaged in continuous, decorous response. Political theorizing is embedded in quotidian acts of response; there is no past action without present consideration, no present possibility without past resonance. For Kelly, Tocqueville is exemplary in avoiding the segmented roles of student and politician (*HC* 232).

Walzer takes the initiative a step further. Kelly's political hermeneuticist proceeds rhetorically; for Walzer, politics *is* hermeneutics: the political writer as "connected critic" is inevitably an interpreter; she not only interprets, she is defined by her historical connection making. The political philosopher who claims to "discover" or "invent" is self-deceived; she must start some place, and the site is her own historical conditions, a thick matrix of customs, beliefs, practices, laws, institutions. In *Interpretation and Social Criticism,* Walzer's definition of prophecy as central political role raises the rhetorical ante to an almost alarming degree. Walzer opposes the beside-the-pointness of the un-situated, "objective" critic to the effectiveness of the connected critic. If Tocqueville is Kelly's model, the prophet Samuel is Walzer's; Walzer does not cast himself as Samuel, but he can deliver Samuel.[34] Both, I would argue, as-sume the contiguity of the belief practices of investigated and investigator, of Their beliefs and Ours. The recognition of the status as belief of the energizing assumptions of the political inquiry community supports the intrication of the investigative belief community and the investigated communities of belief; the refusal to assume the privileged status of the investigative community res-cues the investigator from delusions of jejune, naive notions of applicability. In both Kelly and Walzer there is a distrust of the manipulative author-critic, a distrust of the bookish, academic mode; they view attempts to replace beliefs with academic facts as simply the replacement of a given community's beliefs with current academic beliefs. Peircian open-endedness, then, functions as endlessly self-effacing.[35] The positive hermeneutic saves history from "imagi-nary" certitudes, the description and classification of inert ideas, tables of rela-tions (a classification of "available political languages" is fairly inert). It saves political history from the seduction of demystification as omnibus strategy, the reduction of history to a catalogue of false intentions, betrayals, ideologies.

But Kelly emphasizes the difficulties of an American program, perhaps be-cause of his Tocquevillian irony, perhaps because, like Tocqueville, he must write politically in a highly unstable political context. Notice his critique of William James, Peirce's fellow pragmatist. As an American writer on religion, James is implicated in the problematic of freedom and control that Tocque-ville set forth in *Democracy in America;* but James is intent on the reduction of theology to psychology. Although James deems religious feeling "an absolute addition to the subject's range of life" (*PRC* 114), his notions of belief are nour-ished not simply by Peirce's work but by a dubious recourse to psychical re-search (an American hobby) and mysticism (115). James's bent was the "codifi-cation" of the genius loci, and thus his work underwrites radical pluralism; each person becomes an individual sectarian system. The charge of his pro-gram for politics was negative; James undercuts Tocqueville's "precious conju-gation of religious belief and civic freedom" as "totally irrelevant" (117); Tocqueville, Kelly comments, "would not have been reassured by reading William James" (113).

Yet the vital, positive lesson of the Americans is the intrinsic interest of is-sues of belief, energized knowledge. Peirce's concept of fixation of belief en-ables an account of the practices of the community of inquirers that contests perverse academicism. The strategy of Kelly and Walzer, the correlation of re-ligion and politics, makes clear that the neglect of belief leaves secularized be-liefs, currently even more rhetorically powerful as secularized, unattended. Kelly and Walzer offer a positive hermeneutic in a specific way; both reconsti-tute a historical problematic of considerable interest for current political prac-tices, investigative or not. The concluding chapter of *Politics and Religious Consciousness,* "Faith and Loyalty," is, indeed, a political agenda, though a pessimistic one; faith (religious belief) and loyalty (political belief) are in diffi-culties and in a difficult relation with each other. Perhaps the pessimism should be glossed by the short elegiac section on Parnassian liberalism, "The Sadness of Tocqueville," in the last chapter of the *Humane Comedy,* a passage that considers the retreat as a calculated evasion of "mediocrity," of a broken career (225). But here Kelly's account recommends for us a balance of virtue and value: irony "should be included in any taxonomy of liberal virtues" (230) as an essential poise; liberty should be prized as "non-ironic value" (231).[36] This would be a stripped-down hermeneutic career perhaps. Yet it is neither a full Parnassian retreat to Culture Criticism, nor merely a conservative fixation on an authorizing past; rather, it is a career in which ironic modesty makes tol-erable "a rummage among the ruins" of faith and loyalty (*PRC* 276), a "rum-mage" required for the excavation and application of liberty.

NOTES

1 Hans-Georg Gadamer, *Wahrheit und Methode; Grundzüge einer philosophischen Hermeneutik,* 2d ed. (Tübingen: Mohr, 1965); English translation: *Truth and Method* (London: Sheed and Ward, 1975), 274.

2 Klaus Dockhorn's review appeared in the *Göttingische Gelehrte Anziegen,* 218, nos. 3–4 (1966): 169–206; it is translated partially by Marvin Brown in "Hans-Georg Gadamer's *Truth and Method,*" *Philosophy and Rhetoric* 13 (1980): 160–180; Dockhorn refers to rhetoric as the second *Bildungsweg* on p. 169, to the tripartite definition on pp. 193ff. in the German version. Does Dockhorn "essentialize" rhetoric? I think not; the review is a historical account of the rhetorical tradition as a site of affect theory through the nineteenth century. See as well J. Lohmann's review in *Gnomon* 37 (1965), which also refers to the Rambach citation on p. 713. Helmut Schanze informs me that Dockhorn's review was the stimulus for major rhetoriciz-ing revisions in the second edition of *Truth and Method.*

3 Gadamer, "Rhetorik, Hermeneutik und Ideologiekritik," in *Hermeneutik und Ide-ologiekritik* (Frankfurt am Main: Suhrkamp, 1975), 58. For a translation, see Chap-ter 15 in this volume.

4 Wilhelm Dilthey, "Die Enstehung der Hermeneutik," *Gesammelte Schriften,* vol. 5 (Leipzig: Teubner, 1925): 332–33, 338.

5 Dilthey, "Die Enstehung," 333.

6 C. S. Peirce, "The Logic of Drawing Testimony from Ancient Documents," in *Collected Papers*, vol. 7, ed. Arthur Burks (Cambridge: Harvard University Press, 1958), 89–164.

7 See, in particular, "Some Consequences of Four Incapacities," in *Writings of C. S. Peirce*, ed. Max Fisch et al. (Bloomington: Indiana University Press, 1982), 2:211–42.

8 Peirce, "Reply," *The Monist* 3 (1893): 546, 548.

9 C. S. Peirce, "The Architecture of Theories," *Monist* 1 (1891): 165. It is important to note that Peirce finds morally repugnant the appropriation of Darwin in Darwinist sociopolitical theories; see Peirce, "Evolutionary Love," *Monist* 3 (1893): 178ff.

10 C. S. Peirce, "The Law of Mind," *Monist* 2 (1892): 548ff.

11 Peirce, "Architecture of Theories," 170. On the thesis of continuity, see especially Peirce's "Man's Glassy Essence," "The Doctrine of Necessity Examined," "The Law of Mind." Continuity entails a revisionary psychology: Peirce speaks of the "intrinsic quality as a feeling of an idea" in "Law of Mind," 549; and he claims that "every general idea has the unified living feeling of a person" and that "feelings can never be explained unless we admit that physical events are but degraded or undeveloped forms of psychical events" in "Man's Glassy Essence," *Monist* 3 (1892): 21, 18. Peirce is aware that he is working on the issue of the connection of body and soul; see "The Doctrine of Necessity Examined," *Monist* 2 (1892): 335. Dockhorn's citation of Heidegger is in the German version of the review, p. 186.

12 On the centrality of the principle of growth, see "Law of Mind," 557, and "Reply," 565; in the "Law of Mind," Peirce develops a strong initiative in the definition of the pastness of the past, 535f.: thus, "The present is connected with the past by a series of real infinitesimal steps," 536.

13 C. S. Peirce, "Ideas, Stray or Stolen," *Philosophy and Rhetoric* 2 (1978): 147–55.

14 C. S. Peirce, "How to Make Our Ideas Clear," in *Writings*, 3:263, 265.

15 Peirce, "Reply," 536, 549; his philosophical opponents work in "a world of dreams," 558; "Deduction is really a matter of perception and of experimentation, just as induction and hypothetical inference are; only, the perception and experimentation are concerned with imaginary objects instead of real ones," 534.

16 Peirce, "Reply," 547; "Doctrine of Necessity Examined," 336. There are many references to the spontaneity, variety, and indeterminacy of nature and to the imprecision and uncertainty of thought: see "Doctrine of Necessity Examined," 333–34; 337; "The Architecture of Theories," *Monist* 1 (1891): 165. "Law of Mind," 554, for example, claims that the "uncertainty of the mental law is no mere defect of it, but is on the contrary of its essence."

17 Peirce, "Reply," 565; "Evolutionary Love," 188; cf. "Reply," 549: "What should we suppose *not* to be a product of growth?"

18 Peirce, "Reply," 555; cf. 559: "Reality is the dynamical reaction of certain forms on the mind of the community."

19 Peirce believes that our four incapacities—the nonexistence of pure intuition, the

embeddedness of thought in successive acts, the embeddedness of thought in signs, the futility of asserting the incognizable—invalidate naive progressive accounts; see "Some Consequences of Four Incapacities."

20 Peirce, "Some Consequences," 239. Compare Dockhorn's invocation of Cicero on the dialectical origins of "common conclusions." The source of valid universals, indeed, the source of their validity, lies in the give and take, in the accessible, careful, economically structured arguments of the community: validity is the product of rhetorical competence; see pp. 172ff. in the German version of the review.

21 Peirce, "Law of Mind," 534.

22 George Armstrong Kelly, *Politics and Religious Consciousness in America* (New Brunswick, N.J.: Transaction, 1984); *Mortal Politics in Eighteenth-Century France, Historical Reflections/Réflexions Historiques* 13 (1986); *The Humane Comedy: Constant, Tocqueville, and French Liberalism* (Cambridge: Cambridge University Press, 1992); these editions are cited parenthetically in the text as *PRC, MP,* and *HC,* respectively. Kelly is not a trained rhetorical technician, and his style is too rapid, perhaps because hurried—in the case of *HC,* unfinished. To be sure, anyone with Henry Kissinger as mentor must have been exposed to continuous, excited rhetorical maneuvering.

23 Hannah Arendt, *Between Past and Future: Six Exercises in Political Thought* (New York: Meridian, 1963). Kelly's Tocquevillian perspective of skepticism/faith is a benign, supple trade-off, rather than a malign rigidity of opposition. Kelly, however, as a practicing Anglo-Catholic, found the "fissionable tendency" of Protestantism deleterious; the opposition of religious solidarity/fission is one of well/ill-motivated practice; see *PRC* 199; cf. 183.

24 Thus Kelly's perceptive remark: "There is a touch of William Wordsworth in Lamartine; of Rimbaud there is none," 190.

25 Kelly describes it as "the shifting of the ground of normative political activity from a hidden God to a mythical society," 315–16.

26 Peirce, "Reply," 546.

27 *Sacred* to *profane* is a binary relation; the stipulation of one assumes the other.

28 Peirce, "Some Consequences," 264; "Evolutionary Love," 165.

29 Chapters 3, 4, 10, and 11 in *Mortal Politics* are entirely given over to textual analysis.

30 See, for example, John Guillory's critique of Paul de Man's reductive rhetoric, *Cultural Capital* (Chicago: University of Chicago Press, 1993).

31 Gadamer, "Rhetorik, Hermeneutik, und Ideologiekritik," 72.

32 Gadamer, *Truth and Method,* 275, my emphasis; *Wahrheit und Methode,* 292.

33 Walzer first established his interest in the correlation of religion and politics in his *The Revolution of the Saints* (Cambridge: Harvard University Press, 1965); it has by now become an extraordinarily complex project, immensely sensitive to the issues of application. Surely it is unnecessary to emphasize the continuous, strong presence of American religio-political interactions from the seventeenth-century to the present day as context for this investigative interest.

34 Michael Walzer, *Interpretation and Social Criticism* (Cambridge: Harvard Univer-

sity Press, 1987); see, in particular, Chapter 3, "The Prophet as Social Critic," 69–94. I wish to thank my student Mallory Conklin for first drawing my attention to the similarities of Kelly's and Walzer's programs.

35 Thus Walzer: our moral justifications "are worked out with reference to an actual, not merely speculative, moral discourse: not one person but many people talking," *Interpretation and Social Criticism*, 47. Walzer recalls Dockhorn when he claims interpretation as a "common activity" (83); social criticism is "less the practical offspring of scientific knowledge than the educated cousin of common complaint" (65).

36 Kelly discusses Tocquevillian irony at length, *HC*, 221–23; 227f; he contrasts it with Hayden White's irony as a "vision of puzzled defeat and despair," in *Metahistory* (Baltimore: Johns Hopkins University Press, 1973), 196; Tocquevillian irony is a "purposeful irony," *HC* 230; Kelly speaks of irony as well in *PRC* 201, 241. We must note White's hostility to Tocqueville's irony as "collapse," *Metahistory*, 200. On White's irony, see my article "Irony and Experimentation in Hayden White's Metahistory," *Storia della Storiografia* 24 (1993), 45–57.

Part III

Arguments and Narratives

11

The Uses of Rhetoric:
Indeterminacy in Legal Reasoning,
Practical Thinking, and the
Interpretation of Literary Figures

Wendy Olmsted

Interpretive theory has been unsuccessful in finding a system of rules that can be applied in legal reasoning or in the interpretation of literature. Theorists' aspiration toward such a system of rules and their skepticism that such rules are possible have given rise to much controversy.[1] Rhetoric offers a way out of this impasse because it is an art of reasoning adapted to the particularities of situation and action. This art is reasonable but does not presuppose that, in order to be used intelligently, rules and terms must be determinate (specifiable precisely, repeatable in different situations, and univocal). In fact, the art of rhetoric uses relatively indeterminate language to discover and organize facts and arguments for the sake of judging particularities and informing interpretation. Rhetoricians evaluate degrees and kinds of indeterminacy with respect to how useful they are for a particular inquiry, so that, for them, "the question of determinable meanings in both law and literature is actually a false one. . . . It states alternatives neither of which is possible."[2] The belief that meaning is either univocal or undecidable leads to unnecessary skepticism by absolutizing alternatives and narrowing possibilities for interpretation. In order to propose an alternative to the hard distinction between determinate and indeterminate meaning, I take up a series of examples, moving through progressively less determinate uses of terms, arguments, and figures, showing how each degree and kind of indeterminacy is appropriate for the inquiry it serves.

First, I analyze three main kinds of radical indeterminacy that Paul de Man and Jacques Derrida find in the ambiguous meanings of words, tropes, and binary distinctions, and I distinguish these approaches from a rhetorical point of view according to which meanings of words, distinctions, arguments, and figures are partly determinate and partly open. I argue that whereas de Man and Derrida understand figures to *decenter* thought, a classically derived rhetoric studies how they may *enable* thought. My essay moves from the analysis of terms in practical thinking (for example, in the *Federalist Papers*) and in American case law to arguments in scientific problem solving and argument by analogy in case law to an analysis of the relations of rhetorical argument to figures of thought, and more specifically to the extended simile.[3] Unlike those approaches that subvert meaning by finding figurality in a language that claims to be logical, rhetoric enables us to understand interrelations of argument and figure. Figures are not, as they are in many other approaches, cognitively suspect. Instead, simile, like argument by example, can be used as an indeterminate formulation for discovering more than meets the eye in real or fictional situations.

Because the scope of rhetoric as a method is universal, rhetoric provides a useful method for considering the function of indeterminacy in different sorts of inquiry, including even scientific reasoning, when that reasoning is regarded as an activity performed by a scientist in a concrete decision-making situation. As Richard Rorty has argued, "For the pragmatist [as for the rhetorician, I would suggest], the pattern of all inquiry, scientific as well as moral, is deliberation concerning the relative attraction of various concrete alternatives."[4] Rhetoric uses language to inform decision with regard to matters that vary—that can be otherwise than they are.[5] More or less indeterminate terms, arguments, and figures of thought, such as simile, suggest the considerations to look for in an empirical inquiry, a legal case, a deliberative situation, or a fictional situation without specifying exactly what the inquirer will find.

For classical rhetoric, ambiguity and relative indeterminacy gave *topoi* (rhetorical places), arguments, and figures the flexibility that allowed them to serve as tools of invention and discovery. Cicero wrote that "it is easy to find things that are hidden if the hiding place is pointed out and marked; similarly if we wish to track down some argument, we ought to know the places or topics: for that is the name given by Aristotle to the 'regions,' as it were, from which arguments are drawn."[6] Ambiguous topics functioned within the rhetorical handbooks to guide speakers and writers to considerations and arguments.

For Paul de Man, on the other hand, both the ambiguity of language and its figurality entail loss of control over meaning. De Man uses the (by now well-known) example of Archie Bunker's exclamation "What's the difference?" to illustrate how ambiguity and figurality frustrate the speaker as they confront him with his inability to control the structure of linguistic meaning:

> Asked by his wife whether he wants to have his bowling shoes laced over or laced under, Archie Bunker answers with a question: "What's the difference?" Being a reader of sublime simplicity, his wife replies by patiently explaining the difference between lacing over and lacing under, whatever this may be, but provides only ire. "What's the difference" did not ask for difference but means instead "I don't give a damn what the difference is." The same grammatical pattern engenders two meanings that are mutually exclusive: the literal meaning asks for the concept (difference) whose existence is denied by the figurative meaning. As long as we are talking about bowling shoes, the consequences are relatively trivial; Archie Bunker, who is a great believer in the authority of origins (as long, of course, as they are the right origins), muddles along in a world where literal and figurative meanings get in each other's way, though not without discomforts.[7]

De Man argues that Archie Bunker's anger when he is misunderstood "reveals his despair when confronted with a structure of linguistic meaning that he cannot control and that holds the discouraging prospect of an infinity of similar future confusions, all of them potentially catastrophic in their consequences."[8]

De Man also characterizes language as indeterminate insofar as it is tropological. Tropes decenter or undermine discourse that claims implicitly or explicitly to be determinate and literal. For example, philosophical definitions can be deconstructed, revealing the hidden metaphor that underlies them. Philosophical discourse is a "figural discourse or translation, and, as such, creates the fallacious illusion of definition."[9] De Man's analysis of John Locke is a case in point. He refers to the atomist's definition of motions as "a passage from one place to another." De Man reads the proposition not as a definition but as a translation, on the grounds that it is equally valid to say that "passage is a motion." *Passage* and *motion* are translations of each other; *to translate,* in turn, translates the Greek *metaphorein.* Definition is thus reduced to metaphor, an indeterminate trope.

Finally, Derrida undermines distinctions like those between nature and culture, male and female, speech and writing by arguing that the left-hand terms in each pair are hierarchically superior to the right-hand terms. He then reverses the hierarchy by showing that the right-hand term is really prior, that nature depends on culture and speech on writing. So he also undermines the distinction between nature and culture by referring to what Claude Lévi-Strauss calls "a scandal: something which no longer tolerates the nature/culture opposition he (Lévi-Strauss) has accepted and which seems to require at one and the same time the predicates of nature and those of culture. This scandal is the incest prohibition. The incest prohibition is universal; in this sense one could call it natural. But it is also a prohibition, a system of norms and interdicts; in this sense one could call it cultural."[10] Derrida suggests that because he can find a phenomenon that is both natural and cultural, the distinction between nature and culture is called into question. Derrida's undermining of the categories of nature and culture depends on the belief that distinctions must be precise, that they must divide sharply and unambiguously the phenomena they seek to distinguish in order to be distinctions at all. John Searle argues that deconstruction presupposes the positivistic belief that unless a distinction or a set of terms admits of rigorous internal boundary lines, it does not hold.[11] Only if we believe that terms and distinctions must be rigid do we feel shocked or liberated when we discover that the distinction is ambiguous or characterizes phenomena as indeterminate. Searle argues, on the contrary, that "it is a condition of the adequacy of a precise theory of an indeterminate phenomenon that it should precisely characterize that phenomenon as indeterminate; and a distinction is no less a distinction for allowing for a family of related, marginal cases."[12] Underminings really only undermine if one believes that distinctions must be rigid and must refer to clearly differentiable phenomena to be true or useful. Yet there are kinds of thinking in which determinate terms and distinctions are not only impossible but undesirable; terms themselves must often be ambiguous in order to function well.

Terms and distinctions that are used to inform decision about matters that can be otherwise are at once relatively determinate and relatively indeterminate. In the framework of a rhetorical method as I have defined it, "relatively determinate" refers to what has been agreed upon and "relatively indeterminate" to what is still ambiguous and open to discussion. So if everyone agrees that a person has killed someone, no one considers or deliberates about it: yet we might deliberate about whether the killing was a crime or was committed in self-defense. So also relatively indeterminate terms or *topoi* have an agreed upon, but ambiguous, meaning that directs thought toward considerations without specifying them exactly. For example, the terms *safety, welfare,* and *union* in the first essay of the *Federalist Papers* function as relatively indeterminate *topoi. Safety* and *welfare* formulate the ends everyone desires without specifying exactly what those ends are; the succeeding essays fill in the ambiguous topic by considering security, ways of protecting against dangers arising from domestic causes, ways of protecting against the violation of treaties, and issues of national defense. The essays move from limited indeterminacy to determinacy. Some of the writers use topics to indicate the general kind of purpose they have in mind at the beginning; the text then fills in that meaning until it is determinate by the end. Yet not all speeches or writings are constructed so as to arrive at determinate meanings for their terms. Speeches and writings also use ambiguous language to articulate conflicting or evolving purposes and to generate open-ended inquiries. Intelligent use of terms and distinctions requires one to leave the indeterminate appropriately ambiguous and not to seek for an accuracy greater than a particular inquiry will admit.

Terms, relations, and figures of thought are relatively and positively indeterminate when they are sufficiently ambiguous that their meanings can change as they are brought to bear on new situations. In case law, for example, in the distinction between "inherently dangerous things" and "things not of themselves dangerous," terms changed their meanings and their relations to one another as they were used to classify a changing set of objects—loaded guns, defective lamps, defective coaches, and, finally, defective automobiles.[13] Early in the process, the distinction between "inherently dangerous things" and "things not of themselves dangerous" became clear, and loaded guns, defective guns, poison, and hair wash were considered to be things in their nature dangerous, whereas a defective lamp was a thing which became dangerous by an unknown latent defect.[14] As new situations and problems arose, ideas about the meaning and importance of "inherently dangerous" shifted. Later the rule was that "if the nature of a thing is such that it is reasonably certain to place life and limb in peril, when negligently made, it is then a thing of danger." As Edward Levi formulates it, "what was only latently dangerous in *Thomas v. Winchester* . . . became imminently dangerous or inherently dangerous, or, if verbal niceties are to be disregarded, just plain or probably dangerous." The meaning of "inherently dangerous" broadened to include scaffolds and coffee urns, that is, to include the "latently dangerous." Thus, the meanings of both terms had changed. Levi traces the evolution of legal terms to show how meanings evolve as they are brought to bear on new situations. Legal concepts need this ambiguity and flexibility because changing circumstances raise new problems for judgment. A vehicle might not be thought of as inherently dangerous when one had a coach in mind; automobiles present a different problem and may change the way one uses terms and the way the terms mean. The terms "inherently dangerous" and "latently dangerous" directed investigations into various defective things; yet those terms did not define exactly what sort of danger the court discovered in those things. Instead of taking a formulation as explicit and fixed, on the one hand, or as radically indeterminate, on the other, interpreters can use it as an instrumentality for exploring a situation.

RHETORICAL TERMS AND ARGUMENTS IN LAW: ARGUMENTS

In the case of arguments as in the case of terms, *indeterminacy* is relative and functions in relation to what is determinate; both together allow for an openness that facilitates inquiry. Determinacy and indeterminacy work in two interrelated ways in argument. First, because argument presupposes the ability to relate one term to another in a controlled way, the mode of relation between terms can be determinate, that is, linked according to a carefully defined logical relation (as in "A is one half of B") or relatively indeterminate (as in "the father is related to his son as a king to his subject"). In the second example the relations between terms are ambiguous. Second, arguments may be determinate or indeterminate in how they attach to situations, circumstances, or nature. So the formula $f = ma$, attaches to well-defined aspects of a ball rolling down an inclined plane: one can identify and interrelate the force, mass, and acceleration in an exact way. However, as Thomas Kuhn argues in his postscript to *The Structure of Scientific Revolutions,* when students study a pendulum or the descent of water in a tank, they will have to modify the formula in order to attach it to features that are similar but not identical to the inclined plane situation.[15] Thus, even here, where one is, in a sense, working with determinate formulas (that is, formulas in which terms are related in exactly specified ways), students encounter an area of indeterminacy insofar as they seek for similar but not identical features in the pendulum situation and are able to change the formula to accommodate to the difference in the new situation. I call such formulations that persons change in light of problems they are considering "instrumentalities." Instrumentalities allow for some degree of modification as they are used in relation to nature or other objects of study.

In order to suggest the continuum of degrees and kinds of indeterminacy one may find in arguments, I would like to take up a series of examples, proceeding from the least to the most indeterminate. We shall find that absolute judgments concerning indeterminacy give way to more specific rhetorical evaluations concerning whether an argument is appropriately indeterminate for the inquiry it serves.

In the following analysis I focus on instances of argument by example or analogy, one of the two main forms of rhetorical argument (and the form that occurs most often in modern law), and analogical figures (including simile) that are closely related to argument by example.[16] Argument by example allows the inquirer to look at one example in light of another, adjusting his or her understanding of the first as he or she probes the second. The inquirer juxta-poses examples in a discovery process that finds considerations for judgment concerning things that can be otherwise than they are. Yet the degree to which an inquirer can adjust formulations and arguments varies within a field or type of inquiry.

In general, argument by example or by analogy works not by relating an ex-ample (the "part" in the following quotation) to a general premise (the "whole") but by relating one example to another, when "both come under the same genus, but one of them is better known than the other." Argument by ex-ample is "neither the relation of part to whole, nor of whole to part, nor of one whole to another whole, but of part to part, of like to like, when both come under the same genus, but one of them is better known than the other. For ex-ample, to prove that Dionysius is aiming at a tyranny, because he asks for a bodyguard, one might say that Pisistratus before him and Theagenes of Megara did the same, and when they obtained what they asked for made themselves tyrants."[17]

Argument by example resembles faulty induction in that one reasons from the case of Pisistratus to the case of Dionysius. Yet no general rule about body-guards is sought for its own sake, as in induction.[18] Instead, one may use the ex-ample of Pisistratus to examine the situation of Dionysius, discovering how probable or improbable it is that Dionysius seeks to be a tyrant. Similarly, someone evaluating a case of a defective automobile might use a related case concerning a defective coach in order to find similarities and differences rele-vant to judgment. Argument by example has a heuristic function; it helps one discover relevant considerations that in turn become a source of persuasion. In case law, "similarity is seen between cases; next the rule of law inherent in the first case is announced; then the rule of law is made applicable to the sec-ond case."[19] Because the process of reasoning involves adjusting the rule in light of what one sees in the cases, it is relatively indeterminate. In other words, lawyers and judges do not merely apply known terms and rules to new cases; they can adjust words and rules to fit new cases or they can invent new words and rules. Thus, a lawyer persuades not only by finding relevant consid-erations but by persuading that certain words or interpretations of words are decisive. I have already considered how legal terms change as they are used in relation to specific cases. Now I wish to emphasize that argument by example also has flexibility. Instead of applying a known rule to diverse facts or diverse cases, legal reasoning first determines what "facts will be considered similar to those present when the rule was first announced"; "the finding of similarity or difference is the key step in the legal process."[20] This finding of similarity or difference is an act of rhetorical discovery.

Inquiries differ in the kinds of formulations they use to guide reasoning by example and in the degree of indeterminacy they find useful. Earlier I referred to the fact that although a scientific formula like $f = ma$ defines the relation between terms and the meaning of terms themselves in a specifiable way, students also need to use reasoning by analogy to attach the formulation to nature. They discover similarities between the operation of forces and masses in the case of the inclined plane and in the case of pendulums; they learn how to see two problems as alike in relevant respects.[21] Knowing a formula like $f = ma$ means using it to explore nature. The student learns to do this by seeing his problem "as like a problem he has already encountered." "Having seen the resemblance, and grasped the analogy between two or more distinct problems, he can interrelate symbols and attach them to nature in the ways that have proved effective before. The law-sketch, say $f = ma$, has functioned as a tool, informing the student what similarities to look for, signaling the gestalt in which the situation is to be seen. The resultant subject for $f = ma$, or some other symbolic generalization, is, I think, the main thing a student acquires by doing exemplary problems."[22]

The problem here, as in other kinds of reasoning by example, is that the student does not encounter identical situations; he or she has to *learn* to see situations as alike in relevant respects. But the law schema $f = ma$ only tells students what to look for; it does not tell them exactly how and in what form they will find it.

Once students have seen the two problems as alike, they may need to learn how to modify a formula, using it as an instrumentality for understanding free fall or the pendulum. For the case of free fall, $f = ma$ becomes

$$mg = m \frac{d^2s}{dt^2}.$$

For the simple pendulum, it is transformed to

$$\sin \theta = ml \frac{d^2\theta}{dt^2}.$$

Students are learning $f = ma$ by using it; they are also learning to design appropriate versions of $f = ma$. Knowing $f = ma$ means being able to adapt it to fit different situations. At the same time, adaptation of the formula operates within constraints; $f = ma$ functions as a law schema to guide investigation of nature and the design of a different formulation.

Whereas the law schema guides the investigative activity in the example from Kuhn, in legal reasoning relatively indeterminate terms help to organize reasoning in case law, statutory law, and constitutional law. In case law, the terms to be used in reasoning are not stated in a statute; they arise out of the process of case-to-case reasoning. I have discussed the way Levi's analysis of reasoning by example illustrates how one case is juxtaposed to another in order to find a general term for what is at stake in the second case.[23] Analogizing helps establish what in the first case is helpful in understanding and evaluating the second. The example is relatively indeterminate insofar as it directs inquiry without defining exactly what is to be discovered.

The discovery of similarity and difference is crucial to the reasoning process; yet there seems to be no general rule that tells what similarity is decisive or how to rank similarities according to importance and degree. The problem is "when will it be just to treat different cases as though they were the same."[24] The adversary system is designed to facilitate the doing of what is just by ensuring that differences as well as similarities are urged and that competing examples are presented.

Yet even in case law, finding similarity and difference is not enough; the process of reasoning cannot get going until terms are invented or taken from past cases and reapplied to the present. There are three stages to the process: the first, in which the court fumbles for a term (a word); the second, in which the term is more or less fixed, and reasoning by analogy continues to classify cases inside and outside it; and the third, when the term breaks down, and reasoning by example moves beyond what is suggested by it.

Levi's analysis of the early stages of the development of the term "inherently dangerous" illustrates how reasoning by example helps to discover relevant factors in the cases and determines further the meaning of legal terms. Levi cited *Dixon v. Bell*, in which an owner of a gun sent a servant girl for the gun; it went off and shot the plaintiff's son, injuring the son. It was judged that the defendant—the owner of the gun—showed want of care and that the gun was left in a dangerous state; and damages were awarded. In a later case (*Langridge v. Levy*), the defendant knowingly sold a father a defective gun, which blew up in his son's (the plaintiff's) hand. There was also the case of a defendant who provided a defective coach that broke and lamed the plaintiff, a coachman (*Winterbottom v. Wright*), and the case of a defendant, a storekeeper, who sold lamps others had assembled. The buyer's wife was hurt when one of the lamps exploded (*Longmeid v. Holliday*).

In all these cases there is someone (A) who owns, sells or provides a thing (B) to someone else. Someone (C) related to the latter person is injured by the thing, which is in some way dangerous. The form can be roughly schematized as A/B/C :: D/E/F. Questions are raised as to whether the defendant knew or should have known about the danger (the character of A), what the relation of the defendant to the plaintiff is ("/" as direct dealing, etc.), what the nature of the action affecting them both is ("/" as fraud) and whether the thing in question ("B") is dangerous in itself or only when another action intervenes to make it dangerous. These questions are interrelated. If a thing is only latently dangerous, perhaps the defendant could not be expected to know it was dangerous. Such determinations are made by relating the case (A/B/C) to another (D/E/F), further defining the elements and "/" relations in light of one's understanding of the "::" relation. Here reasoning by example serves as a resource for raising considerations similar to those mentioned above. But only when a general term is discovered that expresses what is important from a particular point of view can a decision be made. When agreed upon, the term, like the student's formula, functions as an instrumentality, directing thought to certain aspects of the situation to be resolved. As reasoning by example continues to classify cases inside and outside the term, the term becomes more determinate. Eventually, it breaks down; its meaning becomes too fixed (too determinate!) or is felt to be inappropriate to the changed circumstances. Distinctions felt to be important earlier may cease to be made later. Reasoning by example has moved beyond what is suggested by the word.

In case law there may also be fumbling in an early stage because of the difficulty of finding a word; here the situation is too indeterminate. Later the court may be influenced by the existence of a ready concept. In the first situation, the court must struggle for a formulation: "It may be objected that this analysis of legal reasoning places too much emphasis on the comparison of cases and too little on the legal concepts which are created. It is true that similarity is seen in terms of a word, and *inability to find a ready word to express similarity or difference may prevent change in the law.* The words which have been found in the past are much spoken of, have acquired a dignity of their own, and to a considerable measure control results. As Judge Cardozo suggested in speaking of metaphors, the word starts out to free thought and ends by enslaving it."[25]

The finding of general terms is important, even in case law, but they do not become frozen rules. As I read Levi's account of the development and evolution of the notions of things dangerous in themselves and things imminently dangerous, it seems to me that throughout the process there is a continuous development and modification of judgment about what is important or what needs to be taken into account when affixing (or not affixing) responsibility for guns that blow up, lamps that explode, and defective carriages. Levi emphasized the case-to-case nature of the reasoning. I wish to note that the fashioning of a general term like "inherently dangerous" marks a moment at which some aspect of the cases being compared is thought to be crucial from a particular point of view. Adhering to old words may produce decisions that do not express the present values of the community. The relative indeterminacy of reasoning by example and of the terms used in connection with it is crucial to the legal process because the law is concerned with particular situations that change through time. The inability to formulate a term may prevent a certain range of considerations from being raised and so may prevent change. The legal understanding of a single case can change when that case is set next to a later one; reasoning by example may allow new considerations to emerge.

The examples from law and science suggest that the degree and kind of indeterminacy of rules and terms depends upon how formulations are used to direct observations and how susceptible they are to modification when further facts and relations are discovered. $F = ma$ exerts a tight constraint over what features are relevant and how they are to be related; we might wish to call it determinate. Yet using the formula implies a capacity for seeing similarity in difference. Legal analogies and concepts are more ambiguous and more flexible. Yet they need to be sufficiently determinate to direct judgment. Inability to find a word may obstruct the process of judgment, because relevant features of a case cannot be discerned and characterized without the use of a general term. Too determinate a concept can become useless in new cases or in the face of changing public values.

Classical rhetoricians would have called the relatively indeterminate legal terms *topoi*, "places" useful for finding the materials and arguments that function as proofs.[26] The development of a modern rhetoric capable of relating the structures of topics and arguments in different areas of reasoning allows us to understand better how words and arguments can be used most skillfully to discover factors in particular situations. The next section will deal with the relation between relatively indeterminate arguments and such figures of thought as simile.

THE RELATION OF RHETORICAL ARGUMENT TO FIGURES
OF THOUGHT: SIMILE

Rhetoric enables us to understand the interrelation of argument and figure and frees us from the necessity of opposing the definitional to the figural or of "deconstructing" one by reducing it to the other. The deconstructionist move of finding hidden tropes in discourse that purports to be logically sound presupposes that tropes are themselves inherently undermining or cognitively suspect. This position is a far cry from the classical rhetorical view that figures of thought function to *enable* thought. Figures of simile and metaphor, like arguments by example, can be used as relatively indeterminate tools for finding more than meets the eye in real or fictional situations. This close interconnection between thought and figure becomes more apparent when we perform a thought experiment in which we imagine ourselves as speakers searching for arguments and figures that will allow us to interpret a situation. For example, if one were having difficulty in formulating the dangerous character of a friendship, one might search for an example similar in its structure and moral tones to the existing situation: "Yes, John is your friend, just as Iago was a friend to Othello." Suddenly, possible features of John's "friendship" stand out vividly, whereas they might otherwise have been difficult to capture in words. Argument by example can be used in very informal ways.

Similarly, hearers and readers can use both arguments by example and figures as relatively indeterminate tools for organizing the ideas about a situation and for testing its meaning. Imagine a woman in labor who is told by a nurse, "Pant like a puppy." The power of the simile is greater than the instructions "inhale and exhale in quick, loose breaths." Why is it greater and how does the woman use the simile as an instrumentality? The woman thinks of a rhythm of breathing by using the puppy as an example; she then imitates the rhythm and shallowness of the diagram she has created and so relates the puppy's breathing to her own.[27] Thus, her interpretation of the relatively indeterminate expression is complex. The meaning of the nurse's sentence includes the semantic meaning according to which the sentence makes sense, as well as an additional intended meaning, that the nurse means it as a suggestion to help breathing. In order to be helpful, the nurse has given the woman an instrumentality for thinking about how to breathe well.

"Pant like a puppy" gives the woman a diagram to think about, and in imitating the puppy's action she thinks about its breathing and her own until she can breathe more effectively for labor. Technically, she is using the image of the puppy as an individual diagram—that is, as an "object of experience in so far as some quality of it makes it determine the idea of an object."[28] She uses the puppy as a kind of clue to the relaxed, quick breathing that would help her in labor. In a sense, she does not really know how a puppy pants; she thinks about it and tries a few different ways, not with the idea of achieving a determinate interpretation of "Pant like a puppy" but with the purpose of learning how she might breathe effectively in this particular situation. The diagram is relatively indeterminate in that it directs her activity while her interpretation changes and grows. This relative indeterminacy is constructive, not destructive, as it might be considered in other approaches.

Communication in this situation is not simply a conveying of a message. The aim of interpretation is not to reconstruct exactly what the speaker meant by "Pant like a puppy," because the hearer may use the simile to evolve a way of breathing more effective than that intended by the speaker. Nor does the diagram determine interpretation, although it directs the woman's thoughts about breathing. The woman does not try to pant exactly like a puppy, indiscriminately repeating every element of the puppy's actions; she decides what she needs as she goes. Her idea of the puppy's breathing directs her efforts at trying different ways to breathe: her efforts are not random because the analogue excises some possibilities as unlikely to prove helpful. The woman aims to use the diagram of a puppy panting as an instrumentality for discovery, and she is willing to alter her diagram, her idea of a puppy's breathing and of her own breathing, in light of her developing understanding.

Too often rhetorical terms, arguments, and figures are treated either as if they have a fixed nature capable of serving particular purposes or as inherently and radically indeterminate. Yet, in practical decision-making activities, language needs to be flexible and to leave room for interpreters to adjust meaning to situation. Moreover, interpretation of "poetic" similes involves some of the same flexibility and rhetorical skill one needs in practical situations. Reductions of cognitive works to indeterminate "rhetorics" or "poetics" underestimate the strong ties between practical and poetic thinking. For example, extended similes, traditionally thought of as the most "poetic" of metaphors, usable only in moments of inspiration, invite their hearers and readers to test and refine interpretation in a fashion analogous to that in which the lawyer uses argument by example in case law or the woman uses a phrase to direct her actions in labor. When the *Iliad* compares the motion of men moving into battle to that of waves breaking on a beach, it invites the interpreter to find a resemblance of relations between the motion of men and the motion of waves:

> As when along the loud-sounding beach, waves of the sea
> are stirred up by the moving Zephyr, pressing one after another,
> and first one rises in crests on the sea, but then
> breaking on the land it roars and around the curve of the high cliff
> it breaks and spits forth foam
> So then the phalanxes of Danaans pressing on one after another
> moved ceaselessly into battle.
> Each leader commanded his men and they went in silence.—*Iliad* 4.422–29.[29]

If the reader uses the analogical connection (::) to find a possible way of relating the patterns in simile proper (as waves break and roar) and its narrative counterpart (so Danaans press and are silent), he or she might use the relation between the waves breaking on the land to project conflict into the narrative situation (A/B/C :: a/b/c), understanding that the forceful motion of the Danaans will break at the moment they meet an obstacle in the enemy. The simile would then anticipate the narrative, predicting an action. Readers could further understand such a simile as situating battle energy in terms of a blindly passive yet deeply powerful natural motion that may somehow underlie or go beyond purposeful human action. They might then relate this deeper interpretation they have discovered to the relevant portion of the narrative, changing their apprehension of both by their assessment of each in terms of the other. The reader uses the pattern of waves to understand the men in the narrative as engulfed by a powerful, repetitive motion, one that emerges as simile and narrative are thought together. At the same time, the difference between the roar of the waves and the quiet of the Danaans undercuts the reader's expectation of similarity. Whereas general terms and formulas help guide the reasoning process in the legal and scientific examples, a grasp of the whole configuration of an action or event guides discovery of similarity and difference in the extended simile. The configuration of the waves breaking on the land is relatively indeterminate until the reader relates it to the men moving into battle and determines further the patterns that shape the two events.

Elaborate, disanalogous similes like the lion simile in Homer's *Iliad*, book 20, are more relatively indeterminate than the simile about the waves and the men and offer more perplexing, challenging occasions for analogical interpretation. The simile presents a miniature story about a lion being hunted by men and leaves partly undetermined how that story may be related to its counterpart in the narrative:

> First Aineias came to threaten him [Achilleus]
> shaking his heavy helmet, and he held the eager shield
> before him, and shook his bronze spear.
> The son of Peleus rose up against him like a lion,
> rapacious, whom men desire to kill,
> gathering the whole deme. And he comes at first,
> paying no heed, but when some one of the swift young men
> wounds him with a spear, he crouches, jaws yawning, and foam comes
> from his teeth, and the courageous heart groans in his chest.
> With his tail he lashes his ribs and flanks on both sides,
> and his heart drives him to fight,
> and, his eyes glaring with fire [*menos*], he is borne on (to see)
> if he might kill some one
> of the men, or be killed himself in the crowd first.
> So the energy [*menos*] and brave courage [*thumos*] drove
> Achilleus to go against great-hearted Aineias.—*Iliad* 20.162–77

The simile story is more detailed than the analogous battle situation and yet does not make clear how a reader or hearer might relate the simile story and the battle event or how he or she might determine what is being related (the wounding of the lion? his anger? the whole story of the lion?) to what (to Achilleus? to his rage? to the energy that drives him on against Aineias?).

The reader brings the simile into relation with its counterpart action in the narrative, understanding the account of the battle event in terms of the story of the lion. The interrelating of the two allows the reader to determine further what should be related to what. Some similes can be used to discover a structural parallelism so that reader uses an A/B/C (here, the approach and wounding of the lion and his resulting fury) to articulate and dramatize a similar structure of actions D/E/F in the narrative (perhaps the approach and wounding of a hero and his resulting anger).

Because the process of determining similarity and difference is not guided by a general term like "inherently dangerous" that defines what is important from a certain point of view but, instead, is guided by the simile story as a whole, the interpreter can engage in a kind of free play, a process of balancing out the various elements of the story in relation to the human action. For example, the reader of the lion simile may take in the whole story of the lion who approaches, is wounded, and becomes infuriated, lashing his tail and foaming at the mouth until he seeks to kill, his eyes burning with the fire of his anger and energy. The energy and fire that occur at the end of this sequence of events take on a newly distinctive meaning by their placement within the mini-narrative sequence. The story consolidates our interpretation of that energy and fire. We can then use that idea of energy and fire to construe the intensity and quality of Achilleus's energy. We need not see them as literal "resemblances." Readers adjust the way they "take" the analogy in light of their explorations of the poem. Here we come closest to the kind of indeterminacy in which language can be detached from a specific reference and its interconnections explored and redefined. Nevertheless, this process need not be understood as being in opposition to the process of case-by-case reasoning or the more informal use of argument by example in ordinary speech.

In fact, we must resist the temptation to praise indeterminacy as the chief condition for freedom and the opening of possibilities, although it is commonly taken to be so. The power of the simile to create expectations and direct attention toward the human action in battle (that is, its relative determinacy) allows the reader to discover something further than would otherwise be evident (men in the narratives as engulfed by a powerful, repetitive motion). In addition, the account of human action corrects projection, allowing the audience to modify its view. (Achilleus does not behave exactly like the lion; difference is as important as similarity.)

My analysis of arguments and figures has shown that rhetoric offers a way of considering the function of indeterminacy without falling into the rigid dis-

tinctions between what is determinate (precisely definite, univocal and repeatable) and what is indeterminate (ambiguous and figurative) that undermine the possibility of thought. Rhetoric, as the art of discovering considerations in situations where more than one possibility is available, understands
argument and figure not as opposed categories but as closely interrelated
functions, often complementing or supplementing each other in reasoning activity. Rhetoric uses and understands terms, arguments, and figures as capable
of sustaining degrees of ambiguity, depending upon the purpose of the thinker
and the nature of what is to be decided.

The question of whether meaning is determinable in law and literature has
generated much controversy; yet insofar as the question leads us to choose between two impossible alternatives, in which meaning is either objective and
determinable or inherently unstable and indeterminable, it forecloses discovery. The aspiration toward a system of known rules and the skepticism that
such rules are possible create an impasse. Rhetoric offers a way out of this impasse because it is an art of reasoning that adapts rules to the particularities of
situation and action. Rhetoric uses ambiguous or relatively indeterminate
terms, arguments, and figures to discover and organize considerations for the
sake of judging particularities. Meanings of terms and relations change as they
are brought to bear on new situations.

  Fields vary in the kind and degree of indeterminacy their terms, arguments, and figures need in order to function well. Examples from mechanics,
law, and literature suggest that the degree and kind of indeterminacy of rules
and terms depend upon how formulations are used to direct observation and
how susceptible they are to modification when further facts and relations are
discovered. Rhetoric allows us to discern a continuum of degrees and kinds of
indeterminacy, freeing us from the necessity of opposing absolutely determinate rules that control reasoning to a destructive, radical indeterminacy of language that undermines the possibility of coherent thought.

NOTES

  I wish to thank William Olmsted, Paula Schiller, and David Smigelskis for their
comments on a draft of this article. My mistakes, of course, remain my own. Thanks
also go to Dennis Hutchinson for helpful references.

  1 For a good characterization of positions on this issue in literary criticism and law, see
    Sanford Levinson, "Law as Literature," *Texas Law Review* 60, 3 (March 1982):
    373–403. See also the responses of Gerald Graff, "'Keep off the Grass,' 'Drop
    Dead,' and Other Indeterminacies: A Response to Sanford Levinson," in the same

issue: 405–13, and James Boyd White, "Law as Language: Reading Law and Reading Literature" in the same issue: 415–45. The articles by Levinson and Graff are revised and reprinted in *Interpreting Law and Literature: A Hermeneutic Reader*, ed. Sanford Levinson and Steven Mailloux (Evanston, Ill.: Northwestern University Press, 1988), 155–73 and 175–80.

2 White, "Law as Language," 416. The most sustained defense of determinacy of meaning in interpretation is E. D. Hirsch, Jr., *Validity in Interpretation* (New Haven: Yale University Press, 1967). For a brief history of legal analyses of how terms function in American law, see Elizabeth Mensch, "The History of Mainstream Legal Thought," in *The Politics of Law: A Progressive Critique*, ed. David Kairys (New York: Pantheon, 1982), 26–39. Other law professors and literary critics have decried the sharp distinction between determinacy and indeterminacy; see Robert Weisberg, "The Law-Literature Enterprise," *Yale Journal of Law and the Humanities* 1 (December 1988): 43 and note 146.

3 For the analogy between rhetoric and modern American law, see James Boyd White, *Heracles' Bow: Essays on the Rhetoric and Poetics of the Law* (Madison: University of Wisconsin Press, 1985), 28–48, especially 41, where White writes that to see law rhetorically is to see "its ambiguities as ways of at once defining and leaving open the topics of conversation." Statutes can be viewed as "establishing a set of topics, a set of terms in which those [conversational] topics can be discussed." For an analysis of "rhetorical hermeneutics" as a therapy for theoretical literary discourse, see Steven Mailloux, "Rhetorical Hermeneutics," in *Interpreting Law and Literature*, 345–62, esp. 354ff., and idem, "Articulation and Understanding: The Pragmatic Intimacy Between Rhetoric and Hermeneutics," Chapter 18 in this volume.

4 Richard Rorty, *Consequences of Pragmatism* (Minneapolis: University of Minnesota Press, 1982), 163–64.

5 Aristotle, *Art of Rhetoric*, trans. J. H. Freese (Cambridge: Harvard University Press, 1975), 1.2.12.1357a 3. Three good, brief modern statements of the nature and function of rhetoric are Hanna Holborn Gray, "Renaissance Humanism: The Pursuit of Eloquence," *Journal of the History of Ideas* 24 (1963): 500; Victoria Kahn, *Rhetoric, Prudence, and Skepticism in the Renaissance* (Ithaca: Cornell University Press, 1985), esp. the introduction and chapter 2: "Humanist Rhetoric"; and Kahn, "Humanism and the Resistance to Theory," in *Literary Theory/Renaissance Texts*, ed. Patricia Parker and David Quint (Baltimore: Johns Hopkins University Press, 1986), 373–96 (reprinted as Chapter 7 in this volume).

6 Cicero, *Topica*, trans. H. M. Hubbell (Cambridge.: Harvard University Press, 1968), 386–87. See Aristotle, *Rhetoric* 1.2.8.1356b.

7 Paul de Man, *Allegories of Reading: Figural Language in Rousseau, Nietzsche, Rilke, and Proust* (New Haven: Yale University Press, 1979), 9.

8 Ibid., 10.

9 Paul de Man, "The Epistemology of Metaphor," *Critical Inquiry* 5 (1978): 17.

10 Jacques Derrida, "Structure, Sign and Play," in Derrida, *Writing and Difference*,

trans. Alan Bass (Chicago: University of Chicago Press, 1978), 253. Also in *The Structuralist Controversy: The Languages of Criticism and the Sciences of Man*, ed. Richard Macksey and Eugenio Donato (Baltimore: Johns Hopkins University Press, 1972), 253.

11 John R. Searle, "The Word Turned Upside Down," *New York Review of Books* 31, no. 16 (1983): 74–79.

12 Ibid., 79.

13 Strictly speaking, the terms were used to examine the objects in relation to those who sold them, those who used them, and those who were injured by them. As we shall see later, terms function in case law in relation to a process of reasoning by example or by analogy. See below. It can be misleading to consider the terms and distinctions in relation to objects such as loaded guns and defective lamps in abstraction from the process of comparing cases (not just things), inasmuch as the dangerousness of a thing may be related to how it is used and by whom. Melvin Eisenberg treats reasoning by example as a processing of reasoning that is about things rather than cases, and he abstracts the things not only from their cases but from the process of reasoning and of using terms and rules. Melvin Aron Eisenberg, *The Nature of the Common Law* (Cambridge: Harvard University Press, 1988), 86. I would argue that example refers not just to a thing like a radial saw but to a case in which someone gives or sells something to someone else who is injured by it or whose relative is injured.

14 Edward H. Levi, *An Introduction to Legal Reasoning* (Chicago: University of Chicago Press, 1949), 13ff.

15 Thomas S. Kuhn, *The Structure of Scientific Revolutions*. International Encyclopedia of Unified Sciences, 2d ed. (Chicago: University of Chicago Press, 1962, 1970), 190.

16 Aristotle calls argument by example one of the two main forms of rhetorical argument; the other form is the enthymeme; *Rhetoric*, I.2.8 and II.20.1.2.

17 Aristotle, *Rhetoric*, 1358a.

18 Aristotle seems to have two notions of reasoning by example in mind, one that emphasizes example as providing support for an argument, the other as functioning in invention. Gerald A. Hauser, "The Example in Aristotle's *Rhetoric*: Bifurcation or Contradiction?" *Philosophy and Rhetoric* 1 (1968): 78–90, and Hauser, "Aristotle's Example Revisited," *Philosophy and Rhetoric* 18 (1985): 171–80. Hauser's treatment of *epagoge* in the second article as a "form of discovery" is of particular interest, emphasizing as it does the ability of *epagoge* "to spark as noetic insight whereby the *archai* are grasped," p. 174. Aristotle refers the reader to the *Topics*, a work on invention, to understand the difference between example and enthymeme; I.2.1356b.

19 Levi, *Introduction to Legal Reasoning*, 2. For an effort to understand reasoning by analogy as similar to reasoning from precedent or principle, see Eisenberg, *Nature of the Common Law*, 83 ff. Notice, however, that Levi argues that the rule of law is announced *after* one case is set next to another by the process of reasoning by exam-

ple. Thus, one does not know the appropriate rule from an analysis of a single case. For an analysis of the relation between common-law rules and reasoning by analogy, see Steven J. Burton, *An Introduction to Legal Reasoning* (Boston: Little, Brown, 1985), 25–40 and 59ff. Burton comments: "The form of expression that purports to treat the results in common law cases as a consequence of preexisting rules . . . does not reflect accurately the process of common law," 36. For a discussion of *stare decisis* and the issue of how courts decide which precedents to follow, see David Kairys, "Legal Reasoning," in *Politics of Law*, 11 ff.

20 Levi, *Introduction to Legal Reasoning*, 2.

21 Kuhn, *Structure of Scientific Revolutions*, 189.

22 Ibid.

23 Levi, *Introduction to Legal Reasoning*, 1.

24 Ibid., 3.

25 Ibid., 8, emphasis added.

26 See the reference above to Cicero's formulation concerning the topics; *Topica*, 386–87. Aristotle, *Rhetoric*, 1.2.8.1356b. See also note 5, above.

27 *Diagram* refers here to C. S. Peirce's distinction of iconic signs into images, diagrams, and metaphors: "Those which partake of simple qualities . . . are *images*, those which represent the relations, mainly dyadic, or so regarded, of the parts of one thing by analogous relations in their own parts, are *diagrams*, those which represent the representative character of a representamen by representing a parallelism in something else are *metaphors*," *Collected Papers*, ed. Charles Hartshorne and Paul Weiss, 6 vols. (Cambridge: Harvard University Press), 2:277.

28 Ibid.

29 Homer, *Iliad*, ed. D. B. Munro, vol. 1 (4th ed., rpt., Oxford: Clarendon Press, 1960), my translation.

12

Charity, Obscurity, Clarity: Augustine's Search for Rhetoric and Hermeneutics

David Tracy

Rhetoric and hermeneutics have rediscovered each other in our postmodern period. In classical modernity both had seen their range narrowed and their importance as intellectual disciplines denied. Modern rationality felt free to diminish, even dismiss, both rhetoric and hermeneutics because each resisted the famous separations enforced by modernity: thought from feeling (dissociation of sensibility); content from form; theory from practice. Rhetoric could be reduced to issues understood as separate from and unimportant to modern theory: first, practical reason and its topical thinking; second, the forms of thought and the tropes informing all reason; third, the reasonableness of emotions, feelings, moods, passions. Rhetoric, in sum, became "mere rhetoric"—a rhetoric of form and style for secondary labors in the vineyard of rationality. Hermeneutics was also reduced to external traditions (especially biblical) and seemingly secondary issues (such as understanding in historical context with attention to both form—composition, genre—and style). Hermeneutics, for modernity, should have returned to its biblical and classicist origins and ceased to influence such modern enterprises as theory formation or historical-critical methods.

Postmodernity has not merely released new methods (poststructuralism, critical theory, feminist theory, cultural studies, the new historicism, and the like) but has also retrieved and rethought two classical premodern methods: rhetoric and hermeneutics.[1] Each of these methods has, in the late twentieth century, recovered its former range in new and classical forms. Rhetoric, for any thoughtful person, once again means not "mere rhetoric" but the range of disciplines appropriate to analyze all the acts and arts of persuasion. The new rhetorics of invention include the full range of classical rhetoric—*logos, ethos,* and *pathos.* There are fruitful debates between those (like Stephen Toulmin) concerned to recover and rethink rhetorical practical reason and arguments, including the topics, and those more explicitly postmodern thinkers (like Paul de Man) concerned to retrieve and radicalize the tropes. These thinkers are joined in debate with a still wider circle of rhetorical thinkers (for example, Wayne Booth) concerned to rethink the full range of rhetoric—in cryptic form, both the topics and the tropes.

Hermeneutics is a discipline that develops in times of cultural crisis when the classical resources of a tradition seem in doubt: the Stoic interpretation of the Homeric poems through allegory; the classical Jewish and Christian allegorical methods for reading the Bible; the rethinking of the primacy of the literal sense of the Bible in Luther; the retrieval of classical hermeneutics in the Renaissance; the development of a romantic hermeneutics of empathy from Friedrich Schleiermacher through Wilhelm Dilthey; and even the contemporary (and, to an extent, postmodern) development of an anti-Enlightenment hermeneutics in Hans-Georg Gadamer.[2]

In the late twentieth century, hermeneutics has left its confinements to either biblical or classical texts, thanks to the extraordinary achievements of Gadamer and the developments and critiques of Gadamer's position by Paul Ricoeur (the latter especially on the role of explanatory theories in hermeneutical understanding and the need for various hermeneutics of suspicion and critique as well as hermeneutics of retrieval). In its most interesting and important contemporary forms, hermeneutics has expanded its range beyond biblical texts and even beyond texts themselves, to all action, while it also maintains its central focus on understanding as the ontological character of human being, as well as its emphasis on manifestation or disclosure-unconcealment (not correspondence) as the primordial character of truth.

There is now an expansive range to both contemporary hermeneutics and contemporary rhetoric. Hermeneutics is focused principally on the understanding, employing models of conversation and manifestation. Rhetoric (or, as Booth nicely names it, rhetorology) is focused principally on persuasion, on models of argument, and on invention or discovery by means of both topical arguments and the tropes. Both disciplines resist reification into a single definition or method. Each discipline bears the signs of lively internal debate, indeed, conflict of interpretations. Each discipline provides distinct but related critiques of Enlightenment models of rationality and thereby opens its expansive understanding to both postmodern concerns and methods and to premodern resources. Each discipline has maintained its characteristic focus of attention while finding itself drawn toward the other, sometimes overlapping, sometimes conflicting. Hermeneutical understandings of truth as manifestation, for example, inevitably find themselves entangled with rhetorical reflections on persuasion. Rhetorical debates on topical argument inevitably find themselves paying attention to hermeneutical models of conversation as a wider category for inquiry than argument alone. Indeed, the elective affinities and family resemblances of hermeneutics and rhetoric suggest the need for the kinds of both flexibility and distinctiveness that thinkers in each discipline find it more and more necessary to maintain toward the other.

It now seems clear that hermeneutical thinkers must both acknowledge and engage rhetorical theories and vice versa. Otherwise, the common fate both disciplines endured in classical modernity could visit them again; otherwise, the fate of a classical text like Augustine's fine *De doctrina christiana* could await all rhetorical and hermeneutical texts.[3]

Religion, with its rhetoric of limits and ultimacy,[4] can provide an exceptionally clear test case of the need to employ both hermeneutics and rhetoric when studying any phenomenon. And Augustine, one of the great rhetorical thinkers of the West and the single most important Western Christian hermeneut of the Bible, is a splendid test case for religious studies, as well as for humanistic studies more widely, allowing us to examine the roles that both rhetoric and hermeneutics play. Judged strictly in terms of the reception of *De doctrina christiana* in Western culture, Augustine might have written two texts; books I, II and III on hermeneutics for the Bible; and book IV on rhetorical style. The fact is that Augustine wrote a single book, on both hermeneutics and rhetoric. That text shows how these two great disciplines of inquiry are both distinct and (to employ Hegel's favorite adverbs) always already related.

Any theologian who writes as well as Augustine did is, ironically, always in danger of being misunderstood by theological practitioners of the "plain style," or by those who practice what the ancients named dialectics. Not until the late twentieth-century revival of both rhetoric and hermeneutics have the limitations of dialectic been acknowledged in, or the persuasive power of rhetoric readmitted to, the conversations of philosophers and theologians. To the purely dialectical mind, a rhetoricized theology can seem a halfway house to "true" theology. This dialectical self-deception belies both the rhetoric in all dialectical arguments and the argumentative force of all good rhetoric.

Augustine never explicated his full rhetorical theory. However, he did leave us *De doctrina christiana,* a text that is too often hurried through by theologians anxious to move on to Augustine's more speculative and more polemical writings. This will not do.

Only in *De doctrina christiana* does one find Augustine's clearest statement of both his hermeneutics and what he left us of his rhetorical theory.[5] Too often Augustine's theory of rhetoric has been read through the strictly neo-Aristotelian eyes of modern rhetoricians. Then he is thought to be concerned solely, or at least principally, with "style" rather than with rhetorical "content," that is, rhetorical *inventio* as the discovery of true topics and arguments. This is a serious misreading. Augustine, to be sure, is deeply concerned with style. But he is equally concerned with both a rhetoric of *inventio* and a hermeneutics for reading Scripture. However, the Augustinian understanding of *inventio* can be understood only in his theological terms, not in solely philosophical terms. Augustine continues to persuade, to instruct, delight, and move, because he also developed rhetorical and theological principles of discovery or *inventio.*

Before interpreting Augustine's text, however, there are three background issues worth noting: the first two suggest possible difficulties with the text itself; the third, with the history of its interpretation. All three demand attention if an interpreter is to explicate the partly explicit, partly implicit theories of Christian hermeneutics and rhetoric in this text, the work of a former professor of rhetoric in the cosmopolitan capitals of Milan and Rome, who became a Christian bishop-rhetorician in the provincial city of Hippo.

The first issue is both the most obvious and hermeneutically the most central: the strange combination of simplicity and complexity in *De doctrina christiana.* On the one hand, this influential text seems far less complex in its analysis of rhetoric than the texts of either Plato or Aristotle or even of Augustine's own major mentor, Cicero. *De doctrina* is also far less complex a text than other texts by Augustine himself: not only the *Confessions, The City of God,* and *On the Trinity* but also some of his commentaries on Genesis, the Gospel of John, and the Psalms. On the other hand, *De doctrina christiana* (henceforth *DDC*) remains a quintessential Augustinian text, for the hermeneutical and rhetorical theories on the relation of theology and culture in *DDC* constitute a central clue for reading other Augustinian texts.

The problem of the text is further complicated by the question of whether it in fact constitutes a whole. The circumstances of *DDC*'s origins and completion over a twenty-year period are important here. After Augustine resigned as professor of rhetoric following his conversion to Christianity, he desired to remain a contemplative (more exactly, a Christian Platonist contemplative) in the company of a few like-minded friends. He hoped to produce dialogues like those he had written at Cassiciacum (*De dialectica, De musica, De magistro, De ordine,* and the like). It is important to recall that Augustine's conversion to Christianity was the final stage in a prolonged journey of conversion: the first conversion was to philosophy itself—a search for true wisdom by means of his struggles with Cicero's now lost *Hortensius*—while the second was to the realm of the "invisible," the "intelligible," the "spiritual," via "some writings of the Platonists."[6]

In his early years as Christian convert, priest, and eventually bishop, Augustine never lost sight of the importance of these first two moments in his journey. Like his rhetorical mentor, Cicero, Augustine tried to be faithful to the rhetorical search for both wisdom and eloquence. Like his Platonist contemporaries and against his own earlier materialist instincts, Augustine wished, above all, to contemplate the truths of Christianity through a spiritual hermeneutics. To Augustine the example of the sermons of Ambrose in Milan demonstrated that this ideal—at once rhetorical and hermeneutical—could be made actual: a spiritual (Platonist) reading of the Scriptures and all Christian doctrine (the hermeneutics), which precisely as such could teach, move, and delight other, like-minded searchers for wisdom and eloquence (the rhetoric). Christian theology, as philosophically true wisdom and true eloquence, was the now-achievable goal of the search of seekers for wisdom and happiness. With this goal in mind, Augustine intended to write reflections on each of the liberal arts by composing dialogues with his small group of Christian Platonist friends. Except for *De musica* and certain parts of his *De dialectica,* however, these early texts are now lost. The extant dialogues of that early period (especially *De ordine* and *De magistro*) show the promise of that desired, unfulfilled life of communal contemplation.

Why Augustine returned to North Africa, and especially to the provincial town of Hippo, remains something of a mystery to his biographers. But whatever else that his attempt to return home meant, Augustine clearly desired to continue the *otium liberale* (the leisured life) with a small circle of friends in order to understand what he had come to believe. The ideal that shaped Western Christian thought for centuries finds its roots in Augustine's use of both hermeneutics and rhetoric throughout his life: "Believe in order to understand: understand in order to believe."

The ideal remained. But these early hopes for the *otium liberale* proved illusory. For Augustine was elected (*forced* seems the more exact verb) by the acclamation of the people to become first priest, then bishop of Hippo. As bishop of an often unruly people, he found himself with a new set of problems. Augustine was too keen a rhetorician not to realize that he now had a different audience: the remarkably diverse congregation of Hippo.

This shift of audiences is a major impetus behind the emergence of *De doctrina christiana.* Augustine began to write this text shortly after he became bishop in 396. For Augustine ceased writing *DDC* in 397 at book III, paragraph 35 (in the midst of his hermeneutical discussion of the "rules for interpretation of the Scriptures by Tyconius"). And the difficulties of interpreting *DDC* increase when we realize that Augustine was also writing the *Confessions*—the classic Christian rhetoric of conversion—during this period. Is this simultaneity merely a historical accident of a prolific writer? Or does it suggest that Augustine needed both the *Confessions* and *De doctrina christiana* to express his full rhetorical theology at this crucial moment of transition in his life? The rest of the text of *De doctrina christiana,* moreover, was not completed until 427, which is to say, not until after Augustine's intense struggles and troubled (and often troubling) writings against the Donatists and, later, the Pelagians. However, it is difficult to find in the post-427 additions to *DDC* the later, deeply pessimistic Augustinian vision of the human situation: that theological vision was forged in response to the situation with the Pelagians. It is a tragic vision of humanity, which has seemed to many commentators (including Pelagius and Julian of Eclanum) to cancel out the relative optimism (especially on free will) of Augustine's earlier Platonic dialogues.

Given the shifts from pre-Hippo Augustine to post-Hippo Augustine, it is amazing that the text of *De doctrina christiana* does form so coherent a whole. In fact there are few references in the remainder of book III and book IV to the bleak anti-Pelagian vision of human perversity. Not even in his *Retractions,* written near the end of his life, does Augustine find it necessary to call into question the relative optimism about "pagan culture" that is found in *De doctrina.* Despite the significant interruption in the writing, the text nonetheless constitutes a coherent whole, thereby disclosing whatever we can learn of Augustine's unwritten rhetorical theory, as it explicitly discloses his most basic position on both biblical hermeneutics and on the hermeneutical relation of theology and culture.

What *DDC* does not address, however, also deserves mention. First, although it includes apologetic elements, it is not a rhetoric of Christian apologetics. Augustine's earlier dialogues seem more appropriate candidates for this role. Second, *DDC* is also not a rhetoric of conversion. The *Confessions*—which, to repeat, Augustine was writing both before and after he broke off the writing of *DDC*—remains the classic text in Augustine's oeuvre for understanding the rhetoric of conversion. Indeed, some commentators have even suggested that in the course of writing *DDC,* Augustine discovered that he needed a rhetoric of conversion in order to complete his Christian rhetorical theory—hence the *Confessions.* This hypothesis seems to me fruitful. But even if a fuller Augustinian theory of religious (here Christian) rhetoric does need an explicit rhetoric of conversion-confession, that fact only suggests the incompleteness of *DDC* as the locus of Augustine's full theological rhetoric, not the incorrectness of the theological-rhetorical theory actually present there. But this is to get a bit ahead of the story. We need first to see the final hermeneutical complication for any interpretation of the text before risking an interpretation of this seemingly straightforward text.

The third complication is, indeed, the complex and conflictual history of the effects of *De doctrina christiana.* As mentioned earlier, given the conflicts of readings, *DDC* might as well have been two texts. As modern hermeneutics since Gadamer argues,[7] the history of the effects of a classic text (that is, its history of interpretations or readings) cannot be separated from the reader's reading of the text itself. Any later reading must, therefore, also address this history as not simply an external problem for a full reading. In one sense, any Western Christian thinker (and a good number of post-Christian secular thinkers) is a part of the history of the effects of the texts of Augustine. Indeed, one need only read any Eastern Orthodox (non-Augustinian) Christian thinker to understand the profoundly Augustinian character pervading the family quarrels of Western Christians: Catholic versus Protestant and Liberal versus Neo-Orthodox.

If we attend to the history of readings of *DDC,* the problem of the unity of the text occurs on new grounds. The first text (books I–III) is one of the crucial texts in Western biblical hermeneutics, the text that employs Eastern allegorical methods in a Western anthropocentric (rather than Eastern cosmocentric) manner. This text gave the major impetus to Western theological figurative readings of the Scriptures. In more general cultural terms, this text also provided the major impetus to a rhetorical defense of "obscurity" as an intellectual value. For the medieval Augustinians a defense of obscurity was largely a defense of symbolic-religious texts. For moderns since the time of Petrarch, Boccaccio, and Erasmus (rhetorical thinkers all) through the romantics and the modernists to the rhetorical theorists of the late twentieth century, a defense of obscurity has become a claim to the priority of the poetic and symbolic over the conceptual, the propositional, and, in that limited sense, even the literal sense beloved by dialectics.

Augustine was not simply an Alexandrian hermeneut with a strong (indeed too strong) emphasis on the allegorical sense of Scripture. Indeed, in *DDC* and elsewhere Augustine provides one of the great defenses of the literal sense of Scripture. This is the case even if a modern reader suspects that Augustine's Christian Platonist heart is elsewhere, given his equally strong rhetorical defense of the spiritual, allegorical sense of Scripture. Augustine, to be sure, does not argue for the literal sense in the manner of his later and very different admirers, Thomas Aquinas and Martin Luther.[8] Rather, Augustine's rhetorical sense of the importance and value of obscurity in both the literal and the spiritual senses of the Scriptures led him to defend an important hermeneutical principle: to revise the New Testament tradition of typological reading in such a manner that the interpreter could, in principle, honor both the literal and the spiritual senses of the scriptural texts.[9] As Hans Frei justly argues, Augustine did envisage the world as it was formed by the historylike and realistic narratives rendered in the biblical stories as the history of salvation.[10] In that post-Augustinian sense, Augustine could be said to accord a certain priority to the literal sense as the plain sense of the Christian community. At the same time, Augustine's additional interests—here again at once rhetorical and hermeneutical—lay elsewhere. Assuming the community's affirmation of the plain sense of Scripture and assuming the traditional typological mode of scriptural hermeneutics, how could a Christian interpreter honor and control the reading of both the literal and the spiritual senses of the text whenever the obscurity of the text itself demanded such further reflections (as, for Augustine, the Bible often did)? Here the history of the readings of books I–III fruitfully shows that Augustine's defense of rhetorical obscurity in the text, as promoting both wisdom and eloquence allied to a necessary hermeneutical plurality of readings of any obscure text, is the one sure clue to the heart of Augustinian biblical and cultural hermeneutics, as well as central to his rhetorical theory.

The "second" text (book IV) is often cited by historians of rhetoric as a major influence of a different sort, namely, the narrowing of Western rhetorical interests to concerns of style alone. On that reading, book IV and its profound influence on Christian preaching and rhetoric is charged with no little of the blame for the removal of philosophical *inventio* from the rhetorical tradition in favor of an overconcern with style—an overconcern that is always in danger of sliding into "mere rhetoric." A strange charge to post on the door of the Ciceronian professor of rhetoric of Milan and Rome—or even to post on the door of the beleaguered bishop of Hippo!

The charge would hold if all we could learn from *DDC* about Augustine's rhetoric were to be found in book IV. But what if the text really does constitute a whole? What if books I–III (if largely implicitly) give Augustine's new suggestions not only for hermeneutics but also for Christian theological *inventio?* What if the hermeneutical concerns of books I–III constitute a new form of philosophical-theological *inventio* that suggests new topics and new forms of argument for the new Christian reading of both the old classics (the liberal arts) and the new classics (the Scriptures)? Then the Augustinian *inventio* would constitute the emergence—*at once* hermeneutical and rhetorical—of a new model for the relation of Christianity and culture. The Augustinian model formed medieval and Renaissance culture and continues to inform much contemporary Christian theology. On this reading, the text of *De doctrina christiana* must be read as a whole.[11] On this reading, moreover, the Augustine of *DDC* never suffered the nightmare that affected the conscience of his contemporary and friend Jerome, who dreamt that at the Last Judgment he declared himself a Christian only to have Christ condemn him as a Ciceronian. Nor did the Augustine of *DDC* share the belief of his North African forensic-rhetorican predecessor Tertullian that the question What has Athens to do with Jerusalem? was purely rhetorical, to which the expected answer was, Nothing. In contemporary language, the question of *DDC* is: What has a hermeneutics of Scripture to do with a rhetoric of both invention and style? In Augustine's own context the question is: What have books I–III to do with book IV? Or even, What does the Ciceronian professor of rhetoric of Milan and Rome have to do with the bishop of Hippo?

RHETORICAL *INVENTIO* AS HERMENEUTICS

I shall begin with this line from book I: "There are two things necessary to treatment of the Scriptures: a way of discovering those things which are to be understood, and a way of teaching what we have learned. We shall speak first of discovery and second of teaching (I, I)."

In one sense, Augustine places the reader in medias res in a pursuit of principles for interpreting the Scriptures. More exactly, we are quickly informed that in order to understand the Scriptures we must pay attention to two related realities: things (*res*) and signs (*signa*). There follow brief examples of this distinction—for example, the thing, stone, in contrast to the stone on which Jacob placed his head: the latter is both a thing and a sign, that is, a thing used to signify something else. As influential and complex as his theory of signs will prove to be, however, one principally finds in book I Augustine's characteristic insistence that in order to understand signs at all, we must first understand things.

But this typical move leads just as swiftly to another famous Augustinian distinction: between *frui* (to enjoy) and *uti* (to use). Both of these realities, in turn, are quickly related to our loves and desires. What is going on here? As the next chapters (III–XXXIV) suggest by their frequent if abbreviated Augustinian excursions into dialectic and rhetoric (many of the chapters are, in fact, capable summaries of arguments from his earlier dialogues), what we find in book I, in the most general terms, is the fundamental discovery (and "method of discovery") informing Augustine's entire thought: the reality of love (*caritas*) intended to function as a kind of foreknowing. Simultaneously, we find that Augustine, the Christian convert-rhetor, has not and will not abandon his first two conversions (to rhetorical philosophy as the search for wisdom and to the realm of the intelligible, invisible, immutable, spiritual) after his Christian conversion—even after his forced assumption of duties as bishop-preacher at Hippo.

The distinction between *frui* and *uti* itself is clear: "To enjoy something is to cling to it with love for its own sake. To use something, however, is to employ it in obtaining that which we love, provided it is worthy of love" (I, IV). In the next chapter this distinction is quickly linked with the search for true things: "The things which are to be enjoyed are the Father, the Son, and the Holy Spirit, a single Trinity, a certain supreme thing common to all who enjoy it, if, indeed it is a thing and not rather the cause of all things, or both a thing and a cause" (V).

This seems clear enough, save for the fact that, as Augustine knows, it still leaves us with the problem of how we are to know God, the supreme reality. Augustine insists that we can discover God only if God gives us the grace (gift-power) for the discovery. A finely Augustinian paradox ensues: God must give us the grace to discover God, and yet we are inexorably driven and called to that discovery both before and after grace comes as pure gift. *De doctrina christiana* is presumably written for an audience that is already in some sense converted yet that still needs to discover how to understand the supreme reality who converted them and thereby allowed them to find new principles of invention (Believe *in order* to understand).

At the same time, one cannot help noticing that another audience also seems to surface in the speculations and arguments of book I: people who have not converted to Christianity, as well as the converted Christians who remain unconverted in certain aspects—in other words, those who need to understand in order to believe. What a rhetorical thinker with this kind of intellectual problem most needs is a new form of invention by means of which to discover the new places (*topoi*) where arguments can be found. To provide a full rhetorical theory, Augustine's principle of rhetorical invention must also prove a matter of transformational *ethos*. That *ethos* will, in the Augustinian vision, necessarily be complex, at the same time respecting our desire (*eros*) for wisdom and happiness while honoring, above all, the fact that only God can give us the living gift of grace as the gift of love (*agape*), the gift that will turn us around (*conversio*) to see the truth of things and thereby to transform both our understanding and our wills by reordering both rightly. Contrary to many readings, I contend that Augustine did develop a rhetoric of invention. But his notion of invention here is necessarily neither Platonic nor Aristotelian nor even Ciceronian. Augustinian invention is necessarily theological (which includes, but cannot be confined to, philosophical invention). His principal audience is a Christian interpreter who wishes to know how to interpret the Scriptures correctly. Thus the paradox or at least the complication that a proper hermeneutics is simultaneously a new rhetoric of discovery or invention. For only that kind of invention will allow Christians to know how to find the new topics revealed by the supreme reality, God, in the true signs of the Scriptures.

Nor does Augustine disappoint his readers. Unlike in some of his later writings (think of the *massa damnata* motif of the anti-Pelagian writings on sin and grace, or even *The City of God* on how the "virtues" of the pagans become "splendid vices"), grace in *De doctrina christiana* does not simply confront nature in order to force us to acknowledge our perversity, evil habits, sins. Rather, the references to such perversity and the allusions to our human, willful genius at trapping ourselves by means of our habits seem to function in *DDC* as unsettling but not disabling moments in a larger, theologically transformational context.

The key to a true interpretation is *caritas:* the transformation of our *eros* by God's *agape* of grace provides, for Augustinian hermeneutics, a new way of foreknowing.[12] This hermeneutics also frees us to a true rhetoric of invention. The discovery of the true wisdom of our desires and strivings for wisdom and happiness is grounded in a discovery of the true way to interpret (and thereby argue from) the signs of Scriptures, the new classics of the converted ones. In Augustine's mature theological understanding, the Fall caused a rupture between our knowledge of reality and our use of signs. Even in his earlier theories on signs and things, it is clear from his rhetorical thought that we can read signs correctly only if we somehow already understand the realities to which they refer. Hermeneutically construed, Augustine's principle can be stated this way: we must have some preunderstanding of the subject matter in order to interpret the signs in texts correctly. On this reading, therefore, Augustine's position in book I is not dependent on either his implicit philosophical position on sense and reference nor on his theological reading of the Fall as causing the rupture of signs from things, things that he believed he had found in his own long and often tortured route to conversion and in his postconversion, lifelong convalescence. As important as these principles are for the implications of Augustine's fuller theory of signs and things, they do not determine the fundamental Augustinian position, at once a hermeneutics and a rhetoric of *inventio,* in book I. For that, we need only to understand, at least initially, that we must have some understanding of the *res* (the subject matter) if we are to understand signs at all. But how can we have a true understanding? This is Augustine's basic problem in book I.

The highly abbreviated reflections of book I can be considered, therefore, both dialectically and rhetorically. There are rhetorical and dialectical arguments on why God alone (as true *res*) can be truly enjoyed and can only be truly enjoyed by one who has been given the grace from that same God to enjoy that supreme thing. These arguments (most of them, to repeat, summaries of the dialectical and rhetorical arguments of his earlier dialogues) take up familiar Christian Platonist themes. The drive to true wisdom is the drive to enjoy the invisible and the immutable, and it is only fulfilled if the immutable discloses itself. The drive to true happiness for our highly mutable wills meets two chief obstacles: the multiplicity (and thereby internal conflict) of our desires and the traps we set for ourselves when we—perversely—enjoy what we should use (all mutable things, especially ourselves) and use what we should enjoy (the immutable, the invisible, the eternal supreme reality, God).

These two drives to wisdom and happiness constitute the fundamental *eros* that at once impels us and traps us. Only through the gift of the self-revelation of the immutable in the Incarnation could we discover true wisdom and true happiness. For only then could we enjoy what is to be enjoyed (God) and love all else by using it for the sake of that love-enjoyment of God. For Augustine, even the neighbor is to be loved as "used," that is, for the sake of God.[13]

But faith and hope for the converted make possible a transformation of the self that allows a new search for the true discovery of wisdom and happiness. That transformation is *caritas:* because God's grace as the love gift of *agape* is freely given, it frees the *eros* of our essential drive to wisdom and happiness to the new Augustinian synthesis of *caritas* and, therefore, to new possibilities for the discovery of true wisdom and true happiness. This transformational principle of *caritas* seems to suggest that, for Augustine, rhetorical discovery (*inventio*) is entirely a matter of the proper *ethos.* But even aside from the notorious (or, at least, anti-Quintillian) problem of the preacher who does not practice what is preached (book IV), this reading based solely on *ethos* does not hit the mark in explaining how *caritas* also transforms the *logos* of the Christian rhetorican to the discovery of true understanding.

Caritas is needed, to be sure, to transform the *ethos* of the rhetor. But *caritas* is also another kind of clue, one more related to *logos,* and thereby to *inventio,* than to *ethos.* For *caritas,* as a new mode of foreknowing, formulated as the principle of "love of God and love of neighbor," becomes the means by which new wisdom is born. Faith for Augustine can now be understood as a "wisdom born of *caritas.*" *Caritas,* formulated as a transformational principle, transforms both *ethos* and *logos.* *Caritas* becomes the means to discover the true meaning of (and thereby the *topoi* or "places" for true arguments from) the new classics—the Scriptures. Yet however new these biblical classics may be for the educated of antiquity, the biblical texts will be classic only because they are the authoritative signs of the self-manifestation of the true *res,* the supreme thing or cause of all things, God. These signs, as books II and III show, will yield their true meaning (and their new topics) solely to the one who has grasped (or, more accurately, been grasped by) the true *res*—that is, to the person who knows this divine reality by knowing that the central topic of both the Scriptures and our desires must be the love of God and love of neighbor. The hermeneutical *caritas* principle of Augustine, moreover, is clearly christomorphic but still more clearly radically theocentric.

So much is this the case that Augustine does not hesitate to reach a conclusion that would upset many a Christian today: "Thus a man supported by faith, hope, and charity, with an unshaken hold upon them, does not need the Scriptures except for the instruction of others. And many live by these things in solitude without books" (I, XXXIX). So central is the *res* of God for both *ethos* and *logos* that true Christians could live without the *signa* (the words of Scripture). And yet we have these signs and they will help us to discover true wisdom, provided we keep clearly in mind the fundamental hermeneutical principle of Augustine: the love of God and the love of neighbor. *Caritas,* then, as both *ethos* and *logos,* will also prove to be the central new rhetorical principle of discovery (*inventio*) for both the signs of *eros* in the search for true wisdom in the classics of the pagans and the signs of *agape* in the new classics, the Scriptures. As a transformative (and not purely confrontational) principle, moreover, Augustinian *caritas* will allow the Christian rhetor to continue to learn from the wisdom of the pagan classics even while interpreting the new wisdom of the Scriptures. Athens (and Milan and Rome), it seems, still have a great deal to do with Jerusalem (and Hippo). For theology and culture are reunited under the new principle of Augustinian invention: love of God and love of neighbor.[14]

ON DISCERNING THE SIGNS OF THE NEW CLASSICS: A DEFENSE OF OBSCURITY AND PLURALITY

Book I, therefore, has been concerned with "things," especially the supreme thing, God, and the principle (as both *ethos* and *logos*) by means of which Christian interpreters can find principles of discovery for true wisdom and true happiness (*caritas*). But God, we have also been informed, has revealed

Godself through certain signs. The supreme sign of that self-revelation (that is, the incarnation) is mentioned in book I. Curiously, however, Augustine does not dwell upon the incarnation when he comes to reflect upon signs themselves. But we should recall that the *caritas* principle represents, for Augustine, precisely what the incarnation as sign reveals about what has happened to us through the incarnation. Indeed, the principle of love of God and love of neighbor is what Augustine consistently employs when he engages in a Christian typological (and, in that sense, christological) reading of the figurative signs of the Old Testament.

It does no injustice to Augustine's relative silence on the incarnation as the supreme sign of the supreme *res* to suggest that his fundamental theological presupposition on signs in *DDC* and elsewhere can be restated in modern theological-hermeneutical terms. That presupposition is this: for the Jew and the Christian (the Muslim is, significantly—hermeneutically—different here), the relation of the "texts" of the Scriptures and the "events" to which those texts bear authoritative (canonical) witness is one in which the revelation occurs in events of divine self-disclosure (e.g., Sinai or the incarnation) to which the biblical texts bear witness. The revelatory events are both historical (e.g., they concern Jesus of Nazareth) and transhistorical (e.g., the divine self-disclosure in Jesus the Christ). The texts, the Scriptures, are not the revelation but the authoritative witness to the original revelation. The Christian confession is "We believe *in* Jesus Christ *with* the apostles." The texts of the New Testament are the texts of apostolic witness to the revelation of God in the event and person of Jesus Christ. This revelation continues, in the understanding of the Christian community, by being re-presented through the primary signs of word (proclamation) and sacrament (the sign that makes present what it signifies).

To translate this contemporary Christian theological hermeneutic into the terms of books II and III: Augustine's principal concern is to discover how the authoritative signs of witness (the Scriptures) are related to the supreme sign (incarnation) of the supreme *res* (God). Book I has articulated the needed new Christian rhetorical principle of discovery, *caritas*. For Augustine, this principle is what Christian interpreters should use to interpret the authoritative texts of the Scriptures, i.e. these word-signs of witness to that supreme sign-event of the self-disclosure of the supreme *res*. To read the Scriptures as scripture is to read them theologically through the christomorphic and theocentric Augustinian principle of *caritas*. The signs of the New Testament may be read directly by means of this principle. The Old Testament should be read, for Augustine, typologically. Both testaments, for Augustine, should be read both literally and spiritually, depending on the nature of the written signs involved and the interpreters' knowledge of "true things" through the central principle of love of God and love of neighbor.

Yet even if we grant all these Augustinian terminological and hermeneutical-theological presuppositions, any reader of the Scriptures realizes, with Augustine, that the interpreter still finds a host of difficulties in interpreting the word-signs of Scripture. Some of these difficulties can be treated, as they are by Augustine, with relative ease. For example, we can distinguish between natural and conventional signs. We can also take commonsense methods in dealing with many of the problems of "unknown signs." As an obvious example, we can learn the original languages of the Bible. Augustine, in fact, knew little Greek and probably no Hebrew. Hence his great concern in *DDC* with using the best Latin translation. Other Augustinian methods of textual discernment (such as his Pythagorean love of numbers and music) strike most contemporary interpreters of Scriptures as a part of the common sense of Augustine's late classical culture but rarely of ours.

Augustinian methods like rhetorical analyses of the tropes in the Scriptures live on in new forms in many contemporary historical-critical and literary-critical interpretations of the Scriptures. Still other suggestions (such as the importance of context and the relation of parts to the scriptural whole) were standard *topoi* in scriptural interpretation before Augustine and have remained so, in modified forms, ever since (e.g., form-critical analysis of context or redactional analysis of the whole of an individual gospel in order to understand the parts). Augustine's own candidate for a theocentric principle of understanding the *res* (namely, the principle of love of God and love of neighbor) survives, at best, as but one candidate among several for that much-disputed theological role.[15]

These Augustinian analyses are important but familiar. However, three characteristically Augustinian positions in books II and III practically had a life of their own in the history of their reception. They demand, by their novelty, further reflection.

The first question is how to value and understand "ambiguous" signs of the Scriptures, especially how to discern "figurative" from "literal" senses of particular texts. To treat the latter problem first: Augustine is both clear and consistent in his use of the *caritas* principle as the chief way to distinguish the literal sense and the figurative sense of particular passages (e.g., III, X: "Therefore a method of determining whether a location is literal or figurative must be established. And generally this method consists in this: that virtuous behavior pertains to the love of God and one's neighbor; the truth of faith pertains to a knowledge of God and one's neighbor"). So we do possess a principle ("generally") that can help us discover the true meaning of difficult passages.

But we also have a hermeneutical principle that defends not only figurative meanings but the ambiguity and obscurity often present in the Scriptures; this very obscurity, which often gives rise to this difficult issue of what is literal and what is figurative, must be established. And generally this method consists in this: whatever appears in the divine word that does not literally pertain to virtuous behavior or to the truth of faith you must take to be figurative.

Throughout books II and III (and, under a new form, in book IV's defense of the "true eloquence" of the Scriptures), we find Augustine providing one of his most characteristic hermeneutical and rhetorical moves: a restatement of the defense of obscurity and ambiguity that appears as a common topic in the Greek fathers. Among several examples, consider the discussion in book II, chapter VI. We are informed there (in the midst of Augustine's fascinating interpretation of the teeth and shorn sheep metaphors in the Song of Songs) that there are both good negative reasons for scriptural obscurity and good positive reasons. Negatively, these obscure passages help conquer our pride through hard work. They discipline our natural disdain for what seems obvious. Indeed, Augustine does not doubt that God has provided these obscurities for such discipline.

Positively, those obscure words and passages are wise (and, later, eloquent) because "no one doubts that things are perceived more readily through similitude and that what is sought with difficulty is discovered with more pleasure." This is a debatable rhetorical principle, which will free Augustine from his earlier preconversion disdain for the "vulgarity" and "obscurity" of the Scriptures. In sum, the principle of a new formal value of obscurity and ambiguity allows Augustine to argue for the Scriptures as the new classic signs—wiser (a matter of *logos*) and even more eloquent than his own beloved pagan classics. Just as *caritas* can transform human *eros,* so, it seems, can scriptural obscurity paradoxically transform Augustine's earlier preconversion rhetorical assessment of the status of these scriptural signs in relation to the "clearer" signs of the pagan classics. This same rhetorical principle of obscurity as a value, as noted above, will live a strange afterlife in the Augustinian humanists and rhetorical theorists of the Renaissance (Petrarch, Boccaccio, and Erasmus). In yet another sea change, the Augustinian principle will find life among romantics and modernists under the rubric of the priority of the symbolic (obscure-ambiguous) over the conceptual, prepositional, literal—an ironic twist, surely, to Augustine's defense of scriptural obscurity.

With regard to the second issue, this defense of obscurity can also illuminate another aspect of the Augustinian program—the famous suggestion (borrowed from Irenaeus) of book II, chapter XL, about stealing Egyptian gold. This Old Testament trope is used by Augustine in his insistence that even in the new rhetorical situation where the Scriptures are not the primary classics, the Christian rhetor can still use the classics of the pagan liberal arts. Indeed, those disciplines, like the gold and silver of the Egyptians stolen by the departing Israelites, belong to the new Israelites (i.e., the Christians) because these disciplines were not invented by the pagans, after all. Rather, the liberal arts were discovered, on this reading, as already existing by the grace of the God who created them. Christians need not reject these treasures (pace Tertullian and Jerome) because, as the new Israelites, they already own all of the liberal arts.

The classics of Scripture are, for Augustine, both wiser and more eloquent than the pagan classics, for the Scriptures alone are the signs of witness to the direct self-disclosures of the divine. Still, the Christian rhetor, informed by the Scriptures themselves through this new interpretation of the figurative meaning of the Israelite theft of Egyptian gold and silver, can now freely use these pagan treasures as his or her own. The original biblical image and the Christian analogical argument derived from it may be more than a little strained. But if one considers the Tertullian option and the positive history of the effects of this surprising theft imagery, latter-day rhetoricians, hermeneuts, and theologians must agree that Augustine's figurative reading of scriptural obscurity allowed the gold and silver of the liberal disciplines to find a new life in medieval Christianity and, through the medieval Christians, in the late twentieth century in the West.

A final topic on how to interpret the signs of the Scriptures is also worth noting, namely, Augustine's defense of a plurality of readings of the Scriptures (book III, chapter XXVII). What is hermeneutically interesting here is that Augustine does not allow the author's meaning in the Scriptures to determine the meaning of the text. God, as the supreme author, can use the human author to state a meaning that even he or she did not understand but which a reader (e.g., Augustine) could then discern. ("And certainly the Spirit of God, who worked through that author, undoubtedly foresaw that this meaning would occur to the reader or listener.")

This theological hermeneutics provides for a remarkable flexibility of meaning of the scriptural texts and for a genuine plurality of readings. That plurality, moreover, was bound to increase once Augustine's own principle of *caritas* was also questioned. In sum, the more one moves into books II and III, the more flexible do Augustine's hermeneutical and rhetorical principles of book I become in practice: the ambiguity and obscurity of the scriptural signs are defended; the figurative begins to play almost as great a role as the literal sense (in contrast to Augustine's later disciples, Aquinas and Luther); the pagan classics of liberal disciplines will continue to play a role for Christian interpreters and thereby provide more readings still; and, finally, because God is the ultimate author of these texts, any hermeneutical primacy accorded the "author's intention" becomes relatively unimportant. The "signs" of books II and III will be dependent, of course, on the *res* of book I. But as the Augustinian theological rhetoric of invention became more and more questionable, both within later Christian readings of the Scriptures and in secular interpretations on the scriptural texts, some modern hermeneut-turned-rhetoricians have been tempted to find the hermeneutical principles of books II and III as the true wisdom for rhetorical discovery of the signs of Augustine's own text. This would leave books I, II, and III as a theologically truncated but still a hermeneutically interesting text. That new text would bear strong family resemblance to Gadamer's hermeneutics and to suggestions that modern rhetorical theory needs hermeneutics for its own process of *inventio*. On that reading, modern hermeneutics would be construed as ancient rhetoric historicized. But that is, to be sure, another story—and one perhaps best entitled "The Revenge of the Egyptians." It is not, however, Augustine's story, in which rhetoric and hermeneutics form a genuine whole.

ELOQUENCE AND CLARITY

If books I–III present Augustine's discussion of rhetorical-theological *inventio* for discovering true wisdom by means of correct hermeneutical principles of interpretation for the new classics, then the familiar suggestion that the (narrowly) rhetorical interests of *DDC* may be found *only* in book IV, on style, becomes highly unlikely. In fact, the truth is quite the contrary. On the present reading, the analysis in book IV of the need for the preacher to instruct, delight, and move (i.e., persuade to action) suggests that rhetorical instruction, as first in this series, always needs principles of both interpretation *and* invention: hence the hermeneutics and rhetoric of books I–III. Augustine is, to be sure, greatly concerned with style (or styles—subdued, temperate, and grand) and does stretch Cicero a good deal in chapter XVII in order to link his styles directly to the "teach, delight, persuade" motifs of Cicero. I admit that the opening sentence of book IV, chapter II, is somewhat disconcerting for my reading of *DDC* as providing a full rhetorical theory of *inventio* united to a full hermeneutics for the interpretation of Scriptures. The sentence seems to suggest a somewhat sophistic understanding of rhetoric—indeed, one that Augustine's own earlier antisophistic remarks seemed firmly to exclude. Yet the rhetorical thrust of the chapter (as well as Augustine's reluctance to explicate his full rhetorical theory either here or elsewhere) suggests that the rhetoric of instruction (and thereby invention) remains his central rhetorical concern.

More exactly, the now-familiar Augustinian motifs return, on this reading, in new guises: e.g., the true wisdom of the new classics has also become true eloquence (especially in Paul and Amos). Still, the preacher of biblical wisdom and eloquence must not try to imitate the obscurity-profundity of the Bible.

But why not—especially given Augustine's own plea for preachers to "imitate" classical models of eloquence as, in effect, a partial replacement for lack of formal rhetorical training? The reason seems clear enough: the preacher is not the inspired author of Scripture who can be used by God to speak obscure truths that even the author need not understand. Rather, the preacher is the *interpreter* of this true wisdom and eloquence. As interpreter, the preacher should not presume to imitate scriptural obscurity; the preacher should instead render biblical obscurity clear for the instruction, delight, and persuasion of the congregation. The preacher needs rhetorical and hermeneutical principles of interpretation of the Scriptures in order to instruct clearly (books I–II). The preacher also needs some knowledge of "styles" (acquired, e.g., through imitation of classical styles or through rhetorical education in style) in order to delight the congregation and thereby hold their attention and to move them—persuade them—to action.

But above all, as interpreter of often obscure scriptural passages, the preacher must strive for clarity. Clarity alone can instruct the mixed audience that needs the true wisdom and eloquence of Scripture. Only such clear instruction can properly use whatever other rhetoric is both available and necessary (e.g., to delight and to move). Augustine is never "merely rhetorical" or principally concerned with a rhetoric of style, even in book IV. This is the case at least insofar as delighting and moving are controlled by the demands of instruction and *inventio;* and invention is specified by the demands of the discovery of the rules for true hermeneutics for the Scriptures in books I–III.

Perhaps Augustine, the former professor of rhetoric, might even agree that my interpretation of the rhetorical and hermeneutical theories sometimes obscured in the signs of his text is unforced. What the bishop of Hippo might think of his latter-day theological descendants is a more unsettling question, best left for another day. And yet whatever the answer to that second question, some of Augustine's rhetorical principles seem to live in new forms in the late twentieth-century rhetorical context: theological charity becomes, for example, Wayne Booth's hermeneutical model of the text as "friend"; scriptural obscurity becomes the "priority of the poetic" in modern and postmodern hermeneutics and literary criticism; the divine impetus to a plurality of readings not determined by the author's meaning becomes the loss of the author in some deconstructionism; the demand for clarity in communication becomes arguments over the relation of a rhetoric of invention (*logos*) to a rhetoric of delight (*pathos*) and a rhetoric of *ethos*—and all three to a fuller rhetoric of persuasion in contemporary rhetorical debates on the relations of the topics and the tropes. What Augustine might add to those arguments rises or falls, I suggest, on whether we read *De doctrina christiana* as one text or two. If one seeks Augustine's apologetic rhetoric, one should read his early dialogues. If one desires his rhetoric of conversion one must turn to the *Confessions*. But if one wishes to find Augustine's rhetoric of *inventio* as a key moment in any Christian persuasion to action, and if one wishes to see how Augustine correlated hermeneutics and rhetoric into a coherent whole without loss of the distinctiveness of either, then *De doctrina christiana* is the classic Christian text.

NOTES

1 On rhetoric for a postmodern reading of the Bible, see the Bible and Culture Collective, *The Postmodern Bible* (New Haven: Yale University Press, 1995).

2 For more on these matters, see David Tracy, *Plurality and Ambiguity: Hermeneutics, Religion, Hope* (San Francisco: Harper, 1987).

3 Saint Augustine, *On Christian Doctrine [De doctrina christiana]*, trans. D. W. Robertson, Jr. (Indianapolis: Bobbs-Merrill, 1958). The translations throughout are Robertson's.

4 See, for example, Kenneth Burke, *The Rhetoric of Religion: Studies in Logology* (Berkeley: University of California Press, 1961).

5 On the discussion of the relation of Augustine's rhetoric to Greek and Roman models, see James J. Murphy, *Rhetoric in the Middle Ages: A History of Rhetorical Theory from St. Augustine to the Renaissance* (Berkeley: University of California Press, 1974); Richard McKeon, "Rhetoric in the Middle Ages," *Speculum* 1 (1926): 1–32; Maurice Festard, *St. Augustin et Cicéron*, 2 vols., Etudes Augustiniennes (Paris: Aubier, 1958). For the Greek and Roman models, see George Kennedy, *The Art of Persuasion in Greece* (Princeton: Princeton University Press, 1963); idem, *The Art of Rhetoric in the Roman World* (Princeton: Princeton University Press, 1972).

6 Robert O'Connell, *St. Augustine's Confessions: The Odyssey of Soul* (Cambridge: Harvard University Press, 1969); idem, *St. Augustine's Early Theory of Man, A.D. 386–391* (Cambridge: Harvard University Press, 1968).

7 Hans-Georg Gadamer, *Truth and Method*, 2d rev. ed., trans. Joel Weinsheimer and Donald G. Marshall (New York: Continuum, 1993).

8 For an account of this argument, see "Rhetoric and the Politics of the Literal Sense in Medieval Literary Theory: Aquinas, Wyclif, and the Lollards," by Rita Copeland, Chapter 16, this volume.

9 For more on these matters, see James Preus, *From Shadow to Promise: Old Testament Interpretation from Augustine to Young Luther* (Cambridge: Belknap Press, 1969); and Henri de Lubac, *Exégèse médiévale*, 3 vols. (Paris: Aubier, 1968).

10 Hans Frei, *The Eclipse of Biblical Narrative: A Study of Eighteenth- and Nineteenth-Century Hermeneutics* (New Haven: Yale University Press, 1974), 1–3.

11 I use the book-chapter format (cited in the text as, e.g., I, I) to facilitate use of both Robertson's fine English translation and the original Latin. The latter may be found in J-.B. Migne, ed., *Patrologia cursus completus*. Series Latina (Paris: Migne), vol. 34, and in S. Aurelei, *Augustini de doctrina christiana libros quatuor*, ed. H. J. Vogels, Florilegium Patristicum, Fasc. XXIV (Bonn, 1930). Citations in the text are to these editions.

12 The best modern study of *caritas* is John Burnaby, *Amor Dei: A Study of the Religion of St. Augustine* (London: Hodder and Staughton, 1938).

13 See Anders Nygren, *Agape and Eros* (New York: Harper and Row, 1969), 449–563, esp. 539–43.

14 The classic study is Henri-Irénée Marrou, *Saint Augustin et la fin de la culture antique* (Paris: E. D. Bocard, 1949); see also Ragnar Holte, *Béatitude et sagesse: St. Augustin et le problème de la fin de l'homme dans la philosophie ancienne* (Paris: Etudes Augustiniennes, 1962). These works should be read in conjunction with the fine biography by Peter Brown, *Augustine of Hippo: A Biography* (Berkeley: University of California Press, 1969).

15 For an analysis see David Tracy, *The Analogical Imagination: Christian Theology and the Culture of Pluralism* (New York: Crossroad, 1981), 233–339; Robert M. Grant with David Tracy, *A Short History of the Interpretation of the Bible* (London: SCM, 1984), 174–87.

13

Rhetoric, Hermeneutics, and the Interpretation of Scripture: Augustine to Robert of Basevorn

Donald G. Marshall

Rhetoric and hermeneutics find common ground in their suspicion of philosophy and grammar. In *De oratore* Cicero brings out the complex relations between rhetoric and philosophy by means of a dialogue.[1] When Crassus claims that the orator must possess far-reaching knowledge and culture, Scaevola objects that knowledge is the philosophers' domain, and they have already demonstrated that orators are ignorant (1.41–44). Crassus replies that this is a familiar theme among the Greeks, but when Plato is eloquent against eloquence, he exhibits a failure of self-comprehension. The orator cannot be potent without having grasped the subject he discusses (1.48). Unlike the philosophers, who "debate these subjects in their holes and corners, to pass an idle hour" (1.56), the orator develops with full weight and charm (*cum omni gravitate et iucunditate*) the themes philosophers dispute "in a sort of thin and bloodless style" (*tenui quodam exsanguique sermone*) (1.57). The orator's culture is not entangled in technicalities nor based on abstract reflection nor aimed at a self-centered wisdom but synthesized into *humanitas* manifest as prudence applicable in the hurly-burly of public affairs and offered to the common sense of ordinary people. The philosopher's knowledge is subsumed by the orator's eloquence (3.143).

Quintilian, although he speaks more as a schoolmaster, confirms Cicero by arguing that philosophy has annexed fields of knowledge rashly abandoned by oratory.[2] The teacher of rhetoric must not lazily shirk his duties and hand over core subjects to the grammarian (2.1.2). The control Quintilian wishes the rhetorician to exert is manifest in the compendium of grammar with which the *Institutio oratoria* begins. This is no trivial subject but the foundations of oratory, which will collapse if they are ill laid (1.4.5). The grammarian has his proper field, but the rhetorician must check grammar's tendency to usurp branches of knowledge that belong to oratory. The rhetorician must ensure that the student is not bewildered amid proliferating grammatical technicalities nor forced to linger at what is only a preparatory stage.

Hermeneutics has likewise rooted itself in historical realities and an existential analysis that claims broad applicability without recourse to conceptual universals and the scholastic architecture of systematic reasoning. Hans-Georg Gadamer recovers the guiding concepts of the humanist tradition— "*Bildung* (culture)," "*sensus communis,*" "judgment," and "taste"—in their continuing relevance to the human sciences, even if humanists cannot offer "any epistemological justification" for them.[3] Even more forcefully, in the transition from Edmund Husserl's concept of "life" to Heidegger's analysis of understanding as the existential structure of *Dasein,* Gadamer discerns the overcoming of foundationalist metaphysics by reconceiving the whole idea of grounding itself (*TM* 242–64). Equally, Gadamer rejects the view of language, which is that of structural linguistics, as "something wholly detached from the being of what is under consideration" (*TM* 416): "a word is not a sign coordinated to the thing ex post facto," nor is it "a sign that one selects, nor is it a sign that one makes or gives to another" (*TM* 417). Rather, the word belongs to the thing, so that "Being that can be understood is language" (*TM* 474). Grammar is a false abstraction insofar as it reduces language to an arbitrary structure with a merely internal logic.

Hermeneutics and rhetoric both keep in the center of their attention the close connection between language and practical life in human affairs. But this apparent parallel may conceal an irreducible tension. For despite the expansiveness of Heidegger's concept of understanding, hermeneutics loses itself unless it remains rooted in the interpretation of texts. Rhetoric, on the other hand, has been concerned since antiquity with controlling situations. This concern is the core of the tangled line of thought that runs from Aristotle's conception of the "topic" to Hermogenes' concept of "stasis." In the *Rhetoric,* Aristotle struggles to discriminate materials peculiar to specific subject matters from patterns of thinking common to all.[4] Aristotle does not bring his discussion to sharp clarity, but for my purposes here, it seems close enough that his aim is to examine the materials that go into intelligent speaking about variable human affairs oriented toward judgments or decisions that issue in action. The notion of topic goes beyond a list of subjects that keep coming up in speaking and tries to grasp the intelligible structure of affairs that is the reason experience falls into regular patterns. In order to grasp all possible means of persuasion, it is necessary to find this structure without abstracting so far from affairs that the speaker loses sight of speaking's orientation toward action, not speculation (*theoria*). The point here is to enable the orator to grasp not just the specific facts under discussion but what is at issue in specific circumstances, and to put what is at issue in a light that will convince the auditors to act in a specific way (*pistis*).

In book 3 of the *Institutio oratoria*, Quintilian tackles the same problem. An orator must address a question arising either from what is written (law) or what is not written (3.5.4). Although Quintilian gives some attention to questions of interpreting written law, he is expansive in reviewing the myriad terms and theories for analyzing "the facts" or states of affairs addressed in legal and political oratory. Undoubtedly Quintilian is proving his bona fides as a professor by bristling with erudition. But characteristically he asserts the need for common sense to restrain the luxuriance of technicalities. With witty self-reflectiveness, he keeps in view his topic, namely, the subject of topics, and strives to help his readers see that the point is that speaking must have a point. Whether this is called *stasis* or *status* or *quaestio* or *constitutio* or *caput* is not the point (3.6.2). Rather, it is to focus on the point at issue (*primam causarum conflictionem*, 3.6.4) and to grasp in any specific case the cause, the point for the judge's decision, and the central argument (*causa, iudicatio, continens*, 3.6.104 and 3.11.1). The proliferation of theories and terms only shows how difficult it is to demonstrate in specific but general terms the difference between talking at random and talking that sticks to the point. Quintilian offers a nicely practical test: the basis is "that which I should say, if I were confined to one single line of argument" (3.6.11). He analyzes an example involving inheritance law (3.6.96ff.). But whatever the complexities, the placing of this discussion early in the *Institutio oratoria* testifies to Quintilian's conviction that rhetoric is concerned first of all to analyze and grasp the inner, intelligible structure of complex human situations not to focus on the subdivisions of speeches or the details of style—topics he addresses at length and that tended historically to bear the bell away from this more fundamental issue.

The place in antiquity where we can see most revealingly the tension between a rhetorical analysis oriented toward situations and the demands of a hermeneutic oriented toward interpreting texts is in Augustine. Like Quintilian, he was a professor of rhetoric and so, perhaps, more absorbed in the theory than in the practice of rhetoric. At least Augustine's *Confessions* focuses more on his philosophical and theological inquiries, unlike Cicero's *De oratore*, with its vivid narratives of great triumphs of public speaking. This may somewhat obscure the work's issue in a way that has contributed to the longstanding perplexity over the final three books. For if the issue is Augustine's spiritual quest, which culminates in his conversion in book 8, together with its shapely coda of his mother's last days in book 9 and his confession of sin in book 10, why do we go on to three books of tortuous and abstractly impersonal exposition of Genesis and philosophical analysis of such matters as the nature of time, the multiple meanings of Scripture, and how an earth "without form, and void" (Gen. 1.1) can exist?

There are, however, indications of the connection of these books to what precedes. The *Confessions* opens with desire to praise God, who is the harbor of the restless human heart.[5] Yet to call on God, people must first believe, and "How shall they believe without a preacher?" Augustine calls on God by the faith he has received "by the humanity of thy Son, and by the ministry of thy preacher." This beginning bears fruit in book 11, where Augustine commits all his time to confessing first, all the variegated experiences by which God "hast brought me up to be a preacher of thy word, and a dispenser of thy Sacrament unto thy people" (11.2; p. 211); and second, 'Whatsoever I shall find in thy books" (11.2; p. 213). And in fact the verb *confiteor* runs all through these final three books, so that the entire work is "a sacrifice of confession" (*sacrificium confessionis*) vowed to God (12.14; p. 345). In books 11–13 Augustine is confessing neither his sins nor even his life but rather the meaning God enables him to find in Scripture. That discovery of meaning is the foundation of his ability to respond to God's call to the ministry. The *Confessions* leads up not to Augustine's conversion but to the dawn of his new life as a preacher.

The contrast between this vocation and that of the traditional orator seems quite sharp. It was, after all, rhetoric that short-circuited Augustine's early move toward Christianity. Reading Cicero's *Hortensius* (a work that has not come down to us), Augustine fell into the error Crassus deplored in the *De oratore*. He took to heart its exhortation to philosophy and turned in revulsion from the wordy ambition of the orators. Yet when his sudden love of wisdom led him to read Scripture, rhetoric took its vengeance on its wayward son. The style of Scripture was so poor in comparison to Cicero's eloquence that Augustine was turned back once more to words and away from the matter they ought to contain (3.4–5). His feet returned to the right path only when Ambrose's distinction between the letter and the spirit (echoing 2 Cor. 3.6; 6.3–5, esp. p.

279) opened him to the authority of the Bible rightly understood. And in fact, books 11–13 rely on the resources of Augustine's philosophical training rather than on rhetoric. The intricate analysis of time exhibits the possibility of unfolding meaning from the text (Gen. 1.1) not by conferring with the author—and even in ignorance of the original language—but through insight into the truth the text expresses, understood with the help of God, who is truth (11.3, pp. 215–17).

It is not relevant here to follow in detail the train of Augustine's thought as he turns over issues dialectically, following up philosophical *quaestiones* (e.g., 11.30, p. 281) with debates both with opponents and within his own soul. It is more pertinent to note that this method runs into an impasse in book 12 because even adhering to truth allows different interpreters to come up with many meanings for the same scriptural passage. Augustine refuses to fall back on the author's intention as a controlling criterion, for our insight into truth is more certain than our insight into the author's mind (12.24, p. 345), and in any case, either the author may have meant everything the reader discovers (12.31, p. 367) or, a fortiori, God foresaw all the meanings He would reveal to readers by means of the text throughout the ages, even if the author was cognizant of only one (12.32, p. 369). Augustine thus reviews a multitude of possible interpretations of Genesis 1.1, all true (12.28–29). Although "a narrow scantling of language" thus overflows "into streams of clearest truths," much to the benefit of "many who were to preach upon it" (12.27, pp. 353–55), nevertheless such a pent-up fountain creates a problem. For there results simply too much to say—so many pages on so few words that his own strength and long ages would be insufficient "to go over all thy books in this manner" (12.32, pp. 369–71). Hence, Augustine prays, "Give me leave therefore brieflier now to confess unto thee concerning them." His solution is "to make choice of some one true, certain, and good sense that thou shalt inspire me withal, even if many such senses shall offer themselves unto me (where many safely may)." It will still be best if what Augustine confesses is faithful to Moses' meaning (*ea fide confessionis meae*), for that is what he must strive to do; but at least he can pray to speak the truth God speaks to his inner ear (a repeated phrase, e.g., 12.11, pp. 305, 307; 12.15, pp. 315, 321), just as God spoke truth to Moses.

This transition leads to a different approach to Scripture in book 13, one unavailable to ancient philosophical dialectic. We can call the method allegorical, if we do not allow that term's modern literary meaning to mislead us. For this is not a question of an abstract meaning conveyed through concrete images. Instead, Augustine brings together the two halves of Christian Scripture, the Old Testament and the New. The account in Genesis of creation becomes the framework on which to hang thoughts about the Trinity, baptism (the waters), the Lord's Supper (the creation of birds and fishes), works of charity (be fruitful, increase and multiply), and so on. It is especially significant that in these meditations, a tiny fragment of the Old Testament is unpacked with the help of a string of New Testament citations, chiefly from the epistles. This is not conventional typology, relating events of Israelite history to the life of Jesus, but more doctrinal, ethical, and anthropological. It is by no means Augustine's only way of treating Scripture, but the method here provides a commentary that synthesizes Scripture while turning it toward present-day application. If we have not, then, quite completed a path from philosophical disputation to sermon, we are on the brink of that destination. And rhetoric played no apparent role in getting us there.

Suspicion of rhetoric is manifest in Augustine's *On Christian Doctrine*. Augustine finds himself conceding that if speakers are not just to teach but also move hearers, they need forceful resources for speaking.[6] But he immediately takes it back: whoever speaks wisely benefits hearers, even if eloquence might increase the benefit; but whoever speaks merely eloquently does positive harm (4.5., p. 121). But wisdom is proportional to proficiency in Scriptures (4.5, p. 122). It is better to read, understand, and memorize Scripture than to waste time studying eloquence. Augustine returns to lick an old sore. He knows Scripture does not meet the rhetorical standards of eloquence but he cannot bear to let the charge pass unanswered. He insists he can show eloquence in Scripture, but he dislikes doing so: "But those things in that eloquence which our authors have in common with pagan orators and poets do not greatly delight me" (4.6, p. 124). Gritting his teeth, he proceeds to his demonstration. First Paul and the prophets are quoted and analyzed for the presence of balanced members, periodic rhythm, and even a climactic sequence of clauses (4.7). Scriptures are later dragooned into supplying examples of the plain, moderate, and grand styles (4.20), and the presence of the same levels in Cyprian and Saint Ambrose shows that the faithful can become "proficient in the knowledge of divine and salutary truths" by reading the Scriptures (4.21, p. 153). To be sure, Scripture style lacks rhythmic closings, but although these rhythms are "so highly regarded and taught in the schools of grammarians or rhetoricians . . . it pleases me more to find them very rarely in the writings of our authors" (4.20, pp. 149–50). Augustine's revulsion from the niceties of rhetorical style bears positive fruit, however, when he redefines eloquence. Instead of an almost magical and autonomous power of language, an utterance is eloquent whenever "it should not have been said in any other way" (4.6, p. 123). The compulsion eloquent language answers to is, of course, God's truth, and hence the speakers should pray that God will grant them what to say and the means of delivering it with results profitable to the hearers (4.30, p. 168).

Augustine's insuperable distrust of rhetoric contrasts vividly with his enthusiasm for allegorical interpretation. He cites Canticles 4.2, "Thy teeth are as flocks of sheep, that are shorn, which come up from the washing, all with twins, and there is none barren among them." It seems obvious to Augustine that this verse speaks about the saints, whom he contemplates "more pleasantly when I envisage them as the teeth of the Church cutting off men from their errors and transferring them to her body after their hardness has been softened as if by being bitten and chewed" (2.6, pp. 37–38). We are back to rhetoric versus Saint Ambrose, and though Augustine can see that the antithesis is false and reductive, he cannot help it: "It is a mark of good and distinguished minds to love the truth within words and not the words" (4.12, p. 136).

The restless reversals in his appraisal of rhetoric, however, betray a problem Augustine cannot resolve consciously, namely, a deep indebtedness to rhetoric that he cannot shed. He is most intensely negative when he is thinking about style—an indicator of the fact that for an ancient rhetorician, style was the man, that is, style was rooted in and expressed a whole way of life, a system of values that Augustine could see must be destroyed and supplanted by Christianity. *On Christian Doctrine* begins with the assertion that "there are two things necessary to the treatment of the Scriptures: a way of discovering those things which are to be understood, and a way of teaching what we have learned" (1.1, p. 7). In 396–397, just before he wrote the *Confessions,* Augustine completed the first three books, on interpretation—how to discover what Scripture teaches—and then set the work aside. He was then apparently distracted from the work and returned to it only in 426–27. At that point, he quoted again his opening promise and announced his intention, "with the help of God," of concluding "everything with one book" on teaching, that is, on how to convey in language suited to address a congregation the truth a preacher had discovered in Scripture (4.1, p. 118). On this conscious, surface level, rhetoric is no help in interpretation, and in its implicit cultural commitment it is a dangerous ally in the task of public proclamation.

Yet the whole antithesis of discovering meaning versus putting it into public discourse is itself rhetorical—the ancient duo of *res* and *verba,* subject matter and language, thing and words. And the first book in particular is an extraordinarily subtle meditation on what the *res,* the substance of Scripture, really is. Augustine explains that all doctrine, all teaching "concerns either things or signs" but adds that "things are learned by signs" (1.2, p. 8). Things are defined by not being employed to signify something else. But some things do signify something else, for example, the wood Moses cast into bitter waters to dispel their bitterness, which wood is a sign of the Cross. Words are also things, but their whole being consists in their being used to signify. Augustine is thus evading a reductive opposition here and pointing to a complex relation of things to meanings and signs to things. Instead of pursuing this thought, however, he begins to speak of the right uses of things: some are to be enjoyed, some to be used, some to be both enjoyed and used (1.3, p. 9). What is enjoyed is loved for its own sake; what is used is used to obtain something else—ultimately, to obtain what is enjoyed. Our life is a journey toward home, and we must use the things of this world to help us toward the only thing worthy of being enjoyed for itself, God. In order to stick to the way home, we must be cleansed of whatever distracts us or blinds the inward eye that guides us. Our choice is one of conforming ourselves to this world, to something lower; or to God, our Creator. We are enabled to conform to God through the help of a healer, Christ, who shows us the way and who is the way. We progress along the prescribed road of the affections insofar as we conform ourselves to truth. We do so by following the law of love, which is twofold: to love God and to love our neighbors. Thus each of us will become a whole and unprejudiced evaluator of things (*rerum integer aestimator*, 1.27, p. 23). We shall be able to understand the *res,* the thing or substance, of Scripture: "The sum of all we have said since we began to speak of things thus comes to this: it is to be understood that the plenitude and the end of the Law and of all the sacred Scriptures is the love of a Being which is to be enjoyed and of a being that can share that enjoyment with us" (i.e., love of God and of neighbor; 1.25, p. 30). This becomes a criterion of interpretation: "Whoever, therefore, thinks that he understands the divine Scriptures or any part of them so that it does not build the double love of God and of our neighbor does not understand it at all. Whoever finds a lesson there useful to the building of charity, even though he has not said what the author may be shown to have intended in that place, has not been deceived, nor is he lying in any way" (1.36, p. 30). The conception of truth here involves a dynamic process of a community life gradually altered toward a shared goal. Meaning is no propositional content but is already oriented toward its application within the life of the Church, the preacher's audience.

A related point can be made about the conception of language that Augustine expounds in book 2. Here he turns his attention from *res* to *signa* and distinguishes natural signs, such as smoke for fire, where the relation between the sign and what it shows occurs without any intending consciousness, and conventional signs, where the relation between sign and thing signified depends on a living creature who uses the sign to convey its inward spiritual life to his or her fellows (2.1–2, pp. 34–35). Within this broad framework, Augustine can investigate what knowledge of signs may be needed to understand

Scripture and how that knowledge can be obtained. It follows that conventional signs assume meaning within a human community; to use the sign to signify entails joining the community within which it signifies. Hence, signs belonging to any community that is inconsistent with Christian life must be avoided. Those who investigate arts like astrology to divine the future are presumptuous and ally themselves with devils: "All arts pertaining to this kind of trifling or noxious superstition constituted on the basis of a pestiferous association of men and demons as if through a pact of faithless and deceitful friendship should be completely repudiated and avoided by the Christian" (2.23, p. 59). Again, I shall not pursue Augustine's analysis exhaustively. My point is simply that this conception of language as firmly rooted in community and thus saturated implicitly in the values of the life that discourse sustains is profoundly rhetorical. It is far from those philosophical, epistemologically formulated anxieties over how to guarantee a proper relation of word to thing. This is not to say that one cannot find complex understandings of language in philosophers, only to point to a subtle debt to rhetoric in Augustine's thinking at this point.

What is important about these examples for my argument here is that a rhetorical way of thinking leads toward hermeneutic insights into the meaning and language of texts at a deep structural level. Nor is this unique to this early book of *On Christian Doctrine*. Rhetorical maneuvers permeate, for example, a sermon preached shortly after Christmas, perhaps in 417.[7] Augustine begins: "My dear people, may He fulfill your expectation who has awakened it!" (*S* 21). Apparently, he had promised this sermon in an earlier one, but he stresses that his promise and its present fulfillment come from God, for in making that promise the preacher petitioned God and is now redeeming it in debt to Him, who gives the preacher everything he says. The complex paradoxicality of this thought is typical of elaborate rhetorical forms of politeness, but it bears the weight of Augustine's theory of preaching. He goes on to recall the subject he promised, which the audience will remember: the solution of a certain question. At the time, the large audience may have been interested only in the festivities celebrated on Christmas. But those who returned to listen have come to hear this sermon and to have the problem solved. Hence, Augustine is not speaking "to hearts that are deaf, nor to minds that are bored; and this your eager expectation is actually a prayer for me" (*S* 21). The play in this exordium on prayer, expectation, and God's fulfillment of them turn rhetorical convention to hermeneutic purpose.

A similar aim is at work in certain stylistic devices. Those who have come to hear the sermon have chosen it over public spectacles being staged at the same time. And yet they have also chosen a spectacle. For Christ made himself a

spectacle: "Hear how" (*S* 22). His sufferings showed what the prophet pre-
dicted, and men made him a spectacle in their fury. Likewise, the martyrs
were "made a spectacle to the world," as the apostle Paul says. But this is a spiritual spectacle for those who look with the eyes of faith: "A grand spectacle is
here offered to the eyes of the heart—a soul unscathed while the body is torn
to pieces" (*S* 23). Those who are present in church are interested spectators of
the things that are read. Through the words, they see the substance, without
which the words are meaningless. And so forth. Augustine is elaborating a circumstance in a rhetorical manner that brings out doctrine. Likewise, antitheses and paradoxes structure scriptural doctrine. Jesus has subjugated kings,
"not by a haughty army, but by a derided Cross; not by the fury of the sword,
but by hanging on the Wood; by suffering physically, by toiling spiritually"
(*S* 24). Throughout these opening pages, Augustine builds up an antithetical
play on an intertwined series of terms: physical spectacle/spiritual spectacle, hounding/being hounded, overcoming-beating/being overcome-beaten.
Rhetorical style and hermeneutic content are here inseparable.

The entire sermon is organized like a legal disputation. The problem Augustine has promised to solve is a *quaestio,* the sort of issue debated in a school
of rhetoric. It concerns the apparent discrepancies in the genealogy of Jesus
given by Matthew and Luke. Augustine's answers are ingenious, and they are
offered to relieve the perplexity and scandal of the less ingenious members of
his congregation. They would suffer no pain "if it were not for the agitation of
these pettifoggers. For when heretics make their false charges, the little ones
become very much disturbed" (*S* 36). "Thus," Augustine asserts, "this problem and the malice that proposes it is disposed of; for clear reasoning has demonstrated" a plausible solution (*S* 59). Having cleared away several puzzles,
Augustine can address one more, while calling again, as he does several times
in the sermon, for the audience's attention: "I beg you, do listen to this atten-
tively, as the Lord sees fit to assist us; your minds are now at ease and do not
have to contend with trumped-up charges" (*S* 65). The sermon has much the
form, therefore, of a legal defense against false charges, even though its content is the apparently philosophical one of resolving a *quaestio* through disputation (and in fact the sermon frequently adopts a question-and-answer format). The epilogue makes the hermeneutic intention clear:

> And so, whatever else there is to be said regarding these hidden treasures among
> God's mysteries [that is, deeper meanings in Scripture], this is for others who are
> more diligent and more worthy than we, to bring out. At all events, we have spoken
> on this subject to the best of our ability, as the Lord assisted us and inspired us, and

as the limitations of time permitted us. If there be anyone among you who has a pro-founder grasp of this, let him knock at the door of Him from whom we, too, receive what we are able to grasp, what we are able to say. But this do keep in mind before all else—you must not lose your composure over matters in Sacred Scripture which you do not yet understand; and when you do understand them, you must not feel conceit. What you do not understand, treat with reverence and be patient; and what you do understand, cherish and keep. (S 70)

Although many scholars have pointed out the highly rhetorical style of Augustine's sermons and attributed his effectiveness as a preacher to the audience's responsiveness to these devices, I am arguing here for a deeper interconnection of rhetorical manner with the scriptural, hermeneutic substance of this sermon—an interconnection that, perhaps, Augustine himself might have been somewhat reluctant to acknowledge.

In this chapter, I have been able only to broach the large and complex topic of the relation between rhetoric, a well-recognized subject in classical antiquity, and hermeneutics, one that remained largely implicit until the classical world came into confrontation with Christianity and with Jewish exegetical practices embedded in Christian Scriptures. I would like to close by leaping forward a millennium beyond Augustine and discussing briefly Robert of Basevorn's fourteenth-century work, *The Form of Preaching*.[8] This strange work presents many puzzles. Like many medieval treatises, antiquity appears here so transformed that familiar terms become completely bewildering. Nevertheless, I think at least some light is shed by thinking about the interplay between rhetoric and hermeneutics.

Robert's treatise supports instruction in composing a sermon according to the "method of the Parisians," an innovative style of astonishing intricacy. After some preliminaries, Robert comes to the question of the "invention of the theme" for a sermon (chaps. 15–23, pp. 133–45). For Robert, the theme is a biblical text. It is chosen not in relation to an actual situation but in relation to the ecclesiastical calendar—the feast or saint's day. The precise text in the accepted translation must be followed, although slight changes may be permitted.

A proper theme must then be divided, always into "three statements, or the equivalent of three" (chap. 19, p. 138). As an example, Robert dissects the theme "God sent His Son made of a woman, made under the law, that He might redeem them who were under the law." The whole can be divided into three: "(1) There is noted in the doctor a generously-expended sublimity because it says God sent His Son. (2) There is shown how virtuously-shown humility heals because it says *made of a woman made under the law*. (3) There is shown how fruitfully-extended utility is derived, because it says *that he might redeem them who were under the law*" (chap. 19, pp. 138–39). The division is, however, ramified. Thus, in part 1, the trio *sublimity, expended,* and *generously* parallel *God, He sent,* and *His Son.* It would be ideal to confirm this trio "by one authority in which verbally there are the three: *God, sent,* and *Son* and that in the sentence such great nobility is communicated to us. But because such authorities are difficult to find, themes of so many words are not commonly accepted" (chap. 19, p. 139).

The rhetorical notions of "invention" and "division" are here being transformed in a striking way. In a rhetorical context, invention brings to bear resources for finding issues at stake in actual or imagined sets of facts. These issues provide subject matter for a speech. Division assists this process by clarifying both the structure of the controversy and the relation of that structure to the structure of the speech. Thus, Cicero suggests that following one form of partition, we show "in what we agree with our opponents and what is left in dispute." This helps the auditor see what to fix his or her attention on. The other form surveys briefly and methodically "the matters which we intend to discuss," helping the auditor "hold definite points in mind" and see when "the oration will be over."[9] The orientation here is toward the speech as a means of analyzing a real situation so that it becomes perspicuous for the judgment of the auditor.

Robert's transformation focuses entirely on the manipulation of verbal materials. "Division" encompasses techniques for building links between the subdivisions of the theme and certain other materials the preacher wishes to draw in, especially "authorities" (other biblical citations). Thus, the theme about a learned man, "the intelligent minister is acceptable to the king," can be divided into the ideas of mental perfection (intelligent), spiritual humility (minister), and brotherly kindness (acceptable to the king). Suppose one wishes to confirm the connection between "intelligent" and "mental perfection": "It sometimes happens that an authority which fits the force of a word cannot occur. There must then be added another determinant which the authority will fit. For example, suppose that I cannot find an authority proving that intelligent things include mental perfection. I must then add another determinant by means of some adjectives, or in some other way, so that it may be stated thus: first, rational perfection is shown to be severely punished in those abusing it." And Robert can then cite the Wisdom of Solomon 6.2–6, which confirms the latter point and from which he can infer his way back to the connection he wished to make (chap. 33, pp. 160–61).

Following division comes "the Declaration of Parts" (chap. 34, p. 162).

Robert recognizes various kinds of wholes. Thus, "the intelligent minister is acceptable to the king" can be broken into parts of a virtual whole: first, "the splendor of truth by which one is celebrated in the power of vision" (= intelligence); second, "the course of purity by which one lives with affection" (= minister); which affection "provides us with hope for the sweetness of charity by which one is actually rewarded" (= acceptable to the king). The first two, vision and feeling/affection, are equivalent to "reason and will" and hence parts of a virtual whole, the soul. Or again, faith disposes; for knowledge of truth (= intelligence); hope adds certitude by a life of purity (= minister); and charity makes an end with a reward of eternity (= acceptable to the king). Now a theological virtue "is some universal whole, that is, a genus containing Faith, Hope, and Charity, as parts of an universal whole" (chap. 34, p. 162).

The rhetorical equivalent here is the *narratio,* laying out the facts in an orderly way that is susceptible to the orator's persuasive analysis. Once again, a division of speechmaking oriented toward a state of affairs has been transformed into a process for generating verbal connections to expand the theme. What Robert seems to be interested in is various ways of synthesizing the parts into which the theme has been divided, whether by grammatical or logical maneuvers or according to the physical properties stated by the theme (as when "I leave the world and go to the Father" is "declared" into the point from which, the point to which, and the mobility of form between, that together constitute motion; chap. 34, p. 166). The coherence that results, however tight and impressive, begins from verbal material and remains verbal, without reference to the intelligible structure of a specific state of affairs.

It seems unnecessary to belabor the point. This perspective may shed light on some of what Robert says, although much of it remains—at least to me— rather baffling. In its potential to produce elegantly structured discourses that, almost incidentally, might illuminate the realities of human life, Robert's treatise seems to represent a kind of extreme in the simultaneous use and subordination of rhetoric to the task of generating discourses not out of situations but out of texts. That function may have been carried so far that here even hermeneutics has been subordinated to the demands of structure to be achieved in the interpreting text, the sermon. What other forms of interaction between rhetoric and hermeneutics may be found in the historical record remains an open question—one might mention Judah Messer Leon's *Book of the Honeycomb's Flow* (printed 1475/76), a treatise that both serves as a textbook of rhetoric using Hebrew Scripture for examples and also argues "that the fundamental principles of the 'science of Rhetoric' are included in, and could best be learned from, the Hebrew Bible."[10] Here hermeneutics interprets Scripture to yield rhetoric instead of using rhetoric to interpret Scripture. Although the different orientations of rhetoric and hermeneutics—to practical states of affairs versus texts—guarantees a certain tension, the inevitability through two millennia of Western history that those rigorously trained under the dominant regime of rhetoric would deploy its resources in their efforts to elicit meaning from texts, especially sacred texts, assures a complex relation between the two fields that deserves mapping.

NOTES

1 Cicero, *De oratore,* trans. E. W. Sutton and H. Rackham, 2 vols. (Cambridge: Harvard University Press, 1942). Further references will be to this edition and cited parenthetically in the text.

2 Quintilian, *Institutio oratoria,* trans. H. E. Butler, 4 vols. (Cambridge: Harvard University Press, 1920–22), 1.10.2. Further references will be to this edition and cited parenthetically in the text.

3 Hans-Georg Gadamer, *Truth and Method,* 2d rev. ed., trans. Joel Weinsheimer and Donald G. Marshall (New York: Crossroad, 1989), 3–42; the phrase quoted occurs on p. 9. Further references will be to this edition and cited parenthetically in the text as *TM* and page number.

4 Aristotle, *The 'Art' of Rhetoric,* trans. John Henry Freese (Cambridge: Harvard University Press, 1926), 1.2.22.1358a37ff. Further references will be to this edition and cited parenthetically in the text. The concern here is "topics." See also William M. Grimaldi, "The Aristotelian *Topics,*" and Donovan J. Ochs, "Aristotle's Concept of Formal Topics," in *Aristotle: The Classical Heritage of Rhetoric,* ed. Keith V. Erickson (Metuchen, N.J.: Scarecrow, 1974), 176–93 and 194–204.

5 Augustine, *Confessions,* trans. William Watts, 2 vols. (Cambridge: Harvard University Press, 1912), 1.1. Citations in the text give book and chapter followed by page number. I have also consulted *Confessions,* ed. James J. O'Donnell, 3 vols. (Oxford: Clarendon Press, 1992).

6 Augustine, *On Christian Doctrine,* trans. D. W. Robertson, Jr. (Indianapolis: Bobbs-Merrill, 1958), 4.4, p. 121. Citations in the text give book and chapter followed by page number.

7 Augustine, *Sermons for Christmas and Epiphany,* trans. Thomas Comerford Lawler, Ancient Christian Writers, no. 15 (Westminster, Md.: Newman Press, 1952). For the date, see p. 190n1. Further references will be to this edition and cited parenthetically in text as *S* and page number. The work would probably have taken at least two hours to deliver—not impossible for a speech of this time period but perhaps improbable enough to suggest that this is a treatise in sermon form.

8 Robert of Basevorn, *The Form of Preaching,* trans. Leopold Krul, in *Three Medieval Rhetorical Arts,* ed. James J. Murphy (Berkeley: University of California Press, 1971), 109–215. Citations in text give chapters in Basevorn's text and page numbers

in Murphy. My limited purpose here does not require a review of the extensive scholarly literature on the *ars praedicandi*. A brief comment and introductory bibliography can be found in Thomas M. Conley, *Rhetoric in the European Tradition* (Chicago: University of Chicago Press, 1990), 96–97 and 102–3, or James J. Murphy and Martin Camargo, "The Middle Ages," in *The Present State of Scholarship in Historical and Contemporary Rhetoric,* ed. Winifred Bryan Horner (rev. ed.; Columbia: University of Missouri Press, 1990), 51–52 and 65.

9 Cicero, *De inventione,* trans. H. M. Hubbell (Cambridge: Harvard University Press, 1949), 1.22.31.

10 Issac Rabinowitz, introduction to Judah Messer Leon, *The Book of the Honeycomb's Flow,* ed. and trans. Isaac Rabinowitz (Ithaca: Cornell University Press, 1983), lii.

14

Hermes' Rhetorical Problem: The Dilemma
of the Sacred in Philosophical Hermeneutics

Allen Scult

The convergence of rhetoric and hermeneutics around what I shall call Hermes' rhetorical problem is evident in both the tradition of sacred hermeneutics and philosophical hermeneutics after Heidegger.[1] Because philosophical hermeneutics grows out of sacred hermeneutics, which is itself rooted in reflection on the complexities of interpreting Scripture, let us begin with a scriptural passage in which we find an early and influential manifestation of the problematical convergence of rhetoric and hermeneutics.

> Now Moses, tending the flock of his father-in-law Jethro, the priest of Midian, drove his flock into the wilderness, and came to Horeb, the mountain of God. An Angel of the Lord appeared to him in a blazing fire out of a bush. He gazed and there was a bush all aflame, yet the bush was not consumed. Moses said, "I must turn aside to look at this marvelous sight, why doesn't the bush burn up?" When the Lord saw that he had turned aside to look, God called to him out of the bush: "Moses, Moses!" He answered: "Here I am."[2]

Notice that this unique face-to-face encounter between God and Moses begins with a fair amount of earthbound indirection. Not only does the angel appear first but its appearance is mediated through the burning bush—a rare phenomenon, perhaps, but nonetheless an earthly one. Yet then the bush burns without being consumed by the fire, surely an otherworldly occurrence. Moses, not God, is the first to actually "speak," by responding with astonishment to the sight of the bush. Only when God sees that Moses' attention is focused on the miraculous sight does he actually call to him. Moses answers without hesitation, "Here I am."

Because Moses grew up as an Egyptian, this is his first experience with the god who will later make himself known as Yahweh. Thus the "presencing" of one to the other is problematical. Yahweh's capacity to speak meaningful words to Moses, even to reveal his own name, must somehow be preceded by Moses' willingness to attend to him as a speaking presence. This problem is solved narratively by having Yahweh begin this presencing in the form of a concrete and material entity, a form that also somehow reflects an origin beyond itself. Only after Moses responds to the otherworldly dimension of the experience can God begin to speak. With God's call, "Moses, Moses," and Moses' direct and obedient response to that call, the exchange becomes more or less localized in earthly discourse. The problem of introducing a transcendent being to a being who lives within the limits of language has been temporally resolved.

But when Moses is charged with communicating God's words to the people, the problem resurfaces. What should he do now? Should the people be brought to the bush and the experience repeated (at best a cumbersome way to carry a religious tradition forward)? If not, how does Moses represent the experience in a way that is both believable and meaningful to the people and, at the same time, faithful to the nature and import of the original event? The problem is further compounded by the fact that future audiences will become less and less responsive to miraculous occurrences. The more common response to these occurrences will be to bring them into the realm of the commonplace through scientific explanations. What is a divine messenger to do?

At this stage, the problem is the classic rhetorical one of "adjusting ideas to people and people to ideas."[3] But in its earlier form the problem is also definitively rhetorical and endemic to the experience of understanding. Even before Moses must relay his own hermeneutical experience in terms appropriate to a wider audience, he must himself be able to "understand" the experience of God's presence in order to undergo it. And so his attention must be somehow aroused and made ready to be "appropriately" affected by a strange and uncanny event that will change the course of his life.

These two rhetorical moments are intertwined. Before Moses could convey God's words to the Israelites, he first had to be positioned to undergo the experience of God's speaking. This positioning involved a symbolic act intended to evoke a particular response from Moses. Though not exactly linguistic, nor precisely persuasive, this call to attention had the rhetorical function of inducing a particular sort of responsive readiness in Moses.[4] Having rhetorically prepared the way for Moses to undergo the experience, the narrative must then deal with the problem he faces in readying the people to hear God's word. As with Moses' experience at the bush, God's word can be communicated meaningfully to the people only if they are ready to hear.[5]

One sees a parallel manifestation of the earlier phase of the problem in Heidegger's philosophical hermeneutics, where again a similar sort of prior understanding is a prerequisite to *Dasein*'s hermeneutical task.[6] Before *Dasein* is able to understand anything about Being, it must first be made capable of undergoing the sort of experience in which Being makes its appearance. Human *Dasein* must be "shown" the possibility of this appearance and become engaged by this possibility, as Moses was shown the burning bush and responded to it with rapt attention. Only then can the transcendent be "heard"; only then can hermeneutical experience proceed.

This need to engage the attention of the "auditor" in the presencing of Being as a prerequisite to understanding might be called, following Heidegger, the primordial relation between rhetoric and hermeneutics.[7] As with the experience of the bush, it would seem to be a wordless rhetoric or, at most, a rhetoric on the way to words.[8] But as we shall see, wordless though it may be, the phenomenon I am pointing to is unmistakably rhetorical in Heidegger: it serves to "address" the individual in a powerfully evocative way—powerful enough to induce a capacity for experience he did not know he had. Heidegger himself refers to this primordial rhetorical moment as a "call."[9] The rhetorical character of this call is suggested even more pointedly by Heidegger in the essay on Parmenides: "What happens in *Phasis* and in *Logos*? Could the gathering-calling-saying which reigns in them be that bringing which brings forth a shining?"[10] The word *shining* here suggests the coming to light, the shining forth of a phenomenon. And it is precisely the "lighting" of what is (*das Lichtung des Seins*)[11] that is the *Sache,* or subject matter, of Heidegger's phenomenology. We might say, therefore, that it is the primordial rhetoric that calls one to the brink of understanding that Heidegger is attempting to reproduce in his hermeneutical phenomenology and that is in fact the core phenomenon of his phenomenology.

It is this primordial rhetoric that messengers from Moses to Heidegger have sought to reiterate. But how does one reiterate the wordless call that gives understanding without posing as the godhead who originates the gift? This is Hermes' rhetorical problem writ large, and I shall show that it is precisely this problem, conceived as rhetorical (though of course Heidegger does not use that word), that plagues Heidegger's phenomenological project.

Furthermore, we shall see that it is Heidegger's reluctance to explicitly face Hermes' rhetorical problem as a self-implicating ethical question of his own rhetorical style—that is, his public construction of himself as a philosopher—that eventually restricts the reach of his phenomenology. Heidegger, assuming that his phenomenological method was rigorous enough to offset the self-implicature of his way of speaking, stopped short of examining the relation between rhetoric and hermeneutics in his own discourse. One might say that a similar methodological presumption underlies Plato's argument for Socratic dialectic as the master hermeneutical discourse. The dialectic was supposedly so rigorous that Socrates' rhetorical moves could be seen as an "inert ingredient," interfering not at all with the direct apperceptions of his dialectical method.

Because Plato and Heidegger were also excellent rhetoricians, we might add another reason for their reluctance to reflect on their rhetoric: it would have interfered with the effectiveness of their own discourse. As Aristotle suggests, the best rhetoricians conceal their art from the audience.[12] This concealment becomes especially important for those philosophers who come to take their missionary role as Hermes seriously. Plato was committed to altering the course of philosophy, and his success in this regard is ironically responsible for Heidegger's rhetorical zeal to call philosophy back to true "thinking" as it was practiced by the pre-Socratics. Heidegger makes the rhetorical mission of his hermeneutical phenomenology explicit in a number of places, perhaps none so vivid as his expressed attempt in *What Is Called Thinking?* to find the language appropriate to the call of Being in order to reiterate the call and bring philosophy back to thinking.[13]

Thus we see that Hermes' rhetorical problem doubles back on itself, when one considers the multileveled convergence of rhetoric and hermeneutics as it obtains in both the scriptural and philosophical traditions. We continue our exploration of the convergence as it emerges in Saint Augustine, for the way he treats rhetoric in his scriptural hermeneutics provides an instructive backdrop for our examination of a parallel move in Heidegger's project.

SACRED RHETORIC IN AUGUSTINE'S HERMENEUTICS

For Augustine, truly understanding Scripture involves the realization that its rhetoric is essentially different from our own: that is, the means by which Scripture makes itself understood, its manner of speaking, remains beyond the reach of our own speaking to imitate, and beyond our understanding to comprehend. Indeed the impossibility of fully comprehending and articulating the experience of understanding Scripture is what lends Scripture its hermeneutical identity. Understanding Scripture necessarily entails recognizing the limits of that understanding, and those limits are defined by the inaccessibility of the text's rhetoric.[14]

One might even say that sacred texts viewed in this way are defined by the very ineffability of their most essential meanings. We can experience those meanings only through the divinely inspired discourse whose rhetorical genius it is to know precisely what to withhold and how to withhold it. An ability to comprehend how the discourse is able to do this, let alone an ability to articulate this comprehension, would "make us like gods,"[15] knowing only what the divine consciousness that informs the discourse can know. This ineffable depth of meaning creates the space in which sacred texts do their peculiar rhetorical work, which by its nature is untheorizable and unknowable in any other discourse.

The Old Testament makes this point in a rigorously explicit way further on in the burning bush episode. Moses expresses what might be called rhetorical anxiety at the thought of communicating God's message to the people. "What shall I say when they ask for your name?"[16] At this point in the transaction, God withholds his name, thereby withholding intimate knowledge of his nature. Instead of a name, God rhetorically inscribes his identity in the mystery of *Ehyeh asher Ehyeh,* usually rendered "I am that I am," but essentially untranslatable. Thus knowledge of God's nature, the sacred core of all that human beings might understand, is left hidden in a nugget of sublimely indeterminate rhetoric. Not only are "his ways not our ways," but his discourse likewise is irretrievably removed from our discourse. The secrets hidden in God's speech will serve as a propaedeutic to the endless hermeneutical meditations that constitute Israel's vocation. Human understanding will be defined by the rhetorical mystery that stands guard at its limits.

Augustine thus stands in a long line of those who carry on Hermes' mission as divine messenger and whose task is to transmit the message of the gods in a way that preserves the sanctity, the heavenly otherness, of their discourse. The sacred might even be said to be defined hermeneutically by the impossibility of human discourse to fully comprehend it or, more specifically, by the incapacity of human discourse to explain the rhetorical function of the sacred, its way of making itself known. The sacred is thus left with a depth of ineffability that humanly constructed discourse cannot and should not try to penetrate.

And so there is good reason why, throughout its history, hermeneutical reflection has been preoccupied with sacred texts. And when it attempts to find a more secular metonym for the sacred, as Hans-Georg Gadamer does with his notion of the classic,[17] hermeneutical thought begins to confound postmodern sensibilities: Why does Gadamerian hermeneutics privilege classical texts? There is a link to the tradition of sacred hermeneutics here that is essential to Gadamer's argument but that is not explicitly discussed.

I would suggest that any matter or *Sache* worthy of hermeneutical reflection engages our attention, evokes our deepest capacity to listen, by a means that is reminiscent of the ineffable rhetorical work of the sacred. One might say that this leads to the experience of the hermeneutical object as sacred, even though in secular hermeneutics we avoid the term. But the way such a text carries out the rhetorical function of making known its meaning remains a mystery that continually engages our hermeneutical desire. The originary hermeneutical experiences generated by such texts show themselves worthy of reflection precisely because the manner of their showing remains hidden. They are able to make themselves known to us without our understanding how, and so our desire to understand is further prompted.

But as philosophical hermeneutics after Heidegger attempts to detach the *Sache* of its reflection from sacred texts, it also cuts itself off from the ineffable rhetorical mystery in which hermeneutical reflection was rooted. Without this sense of the ineffable, the insistence on reading certain texts as paradigmatic of the hermeneutical experience (as in Heidegger's reading of the pre-Socratics and the modern German poets, for example) seems like a clear case of privileging. As we shall see, Heidegger may be indirectly responsible for this cutoff and the resulting confusion, owing to changes (early and late) in his own management of Hermes' rhetorical problem and its relation to the sacred.

But first, to recapitulate: it is the ineffable depth of certain discourses, the inaccessibility of their rhetoric, that makes understanding them both worthwhile and problematic. Hermeneutical activity is elicited by the mysterious rhetoric that both reveals and conceals what we wish to understand. At the same time the rhetoric makes the meaning seem powerfully true for us—so much so that we may experience ourselves as somehow "belonging" to it. Yet its manner of speaking this "truth" also keeps us at a respectful but frustrating distance. The hermeneutical desire of the interpreter is deepened by the challenge of bringing the discourse into closer range by removing some of the rhetorical shadows that cloud the original. But in the very act of bringing it close, that is, in shedding her own rhetorical light on the shadows of the original, the interpreter may reduce the originary hermeneutical experience to something less than it is. She might "tame it," to borrow a phrase from Antoine St. Exupéry, and so dilute its endogenous, primordial rhetorical force. Perhaps the most evident slippage occurring in this dilution is the sacred sense of mystery surrounding the primordial rhetorical force of the original.

On the other hand, by trying to preserve that rhetorical force in the hermeneutical experience he gives to his own readers, the interpreter is himself in danger of posing as the originary giver of truth and so shifting the burden of Hermes' rhetorical problem to his readers, who are left to decide whether to read his text as sacred. As we shall see, this second-generation version of Hermes' rhetorical problem is precisely what confronts some of the less-than-faithful as they read Heidegger, especially his later writings.

HEIDEGGER'S FIRST ENCOUNTERS WITH THE PROBLEM

In his early work Heidegger faces Hermes' dilemma head on. Beginning with his *Habilitationsschrift* and continuing through the seminars of the early twenties, Heidegger was engaged in negotiating the difficult transition between his early intellectual work as a "Christian theologian" and his life-long effort to construct a hermeneutical phenomenology. The transition was not easy. His *Habilitationsschrift* is replete with celebrations of what we might call the rhetorical vitality of medieval mysticism. How could philosophy leave such powerfully evocative experiences behind—experiences that seem to ground so much that is worthwhile and authentic in human thought? But this seemed to be the cost of doing philosophy after the manner of Edmund Husserl. Even though Husserl had begun to revitalize philosophy through his phenomenology, he still kept the sacred at arms' length and felt strongly that in order to engage in serious philosophy, Heidegger needed to do the same.[18]

As Heidegger began to move into his philosophical maturity, however, he found philosophy disconnected from the experience of the sacred to be theoretical and lifeless. *Ent-leben,* he called it.[19] In the twenties, with his theological experience still fresh and thinkable, Heidegger set about the task of bridging the gap between the untheorized vitality of medieval mysticism and the overly theorized *Ent-leben* of modern philosophy. In Heidegger's own words, "Philosophy as a rationalistic system detached from life is powerless, mysticism as an irrationalistic experience is aimless."[20]

As Heidegger was thinking his way from theology to philosophy, he began to see important resemblances between the kinds of experiences the mystics had identified with the sacred, and the originary, life-constructing, intuitive experiences Husserl's phenomenology had tried to uncover. Heidegger was sure that this resemblance had a form that could be hinted at and indicated but not fully articulated. There was something, an *Ur Etwas,* that gave such experiences their powerful immediacy, their sense of "the in-itself of the streaming experience of life."[21] Like the revelation at Sinai, life-as-it-is befalls us, is given to us, as a "properizing event" [*Ereignis*].22 It "appropriates" us as we allow ourselves to be appropriated by it.

The quality of lived experience comes to us as a result of the "givenness" of what is. In this quality of experienced givenness, Heidegger sees the missing link between the mysterious power of sacred revelation and the ontological force of "hermeneutical intuition."23 Hermeneutical intuition comes to us in a way that is reminiscent of the revelation at Sinai. Both experiences seem to descend with an overwhelming sense of a truth not of our own making. Perhaps it is Heidegger's recognition of the resemblance between the untouched otherness of hermeneutical intuition and the *Ganz Andere* of the sacred that eventually leads him, in *Being and Time* and afterward, to speak of the relation between Being and Truth with an ambiguous hint of their shared a priori otherworldliness.24

Yet Heidegger is completely unambiguous in his insistence that the primordial *es gibt* of hermeneutical intuition that gives us lived experience is very much of this world. Indeed, the phenomenon of givenness accounts for the seemingly impersonal, yet irresistibly forceful "worlding" of the world. In his early work, Heidegger identifies the force that induces our lived experience as the *modus essendi:* "The *modus essendi* is the experienceable as such, is in the absolute sense whatever stands over against consciousness, the 'robust' reality which irresistibly forces itself upon consciousness and can never nor again be put aside and eliminated."25

We are now ready for at least a preliminary formulation of Hermes' rhetorical problem as it is manifested in Heidegger's negotiation of the transition from theology to phenomenology. Heidegger seems to share with Augustine an awestruck sense of the otherness of originary hermeneutical experience. He also believes it to be a profound mistake to try to comprehend that experience in the earthly rhetoric of traditional philosophy. But he begins to diverge from Augustine in his understanding of the transcendence that characterizes that otherness. Though experienced as other, transcendence is of this world: "The Dasein is the transcendent being. Objects and things are never transcendent. The original nature of transcendence makes itself manifest in the basic constitution of being-in-the-world."26

This paradoxical notion of transcendence as characteristic of *Dasein's* being-in-the-world opens up the space of *Mitsein,* the "being-with" but nonetheless "non-relational" frame of *Dasein's* hermeneutical intuition.27 This moment of *aporia,* wherein *Dasein* experiences a contradictory non-relational being-with, Heidegger identifies with the primordial discourse that gives understanding: "Discourse (*Rede*) is existentially equiprimordial with state-of-mind and understanding. The intelligibility of something has always been articulated, *even before* there is any appropriative interpretation of it."[28] The "world" we interpret is given to us as already meaningful (but not meaningful enough!). This giving takes place through a primordial discourse that is amenable to linguistic interpretation but that is itself not yet language as we know and speak it. (The similarity to *Ehyeh asher Ehyeh* is striking.) The dialogical, languagelike quality of the primordial *Rede* Heidegger indicates metaphorically as a "being-with." The metaphor is given even more distinct rhetorical contours in another passage, in which "being-with" acquires the character of "friend" (not an unfamiliar metaphor in rhetorical epistemology):[29] "Indeed, hearing constitutes the primary and authentic way in which Dasein is open for its ownmost potentiality-for-Being as in hearing the voice of the friend whom every Dasein carries with it. Dasein hears because it understands. As a Being-in-the-world with others, a Being which understands, Dasein is 'in thrall' to Dasein-with and to itself."[30]

The rhetorical challenge, so to speak, of Heidegger's early phenomenology is how to describe the in-the-world but nonetheless transcendent phenomenon of the originary hermeneutical experience of *Hören*. Augustine and the tradition of sacred hermeneutics had, for the most part, been content with a kind of epideictic celebration of the experience: the message itself might be interpreted; but the manner in which the message made itself understood necessarily remained a mystery, to be appreciated only from afar.

But in order to forge the link between the sacred and the factical, Heidegger had to reinvent, to reinscribe in language amenable to philosophy the mysteriously ineffable rhetoric that transmits the transcendent as lived experience. The true task of phenomenology was to confront anew, in secular terms, Hermes' rhetorical problem: to render the impossible to articulate but nonetheless "there-being" of factical experience. How is our being-in-the-world situated with the definitive force of a *Da? Was ist in es gibt?* We see immediately in these easily satirized Heideggerianisms the immense difficulty of communicating the givenness of facticity without implying a divine giver. And, indeed, some critics are forever reading Heidegger's ontology as ontotheology. How can one have what appears to be an epideictic celebration of the mysteries of existence and call it philosophy?

Heidegger's attempt to build a philosophical bridge to the sacred is founded on his insistence that the experience of the sacred is but an example of the sort of originary hermeneutical experience that lends facticity to the life of human being. Heidegger's association of facticity with the sacred corresponds to Friedrich Schleiermacher's insight that the interpretation of sacred texts is an instance, albeit a paradigmatic one, of the universal human experience of understanding.[31] But as we have already seen, this broadening of the scope of hermeneutics brings with it a distinction that smacks of privilege: some texts "mean" more powerfully than others. As Gadamer puts it: "We all know that there are words that function merely as signals, and then there are other words . . . that bear witness themselves to that which they communicate. These words are, so to speak, proximate to something that is; they are neither replaceable nor exchangeable, a 'Da,' that discloses itself in its own act of speaking."[32]

Corresponding to the texts that bring us such words, some experiences are given to us as "more real" than others. These are the factical experiences that situate us most firmly as the individual human beings we are. In a letter to Elizabeth Blochmann (an early correspondent who was also interested in Schleiermacher), Heidegger refers to such privileged experiences as "gifted moments":

> We must be able to wait for high-pitched intensities of meaningful life, and we must remain in continuity with such gifted moments, not so much to enjoy them as to work them into life, to take them with us in the onrush of life and to include them in the rhythms of all oncoming life. And in moments when we immediately feel ourselves and are attuned to the direction in which we vitally belong, we cannot merely establish and simply record what is clearly had as if it stood over against us like an object. The understanding self-possession is genuine only . . . in a vehement life becoming aware of its own directedness, which is not theoretical, but a total experience.[33]

I am characterizing as rhetorical the isomorphism that Heidegger found between the force of the factical and the power of the sacred to induce the truth-giving immediacy of lived experience. By literally hearing and responding to the words contained in Scripture, the religious mystic merges his own experience with that of his forebears and thus reenacts the essential unity between himself and the divine. As Heidegger reads Meister Eckhardt, insofar as we have being it is anchored precisely in the "transcendent primal relationship of the soul to God."[34] Thus it is with *Dasein*. The experience of facticity that gives *Dasein* the opportunity for authenticity ignites the spark of essential unity between *Dasein*'s hermeneutical quest and Being. By responding to the originary *Ruf* or "call," *Dasein* is situated to become itself authentically.[35]

The *Ruf* that situates *Dasein* to become itself is highly motivated. Heidegger, in his early formulations of the concept of *Dasein*, comes to focus again and again on the interrelated notions of situation and motivation—notions that irresistibly catch a rhetorician's attention. Though it may be that "Language is the House of Being," that "isness" comes to us through a primordial rhetorical making known of our situated being-in-the-world. Early on Heidegger identifies *Dasein* with the experienced situatedness of the I, *das Situation-Ich*.[36] Human beings are situated, motivated to become an "I," through their experience of a primordial, situating evocation of their being. But how to describe that evocation as the subtle rhetoric it is—articulated just meaningfully enough to leave us stranded on a narrow ridge between a full realization of our potentiality-for-being on the one side and the abyss of nothingness and despair on the other?

The rhetorical task of Heidegger's hermeneutical phenomenology is somehow to show this primordial showing without bringing it to inauthentic articulation—in other words, to show life as it is given to *Dasein* to understand, as "Life in and for itself." This means a rhetorical enactment that denies itself the sort of adaptation characteristic of rhetoric. The originary *Ruf* must be faithfully rendered in its own *Rede*, a discourse that is not ours to fully have. But at the same time it cannot be left in the rarefied transcendent language of the sacred: *Ehyeh asher Ehyeh* is not philosophy! Here Heidegger begins to step delicately where Augustine feared to tread.

THE *FORMALE ANZEIGE* AS THE RHETORICAL ENACTMENT OF HEIDEGGER'S PHENOMENOLOGY

Heidegger's early attempts to render the ur-discourse of lived experience are conceptualized in his notion of the *Formale Anzeige* (usually translated "formal indication").[37] Here is one of the earliest yet fullest articulations of the concept: "It is out of this preworldly vital something that the formal objective something of knowability is first motivated, a something of formal theorization. The tendency into a world (that of *es weltet*) can be theoretically deflected before its demarcation and articulation as a world. Thus the universality of the formally objective appropriates its origin from the in-itself of the streaming experience of life."[38] The "in-itself of the streaming experience of life" is the not-yet-differentiated primordial something through which the self-interpreting *Dasein* becomes an individual human being. Heidegger intends to point here to "the basic trait [*Zug*] of life to live out toward something, to 'world out' [*auszuwelten*] into particular lifeworlds."[39] The methodological task of the *Formale Anzeige* is to ensure a "formally objective" rendering of this phenomenon.

The possibility of a phenomenological rendering of the primordial rhetoric that "motivates" lived experience thus depends on the rigor and precision of the *Formale Anzeige*. Although this suggestive idea defines the method appropriate to Heidegger's hermeneutical phenomenology, the method itself remains incompletely articulated. To overly thematize the *Formale Anzeige* would simply return phenomenology to the theoretically distant *Ent-leben* of philosophy, and so Heidegger says little *about* the *Formale Anzeige*, perhaps leaving us to suppose that the rest of his work simply demonstrates it. I shall return to this point momentarily, but the need for restraint in discussing the *Formale Anzeige* does make my task quite delicate at this point: How to develop the concept, how to say something meaningful—presumably new things— about it, without saying too much?

First, the *Formale Anzeige* constitutes what I have called the rhetorical task of hermeneutical phenomenology: that task is to render discursively the originary *Ruf* of hermeneutical experience without being drawn into either thematizing it into the traditional theoretical rhetoric of philosophy on the one hand, or simply leaving it as undigested mystical gibberish on the other. As the passage from Heidegger suggests, perhaps the first and most important guideline in using the *Formale Anzeige* is not to overparticularize it. The form of the originary motivating discourse must be captured, "read off," the original before it reaches particular instantiation in an individual history. The appropriate rendering of the *Formale Anzeige* is thus distinguished by what might be called its rhetorical restraint. It stops itself before it falls into the particular. Once past the fail-safe point, rhetoric becomes "mere rhetoric," an attempt to essentialize the particular as if it represented Being itself. This rhetorical overkill is characteristic of our "fallenness." Indeed, it might be said that Heidegger's tacit disapproval of rhetoric (identified later as "language under the dictatorship of the public realm")[40] is due precisely to its association with the essentializing temptations of fallenness. The almost irresistible impulse to give particular content to the universalizing, if not universal form, of the hermeneutical situation, to tie Being down to a particular way of being, is the downfall of rhetoric as philosophers since Plato have deprecated it. But the *Formale Anzeige* represents the possibility of a philosophical rhetoric that captures the motivating directional force, the decidedly rhetorical *Zug*, which situates Dasein to pursue its course toward the particular before that particularity is articulated in the life of an individual.

The exercise of this rhetorical restraint is crucial to the success of Heidegger's phenomenology. There is a kind of a derivative, third-person quality to existence as it is lived in particular lives. This is the inauthentic everydayness of *das Man* as distinguished from life as it is given to the Dasein within *das Man*. Heidegger sees the task of phenomenology as returning philosophy to authenticity by refocusing its attention on the Dasein within *das Man*, Dasein "before the Fall." In Heidegger's words, "Philosophy is a fundamental manner of living itself, such that philosophy, in each case, authentically retrieves life, taking it back from its downfall, a taking back which, as a radical searching, is life it-self."[41]

But the more one sheds the trappings of the particular, the less one is able to communicate one's insight to a wider community. As Heidegger pursues the *Formale Anzeige* by way of authentically rendering the primal motivating ur-stream of life, his rhetoric becomes more inaccessible and the farther up the mountain he himself retreats. A kind of sublime isolation characterizes Hei-degger's later work. His readers are not so much addressed as called upon to observe the master in meditative solitude. Heidegger no longer speaks of the *Formale Anzeige*. He hardly speaks of method at all, as his writings become more overtly autobiographical. Perhaps he means for his own prose to reenact the formal power of his original insight rather than to further interpret it. And so, for some, Heidegger's voice assumes an authority beyond Augustine's and perhaps even his own proscriptions: he becomes more the giver of revelation than its interpreter. Instead of continuing to grapple with Hermes' rhetorical problem, Heidegger assumes the voice of the godhead. He seems to have gone beyond the *Formale Anzeige* and reframed the rhetorical task of phe-nomenology as fully reiterating the primordial call underlying hermeneutical experience. In the later writings, the phenomenological search for the this-worldly call of conscience is replaced by a more cosmically far-reaching search for the "call of Being."[42] And the "task of thinking at the end of philosophy" be-comes to "think *Aletheia,* unconcealment, as the opening which first grants being and thinking and their presencing to and for each other."[43] Heidegger is claiming that phenomenology must capture the rhetorical force of the primor-dial ur-discourse as the transcendently mysterious rhetoric it is: "To let that which shows itself be seen from itself in the very way in which it shows itself from itself."[44]

Understanding always comes rhetorically packaged. To quote again Hei-degger's wonderful formulation of this idea: "Hermeneutics means not just the interpretation but, even before it, the bearing of message and tidings."[45] In other words, the experience of understanding comes to us already expressed, already interpreted, already meaningful. This already expressed quality we have designated the primordial relation of rhetoric to hermeneutics. It is the mysterious originary showing of Being, a showing that carries with it a vaguely recognizable but unspeakable intentionality.[46] But what gives existence its "in-tentional directionality," and how is it given? This line of questioning seems to pursue the phenomenon of hermeneutical experience beyond the mystery of rhetorical inaccessibility that always kept the interpreter in the sacred tradi-tion at an appropriate distance from the biblical text. God's word always re-quired interpretation, but the task of interpretation was merely to recover the meaning that was already there, expressed in the saying. How the saying came to mean as it did lay beyond the capacity of interpretation.

The early Heidegger, like Augustine, warns against attempting fully to theorize and thus presume fully to reiterate the voice of originary meaningfulness. But the Heidegger of *Being and Time* and thereafter suggests that it is the task of phenomenology to bring that voice out into the open: to show it to us as it was shown to him, thus exposing the hidden dimension of its original showing. Heidegger seems to be suggesting that his own ear is so well attuned to the voice of Being, and his phenomenological method so well-honed, that he can visually (verbally) render the rhetorical manner of its showing beyond what is accessibly apparent in the original. Hubert Dreyfus brings this claim to a fine point: "The subject of phenomenology must be something that does not show itself but can be made to show itself."[47] Heidegger can force the nameless out of hiding![48] He is not the first to commit this transgression. Probably not the last. Richard Rorty characterizes Heidegger's widest turn this way: "Heideggerise is only Heidegger's gift to us, not Being's gift to Heidegger."[49]

Gadamer is not so quick to judge. He suggests that as Heidegger's phenomenology unfolds, Heidegger himself continues to struggle with Hermes' rhetorical problem. Although Heidegger no longer speaks of the *Formale Anzeige,* his work continues to give us what might be called formal indications of a method, a way of comporting ourselves in relation to the originary discourse that gives understanding. This way of comporting is not so much thought as modeled by the later Heidegger. In Heidegger's own language, he shows us the way. The way in this case requires a rhetoric whose force might be similar to the original but whose task is different. Gadamer characterizes Heideggerise thus: "Perhaps it was not to be avoided that this thinker's language often resembles a tormented stammering, for it is a language struggling to awaken from the forgetfulness of being, and to think only that which is worthy of thought."[50]

For philosophers the forgetfulness of being is manifested in their forgetfulness of the deficiencies of philosophical language. By presuming that its language is adequate to the task, philosophy loses sight of the rhetorical problematic that surrounds the originary givenness of human understanding.

So the formal indication of Heidegger's later rhetoric is interpreted by Gadamer to be self-reflexive.[51] Heidegger means to tease himself out of his own philosophical forgetfulness, as we stand by to observe and perhaps pick up on the awakening. Thus, for Gadamer, the rhetorical task of Heidegger's later phenomenology remains faithful to the mission first conceived in his *Habilitationsschrift:* to bring philosophy back from its long sleep of *Ent-*

leben by restoring the rhetorical problematic that inheres in our linguistic situatedness.

It seems that we are left with the question of whether to read Heidegger with
Gadamer or with Rorty. Is Heidegger giving us the language of Being or the
being of Heidegger in language?

There are some momentous choices to be made here on the side of both author and auditor. Heidegger had to decide how strongly to assert his claims.
We must decide how strongly to let ourselves hear them. These choices interact with each other to create the experience of reading Heidegger. This interaction is not dissimilar from the choice that the author himself might have
made about how strongly to hear the original. Surely, strongly enough to be
"appropriated" by it. But how strongly should Heidegger assert the otherness
of this hearing experience to his auditors? This rhetorical-hermeneutical circle is complex and delicate. Rorty, I think, oversimplifies it.

Rorty chooses to hear Heidegger as "just" another philosopher. But Heidegger himself asked to be heard differently. Early on, he expressed this desire to his student Karl Löwith with ambiguous humility: "[It would be] a fundamental mistake to measure me (hypothetically or not) against figures such
as Nietzsche, Kierkegaard, or any of the other creative philosophers. Such is
not to be prohibited, but then it must be said that I am not a philosopher, and
am only deluding myself to believe that I could be something comparable. I
am a Christian theologian."[52]

Later, Heidegger would reenact this denial with a stronger assertion of
what he *is* doing, namely, thinking, and he would identify himself, not at all
humbly, with the true thinkers who began it all: "Heraclitus and Parmenides were not yet 'philosophers.' Why not? Because they were the greatest
thinkers."[53]

Through the sheer rhetorical force of his vision, Heidegger means to return
us to the this-world transcendency of thinking before it became sedimented as
philosophy. In his later essays, Heidegger explicitly charges his readers to
themselves "come to the experience of language," presumably by following his
lead.[54] Heidegger's rhetoric holds out for his readers the possibility of the rebirth that he, himself, underwent forty years earlier. In responding to Heidegger's offering, one may follow Heidegger on the path of thinking and thus
begin anew: "With the end of philosophy thinking is not also at its end, but in
transition to another beginning."[55]

How might we characterize the rhetorical stance of the later Heidegger? It
surely goes beyond the restraint demanded by the *Formale Anzeige*. The primarily rhetorical urge to *bear the message* of the original has overtaken the pri-

marily hermeneutical urge to render its phenomenological contours. Philosophy has given way to the rhetorical temptations of prophecy. Here Heidegger goes against the advice of Augustine and tries to reenact the eloquence of the original, rather than simply to interpret it. Heidegger's rhetorical presumption shifts the burden of choice to us to read his phenomenology with Gadamer or with Rorty—as ontology or ontotheology; as a rhetorically framed, but nonetheless originary and authentic rendering of the universal form of hermeneutical experience, or merely as one philosopher's rhetorical version of his own particular hermeneutical experience posing as something more. I think the question of how to read Heidegger comes down to a deeper question regarding the proper relation between hermeneutics and rhetoric in philosophy. Ought the philosopher to practice the humility prescribed by Augustine and the early Heidegger and make no claims for the ontological reach of her own discourse? Taking this route, we would lose sight of Heidegger on the way up the mountain and would have difficulty finding our way with Gadamer to Heidegger's other beginning. Rather than a philosophy in an aggrandized form reminiscent of its glorious beginnings, we would be left with a philosophy cut down to size, as in Wittgenstein: "merely" a description of the language games we play and ultimately itself just another language game. On this view, no matter what the philosopher thinks she has captured inside, the rhetorical packaging of hermeneutics must itself be laid bare as the rhetoric it is. For whatever reason, Heidegger's own philosophical rhetoric never seemed to reach this level of self-reflexivity.

After warning us that "in the realm of thinking there can be no assertions,"[56] Heidegger seems to leave it to his interpreters to circumvent the contradictions of his own discourse. Perhaps no other interpreter does this as gracefully as John Caputo: "Because *Being and Time* is itself made up of assertions which are meant to have disclosive power and to be drawn from primordial sources, it is also exposed to the danger that its own assertions may simply get passed along and emptied of their originary force. The task of the reader here is not to hold himself exempt from uncovering what these assertions disclose."[57]

It was Augustine who suggested that the disclosive power of scriptural rhetoric must be protected by the deference of interpreters in reading it—that its eloquence cannot and should not be bound by the same rules as our own. As Augustine said of the writers of Scripture: "Thus there is a kind of eloquence fitting for men most worthy of the highest authority. Nor does any other kind become them. Nor is that kind suitable for others. It is suited to them and the more it seems to fall below others, the more it exceeds them. Where I do not understand them, their eloquence appears to me to be less . . . [but it is a kind] of eloquence through which our understandings should be benefited not only by the discovery of what lies hidden but also by exercise."[58]

Does Heidegger *merit* such hermeneutical respect? Perhaps at this point, as our inquiry draws to a close, we might reframe the question thus: Does Heidegger's rhetoric *induce* the requisite respect? Insofar as rhetoric finds its end in judgment, the rhetorical and the ethical must inevitably intersect. And as Hermes' rhetorical problem is passed from Heidegger to his readers, judging the merit of Heidegger's "saying" becomes enormously complicated. Not only does the rhetorical comportment of Heidegger's phenomenological discourse change before and after *Being and Time* in ways this chapter has tried to trace, but it seems obvious that, especially for some months in 1933, Heidegger himself overparticularized his rendering of "the call," and, of course, his tragic inscription must stand. But then there were those other moments, especially in the twenties, when the call seemed to shine forth brightly and clearly in a lighting more appropriate to it. Perhaps the virtue of studying philosophical hermeneutics from the perspective of Hermes' rhetorical problem is that it enables us to trace the changing relation between rhetoric and hermeneutics as it unfolds through time and, perhaps most interestingly, through the words that marked the way in the philosophical life of a most gifted Hermes.

NOTES

1 Hermes, the messenger god, is conventionally conceived of as standing behind the etymological root of *hermeneutics*. See, for example, Martin Heidegger's version of the derivation in "A Dialogue on Language," in his *On The Way to Language*, trans. Peter Hertz (San Francisco: Harper and Row, 1982), 29. My description of Hermes' task as problematically "rhetorical" will become clear as the chapter proceeds.

2 Exodus 3:1–3. This translation, as well as all other translations from the Bible, is from the Jewish Publication Society's *Torah* (Philadelphia: Jewish Publication Society, 1962).

3 This definition of rhetoric is likewise "classical," as noted in a landmark essay by Donald Bryant, "Rhetoric: Its Functions and Its Scope," *Quarterly Journal of Speech* 39 (1953): 401–24.

4 This account, somewhat broader than Bryant's, of the basic rhetorical function, is from Kenneth Burke: "A symbolic means of inducing cooperation in beings that by nature respond to symbols" (*A Rhetoric of Motives* [Berkeley: University of California Press, 1969], 43). The use of more than one definition for *rhetoric* is consistent with the ongoing attempt in contemporary rhetorical theory to capture the richness of the idea of rhetoric in Greek philosophy, especially in Aristotle.

5 Thus, what I want to call Hermes' rhetorical problem reproduces itself in ever-more challenging configurations, inasmuch as the hermeneutical/rhetorical task of

"bearing a message" (see Heidegger's definition of hermeneutics as "the bearing of message and tidings" in "A Dialogue on Language," 29) finds itself further and further removed from the original experience of revelation. It seems that the greater the distance from the original event of revelation, the more difficult becomes the task of mimetically reproducing the rhetorical force of God's word.

6 See Martin Heidegger, *Being and Time,* trans. John Macquarrie and Edward Robinson (New York: Harper and Row, 1962), 36ff.

7 Heidegger's fullest discussion of the "primordiality" of the phenomenon I am identifying as rhetorical is in *Being and Time,* 261ff.

8 I realize that I am taking some license here in calling the event of the bush primordial, but as the chapter proceeds I think it will become clear that, in the biblical scheme, the bush is a narrative metonym for what I am discussing: the primordial rhetoric that calls human beings to their most profound moments of understanding.

9 I am referring to the "call of conscience." In his first reference to the call in *Being and Time,* Heidegger glosses the term with even stronger indications of its rhetorical character. He calls it a voice (313), a mode of discourse, an appeal, and a summoning (314).

10 Martin Heidegger, "*Moira,*" originally part (though undelivered) of the lecture course entitled *Was Heisst Denken?* included in his *Early Greek Thinking,* trans. David Farrell Krell and Frank A. Capuzzi (New York: Harper and Row, 1975), 93.

11 Heidegger's later suggestion of what he would have called *Sein und Zeit.* See John Caputo, *The Mystical Element in Heidegger's Thought* (New York: Fordham University Press, 1986), xiii.

12 Aristotle's *Rhetoric,* book III, 1414b: "As a result, authors should compose without being noticed" (*Aristotle: On Rhetoric: A Theory of Civic Discourse,* trans. George Kennedy [New York: Oxford University Press, 1991]).

13 A recollection of Gadamer's is even more indicative of Heidegger's rhetorical view of the call: "When he [Heidegger] wrote to Löwith 'I am a Christian Theologian,' he must have meant that he wanted to defend the true task of theology, that is 'To find the word that is capable of calling one to faith and preserving one in faith,' against the appropriated Christian spirit of today's theology. (I heard him use these words in a theological discussion in 1923.)." Gadamer goes on to say: "But this [finding the words that call one to faith] was also a task for thinking." Hans Georg-Gadamer, *Heidegger's Ways,* trans. John W. Stanley (Albany: State University of New York Press, 1994), 175.

14 Augustine discusses the sui-generis character of scriptural rhetoric in section VI of book IV of *De doctrina christiana,* trans. D. W. Robertson, Jr. (Indianapolis: Bobbs-Merrill, 1958), 123. Here, he describes the peculiar eloquence of Scripture as marked by its "obscurity."

15 Genesis 3:4, 22.

16 Exodus 3:13.

17 See, especially, Hans-Georg Gadamer, *Truth and Method,* 2d ed., trans. Joel Weinsheimer and Donald G. Marshall (New York: Continuum, 1993), 285ff.

18 In a letter to Paul Natorp recommending the Catholic Heidegger for a faculty position at Marburg, Husserl assures Natorp that Heidegger has "freed himself from dogmatic Catholicism" and is now "my most valuable philosophical co-worker" (quoted in Theodore Kisiel, *The Genesis of Heidegger's* Being and Time [Berkeley: University of California Press, 1993], 75).

19 *Ent-leben* may be translated "unliving" and is contrasted to the "'living through' (*Er-leben*) of experience in the full sense"; cf. Kisiel, *Genesis,* 46.

20 From Heidegger's *Habilitationsschrift,* quoted in and translated by Kisiel, *Genesis,* 71.

21 Martin Heidegger, *Zur Bestimmung der Philosophie* (Frankfurt am Main: Vittorio Klostermann, 1987), 116 (hereafter referred to as *ZBP*), quoted in and translated by Kisiel, *Genesis,* 47.

22 *ZBP,* 75, quoted in Kisiel, *Genesis,* 46.

23 *ZBP,* 116, quoted in Kisiel, *Genesis,* 51.

24 Cf. Heidegger, *Being and Time,* 272: "Being and truth 'are' equiprimordially."

25 From the *Habilitationsschrift,* quoted in and translated by Kisiel, *Genesis,* 47.

26 Martin Heidegger, *Basic Problems of Phenomenology,* trans. Albert Hofstadter (Bloomington: Indiana University Press, 1982), 300.

27 Heidegger, *Being and Time,* 308: "The ownmost possibility is *non-relational.* . . . Dasein is authentically itself only to the extent that, as concernful Being-alongside and solicitous Being-with, it projects itself upon its ownmost potentiality-for-Being rather than upon the possibility of the 'they self.'"

28 Heidegger, *Being and Time,* 203 (emphasis added).

29 I am thinking here of Aristotle's notion of *Homonoia* or political friendship. An insightful examination of its relevance to rhetoric may be found in Ronald Beiner, *Political Judgment* (Chicago: University of Chicago Press, 1983), 20.

30 Heidegger, *Being and Time,* 206.

31 For a helpful explication of this important shift in hermeneutics, see Joel Weinsheimer, *Philosophical Hermeneutics and Literary Theory* (New Haven: Yale University Press, 1991), 2ff.

32 Gadamer, *Heidegger's Ways,* 24.

33 Heidegger, letter to Elizabeth Blochmann, quoted in Kisiel, *Genesis,* 112–13.

34 Heidegger, from the dissertation, quoted in and translated by Kisiel, *Genesis,* 71.

35 "What makes a call upon us that we should think and, by thinking, be who we are?" See Martin Heidegger, *What Is Called Thinking?* trans. J. Glenn Gray and Fred D. Wieck (New York: Harper and Row, 1968), 121.

36 Heidegger, *ZBP,* 206, quoted in Kisiel, *Genesis,* 64; Kisiel explains that *das Situation-Ich* is "a clear precursor of Dasein."

37 My understanding of the *Formale Anzeige* is much indebted to Daniel O. Dahlstrom, "Heidegger's Method: Philosophical Concepts as Formal Indications," *Review of Metaphysics* 43 (1994): 775–95.

38 Heidegger, *ZBP,* 116, quoted in Kisiel, *Genesis,* 51.

39 Kisiel, *Genesis,* 51.

40 Martin Heidegger, "Letter on Humanism," trans. Frank Capuzzi and J. Glenn Gray, in *Heidegger: Basic Writings,* ed. David Farrell Krell (New York: Harper and Row, 1977), 197.

41 Martin Heidegger, *Phänomenologische Interpretationen zu Aristoteles, Gesamtausgabe* 61 (Frankfurt am Main: Vittorio Klostermann, 1985), 80, quoted in and translated by Dahlstrom, "Heidegger's Method," 787.

42 See especially *What Is Called Thinking,* 242ff.; and *Early Greek Thinking,* 89ff. In the later writings, Heidegger uses synonymously far-reaching terms such as "the claim of Being"; see *Early Greek Thinking,* 27, 39; also his discussion of *logos* as the "Saying" of Being, 77.

43 Martin Heidegger, "The End of Philosophy and the Task of Thinking," in *Basic Writings,* 387.

44 Heidegger, *Being and Time,* 58. Notably, in this same passage, Heidegger makes reference to Husserl's notion of "the things themselves," suggesting that his method of rendering the primordial discourse is able to reach back far enough to touch the "Holy Grail" of phenomenology.

45 Heidegger, "Dialogue on Language," 29.

46 For an enlightening exploration of the relation between Heidegger's phenomenology and Husserlian intentionality, see Kisiel, *Genesis,* 30–32.

47 Hubert Dreyfus, *Being-in-the-World: A Commentary on Heidegger's Being and Time, Division I* (Cambridge: MIT Press, 1991), 32.

48 Cf. *Being and Time,* 59–60: "What is it that must be called 'a phenomenon' in a distinctive sense. . . . It is something that lies hidden, in contrast to that which proximally and for the most part does show itself. . . . And just because the phenomena are proximally and for the most part not given, there is need for phenomenology."

49 Richard Rorty, "Wittgenstein, Heidegger, and the Reification of Language," in his *Essays on Heidegger and Others* (Cambridge: Cambridge University Press, 1991), 63.

50 Gadamer, *Heidegger's Ways,* 25.

51 Heidegger himself suggests a similar self-reflexive transformation as the function of the formal indication. See Dahlstrom, "Heidegger's Method," 787, 794–95.

52 Heidegger, quoted in Dahlstrom, "Heidegger's Method," 170.

53 Martin Heidegger, *What Is Philosophy?* trans. William Kluback and Jean T. Wilde (Pfullingen: Verlag Günther Neske, 1956), 52–53.

54 Heidegger, "The Way to Language," in *On The Way to Language,* 119.

55 Martin Heidegger, "Overcoming Metaphysics," in *The End of Philosophy,* trans. Joan Stambaugh (New York, Harper and Row, 1973), 96.

56 Heidegger, quoted in John Caputo, *Radical Hermeneutics: Repetition, Deconstruction, and the Hermeneutic Project* (Bloomington: Indiana University Press, 1987), 196.

57 Caputo, *Radical Hermeneutics,* 76.

58 Augustine, *On Christian Doctrine,* 123.

Part IV

Civic Discourse and Critical Theory

15

Rhetoric, Hermeneutics, and Ideology-Critique

Hans-Georg Gadamer

Translated by G. B. Hess and R. E. Palmer

Philosophical hermeneutics takes as its task the opening up of the hermeneutical dimension in its full scope, showing its fundamental significance for our entire understanding of the world and thus for all the various forms in which this understanding manifests itself: from interhuman communication to manipulation of society; from personal experience by the individual in society to the way in which he encounters society; and from the tradition as it is built of religion and law, art and philosophy, to the revolutionary consciousness that unhinges the tradition through emancipatory reflection.

Despite this vast scope and significance, however, individual explorations necessarily start from the very limited experiences and fields of experience. My own effort, for instance, went back to Dilthey's philosophical development of the heritage of German romanticism, in that I too made the theory of the *Geisteswissenschaften* (humanistic sciences and social sciences) my theme. But I hope to have placed it on a new and much broader footing linguistically, ontologically, and aesthetically; for the experience of art can answer the prevailing presumption of historical alienation in the humanistic disciplines, I believe, with its own overriding and victorious claim to contemporaneousness, a claim that lies in its very essence. This should be evident already from the essential linguisticality of all human experience of the world, which has as its own way of fulfillment a constantly self-renewing contemporaneousness. I maintain that precisely this contemporaneousness and this linguisticality point to a truth that goes questioningly behind all knowledge and anticipatingly before it.

And so it was unavoidable that in my analysis of the universal linguisticality of man's relation to the world the limitations of the fields of experience from which the investigation took its start would unwittingly predetermine the result. Indeed, it paralleled what happened in the historical development of the hermeneutical problem. It came into being in encounter with the written tradition that demanded translation, for the tradition had become estranged from the present as a result of such factors as temporal distance, the fixity of writing, and the sheer inertia of permanence. Thus it was that the many-layered problem of translation became for me the model for the linguisticality of all human behavior in the world. From the structure of translation was indicated the general problem of making what is alien our own. Yet further reflection on the universality of hermeneutics eventually made clear that the model of translation does not, as such, fully come to grips with the manifoldness of what language means in man's existence.[1] Certainly in translation one finds the tension and release that structure all understanding and understandability, but it ultimately derives from the universality of the hermeneutical problem. It is important to realize that this phenomenon is not secondary in human existence, and hermeneutics is not to be viewed as a mere subordinate discipline within the arena of the *Geisteswissenschaften*.

The universal phenomenon of human linguisticality also unfolds in dimensions other than those that would appear to be directly concerned with the hermeneutical problem, for hermeneutics reaches into all the contexts that determine and condition the linguisticality of the human experience of the world. Some of those have been touched upon in my *Truth and Method,* for instance, the *wirkungsgeschichtliches Bewusstsein* (consciousness of effective history, or the consciousness in which history is ever at work) was presented in a conscious effort to shed light on the idea of language in some phases of its history. And of course linguisticality extends into many different dimensions not mentioned in *Truth and Method*.[2]

In rhetoric, linguisticality is attested to in a truly universal form, one that is essentially prior to the hermeneutical and almost represents something like the "positive" as over against the "negative" of linguistic interpretation. And in this connection the relationship between rhetoric and hermeneutics is a matter of great interest.[3] In the social sciences, one finds linguisticality deeply woven into the sociality of human existence, so that the theorists of the social sciences are now becoming interested in the hermeneutical approach. Preeminently, Jürgen Habermas has recently established a relationship between philosophical hermeneutics and the logic of the social sciences in his significant contribution to the *Philosophische Rundschau*,[4] evaluating this relationship from within the epistemological interests of the social sciences. This relationship too raises important questions as to the proper interests and purposes of hermeneutical reflection as compared with those characteristic of the sciences and social sciences.

It seems advisable, then, if not imperative, to take up the question of the interdependence of rhetoric, hermeneutics, and sociology as regards the universalities that run through all three and to try to shed some light on the various kinds of legitimacy possessed by these elements. This endeavor is the more important in view of the fact that the claim to being strictly a science is in all three cases rendered rather ambiguous because of an obvious relationship to *praxis*. Of course, this relationship applies most openly and clearly to rhetoric and hermeneutics; but it also applies to sociology, as we shall see presently.

For it is clear that rhetoric is not mere theory of forms of speech and persuasion; rather, it can develop out of a native talent for practical mastery, without any theoretical reflection about ways and means. Likewise, the art of understanding, whatever its ways and means may be, is not dependent on an explicit awareness of the rules that guide and govern it. It builds, as does rhetoric, on a natural power that everyone possesses to some degree. It is a skill in which one gifted person may surpass all others, and theory can at best only tell us why. In both rhetoric and hermeneutics, then, theory is subsequent to that out of which it is abstracted; that is, to *praxis*.

Historically it is worthy of note that while rhetoric belongs to the earliest Greek philosophy, hermeneutics came to flower in the romantic era as a consequence of the modern dissolution of firm bonds with tradition. Of course, hermeneutics occurs in earlier times and forms, but even in these it represents an effort to grasp something vanishing and hold it up in the light of consciousness. Therefore, it occurs only in later stages of cultural evolution, like later Jewish religion, Alexandrian philology, Christianity as inheriting the Jewish gospel, or Lutheran theology as refuting an old tradition of Christian dogmatics. The history-embracing and history-preserving element runs deep in hermeneutics, in sharp contrast to sociological interest in reflection as basically a means of emancipation from authority and tradition. Reflection in rhetoric, like that in hermeneutics, is a meditation about a *praxis* that is in itself already a natural and sophisticated one. I should like to recall something of the early history of both rhetoric and hermeneutics in order to characterize and compare the scope and functions of the two fields.

RHETORIC AND HERMENEUTICS

The first history of rhetoric was written by Aristotle, and we now possess only fragments of it. It is clear, however, that basically Aristotle's theory of rhetoric was developed to carry out a program originally projected by Plato. Plato, going back behind all the shallow claims put forward by the contemporary teachers of rhetoric, had discovered a genuine foundation for rhetoric that only the philosopher, the dialectician, could carry out: the task is to master the faculty of speaking in such an effectively persuasive way that the arguments brought forward are always appropriate to the specific receptivity of the souls to which they are directed. Certainly this statement of the task of rhetoric is theoretically enlightening, but implicit in it are two Platonic assumptions: first, that only he who has a grasp of the truth (i.e., the ideas) can unerringly devise the probable *pseudos* of a rhetorical argument; second, that one must have a profound knowledge of the souls of those one wishes to persuade. Aristotelian rhetoric is preeminently an expansion of the latter theme. In it is fulfilled the theory of the mutual accommodation of speech and soul demanded by Plato in the *Phaedrus,* now in the form of an anthropological foundation for the art of speech.

Rhetorical theory was a long-prepared-for result of a controversy that represented the breaking into Greek culture of an intoxicating and frightening new art of speaking and a new idea of education itself: that of the Sophists. At that time an uncanny new skill in standing everything on its head, the Sicilian art of oratory flowed in on the straitlaced but easily influenced youth of Athens. Now it became paramountly necessary to teach this new power (this great ruler, as Gorgias had called oratory) its proper limits—to discipline it. From Protagoras to Isocrates, the masters of rhetoric claimed not only to teach speaking but also the formation of a civic consciousness that bore the promise of political success. Yet it was Plato who first created the foundations out of which a new and all-shattering art of speaking (Aristophanes has depicted it for us blatantly enough) could find its limits and legitimate place.

The history of understanding is no less ancient and venerable. If one acknowledges hermeneutics to exist wherever a genuine art of understanding manifests itself, one must begin, if not with Nestor in the *Iliad,* then at least with Odysseus. One can point out that the new philosophical movement represented by the Sophists was concerned with the interpretation of sayings by famous poets and depicted them very artfully as pedagogical examples. Certainly this was a form of hermeneutics. Over against this, one can place the So-cratic hermeneutics.[5] Still, it is far from a full-fledged theory of understand-ing. It seems, rather, to be generally characteristic of the emergence of the "hermeneutical" problem that something *distant* has to be brought close, a certain strangeness overcome, a bridge built between the once and the now. Thus hermeneutics, as a general attitude over against the world, came into its own in modern times, which had become aware of the temporal distance sep-arating us from antiquity and of the relativity of the lifeworlds of different cul-tural traditions. Something of this awareness was contained in the theological claim of Reformation biblical exegesis (in the principle of *sola scriptura*), but its true unfolding came about only when a "historical consciousness" arose in the Enlightenment (although it was influenced by the novel insights of Jesuit chronological information) and matured in the romantic period to establish a relationship (however broken) to our entire inheritance from the past.

Because of this historical development of hermeneutics, hermeneutical theory oriented itself to the task of interpreting expressions of life that are fixed in writing, although Schleiermacher's theoretical working out of herme-neutics included understanding as it takes place in the oral exchange of con-versation. Rhetoric, on the other hand, concerned itself with the impact of *speaking* in all its immediacy. It did, of course, also enter into the realm of ef-fective *writing*, and thus it developed a body of teaching on style and styles. Nevertheless, it achieved its authentic realization not in the act of reading but in speaking. The phenomenon of the orally read speech occupies an in-be-tween, a hybrid, position: already it displays a tendency to base the art of speaking on the techniques of expression inherent in the medium of writing, and thus it begins to abstract itself from the original situation of speaking. Thus begins the transformation into poetics, whose linguistic objects are so wholly and completely art that their transformation from the oral sphere into writing and back is accomplished without loss or damage.

Rhetoric as such, however, is tied to the immediacy of its effect. Now the arousing of emotions, which is clearly the essence of the orator's task,[6] is effec-tual to a vastly diminished degree in written expression, which is the tradi-tional object of hermeneutical investigation. And this is precisely the differ-ence that matters: the orator carries his listeners away with him; the convincing power of his arguments overwhelms the listener. While under the persuasive spell of speech, the listener for the moment cannot and ought not to indulge in critical examination. On the other hand, the reading and inter-preting of what is written is so distanced and detached from its author—from his mood, intentions, and unexpressed tendencies—that the grasping of the meaning of the text takes on something of the character of an independent productive act, one that resembles more the art of the orator than the process of mere listening. Thus it is easy to understand why the theoretical tools of the art of interpretation (hermeneutics) have been to a large extent borrowed from rhetoric.[7]

Where, indeed, but to rhetoric should the theoretical examination of interpretation turn? Rhetoric from oldest tradition has been the only advocate of a claim to truth that defends the probable, the *eikos* (verisimilar), and that which is convincing to the ordinary reason against the claim of science to accept as true only what can be demonstrated and tested! Convincing and persuading, without being able to prove—these are obviously as much the aim and measure of understanding and interpretation as they are the aim and measure of the art of oration and persuasion. And this whole wide realm of convincing "persuasions" and generally reigning views has not been gradually narrowed by the progress of science, however great it has been; rather, this realm extends to take in every new product of scientific endeavor, claiming it for itself and bringing it within its scope.

The ubiquity of rhetoric, indeed, is unlimited. Only through it is science a sociological factor of life, for all the representations of science that are directed beyond the mere narrow circle of specialists (and, perhaps one should say, insofar as they are not limited in their impact to a very small circle of initiates) owe their effectiveness to the rhetorical element they contain. Even Descartes, that great and passionate advocate of method and certainty, is in all his writings an author who uses the means of rhetoric in a magnificent fashion.[8] There can be no doubt, then, about the fundamental function of rhetoric within social life. But one may go further, in view of the ubiquity of rhetoric, to defend the primordial claims of rhetoric over against modern science, remembering that all science that would wish to be of practical usefulness at all is dependent on it.

No less universal is the function of hermeneutics. The lack of immediate understandability of texts handed down to us historically, or their proneness to be misunderstood, is really only a special case of what is to be met in all human orientation to the world as the *atopon* (the strange), that which does not "fit" into the customary order of our expectation based on experience. Hermeneutics has only called our attention to this phenomenon. Just as when we progress in understanding the *mirabilia* lose their strangeness, so every successful appropriation of tradition is dissolved into a new and distinct familiarity in which it belongs to us and we to it. They both flow together into one owned and shared world, which encompasses past and present and which receives its linguistic articulation in the speaking of man with man.

The phenomenon of understanding, then, shows the universality of human linguisticality as a limitless medium that carries *everything* within it—not only the "culture" that has been handed down to us through language, but absolutely everything—because everything (in the world and out of it) is included in the realm of "understandings" and understandability in which we move. Plato was right when he asserted that whoever regards things in the mirror of speech becomes aware of them in their full and undiminished truth. And he was profoundly correct when he taught that all cognition is only what it is as recognition, for a "first cognition" is as little possible as a first word. In fact, a cognition in the very recent past, one whose consequences appear as yet unforeseeable, becomes what it truly is for us only when it has unfolded into its consequences and into the medium of intersubjective understanding.

And so we see that the rhetorical and hermeneutical aspects of human linguisticality completely interpenetrate each other. There would be no speaker and no art of speaking if understanding and consent were not in question, were not underlying elements; there would be no hermeneutical task if there were no mutual understanding that has been disturbed and that those involved in a conversation must search for and find again together. It is a symptom of our failure to realize this and evidence of the increasing self-alienation of human life in our modern epoch when we think in terms of organizing a perfect and perfectly manipulated information—a turn modern rhetoric seems to have taken. In this case, the sense of the mutual interpenetration of rhetoric and hermeneutics fades away and hermeneutics is on its own.

HERMENEUTICS AND THE SOCIAL SCIENCES

It is in keeping with the universality of the hermeneutical approach that hermeneutics must be taken into account with regard to the logic of the social sciences and especially in relation to the intentional alienation and distancing present in sociological methodology. Jürgen Habermas in his article on the subject worked with my analysis of the *wirkungsgeschichtliches Bewusstsein* and the model of translation as both were given in *Truth and Method* with the hope that they could help to overcome the positivistic ossification of sociological logic and move sociological theory beyond its historical failure to reflect upon its linguistic foundations. Now Habermas's use of hermeneutics stands on the premise that it will serve the methodology of the social sciences. But this premise is, in itself, a prior decision of greatest significance, for the purpose of sociological method as emancipating one from tradition places it at the outset very far from the traditional purpose and starting point of the hermeneutical problematic, with all its bridge building and recovery of the best in the past.

Admittedly, the methodical alienation that comprises the very essence of modern science is indeed to be found also in the *Geisteswissenschaften,* and the title of *Truth and Method* never intended that the antithesis it implies should be mutually exclusive.[9] But the *Geisteswissenschaften* were the starting point of my analysis in *Truth and Method* precisely because they related to experiences that have nothing to do with method and science but lie beyond science—like the experience of art and the experience of culture that bear the imprint of their historical traditions. The hermeneutical experience as it is operative in all these cases is not in itself the object of methodical alienation but is directed against alienation. The hermeneutical experience is prior to all methodical alienation because it is the matrix out of which arise the questions it then directs to science. The modern social scientists, on the other hand, insofar as they recognize hermeneutical reflection as unavoidable, nevertheless advance the claim (as Habermas has formulated it) of raising understanding up out of a prescientific exercise to the rank of a self-reflecting activity by "controlled alienation"—that is, through "methodical development of intelligence."[10]

It has been the way of science from its earliest stages to achieve through teachable and controllable ways of proceeding what individual intelligence would also occasionally attain, but in unsure and uncheckable ways. But is this way to be absolutized and idolized? Is it right that social scientists should believe that through it they attain human personal judging and practice? What kind of understanding does one achieve through "controlled alienation"? Is it not likely to be an alienated understanding? Is it not the case that many social scientists are more interested in using the sedimented truisms inherent in linguisticality (so as to grasp "scientifically" the "real" structures, as they define them, of society) than in really understanding social life? Hermeneutical reflection will not, however, allow a restriction of itself to this function, which is immanent in the sciences. And most especially, it will not be deterred from applying hermeneutical reflection anew to the methodical alienation of understanding practiced by the social sciences, even though it exposes itself to positivistic detraction.

But let us examine first how the hermeneutical problematic applies within social scientific theory and how it would be seen from that vantage point. Habermas sees in its analysis of historicity one of the principal values of hermeneutics for social theory. So it is the claim of hermeneutics that the idea of *Wirkungsgeschichte* (effective history) furnishes a means of access to the realm of objects treated by sociology. The *wirkungsgeschichtliches Bewusstsein* (consciousness of effective history) seeks to be aware of its prejudgments and to control its own preunderstanding; and thus it does away with that naive objectivism that falsifies not only the positivistic theory of science but also any project of laying either a phenomenological or language-analytical foundation for sociology.

Yet the question arises as to what hermeneutical reflection really does. Habermas answers this question in reference to universal history, a goal that unavoidably lifts itself out of the multiple goals and conceptions of goal in social actions. He asserts that if hermeneutical reflection were simply satisfied with general considerations, such as that nobody is able to reach beyond the limitedness of his own standpoint, then it would be ineffectual. The claim to a material philosophy of history may be contested by such a consideration, but historical consciousness nevertheless constantly will project an anticipated universal history. What is the good, after all, Habermas asks, of knowing merely that a projected futurity cannot be other than preliminary and essentially provisional? So, where it is effective and operational, what does hermeneutical reflection do? In what relationship to the tradition of which it becomes conscious does this "historically operative" reflection stand?

My thesis is—and I think it is the necessary consequence of recognizing the operativeness of history in our conditionedness and finitude—that the thing hermeneutics teaches us is to see through the dogmatism of asserting an opposition and separation between the ongoing, natural "tradition" and the reflective appropriation of it. For behind this assertion stands a dogmatic objectivism that distorts the very concept of hermeneutical reflection itself. In this objectivism the understander is seen—even in the so-called sciences of understanding like history—not in relationship to the hermeneutical situation and the constant operativeness of history in his own consciousness, but in such a way as to imply that his own understanding does not enter into the event.

But this is simply not the case. Actually, the historian—even the one who treats history as a "critical science"—is so little separated from the ongoing traditions (for example, those of his nation) that he is really *himself engaged* in contributing to the growth and development of the national state. He is one of the "nation's" historians; he belongs to the nation. And for the epoch of national states, one must say: the more he may have reflected on his hermeneutical conditionedness, the more national he knows himself to be. J. F. Droysen, for instance, who saw through the "eunuch-like objectivity" of the historian in all its methodological naïveté, was himself tremendously influential for the national consciousness of bourgeois nineteenth-century culture. He was, in any case, more effective than the epical consciousness of Leopold von Ranke, which was inclined to foster the nonpoliticality appropriate to an authoritarian state. To understand, we may say, is itself a kind of happening. Only a naive and unreflective historicism in hermeneutics would see the historical-hermeneutical sciences as something absolutely new that would do away with the power of "tradition." On the contrary, I have tried to present in *Truth and Method,* through the aspect of linguisticality that operates in all understanding, an unambiguous demonstration of the continual process of mediation by which that which is societally transmitted (the tradition) lives on. For language is not only an object in our hands, it is the reservoir of tradition and the medium in and through which we exist and perceive our world.

To this formulation Habermas objects that the medium of science itself is changed through reflection and that precisely this experience is the priceless heritage bequeathed us by German idealism out of the spirit of the eighteenth century. Habermas asserts that although the Hegelian procedure of reflection is not presented in my analysis as fulfilled in an absolute consciousness, nevertheless my "idealism of linguisticality" (as he calls it)[11] exhausts itself in mere hermeneutical appropriation, development, and "cultural transmission," and thus displays a sorry powerlessness in view of the concrete whole of societal relationships. This larger whole, says Habermas, is obviously animated not only by language but by work and action; therefore, hermeneutical reflection must pass into a criticism of ideology.

In taking such a position, Habermas is tying directly into the central motif in sociological interest in gaining knowledge. Rhetoric (theory) stepped forward against the bewitching of consciousness achieved through the power of speech, by differentiating between the truth and that which appears to be the truth (and which it teaches one to produce). Hermeneutics, being confronted with a disrupted intersubjective understanding, seeks to place communication on a new basis and, in particular, to replace the false objectivism of alienated knowing with new hermeneutical foundations. Just as in rhetoric and hermeneutics so also in *sociological reflection,* an emancipatory interest is at work that undertakes to free us of outer and inner social forces and compulsions simply by making us aware of them. Insofar as these forces and compulsions tend to legitimate themselves linguistically, Habermas sees the critique of ideology as the means of unmasking the "deceptions of language."[12] But this critique, of course, is in itself a linguistic act of reflection.

In the field of psychoanalytical therapy, too, says Habermas, we find the claims for the emancipatory power of reflection corroborated. For the repression that is seen through robs the false compulsions of their power. Just as in psychotherapy it is the goal to identify through a process of reflective development all our motives of action with the real meaning to which the patient is oriented (this goal is, of course, limited by the therapeutic task in the psychoanalytic situation, which therefore itself represents a limiting concept), so in social reality also (as Habermas would have it) hermeneutics would be at its best when such a fictitious goal situation is operative. For Habermas, and for psychoanalysis, the life of society and the life of the individual consist in the interaction of intelligible motives and concrete compulsions, which social and psychological investigation, in a progressive process of clarification, appropriates in order to set man, the actor and agent, free.

One cannot dispute the fact that this sociotheoretical conception has its logic. The question we must ask ourselves, however, is whether such a conception does justice to the actual reach of hermeneutical reflection: Does hermeneutics really take its bearings from a limiting concept of perfect interaction between understood motives and consciously performed action (a concept that is itself, I believe, fictitious)? I maintain that the hermeneutical problem is universal and basic for all interhuman experience, both of history and of the present moment, precisely because meaning can be experienced even where it is not actually intended. The universality of the hermeneutical dimension is narrowed down, I think, when one area of understood meaning (for instance, the "cultural tradition") is held in separation from other recognizable determinants of social reality that are taken as the "real" factors. But is it not true that we can understand precisely *every* ideology as a form of false linguistic consciousness, one that not only might show itself to us as a conscious, manifest, and intelligible meaning but also might be understood in its "true" meaning? Take for example the interest in political or economic domination. In the individual life, the same thing applies to unconscious motives, which the psychoanalyst brings to conscious awareness.

Who says that these concrete, so-called real factors are outside the realm of hermeneutics? From the hermeneutical standpoint, rightly understood, it is absolutely absurd to regard the concrete factors of work and politics as outside the scope of hermeneutics. What about the vital issue of prejudices with which hermeneutical reflection deals? Where do they come from? Merely out of "cultural tradition"? Surely they do in part, but what is tradition formed from? It would be true when Habermas asserts that "hermeneutics bangs helplessly, so to speak, from within against the walls of tradition,"[13] if we understand this "within" as opposite to an "outside" that *does not enter* our world—our to-be-understood, understandable, or nonunderstandable world—but remains the mere observation of external alterations (instead of human actions). With this area of what lies outside the realm of human understanding and human understandings (our world), hermeneutics is not concerned. Certainly I affirm the hermeneutical fact that the world is the medium of human understanding or not understanding, but it does not lead to the conclusion that cultural tradition should be absolutized and fixed. To suppose that it does have this implication seems to me erroneous. The principle of hermeneutics simply means that we should try to understand everything that can be understood. This is what I meant by the sentence: "Being that can be understood is language" [*Truth and Method*, p. 474].

This does not mean that there is a world of meanings that is narrowed down to the status of secondary objects of knowledge, mere supplements to the economic and political realities that fundamentally determine the life of society. Rather, it means that the mirror of language is reflecting everything that is. In language, and only in it, can we meet what we never "encounter" in the world because we are ourselves it (and not merely what we mean or what we know of ourselves). But the metaphor of a mirror is not fully adequate to the phenomenon of language, for in the last analysis language is not simply a mirror. What we perceive in it is not merely a "reflection" of our own and all being; it is the living out of what it is with us—not only in the concrete interrelationships of work and politics but in all the other relationships and dependencies that comprise our world.

Language, then, is not the finally found anonymous subject of all social-historical processes and action, which presents the whole of its activities as objectifications to our observing gaze; rather, it is by itself the game of interpretation that we all are engaged in every day. In this game nobody is above and before all the others; everybody is at the center, is "it" in this game. Thus it is always your turn to be interpreting. This process of interpretation takes place whenever we "understand," especially when we see through prejudices or tear away the pretenses that hide reality. There, indeed, understanding comes into its own. This idea recalls what we said about the *atopon,* the strange, for in it we have "seen through" something that appeared odd and unintelligible: we have brought it into our linguistic world. To use the analogy of chess, everything is "solved," resembling a difficult chess problem, where only the definitive solution makes understandable (and then right down to the last piece) the necessity of a previous absurd position.

But does this mean that we "understand" only when we see through pretexts or unmask false pretensions? Habermas's Marxist critique of ideology appears to presuppose this meaning. At least, it seems that the true "power" of reflection is evident only when it has this effect, and its powerlessness, when one would remain occupied with the supposed phantom of language and spin out its implication. The presupposition is that reflection, as employed in the hermeneutical sciences, should "shake the dogmatism of life-*praxis*." Here indeed is operating a prejudice that we can see is pure dogmatism, for reflection is not always and unavoidably a step toward dissolving prior convictions. Authority is not always wrong. Yet Habermas regards it as an untenable assertion, and treason to the heritage of the Enlightenment, that the act of rendering transparent the structure of prejudgments in understanding should possibly lead to an acknowledgment of authority. Authority is by his definition a dogmatic power. I cannot accept the assertion that reason and authority are abstract antitheses, as the emancipatory Enlightenment did. Rather, I assert that they stand in a basically ambivalent relation, a relation I think should be explored rather than our casually accepting the antithesis as a "fundamental conviction."[14]

For in my opinion this abstract antithesis embraced by the Enlightenment is a mistake fraught with ominous consequences. In it, reflection is granted a false power, and the true dependencies involved are misjudged on the basis of a fallacious idealism. Certainly, I would grant that authority exercises an essential dogmatic power in innumerable forms of domination: from the ordering of education and the mandatory commands of the army and government all the way to the hierarchy of power created by political forces or fanatics. Now the mere outer appearance of obedience rendered to authority can never show why or whether the authority is legitimate, that is, whether the context is true order or the veiled disorder that is created by the arbitrary exercise of power. It seems evident to me that *acceptance* or *acknowledgment* is the decisive thing for relationships to authority. So the question is On what is this acknowledgment based? Certainly such acceptance can often express more a yielding of the powerless to the one holding power than true acceptance, but really it is not true obedience and it is not based on authority but on force. (And when anyone in an argument appeals to authority, he only pretends.) One need only study the processes of forfeiture and decline of authority (or its rise) to see what authority is and that out of which it lives and grows. It lives not from dogmatic power but from dogmatic acceptance. What is this dogmatic acceptance, however, if not that one concedes superiority in knowledge and insight to the authority, and for this reason one believes that authority is right? Only on this crucial concession, this belief, is acceptance founded. Authority can rule only because it is freely recognized and accepted. The obedience that belongs to true authority is neither blind nor slavish.

It is an inadmissible imputation to hold that I somehow meant there is no decline of authority or no emancipating criticism of authority. Of course, whether one can really say that decline of authority comes about *through* reflection's emancipatory criticism or that decline of authority is expressed in criticism and emancipation is a matter we shall leave aside (although we may say that it is perhaps a misstatement of the genuine alternatives). But what is really in dispute, I think, is simply whether reflection always dissolves substantial relationships or is capable of taking them up into consciousness.

In this regard, my presentation in *Truth and Method* of the teaching and learning process (referring principally to Aristotle's *Ethics*) is taken by Habermas in a peculiarly one-sided way. For the idea that tradition as such should be and should remain the only ground for acceptance of presuppositions (a view that Habermas ascribes to me) flies in the face of my basic thesis that authority is rooted in insight as a hermeneutical process. A person who comes of age need not—but he also, from insight, can—take possession of what he has obediently followed. Tradition is no proof and validation of something, in any case not where validation is demanded by reflection. But the point is this: Where does reflection demand it? Everywhere? I would object to such an answer on the grounds of the finitude of human existence and the essential particularity of reflection. The real question is whether one sees the function of reflection as bringing something to awareness in order to confront what is in fact accepted with other possibilities—so that one can either throw it out or reject the other possibilities and accept what the tradition de facto is presenting—or whether bringing something to awareness *always dissolves what one has previously accepted.*

The concept of reflection and bringing to awareness that Habermas employs (admittedly from his sociological interest) appears to me, then, to be itself encumbered with dogmatism and, indeed, to be a misinterpretation of reflection. For from Husserl (in his doctrine of anonymous intentionalities) and from Heidegger (in demonstration of the ontological abridgment evident in the subject-object concept in idealism), we have learned to see through the false objectification inherent in the idealist conception of reflection. I would hold that there is most certainly an inner reversal of intentionality in reflection, which in no way raises the thing meant to a thematic object. Franz Brentano, using Aristotelian insights, was aware of this fact. I would not know, otherwise, how the enigmatic form of the being of language could be grasped at all. Then one must distinguish "effective reflection" (*die "effektive" Reflexion*), which is that in which the unfolding of language takes place, from expressive and thematic reflection, which is the type out of which Occidental linguistic history has been formed.[15] Making everything an object and creating the conditions for science in the modern sense, this latter type of reflection establishes the grounds for the planetary civilization of tomorrow.

Habermas defends with extraordinary emotion the sciences of experience against the charge of being a random game of words. But who, from the vantage point of having the technical power to place nature at our disposal, would dispute their necessity? The researcher might disclaim the technical motivation of his work and defend his relationship to pure theoretical interests—with full subjective justification. But nobody would deny that the practical application of modern science has fundamentally altered our world, and therewith also our language. But precisely so—"*also* our language." This by no means suggests, however, what Habermas imputes to me: that the linguistically articulated consciousness claims to determine all the material being of life-practice. It suggests only that there is no societal reality, with all its concrete forces, that does not bring itself to representation in a consciousness that is linguistically articulated. Reality does not happen "behind the back" of language;[16] it happens rather behind the backs of those who live in the subjective opinion that they have understood "the world" (or can no longer understand it); that is, reality happens precisely *within* language.

Obviously this fact makes the concept of "natural situation" discussed by Habermas highly questionable.[17] Marx had already persuasively held that this concept was the counter-idea to the working world of modern class society, but Habermas willingly uses it in his reference not only to the "natural substance of tradition" but also to "the causality of natural patterns." I believe it is pure romanticism, and such romanticism creates an artificial abyss between tradition and the reflection that is grounded in historical consciousness. However, the "idealism of linguisticality" at least has the advantage that it does not fall into this sort of romanticism.

Habermas's critique culminates in questioning the immanentism of transcendental philosophy with respect to its historical conditions, conditions upon which he himself is dependent. Now this is indeed a central problem. Anyone who takes seriously the finitude of human existence and constructs no "consciousness as such," or "intellectus archetypus," or "transcendental ego" to which everything can be traced back will not be able to escape the question of how his own thinking as transcendental is empirically possible. But within the hermeneutical dimension that I have developed I do not see this difficulty arising.

The well-known young theologian Wolfhart Pannenberg has presented a highly useful discussion of my book in his article "Hermeneutics and Universal History,"[18] which relates to the question of immanentism but more particularly to the question of whether my philosophical hermeneutics necessarily but unconsciously rehabilitates the Hegelian concept of universal history (such as in the concept of fusion of horizons, where the ultimate horizon is, says Pannenberg, implied or presupposed in the direction of every individual event of fusion). In particular, his discussion brought home to me the vast difference between Hegel's claim to demonstrate the presence of reason in history and the conceptions of world history, those constantly outstripped conceptions, in which one unconsciously always behaves like the latest historian.

Hegel's claim to a philosophy of world history can certainly be disputed. Hegel himself knew how finite it was and remarked that the feet of his pallbearers could already be heard outside the door,° and one finds that behind all the disavowals of world history the goal, the end-thought, of freedom possessed a compelling evidentness. One can as little get beyond this as one can get beyond consciousness itself.

But the claim that every historian must make and operate within, namely, to tie the meaning of all events to today (and, of course, to the future of this today), is really a fundamentally more modest one than asserting a universal history or a philosophy of world history. Nobody can dispute that history presupposes futurity, and a universal-historical conception is unavoidably one of the dimensions of today's historical consciousness from a practical point of view or for practical purposes ("In praktischer Absicht"). But does it do justice to Hegel to want to reduce him to the limitations implied by this pragmatic interpretive requirement that the present demands? "In praktischer Absicht"—nobody today goes beyond this claim, for consciousness has become aware of its finitude and mistrusts the dictatorship of ideas or concepts. Even so, who would be so foolish as to try to reduce Hegel to the level of practical purposes? I certainly would not, even while criticizing his claims to a philosophy of universal history. So on this point I think there is really no dispute between Pannenberg and myself, so far as I understand him. For Pannenberg does not propose to renew Hegel's claim either. There is only the difference that for the Christian theologian the "practical purpose" of all universal historical conceptions has its fixed point in the absolute historicity of the Incarnation.

All the same, the question of universality remains. If the hermeneutical problematic wishes to maintain itself in the face of the ubiquity and universality of rhetoric, as well as the obvious topicality of critiques of ideology, it must establish its own universality. And it must do so especially over against the claims of modern science to universality, and thus to its tendency to absorb hermeneutical reflection into itself and render it serviceable to science (as in the concept, for instance, of the "methodical development of intelligence" Habermas has in mind). Still, it will be able to do so only if it does not become imprisoned in the impregnable immanence of transcendental reflection but rather gives account of what its own kind of reflection achieves. And

---

°Gadamer expresses this more picturesquely with a quote: "Die Füsse derer, die dich hinaustragen, sind schon vor der Türe." [Translators' note]

it must do it not only within the realm of modern science but also over against this realm, in order to show a universality that transcends that of modern science.

ON THE UNIVERSALITY OF HERMENEUTICAL REFLECTION

Hermeneutical reflection fulfills the function that is accomplished in every bringing of something to a conscious awareness. Because it does, it can and must manifest itself in all our modern fields of knowledge, especially science. Let us reflect a bit on this hermeneutical reflection. Reflection on a given pre-understanding brings before me something that otherwise happens *behind my back*. Something, but not everything, for what I have called the *wirkungs-geschichtliches Bewusstsein* is inescapably more *being* than consciousness, and being is never fully manifest. Certainly, I do not mean that such reflection could escape from ideological ossification if it does not engage in constant self-reflection and attempts at self-awareness. Thus, only through hermeneutical reflection am I no longer unfree over against myself but rather can deem freely what in my preunderstanding may be justified and what unjustifiable.

And also only in this manner do I learn to gain a new understanding of what I have seen through eyes conditioned by prejudice. But this implies, too, that the prejudgments that lead my preunderstanding are also constantly at stake, right up to the moment of their surrender—which surrender could also be called a transformation. It is the untiring power of *experience* that in the process of being instructed, man is ceaselessly forming a new preunderstanding.

In the fields that were the starting points of my hermeneutical studies—the study of art and the philological-historical sciences—it is easy to demonstrate how hermeneutical reflection is at work. For instance, consider how the autonomy of viewing art from the vantage point of the history of style has been shaken up by hermeneutical reflection (1) on the concept of art itself, and (2) on concepts of individual styles and epochs. Consider how iconography has pressed from the periphery to the forefront, and how hermeneutical reflection on the concepts of experience and expression has had literary-critical consequences (even in cases where it becomes only a more conscious carrying forward of tendencies long favored in literary criticism). Although it is, of course, evident how the shake-up of fixed presuppositions promises scientific progress by making new questions possible, it should be equally evident that this applies in the history of artistic and literary styles. And we constantly experience what historical research can accomplish through becoming conscious of the history of ideas. In *Truth and Method* I believe I have been able to show how historical alienation is mediated in the form of what I call the fusion of horizons.

The overall significance of hermeneutical reflection, however, is not exhausted by what it means for and in the sciences themselves. For all of the modern sciences possess a deeply rooted alienation that they impose on the natural consciousness and of which we need to be aware. This alienation has already reached reflective awareness in the very beginning stages of modern science in the concept of *method*. Hermeneutical reflection does not desire to change or eliminate this situation; it can, in fact, indirectly serve the methodological endeavor of science by making transparently clear the guiding preunderstandings in the sciences and thereby open new dimensions of questioning. But it must also bring to awareness, in this regard, the price that methods in science have paid for their own progress: the toning down and abstraction they demand, through which the natural consciousness still always must go along as the consumer of the inventions and information attained by science. One can, with Wittgenstein, express this insight as follows: The language games of science remain related to the metalanguage presented in the mother tongue. All the knowledge won by science enters the societal consciousness through school and education, using modern informational media, though maybe sometimes after a great—too great—delay. In any case, this is the way that new sociolinguistic realities are articulated.

For the *natural* sciences, of course, this gap and the methodical alienation of research are of less consequence than for social sciences. The true natural scientist does not have to be told how very particular is the realm of knowledge of his science in relation to the whole of reality. He does not share in the deification of his science that the public would press upon him. All the more, however, the public (and the researcher who must go before the public) needs hermeneutical reflection on the presuppositions and limits of science. The so-called humanities, on the other hand, are still easily mediated to the common consciousness, so that insofar as they are accepted at all, their objects belong immediately to the cultural heritage and the realm of traditional education. But the modern social sciences stand in a particularly strained relationship to their object, the social reality, and this relationship especially requires hermeneutical reflection. For the methodical alienation to which the social sciences owe their progress is related here to the human-societal world as a whole. These sciences increasingly see themselves as marked out for the purpose of scientific ordering and control of society. They have to do with "scientific" and "methodical" planning, direction, organization, development—in short, with an infinity of functions that, so to speak, determine from outside the whole of the life of each individual and each group. Yet this social engineer, this scientist who undertakes to look after the functioning of the machine of society, appears himself to be methodically alienated and split off from the society to which, at the same time, he belongs.

But is man as a political being the mere object of the techniques of making public opinion? I think not: he is a member of society, and only in playing his role with free judgment and politically real effectiveness can he conserve freedom. It is the function of hermeneutical reflection, in this connection, to preserve us from naive surrender to the experts of social technology.

Of course, a hermeneutically reflective sociologist like Habermas cannot conceive himself in these shallow terms of social engineering. Habermas's lucid analysis of social-scientific logic has resolutely worked out the authentic epistemological interest, which distinguishes true sociologists from technicians of social structure. He calls it an *emancipating interest* (what a contrast to the interest of the social engineers!), which takes reflection alone as its objective. He points in this regard to the example of psychoanalysis. And it is in psychoanalysis, as a matter of fact, that hermeneutical reflection plays a fundamental role. This is because, as we have emphasized earlier, the unconscious motive does not represent a clear and fully articulatable boundary for hermeneutical theory: it falls within the larger perimeter of hermeneutics. Psychotherapy could be described as the work of "completing an interrupted process of education into a full history (a story that can be articulated in language)," so in psychotherapy, hermeneutics and the circle of language that is closed in dialogue are central. I think I have learned this fact, above all, from Jacques Lacan.[19]

All the same, it is clear that even this is not the whole story, for the psychoanalytic approach turns out not to be universalizable even for the psychoanalyst himself. The framework of interpretation worked out by Freud claims to possess the character of genuine natural-scientific hypotheses, that is, to be a knowledge of acknowledged laws. This orientation inevitably shows up in the role that methodical alienation plays in his psychoanalysis. But although the successful analysis wins *its* authentication in its results, the claim to *knowledge* in psychoanalysis must not be reduced to mere pragmatic validation. And this means that psychoanalysis is exposed again to another act of hermeneutical reflection, in which one must ask: How does the psychoanalyst's special knowledge relate to his own position within the societal reality (to which, after all, he does belong)?

The psychoanalyst leads the patient into the emancipatory reflection that goes behind the conscious superficial interpretations, breaks through the masked self-understanding, and sees through the repressive function of social taboos. This activity belongs to the emancipatory reflection to which he leads his patient. But what happens when he uses the same kind of reflection in a situation in which he is not the doctor but a partner in a game? Then he will fall out of his social role! A game partner who is always "seeing through" his game partner, who does not take seriously what they are standing for, is a spoilsport whom one shuns. The emancipatory power of reflection claimed by the psychoanalyst is a special, rather than general, function of reflection and must be given its boundaries through the societal context and consciousness, within which the analyst and also his patient are on even terms with everybody else. This is something that *hermeneutical reflection* teaches us: that social community, with all its tensions and disruptions, ever and ever again leads back to a common area of social understanding through which it exists.

Here, I think, the analogy Habermas suggests between psychoanalytical and sociological theory breaks down, or at least raises severe problems. For where are the limits of this analogy? Where does the patient relationship end and the social partnership in its unprofessional right begin? Most fundamentally: Over against what self-interpretation of the social consciousness (and all morality is such) is it appropriate to inquire *behind* that consciousness—and when is it not? Within the context of the purely practical, or of a universalized emancipatory reflection, these questions appear unanswerable. The unavoidable consequence to which all these observations lead is that the basically emancipatory consciousness must have in mind the dissolution of all authority, all obedience. This means that unconsciously, the ultimate guiding image of emancipatory reflection in the social sciences must be an anarchistic utopia. Such an image, however, seems to me to reflect a hermeneutically false consciousness, the antidote for which can only be a more universal hermeneutical reflection.

NOTES

Bracketed information has been supplied by the editors.

1 Thus what O. Marquard (Heidelberger Philosophiekongress, 1966) calls "das Sein zum Texte" does not at all exhaust the hermeneutical dimension unless the word *Texte* is taken not in the narrow sense but as "the text that God has written with his own hand," i.e., the *liber naturae*, which consequently encompasses all knowledge from physics to sociology and anthropology. And even in this case the model of translation is implied, which is not fully adequate to the complexity of the hermeneutical dimension.

2 See Johannes Lohmann, *Philosophie und Sprachwissenschaft* [Berlin: Duncker and Humblot, 1965], and his review of my book in *Gnomon* 37 (1965): 709–18. Lohmann's treatment may be seen as a greatly expanded application of what I had briefly sketched as the imprint of the concept of *Sprache* (language in Occidental thought). He traces "the emergence of the concept (*Begriff*) as the intellectual vehicle by which given objects are momentarily subsumed under one cogitated form" (714). He recognizes in the stem-inflecting verbs of Old Indo-Germanic the grammatical expression of this idea, especially in the copula. From this, he says, we can deduce the possibility of theory, which is a creation peculiar to the Occident. The significance of this is more than historical; it also extends into the future. Not only does Lohmann take the transition from stem-inflecting to word-inflecting language types to interpret the history of thought in the Occident by showing the development of language forms, he shows that this latter-day development to word-inflecting types makes possible science in the modern sense—science as the rendering disposable to us of our world.

3 I have considered some aspects of this in *Warheit und Methode* [*Truth and Method*, 2d rev. ed., trans. Joel Weinsheimer and Donald G. Marshall (New York: Continuum, 1989)] but they can be greatly expanded; see, for instance, the extensive supplements and corrections contributed by Klaus Dockhorn to the Göttingen *Gelehrten-Anzeigen*, 218, nos. 3–4 (1966), 169–206.

4 Jürgen Habermas, ["Zur Logik der Sozialwissenschaften"], *Philosophische Rundschau* (hereafter *PhR*) 14, no. 5 (1967), 149–80. See also his more recent book, *Knowledge and Human Interests* (Boston: Beacon Press, 1972).

5 Hermann Gundert has done this in his contribution ["Die Simonides—Interpretation in Platons Protagoras"] to *Hermeneia* [(Heidelberg: C. Winter], 1952), a festschrift for Otto Regenbogen.

6 Klaus Dockhorn has shown, with profound scholarship, in *Gelehrten-Anzeigen,* the extent to which the arousing of emotions has been considered the most important means of persuasion from Cicero and Quintilian to the political rhetoric of the eighteenth century in England.

7 I discussed this in my book [*Truth and Method*], and Dockhorn, *Gelehrten-Anzeigen,* has carried out the exploration on a much broader basis.

8 Henri Gouhier in particular has shown this in his "La résistance au vrai," [in *Retorica e Barocco*], ed. E. Castelli (Rome: [Fratelli Boca], 1955).

9 In this regard see the preface to the second edition (1965).

10 Cf. Habermas, *PhR,* 172–74.

11 Ibid., 179.

12 Ibid., 178.

13 Ibid., 177.

14 Ibid., 174.

15 On this point I am agreeing with Lohmann in *Philosophie und Sprachwissenschaft.*

16 Habermas, *PhR,* 179.

17 Ibid., 173–74.

18 Wolfhart Pannenberg, "Hermeneutik und Universalgeschichte," *Zeitschrift für Theologie und Kirche* 60 (1963): 90–121. English translation: Paul J. Achtemeier in *History and Hermeneutic,* ed. Robert W. Funk and Gerhard Ebeling (New York: Harper and Row, 1967), 122–52.

19 See the collection of Lacan's writings now published as *Ecrits* (Paris: Editions du Seuil, 1966).

16

Rhetoric and the Politics of the Literal Sense
in Medieval Literary Theory:
Aquinas, Wyclif, and the Lollards

Rita Copeland

It is well known that late medieval literary theory owes much to Aquinas's reconciliation of human rhetoric with the divine revelation of truth in the text of
Scripture. Aquinas and those theorists who followed his method accomplished this rapprochement by redrawing the boundaries between the literal
and the spiritual senses of Scripture and assimilating rhetorical language to
the literal sense. Aquinas's critical move has been much studied for its impact
on the exegetical theory and practice of the thirteenth and fourteenth centuries, especially for its new emphasis on the contributions of human authors to
Scriptural discourse. But at what cost to rhetoric was this remarkable synthesis
achieved? Medieval attempts to reconcile rhetorical figures and tropes with
the literal sense left many conflicts about the status of rhetoric unresolved. I
would like to consider how the role of rhetoric was reconfigured as theories of
the literal sense evolved from the relatively restricted context of clerical academic theory to the popular polemics of Wycliffite hermeneutics. I suggest
here that scholastic efforts to legitimize the language of human rhetoric by
containing it within the fixed domain of the literal sense represented an impossible solution to what was already an impossible problem. How can rhetorical

language, the inherent nature of which is indirection and ambiguity, have a place in the truthful discourse of Scripture? The internal contradictions of the scholastic synthesis were reopened and brought to the foreground in the dissenting hermeneutics of the Lollards, where the literal sense became a site of political contest. In the second part of this chapter I shall consider how Wycliffite critical theory drives a new wedge between rhetoric and the literal sense by representing rhetoric as a constraint from which the open, literal meaning of the text must be liberated.

The major assumptions of scholastic criticism on figurative language in the Bible emerge out of early medieval thought about figurative discourse. Bede's treatise *De schematibus et tropis* represents a midpoint, both chronologically and theoretically, between antique and high medieval articulations of the relation between scriptural symbolism and rhetorical language—what Bede calls *allegoria in factis* and *allegoria in verbis*.[1] As Armand Strubel shows, Bede advances on Augustine's semiotics by explicitly introducing and considering the place of rhetorical figuration in Scripture.[2] In *De doctrina christiana* 2.10.15, in his discussion of the *signum proprium* and the *signum translatum,* Augustine certainly infers the existence of a level of rhetorical figuration in Scripture, but he does not pursue this question and does not develop a theoretical explanation for a relation between *signa translata* (things that symbolize other things, such as the ox that is understood to stand for the evangelist; see Deut. 25: 4 and 1 Cor. 9: 9), and the indirection or doubleness that characterizes rhetorical tropes. In *De Trinitate* 15.9.15 he seems to deny the trope allegory its rhetorical-linguistic claims, defining it instead as that which is found, not in words but in historical events themselves.[3]

While drawing on Augustinian sign theory, Bede locates his whole discussion of figurative meaning under the aegis of rhetoric. His definition of the trope is consistent with ancient and early medieval rhetorical and grammatical treatments of the term: "Tropus est dictio translata a propria significatione ad non propriam similitudinem ornatus necessitatisve causa" (A trope is an expression which has been transferred from its proper meaning and understood in a sense which it does not have, either from necessity or for sake of ornamentation).[4] In this system, allegory is the master trope, defined also in traditional rhetorical-grammatical terms as that "which means something other than what it says" (quo aliut significatur quam dicitur).[5] But under the influence of Origen and Augustine, Bede introduces a dialectical doubling of the levels of allegorical operation: "Notandum sane quod allegoria aliquando factis, aliquando verbis tantum modo fit" (It is important to observe that allegory is sometimes historical and sometimes purely verbal).[6] According to Bede at this point in his exposition, purely verbal allegory, or *allegoria in verbis,* is distinguished from historical or factual allegory, *allegoria in factis,* on the basis of one important principle: figuration may function at several levels and in several modes in the text of Scripture, but allegory in its purely rhetorical form has no "proper" or "literal" sense of its own. In the example given from Isaiah 11: 1, "There shall come forth a rod out of the root of Jesse, and a flower shall rise up out of his root," the root, rod, and flower may be likened, for the purpose of interpretation, to the house of David, the Virgin, and Christ, but they have no literal and, in this sense, historical meaning, because the enunciation has no necessary referent in reality. The verbal images bear only a contingent poetic (what we can loosely call metaphorical) resemblance to spiritual truths. Unlike *allegoria in factis,* in which a historical fact in Scripture (such as Abraham's two sons) can also point beyond itself in typological fashion to another meaning (in this case to symbolize the Old and New Testaments), *allegoria in verbis* has no facticity of its own but exists purely as a rhetorical figure to point beyond itself.[7] As Calvin Kendall puts it, verbal allegory is not bivalent in the way that factual allegory is because the meanings of verbal allegory are to be found only in the interpretations placed on it.[8] The human imagination constructs a contingent relation of resemblance or similitude between the verbal image and historical-theological realities.

But Bede also seems to lose the force of the distinction he makes between verbal and historical allegory by allowing verbal allegory (and in this sense, rhetorical tropes in general) a place among the various spiritual levels of Scripture. In the next portion of his exposition, where he offers a version of the traditional four senses of scriptural interpretation (historical and typological prefiguration, and the moral and anagogical senses), he permits *allegoria in verbis* to perform the same function as historical allegory by asserting that it can express figuratively the moral and anagogical senses of Scripture. Here he confuses the very issue that he had earlier set out to clarify, for he has inserted human rhetoric (*allegoria in verbis,* with its unidimensional and merely contingent value) into the polyvalency of facts, the multiple theological referents that can only be produced and designated within the sacred economy of salvation.[9] Thus Bede actually makes it difficult to differentiate, along absolute lines, the valences of human rhetoric and of events that have spiritual meanings (what Augustine calls *signa translata,* things used as signs of other things).

One way to describe the ambiguities that arise in Bede's influential account is that he is struggling to establish a rapport or even point of contact between two entirely different terminological and theoretical systems: on the one hand, the classical rhetorical program of tropes and figures and on the other hand, the Alexandrian hermeneutical system of the three or four levels of scriptural meaning and interpretation. He attempts to achieve this rapport by doubling one rhetorical category, the master trope allegory, into the pair *allegoria in verbis* and *allegoria in factis*. Verbal allegory, one half of this new pair, he retains under the category of rhetoric; the other new entity, factual or historical allegory, he transfers over to the Alexandrian hermeneutical system, in which the historical sense gives way allegorically to the tropological and anagogical senses.

But the legacy of Bede's attempt to define the function of rhetoric and reconcile the two systems is some confusion among later exegetes rather than a sense of progress toward clarity. The best-known example of this is the attempt by Peter of Poitiers (fl. 1167–1205), in his *Allegoriae super tabernaculum Moysi*, to accommodate Bede's terminology to contemporary thinking about the importance of the literal sense which was stressed by the Victorine masters Hugh and Andrew. Exegetes continually faced the question of whether they would include metaphor in the historical-literal sense and whether prophecy could refer literally to Christ or should be understood as belonging among the mystical senses of Scripture.[10] Peter distinguishes between two classes of signification. In the first, words signify things, either immediately or indirectly, through metaphor, the equivalent of Bede's *allegoria quae verbis fit*. In the second class, things signify things, which corresponds with *allegoria in factis*. But in discussing this second class, historical symbolism, he returns to Bede's definition of *allegoria in verbis* and the example of the root, rod, and flower as allegories of Jesse's race, the Virgin, and Christ. Here he adds an uncomfortable note: "Quidam tamen dicunt hoc esse historiam per metaphorice transsumpta verba narratam" (others, however, consider this to be a metaphorical representation of history).[11] Peter wants to include this example under historical prophecy, and unlike Bede, he seems to think that the presence of verbal allegory does not by itself bar a text from operating through the primary literal sense. Whereas Bede cannot allow verbal allegory any literal referent, Peter of Poitiers, along with his Victorine predecessors as well as such later figures as Stephen Langton, thinks of prophetic metaphor as part of the literal sense, which is the foundation of the text.[12]

The struggles that we see in Bede and among twelfth-century exegetes to define the place of poetic metaphor and other tropes underscore the problems that the claims of rhetoric posed as soon as there was any attempt to account theoretically for its contribution to the construction of meaning in sacred language. Augustine's influential semiotics in the *De doctrina christiana* skirts the issue. Bede broaches it directly; but his basic assumption that rhetorical figuration chiefly serves an ornamental rather than instrumental function in discourse, that it is a "clothing" and "adornment" rather than the substance of speech, impairs his analysis, for on this assumption he is forced to dissociate rhetorical language from any realm of truth, historical or theological.[13] In *The Friar as Critic*, Judson Allen reviews twelfth-century debates about the literal sense and their implications for thirteenth- and fourteenth-century literary criticism. His explanation of the literal sense, that it "consists of the things to which words refer," summarizes the arguments of theorists like Hugh of St. Victor who seek a way to resolve the problems that arise from Augustine's silence and Bede's ambiguity and to reinstate the referential value of figurative discourse.[14] Hugh intimates this problem when he criticizes those who read only the spiritual sense, for "then the metaphors and similes, which educate us spiritually, would have been included in the Scriptures by the Holy Spirit in vain."[15] Allen proposes that in these contexts involving both sacred texts and secular poetry, the "literal" sense means, in effect, the "literary" sense, the poetic surface, which has an almost integumental exteriority and which constitutes the most reductionist form of meaning.[16] But Allen's explanation, elegant and powerful as it is, does not address the difficulties that arise out of the theoretical desire to locate and confine rhetoric within the literal sense, especially the critical conflicts this produces in late medieval polemic about the role of the literal sense as the purveyor of true meaning.

Aquinas's positive contribution to this long debate consists not in the introduction of new ideas but in the careful attention he gives to achieving some theoretical consistency among many competing ideas. In his discussions in the *Summa theologiae* and the *Quaestiones quodlibetales* 7 he seeks to clarify the difference between metaphor (including the difficult category of prophetic metaphor) and the various spiritual senses of Scripture. He accomplishes this by articulating principles that had been grasped by earlier writers, notably Hugh of St. Victor, but that were not before so precisely expressed.

Aquinas explains the relation between *allegoria in verbis* and *allegoria in factis* by making a strict demarcation between the domain of words, which are instituted by humans, and that of things or events of history, which God alone creates and to which he assigns meaning. Scripture can thus have multiple senses, because words constitute the literal sense, and the things to which words refer can give way to a multiplicity of spiritual senses.

> Manifestatio autem vel expressio alicujus veritatis potest fieri de aliquo rebus et verbis; inquantum scilicet verba significant res, et una res potest esse figuras alterius. Auctor autem rerum non solum potest verba accommodare ad aliquid significandum, sed etiam res potest disponere in figuram alterius: et secundum hoc in sacra Scriptura manifestatur veritas duplicitur. Uno modo secundum quod res significantur per verba: et in hoc consistit sensus litteralis. Alio modo secundum quod res sunt figurae aliarum rerum; et in hoc consistit sensus spiritualis, et sic sacrae Scripturae plures sensus competunt.

[The manifestation or expression of these truths can be accomplished either through words or things; that is to say, words signify things, and one thing can be a figure of another thing. Now the author of all things has the power not only to use words to designate things, but to order things in such a way that they serve as figures of other realities; and in this way sacred Scripture manifests truth in a double fashion. At one level, things are signified through words: and this is what constitutes the literal sense. At the second level, things serve as figures of other things; and this constitutes the spiritual sense. And so sacred Scripture can produce multiple senses.][17]

This effectively clears away the ambiguity of Bede's formulation, for the valences of words are entirely distinguished from the valences of facts. Words themselves cannot supply the spiritual senses of Scripture: only the facts, the historical events ordained by God and "subject to his providence" are endowed with spiritual and mystical significances beyond themselves.[18] Moreover—and this is Aquinas's definitive answer to the difficulties encountered by earlier generations of exegetes—there are really only two senses of Scripture, the literal and the spiritual (the spiritual can be multiplied according to the Alexandrian divisions of moral, allegorical, and anagogical). The distinctions are clear: the words of Scripture pertain, always and entirely, to the literal sense. There is no slippage, such as Bede allows, of *allegoria in factis* into the domain of linguistic phenomena: "Manifestatio autem quae est per verba, facit sensum historicum sive litteralem; unde totum id ad sensum litteralem pertinet quod ex ipsa verborum significatione recte accipitur" (The manifestation [of truth in Scripture] that is accomplished through words produces the historical or literal sense; thus all that is properly understood from the signification of words pertains to the literal sense; *Quaestiones quodlibetales* 7.16.15). Words point to things literally, and those things—events, objects, and facts—are ordained to yield up higher truths. This recalls Hugh of St. Victor's effort, especially in the *Didascalicon,* to save the literal sense.[19] As Aquinas puts it, everything is grounded in the literal sense, which is the necessary vehicle of our perception of things and their higher meanings: "Illa vero significatio qua res significatae per voces, iterum res alias significant, dicitur sensus spiritualis, qui super litteralem fundatur, et eum supponit" (That meaning, however, whereby the things signified by the words in their turn also signify other things, is called the spiritual sense; it is based on and presupposes the literal sense).[20]

But there is a further dimension to this reasoning: words pertain only to the literal sense, and all that is comprised in linguistic use is part of the literal sense. Thus even rhetorical figures—metaphor, fictive similitude, and parable or rhetorical allegory—as linguistic phenomena are assimilated to the literal sense: "Significare autem aliquid per verba vel per similitudines fictas ad significandum tantum ordinatas, non facit nisi sensum litteralem" (Signifying something through words or through fictive similitudes whose purpose is to signify something, produces nothing but the literal sense; *Quaestiones quodlibetales* 7.6.16). This of course provides an important solution to Bede's inference that rhetorical allegory, *allegoria in verbis,* has no literal application, a position that later exegetes found difficult to accept, especially in the case of prophetic metaphor. Aquinas reverses Bede on this: Aquinas's view is that *allegoria in verbis* is a linguistic phenomenon and thus must have a literal reference. The *Summa* offers a supplemental explanation of this: "Sensus parabolicus sub litterali continetur, nam per voces significatur aliquid proprie et aliquid figurative. Nec est litteralis sensus ipsa figura, sed id quod est figuratum" (The parabolical sense is contained in the literal sense, for words can signify something properly and something figuratively; in the last case the literal sense is not the figure of speech itself, but the *object it figures* [emphasis mine]; *Summa theologiae* 1.1.10 ad 3).

Thus in a metaphorical expression the immediate sense is not the figure itself, but what the figure represents.[21] As Umberto Eco puts it, "Parabolic sense . . . is the meaning of a verbal or pictorial image which is so appropriate and so well proportioned to its sense that it proclaims itself to be at one with it."[22] Aquinas's example is that when Scripture speaks of God's "arm," the literal sense of this figure of speech is not that God has a physical limb but that God has the power that is typically ascribed to an arm, that of doing and making (*Summa theologiae* 1.1.10 ad 3).

It is this argument and its consequences, the assimilation of rhetorical figuration to the literal sense, that raises profound and, I think, irresolvable problems for the status of rhetoric in Aquinas's system. Aquinas offers a clear picture of the function of rhetorical figuration in the domain of the literal sense: rhetoric is reduced to a system of signs the only purpose of which is to yield up meaning: "Fictiones poeticae non sunt ad aliud ordinatae nisi ad significandum; unde talis significatio non supergreditur modum litteralis sensus" (Poetic fictions have no purpose except to signify; and such signification does not go beyond the literal sense; *Quaestiones quodlibetales* 7.6.16). On this view we must enlarge our definition of the literal sense: by the literal sense Aquinas understood every signification that has its immediate origin in words or poetic fictions of which the only raison d'être is to serve as signs.[23]

This is a purely mechanical view of rhetorical language. It is strikingly close to Goethe's view of allegory as a rhetorical convention, in counterdistinction to the symbol, which represents the premier expression of romanticism's organic aesthetic. For Goethe, allegory (as the master trope of rhetoric) works by signifying directly; its only purpose, as Tsetvan Todorov puts it, is "to transmit a meaning." It offers "an instantaneous passage through the signifying face of the sign toward knowledge of what is signified."[24] According to Goethe, "There are . . . works of art that sparkle by virtue of reason, wit, gallantry, and we include in this category all allegorical works as well; of these latter we expect the least, because they destroy our interest in representation itself, and shove the spirit back upon itself, so to speak, and remove from its field of vision all that is truly represented. The allegorical differs from the symbolic in that what the latter designates indirectly, the former designates directly."[25]

Unlike the symbol, which Goethe describes as exceeding and defying any rational attempt to articulate and exhaust its organic potential for creating meanings, allegory as a rhetorical trope is finite in its meanings and reducible to a simple code to which we need only the interpretive key: "In [allegory] there is more of accident and caprice, inasmuch as the meaning of the sign must be first communicated to us before we know what it is to signify; what idea, for instance, is attached to the green colour, which has been appropriated to hope?"[26] We see this principle in Aquinas's understanding of rhetorical figuration or the parabolic sense. Scriptural parable, including prophetic metaphor, is an established and conventional code, a system of poetic usages that can be unlocked by any trained reader. Thus the goat of Daniel 8 can be understood immediately as a poetic similitude standing for Christ; it is part of a stock of poetic conventions that can be decoded once we know what significance to attach to them.[27] For Aquinas, as for Goethe nearly five hundred years later, rhetoric is reducible to a purely mechanical and conventional function. We should not decontextualize the positions of these two important theorists, as if their similarities with one another were a mere coincidence or curiosity; on the contrary, the scholastic theologian and the romantic aesthetician represent points on a historical continuum of rhetoric's gradual but perceptible debasement to a merely conventional and arbitrary function—the dynamics of which were set in motion in the early Christian era and various expressions of which are to be found up through the early modern period.[28] But my interest in this comparison is more specific, for I use it to point up an important difference between the two that returns us to the particular problematic of Aquinas's system. Whereas for Goethe the instrumentalizing of rhetoric serves as grounds for a virtual rejection of it as too mechanical an operation, for Aquinas the instrumentalization of rhetoric represents the only way of saving and preserving it. Aquinas's assimilation of rhetorical figuration to the literal sense is a way of ensuring a legitimate place for rhetoric by containing its threat of proliferating and unstable reference.

In his classic essay "The Resistance to Theory," Paul de Man argues that the contested status of literary theory in the modern academy, what he calls the resistance to theory, is "a resistance to the use of language about language," a resistance, in effect, to reading rhetorically.[29] As a rhetorical inquiry, theory is concerned not with the meaning or the value of texts but with "the modalities of production and of reception of meaning" (7); it is more interested in "language as a system of signs and of signification . . . than as an established pattern of meanings" (9). De Man argues that literary theory in the modern academy has the same contested role that rhetoric had in the late classical and medieval trivium. The trivium as a whole constitutes one of the most traditional and general linguistic models, for each of its sciences—grammar, rhetoric, and dialectic—deals with the operations of language from different epistemological perspectives (13–15) . What de Man brilliantly articulates here is the historically uncertain status of rhetoric as a scientific language that deals with the unfixing of linguistic reference: rhetoric deals with devices of persuasion, the most visible and characteristic of which are tropes and figures, which operate by "turning" or "transferring" words from their proper significance. The threat that rhetoric always poses is to unfix the stable referentiality that the other trivium sciences, grammar and dialectic, promise. Its relation with grammar, with which it shares the study of figures of speech, is particularly strained, for where grammar offers a prescriptive and determinate knowledge of linguistic codes, rhetoric's interest in the tropological dimension of speech undoes or destabilizes grammar's claim to making language a transparent medium (15–17).

De Man's articulation of the kind of threat rhetoric poses to ideal claims of fixed referentiality can help us discover what is at stake in Aquinas's placement of rhetorical language within the strictly delimited realm of the literal sense. It illuminates the conflict between the determinacy of grammatical knowledge and the slipperiness of rhetorical usage. For Aquinas, to locate rhetorical figures and tropes in the literal sense is effectively to incorporate rhetoric within the secure boundaries of grammar because grammar, or grammatical exposition, is associated with the literal sense, the letter and the surface meaning, as we find in Hugh of St. Victor's *Didascalicon* (book 6, chap. 8). The purpose of Aquinas's move is to save rhetoric as a component of scriptural discourse by taming it, confining it within the fixed boundaries of literal, grammatical exposition. The power of rhetorical doubleness, its inherent capacity to turn language away from its proper signification, can be contained if it is incorporated into the literal sense, which is, by definition, always manageable and open. If rhetorical language can be identified with the literal sense, its meaning should become plain. In this way, rhetoric is returned to the ordered control of a stable, authoritarian system of exposition.

It is necessary for Aquinas to preserve rhetorical figuration and validate its place in scriptural discourse. Earlier exegetes like Bede had of course demon-strated the presence of figures and tropes in Scripture; but for Aquinas's theo-logical system as a whole it is also important to offer a substantive explanation as to why Scripture uses rhetorical language. At the beginning of the *Summa theologiae* he takes up the question of whether Scripture uses metaphors, si-militudes, and other forms of poetic representation, explaining and validating their place in Scripture according to the terms of the larger Aristotelian princi-ples of sensory cognition that inform his doctrine. Human knowledge begins in corporeal sense, and poetic metaphors constitute sensory modes of repre-sentation that give us access to the higher "world of intelligence through the world of sense" (1.1.9, responsio). But while the presence of rhetorical figures in Scripture may be justified on these grounds, it is still necessary to explain how they work in sacred writing and to address the difficulties that had chal-lenged earlier exegetes about how tropes are to be understood in Scripture. It is important here to note that Aquinas admits the opaque nature of rhetorical language. In describing metaphorical usage he invokes a language of bodily disguise, veils, or wrappings, descended from ancient rhetorical and philo-sophical discourse about the integumental character of figures and tropes:

> Conveniens est sacrae Scripturae divina et spiritualia sub similitudine corporalium tradere. . . . Unde convenienter in sacra Scriptura traduntur nobis spiritualia sub metaphoris corporalium; et hoc est quod dicit Dionysius. . . . Impossibile est nobis aliter lucere divinum radium, nisi varietate sacrorum velaminum circumvela-tum. . . . Radius divinae revelationis non destruitur propter figuras sensibiles, qui-bus circumvelatur, ut dicit Dionysius.

> [Holy Scripture fittingly delivers divine and spiritual realities under bodily guises. . . . Congenially, then, holy Scripture delivers spiritual things to us beneath metaphors taken from bodily things. Dionysius agrees, *The divine rays cannot en-lighten us except wrapped up in many sacred veils.* . . . Dionysius teaches in the same place that the beam of divine revelation is not extinguished by the sense im-agery that veils it.] (*Summa theologiae* 1.1.9 responsio-ad 2)

With the acknowledgment of rhetoric's opacity, its ambiguity or double-ness, comes a method of stabilizing it and restricting its multiple valences. To save rhetoric, Aquinas deforms it: he suppresses the basic capacity of meta-phor to mean two things at once. In the example of the arm of God, cited above from 1.1.10 of the *Summa*, Aquinas explains that the literal sense is not the fig-ure but what is figured, so that the literal sense of the metaphor is not that God has an arm but that he has the power of doing and making commonly ascribed to a human arm. On this reading, we move immediately, in a reductive and me-chanical way, to the paraphrasable content of the metaphor. In New Critical terminology we would say that this reading moves immediately to the tenor, leaving the vehicle behind. Of course this makes rhetorical language a transparent passage to meaning. Thus the threat of rhetorical doubleness and unstable ambiguity is dehorned: rhetoric becomes a manageable linguistic system whose only purpose is to yield up meanings, after which its value is spent. The literal sense, as Aquinas tells us, contains nothing false (*Summa theologiae* 1.1.10 ad 3). With the literal sense thus elevated, rhetoric is tamed and redeemed.

An important corollary of these arguments is that the literal sense represents the intention of the author (*Summa theologiae* 1.1.10 responsio). Aquinas's exegetical successors, notably Nicholas of Lyre, also develop this premise.[30] It is necessary on theological and philosophical grounds for Aquinas to assign the literal sense, with its metaphorical significations, to the intention of the human author, for this maintains a strict hierarchical separation between the verbal realm of the human author and the symbolic realm of the divine author.[31] Authorial intention is the link between rhetoric and the literal sense. It is the principle for authenticating the meaning or meanings of the literal sense because it is possible, according to this rule, for the literal sense to have multiple meanings, insofar as the human author understood and intended such a multiplicity (*Summa theologiae* 1.1.10 ad 1; *Quaestiones quodlibetales* 7.6.14 ad 5).[32] Aquinas is careful to establish the validity of the literal sense as the ground of all arguments to be drawn from Scripture, and to this end he uses intention to rule out the possibility of doubleness or ambiguity of meaning; for the things signified by words, according to the intention of the human author, may in turn reveal further significances (*Summa theologiae* 1.1.10 ad 1). It is in the spirit of such a concern to suppress any hint of ambiguity in the literal sense that later exegetes, among them Nicholas of Lyre and Richard Fitzralph, introduce the notion of a double literal sense (*duplex sensus litteralis*), of which one part is a "proper" sense, and the other part a metaphorical one: both kinds of signification represent the author's intention.[33]

But while the theological and exegetical rationales may be coherent, the system strains against the very nature of rhetoric. At its root, rhetoric and its tropological dimension is about the impossibility of there being a manifest, plain truth. The attempt to anchor the verity of the literal sense in the principle of intention is especially telling in the deformation of rhetoric that it involves. Intention is the most flexible and expedient of rhetorical concepts, adaptable and attributable in any circumstances. What we see here is the conflict between the desire to acknowledge the human-produced rhetoricity of Scripture and the need to suppress the doubleness, ambiguity, and referential instability that rhetoric always implies.

This is the contradiction that John Wyclif and his followers expose and challenge. What is often seen as their return to a stern and severe realism is also the basis of their acute recognition of the impossibility of assimilating rhetoric to the openness of the literal sense. Wyclif confronts the real pressures that rhetoric exerts on meaning, and I suggest that he understands far better than Aquinas the force of rhetoric as discursive interference and indirection. It is because he recognizes the destabilizing power of rhetoric that he resists it. He does not open his system to accommodate the claims of rhetoric, nor does he seek to relieve rhetoric of the danger that it bears by trying to make peace between rhetoric and the literal sense. He assesses rhetoric for what it is, and on these grounds rejects it utterly as an element in the language of Scripture. Unlike Aquinas, who wants to save rhetoric by changing its character, Wyclif has no investment in the preservation of rhetoric as a necessary corporeal approach to the *invisibilia* of divine truth; but in denying the role of rhetoric in Scripture he negatively affirms the true nature of rhetoric.

Wyclif's polemics on the nature of scriptural language, as set forth in his treatise *De veritate sacrae scripturae,* are not directed against Aquinas or such Thomistic theorists as Lyre and Fitzralph: the objects of his attack are the "logic choppers" and "geomancers" of the fourteenth-century schools, Nominalist thinkers such as William of Ockham and Robert Holkot. More generally, he is derisive of the quick fashion changes of academic theory.[34] But in terms of the role of rhetoric, Wyclif's position is strongly differentiated from that of Aquinas. Wyclif seeks to reconcile the undeniable presence of figurative language in Scripture with the necessary assumption of Scripture's literal truth. He does so by declaring the language of Scripture to be a singular system, governed by its own particular linguistic logic, which he calls the *vis* (or *virtus*) *sermonis*. Aquinas had also declared Scripture to be unique in having both a literal and a spiritual sense, but on Aquinas's view, human rhetoric still has a place in sacred language. For Wyclif, however, human eloquence, or rhetoric, is outside the domain of Scripture. Nothing that we recognize as figurative or rhetorical in ordinary speech has any claim on the linguistic functions of scriptural eloquence: "Quod ista est vera de virtute sermonis secundum quamlibet eius partem et quod professores scripture sacre debent sequi eam in modo loquendi quoad eloquenciam et logicam plus quam aliquam alienam scripturam gentilium (On account of the *virtus sermonis* Scripture is true in each and all of its parts, and the exponents of sacred Scripture ought to follow its particular mode of speaking, insofar as eloquence and logic are concerned, more than any other worldly writing; 1: 2/7–10).

On these grounds alone can the true meaning of Scripture be said to be contained in the literal sense. If Scripture uses figurative language, those figures are not to be judged "improper" by the standards applied to ordinary rhetoric, for such rhetoric is now outside the parameters of scriptural usage. The literalism of Scripture can only be absolute by virtue of the categorical exclusion of human rhetoric:

> Et hinc ecclesia et sancti doctores post exposicionem sensus scripture concedunt verissime de virtute sermonis, quod Cristus est "agnus, ovis, vitulus, aries, serpens, leo, vermis," sed ad sensum misticum, qui est ut plurimum literalis. nec moveat dictum Augustini capitulo sexto quarti libri De Doctrina cristiana, quo dicitur quod "nec ipsos autores decet alia eloquencia nec alios ipsa." hoc enim est verum ad verba, cum quilibet rethor habet propriam eloquenciam, sed sensus est, quod illa eloquencia non decet alios autentice, sed imitatorie.

> [For this reason the Church and the sacred doctors concede most reasonably, after the exposition of the sense of Scripture, by *virtus sermonis,* that Christ is lamb, egg, calf, ram, serpent, lion, worm, but according to the mystical sense, which is the most literal sense. The dictum of Augustine should stand, where he says in chapter 6, book 4 of *De doctrina christiana,* that "no other eloquence befits these authors, nor this eloquence any other authors." The words of this are true, for any speaker has his own eloquence; but the sense is that this eloquence befits no other authors naturally, but only by imitation; 1: 5/1–11.]

Ordinary eloquence, the medium of "other authors," has no purchase on scriptural discourse, the realm in which "these authors" operate. Just as human rhetoric is inappropriate to God, so divine eloquence is not fitting to human usage. The very question of "proper" as opposed to "improper," as applied to figures of speech, is dialectically doubled here: the "impropriety" of figurative language, in which an attribute that is not "proper" to an entity is linked with it rhetorically through the indirectness of allegory or metaphor, becomes, in Wyclif's system, an inappropriate or "improper" understanding of scriptural language. Scriptural language is always "proper" or literal, and its very nature or "property" is for the literal to be identical with the mystical sense, as governed by the "propriety" of the *vis sermonis.* The *vis sermonis* is to be understood as the authorial intention of scriptural speech, and hence as God's intention as author of Scripture (see *De veritate sacrae scripturae,* 1: 43/17ff.).[35] The distortive effect of rhetoric is now banished from the domain of Scripture, not because Scripture uses no figures but because God uses a language that defies human rules, a language in which the "improper" is always "proper" or literally true by virtue of his intention.[36] On the terms of the *vis sermonis,* figurative usages are both stylistically "fitting" and ontologically "proper." The author of Scripture uses a fitting rhetoric, not the common rhetoric of pagan usage.[37]

Rhetoric is now completely external to the body of Scripture. The necessary and absolute literalism of Scripture cannot accommodate rhetoric in any form, not even a rhetoric, as Aquinas would have it, stabilized and purged of its indirectness. Wyclif does not seek to work any changes on rhetoric: he simply excludes it from the picture. The domain of the literal sense, governed by the *vis sermonis,* is enlarged to occupy and encompass the territory vacated by a now irrelevant, mundane rhetoric. Always immanent in the literal sense is the divine authorial intention, which confers a comprehensive wisdom on the literal so that it can never be mistaken for the false or commonplace. Indeed, any misreading of the literal sense is the result of false intention on the part of the reader, who may use the interpretation of Scripture to advance vain or selfish interests.[38] Here we can see how the mechanism of distortion, indirection, and ambiguity has been relegated to a place outside the text: the capacity for rhetorical equivocation now resides entirely in the bad intentions of certain readers who wilfully and cynically impose indeterminate readings upon the text and purvey such equivocations as authentic (see *De veritate sacrae scripturae* 1: 36/20–22, 111/2–5, 12–19).

In Lollard polemic on scriptural interpretation, we see the radical effects of Wyclif's removal of rhetoric from the literal sense. Lollard theory tries to liberate reading along political lines, first by postulating the integrity and hence translatability of the literal sense and second, by directing attention to the accessibility of meaning itself. A treatise on biblical translation presents a realist case for theorizing meaning as outside the possession of language:

> Sithen that the trouthe of God stondith not in oo langage more than in another, but who so lyueth best and techith best plesith moost God, of what langage that euere it be, therfore the lawe of God writen and taught in Englisch may edifie the commen pepel, as it doith clerkis in Latyn, sithen it is the sustynance to soulis that schulden be saued. And Crist comaundid the gospel to be prechid, for the pepel schulde lerne, kunne it and worche therafter. Whi may we not thanne writ in Englische the gospel and al holy scripture to edificacioun of cristen soulis, as the prechour schewith it truly to the pepel? For, if it schulde not be writen, it schulde not be prechid.[39]

This realist position, that the particulars of language are not constitutive of meaning, is written into Lollard justifications of their linguistic medium. As a tractate on secular rulers puts it, "witte stondis not in langage but in groundynge of treuthe, for tho same witte is in Laten that is in Grew [Greek] or Ebrew, and trouthe schuld be openly knowen to alle manere of folke."[40] In Scripture, the "truth of God" that stands outside the domain of linguistic particulars is the literal sense which the divine author intended.

The opposing argument, that meaning is bound by language, is of course what Archbishop Thomas Arundel employs in the Oxford *Constitutiones* of 1407, where he determines that "it is dangerous, as St Jerome declares, to translate the text of Holy Scripture out of one idiom into another, since it is not easy in translations to preserve the same meaning in all particulars."[41] Arundel's reductive appropriation of Jerome's views on translation makes an opportunistic case for a rhetorical idea of the text, in which the particularity of idiom contains and defines the meaning. As Jerome says, rhetorical figuration presents one of the greatest obstacles to idiomatic translation in general.[42] The orthodox construction of the problem of translation, as represented by Arundel, forces Lollard theory into its most radical, but also most productive, extreme. If the literal sense, which is what the author intended, includes the idiomatic particulars of rhetorical language, then it would be impossible to translate from one language to another without losing the literal sense. Thus the Lollards must theorize rhetoric as not of the literal sense, for otherwise the literal sense—and hence the sacred text as a whole—would be untranslatable. This places the Lollards in the interesting position of affirming classical (especially Ciceronian) views of the discursive power of rhetoric to shape meaning and indeed to distort it. But rather than attempting to accommodate rhetoric by denaturalizing and disempowering it, as scholastic criticism had done, the Lollards refuse rhetoric any place in the language of Scripture. In this they reproduce Wyclif's arguments on the *vis sermonis*. A Lollard sermon dealing with the Eucharist draws its explanation of linguistic signification from *De veritate sacrae scripturae:* "And so yiue we God leue to speke as him likith, al if we speken not ay so bi this same autorite. These wordis that God spekith schulde we algatis graunte, and declare hem to trewe vndirstonding."[43] Where Lollard writing does give attention to the nature of figurative speech in Scripture, as in chapter 12 of the *Prologue* to the Wycliffite Bible, the governing assumption is still this Augustinian dictum of the special character of divine eloquence.[44]

But Wyclif's distinction between the terms of human and divine discourse assumes another dimension in Lollard polemic about vernacular translation. For the Lollards, rhetoric is not simply theoretically incommensurate with the idea of a divine intention that manifests itself in a coherent literal sense. It also represents for them a very real threat of linguistic disempowerment. If rhetorical troping, with all of its idiomatic particularity, is constitutive of the literal sense, it would confine the sacred text within the Latin of the Vulgate. Rhetoric would become a linguistic prison, an insurmountable barrier to the Lollard objective of opening the text to the linguistic accessibility of the vernacular. One of the most important theoretical projects of the Lollards is to challenge the fiction of the immanent and hence universal authority of Latin, the fiction that underwrites the hegemony of the Vulgate. Wyclif's arguments about the *vis sermonis* serve the Lollards' purpose here: truth is constructed outside the terms of human language, and human language is at best a conveyor, never a repository, of truth. Indeed, the stability of meaning cannot depend on particularities of language that would unfix meaning. This is the theoretical claim that entitles diverse languages to a singular truth and that grounds the Lollard project of a vernacular Scripture. For the Lollards, to disempower rhetoric by excluding it from the literal sense is to empower the vernacular as an authoritative linguistic medium. It is no less than a liberation of the literal sense from the false bonds of a particular language, and thereby the liberation of reading itself.

In this context, then, rhetoric becomes a constraint from which both the text and the act of reading must be freed. Lollard theoretical writing creates a nexus of meanings around the idea of openness.[45] "Open" is applied to the scriptural text itself, denoting clarity of meaning and of grammar in the translation. The *Prologue* to the Wycliffite Bible asserts that the best kind of translation is "aftir the sentence and not oneli aftir the wordis, so that the sentence be as opin either openere in English as in Latyn, and go not fer fro the lettre; and if the lettre mai not be suid in the translating, let the sentence euere be hool and open, for the wordis owen to serue to the entent and sentence, and ellis the wordis ben superflue either false."[46] Translating only according to the words risks fragmenting and distorting the "open sentence," which has an innate integrity. On these lines "open" is identified with truthfulness, as in the translator's declaration that "I purposide with Goddis helpe to make the sentence as trewe and open in English as it is in Latyn, either more trewe and more open than it is in Latyn."[47] By extension, the text is also "open" to future translators who may express "the trewe sentence and opin of holi writ," for "where oon seid e derkli, oon either mo seiden openli."[48] In this sense of an unfinished and ongoing collective project, neither one version of the text nor one translator has a monopoly on the open truth of Scripture. Even the Augustinian principle of charity, which is invoked as the rule for reading what is both "hidden" and "open" in Scripture, constitutes an exegetical economy of openness, for "he that hooldith charite in vertues, either in goode condiscouns, hooldith bothe that that is opyn and that that is hid in goddis wordis."[49] Charity is both of the text and metatextual, common to all readers but possessed by no one reader. This metaphysic of openness is thus linked to the idea of an open text as a communal and collective social practice that admits a multiplicity of languages and readers. By this logic, "open" also takes on its political inflection of public rights and common accessibility. Implicit in the idea of openness is antielitism, as in the *Prologue* writer's endorsement of Nicholas of Lyre's *Postilla:* "Heere Lire rehersith the sentence of seint Austyn, and of Isidre in these

reulis, and declarith hem opinly by holy scripture and resoun, and countrith
not Austin, but declareth him ful mychel to symple mennis witt."[50] "Simple
men's wit" becomes the abiding standard, the "open" measure, for who should
be allowed to read Scripture.

The literal sense is the site of openness in every sense, grammatical, hermeneutical, and political. The text itself is open in the sense that it is not "possessed" from within by the conflicting and potentially disruptive force of rhetoric. An open text does not require elaborate clerical mediation and
explanation. Conversely, the "closing" of the text is something that is done to it
against its nature. The idea of "closed" also has both a hermeneutical and political inflection. As the *Prologue* declares, the Bible is withheld and monopo-
lized by "covetous clerks" fearful of losing the textual privilege of their class:
"For though couetouse clerkis ben woode by simonie, eresie, and manye oth-
ere synnes, and dispisen and stoppen holi writ, as myche as thei moun, yit the
lewid puple crieth aftir holi writ, to kunne it, and kepe it, with greet cost and
peril of here lif."[51] Such covetous possession of Scripture also takes the form of
hermeneutical dominion and obstruction: clerks "prechen sumwhat of the
gospel, and gloson it as hem liketh."[52] Most important, the wilful closing or
mystification of the text through false exegesis is represented in terms of rhetorical obfuscation: according to the English version of the *Vae octuplex* sermon, "summe prechen fablis and summe veyne storyes, somme dockon hooly
wryt and somme feynon lesyngus; and so lore of Godis lawe is al put obac."[53]
This veiling of meaning through ambiguity or indirection ("fables," "vain stories," "lies") is a distortion imposed from outside the text, almost like an integ-
ument externally manufactured by false intentions and laid over the true literal sense. A Lollard tract known as "The holi prophet David saith" attacks the
elaborate systems of exposition associated with the friars in terms that clearly
mark a distinction between literal truth and external mechanisms of rhetorical
"colours": "Thei takyn the nakid vndirstondynge bi presumcion of mannes
witt, and bryngen forgt pride veynglorie and boost, to coloure here synnes and
desceiue sutilli here negebours."[54] The false readers of Scripture seek to color
or veil their own sins with subtle deception; but there is also an echo here of
the false work of rhetorical figuration which colors the naked or literal text
with subtle ambiguities (the *colores* of rhetoric). Rhetoric is now outside the
text: rhetoric hides the open (naked) text, and it is the tool of unscrupulous
readers. The naked text has its own internal coherence, and rhetoric is something that is belatedly done to Scripture. Thus, for the Lollards, the linking of
intention to rhetoric is a sign of false hermeneutical intention. The divine author of Scripture does not intend rhetorical ambiguity.

Lollard polemic succeeds so well in externalizing rhetoric from Scripture, banishing it to a secondary domain of false intention outside the true text, that the paradigm can be taken up by Lollard adversaries, who in their turn characterize the literal exposition of the Lollards as a false rhetoric imposed on the text. What the Lollard opponents object to is the supposed Lollard preference for literal over mystical exposition (an inaccurate charge, as a glance at any Lollard biblical exposition shows). But in the polemical discourse of orthodox prosecutors, literalism occupies the same structural position as rhetorical indirection does in Lollard polemic. In 1395 John Croft, a Herefordshire squire, had to take an oath foreswearing any contact with the Lollard heresy, including "English books extracted wickedly (*sinistre*) from sacred Scripture according to the naked text (*nudum textum*) by those commonly known as Lollards," who "try not only to beguile our simplicity, but even more, cause perverse people to deviate stubbornly from the sound and true understanding of sacred Scripture and revealed truth and the orthodox faith."[55] We see how the naked text itself has become somehow the false coloring belatedly imposed on scriptural truth, the vehicle of perverse hermeneutical intention. In the heresy proceedings against William Swynderby, who was brought before John Trefnant, bishop of Hereford, in 1390, the Lollards are condemned for expounding sacred Scripture to the people "ad litteram more moderno aliter quam spiritus sanctus flagitat, ubi vocabula a propriis significacionibus peregrinantur et novas divinari videntur, ubi non sunt iudicanda verba ex sensu quem faciunt sed ex sensu ex quo fiunt" (according to the letter in the new way, otherwise than as the Holy Spirit commands, where the words stray from their proper signification and seem to be newly divined, where the words are judged, not from the sense that they make but from the sense from which they are made).[56] Here the language of censure directed against literal exposition exactly mirrors Lollard condemnation of rhetorical distortion, the vain fables that estrange words from their proper meaning. It hardly matters that rhetoric means an entirely different thing to each camp, that the Lollards see it as an obstruction of the literal sense and that their adversaries see it as an obstructive and perverse literalism. For both, rhetoric is perceived to be outside the text, where it becomes the attribute of the enemies of scriptural truth, the appeal used by false and wayward intentions.

If rhetoric is always a destabilizing force, it can never be comfortable in its relation with the literal sense. In the critical debates I have traced here, from the scholastic attempt at a synthesis to the Wycliffite confutation of any such accord, the status of rhetoric undergoes radical change: from something to be contained and delimited, its role in scholastic theory, to something that contains or imprisons and must be resisted, its avatar in Wycliffite polemic. Moreover, once rhetoric is divorced from the literal sense, it no longer needs to be justified by any linkage with authorial intention; in this dissociated state, it acquires a new value, linked now with false and belated hermeneutical intention. At the root of this is the idea that medieval criticism distrusts rhetoric for its power to undo the truth claims of any discourse, and theories of the literal sense must either denature or demonize rhetoric in order to maintain their claims to coherence. To read this phase of medieval critical theory from the perspective of rhetoric's fortunes is to read a history of unresolved and contradictory relations. But there is one powerful conclusion that can be drawn from this history of rich contradiction: rhetoric is precisely what is political about the literal sense. If the literal sense is always the site of contest over control of the text, rhetoric is the means of that control; and it is the regulation of rhetoric, whether through accommodation or resistance, that determines what is literal about the literal sense.

NOTES

1 See Armand Strubel, "'Allegoria in factis' et 'allegoria in verbis,'" *Poétique* 23 (1975): 342–57.

2 Although Bede's *De schematibus* has been classified as both a rhetorical and a grammatical treatise, his concern is with a body of figures traditionally associated with rhetoric. By late antiquity, however, the figures of speech could be treated under grammar, as in Donatus's *Barbarismus*, or under rhetoric, as in Martianus Capella's *De nuptiis Mercurii et Philologiae* 5, or under both, as in Isidore's *Etymologiae* 1–2. See the discussions about classifying Bede's treatise in Martin Irvine, "Bede the Grammarian and the Scope of Grammatical Studies in Eighth-Century Northumbria," *Anglo-Saxon England* 15 (1986): 36, and James J. Murphy, *Rhetoric in the Middle Ages* (Berkeley: University of California Press, 1974), 77. See also the excellent study of Bede's indebtedness to late-classical rhetoric by Roger Ray, "Bede and Cicero," *Anglo-Saxon England* 16 (1987): 1–15. Ray suggests that Bede may have known Cicero's *De inventione*.

3 "Sed ubi allegoriam nominauit apostolus non in uerbis eam reperit sed in facto cum ex duobus filiis Abrahae, uno de ancilla, altero de libera, quod non dictum sed etiam factum fuit duo testamenta intellegenda monstrauit," *De Trinitate* (15.9.5), ed. W. J. Mountain, *Corpus Christianorum Series Latina* 50 (Turnhout, Belgium: Brepols, 1968).

4 Text and translation from Calvin Kendall, ed. and trans., *Libri II De arte Metrica et De schematibus et tropis; The Art of Poetry and Rhetoric,* Bibliotheca Germanica, ser. nova, vol. 2 (Saarbrücken: AQ-Verlag, 1991), 168, 169. Cf. Isidore, *Etymologiae* 1.37.1; *Ad Herennium* 4.31.42; Quintilian, *Institutio oratoria* 8.6.1.

5 Kendall, *Libri II De arte Metrica et De schematibus et tropis,* 192, 199; and see Kendall's introduction, 24.

6 Kendall, ibid., 196, 201.

7 See Strubel, "'Allegoria in factis' et 'allegoria in verbis,'" 351; and Johan Chydenius, "La théorie du symbolisme médiéval," *Poétique* 23 (1975): 329. Irvine's account of this problem assumes a greater similarity between Bede and Augustine's *De doctrina christiana* than does Strubel's; see "Bede the Grammarian," 37.

8 Kendall, introduction, *Libri II De arte Metrica et De schematibus et tropis*, 27.

9 Strubel, " 'Allegoria in factis' et 'allegoria in verbis,'" 352: "Bède reprend ici, à l'intérieur des distinctions qu'elle fait naître, l'opposition *allegoria in factis* et *in verbis*. Or l'étagement des sens n'est possible qu'à l'intérieur de *l'allegoria in factis*. Si on y introduit *l'allegoria in verbis*, comme le fait Bède, on la place du côté du sens spirituel."

10 Beryl Smalley, *The Study of the Bible in the Middle Ages* (Oxford: Oxford University Press, 1952: reprint Notre Dame, Ind.: University of Notre Dame Press, 1978), 232; on Hugh and Andrew of St. Victor, see 83–263.

11 Peter of Poitiers, in P. S. Moore and J. A. Corbett, eds., *Allegoriae super tabernaculum Moysi* (Notre Dame, Ind.: Notre Dame University Press, 1938), 100–102. See also the editors' discussion of this crux in their introduction, pp. xix–xxiii, where they find the distinction between allegory and history recounted metaphorically to be ambiguous. See also Smalley, *Study of the Bible*, 232; and Chydenius, "La théorie du symbolisme médiéval," 329–30.

12 See Smalley, *Study of the Bible*, 233–34; and Beryl Smalley, "Stephen Langton and the Four Senses of Scripture," *Speculum* 6 (1931): 60–76.

13 "Quod grammatici Grece 'schema' vocant, nos habitum vel formam vel figuram recte nominamus, quia per hoc quodam modo vestitur et ornatur oratio" (Scholars call an artificial arrangement of words a schema in Greek; speakers of Latin properly call such an arrangement a 'habit,' or an 'adornment,' or a 'figure,' because in this way language is so to speak clothed and adorned), Kendall, *Libri II De arte Metrica et De schematibus et tropis*, 168, 169. On the debasement of rhetoric to a merely ornamental function, see the account of the crisis of oratory that led to the Second Sophistic and rhetoric's later decline in Tzvetan Todorov, *Theories of the Symbol*, trans. Catherine Porter (Ithaca: Cornell University Press, 1982), 60–83.

14 Judson Boyce Allen, *The Friar as Critic* (Nashville, Tenn.: Vanderbilt University Press, 1971), 11.

15 Hugh of St. Victor, *De scripturis* 5.13, P.L. 175. Translation quoted from Smalley, *Study of the Bible*, 93–94.

16 Allen, *Friar as Critic*, 26–27.

17 Aquinas, *Quaestiones quodlibetales* 7.6.14. Text from the Parma edition, vol. 9 (Parma: Fiaccadori, 1859; reprint New York: Musurgia, 1949), my translation. Further references will be to this edition and will be cited parenthetically in the text. On this passage see P. Synave, "La doctrine de Saint Thomas d'Aquin sur le sens littéral des Ecritures," *Revue biblique* 25 (1926): 41. Compare also *Summa theologiae* 1.1.10 responsio.

18 "Sicut enim homo potest adhibere ad aliquid significandum aliquas voces vel aliquas similtudines fictas, ita Deus adhibet ad significationem aliquorum ipsum cur-

sum rerum suae providentiae subjectarum," Aquinas, *Quaestiones quodlibetales* 7.6.16. See Mark D. Jordan, *Ordering Wisdom: The Hierarchy of Philosophical Discourses in Aquinas* (Notre Dame, Ind.: Notre Dame University Press, 1986), 29–30.

19 Hugh of St. Victor, *Didascalicon,* ed C. H. Buttimer (Washington, D.C.: Catholic University of America Press, 1939), book 6, chaps. 1–4.

20 Aquinas, *Summa theologiae* 1.1.10. Text from Parma edition (Parma: Fiaccadori, 1852; reprint New York: Musurgia, 1948), vol. 1; translation from Blackfriars edition, ed. and trans. Thomas Gilby (New York: McGraw-Hill; London: Eyre and Spottiswode, 1964), vol. 1. All further citations from these editions will be noted parenthetically in the text.

21 See Albert Blanche, "Le sens littéral des Ecritures d'après Saint Thomas d'Aquin," *Revue Thomiste* 14 (1906): 194; cf. Strubel, "'Allegoria in factis' et 'Allegoria in verbis,'" 355.

22 Umberto Eco, *The Aesthetics of Thomas Aquinas,* trans. Hugh Bredin (Cambridge: Harvard University Press, 1988), 153.

23 Blanche, "Le sens littéral des Ecritures," 194.

24 Todorov, *Theories of the Symbol,* 201.

25 J. G. von Goethe, "On the Objects of the Plastic Arts," quoted in Todorov, *Theories of the Symbol,* 199.

26 J. G. von Goethe, *Theory of Colours,* quoted in Todorov, *Theories of the Symbol,* 202.

27 Aquinas, *Quaestiones quodlibetales* 7.6.15 ad 1; see Eco, *Aesthetics of Thomas Aquinas,* 154; cf. Strubel, "'Allegoria in factis' et 'Allegoria in verbis,'" 355.

28 In addition to the classic study by Todorov, *Theories of the Symbol,* see also the essay by Gérard Genette, "Rhetoric Restrained," in Genette, *Figures of Literary Discourse,* trans. Alan Sheridan (New York: Columbia University Press, 1982), 103–26; and C. Jan Swearingen, *Rhetoric and Irony* (New York: Oxford University Press, 1991).

29 Paul de Man, "The Resistance to Theory," *Yale French Studies* 63 (1982): 13. Further references will be cited parenthetically in text.

30 See A. J. Minnis, "'Authorial Intention' and 'Literal Sense' in the Exegetical Theories of Richard Fitzralph and John Wyclif," *Proceedings of the Royal Irish Academy* 75 (1975): 1–31.

31 See Jordan, *Ordering Wisdom,* 30.

32 See Synave, "La doctrine de Saint Thomas d'Aquin," 58–59. On the further implications of this principle of intention, see C. Spicq, *Esquisse d'une histoire de l'exégèse latine au moyen âge,* Bibliothèque Thomiste 26 (Paris: Vrin, 1944), 251.

33 Minnis, "'Authorial Intention' and 'Literal Sense,'" 4–10; A. J. Minnis and A. B. Scott, eds., with the assistance of David Wallace, *Medieval Literary Theory and Criticism c. 1100–c. 1375: The Commentary Tradition* (Oxford: Oxford University Press, 1988), 205–6; G. R. Evans, *The Language and Logic of the Bible: The Road to Reformation* (Cambridge: Cambridge University Press, 1985), 43–47.

34 Minnis, "'Authorial Intention' and 'Literal Sense,'" 13–17; on "geomancers" and the "modern generation," see John Wyclif, *De veritate sacrae scripturae,* ed. Rudolf Buddensieg (London: Wyclif Society, 1905), 1: 114/20–25; on the modishness of Oxford debate, see 1: 54/6ff. For an overview of Wyclif's scriptural theories, see Michael Hurley, "'Scriptura sola': Wyclif and His Critics," *Traditio* 16 (1960): 275–352, esp. 293–98.

35 G. R. Evans, "Wyclif on Literal and Metaphorical," in Anne Hudson and Michael Wilks, eds., *From Ockham to Wyclif, Studies in Church History,* Subsidia 5 (Oxford: Oxford University Press, 1987), 259–66, esp. 263–65.

36 Evans, "Wyclif on Literal and Metaphorical," 263; David Lyle Jeffrey, "Chaucer and Wyclif: Biblical Hermeneutic and Literary Theory in the XIVth Century," in Jeffrey, ed., *Chaucer and Scriptural Tradition* (Ottawa: University of Ottawa Press, 1984), 109–40, esp. 115–23.

37 See Gustav Adolf Benrath, *Wyclifs Bibelkommentar,* Arbeiten zur Kirchengeschichte 36 (Berlin: De Gruyter, 1966), 64.

38 Jeffrey, "Chaucer and Wyclif," 122; see the text of Wyclif's *postilla* on Luke 9 printed in Benrath, *Wyclifs Bibelkommentar,* 364.

39 Treatise on biblical translation, in Anne Hudson, ed., *Selections from English Wycliffite Writings* (Cambridge: Cambridge University Press, 1978), 107 (hereafter cited as *SEWW*). Here and throughout, "th" is substituted for the letter "thorn" and "gh" and "y" are substituted for the letter "yogh," as appropriate.

40 Tractate on secular rulers, in Hudson, ed., *SEWW,* 127.

41 *Constitutiones,* text in D. Wilkins, ed., *Concilia Magnae Britanniae et Hiberniae* (London, 1737), 3: 317; translation quoted from Herbert B. Workman, *John Wyclif: A Study of the English Medieval Church* (Oxford: Clarendon Press, 1926), 2: 194.

42 See Jerome's preface to his translation of Eusebius's *Chronicle* in J. K. Fotheringham, ed., *Eusibii Pamphili chronici canones latini* (London: Milford, 1923), 1/12a–25b. For Jerome's views on biblical translation, see Epistle 57 to Pammachius in I. Hilberg, ed., *S. Eusebii Hieronymi opera, epistularum pars I,* Corpus Scriptorum Ecclesiasticorum Latinorum 54 (Vienna: Tempsky, 1910), 508–10. Interestingly, Jerome says that the Bible demands close literal translation rather than idiomatic rendering.

43 Sermon on the Eucharist, in Hudson, ed., *SEWW,* 114 and notes, 194; cf. Wyclif, *De veritate sacrae scripturae* 1: 5/10–11.

44 See Josiah Forshall and Frederic Madden, eds., *The Holy Bible, Made from the Latin Vulgate by John Wycliffe and His Followers* (Oxford: Oxford University Press, 1850), 43–48.

45 I owe the idea of considering the multiple connotations of the word *open* to Ralph Hanna, "The Difficulty of Ricardian Prose Translation: The Case of the Lollards," *Modern Language Quarterly* 51 (1990): 319–40.

46 *Prologue, The Holy Bible,* chap. 15; Forshall and Madden, eds., *The Holy Bible,* 57. Cf. the discussion immediately following on making the "sentence open" through grammatical equivalences between Latin and English.

47 Ibid.

48 Ibid., 57, 59.

49 Ibid., 46. Cf. the invocation in the *Prologue* of the traditional scholastic principle that the literal sense is the foundation and standard of all meaning in Scripture: "And worschipfully and heelfully the Holy Goost mesuride so holy scripturis, that in opyn placis he settide remedie to oure hungir, and in derk placis he wipte awey anoies; for almest no thing is seyn in tho derknessis, which thing is not founden seid ful pleynly in other placis" (ibid., 50).

50 Ibid., 55.

51 Ibid., 57. On the question of "covetous clerks" and closed access to books, see Richard H. Rouse and Mary A. Rouse, "The Franciscans and Books: Lollard Accusations and the Franciscan Response," in Hudson and Wilks, eds., *From Ockham to Wyclif,* 369–84.

52 Treatise on biblical translation, in Hudson, ed., *SEWW,* 107.

53 *Vae octuplex* sermon, in Pamela Gradon, ed., *English Wycliffite Sermons,* vol. 2 (Oxford: Oxford University Press, 1988), 366–67. Text also in Hudson, ed., *SEWW,* 75.

54 "The holi prophet David saith," in Margaret Deanesly, *The Lollard Bible* (Cambridge: Cambridge University Press, 1920; reprint, 1966), 447.

55 From John Croft renunciation, in W. W. Capes, ed., *Registrum Johannis Trefnant, Episcopi Herefordensis.* Canterbury and York Series 20 (London: Canterbury and York Society, 1916), 148, my translation.

56 From William Swynderby proceedings, in Capes, ed., *Registrum Johannis Trefnant,* 232, my translation. On the place of the *faciunt/fiunt* distinction in other hermeneutical controversies, see Karlfried Froehlich, "'Always to Keep the Literal Sense in Holy Scripture Means to Kill One's Soul': The State of Biblical Hermeneutics at the Beginning of the Fifteenth Century," in Roy Miner, ed., *Literary Uses of Typology from the Late Middle Ages to the Present* (Princeton: Princeton University Press, 1977), 20–48, esp. 35–38. I wish to thank Dr. Kantik Ghosh for information on this point.

17

Reason and Rhetoric
in Habermas's Theory
of Argumentation

William Rehg

The late twentieth century presents an especially hostile environment for comprehensive accounts of reason. Precisely at a time when the dangers of social fragmentation and cross-cultural misunderstanding are becoming increasingly evident, the common bases for social integration and rational conflict adjudication seem to be disappearing in a postmodern, multicultural melee. The pluralization of worldviews and disenchantment with grand narratives, the suspicion of hasty ethnocentric generalization, and even the disciplinary specialization of inquiry itself encourage a general retreat into forms of relativism or narrow empiricism. As a result, it has become increasingly difficult to maintain a link between critical social theory, with its intimations of human emancipation and social reconciliation, and the continued project of an enlightened reason.

The theory of communicative action developed by Jürgen Habermas and others represents one of the better-known responses to this challenge. Rather than abandon the project of enlightenment and resort to irony or *aporia*, Habermas has attempted to provide a communicative conception of rationality that abandons the pretensions of Enlightenment foundationalism without surrendering critical, nonrelativistic standards for social critique.[1] Habermas turns to the analysis of communication and discourse to show how a comprehensive concept of reason can still speak to us. More specifically, he links rationality with the ability of language users to raise and justify validity claims of various sorts, such as claims to truth, to normative rightness, to authenticity, and so forth. The theory of communicative action must therefore prove itself not only as an account of communication but as a theory of argumentation (or discourse) as well.

Can Habermas's theory of argumentation meet the contemporary challenges to a normative account of reason? At least two broad trends characterize many of the attempts to provide a more sophisticated conception of argumentative rationality. On the one hand, there has been a wide recognition that the Enlightenment fixation on formal deductive logic and evidential certitude is too narrow to capture the rationality of argumentation and inquiry.[2] On the other hand, rhetorical aspects of argument have been accorded more importance than the ancillary status that rhetoric often received in earlier approaches.[3] Although Habermas is in step with the first trend, his attitude toward rhetoric appears ambivalent. It thus comes as no surprise that Thomas B. Farrell's critical appropriation of Habermas for rhetorical theory should be considered provocative if not dubious.[4] If, as these trends suggest, a plausible account of reason must take rhetoric seriously, then such reactions indicate a weak spot in Habermas's theory.[5] In the present chapter, then, I would like to redress this weakness by showing how Habermas's theory of argumentation, even while it contains an ideal moment that is strongly universalist and cognitivist, is open to the rhetorical features of argument in a nontrivial sense.

Habermas's theory of argumentation is heavily indebted to Stephen Toulmin's efforts to move philosophy beyond its narrow focus on formal logic.[6] If one is interested in the normative analysis of argumentation as it is employed in the different disciplines (as well as in everyday life), then formal deductive logics are of limited usefulness, for deductive, or "analytical," arguments are simply not informative: the conclusion adds nothing to what was already in the premises. The informative argumentation that guides real inquiry and decision making must rather rely on the "substantial logics" by which arguers draw conclusions that go beyond the available data, strictly speaking. Scientific induction is one of the best-known examples of a substantial logic, but one could easily find examples from other fields, such as law. Without going into details, the important point for our purposes is this: the fact that substantial logics do not adhere to demonstrative canons does not imply a lack of normative standards for good arguments.

But if formal logic does not supply all the criteria, then what does? Toulmin looked to standards specific to the field of inquiry or institution. The difficulty with this strategy is that even if it does manage to avoid an outright relativism, it still leaves one too much at the mercy of historical and institutional accident.[7] Although institutional goals certainly shape argumentation, a social critique of institutions requires further, nondeductive standards of rationality that are immanent to argumentation.

To specify these standards it helps to distinguish different aspects or levels of argumentation. Here Habermas is in line with attempts in argumentation theory to provide a more differentiated set of perspectives on argument. Besides the formal and substantial logics of argument, which generate individual arguments (premises and conclusion) as logical "products," one can also speak of argument as a dialectical procedure or method, as a rhetorical process of communication, and perhaps even as an institutionally organized endeavor to fulfill specific societal functions.[8] Let me first recapitulate Habermas's understanding of the first three levels, which he broadly associated with divisions in the Aristotelian organon.[9]

At the logical level, one is concerned with the construction of "cogent arguments that are convincing in virtue of their intrinsic properties and with which validity claims can be redeemed or rejected."[10] This level primarily has to do with the semantic and syntactic relations between conclusion and supporting evidence and claims. The standards are thus provided by the criteria for sound arguments: noncontradiction and consistency in the application of predicates and expressions are some of the specific criteria Habermas adduces.[11] Presumably these criteria cannot be limited to deductive validity but must also include criteria for good informal and inductive arguments.

At the dialectical level, arguers engage in a "ritualized competition for the better arguments." This is thus a "form of interaction" organized as a "cooperative division of labor between proponents and opponents" who are seeking the truth.[12] As dialecticians, participants must step back from the pressures of action, adopt a hypothetical attitude toward the validity claim at issue, and then "test with reasons, and only with reasons, whether the claim defended by the proponents rightfully stands or not."[13] The standards at this level include "everything necessary for a search for truth organized in the form of a competition." Specifically, Habermas includes rules of relevance and rules for the introduction of claims, as well as the broad requirement that speakers maintain only what they believe.[14] Naturally, as Toulmin suggests, many such rules will vary according to the particular institution, but this does not mean that one should move immediately to an institutional level of analysis. Against Toulmin, Habermas maintains that the theorist should first attend to more abstract differences among types of validity claims.[15] How one dialectically tests a truth claim about the empirical world, for example, should differ, at least in some respects, from how one would test a moral claim or an aesthetic claim. Although institutional contexts will further specify and restrict what counts as the appropriate form of testing, institutions may not arbitrarily ignore different dimensions of validity. Habermas thus insists that the dynamics of a given institution—for example, the legitimacy of legal institutions—are better understood within the broad heuristic framework provided by a theory of communicative action.[16]

At the rhetorical level, finally, Habermas construes argumentation as a process of communication in which arguers seek to gain the assent of a universal audience. To be meaningful for rational dialogue, such assent should be free and uncoerced. Hence the relevant standards of good argumentation at this level are the general pragmatic presuppositions that Habermas had earlier formulated as the "ideal speech situation": "Participants in argumentation have to presuppose in general that the structure of their communication, by virtue of features that can be described in purely formal terms, excludes all force—whether it arises from within the process of reaching understanding itself or influences it from the outside—except the force of the better argument (and thus that it also excludes, on their part, all motives except that of a cooperative search for the truth)."[17]

Besides the exclusion of coercion, these presuppositions also include standards of openness (no competent speaker may be excluded from argumentation, and all participants should have an equal opportunity to contribute arguments, raise questions, and the like).[18] Habermas now recognizes that the metaphor of an ideal speech situation was somewhat unfortunate, for these presuppositions are not meant to describe an empirically realizable situation. Rather, they spell out regulative ideas or "idealizations": if participants in argumentation are to consider a consensual outcome rational, then they must suppose that it is not simply an effect of coercion or hidden compulsions. If it later turns out that this supposition was false, then they have grounds for reopening the discussion.[19]

I shall come back to Habermas's association of these idealizations with rhetoric. For the moment we can summarize Habermas's account as broadly distinguishing the three levels by the kinds of activity and corresponding standards each involves: at the level of logic, the activity is one of linguistic construction; at the level of dialectic, the activity is a kind of competition; and at the level of rhetoric, it is a process of communication. Note that these activities are not separate: in presenting an argument, a participant is simultaneously competing with other disputants and communicating with an audience. The relevant criteria for good argumentation can be distinguished according to these levels of activity. Hence, the standards governing the first level are logical and semantic in character. At the second level, standards presumably arise from the type of issue and validity claim or claims at stake (for instance, criteria of relevance, burdens of proof); one might also point to standards of "responsiveness," as I note later. Finally, at the third level, the standards appear to be oriented largely by ideals of free and equal participation. Here too one can see how levels or aspects of argumentation are interrelated: how one defines the idealized audience at the rhetorical level partly depends on the type of issue and what validity claims are at stake.[20]

Although Habermas's analysis raises a host of questions, here I am primarily concerned with its problematic view of rhetoric. Indeed, one might wonder whether Habermas's account has characterized a rhetorical level at all. After all, the concept of an ideal "universal audience" is precisely what Chaim Perelman linked with deductive logic and evidential certitude;[21] Joseph Wenzel sees such idealizations as part of dialectic and finds it odd that Habermas connects them with rhetoric.[22] Moreover, Habermas's highly idealized understanding of rhetoric would appear at cross purposes with traditional views of rhetoric, which generally focus on the means of effective persuasion for specific occasions and particular audiences. In order to address these difficulties, it is first necessary to elaborate some of the internal relations between the levels of argumentation.

We can gain a somewhat more precise understanding of how the three levels are both distinct and related if we examine how, starting with logic, each requires the next in an account of argumentative cogency.

Logic and Dialectic   If we consider the logical level as having to do with the production of individual arguments (conclusions based on a set of supporting claims), then even logically compelling demonstrations do not automatically compel rational assent in the broader process of argumentation. If you confront me with a valid deduction based on premises I have accepted as true, I may well have to grant that your conclusion follows from the premises—yet I could still dispute your claim. I could maintain, for example, that your deduction neglects further relevant considerations or that the premises, though true as far as they go, lack sufficient precision or nuance. Soundness at the logical level presupposes that questions regarding relevance, required degree of precision, and even the appropriate system of logic have already been settled in a broader argumentative context.

Toulmin's account of argumentation illustrates the importance of such questions insofar as they bear on premises. Indeed, in his initial appropriation of Toulmin, Habermas primarily focused on "substantial" argumentation at the level of those premises that provide the general "warrants" for drawing conclusions from a set of data. Because these warrants usually rest on a broad range of inductive and casuistic evidence (the "backing"), substantial argumentation is cogent not in virtue of demonstrative compellingness but because there is enough backing to make it possible to assent to the conclusion as plausible.[23] Reasonable assent thus presupposes a critical examination of the backing for the conclusion, if necessary to the point of assessing the very categorial framework in which the backing is formulated.[24]

We can thus distinguish the two levels of logic and dialectic as follows: *As a logical endeavor,* I construct an argument for a claim p by appealing to a range of supporting evidence that, when formulated as a set of premises, should allow a valid inference to p. The logical structure of my argument is evident in the consistency of my supporting evidence, the fact that the same conceptual system is used both to describe evidence and formulate the conclusion p, and so forth. But if this argument is to be cogent in argumentation, it must be open to—indeed it must presuppose—a *dialectical testing* in which its support and conceptual assumptions are submitted to further questioning. Cogency, in other words, cannot be fully explicated at the level of logical relations as such: a cogent argument does not stand by itself by virtue of its logical relations to its supporting premises but only in relation to competing arguments and the questions they raise. The inability to achieve argumentative closure at the level of logic forces one to bring in dialectical criteria.

We need not tarry over the problems involved in identifying and distinguishing more specific norms and criteria of logic and dialectic.[25] Of greater concern here is the relation between dialectic and rhetoric. To get at this relation it helps to summarize the central dialectical criteria for cogent argumentation in a simple but versatile standard: an argument is dialectically cogent if its proponents can answer all further relevant questions. This standard is at least broadly compatible with Habermas's description of the dialectical level as a competition for the better argument, and, as we shall see, it further illuminates his analysis of argumentation.[26] Cogency, then, requires not only that an argument be logically consistent but that it also have the capacity to withstand (or absorb) relevant objections and counterarguments. This involves a range of activities: the critical examination of the evidence and supporting premises for a position, the search for further relevant data, and the assessment of objections and competing arguments, to name a few. Thus, good argumentation is not simply logically sound; it is, to use Alvin Goldman's term, "responsive" to as many relevant considerations as possible.[27]

This raises the question of what counts as a relevant question. I can address this only indirectly, by clarifying the intersubjectivity connected with this notion of dialectic. We shall then be in a position to understand the relation between dialectic and rhetoric.

Excursus: Intersubjectivity and Argument   The dialectical process is generally a social, cooperative endeavor (organized as a competition), although it can also occur within the individual who rehearses potential questions and objections in an attempt to arrive at a cogent argument. But is it essentially dialogical in some deeper sense? Rather than become entangled in the controversies surrounding consensus theory, I would like to pose a relatively straightforward question suggested by the foregoing analysis: for a given problem or controverted issue, can the single, competent individual working alone know that all relevant questions have been answered, or is cooperation with others required?

For certain simple problems the answer may well be "yes." I can, as an individual and in my own head, not only certify the evidence and logical operations that lead to an answer but also assure myself that I have answered all the relevant further questions connected with the problem's solution. Naturally, mistakes are possible, and I am advised to have others check my reasoning. But the intersubjective acceptability of the result seems to be grounded in *each individual's competence* to recapitulate the reasoning that leads to the solution. Even though the individual is fallible, and even though the individual owes the categorial framework and skills for solving the problem to a social context, the specific arguments by which a solution is arrived at and certified seem to rest on common but individually held competences. One might say that argumentation in such cases is "monological."

The solution of more complex problems, however, is essentially cooperative, or dialogical. This particularly seems to be the case in science, where the collection of relevant data and certification of the vast supporting evidence and claims require a group effort. One can argue that it holds for moral issues as well, if the solution of moral conflicts must embody a respect for persons as autonomous.[28] In such cases, one can say that intersubjective acceptability is grounded in a cooperative group competence. As an individual reasoner, I cannot in principle guarantee or validate a solution by myself alone. Note that this goes beyond mere fallibility. It involves an essential limitation in the individual's reasoning capacity. It follows that a critical, dialectical testing of a proposition essentially refers to a competent audience of engaged participants in argumentation.

Dialectic and Rhetoric   The intersubjective character of complex argumentation and inquiry has a number of implications. To begin with, intersubjectivity moves the assessment of relevance beyond the individual reasoner. As

we have seen, the general dialectical standard for assessing cogent argumentation is responsiveness, the extent to which a given position is able to answer all
relevant questions, so that the argument either defeats or absorbs all objections and counterarguments. From a monological standpoint, this standard is
internal to the structure of arguments and counterarguments on an issue, for it
provides a way of assessing the relevant conceptual and empirical resources
that can be brought in support of a given claim. But once a dialogical standpoint becomes necessary, the raising and answering of relevant questions becomes a social, cooperative process whose success crucially depends on the capacities and dispositions of the participants (or audience) and on the process
of communication itself.

Second, this intersubjectivity opens the door to process considerations and
thence to rhetoric. As already noted, the need for dialogue is most obvious
with complex issues, where no single participant can survey the whole range of
relevant considerations and vouch for the invulnerability of a given solution or
consensus. This means that, from a participant perspective, responsiveness
cannot be separated from the *intersubjective process of argumentation*. That
is, in considering a solution to be rational, participants must rely in part on process considerations—the openness of their argumentation to competent
speakers from different perspectives, the quality of their participation and
ability to listen to one another's views, and so on. Insofar as the process of argumentation has approximated certain idealizations, participants have more
confidence that the current consensus on an issue reflects the most probable
opinion. Each participant's confidence in a consensus is based not just on an
assurance that his or her own questions have been answered—and not simply
on the fact that no one else has any further questions—but on participatory
conditions that should have allowed everyone's questions to be raised and answered.

In touching on issues of communication, the dialectic of question and answer leads into the area of rhetoric. Thus, Habermas's identification of rhetoric with audience idealizations has some plausibility. However, it leaves us
with a concept of rhetoric that seems little more than the shadow cast by dialectic: such idealizations are hardly the highly contextualized devices that have
been traditionally associated with rhetoric, such as character appeals, emotional arguments, stylistic flourishes, and so on. To be sure, Habermas's account does not rule out the auxiliary use of such devices, so long as they remain
subject to the standards developed above; rhetorical devices may even be required for the effective transmission of good arguments. But they remain extrinsic to rational argumentation as such.

The strength of Habermas's approach lies in the clear critical standards it provides for argumentation. To summarize from the participant perspective: at the logical level, I must consider the position and its arguments to be self-consistent. At a dialectical level, I must judge that the position can be defended by arguments that can either answer or show promise of answering all the relevant questions better than competing positions do. If this judgment is my own, it will largely be predicated on my experience of actual debates, which give me a sense of the arguments for different positions and their relative capacity to answer my questions and meet others' objections. Finally, at a rhetorical level, I must assume that my assent has not been merely the result of internal psychological compulsions or external social pressures. In assessing influential rhetorical devices, I ask whether the rhetoric has played on social or psychological compulsions that are incompatible with my free and equal participation in argument. Related to this, I must assume that I have given counterarguments a fair hearing and that my experience of debates has not been overly narrow or one-sided, so that my views are not based on an ignorance of the better arguments.

These three sets of standards imply, correlatively, three sources for the critique of existing social agreements and disagreements: one could criticize positions for being illogical; for relying on the suppression of relevant considerations; and for issuing from communicatively distorted argumentational processes, in which potential competent participants were excluded or not given a fair hearing, or where serious self-deceptions existed among participants, and so forth. To be sure, one cannot apply these critical standards to real debates without familiarity with the social and institutional contexts of debate and their specific demands. But at the same time, one would be able to approach institutions with a broad set of heuristic criteria for good argumentation. Such criteria provide critical theorists with a certain critical leverage vis-à-vis established institutional conventions, so that they are not simply at the mercy of the institutional status quo.

In accepting such critical standards, however, must we remain so aloof toward a more contextual rhetoric? In fact, just the opposite is suggested by an interesting gap in Habermas's account, a gap that becomes most pronounced when consensus is not achieved. According to Habermas, cogent argumentation does not compel assent in the manner of logical deduction but only makes assent to a claim possible or reasonable. This suggests that, at least in some cases—and particularly in more controverted matters—both assent and dissent may be reasonable options. Both options are so insofar as an open, unconstrained process of discourse has not been able to exclude either option as illogical or clearly inferior in responsiveness. How is it, then, that some participants are *rationally motivated* to accept a claim p and others to reject p, given that everyone has heard the same arguments pro and con? Although both options are reasonable, it is hardly a matter of indifference which side the participants believe—that is, participants in argumentation do not simply feel free to adopt either of the two reasonable options.

The gap, then, lies between the *possibility* of reasonable assent provided by logical and dialectical standards, and *actual* rational motivation. Between such general standards and the participants' actual positions lie the various contextual contingencies that tip the scales in favor of one set of arguments. The question, then, is whether at least some of these contingencies contribute to a rationally motivated position. For example, can participants admit the importance of contextual contingencies associated with their actual hearing of the arguments, the character and rhetorical effectiveness of the particular proponents they encountered? If so, they could assert that logical consistency and dialectical responsiveness in open debate have made it *possible* for them to adopt a given position but that various contingencies traditionally associated with rhetorical effectiveness have led them actually to adopt the position. This opens the door to a normative account of argumentation in which rhetoric plays an intrinsic role.

I now propose a more substantive conception of rhetoric, which would be compatible with Habermas's theory of argumentation. Limitations of space force me to put aside the problems occasioned by his distinction between communicative and strategic action.[29] Furthermore, the unsurveyable smorgasbord of conceptions of rhetoric makes it impossible to consider all the possible links between rhetoric and formal pragmatics.[30] In any case, the cognitive orientation of Habermas's approach—and his difficulties in separating rhetoric and dialectic—recommends a particular range of views for our attention. At one end of the spectrum we find Platonic conceptions, which, if they do not dismiss rhetoric as ornamental at best or deceptive at worst, assimilate it to philosophy and dialectic. Here a strong, objective conception of knowledge leaves little or no room for rhetoric. At the other end are views of rhetoric as an architectonic discipline or ubiquitous enterprise, coextensive with any use of language. Such views are often relativistic, but they need not be. In the spirit of Aristotle, I propose here an intermediate view that acknowledges the intrinsic role of *ethos* and *pathos* in cogent argumentation, without sacrificing the rational standards of logic and dialectic.[31]

To see how such rhetorical devices might constitute an essential aspect of rational motivation, we can begin by recalling the general standard governing dialectical argumentation. What drives the dialectical process of critical testing, of question and answer, is a desire to show that one thesis can answer all the relevant questions better than the opposing thesis can. In most argumentation, however, this is only a regulative ideal. Not only is there no definitive algorithm for determining when the relevant questions have been answered, there are few hard-and-fast criteria for determining which of two positions answers the relevant questions better. In difficult cases, participants disagree over which questions are relevant and what counts as the better answer.

The point is this: an assessment of the support for a claim requires participants to make a judgment in a nontrivial sense. This is the case even when there are no deep theoretical disagreements about standards of relevancy, for participants of different temperaments may form different assessments of how solid the support is for a given claim. As Bernard Lonergan notes, the recognition that all the relevant questions have been answered is not automatic: a competent judge must be neither rash, ignoring further questions, nor indecisive, seeing grounds for doubt where none exist.[32] This problem of judgment becomes even more acute when the standards of relevancy are themselves open to question or when there are competing interpretations of the problem at issue. In such cases, an audience must assess not just two competing sets of arguments but competing interpretations of what argumentation itself should be in a given domain. This seems to be the case, for example, at the point of paradigm shifts in science.[33] In effect, one is asked to make a judgment about what constitutes rationality itself in a given area.

The concept of judgment raises a host of further questions. Proponents of formal pragmatics, dissatisfied with Aristotelian appeals to character and the virtue of prudence, have attempted to provide more formal, argumentation-theoretic analyses.[34] I do not intend that the concept of judgment should replace such analyses. Rather, I am using this concept as a way of supplementing and contextualizing the formal-pragmatic account. The key idea is this: in making a judgment between competing arguments, one takes responsibility for an assessment of competing plausibilities.[35] Employed in this modest way, the concept of judgment allows us to see how certain rhetorical devices contribute to rational argumentation.

If we bring this perspective to the foregoing analysis, we can define argumentation as a process of *cooperative judgment formation*. Properly speaking, rhetorical standards govern the social-psychological context in which this cooperative judgment occurs. Such standards, in other words, spell out the social-psychological conditions of argumentation that foster a responsible judgment on the part of the audience. I use the term *social-psychological* loosely, as a blanket term for those speaker and audience properties that affect the course of argumentation in a particular interpersonal context, as distinct from the immanent properties of arguments themselves. One could interpret the idealized pragmatic presuppositions of argumentation in such terms. Details aside, these presuppositions require that participants be able to consider the full range of arguments, free of psychological and social coercion. It is difficult to see how arguments whose success depends on a manipulation of unconscious compulsions, for example, could be called "cogent" in a normative sense, or how one could consider the hearer's acceptance of such arguments as rationally motivated.

But as regulative ideals, these presuppositions have a largely negative sense, ruling out devices that undermine participant freedom. If argumentation is to issue in judgment, however, then at least two traditional aspects of rhetoric may be positively required in many settings: proofs of the speaker's character (or *ethos*) and appeals to audience emotions (*pathos*).[36] Properly employed, these devices do not circumvent or undermine *logos,* or substantive arguments on the merits, but rather assist in the intersubjective judgment of such arguments. To see this, let us imagine an argument involving two parties, each of whom is on familiar ground, so that each believes its view answers all the relevant questions. One might think, for example, of an argument among doctors and nurses about whether to continue to treat a dying, comatose patient aggressively, on the slim chance of recovery, or whether to scale back treatment. One side may argue that there is hope for recovery (based on the patient's age and statistical evidence on recoveries) and that human life is sacred. The other side could counter with the argument that it is unlikely the patient would wish such treatment and that the resources may be better used elsewhere.[37]

In this case, the parties disagree over the estimation of a number of uncertain facts (chances for recovery, what the patient would wish) and in their moral evaluation (how they rank the moral values of autonomy, life, and social utility). Both sides may well agree about what constitutes the relevant considerations, but they judge the plausibilities differently. Precisely because the problem calls for such a judgment, it is rational for participants to make two kinds of persuasive rhetorical appeals in addition to the arguments themselves.

First, in making a case for one side or the other, participants should show that *as speakers*, that is, as proponents of a position, they are properly disposed to judge the arguments and counterarguments. It becomes more rational for a hearer, particularly an opponent, to take my arguments seriously insofar as my presentation of the arguments gives the hearer evidence of my capacity to judge plausibilities responsibly. This is more or less what Aristotle called a "proof from character"; note that character is not simply a matter of reputation but is given in the process of argumentation itself.[38] I shall come back to this point momentarily. Note first that there are numerous devices for providing such evidence: in published scholarly argumentation, the use of footnotes helps serve this end; the listing of the author's degrees (as in law journal articles) and previous publications would seem to serve a similar end. One also finds it in the use of disclaimers: say, if one doctor in our example were to preface her argument for scaling back treatment by noting how seriously committed she is to the value of life. Such a disclaimer signals to opponents that one is being fair-minded in one's judgment, that one is unlikely to underestimate this or that relevant consideration. The speaker thereby provides the audience with further grounds for taking the speaker's arguments seriously, as the result of a responsible judgment. More generally, this suggests that a speaker's care in the presentation of arguments and counterarguments is not simply a dialectical exercise but also a way of providing an audience with rhetorical grounds for accepting the speaker as a trustworthy judge of the matter.

Thus, appeal to character makes the arguments for a position more cogent, and their acceptance rationally motivated, insofar as it gives hearers grounds for taking the speaker's way of judging plausibilities as likely to be correct. As already noted, according to Aristotle such grounds or "proofs" are primarily displayed in the presentation of substantive arguments, or *logos;* this suggests that one should see them more as a dimension of all substantive argumentation than as a separate type of argument. The above examples of character appeals, however, indicate that this relation to *logos* is a matter of degree, that is, some character proofs are more closely related to the substantive issue than others. Thus, a critical rhetorical analysis must gauge the particular type of character proof for its relation to *logos.* For example, the ability to recap convincingly an opponent's argument before refuting it is internally related to judgment in a way that other proofs of expertise, such as the listing of degrees or past publications, are not. Although these can all instill an audience with greater trust in the speaker—and thus affect how the audience weighs the speaker's substantive arguments—the first method should be more resistant to abuse, and thus more intrinsically creditworthy, than the latter devices. At the same time, given the importance of expertise and specialization in contemporary argumentation, one may not simply dismiss more extrinsic appeals as irrelevant to rational motivation.

In any case, exactly what type of character appeal is considered appropriate, and how significant such appeals are for cogency, will depend in part on the context and argument domain. Character will probably be less important in arguments among persons sharing a single expertise, where each participant has considerable trust in his or her own assessment. In more complex cases, where no single person has a grasp of all the relevant considerations and subarguments, one would expect character proofs to be important. If our comatose patient, for example, suffers from complications that must be assessed by different specialists, then each participant's position will depend on acceptance of the testimony of the various specialists. Each participant's judgment will thus depend not only on the arguments themselves but on assessments of trustworthiness as well.

In complex cases, the cooperative character of argumentation is clear. But note that something analogous can occur even in cases that lack this kind of complexity. That is, even if the doctors in our example have no need of specialists' advice—so that each doctor has something approaching a full grasp of the relevant considerations at stake—it is unlikely that each has grasped every argument equally well. Argumentation would still be essentially cooperative insofar as each participant contributes his or her consideration of aspects that others may have examined only superficially. To use the terms developed earlier, the dialogical outcome would exceed what any single participant was able to achieve monologically in his or her private consideration of the issue. Insofar as a speaker presents me with an assessment of the arguments that differ from my own and gives me grounds to take his or her judgment seriously, I am led dialogically to consider certain aspects of the issue more deeply than I did initially. Presumably, my final judgment—even if it remains the same—should be more rational.[39]

This brings us to the second rhetorical proof, argument from emotion. I am not as concerned here with the use of emotions as arguments or reasons for a conclusion as with the role of emotions in disposing participants to make a responsible judgment—that is, with *pathos* as a dimension of all argumentation.[40] If argumentation issues in the judgment of plausibilities, and if this means steering between rash and indecisive conclusions, then argumentation is more cogent to the extent that it employs rhetorical devices that help the participants (*as auditors*) to achieve a proper frame of mind for judging responsibly. This is already an aspect of *ethos* insofar as fostering a friendliness between speaker and audience involves an emotional quality in the audience that affects its readiness to accept a speaker. But this particular emotion, which is open to abuse, is probably not the most relevant in the present context.

The emotional appeals that are internally related to responsible cooperative judgment are those that help the audience strike a balance between rashness and overcaution in judgment. The specific form such appeals take depends on the particular issue and claims involved. For example, in his famous "Common Ground" address before the 1988 Democratic convention, Jesse Jackson confronted the folk equations of poverty with laziness and success with justice. Part of the rhetorical effect of his speech consisted in his ironic juxtaposition of hard work and the denial of need: the poor "wipe the bodies of those who are sick with fever and pain. They empty their bedpans. They clean out their commodes. No job is beneath them, and yet when they get sick they cannot lie in the bed they made up every day. America, that is not right."[41] The image stirs up a sympathy for the working poor and perhaps outrage over their conditions. If we assume that Jackson intended to reach an audience inclined to identify poverty with laziness, then the appeal to emotion could dispose them to listen to arguments they would otherwise dismiss. More generally, one should expect argumentation over issues of justice to involve similar appeals, given the importance of perspective taking for resolving such issues.

In other contexts, other types of emotions could become relevant. If a polity is considering a momentous political decision, and the speaker believes that the audience is overly inclined to push the decision through without regard for the possible dangers, then stirring up a certain fear of potentially disastrous consequences could facilitate a more rational deliberation. One might argue that such fear is no more than another reason or argument, but my point does not depend on this view. Rather, the appeal to fear should enable participants better to weigh a counterargument, in this case by disposing them to consider certain possibilities more seriously. If the polity still opts for a dangerous policy, then the winning arguments could be considered more cogent precisely because they withstood reflection on the possible consequences. Again, the appeal to emotion placed the audience in the proper emotional frame for responsibly judging an issue on its merits.

The underlying assumption here is that judging plausibilities is not simply a logical operation nor a mechanical procedure of raising and answering objections but also a matter of proper psychological disposition. If this assumption is correct, then it may be rational for a speaker to give an argument a certain emotional pitch, whether through inflection and tone or through more sophisticated rhetorical devices. Especially where practical affairs are concerned, arguments imply decisions with consequences that affect interests. This means that certain emotions are often appropriate: anger over an injustice, fear at a disastrous consequence, hope for a beneficial outcome, and so forth. Insofar as projecting the appropriate emotion along with the reason contributes to the audience's capacity to consider a given reason in greater depth, *pathos* is partly constitutive of cogent argumentation.

There are considerable possibilities for abuse here. But again, one could develop more specific standards that spell out whether a given use of *pathos* contributes to cogency. Along with criteria for character appeals, such standards would concretize the idealizations that Habermas has identified with rhetoric, inasmuch as criteria for *ethos* and *pathos* indicate ways of increasing the participants' ability to consider one another's arguments as free and equal participants. By further developing such rhetorical criteria, one could provide a theory of argumentation with more to say about the context of argumentation as a process of communication. Here one must attend to the concrete speech situation: argumentation involves particular speakers who are attempting to persuade particular hearers to accept a claim on the basis of particular arguments. From a rhetorical perspective, such communication is a process of cooperative judgment formation that involves all three aspects: the immanent qualities of arguments and counterarguments, the rational grounds for trusting other participants' judgments, and each participant's capacity to judge. Whatever improves the quality of arguments themselves, improves the grounds for trusting fellow participants, or improves the participants' capacity to judge plausibilities contributes to cogent argumentation—regardless of whether it issues in consensus.

NOTES

I would like to thank Walter Ong and Walter Jost for their willingness to read and comment on an earlier draft of this chapter.

1 See especially Jürgen Habermas, *Theory of Communicative Action,* 2 vols., trans. Thomas McCarthy (Boston: Beacon, 1984; 1987), hereafter cited as *TCA;* also his *Communication and the Evolution of Society,* trans. Thomas McCarthy (Boston: Beacon, 1979). Habermas developed this theory partly in response to difficulties that undermined his earlier effort, *Knowledge and Human Interests,* trans. Jeremy J. Shapiro (Boston: Beacon, 1971); for an account of his shift away from this earlier approach, see Thomas McCarthy, *The Critical Theory of Jürgen Habermas* (Cambridge: MIT Press, 1978), chaps. 2 and 3. For an overview of Habermas's current project, see Maeve Cooke, *Language and Reason: A Study of Habermas's Pragmatics* (Cambridge: MIT Press, 1994).

2 The two groundbreaking works on the subject both first appeared in 1958: Chaim Perelman and Lucie Olbrechts-Tyteca, *The New Rhetoric: A Treatise on Argumentation,* trans. John Wilkinson and Purcell Weaver (Notre Dame, Ind.: University of Notre Dame Press, 1969); and Stephen Toulmin, *The Uses of Argument* (Cambridge: Cambridge University Press, 1964). For a broad overview of developments in the area of argumentation theory, see Robert J. Cox and Charles Arthur Willard, "Introduction: The Field of Argumentation," in *Advances in Argumentation Theory and Research,* ed. Robert J. Cox and Charles Arthur Willard (Carbondale: Southern Illinois University Press, 1982), xiii–xlvii; see also *Argumentation Theory and the Rhetoric of Assent,* ed. David Cratis Williams and Michael David Hazen (Tuscaloosa: University of Alabama Press, 1990).

3 Kenneth Burke was the seminal thinker in this trend; see, for example, his *Rhetoric of Motives* (New York: Prentice Hall, 1950). Besides Perelman and Olbrechts-Tyteca, see also Wayne C. Booth, *Modern Dogma and the Rhetoric of Assent* (Chicago: University of Chicago Press, 1974).

4 See Thomas B. Farrell, *Norms of Rhetorical Culture* (New Haven: Yale University Press, 1993), and the assessments of Dilip Parameshwar Gaonkar, "The Very Idea of a Rhetorical Culture," and Maurice Charland, "Norms and Laughter in Rhetorical Culture," *Quarterly Journal of Speech* 80 (1994): 333–38 and 339–42.

5 Thus the present chapter may be considered a contribution to the project of linking critical theory and rhetoric, but, in contrast to Farrell, who takes an Aristotelian starting point, I begin with Habermas's theory of argumentation.

6 See especially Toulmin's *Uses of Argument;* Jürgen Habermas, "Wahrheitstheorien," in *Vorstudien und Ergänzungen zur Theorie des kommunikativen Handelns* (Frankfurt: Suhrkamp, 1986), 127–83.

7 Cf. Habermas, *TCA* 1:33–35.

8 The analysis of argument as product, procedure, and process was independently proposed by Joseph Wenzel and Wayne Brockriede. See, for example, Joseph W. Wenzel, "Jürgen Habermas and the Dialectical Perspective on Argumentation," *Journal of the American Forensic Association* 16 (1979): 83–94, and Wayne Brockriede, "Arguing about Human Understanding," *Communication Monographs* 49 (1982): 137–47, esp. 142–143, where Brockriede recaps the theoretical developments. This threefold distinction grew out of an earlier distinction indicated by the difference between an "argument" as a set of utterances or sentences, and "arguing" as an interaction; see Daniel J. O'Keefe, "Two Concepts of Argument," *Journal of the American Forensic Association* 13 (1977): 121–28; Daniel J. O'Keefe, "The Concepts of Argument and Arguing," in *Advances in Argumentation Theory and Research,* ed. Willard and Cox, 3–23. For Habermas's treatment of this distinction, see Habermas, *TCA* 1:25–26 and his "Discourse Ethics: Notes on a Program of Philosophical Justification" in *Moral Consciousness and Communicative Action,* trans. Christian Lenhardt and Shierry Weber Nicholsen (Cambridge: MIT Press, 1990), 87–92.

9 Habermas, *TCA* 1:26.

10 Habermas, *TCA* 1:25.

11 Habermas, "Discourse Ethics," 87. Habermas illustrates the rules at these different levels by drawing on Robert Alexy, "A Theory of Practical Discourse," in *The Communicative Ethics Controversy,* ed. Seyla Benhabib and Fred Dallmayr (Cambridge: MIT Press, 1990), 151–90; note, however, that he reorganizes Alexy's categories, which were not arranged according to the three levels.

12 Habermas, *TCA* 1:25; "Discourse Ethics," 87.

13 Habermas, *TCA* 1:25.

14 Habermas, "Discourse Ethics," 87–88. The rules that Habermas adduces are in significant accord with rules for argumentation outlined by Alvin I. Goldman, "Argumentation and Social Epistemology," *Journal of Philosophy* 91 (1994): 27–49.

15 Toulmin in effect moves directly from his universalist analysis of the logical structures of argumentation to the level of institutions; as a result, his analysis does not do justice to the general structures governing argumentation as dialectical and rhetorical; Habermas, *TCA* 1:35.

16 For an example of such an analysis, see Jürgen Habermas, *Between Facts and Norms: Contributions to a Discourse Theory of Law and Democracy,* trans. William Rehg (Cambridge: MIT Press, 1996).

17 Habermas, *TCA* 1:25.

18 Habermas, "Discourse Ethics," 89.

19 See not only Habermas, *TCA* 1:25, but also Jürgen Habermas, *Justification and Application: Remarks on Discourse Ethics,* trans. Ciarin P. Cronin (Cambridge: MIT Press, 1993), 54–57.

20 See Habermas, *Between Facts and Norms,* chap. 4; also Habermas, *Justification and Application,* chap. 1.

21 Perelman and Olbrechts-Tyteca, *New Rhetoric,* 31–35.

22 See not only Wenzel, "Jürgen Habermas," but also his "The Rhetorical Perspective on Argument," in *Argumentation: Across the Lines of Disciplines,* ed. Frans H. van Eemeren et al. (Dordrecht: Foris, 1987), 101–9, esp. 102. Such difficulties should not surprise us, given the troubled history of the relation between dialectic and rhetoric; see, for example, Lawrence D. Green, "Aristotelian Rhetoric, Dialectic, and the Traditions of 'Antistrophos,'" *Rhetorica* 8 (1990): 5–27; Walter J. Ong, *Ramus, Method, and the Decay of Dialogue* (New York: Octagon, 1974).

23 Habermas, "Wahrheitstheorien," 164.

24 Habermas, "Wahrheitstheorien," 165–74.

25 For a sense of the norms and fallacies one can identify from a dialectical perspective, see Frans H. van Eemeren and Rob Grootendorst, *Argumentation, Communication, and Fallacies: A Pragma-Dialectical Perspective* (Hillsdale, N.J.: Lawrence Erlbaum, 1992), part 2.

26 For a fuller analysis of the import of further relevant questions, see Bernard J. F. Lonergan, *Insight: A Study of Human Understanding,* 3rd ed. (New York: Philosophical Library, 1970), part 1; for the application to scientific argumentation, see my "From Logic to Rhetoric in Science: A Formal-Pragmatic Reading of Lonergan's Insight," in *Communication and Lonergan,* ed. Thomas J. Farrell and Paul A. Soukup (Kansas City, Mo.: Sheed and Ward, 1993), 153–72.

27 Goldman, "Argumentation," 40–43.

28 I have argued this for science in "From Logic to Rhetoric in Science" and for the moral sphere in *Insight and Solidarity: A Study in the Discourse Ethics of Jürgen Habermas* (Berkeley: University of California Press, 1994), part 1.

29 For a critique of Habermas on this point, see Farrell, *Norms,* 188–97; for a sense of how one might respond, see James F. Bohman, "Emancipation and Rhetoric: The Perlocutions and Illocutions of the Social Critic," *Philosophy and Rhetoric* 21 (1988): 185–204.

30 See, for example, Bohman's linking of rhetoric with ideology critique and world-dis-

closure; Bohman, "Emancipation and Rhetoric"; also his "Two Versions of the Linguistic Turn: Habermas's Criticisms of Poststructuralism," in *Habermas and the Unfinished Project of Modernity: Critical Essays on "The Philosophical Discourse of Modernity,"* ed. Marizio Passerin d'Entrèves and Seyla Benhabib (Cambridge: MIT Press, 1996).

31 Mary Margaret McCabe has argued that in his *Rhetoric* Aristotle attempts to steer between this opposition (as represented by Plato's *Gorgias* on the one side and Isocrates on the other); see her "Arguments in Context: Aristotle's Defense of Rhetoric," in *Aristotle's* Rhetoric: *Philosophical Essays,* ed. David J. Furley and Alexander Nehamas (Princeton: Princeton University Press, 1994), 129–65. Cf. also Walter Jost, *Rhetorical Thought in John Henry Newman* (Columbia: University of South Carolina Press, 1989), chaps. 1, 7.

32 Lonergan, *Insight,* 284–87. The importance of judgment has also been noted by Farrell, *Norms,* 72–83; cf. also Hans Blumenberg, "An Anthropological Approach to the Contemporary Significance of Rhetoric," in *After Philosophy: End or Transformation?* ed. Kenneth Baynes, James Bohman, and Thomas McCarthy (Cambridge: MIT Press, 1987), 429–58.

33 On this topic, see Thomas Kuhn, *The Structure of Scientific Revolutions,* 2d ed. (Chicago: University of Chicago Press, 1970); and *Criticism and the Growth of Knowledge,* ed. Imre Lakatos and Alan Musgrave (Cambridge: Cambridge University Press, 1970).

34 See Klaus Günther, *The Sense of Appropriateness: Application Discourses in Morality and Law,* trans. John Farrell (Albany: State University of New York Press, 1993); also Rehg, *Insight and Solidarity,* chap. 7.

35 Here I am stimulated by McCabe's reading of Aristotle; cf. her "Arguments in Context," 155. See also Martin Benjamin, *Splitting the Difference: Compromise and Integrity in Ethics and Politics* (Lawrence: University Press of Kansas, 1990), chap. 5.

36 See Aristotle, *On Rhetoric,* trans. George A. Kennedy (New York: Oxford University Press, 1991), esp. 1.2 and 2.1–17; for brief commentaries, see John M. Cooper, "Ethical-Political Theory in Aristotle's *Rhetoric,*" in *Aristotle's* Rhetoric, ed. Furley and Nehamas, 193–210; and Alan Brinton, "*Pathos* and the 'Appeal to Emotion': An Aristotelian Analysis," *History of Philosophy Quarterly* 5 (1988): 207–19. Cf. also Craig R. Smith and Michael J. Hyde, "Rethinking 'The Public': The Role of Emotion in Being-with-Others," *Quarterly Journal of Speech* 77 (1991): 446–66; for a case illustration, see Craig Waddell, "The Role of *Pathos* in the Decision-Making Process: A Study in the Rhetoric of Science Policy," *Quarterly Journal of Speech* 76 (1990): 381–400; Waddell also brings out the role of *ethos.*

37 I take this case from Benjamin, *Splitting the Difference,* 24–32.

38 See Aristotle, *Rhetoric,* 1.2.4.1356a (Kennedy translation, p. 38).

39 This still abstracts from how a real decision is reached, which is determined at the institutional level of analysis.

40 There is, however, a growing literature on the cognitive character of emotions and

their use as arguments; cf., for example, Robert C. Solomon, "On Emotions as Judgments," *American Philosophical Quarterly* 25 (1988): 183–91; Patricia S. Greenspan, *Emotions and Reasons: An Inquiry into Emotional Justification* (New York: Routledge, 1988); Michael A. Gilbert, "Multi-Modal Argumentation," *Philosophy of the Social Sciences* 24 (1994): 159–77.

41 Jesse Jackson, quoted in Farrell, *Norms,* 259.

18

Articulation and Understanding: The Pragmatic Intimacy Between Rhetoric and Hermeneutics

Steven Mailloux

In the *Cratylus,* Socrates offers this interpretation of a certain familiar word:

> I should imagine that the name *Hermes* has to do with speech, and signifies that he is the interpreter (*hermeneus*), or messenger, or thief, or liar, or bargainer; all that sort of thing has a great deal to do with language. As I was telling you, the word *eirein* is expressive of the use of speech, and there is an often-recurring Homeric word *emesato*, which means "he contrived." Out of these two words, *eirein* and *mesasthai*, the legislator formed the name of the god who invented language and speech, and we may imagine him dictating to us the use of this name. "O my friends," says he to us, "seeing that he is the contriver of tales or speeches (*eirein emesato*), you may rightly call him *Eiremes*." And this has been improved by us, as we think, into *Hermes*.[1]

Behind Plato's pseudo-etymology are the various Greek myths that present Hermes as the messenger of the gods, translator of their meanings to humans, interpreter par excellence. Hermes is also, perhaps not surprisingly, the inventor of speech and language, which Socrates describes as intimately connected with interpretation. In addition, this god of interpretation and language is a contriver, a liar, a trickster, not to be trusted. That is, Hermes is Plato's archetypal Sophist.

But I am getting ahead of myself. Let me begin again by taking a simple lesson from Plato's derivation of *Hermes,* a lesson that forms the thesis of the remarks to follow: I would like to assert the practical inseparability of interpretation and language use, and thus of the discourses that theorize those practices, hermeneutics and rhetoric. In developing this rhetorical hermeneutics, I shall address three problems widely debated within the human sciences: interpretive relativism, cultural incommensurability, and ethnocentric politics. Along the way, I shall call upon Hermes and his near relations to serve as my guides.[2]

The traditions of both rhetoric and hermeneutics address very practical tasks. Hermeneutics deals with interpretation focused on texts; rhetoric with figuration and persuasion directed at audiences. Interpretation can be defined as the establishment of textual meaning, while rhetoric (as figuration and persuasion) might be characterized more pointedly as the political effectivity of trope and argument in culture.[3] Interpretation involves the translation of one text into another, a Hermeslike mediation that is also a transformation of one linguistic event into another, later one. Rhetoric involves the transformation of one audience into another, which is also a psychagogic translation from one position to a different one. These translating and transforming activities relate to each other historically and theoretically in a complex mixture.

Rhetorical theory is to rhetorical practice as hermeneutics is to interpretation. As practices, rhetoric and interpretation denote both productive and receptive activities. That is, interpretation refers to the presentation of a text in speech—as in oral performance—and the understanding or exegesis of a written text; similarly, rhetoric refers to the production of persuasive discourse and the analysis of a text's effects on an audience. In some ways rhetoric and interpretation are practical forms of the same extended human activity: rhetoric is based on interpretation; interpretation is communicated through rhetoric. Furthermore, as reflections on practice, hermeneutics and rhetorical theory are mutually defining fields: hermeneutics is the rhetoric of establishing meaning and rhetoric the hermeneutics of problematic linguistic situations. When we ask about the meaning of a text, we receive an interpretive argument; when we seek the means of persuasion, we interpret the situation. As theoretical practices, hermeneutics involves placing a text in a meaningful context, while rhetoric requires the contextualization of a text's effects.[4]

A rhetorical hermeneutics making the above claims must also admit that the inseparability of rhetoric and interpretation depends on the tropes and arguments used to figure and define the activities it is describing. We can understand this better by examining the traditions that describe these practices.

Again, a Platonic text will get us going; this one is a myth about the close Egyptian cousin to our guide Hermes.

When Phaedrus, in the dialogue that bears his name, asks Socrates to answer his own question—"Do you know how you can act or speak about rhetoric so as to please God best?"—the philosopher responds by recounting an ancient Egyptian legend about the god Theuth (Thoth), who "invented numbers and arithmetic and geometry and astronomy, also draughts and dice, and, most important of all, letters." Presenting the last of these to the god Thamus, Theuth proclaims, "This invention, O king, will make the Egyptians wiser and will improve their memories; for it is an elixir of memory and wisdom that I have discovered." But Thamus chastises the father of writing for thinking he can both produce and judge his own offspring. Instead of aiding one's memory, Thamus argues, writing will discourage its use. "You have invented an elixir not of memory, but of reminding; and you offer your pupils the appearance of wisdom, not true wisdom, for they will read many things without instruction and will therefore seem to know many things, when they are for the most part ignorant and hard to get along with, since they are not wise, but only appear wise."[5]

In his gloss on this myth, Socrates is less concerned with what writing will do to the memory than what it will not do for truth. Unlike the spoken word in dialogue, the written text remains powerless to correct its receiver's misreading: "Every word, when once it is written, is bandied about, alike among those who understand and those who have no interest in it, and it knows not to whom to speak or not to speak; when ill-treated or unjustly reviled it always needs its father to help it; for it has no power to protect or help itself" (275e). For Socrates, then, the myth of Theuth is the story of the use and abuse of a new technology; it is about the lack of interpretive and rhetorical controls that results from written inscription.

But "writing" easily becomes a synecdoche for all textuality, all rhetorical productions open to interpretive reception. For the spoken word is no less written than the one inscribed on a tablet. According to Socrates, "the living and breathing word," the word spoken in dialogue, is also the "word which is written with intelligence in the mind of the learner, which is able to defend itself and knows to whom it should speak, and before whom to be silent" (276a). That is, all words are written, inscribed, in one form or another, and the different forms, the different technologies of their production, are part of the rhetorical context in which they are received. As he often is, Plato's Socrates is quite the sophistic rhetorician here as he three times over follows the paths of Hermes and Theuth: in persuasive skill, rhetorical analysis, and clever trickery.[6]

Skillfully persuasive, Socrates posits a commonsense distinction between speaking and writing. He then analyzes that distinction in terms of the different rhetorical contexts speaking and writing each enters into: the context of dialogue increases the probability that the speaker's point will be made simply because the speaker is there for rhetorical follow-up, whereas the context of reading without the author's presence contains no such backing. But what Socrates cleverly ignores in his persuasive contrast is that the speaker's presence guarantees neither that the intended point will be understood nor, once understood, that it will be accepted. Any rhetoric, spoken or written, is open to interpretive risk. In fact, there are contexts in which a written word provides a much higher probability of interpretive success and rhetorical effectiveness from the author's perspective: contexts in which there is more time for interpretive activity (for reading slowly or rereading) or in which the very written-ness of a text testifies to its authority (scriptures or constitutions).

This rhetorical interpretation echoes Derrida's deconstructive reading of the *Phaedrus:* speech is neither *in principle nor in general* more intimate with some originary source or even with itself than is writing.[7] The distance between a spoken or written word and its producer's intention is a function of the interpretations made in the rhetorical context of the word's reception. This theoretical point is illustrated rather ironically in Plato's myth when Theuth, the creator of writing, loses control of its subsequent evaluation. Thamus challenges Theuth's authority, making arguments against his claim, counterarguments that Socrates appears to accept. I say "appears" because there are some interesting differences between Thamus's arguments and Socrates' interpretation and extension of them. Thamus begins his refutation by attacking Theuth's credibility: "You, who are the father of letters, have been led by your affection to ascribe to them a power the opposite of that which they really possess" (274e). Theuth is unreliable as a judge, Thamus suggests, because of his paternal fondness for his offspring, and thus his words are biased and cannot be trusted. But surely this attack on Theuth's ethos is exactly the kind of argument Socrates dismisses when he accuses his own listener, Phaedrus, of questioning the myth just told on grounds that "it makes a difference who the speaker is" rather than "whether his words are true or not" (275c). Against Socrates, then, Thamus claims it does make a difference who speaks.

But what of Thamus's words themselves, the arguments he makes directly against Theuth's predictions about the usefulness of writing? Here Socrates does not so much contradict Thamus's arguments as give them a radically different turn, proposing a supplemental meaning that is difficult to ground in the myth. The crucial passage in Socrates' gloss is this: "He who thinks, then, that he has left behind him any art in writing, and he who receives it in the belief that anything in writing will be clear and certain, would be an utterly simple person, and in truth ignorant of the prophesy of Ammon [Thamus], if he thinks written words are of any use except to remind him who knows the matter about which they are written" (275c). The second part of this passage, after "prophesy of Ammon," does state one of Thamus's criticisms of writing—that it will not instruct, only remind the reader—but the first part of the passage is hard to connect with anything Thamus says in the myth. He does complain that writing will encourage false pride among the ignorant, but he does not seem to be worried about the lack of clarity or certainty, reliability or permanence in the writing itself. It is Socrates, not Thamus, who introduces the dangers of interpretive relativism.

A rhetorical hermeneutics can almost agree with Thamus's characterization (though not his evaluation) of reading: readers can only understand what they, in some sense, already know. This notion of interpretation sounds counterintuitive only when put so baldly. The point is that successful interpretation depends on the interpreter's prior web of beliefs, desires, practices, and so forth. From this perspective (shared by several rhetorical and hermeneutic theorists), an interpreter's assumptions are not prejudices that distort understanding but the enabling ground of the process. In *Truth and Method*, for example, Hans-Georg Gadamer argues that "if we want to do justice to man's finite, historical mode of being, it is necessary to fundamentally rehabilitate the concept of prejudice and acknowledge the fact that there are legitimate prejudices."[8] Following Heidegger, Gadamer views prejudices, presuppositions, and fore-understandings as the very condition of interpretation. As Joel Weinsheimer explains: "Understanding is projection, and what it projects are expectations that precede the text." Suitable projection or so-called "objectivity in interpretation consists not in the avoidance of preconception but its confirmation; and arbitrary, inappropriate preconceptions are characterized not by the fact that they are preconceptions but only by the fact that they do not work out."[9] Without a reader's preconceptions, interpretation can't even begin. Similarly, Stanley Fish argues that "interpretations rest on other interpretations, or, more precisely, on assumptions—about what is possible, necessary, telling, essential, and so on—so deeply held that they are not thought of as assumptions at all." Or again: "Perception [including reading] is never innocent of assumptions, and the assumptions within which it occurs will be responsible for the contours of what is perceived."[10]

A rhetorical hermeneutics invoking such pragmatist and hermeneutical claims has not yet responded directly to the worries of Plato's Socrates in his gloss on the myth of Theuth. In fact, rhetorical hermeneutics would appear to the foundational Platonist as just another ruse by Hermes' followers, the sophistic rhetoricians. As Socrates puts it in the *Cratylus* before he presents his interpretation of Hermes: Protagoras, the master Sophist, "says that man is the measure of all things, and that things are to me as they appear to me, and that they are to you as they appear to you. . . . But if Protagoras is right, and the truth is that things are as they appear to anyone, how can some of us be wise and some of us foolish?" (386a–c). The Sophist's relativism privileges each person's perceptions (based on each individual's assumptions, beliefs, desires) and thus makes it impossible to judge who is right or wrong, wise or foolish, better or worse. According to Platonists, this is not only ethical relativism but nihilistic solipsism.

We can translate this Platonic charge against the Sophists into the three interconnected problems I have mentioned: relativism, incommensurability, and ethnocentricism. To explore these further, I shall use another Platonic myth, in which my guide makes a brief appearance.

In response to a Socratic question, Protagoras tells the story of how Prometheus stole fire and practical wisdom from the gods and gave them to humans for their survival (*Protagoras,* 321). But as people began to gather in cities, they could not get along for they lacked political virtue (*politike arete*). Fearing their self-destruction, Zeus sent Hermes (another thief!) to bring reverence and justice to humans that they might join together to govern their cities. "Hermes asked Zeus how he should impart justice and reverence among men:—Should he distribute them as the arts are distributed; that is to say, to a favoured few only, one skilled individual having enough of medicine or of any other art for many unskilled ones? 'Shall this be the manner in which I am to distribute justice and reverence among men, or shall I give them to all?' 'To all,' said Zeus; 'I should like them all to have a share; for cities cannot exist, if a few only share in the virtues, as in the arts. And further, make a law by my order, that he who has no part in reverence and justice shall be put to death, for he is a plague of the State.' "[11]

Paul Feyerabend has used this myth to illustrate one of his theses in defense of relativism: "Laws, religious beliefs and customs rule, like kings, in restricted domains. Their rule rests on a twofold authority—on their *power* and on the fact that it is *rightful* power: the rules are *valid* in their domains."[12] Feyerabend means to suggest that his own form of relativism has nothing to do with no-controls, "anything goes" nihilism. In Feyerabend's reading, Protagoras "believed that there had to be laws and that they had to be enforced" but "that laws and institutions had to be adapted to the societies in which they were supposed to rule, that justice had to be defined 'relative to' the needs and the circumstances of these societies." This does not mean, Feyerabend argues, "that institutions and laws that are valid in some societies and not valid in others are therefore arbitrary and can be changed at will" (p. 44).

Feyerabend goes on to connect his relativist reading of the Prometheus-Hermes myth with Protagoras's *anthropos metron* maxim—"Humans are the measure of all things, of those that are that they are; and of those that are not, that they are not"[13]—which Feyerabend interprets as meaning that "the laws, customs, facts that are being put before the citizens ultimately rest on the pronouncements, beliefs and perceptions of human beings and that important matters should therefore be referred to the (perceptions and thoughts of the) people concerned and not to abstract agencies and distant experts" (p. 48). Feyerabend notes the traditional absolutist objection to *anthropos metron*: "Good ideas, procedures, laws, according to Plato, are neither popular ideas, procedures, laws, nor things that are supported by authorities such as kings, wandering bards, or experts; good ideas, procedures, laws are things that 'fit reality' and are true in this sense" (p. 49). There is for the antisophistic objectivist the standard outside all communities, beyond the finite, transcending the human, to which historical communities are responsible and against which their actions and beliefs can be judged absolutely. In contrast, a rhetorical hermeneutics agrees with Feyerabend in rejecting this Platonic picture and argues that all we have to deal with as situated interpreters are the webs of belief and desire that constitute our rhetorical contexts.

Feyerabend later puts forth another thesis compatible with rhetorical hermeneutics: "For every statement (theory, point of view) that is believed to be true with good reasons *there may exist* arguments showing that either its opposite, or a weaker alternative is true" (p. 74). This thesis (and its stronger version, p. 76) can also be related to Protagorean sophistry, the (in)famous *dissoi-logoi* fragment: "Protagoras was the first to say that on every issue there are two arguments opposed to each other."[14] The British Pragmatist F. C. S. Schiller argued that this maxim fit neatly with *anthropos metron* as both emerged from the challenges facing a practicing rhetorician.[15] Feyerabend would no doubt have agreed with Schiller's observation.

Feyerabend, however, develops his argument in a different direction, as he quotes the rhetorical observations made by anthropologist E. E. Evans-Pritchard in his study of the Azande of Central Africa: "'Let the reader consider any argument that would utterly demolish all Zande claims for the power of [their] oracle[s]. If it were translated into Zande modes of thought it would serve to support their entire structure of belief. For their mystical notions are eminently coherent, being interrelated by a network of logical ties and are so ordered that they never too crudely contradict sensory experience but, instead, experience seems to justify them.'"[16] The conclusion Feyerabend draws: "Zande practices are 'rational' because supportable by argument" (p. 74). This appeal to the cultural anthropologist's experience brings us back to the central point of Feyerabend's essay: the relativism he defends is "not about concepts (though most modern versions of it are conceptual versions) but about human relations. It deals with problems that arise when different cultures, or individuals with different habits and tastes, collide" (p. 83).

This collision is precisely the concern of Charles Taylor's provocative essay "Rationality," which also discusses the Zande culture.[17] Taylor provides rhetorical hermeneutics with yet another way of formulating the inseparability of rhetoric and interpretation and at the same time allows another run at the question of cultural relativism. In "Rationality," Taylor attempts to establish a framework for making valid cross-cultural judgments. He does this in several steps, many of which will prove useful to us here. Taylor argues that descriptions can make appropriate transcultural discriminations. He privileges the description that distinguishes between "theoretical" and "atheoretical" cultures, defining "theoretical" as giving an account from a "disengaged perspective." The ancient Greeks invented this form of theory, where "theoretical understanding is related to rationality" and "rational understanding is linked to articulation." Articulation, in turn, means to "distinguish and lay out the different features of the matter in perspicuous order" (pp. 136–37).

A rhetorical hermeneutics would separate out Taylor's useful claims about the intimate relation between theoretical understanding and explanatory articulation from his more problematic assumptions concerning theory as a disengaged perspective. It would extend the claims for an "inner connection" (p. 137) between *theoretical* understanding (reason) and *practical* articulation (giving persuasive accounts) to all forms of understanding and language use. That is, to say it once again, interpretation (establishing meaning) and rhetoric (troping, arguing) are closely connected and mutually defining practices. And furthermore, this relation of understanding and articulation is duplicated again at the level of theory, with accounts of understanding (hermeneutics) being closely related to those of articulation (rhetoric). As Gadamer puts it, "Hermeneutics may be precisely defined as the art of bringing what is said or written to speech again. What kind of an art this is, then, we can learn from rhetoric."[18]

A rhetorical hermeneutics supports Taylor's attempt to develop an integral relation between understanding and articulation but encounters problems when he brings this model to bear on the question of transcultural comparisons. Taylor uses Peter Winch's essay "Understanding a Primitive Society," which, like Feyerabend's, relies for its examples on Evans-Pritchard's study of the Azande. Winch criticizes the anthropologist for assuming a notion of reality independent of language use. "Evans-Pritchard, although he emphasizes that a member of scientific culture has a different conception of reality from that of a Zande believer in magic, wants to go beyond merely registering this fact and making the differences explicit, and to say, finally, that the scientific conception agrees with what reality actually is like, whereas the magical conception does not."[19] Now, Winch does want to preserve the "idea that men's ideas and beliefs must be checkable by reference to something independent—some reality," for to abandon such measures would be, he fears, "to plunge straight into an extreme Protagorean relativism" (p. 308).[20] But Winch holds on to "the check of the independently real" by making the measuring act internal rather than external to a culture's language use. "Reality is not what gives language sense," he writes. "What is real and what is unreal shows itself *in* the sense that language has. Further, both the distinction between the real and the unreal and the concept of agreement with reality themselves belong to our language" (p. 309). Accordingly, Winch makes no value judgments in his cross-cultural comparisons and affirms that "a primitive system of magic, like that of the Azande, constitutes a coherent universe of discourse like science, in terms of which an intelligible conception of reality and clear ways of deciding what beliefs are and are not in agreement with this reality can be discerned" (p. 309).

Winch argues against making evaluative judgments of incommensurable activities within different cultures and advocates simply describing these cultural differences (and perhaps learning from them). Taylor also recognizes a "plurality of standards of rationality" but disagrees with Winch that such recognition disables comparative evaluations between cultures ("Rationality," p. 151). He proposes instead criteria for making valid transcultural judgments of rationality.

The example Taylor gives is a judgment that a theoretical culture (like his own) is superior to an atheoretical culture (like the Azande's). Taylor does not explicitly defend his judgment by claiming that it is disengaged. Rather, he argues only that the culture he judges as (in some respects) superior is so because it has developed an activity—theoretical understanding—that is disengaged. "There is," he claims, "an inner connection between understanding the world and achieving technological control which rightly commands everyone's attention, and doesn't just justify our practices in our own eyes" (p. 147). Theoretical understanding leads to the new science, which leads to a technological advancement that must be recognized as such by everyone. A theoretical culture is superior to an atheoretical one at least in terms of theoretical understanding, scientific knowledge, and technological progress.

To fully understand Taylor's argument, we must retrieve another of his notions, that of articulation. A culture is superior to another in terms of articulated reasons. And reasons are exactly what Taylor gives to support his judgment of the superiority of his culture over the Azande's. However, articulation, like understanding, comes from within a cultural position; it is not disengaged from it. Thus, Taylor articulates reasons for why theoretical cultures are superior to atheoretical cultures, but his reasons arise from within his theoretical culture and address an audience within that same culture. If the rhetorical context were different—if it were, for example, the Zande context posited by Evans-Pritchard—Taylor's articulations, his good reasons, might fail to convince.

At times Taylor seems to acknowledge the inescapably ethnocentric character of his interpretive judgment and its rhetorical support. He notes, for instance, that "there is no such thing as a single argument proving *global* superiority" of one culture over another. There is only local preeminence in terms of one culture's standards, Taylor seems to suggest. "Perhaps the critics are right," he continues, "who hold that we have been made progressively more estranged from ourselves and our world in technological civilization. Maybe this could even be shown as convincingly as the scientific superiority of moderns." Taylor correctly argues that such a rhetorical outcome "would not refute this scientific superiority. It would just mean that we now had two transcultural judgements of superiority; only unfortunately they would fall on different sides" (pp. 149–50). We could understand Taylor to be arguing that cross-cultural judgments can be made but acknowledging that which ones are convincing to whom depends on the relevant cultural context.

But Taylor does not simply object to Winch's position on the inappropriateness of making transcultural judgments of incommensurable activities. Apparently still wishing to defend the possibility of nonethnocentric cross-cultural evaluations, Taylor ends by referring back to the contrast between the beliefs underlying Zande magic and those grounding modern science: "Both offer articulations, they lay out different features of the world and human action in some perspicuous order. In that, they are both involved in the kind of activity which I have argued is central to rationality. But one culture can surely lay claim to a higher, or fuller, or more effective rationality, if it is in a position to achieve a more perspicuous order than another" (p. 150). But the question again is: more perspicuous, more persuasive for whom? That *rhetorical* matter is always culture-specific: what convinces European scientists and their followers might not convince Zande oracles and theirs. Put another way: Winch is correct in positing a plurality of standards of rationality; Taylor is right in disagreeing with Winch that such a plurality disables cross-cultural evaluations; against Taylor, a rhetorical hermeneutics argues that such judgments are always ethnocentrically located within the culture making them.[21] Interpretive judgments and rhetorical articulations are woven together within a culture's social practices even when the topic of articulated judgment is another culture's practices.

Both Winch and Taylor try to avoid the cruder forms of ethnocentricism. As Taylor writes: "Really overcoming ethnocentricity is being able to understand two incommensurable classifications" (p. 145). But this overcoming is partial at best, for it is our own ethnocentric web of beliefs and desires that gives us interpretive purchase on any object of attention, including the texts or classification systems of another culture. The validity of our interpretation is a function of the rhetorical context in which we argue them: who participates in the conversation, when and where, with what purposes, and so on. Part of the rhetorical context for late twentieth-century academic intellectuals is a widespread belief not only in the possible incommensurability of radically different cultures and alien traditions but also in the authoritative ethos of the rhetorical agents speaking from within those cultures and across those traditions. It is to this theme of otherness and agency that I would now like to turn, again calling on a relative of Hermes.

The Fon of West Africa also have a trickster god, Legba, modeled after the Yoruba's Esu-Elegbara.[22] Legba is a linguistic mediator, the creator of magic, the sponsor of divination, a conniving thief and troublemaker who also restores and reconciles. He is the translator among the Fon gods, who speak different languages, and the messenger from gods to humans, empowering oracles to interpret destiny in the divining process. As inventor of magic, Legba "draws into the open the power of all boundaries, opens passageways to new life, and makes transformation possible even as he stimulates conflict." He "lives where separate worlds meet and can move back and forth between them, yet he cannot substitute one for the other." Legba is the Hermeslike deceiver, who translates and transforms. He is a "living limen," a passageway to the other, who "relentlessly enlarges the scope of the human."[23]

If transcultural judgments are always cross-cultural translations, then such interpretations are liminal acts opening up a space in which boundaries are transformed yet paradoxically maintained even as they are crossed. Boundaries are crossed in interpretation when one culture becomes the conversational topic or interpretive object of another; boundaries are maintained as the interpretive act in its rhetorical exchanges figures and persuades within the context of the interpreting culture; and boundaries are moved as interpretation changes the shape—trivially or dramatically—of the culture in which the interpretation is produced and received. To understand an act within a foreign culture, the differences must be found in the margins of our own. A completely other would be unintelligible. But as the marginal comes into focus or even moves toward the center, the boundaries of our horizons can shift and even be expanded by the other within. Another way of putting this: as we interact with other communities, traditions, cultures, we can reweave our webs of belief to take account of the other, and we do this more or less successfully from differing points of view within and outside our own groups.

When Christian missionaries first visited the Fon of Dahomey, they interpreted Legba as the primitive disguise for Satan. In fact, they cited one of the Fon creation myths in support by reading it as a corrupted version of the Adam and Eve story. But the Fon were not persuaded by this interpretation: "The story the missionaries tell about the fruit does not exist here. That Legba gave this fruit, that we do not know. . . . But the missionaries, when they heard our name of Adanhu and Yewa, said our gods and theirs were all the same. They tried to teach us the rest about the beginning of man and woman, but the Dahomeans [the Fon] do not agree. They say this is not their story. They know nothing about Legba trying to give fruit."[24] Here we have an act of resistance to an ethnocentric reading, an example of the Fon's assertion of rhetorical agency and interpretive power. A rhetorical hermeneutics takes account of both the missionaries' interpretation and the Fon's rhetorical opposition. It also attempts to make theoretical sense of these historical events as interrelated acts of understanding and articulation.

In the course of this chapter, I have tried to show how hermeneutics and rhetoric are intertwined and how viewing understanding as articulation contributes to clarifying the theoretical problems of relativism, incommensurability, and ethnocentricism. Let me now sum up and extend a few of these points. I have referred to the inescapability of ethnocentricism but also to a cruder form of ethnocentric activity. Such usages assume that our webs of vocabularies, beliefs, and desires constitute both the power and limits of our rhetorical and interpretive acts. We are agents within and because of our enculturation. I thus agree with Richard Rorty that to see ethnocentricism as "an inescapable condition" is to make ethnocentricity "roughly synonymous with 'human finitude.'"[25] That is, we are never not in a particular culture with a particular set of practices or form of life. Such a situation does not disable but grounds interpretation and evaluation of actions both inside and outside one's culture. A particular ethnos—the particular shape of one's finitude, its time and place, its web of beliefs and desires—provides the historical context in which judgments are made and supported.

A rhetorical hermeneutics claims that this cultural context cannot be completely transcended but it can be slowly and significantly changed. Ethnocentrism is with us always, but its shape can be transformed. A belief within the Western intellectual's ethnos now includes a prohibition on forcefully imposing one's beliefs on other cultures. To borrow Rorty's somewhat ironic formulation, some of us in the West have become "sufficiently leisured and civilized . . . to substitute . . . conversation with foreigners for conquest of them."[26] Our particular form of ethnocentricism explicitly privileges verbal persuasion over physical violence, rhetoric over war, both among groups within our own culture and between our culture and others. Thus, a rhetorical hermeneutics claims simultaneously that all cultures are ethnocentric and that a particular culture might distinguish more or less acceptable forms of ethnocentric activity. A particular ethnos might—and ours does—establish an ethnocentric continuum from "physical conquest" through "cultural imperialism" to "respectful understanding," a continuum that can be used to justify the condemnation of cruder forms of ethnocentric behavior toward other cultures.

We might see the historical development of this continuum within our culture and the embrace of its expansion by a significant segment of academic intellectuals as forming the context for the philosophical and anthropological debates over incommensurability. The notion of "incommensurability" provides a rhetorical resource for explaining or justifying many of the newer stances taken along the ethnocentric continuum. To conclude, I shall point out some meanings of the term that are useful to a rhetorical hermeneutics.

As I have developed it here, incommensurability refers not to an absolute inability to translate between cultures, not to an impervious obstacle blocking the articulated understanding of one culture by another. Rather, to posit incommensurability means accepting that in order to make sense of an alien culture's actions, those actions, including speech acts, must be placed in their own contexts of vocabularies, beliefs, and desires—contexts that may be extremely different, radically other from our own. But to say this is to claim that incommensurability is an interpretive category that enables us to deal with competing modes of intelligibility and communication within and outside our own cultural communities.

This take on incommensurability challenges the view that one culture can be so different from another that cross-cultural communication is in principle doomed from the start. Instead, as Rorty puts it, "our form of life and the natives' [in another culture] already overlap to so great an extent that we are already, automatically, for free, participant-observers, not *mere* observers." Moreover, "this overlap in effect reduces the intercultural case to an intracultural one—it means that we learn to handle the weirder bits of native behavior (linguistic and other) in the same way that we learn about the weird behavior of atypical members of our own culture."[27]

But "incommensurability" is also a shorthand for the rhetorical explanation of why agents from different cultures fail to communicate or make sense of one another's acts. It is a way of describing the historical scene of two actors in interpretive and rhetorical trouble. It marks a strategy for establishing the grounds for how to proceed, what advice to give: Try harder with interpretive translation or give up and go bilingual; continue the attempt to translate a set of alien terms into your own language or learn the other community's language.

Whatever the interpretive process of intra- and intercultural exchanges, the rhetorical outcome depends on how different agents reweave their beliefs and practices as a result of the exchanges. This reweaving constitutes what we call learning. What Evans-Pritchard wrote of the Azande applies to actors in other cultures as well: "In this web of belief every strand depends upon every other strand, and a Zande cannot get out of its meshes because this is the only world he knows. The web is not an external structure in which he is enclosed. It is the texture of his thought and he cannot think that his thought is wrong. Nevertheless, his beliefs are not absolutely set but are variable and fluctuating to allow for different situations and to permit empirical observation and even doubts."[28]

The web is rewoven through interpretation and persuasion and thus change takes place. This view of articulated understanding applies both within and between different cultural communities. As Rorty puts it, "To say that we must work by our own lights, that we must be ethnocentric, is merely to say that beliefs suggested by another culture must be tested by trying to weave them together with beliefs we already have."[29] Rhetorical hermeneutics helps to show how this is so as it argues for the pragmatic intimacy of understanding and articulation both within cultures and between them.

NOTES

I would like to thank Peter Carafiol, Michael Clark, Walter Jost, and Edward Schiappa for their helpful comments.

1 Plato, *Cratylus,* trans. Benjamin Jowett, in *Plato: The Collected Dialogues,* ed. Edith Hamilton and Huntington Cairns (Princeton: Princeton University Press, 1961), 407e–408b. Further references will be to this edition and will be cited parenthetically in the text.

2 Hermes, of course, was also the guide of souls, *psychopompos.* For a fuller discussion of Hermes' mythic roles, see Norman O. Brown, *Hermes the Thief: The Evolution of a Myth* (Madison: University of Wisconsin Press, 1947); Karl Kerenyi, *Hermes: Guide of Souls,* trans. Murray Stein (Dallas: Spring Publications, 1976); and William G. Doty, "A Lifetime of Trouble-Making: Hermes as Trickster," in *Mythical*

Trickster Figures, ed. William J. Hynes and William G. Doty (Tuscaloosa: University of Alabama Press, 1993), 46–65.

3 See my *Rhetorical Power* (Ithaca: Cornell University Press, 1989); and "Rhetorical Hermeneutics Revisited," *Text and Performance Quarterly* 11 (July 1991): 233–48.

4 This paragraph has been adapted from my entry for "Hermeneutics," in the *Encyclopedia of Rhetoric and Composition,* ed. Theresa Enos (New York: Garland, 1996), 16–17.

5 Plato, *Phaedrus,* trans. H. N. Fowler, in *Plato,* vol. 1 (Cambridge: Harvard University Press; London: William Heinemann, 1932), 274b–275b (translation slightly revised). Further references will be to this edition and will be cited parenthetically in the text.

6 See Patrick Boylan, *Thoth, the Hermes of Egypt: A Study of Some Aspects of Theological Thought in Ancient Egypt* (London: Oxford University Press, 1922); and Garth Fowden, *The Egyptian Hermes: A Historical Approach to the Late Pagan Mind,* 2d ed. (Princeton: Princeton University Press, 1993), 22–24.

7 Jacques Derrida, "Plato's Pharmacy," in *Dissemination,* trans. Barbara Johnson (Chicago: University of Chicago Press, 1981), 63–171. Also see Jasper Neel, *Plato, Derrida, and Writing* (Carbondale: Southern Illinois University Press, 1988).

8 Hans-Georg Gadamer, *Truth and Method,* 2d ed., rev. trans. Joel Weinsheimer and Donald G. Marshall (New York: Crossroad, 1989), 277.

9 Joel C. Weinsheimer, *Gadamer's Hermeneutics: A Reading of* Truth and Method (New Haven: Yale University Press, 1985), 166.

10 Stanley Fish, *Doing What Comes Naturally: Change, Rhetoric, and the Practice of Theory in Literary and Legal Studies* (Durham, N.C.: Duke University Press, 1989), 195.

11 Plato, *Protagoras,* trans. Benjamin Jowett, in *The Works of Plato,* ed. Irwin Edman (New York: Modern Library, 1956), 322c–d. Further references will be to this edition and will be cited parenthetically in the text.

12 Paul Feyerabend, "Notes on Relativism," in his *Farewell to Reason* (London: Verso, 1987), 43. Further references will be cited parenthetically in the text.

13 See Plato, *Theaetetus,* trans. H. N. Fowler, in *Plato,* vol. 7 (Cambridge: Harvard University Press; London: William Heinemann, 1921), 152a.

14 Diogenes Laertius, IX.51, trans. Michael J. O'Brien, in *The Older Sophists,* ed. Rosamond Kent Sprague (Columbia: University of South Carolina Press, 1972), 4.

15 F. C. S. Schiller, review of Heinrich Gomperz, *Sophistik und Rhetorik,* in *Mind* 22 (January 1913): 112. For further discussion, see my "Introduction: Sophistry and Rhetorical Pragmatism," in *Rhetoric, Sophistry, Pragmatism,* ed. Steven Mailloux (Cambridge: Cambridge University Press, 1995), 8–14. On the interpretive history of Protagoras's texts, see Edward Schiappa, *Protagoras and Logos: A Study in Greek Philosophy and Rhetoric* (Columbia: University of South Carolina Press, 1991).

16 E. E. Evans-Pritchard, *Witchcraft, Oracles and Magic Among the Azande* (Oxford: Oxford University Press, 1937), 319–20, quoted in Feyerabend, *Farewell to Reason,* 74.

17 Charles Taylor, "Rationality," in *Philosophy and the Human Sciences*, vol. 2 of his *Philosophical Papers* (Cambridge: Cambridge University Press, 1985), 134–51. Further references will be cited parenthetically in the text.

18 Hans-Georg Gadamer, "Hermeneutics as a Theoretical and Practical Task," in his *Reason in the Age of Science*, trans. Frederick G. Lawrence (Cambridge: MIT Press, 1981), 119.

19 Peter Winch, "Understanding a Primitive Society," *American Philosophical Quarterly* 1 (October 1964): 308. Further references will be cited parenthetically in the text. For other hermeneutic discussions of Winch's essay, see Richard J. Bernstein, *Beyond Objectivism and Relativism: Science, Hermeneutics, and Praxis* (Philadelphia: University of Pennsylvania Press, 1983), 97–107, and Gerald L. Bruns, *Hermeneutics Ancient and Modern* (New Haven: Yale University Press, 1992), 4–8.

20 This is clearly a different relativism from the one Feyerabend posits in his interpretation of Protagoras. Also see Winch, "Comment," in *Explanation in the Behavioural Sciences*, ed. Robert Borger and Frank Cioffi (Cambridge: Cambridge University Press, 1970), 254; and his slightly more developed reading of *anthropos metron*, from which he also distances his own position, in Winch, "The Universalizability of Moral Judgments," in *Ethics and Action* (London: Routledge and Kegan Paul, 1972), 168.

21 But cf. Taylor on using "the language of perspicuous contrast" to compare cultures: Charles Taylor, "Understanding and Ethnocentricity," in *Philosophy and the Human Sciences*, 116–33; "Comparison, History, Truth," in *Myth and Philosophy*, ed. Frank Reynolds and David Tracy (Albany: State University of New York Press, 1990), 37–55; and "The Politics of Recognition," in *Multiculturalism: Examining the Politics of Recognition*, 2d ed., ed. Amy Gutmann (Princeton: Princeton University Press, 1994), 66–73.

22 "Esu's most direct Western kinsman is Hermes," writes Henry Louis Gates, Jr., in his survey and interpretation of the "divine trickster figure," who, in passing from Africa to the New World, functions as "the figure of formal language use and its interpretation"; see Gates, *The Signifying Monkey: A Theory of African-American Literary Criticism* (New York: Oxford University Press, 1988), 5, 8, 35.

23 Robert D. Pelton, *The Trickster in West Africa: A Study of Mythic Irony and Sacred Delight* (Berkeley: University of California Press, 1980), 84, 88, 108–9.

24 Fon story-teller, "The First Humans: Missionary Version of Legba Rejected," in *Dahomean Narrative: A Cross-Cultural Analysis*, ed. Melville J. Herskovits and Frances S. Herskovits (Evanston: Northwestern University Press, 1958), 151.

25 Richard Rorty, "Introduction: Antirepresentationalism, Ethnocentrism, and Liberalism," in *Objectivity, Relativism, and Truth*, vol. 1 of his *Philosophical Papers* (Cambridge: Cambridge University Press, 1991), 15. For some pragmatist criticisms of Rorty's pragmatist notion of ethnocentrism, see Giles Gunn, *Thinking Across the American Grain: Ideology, Intellect, and the New Pragmatism* (Chicago: University of Chicago Press, 1992), 94–116.

26 Rorty, "Solidarity or Objectivity?" in *Objectivity*, 25.

27 Rorty, "Inquiry as Recontextualization: An Anti-Dualist Account of Interpretation," in *Objectivity*, 107.

28 Evans-Pritchard, *Witchcraft*, 194–95.

29 Rorty, "Solidarity or Objectivity?" 26. Cf. William James on forming new opinions: James, *Pragmatism: A New Name for Some Old Ways of Thinking* (1907; rpt. Cambridge: Harvard University Press, 1975), 34–36. For an alternative pragmatist account of the rhetorical problems treated here, see Peter Carafiol, *The American Ideal: Literary History as a Worldly Activity* (New York: Oxford University Press, 1991), 162–66; and his " 'Who I Am': Ethnic Identity and American Literary Ethnocentrism," in *Criticism and the Color Line: Desegregating American Literary Studies*, ed. Henry Wonham (New Brunswick: Rutgers University Press, 1996), 43–62.

Contributors

Charles Altieri is professor of English at the University of California, Berkeley.

Gerald L. Bruns is William and Hazel White Professor of English at the University of Notre Dame.

Rita Copeland is associate professor of English at the University of Minnesota, Twin Cities.

Hans-Georg Gadamer is emeritus professor of philosophy at Heidelberg University.

Eugene Garver is Regents Professor of Philosophy at Saint John's University (Collegeville).

Michael J. Hyde is University Professor of Communication Ethics at Wake Forest University.

Walter Jost is associate professor of English at the University of Virginia.

Victoria Kahn is professor of English and comparative literature at the University of California, Irvine.

Michael Leff is professor of communication studies at Northwestern University.

Steven Mailloux is professor of English at the University of California, Irvine.

Donald G. Marshall is professor and head of English at the University of Illinois, Chicago.

Wendy Olmsted is associate professor in the New Collegiate Division and the Humanities Division (Committee on the Ancient Mediterranean World) at the University of Chicago.

Richard E. Palmer is Joseph R. Harker Professor of Philosophy at MacMurray College.

William Rehg is assistant professor of philosophy at St. Louis University.

Paul Ricoeur is the John Nuveen Professor Emeritus in the Divinity School, the department of philosophy, and the Committee on Social Thought at the University of Chicago.

Calvin O. Schrag is the George Ade Distinguished Professor of Philosophy at Purdue University.

Allen Scult is National Endowment for the Humanities Professor of Rhetoric and Communication Studies at Drake University.

Nancy Struever is a professor in the department of history and the Humanities Center at Johns Hopkins University.

David Tracy is Andrew Thomas Greeley and Grace McNichols Distinguished Service Professor of Roman Catholic Studies and professor of theology in the Divinity School and the Committee on Social Thought at the University of Chicago.

Joel Weinsheimer is professor of English at the University of Minnesota, Twin Cities.

Acknowledgments

The following chapters are reprinted (some with change of title or in revised form) with permission from their publishers: Hans-Georg Gadamer, "Rhetoric and Hermeneutics," English translation by Joel Weinsheimer from the German, "Rhetorik und Hermeneutik," in *Gessamelte Werke*, 10 vols. (Tübingen: J.C.B. Mohr, 1985–94), 2:276–91. Paul Ricoeur, "Rhetoric—Poetics—Hermeneutics," from *From Metaphysics to Rhetoric*, ed. Michel Meyer, trans. Robert Harvey (Dordrecht: Kluwer, 1980), 137–51. Gerald L. Bruns, "On the Tragedy of Hermeneutical Experience," from Gerald L. Bruns, *Hermeneutics Ancient and Modern* (New Haven: Yale University Press, 1992). Victoria Kahn, "Humanism and the Resistance to Theory," in *Literary Theory/Renaissance Texts*, ed. Patricia Parker and David Quint (Baltimore: Johns Hopkins University Press, 1986). Wendy Raudenbush Olmsted, "The Uses of Rhetoric: Indeterminacy in Legal Reasoning, Practical Thinking and the Interpretation of Literary Figures," *Philosophy and Rhetoric* 24, no. 1 (1991): 1–24. Copyright © 1991 The Pennsylvania State University Press. Reprinted by permission of the Pennsylvania State University Press. David Tracy, "Charity, Obscurity, Clarity: Augustine's Search for a True Rhetoric," from *Morphologies of Faith: Essays in Religion and Culture in Honor of Nathan A. Scott,* ed. Mary Gerhart and Anthony C. Yu (Atlanta, Ga.: Scholars Press, 1990). Hans-Georg Gadamer, "Rhetoric, Hermeneutics, and Ideology-Critique," from Hans-Georg Gadamer, *Philosophical Hermeneutics,* ed. and trans. David E. Linge, chapter 2: "On the Scope and Function of Hermeneutical Reflection," trans. G. B. Hess and R. E. Palmer (Berkeley: University of California Press, 1976), 18–43. Copyright © 1976 The Regents of the University of California. Rita Copeland, "Rhetoric and the Politics of the Literal Sense in Medieval Literary Theory: Aquinas, Wyclif, and the Lollards," from *Interpretation: Medieval and Modern,* ed. Piero Boitani and Anna Torti (Woodbridge, U.K.; Rochester, N.Y.: D.S. Brewer, 1993).

Index

About *Yale Studies in Hermeneutics*

Yale Studies in Hermeneutics provides a venue for inquiry into the theory of interpretation in all its varieties and domains. Titles in the series seek to expand and deepen our understanding of understanding while explicitly framing and situating themselves within the tradition of recognized hermeneutical thinkers from antiquity to the present.